The Teacher's Grammar *of* English

A COURSE BOOK and REFERENCE GUIDE

Ron Cowan

CAMBRIDGE
UNIVERSITY PRESS
www.cambridge.org

CAMBRIDGE UNIVERSITY PRESS
Cambridge, New York, Melbourne, Madrid, Cape Town, Singapore,
São Paulo, Delhi, Dubai, Tokyo, Mexico City

Cambridge University Press
32 Avenue of the Americas, New York, NY 10013–2473, USA

www.cambridge.org
Information on this title: www.cambridge.org/9780521007559

First published 2008
3rd printing 2010

Printed in the United States of America

A catalogue record for this publication is available from the British Library.

Library of Congress Cataloging-in-Publication Data
Cowan, Ron.
  The teacher's grammar of English : a course book and reference guide / Ron Cowan.
      p. cm.
  Includes index.
  ISBN 978-0-521-80973-3 (alk. paper) -- ISBN 978-0-521-00755-9 (pbk. : alk. paper)
  1. English language--Study and teaching--Foreign speakers. 2. English teachers--
    Training of. I. Title.

PE1128.A2C69347 2008
428.2 ' 4--dc22

                                                              2008007254

ISBN 978-0-521-80973-3 hardback
ISBN 978-0-521-00755-9 paperback

This book is dedicated to the memory of my father,

a pioneer in the field of applied linguistics and

an innovator in the field of foreign language teaching:

J Milton Cowan

Acknowledgements

I would like to express my gratitude to a number of people at Cambridge University Press for their encouragement and help at different stages in the preparation of this book. Deborah Goldblatt guided me through the review process, and Mary Carson solicited evaluations of sample chapters from teacher trainers and ESL/EFL teachers in and outside of the United States. Rob Freire devoted considerable time and energy to insuring that the initial manuscript was completed on schedule.

Other people who were particularly helpful were Carol Boggess (Mars Hill College, North Carolina), who tried out chapters with teachers transitioning to ESL instruction in middle school and provided detailed feedback on their reactions to the material. Howard Williams (Teachers College, Columbia University) read first and second drafts of every chapter and wrote detailed critiques that resulted in many improvements. Kent Lee expanded my knowledge of discourse markers and how they might be incorporated in ESL instruction. Randee Falk did a very fine job of editing the final manuscript and the Glossary.

I am grateful to a number of people who helped me investigate grammatical errors made by English language learners whose native languages I have only a nodding familiarity with. Jinhee Choo and Gabseon Lee helped analyze a corpus of errors made by Korean ESL students and, with Doe Hyung Kim, assisted in formulating the descriptions of frequent errors that appear in several chapters. Michael Leeser (Florida State University) helped me classify the errors in a corpus produced by Spanish ESL students. He and Monica Millan checked the descriptions of Spanish that appear throughout this book. Bob Amorin was kind enough to obtain a small corpus of Portuguese EFL student compositions. My colleague Miao-Fen Tseng (University of Virginia) proposed and ran the experiment on Chinese ESL students' use of English conditionals described in Chapter 19.

Mark Cowan taught his father how to use computer graphics tools to create pages with the illustrations that appeared in earlier versions of these materials. He also stepped in and took the workload off my shoulders whenever I needed extra time for this project. Mitra Cowan shared her experiences learning French in the workplace in Montreal, providing examples of situations that were incorporated in Chapter 6. My wife Mehri displayed infinite patience when the writing of this book limited my participation in real life.

Finally, I am indebted to the hundreds of students in the MATESL program at the University of Illinois who, over the years, cheerfully filled out evaluation forms, sent e-mails and gave verbal assessments of the interest value and comprehensibility of these materials. These were of immense value to me during the writing of the book.

To the Instructor

The Teacher's Grammar of English (*TGE*) evolved out of two courses (a core course and its prerequisite) for ESL/EFL teachers in the MATESL program that I have been teaching at the University of Illinois. Its 26 chapters contain all of the knowledge about English grammar that I feel competent, professional teachers should command, as well as information about discourse structuring principles that affect the occurrence of grammatical structures. In addition, each chapter includes analyses of students' errors based on second language research and practical teaching suggestions on how to address these errors. This book was designed to be suitable as a textbook or as a resource book for teachers in all teacher training courses – including short teacher training programs, certificate programs, and MATESL programs.

Structure of the Book

The first three chapters of *The Teacher's Grammar of English* provide a foundation for the study of grammar and an overview of past and present approaches to teaching English grammar to nonnative speakers. Chapter 1, *Introduction*, reviews basic concepts such as grammatical competence as well as sociolinguistic and discourse related factors that influence language use. Chapter 2, *Grammatical Terms*, is provided for instructors whose students may have minimal knowledge of basic grammatical concepts. If you teach Chapter 2, you should stress that all of the grammatical terms in it will reappear and be elaborated on in subsequent chapters. Students who might be nervous about remembering grammatical concepts can refer to the *Glossary of Grammatical Terms* as needed to refresh their memory. Chapter 3, *Teaching Grammar*, examines the empirical evidence for and against the teaching of grammar to ESL students and provides an overview of past and current instructional practices.

The first three chapters can be viewed as optional, given your time constraints and the composition of your audience. Chapter 1 can be given as a reading assignment and discussed briefly in class. (The convention of marking ungrammatical sentences with an asterisk throughout the book is introduced here, so this symbol will have to be explained if you decide to skip this chapter.) Chapter 2 can usually be completed in two class sessions if the reading assignment guidelines described below are followed. There are two advantages of covering Chapter 3 before beginning subsequent chapters. First, many of the recommendations in the *Suggestions for Teaching* . . . section in the remaining chapters refer to the instructional approaches discussed in Chapter 3. Second, the content in Chapter 3 will equip teachers to better evaluate new ESL/EFL materials and to create effective teaching activities.

Chapters 4 through 26 are each subdivided into three sections. The first section is a discussion of the grammar topic. This discussion sometimes touches on concepts presented in previous chapters, but these are cross-referenced so that, regardless of which chapters you decide to teach, your students will not have difficulty understanding their content. After each main grammar point, a *Summary*, listing important terms and concepts, and one or more *Exercises* are provided to help students review and check their comprehension of the material. The second section, *Problems That ESL/EFL Students Have . . .* , describes specific errors that ESL/EFL students from a variety of L1 backgrounds make in speaking and writing when attempting to use the grammar in the chapter. These errors are documented with data from published research in second language acquisition and data from English learner corpora. An attempt is made to evaluate which errors may be transitory, and hence disappear as students receive more input and attain greater proficiency, and which errors appear to be persistent and, therefore, may warrant pedagogical intervention. The final section, *Suggestions for Teaching . . .* , provides activities for teaching aspects of the grammar topic. The proficiency level of the students who would benefit from each activity is indicated by the labels *beginning*, *intermediate*, and *advanced*.

Each chapter concludes with a list of references for further study on the topic. Several chapters (Chapter 9, *Multiword Verbs*; Chapter 12, *Adjectives and Adverbs*; and Chapter 15, *Indirect Objects*) include an appendix as a reference. A glossary, which lists many of the grammatical terms and includes example sentences, is provided for quick review. An index of terms and words is provided for further reference. An answer key is also included.

Using the Teacher's Grammar of English

To succeed in the language classroom, ESL/EFL teachers should have a good command of the material in the first sections of Chapters 4 through 26. However, it is equally important that they be able to relate this knowledge to the problems that their students have in learning the grammar, and that they try out teaching activities that will promote its acquisition. Hence, the chapters that you choose for your course will have the greatest impact if all three sections of every chapter are related to one another in your instruction. My recommendations for achieving this are described below.

1. Select a sequence of chapters from the *TGE* that fits the time constraints of your course. (See Selecting Content That Meets Your Needs, which follows.) When making your selection, you will want to take into consideration the length of different chapters. Chapters 3, 4, 6, 7, 9, and 15 can each be covered in two 50-minute class periods. With the exception of Chapters 14 and 16, each of the remaining chapters can be covered in three class periods.

2. Read each chapter and decide how the content can be covered in no more than three 50-minute sessions. Determine reading assignments (assigned to be read before each class) of ten to twelve pages for each chapter. In the first section of each chapter, those pages that have accompanying exercises represent the grammatical concepts that ESL/EFL teachers should master. Sections under the heading *Additional Facts About . . .* do not have exercises, and can be assigned for reading or skipped, depending upon time constraints. In the first class period, hand out the reading assignments for the entire course and tell your students that they should be prepared to answer the exercise

questions in class. From time to time, you may wish to have the students write out the answers to some of the exercises to ensure they are doing the reading and to check how well they are mastering the material.

3. Begin each class by going over the exercises that relate to the reading assignment. Call on students to answer the questions. If they have difficulty answering a particular question, coax them to come up with reasons why a particular answer is the best choice. Allow at least 15 minutes for answering questions and discussing any issues relating to them.

4. In the remaining 35 minutes of class, you may wish to engage in any of the following activities:

   • Demonstrate the kinds of grammatical errors that are produced when English language learners with different L1s attempt to use the grammatical structures covered in the reading assignment (use the errors in the *Problems That ESL/EFL Students Have . . .* section). Briefly discuss the possible causes of these errors, and engage the students in a short discussion of whether these errors should be addressed through pedagogical intervention. A primary consideration in making this decision should be whether the errors appear to be transitory or persistent.

   • Use the grammar topics in the assigned reading they have completed as a springboard for a discussion about how they might be taught. I sometimes show examples of how a topic is presented in current textbooks. We evaluate the presentations in light of whether they cover the important points of the grammar and determine whether they could be improved or supplemented with the additional facts presented in the first section of the chapter. These discussions can be helpful in developing teachers' ability to critically evaluate teaching materials and improve them.

   • With the next reading assignment, introduce and explain some aspect of a grammar topic that may be particularly challenging. Do this only with difficult topics and be sure not to teach the entire reading assignment for the next class.

By the end of the second class on a particular chapter, you should have, with the exception of Chapters 14 and 16, completed all of the first section. I have my students read the other two sections – *Problems That ESL/EFL Students Have . . .* and *Suggestions for Teaching . . .* – of each chapter for the third class meeting, but I do not hold them responsible for remembering all of the details in them. This is a fairly easy reading assignment because the material is not as challenging as the content of the first section. If I have already talked about some of the errors in the previous two classes, this assignment gives the students an opportunity to read about the errors again and better understand the causes that have been proposed to explain them. In preparation for the third class meeting, I ask my teachers to examine and evaluate the *Suggestions for Teaching . . .* activities and provide recommendations that might improve those activities. In this chapter, they are also asked to share other approaches to teaching the grammar that they have seen or used. I always devote at least half an hour of the final period to a group discussion led by me evaluating the activities in the *Suggestions for Teaching . . .* section. Although I have never asked my students to try out any of the activities in these sections, some of them have done this and reported back on their results. I am happy to say that these reports have always ranged from favorable to enthusiastic.

Term Project

I assign a term project that involves designing a teaching activity on one of the grammar points covered in the course. The activity may extend beyond one hour of instruction and includes a lesson plan. I have sometimes allowed groups of three students to collaborate on a single project. If time permits, you may wish to have these projects presented in class for the benefit of other teachers. I have included a few of the best projects that I have received over the years in the *Suggestions for Teaching . . .* section of some chapters of *TGE*. The authors are acknowledged in the Endnotes.

Selecting Content That Meets Your Needs

As stated previously, the content in *TGE* is relevant to almost all teacher training courses. This includes those courses devoted to teaching writing skills. Since many instructors may not have the time to cover all of the chapters, suggestions as to which chapters might be most suitable for shorter courses are offered below.

- One-Semester Courses

  For a one-semester course of approximately 14 or 15 contact hours, I would recommend Chapters 3 through 7 and Chapters 10 through 18. These cover most of the key structures that elementary- and intermediate-level students are taught. Teachers who feel that they need to cover more advanced-level grammar might consider replacing some of these with chapters 19 through 21.

- Short Courses (six weeks)

  Short six-week courses for teachers who have little or no experience teaching ESL/ EFL should probably include Chapter 3, since these teachers will need an overview of the debate surrounding the teaching of grammar as well as the survey of current instructional approaches. In addition, I would suggest Chapters 4, 6, 11, 14, and 16, because they cover key grammatical teaching points that every teacher has to deal with, and they address common problems that beginning teachers will encounter. Short courses for more experienced teachers will require a broader spectrum of topics.

- Courses Focusing on the Grammar of Writing

  Chapters 21, 23, 24, and 26 discuss grammatical structures that appear more frequently in written English and relate them to topics included in ESL/EFL composition courses (e.g., topic sentences, topic shift, and discourse/information packaging factors that favor the choice of some structures over others in discourse). These chapters offer a number of ways in which grammatical structures relevant to writing can be incorporated in the teaching of composition.

Contents

CHAPTER 1

Introduction

The Teacher's Grammar of English is designed for teachers of English to speakers of other languages. In discussions of English language teaching, the distinction is often made between *English as a foreign language* (EFL) and *English as a second language* (ESL). These two terms refer to the environments in which the learning of English takes place. In an EFL environment, the language spoken outside the classroom is not English. In an ESL environment, it is. Generally speaking, the kinds of problems that English language learners[1] have and the grammatical progress they make differ depending on which of these environments they find themselves in. This book is designed for ESL and EFL teachers alike. Moreover, English learners and teachers of subjects other than English may also find this text helpful in answering questions about how the English language works.

There is a long tradition of writing so-called prescriptive English grammar books aimed at teaching students how to write in a certain style. These books, often called writer's guides, are intended for native speakers of English, usually first-year university students, and they contain rules, or guidelines, for writing "good sentences." These rules might include the following: *Remove words and phrases that add nothing to the meaning of your sentence. Avoid ending a sentence with a preposition. Use active instead of passive sentences. The Teacher's Grammar of English* does not teach these kinds of prescriptive guidelines. Instead, it describes the different rules that produce grammatical sentences in English, the kinds of problems nonnative speakers have learning these rules, and the ways that teachers can help these students learn and use these rules in speaking and writing.

This opening chapter explains why a good understanding of English grammar is necessary for being an effective ESL/EFL teacher. It defines the concept of grammar and demonstrates what grammatical rules are. Next, it discusses sociolinguistic factors and information structuring that affect the use of English grammar and explains why teachers need to be aware of these principles. Finally, this introduction lays out the organization of the chapters in the rest of the book and shows how to get the most out of those chapters.

WHY DO TEACHERS OF ENGLISH HAVE TO KNOW GRAMMAR?

Both native and nonnative speakers of English teach English to speakers of other languages. Those teachers who are nonnative speakers of English typically realize the benefits of knowing English grammar well. However, teachers who are native speakers often wonder why they have to know a lot about English grammar to teach English. After all, they speak the language fluently. Can't they just go ahead and teach what they speak? The answer is no. If you speak a language, you do not automatically know how it works; that is, you do not necessarily have a *conscious* knowledge of the grammatical rules of the language. You are certainly able to use the rules of your first language because you have a *subconscious* (or *tacit*) knowledge of them, which you acquired as a child by listening to adults speak to you and to each other. This tacit knowledge allows you to produce brand-new grammatical sentences that you have never said or heard before. It also enables you to identify a sentence as ungrammatical and to recognize ambiguous sentences as having more than one possible meaning. However, this does not mean that you are able to explain why a sentence is ungrammatical or why a sentence may have more than one meaning. In short, your tacit, native-speaker knowledge of grammar does not enable you to describe or to teach the rules of grammar to a language learner. For that, you must know the rules consciously.

English language learners want to know how grammar in English works. To them, it is the key to understanding the language and using it to communicate. But even native speakers of English who have gone through a teacher training course may not be able to answer learners' questions such as, "Why can't you change that sentence into a passive sentence?" or "Why can't you say 'He let me to do it'?" If a teacher doesn't know the rules of grammar, the only available answer may be, "Because that's the way it is in English." However, this answer is not especially helpful to students who are looking for accurate, detailed information about English grammar. It simply establishes the teacher as a person who may speak the language correctly but is not equipped to tell students what they want to know about it.

As a teacher, you will likely be asked more questions about grammar than any other aspect of English. Even some of your fellow teachers who lack confidence about their knowledge of English grammar may ask you about points that they are not sure of. For this reason, having an accurate, comprehensive understanding of English grammar will make you feel more confident as a teacher and will also help you garner the respect of your colleagues and students.

You might ask, "But isn't the grammar going to be explained in the students' textbook?" Well, yes; unfortunately, however, some English language teaching textbooks contain misleading, oversimplified, and occasionally inaccurate descriptions of particular grammar teaching points. One of the goals of this book is to equip you to recognize misleading or incorrect grammar descriptions. If you see a faulty explanation in a textbook, you will be able to explain the grammar point more accurately and help your students better understand it. A good knowledge of English grammar will also enable you to evaluate a new textbook. As you examine individual lessons and the way the material in it relates to what has been covered in earlier lessons, you will be better equipped to judge how well the textbook is organized and how comprehensive the coverage of individual grammatical topics is. Some books omit important aspects of grammar that need to be covered, and you can supply this missing information and even prepare lessons that are more effective than those in your textbook. You will also find that a clear understanding of English grammar is a valuable aid in designing a syllabus that meets your students' needs and an important asset in preparing your students for national and international English proficiency tests, such as the TOEFL.

A final reason why teachers of English to speakers of other languages should know grammar is because it is one aspect of adult language learning on which instruction can have a lasting effect. For many years, it was thought that students who began learning a second language after the onset of puberty could never learn to speak it as well as native speakers. Neurological evidence was cited as proof of this.[2] However, recent research indicates that native-speaker ability in grammar can be acquired by people who start learning in their late 20s, and that learners in their 30s can attain a high level of grammatical proficiency.[3] This suggests that, as a teacher, you can make a difference in your students' ability to speak and write grammatical English, even if they are no longer at the age where they "pick up" English naturally. Additional support for the value of grammar instruction can be found in numerous studies that show that it helps students increase their grammatical accuracy (see Chapter 3). Although researchers are not all of the opinion that language courses should be organized around an explicit grammar syllabus, they do tend to agree that attention to grammatical form in a general way is beneficial.

WHAT IS GRAMMAR?

Grammar is the set of rules that describes how words and groups of words can be arranged to form sentences in a particular language. This is the definition of grammar that is perhaps most useful for teachers, and it is the definition that will be used in this book. The grammar of English consists of all the rules that govern the formation of English sentences, and this is precisely what learners of English want to know. In fact, many students will demand that a teacher tell them "what the rule is" even if that teacher has been trained to encourage students to figure out what the rule is on their own.

Understanding how grammar rules work and how the elements in a sentence relate to each other can sometimes be facilitated through the use of diagrams. One kind of diagram that can be found in linguistics textbooks as well as in some grammar textbooks for teachers is called a *phrase structure diagram* (or *phrase structure tree*)[4], illustrated in (1). It shows the linear and hierarchical relationship between the various parts of the sentence *Many students use the Internet.*

Phrase Structure Diagram

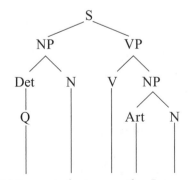

(**1**) Many students use the Internet.

This diagram uses various symbols to represent the larger grammatical groupings in the sentence: S means *sentence*, VP means *verb phrase*, NP means *noun phrase*, and Det means *determiner*. The individual words in (1) are labeled V for *verb*, N for *noun*, Q for *quantifier,* and Art for *article*. (Each of these terms is defined in Chapter 2.) The branches link the higher order elements to the words that make up the sentence.

The phrase structure diagram is just one of many ways to represent the relationships between the various grammatical elements in a sentence, and it can often be complicated to follow. Therefore, this book does not contain phrase structure diagrams, but instead uses a combination of prose descriptions and a simple bracketing system that identifies important words and word groupings within sentences. These brackets are used in the following section and throughout the book wherever necessary.

GRAMMAR RULES IN ENGLISH

Many of the grammar rules discussed in this book move words or groups of words around to create different sentence patterns. They also delete certain words. One example of a grammar rule is *dative movement*, which changes the position of the indirect object, the dative, in a sentence. When applied, as in (2), which has a direct object (DO) after the verb and an indirect object (IO) after the preposition *to*, the rule creates the new sentence pattern shown in (3), in which the positions of the DO and the IO are reversed.

                            DO   *IO*
(**2**) Alan sent [a long e-mail message] to [Susan].

                IO   *DO*
(**3**) Alan sent [Susan] [a long e-mail message].

The dative movement rule does two things as shown in (4): it moves the indirect object to a position before the direct object, and it simultaneously deletes the preposition *to*.

(**4**) Alan sent Susan a long e-mail message ̶t̶o̶ _____.

The dative movement rule is simply a way of stating a relationship between two linear orders or patterns of words that can occur in English. This rule applies only to sentences with verbs such as *send*, *throw*, *give*, and *lend*, and not to sentences with verbs such as *correct*, *mention*, and *report*. (The differences between these two sets of verbs are discussed in Chapter 15.) For now, suffice it to say that the second set of verbs cannot be followed by the IO + DO pattern shown in (3). For instance, if we apply the dative movement rule to (5), with the verb *report*, it will produce the ungrammatical sentence in (6), which is marked with an asterisk. (Throughout this book, an asterisk in front of a sentence indicates that the sentence is ungrammatical.)

                       DO   *IO*
(**5**) They reported [the accident] to [the police].

                       IO   *DO*
(**6**) *They reported [the police] [the accident].

The grammatical error in (6) is one that some English learners make, and it illustrates an important point about grammar rules: certain restrictions are often required to insure that a rule does not produce ungrammatical results. (The dative movement rule and its constraints are considered further in Chapter 15.)

FACTORS AFFECTING GRAMMATICAL CHOICES

Speakers who have successfully internalized the rules of a language and their constraints are said to possess *grammatical competence*. This means that they are able to use the rules of the language automatically to produce grammatical sentences. It also means that they are able to make accurate judgments regarding the grammaticality of the sentences they hear and read. For instance, if you have native-speaker grammatical competence in English, you will be able to identify (6) as clearly ungrammatical. You may not be able to explain what makes it ungrammatical, but you will know that something is wrong with it.

Gaining this kind of competence may well be the most important goal in learning a second language. After all, the ability to produce grammatical sentences is vital for effective communication. Nevertheless, the achievement of grammatical competence does not guarantee that a language learner will be able to communicate effectively and appropriately in every context. This is because several other factors, besides grammaticality, influence the choices that speakers and writers need to make about which grammatical form or structure to use in a given situation. It is important for teachers of English to understand these factors so that they can help their students know when and where it is most appropriate to use the grammatical forms and structures they are learning.

Sociolinguistic Factors

Sociolinguistic factors refer to things like the setting in which a language is used and who the speaker and the interlocutor are. The location, the relationship between the participants, and the medium of communication (e.g., spoken or written language) can affect the choice of grammatical forms and lexical items (*vocabulary*). Different *registers* (i.e., styles of English) are used depending on the setting in which the speaker or writer is attempting to communicate. For example, consider (7), taken from the weekly column of movie critic Roger Ebert. The sentence is a quote from a personal letter received by Ebert.

(7) Jon was very chuffed to hear that you'd picked up on this.[5]

The writer uses a conversational style of English that contains a contraction, *you'd*, for *you had*, and the adjective *chuffed*, a British English slang term meaning "excited" or "pleased." He also uses the idiomatic[6] three-word verb *picked up on*, which means "noticed." This three-word verb is characteristic of conversation, but it will be understood by a much wider audience of native speakers than the slang lexical item *chuffed*. The use of these three grammatical devices – a contraction, an idiomatic three-word verb, and a slang adjective that will be understood by a limited audience – indicates that the social context for which the communication was written is informal, familiar, and personal.

Another writer might choose to remove the conversational tone from the sentence by replacing the contracted form *you'd* with *you had*, the idiomatic *chuffed* with *pleased* or *excited*, and *picked up on* with *noticed*, as shown in (8).

(**8**) Jon was very pleased to hear that you had noticed this.

These changes, especially the removal of the idiomatic *chuffed*, shift the sentence up to a register characteristic of a personal, but more formal, letter, and it can now be understood by more readers. It is possible to make further changes that transform (8) to a slightly more formal register, which is shown in (9). By using the last name of the person who was very pleased, Jon Reynolds, replacing *this* with a direct reference to what was "picked up on," and changing *you* to *your reader*, we get a sentence that might appear in a typical newspaper article or a business letter.

(**9**) Mr. Reynolds was very pleased that your reader had noticed this concealed reference to Mike Royko's fictional character.

Sentence (9) can be shifted to a yet more formal register that approximates the style found in academic prose by changing *your reader* to the more impersonal *the reader* and changing the complement in the sentence (the section following *that*) into the passive voice, as shown in (10).

(**10**) Mr. Reynolds was very pleased that this concealed reference to Mike Royko's fictional character had been noticed by the reader.

An even more impersonal tone can be achieved by deleting the reference to the reader, as in (11).

(**11**) Mr. Reynolds was very pleased that this concealed reference to Mike Royko's fictional character had been noticed.

So we see that by using alternative grammatical forms and lexical items, we can shift the tone from highly informal conversational English to more formal registers. Why is some understanding of the different registers of English important for teachers of English? The reason is that teachers will have to give their students a sense of the circumstances in which certain grammatical constructions are appropriate. If we teach contracted forms of modal verbs (e.g., *I hafta see him* vs. *I have to see him*) or alternative question forms (e.g., *Are you gonna do that?* vs. *Do you intend to do that?*), we must also convey when one or the other form is more appropriately deployed.

One register distinction that is of special concern to teachers of English is the difference between grammar used in conversation and grammar used in written English. It is important for language learners to develop a sense of when a particular sentence structure is appropriate for use in conversation but not appropriate in writing. And it is nearly as important for learners to develop a sense of which sentence structures are favored, for example, in academic articles and which might be better employed in newspaper editorials. Questions concerning the use of specific English grammatical structures in different writing genres can be answered with greater precision today than in the past, due to the appearance of books like the *Longman Grammar of Spoken and Written English* (*LGSWE*) (Biber et al., 1999), which describe the frequency with which different grammatical constructions occur in various registers and genres. The findings in the *LGSWE* are based on data taken from a corpus of over 40 million words representing British and American spoken and written English. The statements made in the chapters that follow regarding how frequently grammatical forms and structures occur in English, and in which registers and genres they most commonly occur, are based on the *LGSWE* corpus. References to pages in the *LGSWE* where a more detailed discussion may be found are included in the Endnotes.

The written/spoken dimension plays a part in English language pedagogy. When students have attained a high-intermediate or low-advanced level of proficiency in many programs, there is usually a greater emphasis on writing skills. And in programs that are preparing students for university coursework, teachers want to know which grammar structures are more prevalent in academic writing so they can emphasize these in their writing instruction. Here the written dimension of English requires further refinement into *academic English* vs. *nonacademic English*. Questions of priority (i.e., which grammar points should be emphasized in an ESL/EFL syllabus because of their high frequency) can be partially answered by corpus data.

Information-Structuring Principles

In this book, we will also look at certain principles that native speakers follow that allow them to interpret and produce sentences that are appropriate within the context of a larger discourse. An example of one of these *information-structuring principles* is the *given–new contract*, which states that in each new sentence that a native speaker of English says or writes, *given* (previously mentioned) information should appear before *new* information (information that has not been mentioned previously). This principle can affect a native speaker's choice of grammatical patterns. For example, earlier we saw that, because of the rule of dative movement, we have two possible patterns, shown in (2) and (3). These two patterns are also shown in (12) and (13), in which the indirect object (IO) for each is the pronoun, *him*.

         DO   *IO*
(**12**) Give [a CD] to [him].

         IO   *DO*
(**13**) Give [him] a [CD].

Most English language teaching textbooks teach or imply that there is no reason to choose one of the above patterns over the other since they are interchangeable in all contexts. However, this is not true. Native speakers will choose one of these two patterns, depending on the previous discourse. If the indirect object is mentioned in a previous sentence, the speaker will choose the pattern in (13), because this puts the given information before the new information contained in the direct object.

In (14), Susan mentions John in the first sentence, so this makes him old information. Pronouns always mark previously mentioned information, so Ann's response would have to be (a), where the IO pronoun *him* comes before the new information, a CD. Response (b) puts the old information in the position of new information, so it will not be chosen. This fact has been demonstrated in large-scale experiments with native speakers.[7]

    (**14**) Susan: You know, I can't figure out what to get John for his birthday. Any ideas?

    (**15**) Ann: a. Give him a CD. You know how much he likes music.
            b. Give a CD to him. You know how much he likes music.

Notice that the given–new contract does not affect the grammatical correctness of the sentences. It is rather a principle that affects our choice of grammatical structures. It is not absolute; rather, it strongly biases a native speaker's decision when more than one syntactic pattern is possible. Both (a) and (b) in (15) are grammatical, but native speakers would invariably choose to continue the discourse with alternative (a), because this sentence conforms to the given–new contract. The pedagogical implication for teaching English is that learners should be exposed to the given–new contract so that they can assimilate it and use it. In this book, we examine other information-structuring principles like the given–new contract and show how they may be relevant to English language pedagogy.

Language Change and Usage

The grammar of a language changes over time. The changes, which often stretch over hundreds of years, are rarely noticed by anyone except linguists; however, some changes can be more generally noticed, and therefore can have consequences for teachers. In this book, we look at some cases of ongoing change that should be addressed by teachers. One of these affects the grammar of conditional sentences such as the one shown in (16).

(16) *If *I would have seen* her, I would have said hello.

This kind of sentence, which is often referred to as a *counterfactual conditional* because the proposition in the *if*-clause did not happen (i.e., I didn't see her), requires the past perfect tense in the *if*-clause. Thus, strictly speaking, the grammatical version of (16) is (17) with the past perfect form, *had seen*, in the *if* clause.

(17) If I *had seen* her, I would have said hello.

However, the version in (16) is becoming more common in spoken American English. You can hear counterfactual conditionals with *would have* in both clauses more and more frequently on television talk shows, often uttered by literate, educated native speakers. The change to *would have* in the *if*-clause is particularly noticeable when the main verb in that clause is *have*. The past perfect tense with the main verb *have* is *had had*, as shown in (18).

(18) If I *had had* more time, I would have visited that old church.

But many native speakers cannot believe that (18) is grammatical and insist instead that (19) is the only grammatical possibility.

(19) *If I *would have had* more time, I would have visited that old church.

The widespread use of *would have* in both clauses of counterfactual conditionals in spoken English is held at bay in written English by editors and teachers wielding blue pencils. It will be interesting to see, however, if this change, which appears to have started in spoken English, will be halted. This kind of ongoing change, where some speakers adhere to the rule embodied in (17) and (18) while an increasing number of other speakers start to use the variation in (16) and (19), presents an interesting challenge to teachers of English, since their students will probably notice the difference and ask if the latter two sentences are grammatical. Even if they do not ask, the teacher or textbook writer should point out the variation and provide students with some guidelines for how to deal with these competing structures when speaking and writing English.

THE ORGANIZATION OF THIS BOOK

Beginning with Chapter 4, each chapter in this book is organized into three major sections. The first section covers the facts about the grammar topic treated in that chapter that one needs to know to be an informed teacher of English. In addition to the grammatical rules, issues relating to meaning and usage (including sociolinguistic factors and information-structuring principles) are treated in this section. For the sake of clarity, invented example sentences are often used to illustrate how specific grammatical rules work. However, you will also find many authentic example sentences that come from newspaper articles and other sources, all of which are referenced in the Endnotes. Sometimes included are facts that are important for the teacher to know in order to answer students' or colleagues' questions but that may not be directly applicable to teaching the grammar topic. These extra pieces of information are found in Additional Facts. Instructors who have a limited amount of time to cover a great deal of material may wish to omit this.

The second major section of each chapter, Problems That ESL/EFL Students Have With . . . , describes recorded grammatical errors that English language learners with different native languages (L1s) typically make when trying to produce sentences that embody the grammar topic. The probable causes of the errors and reasons for their persistence are also discussed. Almost all of these errors are documented in research studies in the area of Second Language Acquisition (SLA) or in corpora of written errors.[8] The specific study or corpus from which an error was taken can be found in the Endnotes and References at the end of each chapter. Some of the errors discussed in these sections have been shown to be highly persistent, occurring in the speech and writing of learners who are about to or have already begun using English as professionals and will receive no more English language instruction. These highly persistent errors are typical of *end-state* or *stabilized grammars* (see Chapter 3), and teachers may wish to take pedagogical action to raise students' awareness of them. The errors that are most likely to have this kind of persistence are indicated, and possible strategies for reducing or eliminating them from the grammar of English language learners are offered.

The third major section of each chapter, Suggestions for Teaching . . . , includes activities for teaching the grammar topic covered in the chapter. This section is divided into two subsections, the first (and shorter) of which indicates the particular points that should be emphasized and describes conventional approaches to teaching them. Potential shortcomings of these approaches may also be mentioned. The second subsection suggests activities that call on students to employ the grammar structures within the context of meaningful communication. An effort has been made to provide a broad range of activities and tasks for use in a variety of settings.

TO THE STUDENT

Throughout the first section of each chapter you will find summary tables that condense the main points that you should understand and retain. Use these to review the section you have just read. The summary tables are not intended to be a substitute for the material in the text. Go back and reread the material on any point in the summary table that you do not feel confident about. After you have done this, go through the exercises that come after the summary table and answer the questions. These are intended to help you determine whether you have mastered the material.

ENDNOTES

[1] While it is quite common to refer to students in ESL/EFL environments as ESL/EFL students, the terms *English language learner* (ELL) and *English learner* (EL) are also used.

[2] See Lenneberg (1967), Curtiss (1977), Johnson and Newport (1989).

[3] See Bialystock and Hakuta (1994) and Birdsong (1992). The most telling piece of evidence that second-language learning may not be limited by a "critical period" comes from Birdsong and Molis's (2001) precise replication of Johnson and Newport's (1989) study with subjects who were native speakers of Spanish. Their results show near-native-like performance by second-language learners in their mid-20s and a few cases of very high performance by learners in their 30s. This evidence also supports the idea that the similarity of a learner's native language to the language being learned (Spanish grammar is relatively similar to English) is an important factor for success in second-language acquisition.

[4] Two widely used textbooks that use phrase structure trees are Morenberg's (2002) *Doing Grammar*, which is designed for use with American college students (native speakers of English) and Celce-Murcia and Larsen-Freeman's (1999) *The Grammar Book*, which is written for ESL/EFL teachers.

[5] *The Answer Man*, F3 News-Gazette, December 29, 2002.

[6] An idiom is a grammatical construction, made up of a fixed group of words, which has its own unique meaning.

[7] For examples, see Haviland and Clark (1974) and Cowan (1995).

[8] Many grammatical errors discussed in this book will be documented from two learner corpora assembled from the compositions of ESL students. One corpus was produced from the written compositions of Korean students. It comprises 241,656 words and includes essays from (1) students in an intensive English program, which prepares them to enter American universities, and undergraduate students in an American university (72,145 words), and (2) graduate students in an American university (169,511 words). There are at least three distinct proficiency levels in this Korean learner corpus. The other corpus was produced by Spanish-speaking ESL students. It has the same proficiency levels as the Korean corpus but comprises only slightly more than 36,000 words.

REFERENCES

Bialystock, E., & Hakuta, K. (1994). *In other words: The science and psychology of second-language acquisition*. New York: Basic Books.

Biber, D., Johansson, S., Leech, G., Conrad, S., & Finegan, E. (1999). *Longman grammar of spoken and written English*. Essex, England: Pearson Education Limited.

Birdsong, D. (1992). Ultimate attainment in second language acquisition. *Language, 68*, 706–755.

Birdsong, D., & Molis, M. (2001). On the evidence for maturational constraints in second-language acquisition. *Journal of Memory and Language, 44*, 235–249.

Celce-Murcia, M., & Larsen-Freeman, D. (1999). *The grammar book: An ESL/EFL teacher's course*, 2nd ed. Boston: Heinle & Heinle.

Cowan, R. (1995). What are discourse principals made of? In P. Downing, & M. Noonan (Eds.), *Word order in discourse* (pp. 29–49). Amsterdam/Philadelphia, PA: John Benjamins.

Curtiss, S. (1977). *Genie: A linguistics study of a modern day "wild child."* New York: Academic Press.

Haviland, S. E., & Clark, H. H. (1974). What's new? Acquiring new information as a process in comprehension. *Journal of Verbal Learning and Verbal Behavior, 13*, 312–521.

Johnson, J. S., & Newport, E. L. (1989). Critical period effects in second language learning: The influence of maturational state on the acquisition of English as a second language. *Cognitive Psychology, 21*, 60–99.

Lenneberg, E. H. (1967). *Biological foundations of language*. New York: Wiley & Sons.

Morenberg, M. (2002). *Doing grammar*, 3rd ed. New York/Oxford: Oxford University Press.

CHAPTER 2

Grammatical Terms

INTRODUCTION

People sometimes make fun of technical terminology, and the creator of this cartoon is no exception. It shows a mechanic using jargon in an attempt to impress (and maybe confuse) a caterer, who promptly uses the same strategy on him. Eventually, they agree to talk in terms they can both understand.

In reality, technical terms are meant not to confuse, but to simplify communication among specialists. As in most other fields of study, grammar has its own terms that allow us to communicate more economically about it. These terms help us to classify words and groups of words in ways that make understanding grammar easier. We could conceivably get along without them, but using these terms makes talking about grammar more efficient. For example, it is much easier to communicate the idea of a direct object by simply saying *direct object* than by saying *the element within a sentence that receives the action described by a verb*.

As you might expect, learning about English grammar will involve becoming familiar with some new terms. These terms will not only help you understand how English works but will also help you explain the details of English grammar to your students. Since you are likely already familiar with many grammatical terms (*noun*, *verb*, *adjective*, *direct object*, etc.), you will need to learn only a limited number of them. This chapter is meant to introduce new terms you may not know and to refresh your memory about grammar terms you already know.

It is not uncommon for there to be two or three terms that are used to refer to the same grammatical construction or rule (e.g., *dative movement* vs. *dative alternation*). An effort has been made in this book to use the most common term in every case. However, other terms that are commonly applied to the same construction or rule are mentioned as well, often in an endnote. All of the grammar terms introduced in this chapter receive more detailed treatment in the chapters that follow.

CONSTITUENT STRUCTURE

In this section, we begin to consider the various *constituents,* or *elements*, that make up sentences in English. A sentence is made up of one or more clauses. In (1) we see a sentence made up of two clauses joined by *and* (a *coordinating conjunction*). Square brackets have been set around each of the clauses to mark them.

> *Clause 1*   *Clause 2*
> (**1**) [My brother ate a hotdog], and [his kids ate pizza].

Each of the clauses in (1) is made up of two major parts, a subject noun phrase (NP) that performs an action and a verb phrase (VP) that describes the action. These subjects and verb phrases can also be bracketed, as shown in (2).

> *NP*   *VP*   *NP*   *VP*
> (**2**) [[My brother] [ate a hotdog]], and [[his kids] [ate pizza]].

We can further identify the words that make up each of these parts. For instance, the subject NP in clause 1 contains the word *my* (a *possessive determiner*) and the word *brother* (a noun). The VP in clause 1 contains a verb, *ate*, followed by an object NP, *a hotdog*, which can also be broken down into its component words, *a* (an article) and *hotdog* (a noun). In (3), each of these elements is bracketed, along with the phrases and words in clause 2.

> (**3**) [[[My] [brother]] [[ate] [[a] [hotdog]]]], and [[[his] [kids]] [[ate] [pizza]]].

The only word that is not bracketed above is the coordinating conjunction *and*. Thus, let's put square brackets around it and label all of the words. We will use the abbreviations PD for possessive determiner, N for noun, V for verb, Art for article, and Conj for conjunction.

> *PD*   *N*   *V*   *Art*   *N*   *Conj*   *PD*   *N*   *V*   *N*
> (**4**) [[[My] [brother]] [[ate] [[a] [hotdog]]]], [and] [[[his] [kids]] [[ate] [pizza]]].

What we have done in (4) is to identify all of the constituents that make up our sentence. As we can see in (4), constituents can have different sizes, and larger constituents are made up of smaller constituents. For example, the largest constituents of (1) are clause 1 and clause 2, linked together by the coordinating conjunction *and*. These clauses, however, consist of smaller constituents called *phrases*, which are made up of even smaller constituents (words). The composition of all of the parts in a unit, such as in (4), or each of the clauses in it, is referred to as the *constituent structure* of that unit. In the sections that follow, we take a closer look at the constituent structure of English phrases and clauses.

PHRASES

A *phrase* consists of a *head element* plus any other required or optional elements that appear alongside the head element. The head element determines which other elements can appear with it. Each of the five types of English phrases is described and shown in (5) through (9). In each sentence, the phrase being described is surrounded by brackets and the head element is in italics. A noun phrase (NP) normally has a noun (N) as its head element.

           PD   N

(**5**) [My *sister*] is sleeping.   *noun phrase*

The head element (called a *head noun*) in (5) is *sister*. This head element is preceded by one of the different kinds of modifiers that can appear with head nouns. The modifier is *my*, a possessive determiner. The NP *my sister* functions as the *subject* of the sentence since it performs the action.

A *verb phrase* (VP) is shown in (6). The head element of this verb phrase is the verb (V) *took*. The verb is followed by an NP (*my keys*), which functions as the direct object of the verb. This object NP is within the VP as shown by the VP brackets that surround the verb and the noun phrase.

           V   NP

(**6**) Helen [*took* [my keys]].   *verb phrase*

Adjectives (Adj) are words that describe properties of something, such as color (*black, white, bright, dark*), size and weight (*big, deep, heavy, light, wide*), and other qualities. An adjective is the head element in an *adjective phrase* (AdjP). It can be preceded by *degree adverbs* (Adv) such as *terribly, extremely, considerably,* and *very*. In (7), the adjective *rude* is preceded by the degree adverb *extremely*.

           Adv   Adj

(**7**) They were [extremely *rude*].   *adjective phrase*

In addition to preceding adjectives, *adverbs* (Adv) supply information about *how, where, when, why,* and *to what extent* some action occurs. Many adverbs end in *-ly*. Like adjectives, adverbs themselves can be preceded by other adverbs. In the *adverb phrase* (AdvP) shown in (8), the adverb *quickly* is the head element.

           Adv   Adv

(**8**) He finished [very *quickly*].   *adverb phrase*

The last type of English phrase is the *prepositional phrase* (PP), which has a *preposition* (Prep) as its head element. Prepositions can indicate many different meanings, including position (*on, in*) and direction (*toward, into, from*). In a prepositional phrase, the head element normally comes before a noun phrase. In (9), the preposition *on* precedes the noun phrase *the table*.

           Prep   NP

(**9**) The keys are [[*on*] [the table]].   *prepositional phrase*

EXERCISE 2.1

Identify each underlined word as a noun, a verb, an adjective, an adverb, a preposition, or a possessive determiner.

Example: Their daughter is a junior in college.

Answer: Their = possessive determiner

1. The governor is speaking to the Senate.
2. He put the keys in the drawer.
3. The tall woman spoke very rapidly.
4. He ran across the bridge and jumped into a red convertible.
5. Jan turned slowly toward her sister.

EXERCISE 2.2

Identify each phrase in square brackets by writing NP, VP, AdjP, AdvP, or PP above it.

              NP   *AdjP*
Example: [The students] are [very happy].

1. Anne bought a [new car].
2. [The young senator] sat [beside the president].
3. His wife spoke [very softly].
4. [The police] [arrested [the two thieves]].
5. My brother is [in the library].
6. Mary is [extremely intelligent].

NOUN PHRASES

Nouns

As we have seen, the head element of a noun phrase is normally a noun. Nouns refer to people, places, and things. Nouns in English are usually classified as *common* or *proper*. *Common nouns* refer to general names for people, places, and things and are divided into two classes: *count* and *noncount nouns* (also called *mass nouns*). Count nouns can be made plural (e.g., *hands*, *tables*), while noncount nouns do not have a plural form (e.g., *stuff*, *clothing*). In some languages, the equivalents of many English noncount nouns are countable. Speakers of these languages are likely to produce errors as in (10).

(**10**) *The police will need a lot of additional evidences.

Collective nouns make up a small group of count nouns in English that refer to a collection, or group, of individual parts or members (e.g., *family*, *committee*, *team*).[1] Unlike other nouns, collective nouns in their singular form may be followed by a singular or plural verb, so that both (11a) and (11b) would be considered grammatical.

(**11**) a. The faculty is meeting next week.
      b. The faculty are meeting next week.

Proper nouns are the names of specific people, places, and things. They can either be singular (e.g., *John*, *Paris*) or plural (*the Parkers*, *the Great Lakes*), and they are usually capitalized.

The table below shows the basic noun types.

COMMON		PROPER
Count	**Noncount**	John
pen　pens	information　*informations	Paris
dish　dishes	stuff　*stuffs	the Great Lakes
Collective		
the Parkers		
family　families		
committee　committees		

Pronouns

The head element of a noun phrase may also be a *pronoun*, a word that refers to a noun that has been previously mentioned. The pronoun *she* in (12) refers back to the noun phrase *a woman* in the previous sentence.

(12) [A woman] got out of the car. [She] was wearing a gray overcoat.

There are different kinds of pronouns, which will be described in greater detail in Chapter 13. *He* is one of a set of *subject personal pronouns*, along with *she*, *I*, and *they*. You are probably familiar with the corresponding set of *object personal pronouns*: *him*, *her*, *me*, and *them*. *You* is both a subject and an object personal pronoun.

Gerunds

A *gerund* is a *present participle* (verb + *-ing*) that can function as the head of an NP. A gerund can appear alone in an NP, as in (13a), or an NP can include more constituents such as *the neighbors* in (13b).

(13) a. [Swimming] is a great form of exercise.
   b. [Inviting the neighbors] was a big mistake.

We can tell that *swimming* and *inviting the neighbors* function as NPs because we can substitute another NP (with a head noun) for each of them. This is shown in (14).

(14) a. [Tennis] is a great form of exercise.
   b. [That invitation] was a big mistake.

Prenominal Modifiers

Prenominal modifiers are words that precede a head noun in a noun phrase. The most common prenominal modifiers fall into two categories: *determiners* and *adjectives*. Each of these categories is discussed briefly below. (For more on determiners, see Chapters 10 and 11. For more on adjectives, see Chapter 12.)

Determiners

Determiners indicate important characteristics about head nouns such as definiteness, indefiniteness, possession, or quantity. There are, thus, several types of *determiners*: *articles*, *demonstrative determiners*, *numbers*, *possessive determiners*, and *quantifiers*.

A. ARTICLES

There are two types of *articles* (Art): *definite* and *indefinite*. The definite article *the* is shown in (15a). The indefinite articles *a* and *an* are shown in (15b) and (15c). Their meanings and the factors that determine the choice of one or the other in speaking and writing are discussed in Chapter 11.

(**15**) a. *The* student arrived late.   *definite article*
     b. *A* student is waiting for you.   *indefinite article*
     c. *An* elephant has escaped.   *indefinite article*

B. DEMONSTRATIVE DETERMINERS

Demonstrative determiners (DemDet) are used to indicate whether something referred to by a noun is near or far away from the speaker.[2] These determiners have singular and plural forms as shown in the following table.

DEMONSTRATIVE DETERMINERS		
	Near	**Far**
Singular	*this* book	*that* book
Plural	*these* books	*those* books

When the forms *this/these* and *that/those* stand by themselves and refer to something already mentioned, they are *demonstrative pronouns*. In (16a) *these* and *those* are demonstrative determiners, but in (16b) *these* and *those* are *demonstrative pronouns*, which refer to a previously mentioned noun – *apples*.[3]

(**16**) a. *These* apples are delicious, but *those* apples over there are sour.
     b. Do you like apples? *These* are delicious, but *those* are sour.

C. NUMBERS: CARDINAL AND ORDINAL

Cardinal numbers (Num), such as *one*, *two*, or *three*, and *ordinal numbers* (Ord), such as *first*, *second*, or *third*, can also appear before a head noun. They often follow some other determiner, as shown in (17b).

(**17**) a. *Six* boys showed up at her doorstep.
     b. *The second* boy was wearing a blue bow tie.

D. POSSESSIVE DETERMINERS

The forms *my*, *your*, *her*, *his*, *its*, *our*, and *their* are *possessive determiners*. They modify nouns that follow them, as in (18a) and the first line of (18b). These possessive determiners should be distinguished from *possessive pronouns*, such as *mine*, *yours*, and *hers*, which do not modify nouns but instead stand by themselves and refer to something already mentioned. For example, in (18b), the possessive pronouns *yours* and *mine* refer to the word *sweater*, which appears in the first line of the exchange.

(**18**) a. Hand me *your* flashlight, please.
     b. Susan: Take *my* sweater.
        Laura: I don't want *yours*, I want *mine*.

E. QUANTIFIERS

Words that describe quantity or extent make up the class of determiners called *quantifiers* (Q). The members of this class include *some, all, many, each, few, much, little,* and *most.* These quantifiers can appear alone before a noun as in (19a) or with *of + definite article,* as in (19b). Quantifiers can also be found with *of + demonstrative determiner,* as in (19c), or with *of + possessive determiner* as in (19d).

(19) a. *Many* passengers arrived early.
   b. *Many of the* passengers arrived on time.
   c. *Many of these* passengers arrived late.
   d. *Many of its* passengers arrived a day late.

Adjectives

As mentioned earlier, adjectives (Adj) are words that describe size, weight, and other properties. We have already seen that they can stand on their own as part of an adjective phrase (AdjP). They can also, however, function as a prenominal modifier in a noun phrase, as in (20).

(20) a. They recently returned from a *long* trip.
   b. We must protect the rights of the *working* man.
   c. Please be sure to deposit the *required* amount.

As illustrated in (20b) and (20c), adjectives are sometimes formed from verbs. In (20b), the adjective *working* is formed from the verb *work,* and in (20c), the adjective *required* is formed from the verb *require.*

EXERCISE 2.3

Identify each underlined word shown by its correct grammatical classification (adjective, definite article, indefinite article, quantifier, demonstrative pronoun, demonstrative determiner, possessive determiner, personal pronoun, possessive pronoun, gerund).

Example: His boss doesn't like him.

Answer: His = possessive determiner; *him* = personal pronoun.

1. I wouldn't buy those oranges if I were you. They look spoiled. But these over here are all very fresh.
2. That bike you are riding looks a lot like mine.
3. All of his friends have moved away.
4. I didn't order this. I ordered the same salad that those people over there are eating.
5. Reading a long paper takes a lot of time.
6. Our car has to be serviced every 5,000 miles. Yours just needs an annual inspection.
7. I don't think she appreciates your comments.

Functions of Noun Phrases

Now that we have looked at the structure of noun phrases, we should examine the functional roles they play in a sentence.

Subjects

A noun phrase can be the *subject* of a sentence, that is, the *agent,* or "doer," that performs the action in a sentence. In (21), the subject NP, *the batter*, carries out the action described by the VP, *hit the ball*.

(**21**) [The batter] hit the ball.

Direct Objects

A noun phrase can also be a *direct object*, or *patient*,[4] the entity that is affected by the action indicated by the verb. The NP bracketed in (22), *the ball*, is the direct object in the sentence.

(**22**) The batter hit [the ball].

Indirect Objects

In (23a) and (23b), the bracketed NPs are *indirect objects*. In (23a), the indirect object, *his daughter*, is the *goal*, or the person to whom the action is directed. In (23b), *his daughter* is the *benefactive*, or the person for whom the action was performed. Indirect objects are discussed in Chapter 15.

(**23**) a. Sam gave [his daughter] an iPod.
b. Sam bought [his daughter] an iPod.

Objects of a Preposition

A noun phrase can also be the *object of a preposition*, as in (24), in which the bracketed NPs each follow a preposition and are part of a prepositional phrase.

(**24**) a. They drove *toward* [the village].
b. The computer is *behind* [the desk].
c. We are meeting *at* [noon].
d. *Over* [the years] we became wiser.

NPs that are objects in a prepositional phrase have different meanings determined by the prepositions that head the phrase. In (24a), the NP *the village* denotes a goal or destination. The NP *the desk* in (24b) denotes a stationary point that marks a position. In (24c), the NP *noon* denotes a specific point on a continuum of time, and the NP *the years* in (24d) denotes a span of time.

Predicate Nominals

A *predicate nominal* is an NP that follows a form of the verb *be* and refers to the subject of a sentence, as shown in (25a) and (25b).

(**25**) a. My mother is [a doctor].
b. We're [taxpayers], and we have rights.

Appositives

An *appositive* is an NP that defines the NP that it follows. In (26), the NP *the capital of the Czech Republic* defines the previous NP *Prague*. Appositives always have commas around them.

(**26**) Prague, [the capital of the Czech Republic], is very beautiful.

EXERCISE 2.4

Identify each underlined NP as a subject, a direct object, an indirect object, an object of a preposition, a predicate nominal, or an appositive.

Example: He parked the car in the parking lot.

Answer: *the car* = direct object; *the parking lot* = object of the preposition *in*

1. Professor Branson, the head of the department, approved the appointment.
2. I think you will find your glasses in the glove compartment of my car.
3. She sent her sister an e-mail.
4. My brother is an anesthesiologist.
5. He hung a large painting over the fireplace.

VERB PHRASES

A *verb phrase* consists of a *main verb*, which is the head of the phrase, any preceding *auxiliary verbs* (discussed later), and any following NPs, PPs, AdjPs, or AdvPs that may be present. A verb phrase is what has been traditionally referred to as the *predicate* in a sentence. In (27), (28) and (29), the brackets for each verb phrase enclose the main verb and all of the elements that follow it.

In (27), the VP consists of the main verb *likes* and an object NP, *fresh strawberries*.

        V   *NP*

(**27**) John [likes [fresh strawberries]].

In (28), the VP shows a VP with an adjective phase (AdjP) following the verb *was*.

       V   *AdjP*

(**28**) She [was [quite happy]].

In (29), the VP contains a prepositional phrase (PP).

      V   *PP*

(**29**) He [slept [on the couch]].

In (30), the verb phrase contains an adverb phrase (AdvP).

      V   *AdvP*

(**30**) She [writes [very slowly]].

Verb Forms

Verbs can take several different forms. For instance, the verb *work* may have the *infinitive* form shown in (31a), in which *work* is preceded by *to*, or it may have the *bare infinitive* form shown in (31b).

(**31**) a. He likes *to work* from home as often as possible.   *infinitive*
      b. Her boss lets her *work* from home.   *bare infinitive*

Verbs can also take a variety of *inflected* forms. Some of these inflected forms are shown in (32).

(**32**) a. She *works* every day.   *inflected for present tense*
      b. He is *working* right now.   *present participle*
      c. I've *worked* there for a long time. *past participle*

In (32a) the ending *-s*, which indicates present tense, third person singular, is added to the *stem,* or *bare infinitive,* form of the regular verb *work* to produce *works.* Endings like this one added to verbs are called *inflections*, and you may often hear or read of verbs being inflected for person (e.g., first person, second person), number (e.g., singular, plural), and tense (e.g., present, past). The present participle (verb + *-ing*) is formed when an *-ing* ending is added to a stem as in *working* in (32b). The *past participle,* shown in (32c), is generally formed by adding an *-en* ending to some verbs (e.g., *taken, eaten, fallen*) and an *-ed* ending to other verbs (e.g., *wanted, called, stopped*). The tensed, present participle, and past participle forms of some verbs are irregular. For example, some verbs do not take the regular *-ed* past inflection. Instead, they either undergo an internal vowel change (e.g., *run* becomes *ran*) or they change their form entirely, (e.g., *be* becomes *was/were* and *go* becomes *went*.)[5]

Auxiliary Verbs

Auxiliary verbs always precede main verbs within a VP. Traditionally, auxiliaries have been called *helping verbs* because they always appear together with a main verb and seem to refine its meaning. Along with inflections on the main verb, they indicate whether the action of the verb is in progress, repetitive, or complete. This is called *aspect. Tense,* which is the time that the action occurs (i.e., present, past, or future) is indicated by inflections on verbs, and on auxiliary verbs, or by modal auxiliary verbs like *will.* (The topics of tense and aspect are covered in Chapter 16.) The auxiliary verbs that contribute to aspect are *be* and *have.* In-progress action requires the use of the auxiliary verb *be* plus a verb with the *-ing* ending (a present participle), as in (33a). This is called the *progressive,* or *continuous,* aspect. Action that is complete (*perfect aspect*) is indicated by use of the auxiliary verb *have* plus a verb with an *-en* or *-ed* ending (a *past participle*), as in (33b).

> (**33**) a. They *are helping* some friends.   *progressive aspect*
> b. He *had* already *looked* at the house.   *perfect aspect*

Modal verbs (also referred to as *modal auxiliaries* or just *modals*) are a specific class of auxiliary verbs that indicate possibility, probability, obligation, ability, or necessity. They include words like *may, might, must, can,* and *should.* Modals appear before other auxiliary verbs and main verbs in the bare infinitive form.

> (**34**) a. They *might come.*
> b. They *may have left* already.
> c. She *could be working* right now.

In (34a), *might* is a modal verb followed by a main verb (*come*) in its bare infinitive form. In (34b), the modal verb *may* precedes the auxiliary verb *have*, which precedes the past participle *left.* In (34c), the modal *could* precedes the auxiliary verb *be*, which precedes the main verb in the present participle form, *working.* (Modal verbs are discussed further in detail in Chapter 14.)

Finally, there is the auxiliary verb *do. Do* is used with a main verb to ask *yes/no* questions as in (35a), to express negation, as in (35b), and to express contradiction, as shown in (35c), where the capitalized *DOES* represents contrastive stress.

> (**35**) a. *Does* he like her?
> b. I know for a fact that he *doesn't* like her.
> c. Speaker A: I'm sure that he *doesn't* like her.
>   Speaker B: Yes, he *DOES* like her!

The auxiliary verb *do* also expresses distinctions involving tense and aspect. For example, the question in (35a) concerns the present and uses *does*. *Did* would be used to ask about the past (e.g., *Did he like her?*). The auxiliary *do* is never used with any form of the verb *be*.

Transitive and Intransitive Verbs

Transitive verbs are verbs that must be followed by a direct object, such as *slapped* in (36a). We know that the verb *slapped* must have a direct object because the same sentence without an object, (36b), is ungrammatical. Verbs may also be *intransitive*; that is, they may not require a direct object, as in (36c), in which the verb *worked* is followed not by an object but by an adverb. If the adverb (*furiously*) were to be removed, however, the sentence would still be grammatical. Adding an object, as in (36d) makes the sentence ungrammatical. Some verbs can be used both transitively and intransitively, as shown in (36e) and (36f).

(**36**) a. The child *slapped* John.   *transitive*
     b. *The child *slapped*.
     c. Karen *worked* furiously.   *intransitive*
     d. *Karen *worked* the job furiously.
     e. The girls *ate* all the pancakes.   *transitive*
     f. The girls *ate* early.   *intransitive*

Ergative Verbs

In (37a), the verb *shatter* is clearly transitive because it is preceded by a subject (*the burglar*) that is an agent capable of carrying out action, and it is followed by an object (*the window*) that experiences the action. However, in (37b), *the window* is now the subject, even though it is not capable of undertaking action. Furthermore, *the window* in (37b) undergoes or is affected by the action expressed in the verb. When the subject itself is affected by the action of the verb, we say that the verb is *ergative*, or *unaccusative*.

(**37**) a. The burglar *shattered* the window.   *transitive*
     b. The window suddenly *shattered*.   *ergative*

Ergative verbs can be divided into two classes: *paired* ergative verbs such as *shatter*, *break*, *bounce*, *boil*, *drop*, and *close*, all of which have a transitive verb counterpart, and *unpaired* ergative verbs such as *appear*, *disappear*, *emerge*, *erupt*, and *die*, which do not have transitive counterparts.[6] Notice that the transitive verb counterpart of a paired ergative verb like *sink* can appear in the passive voice, as shown in (38c).

(**38**) a. The ship *sank*.   *paired ergative*
     b. The submarine *sank* the ship.   *transitive counterpart*
     c. The ship *was sunk* by the sub.   *transitive counterpart in passive voice*

Unpaired ergative verbs do not have transitive counterparts, thus they can never appear in sentences in the passive voice, as (39b) and (39d) show.

(**39**) a. After the party, he fainted.   *unpaired ergative*
     b. *After the party he was fainted.   *unpaired ergative in passive voice*
     c. The accident occurred late last night.   *unpaired ergative*
     d. *The accident was occurred late last night.   *unpaired ergative in passive voice*

Stative vs. Dynamic Verbs

Verbs can also be classified in terms of their inherent *lexical aspect*. Lexical aspect refers to whether a verb describes an action that has duration, like *talk* or *sleep*; whether it describes an action that is *punctual* (happens quickly), such as *notice* or *recognize*; or whether it describes an action that has both duration and culmination, such as *build* or *destroy*. These classifications are useful for explaining the tense and aspect forms a verb can take. Lexical aspect is discussed at greater length in Chapter 16. For now we need to look at one of the most basic classifications of English verbs, one with a profound effect on their grammar.

English verbs can be divided into two categories: *stative* and *dynamic*. *Stative* verbs express a state, rather than an action that is carried out by the subject. *Dynamic* verbs, on the other hand, express actions that a subject can carry out.

Stative Verbs	*Dynamic Verbs*
(**40**) a. He has a book.	He wrote a book.
b. The flag is red and blue.	She unfolded the flag.
c. She knew that man.	She greeted that man.
d. They owned a car.	They bought a car.

One of the direct grammatical consequences of this classification is that stative verbs usually cannot appear in the so-called present progressive and past progressive tenses, but dynamic verbs can. This can be seen when we take the sentences in (40) and try to change them into present and past progressive sentences.

Stative Verbs	*Dynamic Verbs*
(**41**) a. *He is having a book.	He was writing a book.
b. *The flag is being red and blue.	She was unfolding the flag.
c. *She was knowing the man.	She was greeting the man.
d. *They were owning a car.	They were buying a car.

Phrasal and Prepositional Verbs

The term *phrasal verb* is frequently applied to structures that are made up of a verb plus one or two other elements but function as a single unit. In most cases, the verb and the element(s) that appears with it have the same meaning as a single-word verb. For example, the verb + preposition combination *look over* means "examine" in a sentence like *The architect looked over the blueprints*. In Chapter 9, in which these verbs are discussed in detail, we distinguish between *prepositional verbs*, such as *listen to*, where the preposition must remain next to the verb, and *phrasal verbs*, such as *look over* and *look up* (locate in a published document), in which, if the verb takes an object, that object may appear between the two elements of the verb, as shown in (42d).

(**42**) a. He *listened to* the music.
    b. *He *listened* the music *to*.
    c. He *looked up* her address.
    d. He *looked* her address *up*.

Many English language teaching textbooks refer to phrasal and prepositional verbs as *two-word verbs*, and this is, in some ways, an appropriate term. There are, however, three-word verbs as well, which consist of a verb followed by two elements (e.g., *do away with*, *look up to*, *put up with*). These will also be discussed in detail in Chapter 9.

Identify the form of each underlined verb in the sentences as an infinitive, a bare infinitive, a tensed form, a present participle, or a past participle. Identify examples of *be* and *have* as auxiliary verbs and modal verbs. These are not underlined.

Example: He is sleeping right now.

Answer: sleeping = present participle form; *is* = auxiliary verb

1. She let him take it.
2. John tries to write at least two paragraphs every day.
3. She has helped me with my homework many times.
4. They took the shortest route through the mountains.
5. Does he want to do it?
6. I haven't talked to him yet.
7. She may be working on it right now.

Identify each verb shown as stative, transitive, intransitive, paired ergative, or unpaired ergative.

Example: Water boils at 212 degrees Fahrenheit.

Answer: boil = paired ergative verb (transitive counterpart = He boiled some water to make tea.)

1. He knocked the vase off the table and it broke.
2. She hit the ball as hard as possible.
3. They own two cars and a motorcycle.
4. That boy weighs 20 pounds.
5. He died with his boots on, like any good cowboy.
6. The ball rolled off the table and bounced several times.
7. He signed the documents.
8. She ran faster than the other girls.

CLAUSES

Having examined the structure of English phrases and some of the categories of words that make up those phrases, we now turn our attention to the clause, the constituent with which we began our discussion of constituent structure.

The distinction between *independent clauses* and *subordinate* (or *dependent*) *clauses* is fundamental to an understanding of English clause structure. As was mentioned earlier, a clause must have a subject and a verb, and this goes for independent and subordinate clauses alike. Independent clauses, however, can stand alone as sentences, whereas subordinate clauses cannot. In written English, they must always be connected to an independent clause.

In (43a), we see a sentence made up of two clauses. The first clause is a subordinate clause, and it is clear, as shown in (43b), that it cannot stand alone. In contrast, the second clause, an independent clause, could be a sentence on its own, and this is demonstrated in (43c). In sentences like (43a), the independent clause is usually called the *main clause*.

Clause 1 (subordinate)   Clause 2 (independent)

(43) a. [As he was rounding the corner], [John knocked over an elderly woman].

   b. *As he was rounding the corner.

   c. John knocked over an elderly woman.

Coordinate Sentences

Two or more independent clauses can be joined by a coordinating conjunction (also called a *coordinator*) such as *and*, *but*, or *or* to form a *coordinate sentence*. The different forms that coordinate sentences can take are treated in greater detail in Chapter 25.

(44) a. [John likes Alice], *and* [Alice likes John].

   b. [Tom played football], *but* [Fred stayed home].

   c. [Susan must leave], *or* [Mary will do something drastic].

Subordinate Clauses

Subordinate clauses are introduced by special kinds of words. One type of subordinate clause, the *relative clause*, is linked to an NP in the main clause by a *relative pronoun* such as *who*, *whom*, *which*, *whose*, *that*, *when*, *why*, or *where*. The relative pronoun comes after the NP that the clause modifies.

(45) The man [*who* carried the flag] was a veteran of World War II.   *relative clause*

In (45), the main clause is *The man was a veteran of World War II*. The relative clause *who carried the flag*, modifies the subject NP of the main clause, *the man*. Relative clauses are usually embedded in the main clause. They supply extra information about a given NP in the main clause. Relative clauses are discussed in greater detail in Chapter 18.

Most of the other subordinate clauses are introduced by words called *subordinators*. These subordinators show a meaning relationship between the subordinate clause and the entire main clause. For example, the meaning relationship between the subordinate clauses in (46a) and (46b) and the preceding main clauses is one of *reason*; the subordinate clause describes the reason she married him.

(46) a. She married him [*because* she loves him].   *adverbial subordinate clause*

   b. She married him [*so that* she would inherit his fortune].   *adverbial subordinate clause*

   c. He is *as* talented [*as* she is].   *comparative clause*

The types of subordinate clauses shown in (46) are covered in Chapters 23 and 24, respectively.

Complements

Complements (COMP) can be thought of as a type of subordinate clause, since their content is related to the main clause. However, unlike relative clauses, which supply extra information about a noun, and the other subordinate clauses previously mentioned, which have a particular connection to the entire main clause, a *complement* provides information that is necessary to complete the meaning of the verb. Complements are objects of verbs.

The verb determines the grammar of the complement that can come after it. For example, a verb such as *want* can only be followed by a complement that begins with an infinitive. You can say, for instance, *He wants to come*, but you cannot use a complement that begins with a present participle (a *gerund* complement) after *want* because it would result in an ungrammatical sentence, **He wants coming*. Four types of complement clauses can occur after verbs, as illustrated in (47).

(**47**) a. Alice wanted [to come to the party].   *infinitive complement*
b. Joyce enjoys [going to the theater].   *gerund complement*
c. Fred knows [that he must finish the paper].   that *complement*
d. I don't know [how he does it].   *embedded question complement*[7]

Infinitive and gerund complements do not have a visible subject, as can be seen in (47a) and (47b). This is because the subject of the complement is identical to the subject of the verb that the complement follows. For example, we know that the subjects of the complements in (47a) and (47b) are *Alice* and *Joyce*, respectively. Object complements are discussed in much greater detail in Chapter 21.

EXERCISE 2.7

Draw a line under each clause in the sentences and identify it as an independent clause or a subordinate clause. For each subordinate clause, identify it as a relative clause or an adverbial subordinate clause.

Example: John likes opera, and Bill likes the ballet.

Answer: two independent clauses

1. She sold the house because she needed the money.
2. The professors who were chosen by the Nobel committee will travel to Stockholm.
3. Susan stayed home, but Alice went to the basketball game.
4. He grasped her firmly around the waist in order to lift her off the ground.
5. I had never met the guy who sold her the car.

EXERCISE 2.8

Underline each complement in the sentences below and identify it as an infinitive complement, a gerund complement, a *that* complement, or an embedded question complement.

Example: I don't believe that they are going to win.

Answer: that complement.

1. Some of the participants wanted to take a break.
2. We believe that they will come to the reunion.
3. Alan enjoys watching sports on television.
4. I am not sure when he will finish it.
5. She actually enjoys arguing about politics.

CONCLUSION

This chapter does not cover all the grammatical terms that you need to know as a teacher of English to speakers of other languages, nor does it cover all the grammatical terms that you will encounter in the chapters that follow. The aim of this chapter is to provide you with a foundational understanding of some of the basic terms and principles necessary for moving on to learn about the various topics covered in this book. The next chapter is also a preparatory chapter. It contains a good deal of background information about teaching grammar. Once you have completed it, you will be better prepared to examine each of the grammar topics addressed in the remaining chapters.

ENDNOTES

[1] Quirk et al. (1972, 1985) divide collective nouns into three categories: *specific* collective nouns like *committee*, *crew*, *family*, etc.; *generic* collective nouns like *the aristocracy*, *the clergy*, *the intelligentsia*, *the public*, etc.; and *unique* collective nouns like *the Arab League*, *Parliament*, *the United Nations*, *the Vatican*, etc.

[2] These are also called *deictic* determiners. For an explanation of *deixis* see Huddleston (1988), pp. 98–99.

[3] Of course, demonstrative determiners can appear before nouns that refer to something already mentioned or known, as in: *A*: *No, I meant his new novel. B: Oh. You mean that book*.

[4] This is also referred to as a "theme" in some grammars, and a "goal" in functional grammar; see for example Lock (1996:73).

[5] A complete change of form is referred to as *suppletion*. See Huddleston and Pullum (2002), p. 1607, for further examples.

[6] The terms *paired* and *unpaired ergative* verbs are taken from Yip (1995).

[7] This is also called an *interrogative* complement, e.g., McCawley (1988), p. 113.

REFERENCES

Huddleston, R. (1988). *English grammar: An outline*. Cambridge: Cambridge University Press.

Huddleston, R., & Pullum, G. K. (2002). *The Cambridge grammar of the English language*. Cambridge: Cambridge University Press.

Lock, G. (1996). *Functional English grammar: An introduction for language teachers*. Cambridge: Cambridge University Press.

McCawley, J. (1988). *The syntactic phenomena of English*. Chicago: University of Chicago.

Quirk, R., Greenbaum, S., Leech, G., & Svartvik, J. (1972). *A grammar of contemporary English*. London: Longman.

Quirk, R., Greenbaum, S., Leech, G., & Svartvik, J. (1985). *A comprehensive grammar of the English language*. London: Longman.

Yip, V. (1995). *Interlanguage and learnability: From Chinese to English*. Amsterdam: John Benjamins.

CHAPTER 3

Teaching Grammar

INTRODUCTION

The ability to arrange the words of a second language (L2) into meaningful sentences is absolutely basic to communicating in that language. Given this fact, it would seem that adult learners need grammar instruction if they are ever to develop the ability to communicate effectively in an L2. However, this raises an important question: what if adult learners have the ability to learn an L2 grammar without being taught its grammar? In other words, what if adults can learn the grammar of an L2 in the same way that small children learn the grammar of their native language (L1) – by simply being exposed to the speech of native speakers?

The questions posed above highlight a long-standing debate within the language teaching community over whether adult language learners need grammar instruction. The debate is based primarily not on the question of whether learning grammar is important, but on the question of how it is that adult learners best acquire an understanding of L2 grammar. Is grammar best learned "naturally," that is, by simply being immersed in an L2 environment, or does the process require, or at least benefit from, instruction? This is one of the important questions we take up in the sections that follow.

In this chapter we consider evidence that supports the usefulness of teaching grammar to learners of English and the debate over how this should be done. We summarize some current methods and techniques for teaching grammar and also examine issues related to the treatment of learner errors.

WHY TEACH GRAMMAR AT ALL?

For some time, many teachers and second language acquisition (SLA) researchers have recognized that L2 learning seems to be fundamentally different from L1 learning.[1] Some of the basic differences between these processes were summarized by Bley-Vroman (1989). Among the observations made by Bley-Vroman is the fact that L1 learners are always completely successful in learning to speak their language, whereas adult learners often fail in their quest to learn an L2. The fact that success is guaranteed for child learners has been taken as evidence that they are endowed with a specific faculty for learning language. The generally low success rate of adult L2 learners, on the other hand, seems to imply that this language-learning faculty is time sensitive and vanishes as learners reach adulthood.

Bley-Vroman also recognized that L2 learners who do not fail in their effort to learn an L2 can experience varying degrees of success. In other words, different L2 learners reach different levels of proficiency. L1 learners, on the other hand, always reach the same level of proficiency: perfect mastery. This is not what one would expect if L1 and L2 learning were identical processes.

L2 learners commonly attain what is referred to as a *stabilized* L2 grammar (Long, 2003). For instance, recent longitudinal studies, ranging from 5 to 16 years (Han 2000; Lardiere 1998a, 1998b, 2000; Long 2003), reveal that some learners show no improvement in certain basic areas of English grammar, producing errors such as dropping simple present tense *-s* (for third person singular) and plural noun marking, even over a long period of time. These very basic errors continue to occur in the speech of L2 learners who have been in the country from 5 to 25 years, who use the L2 every day, and who have a strong motivation for improving their grammar. These stabilized features never occur in L1 learner grammars.

It has also been noted that part of L2 learners' success in acquiring a new language may be due to *affective* factors, like an outgoing personality and a willingness to take risks, exhibited in ways such as trying to say things in the L2 without worrying about whether they are grammatical. These factors do not appear to play any part in L1 learning. Children always master their native language, regardless of their personality traits.

Given these facts, why would anyone maintain that adult L2 learners learn just like L1 learners and, therefore, do not need any grammar instruction? This is the question we take up in the following section.

The Case Against Teaching Grammar

Beginning in the 1970s, Stephen Krashen developed a theory of L2 learning that rejected the value of teaching grammar. Initially referred to as the Monitor Model but subsequently elaborated as the Input Hypothesis, Krashen's theory holds that there are two processes by which adults obtain knowledge about language. The first is *acquisition*, which is "a subconscious process identical in all important ways to the process that children utilize in acquiring their native language" (Krashen, 1985, p. 1). The second is *learning*, a conscious process that results in *"knowing about a language."* According to Krashen, knowledge obtained by these two types of processes never interacts, and only acquired knowledge can be used in spontaneous conversation in the L2. This theory implies that all facets of grammar instruction are pointless or, as he puts it, "peripheral and fragile" (Krashen, 1993) because, at best, they lead to the accumulation of learned knowledge, which cannot be converted into acquired knowledge. Krashen eventually developed a classroom approach to teaching an L2 referred to as the Natural Approach (Krashen & Terrel, 1983). It involves no instruction about how L2 grammar rules work; rather, its aim is to supply students with opportunities to receive what Krashen refers to as "comprehensible input" – L2 language samples that students can use to figure out the rules of grammar on their own, so that these rules take the form of acquired knowledge.

Many L2 researchers have criticized Krashen's theory. One of the most devastating and detailed critiques came from McLaughlin (1987), who pointed out that, in addition to the fact that the empirical evidence used is of questionable validity, the terms that are the cornerstone of Krashen's theory – *acquisition* and *learning* – are not clearly defined. McLaughlin noted, "It is not possible to tell which process is operating in a particular case. Hence the central claim of the theory, that 'learning' cannot become 'acquisition,' cannot be tested" (p. 56). McLaughlin also listed numerous examples of internal weaknesses and inconsistencies in the theory and pointed out that, unlike most scientific theories, Krashen's Input Hypothesis makes no clear predictions that can be proven or rejected. By proposing concepts while refusing to operationalize them, Krashen makes it impossible for researchers to test their reality and usefulness. McLaughlin also pointed to some disturbing tendencies in Krashen's writings, such as a tendency to ignore empirical research that contradicts his claims.[2] One example is Krashen's statement that grammar instruction has no effect on a learner's acquisition of an L2. The only way for learners to acquire an L2 and work out any errors they have developed, Krashen maintains, is to provide them with more comprehensible input, an excellent source of which is extensive reading for pleasure (Krashen, 1989). In fact, there is a great deal of evidence that contradicts these claims.

The Case for Teaching Grammar

Over the past decade, an abundance of empirical evidence has emerged that shows that classroom instruction in grammar actually results in substantial gains in L2 proficiency. This evidence comes from carefully controlled studies, many of which have been carried out in the classroom. For example, Master (1994) has shown that grammar teaching can effectively improve English learners' accuracy in the use of articles, a grammatical category that is notoriously difficult for many learners of English. Cadierno (1995) and Doughty (1991) have demonstrated that explicit instruction can increase students' accuracy in the production of past tense forms and relative clauses. Additional evidence that instruction that focuses students' attention on grammatical forms promotes the attainment of high levels of accuracy is documented in studies such as Carroll and Swain (1993), Fotos (1993), Lightbown (1991), Lightbown and Spada (1990), and Nassaji and Swain (2000). Furthermore, a number of reviews (R. Ellis, 1990, 1994, 2001; N. Ellis, 1995; Larsen-Freeman & Long, 1991) indicate that grammar instruction affects the ultimate level of proficiency that students attain as well as the rate at which students progress. Finally, an analysis of 49 studies on the effectiveness of instruction by Norris & Ortega (2000) found that grammar instruction produces substantial gains in learning L2 grammar and that these gains hold over time. Furthermore, Krashen's claim that reading for pleasure provides sufficient comprehensible input to promote acquisition is contradicted by two classroom studies (Lightbown, 1992; Lightbown, Halter, White, & Horst, 2002), showing that students who were given oral and written tasks as instruction outperformed students whose learning experience consisted of reading and listening.

In addition to the above studies, there is an extensive body of research on language learning in French immersion programs that argues for the value of grammatical instruction. Immersion programs provide precisely the type of environment that Krashen claims fosters acquisition. The students are given large amounts of meaningful input and have to focus simultaneously on understanding the new language and determining its grammar without any help from the teacher. A series of reports (Hammerly, 1987; Harley, 1989, 1993; Lapkin, Hart, & Swain, 1991; Harley & Swain, 1984, 1985; Swain & Lapkin, 1989) document that students in these immersion classes fall short of achieving accuracy with regard to some grammatical forms. These findings imply that attaining high levels of grammatical accuracy requires some grammar instruction. A number of researchers (Celce-Murcia, Dörnyei, & Thurrell, 1997; R. Ellis, 1997, 2002; Mitchell, 2000) have extended the results of the immersion studies to *communicative language teaching* (described below in greater detail). They found that when a focus on meaning was emphasized at the expense of a focus on grammatical form, classroom instruction did not enable students to attain a high level of *grammatical accuracy* in English.

Today, many SLA researchers have concluded that very little of Krashen's theory of how adults learn an L2 can be supported. Nevertheless, many teachers remain convinced that the Input Hypothesis is viable and that L2 grammar instruction is not useful. The notion that L2 learners do not need grammar instruction resonates strongly with many kindergarten through grade 6 teachers, for instance, who have noted that their students do seem to learn without formal grammar instruction. However, this does not support the Input Hypothesis; rather, it reflects something that has been known for some time – that K–6 children are able to acquire another language with little or no instruction. They require only exposure to the second language in meaningful contexts. Adults, however, no longer have this ability and need help in discovering and internalizing the L2 grammar if they are able to make substantial progress. The results of research cited previously argue that, when teaching adults, adopting a "laissez-faire approach to the development of [grammatical] accuracy in instructed second language, [and] concentrating on only providing opportunities for learners to process rich and comprehensible input" (Doughty, 2003, p. 258) may pose a serious barrier to the learners' development of competence in English.

This book deals primarily with teaching English grammar to nonnative speakers who are postpuberty, or adult, learners. Since the evidence described earlier clearly demonstrates that grammar instruction is important for these learners, we will proceed to consider some of the issues surrounding the best ways to provide such instruction.

EXPLICIT VS. IMPLICIT INSTRUCTION

Although there is general agreement on the value of teaching grammar, for some time it has been debated whether instruction should be *explicit* or *implicit*. In *explicit* grammar teaching, the rules are explained to learners, or the learners are directed to find the rules by looking at linguistic examples, that is, sentences that embody the rules. *Implicit* teaching, on the other hand, "makes no overt reference to rules or forms" (Doughty, 2003, p. 265). Until recently, arguments in favor of one or the other approach were not supported by evidence. But a careful examination of Norris and Ortega's (2000) analysis of 49 studies, referred to earlier, has shown that explicit teaching produces better and longer-lasting learning than implicit teaching.

Most English and foreign language textbooks use a style of explicit grammar teaching called *deductive instruction*, in which different structures are presented and then practiced in different kinds of exercises and activities including memorizing dialogs, reading simplified texts, doing transformation exercises (in which one grammatical structure is converted to another), and getting explicit negative feedback (correction of errors by the teacher). Critics of this traditional "presentation-practice" model believe that it does not result in learning.[3] Long (1997), for one, who refers to this method as *focus on forms*, claims that it teaches more than the learner needs, does not present a realistic model of language use, ignores research findings that show learning is not a "one-time categorical event," and ignores the role of developmental stages in learning. In spite of this harsh criticism, the majority of textbooks today present grammatical rules using some or all of the activities and exercises described above.

The alternative to deductive grammar presentation (within the explicit grammar teaching framework) is *inductive instruction*. This involves having students formulate rules from natural language, and it is perhaps more useful in teaching intermediate and advanced students. An excellent example of how this is done can be found in Carter, Hughes, and McCarthy (2000), *Exploring Grammar in Context*. In order to help students formulate the grammatical rule that constrains the position of adverbs in English sentences, they are given two sentences and asked to guess which one would occur in "real conversation." After judging several pairs like this, students are asked, "*What rules could you make for adverbs with* going to *in the future?*" "*What rules could you make for adverbs with* do / does / did *questions?*" Examples of actual language follow. These are intended to help students formulate the rules that determine the position of different kinds of adverbs in sentences and to relate these discoveries to the use of adverbs in conversation as opposed to writing. To aid the process, the authors provide summaries throughout the book that supply generalizations about the grammar of English adverbs.

It is now generally accepted that either form of explicit instruction is better than no grammar instruction at all. The criticism that Long and others level at the use of explicit instruction in current textbooks is that packaging materials into discrete units, i.e., chapters, gives a misleading impression that students have "learned" a grammatical topic after they have completed the chapter in which it was presented. Long and others know that the explicit presentation and practice is just the beginning, and much more practice will be required before students begin to approach competence. They have pointed to research showing that acquisition of grammar is promoted by instruction that not only stimulates students to reflect on the nature of grammatical rules, but provides opportunities for those rules to be used as part of meaningful conversation in realistic contexts (DeKeyser, 1998). This type of instruction is what Long (1997) has referred to as *focus on form* (as opposed to the *focus on forms* instruction used in many ESL/EFL textbooks). We will now discuss approaches for teaching grammar that continue to compete for teachers' attention.

APPROACHES TO TEACHING GRAMMAR

We begin our survey with three approaches that arose as reactions to prevalent trends in language instruction in the mid-twentieth century. The first of these, *communicative language teaching* (CLT), dominated the field for over two decades. It eschews explicit grammar instruction and emphasizes collaboration among students to achieve meaningful communication.

Communicative Language Teaching

In its purest form, CLT focuses on meaning, with no explicit attention to grammatical form. CLT evolved in reaction to a view of language instruction that relied largely on the development of four language skills—listening, speaking, reading, and writing—and on mechanical drills that manipulated grammatical form with no relation to realistic communication. CLT also grew out of pedagogical trends in Europe (teaching language for special purposes) and the United States in the 1970s and 80s. Some of CLT's popularity during the 1980s was no doubt due to its emphasis on meaningful communication, which was seen to coincide with Krashen's ideas about L2 language learning. One of CLT's founders and strongest champions is a professor of French, Sandra Savignon, who in a (1972) research report and (1983) book proposed that language teaching should foster the development of *communicative competence*[4] in language learners. She defined communicative competence as "the ability to interact with other speakers to make meaning, as distinct from the ability to demonstrate grammatical competence on discrete point tests" (Savignon, 1991, p. 264). In pursuit of this goal, CLT seeks to foster "the collaborative nature of meaning," which involves the participation of other students in the class as well as the teacher. Two important goals of CLT are for students to learn to use feedback to judge the success of their attempts to communicate and to use linguistic forms in the social contexts in which they would be deemed appropriate. Classroom instruction in CLT involves students in unrehearsed communicative activities and games. The choice of these activities and the specific goals of a given lesson are determined by the learner's communicative needs.

In the communicative classroom, teachers must learn to suppress the desire to assist students in producing grammatically accurate communication. The transcript below from Nunan (1989, p. 98) shows CLT in action. A student is telling a story to other students and the teacher. This is a nice demonstration of the collaborative interaction in CLT, but it also reveals some reasons for the reservations that teachers may have about the effectiveness of the method.

(1) Student 1:   China, my mother is a teacher and my father is a teacher. Oh. She go finish, by bicycle, er, go to . . .
Student 2:   House?
Student 1:   No house, go to . . .
Student 2:   School?
Student 1:   My mother . . .
Teacher: Mmm . . .
Student 1:   . . . go to her mother.
Teacher: Oh, your grandmother.
Students: Grandmother.
Student 1:   My grandmother. Oh, yes, by bicycle, by bicycle, oh, is, em, accident (*gestures*).
Teacher: In the water?
Student 1:   In water, yeah. River, yeah, river. Oh yes, um, dead.
Students: Dead! Dead! Oh!

The activity above is focused solely on achieving meaningful communication. Student 2 is trying to help Student 1 achieve a successful outcome, but only the feedback provided by the teacher seems to help. Furthermore, it is hard to imagine that collaborative interaction between the teacher and students will result in any increase in the grammatical accuracy of the storyteller. This has led many language teachers to feel that some focus on grammar is necessary if students are to increase their grammatical competence. The concern that total focus on meaning may result in little or no grammatical development was avoided for many years by citing good scores attained by CLT-trained students on measures of fluency. Unfortunately, many researchers feel that developing objective measures of fluency is as elusive a task as objectively distinguishing between the processes of "acquisition" and "learning." In a *TESOL Quarterly* review of CLT, Savignon (1991) acknowledged teachers' reservations related to the possibility that CLT may not be contributing to the advancement of grammatical competency and cited *task-based language teaching* (TBLT), described later, as a promising development for introducing more emphasis on grammatical form within CLT. CLT still has its advocates, and practically every ESL/EFL textbook produced today claims to embody a "communicative approach." However, the research cited earlier and a greater understanding of SLA and problems that students have acquiring a second language have resulted in what Beale (2002) calls a "growing eclecticism in language pedagogy." Teachers today have not jettisoned the cornerstone of communicative language teaching – having students collaborate in the classroom – but they are reassuming a more active role in the process as "informed decision makers" (Beale, 2002; Kumaravadivelu, 1994). In this more active role, teachers are using a mix of strategies drawn from different theories and classroom research, to focus students' attention on grammatical form, expand grammatical knowledge through speaking and writing, and correct students without interrupting ongoing communication.

Grammar in Context

Teaching *grammar in context* consists of a variety of techniques that can be used to achieve certain goals, rather than a formal method with a series of prescribed steps that should be followed. Grammar in context is a reaction against the "focus on forms" format of traditional language teaching syllabi that present discrete units that focus on a particular grammar point before moving on to another grammar point. Nunan (1998) feels that this "strictly linear approach to language learning, [which entails acquiring] one grammatical item at a time . . . before moving on to the next," is an unrealistic view of how any student learns a second language (p. 101). Instead, he advocates an organic approach that encourages students to "become active explorers of language . . . [and of the] relationships between grammar and discourse" (p. 104).

Some of the operational principles of Nunan's organic method of teaching grammar in context are the following: (1) expose learners to many examples of authentic language; (2) provide them with opportunities to use language that they have not been exposed to or have not practiced in any systematic way; (3) give them opportunities for collaborating with other students and comparing their efforts; and (4) let them revise and compare their final efforts with the language in the original text.

Although Nunan's operational principles for language teaching are not based on any theory of L2 learning or classroom research, they have considerable intuitive appeal to ESL teachers, probably because of his emphasis on providing lots of exposure to authentic language. Nunan's approach has much in common with communicative language teaching in that it relies heavily on collaboration among students and emphasizes implicit grammar instruction. Teaching grammar in context seems to be more suitable for students who have at least an upper-intermediate level of proficiency, since students must possess a sufficient knowledge of grammar to make judgments about "authenticity" and to explain the basis of their judgments.

The next approach to language teaching we will look at offers a way of incorporating tasks as a means of classroom instruction.

Task-Based Language Teaching

The rationale for *task-based language teaching* (TBLT) seems to have several sources: (1) a desire for language instruction relevant to advanced learners who need proficiency for academic, occupational, or vocational purposes (Long, 1997); (2) a feeling that L2 learning does not proceed in the step-by-step process characteristic of language textbooks; and (3) a belief that task-based interaction among learners and teachers promotes real L2 acquisition (Gass & Veronis, 1994; Long, 1997; Prabhu, 1987; Swain & Lapkin, 2001). Some of the basic principles of TBLT are as follows:

- Use realistic tasks in teaching.
- Elaborate on the input given to the student.
- Do not use authentic texts alone.
- Provide the students with rich input (language that is comprehended and promotes the formation of grammar rules).
- Respect and encourage learner syllabi.
- Promote cooperative learning between and among students.

Developing a true TBLT syllabus requires a number of steps. Long (1997) defines seven stages that are necessary for designing, implementing, and evaluating TBLT programs:

1. Conduct a needs analysis.
The teacher examines the L2 communicative needs of his or her students and decides what means are available for meeting those needs. For example, a teacher might decide to design a TBLT unit around certain needs that newly-arrived English learners have, including learning how to buy a bus pass, where to buy appliances, how to shop for groceries, and so on. She or he will discuss these tasks with the students to ensure that they accurately reflect their real-life needs.

2. Classify the target task types.
The teacher classifies the real-life tasks into various types and then identifies the linguistic skills involved in these activities.

3. Derive the pedagogical tasks.
The teacher develops tasks for the classroom that are associated with the real-life tasks. Tasks associated with buying electronic appliances might include listening to TV advertisements and discussing which provide the best bargains, reading advertisements

in weekend bargain sections of newspapers, and role-playing encounters with sales personnel to ask about particular features of appliances and financing conditions.

4. Sequence the tasks so that they form a task-based syllabus.

Long (1997) notes that the sequencing of tasks is done intuitively by the teacher. One obvious possibility for the example we are using is to begin with tasks that prepare the students for shopping (e.g., reading ads, researching products) and move on to tasks relevant to the shopping process itself.

5. Implement the task-based syllabus with appropriate pedagogy.

The students collaborate, in groups and pairs, to carry out the tasks. TBLT interactions allow for the use of negative feedback (correction of errors). But this can be done either overtly by the teacher or unobtrusively by *recasts* of learner errors. (This technique is described in greater detail later.) To use Long's example, if students are omitting the plural *-s* from nouns, the teacher could respond to a student's ungrammatical utterance (e.g., **I need to buy some appliance* or **I want to look at some toaster*) with a recast such as, *"You need to buy some appliances?"* or *"Oh, you want to look at some toasters?"*). Alternatively, the teacher can simply interrupt the conversation and quickly draw attention to the problem. This might involve a very brief explicit statement of the rule. The choice of how this is done is left up to the teacher, who is the expert on what would be the best way to handle a given situation with his or her group of students.

6. Assess the TBLT training by criterion-referenced tests.

In this particular example, assessment could take the form of having the students actually engage in the shopping activities for which they have trained. The ultimate test is whether they can carry out these tasks. It may not be possible to have them actually perform more complex tasks, but activities such as making classroom presentations and writing reports may give a good measure of the level of success attained.

7. Evaluate the program.

This is frequently done by soliciting student feedback about which parts of the TBLT instruction were effective and which areas could stand improvement.

TBLT is becoming more popular with language teachers. It seems to be an excellent way of moving beyond the confines of the grammar presentations contained in textbooks. Two caveats need to be mentioned, however. Some teachers feel that TBLT works better with students who are not beginners. Also, for this method to be effective, teachers must have a reasonably high level of competence in English. Examples and evaluations of the successes and problems encountered by teachers and students in actual TBLT programs can be found in Leaver and Willis (2004). One of the interesting comments made by teachers in some of these programs described in the book was a felt need for some explicit grammar point to be embodied in the tasks as a starting point for the collaboration. The next approach to language teaching we will look at is called *processing instruction*. It is based on a model of second language acquisition.

Processing Instruction

Processing instruction (PI) originated as a result of an observation made by its creator, Bill VanPatten. VanPatten noticed that English native speakers studying Spanish consistently misinterpreted a particular word order in Spanish. English grammar has a basic subject–verb–object (SVO) word order, as does Spanish. But Spanish also permits OVS word order with object pronouns, so the object pronoun *lo* ("him") can appear before a verb in a sentence such as (2).

(**2**) *Lo   sigue   su   madre.*
him   follows   his   mother
"His mother follows him."

VanPatten saw that the English native speakers were invariably applying the SVO English word order to these sentences and interpreting the object pronoun as a subject pronoun. As a result, native speakers would interpret (2) as *He follows his mother.* Errors such as this suggested to VanPatten serious shortcomings in the traditional form of explicit grammar instruction, in which students get a sample of language that illustrates a grammatical rule, *input*, and are then immediately required to produce those samples, *output*. VanPatten argues that this quick progression does not allow learners to make "the form-meaning connection" (VanPatten, 1996) necessary for L2 acquisition. This "form-meaning connection," called *intake*, is a central concept in VanPatten's theory of SLA. *Input* must be noticed and comprehended to become *intake*. The process of converting input to intake, referred to as *input processing*, allows the input to become part of the *developing system* that constitutes the learner's evolving knowledge of the L2. Of course, not all input becomes intake. Just repeating input without making the form-meaning connection does not result in intake. And this is what VanPatten believes happens in traditional language learning. Input that is converted to intake is then available to become *output*, sentences that reflect the learners developing system.

Processing instruction is designed to get students to enhance the chances of input becoming intake. As elaborated in VanPatten (1996), PI involves three stages: (1) learners are given information about a particular linguistic structure (an explicit description); (2) they are then informed about a particular input-processing structure that might negatively affect their ability to make the form-meaning connection; and (3) they are "pushed to process the structure with *structured input*" – input that is manipulated so that the students have a better chance of attending to it. The structured input "pulls the students away from their natural (L1) processing tendencies" toward correct (L2) processing.

In VanPatten's theory of SLA, output, the language produced by students, plays no part in fostering learning. It is simply the product of intake and its integration into the developing system. Hence, richer intake produces better quality output. In fact, on the basis of one study (VanPatten & Oikennon, 1996), VanPatten claimed that explicit explanation could be dropped from PI, since enhancing input is, by itself, shown to be sufficient for promoting both comprehension and production. However, a number of researchers have presented evidence that learner output plays an important role in SLA. We will now examine the arguments for this.

Approaches Based on the Output Hypothesis

The idea that producing language facilitates mastery of L2 grammar was raised by Merrill Swain in the form of the *output hypothesis*. Looking at data from French immersion programs in Canada, Swain (1985) found that L2 learners who received a great deal of comprehensible input in different settings and contexts developed good comprehension; however, their ability to speak and write fell far below this level. Reasons for the disparity were suggested by Gass (1997), who argued that producing utterances requires more attention to grammatical form than input processing does. She noted that, when reading or listening, L2 learners can focus on meaning by using lexical (word) and nonlinguistic (pictures, facial expressions) cues, but that producing oral or written language requires accessing and using L2 grammar rules. The task of producing accurate L2 output must, therefore, facilitate and solidify the evolving grammatical system, the *interlanguage*, of learners more than receptive tasks such as listening and reading, in which input processing is at a premium. Similarly, Swain and Lapkin (1995) argued that in producing L2 output, learners will notice problems and this noticing will "push" them to modify output. The modification of output focuses the learner's attention on syntactic processing, thus it promotes the development of grammatical competence.

The arguments for the importance of output in the development of competence in L2 acquisition have been supported by a number of studies, all of which involve comparing instruction that enhances input with instruction that focuses on production. DeKeyser and Sokalski (2001) found that the relative effectiveness of the two types of instruction depends upon the structure. Input processing works well for teaching things such as verb endings, but complex structures are more effectively taught with output practice.

Nagata (1998), in a study that incorporated computer assisted instruction, found that an output-focused group performed significantly better than an input-focused group on production and comprehension tasks. DeKeyser and Sokalski (2001) examined the results from 82 first-year students and concluded that processing instruction is better for developing comprehension skills, but output practice is better for developing production. Allan (2000), in a study on learning French causative structures, found the same effect, and Izumi's (2002) study of 60 ESL students with various L1s concluded that "no support was found for the hypothesis that the effect of input enhancement was comparable to that of output." Thus, there appears to be a strong case that classroom instruction that emphasizes production improves ESL/EFL students' command of grammar.

DISCUSSION QUESTIONS 3.1

1. What arguments are used to justify the usefulness of communicative language teaching, grammar in context, and task-based language teaching? Are they arguments that appeal to a teacher's common sense, or are they based on classroom research showing the effectiveness of the approach?
2. How do the arguments presented for the usefulness of processing instruction and the output hypothesis differ from those used for the approaches in question 1? Do you find these arguments more or less compelling? Why?
3. What kinds of arguments would convince you to try a particular approach to teaching?

CLASSROOM APPLICATIONS

We turn now to an examination of some of the classroom applications of the approaches to grammar teaching discussed in the previous section. Space limitations prevent a detailed presentation of all of these applications.

Communicative Language Teaching Activities

Classroom instruction in communicative language teaching involves using games, puzzle solving, role-playing, storytelling, discussing ideas, deciding on a course of action, taking a point of view, and making intelligent guesses about a picture shown in conjunction with an oral presentation. A key factor in the communicative classroom is the shift in roles of the teacher and the students from those they play in traditional language teaching. In CLT, the teacher does not direct the classroom activities. Instead, the students work together in small groups or pairs to achieve meaning through interaction, while the teacher steps into the background and is available to guide and to resolve problems that arise in the course of the students' attempts to communicate. This shift in roles has been a source of controversy. Students who are accustomed to traditional teacher-fronted classrooms often feel uncomfortable in this new context when they are asked to express themselves in a language over which they have only a rudimentary control.

Grammar in Context Activities

Nunan uses several kinds of classroom activities to encourage students to explore the relationships between grammar and discourse. In one activity, students are given two conversations on the same topic – one taken from a textbook and one a genuine recorded conversation – and are asked to guess which one is authentic, or natural language. Then they are asked to determine the language that the textbook version is designed to teach and the actual language they would need to use in the authentic version.

In another activity, which Nunan refers to as *information packaging*, the teacher begins by presenting an example of how to combine, or *package*, two sentences on the same topic. Then, students are given a list of sentences that are simplified versions of sentences taken from a paragraph on the same topic as the example and are asked to create a passage by packaging the sentences. Next, they share their passages with each other and note the similarities and differences in the way sentences were packaged. Finally, they revise their passages and then compare them with the original text.

Task-Based Language Teaching

Even if an English language teacher does not go through all seven steps described for TBLT, it is still possible to create tasks that involve the realistic use of specific grammatical rules. These tasks can be "closed," that is, highly structured with only one possible solution, as opposed to "open" unstructured tasks often used in TBLT.

An example of a closed task would be the well-known information gap activity, in which, for example, two students determine whether they have the same picture. Students may not look at their partner's picture but must ask whether it includes a specific element. They take turns asking and answering questions. This task requires them to use the nonreferential *there* structure in questions and answers (e.g., *Is there a chair in your picture? No, there isn't. Yes, there is.*). It is communicative in the sense that the participants must use English to accomplish something, and it promotes an awareness of the form of nonreferential *there* sentences. (See Chapter 7 for coverage of nonreferential *there*.) A closed task is also collaborative, since two students work together to achieve successful communication.

In many cases, students can actually engage in tasks outside the classroom that utilize specific grammar. For instance, after practicing various questions, students can be given the task of asking directions to a particular destination. Generally speaking, for those teachers who wish to focus more specifically on grammatical form within this method, a key requirement is to design tasks that either require or have the possibility of eliciting specific grammatical structures (Ellis, 1995; Fotos, 1993; Loschky & Bley-Vroman, 1993; Mackey, 1999; Nobuyoshi & Ellis, 1993). TBLT research and common sense suggest that students' awareness of a grammatical form is more heightened when task instructions are kept relatively simple (DeKeyser, 1998; Ellis, 2003; Robinson, 1996). The Suggestions for Teaching sections in this book often include collaborative tasks designed to practice specific grammar points.

Enhancing Input

Two classroom applications that shape the input that students must process are input flood and textual enhancement. They are popular with teachers who subscribe to VanPatten's processing instruction.

Input Flood

Input flood is simply supplying students with many instances of targeted grammatical structures. It is a logical classroom application of PI, since it provides repeated instances of structures that will, it is hoped, be noticed and become intake. As Wong (2005, p. 44) points out, input flood can be incorporated in the classroom through stories, which students listen to or read, that have been modified to stress specific grammatical structures, and through the use of the targeted structures in instructions and classroom language.

Although repeated instances of structures would be expected to foster noticing and create some permanent change in student grammars, some studies (e.g., Spada & Lightbown, 1993) have found input flood to have no effect or only a temporary effect. One oft-cited example is a 1993 study by Trahey and White, who employed input flood in an attempt to get their francophone Canadian students to stop making errors like in (3).

(3) *Mary takes often the metro.

This common error results from a difference between French and English in the placement of adverbs. As shown in (4a), French permits adverbs like *souvent*, "often," to occur between the main verb (*prend*) and the direct object (*le métro*). As shown in (4b), it does not permit adverbs between the subject and the verb, the favored position for English.

(4) a. *Marie   prend   souvent   le   métro.*
　　　 *Marie   takes   often   the   metro.
　　 b. **Marie   souvent   prend   le   métro.*
　　　　 Mary   often   takes   the   metro.

Trahey and White had initial success in getting their students to place English adverbs in the position that is not allowed in French, but the change did not last over time.

Spada and Lightbown (1993) conjecture that instruction and feedback, which includes some information about the contrast between the L1 and target L2 structure in the flooded input might produce better results than input flood alone. Wong (2005), takes a similar position. She suggests that input flood can be made more effective if students are required to respond to the input through associated activities such as taking a quiz, answering questions about the flooded input, or performing a task (e.g., reconstructing a story or drawing a picture based on directions).

Textual Enhancement

Textual enhancement refers to the practice of typographically highlighting a particular grammatical structure in a written passage – for example, with capital letters, boldface, underlining, italics, or some combination of these. The purpose is to draw students' attention to the particular structure in the written input. The excerpt in (5) comes from a text by White (1998), who was attempting to determine if textual enhancement would help French elementary-level students learn to use English possessive determiners.

> (5) The king and **his** daughter lived near a dark forest. There was a deep well near the castle. Sometimes the princess would sit by the well and play with **her** ball. Once the princess threw **her** ball into the air, but it did not fall into **her** hands.

Textual enhancement is appealing because it is quite easy for teachers to construct passages such as (5). Structures that especially lend themselves to textual enhancement include noun and verb endings and single-word constituents such as pronouns, determiners, quantifiers, and prepositions.

However, passages must be carefully constructed. As Wong (2005) points out, teachers may construct passages that contain too many different grammatical features and thus reduce the effectiveness of the input. Moreover, although textual enhancement seems like a quick and easy way of providing enhanced input, there is evidence that it often does not promote learning that results in improved production. White's study, referred to previously, showed that students' accuracy with possessive determiners did not differ from that of students with whom textual enhancement was not used. A similar result was obtained by Overstreet (1998). Two studies, Doughty (1991) and Fotos (1994), showed that students using textually enhanced material did make improvements in proficiency. These studies must be weighed, however, against newer studies in which no gains in accuracy were found (Leow, 2001; Izumi, 2002). Until we understand why textual enhancement frequently does not promote learning, teachers should be cautious about embracing it wholeheartedly as a quick and easy method that works.

Output Practice

As we have seen, tasks are one way of providing students with the opportunity to produce language. However, tasks are often open-ended, and there is no guarantee that the output will focus students' attention on problem structures and stimulate them to make judgments that will lead to a restructuring of their grammar. One classroom technique that appears to address this problem is *pushed output*.

Pushed output is a classroom application of the research on the output hypothesis. Swain argued in a series of articles (1995, 2000, 2001) that when L2 learners are encouraged to produce language that is slightly beyond their current level of ability, this "pushes" them to achieve greater accuracy. The language that students produce in these situations is also referred to as pushed output.

A collaborative task that has been used to produce pushed output is the *dictogloss*, or *dicto-comp*, described by Wajnryb (1990). The teacher chooses a text that contains examples of a structure that students do not yet completely command. After reading this text twice, the teacher divides the students into pairs or small groups and asks them to reproduce what they have heard as accurately as possible. For example, if students have had some initial exposure to relative clauses and can produce subject and object relative clauses, as in (6a) and (6b), but do not command prepositional relative clauses, as in (6c), and (6d), a passage for the dictogloss can be chosen or rewritten to contain all four patterns.

(6) a. That is the guy who gave us directions to your house.
    b. The guy who we asked gave us good directions.
    c. The guy who we were talking with gave us good directions.
    d. The guy with whom we were talking knows how to get to your house.

Several classroom studies (Kowal & Swain, 1994; Swain, 2000; Swain & Lapkin, 2001, 2002) suggest that the dictogloss task does result in greater accuracy and causes some students to notice the problems in their output and hence to collaborate with their partners in solving these problems. In view of such studies, the dictogloss is certainly worth consideration as a teaching technique.

DISCUSSION QUESTIONS 3.2

1. For which level of proficiency (beginning, intermediate, advanced) does each technique seem most useful for teaching English learners? Do any of the techniques seem useful for teaching students at every level? Explain your answers.
2. Which techniques do you believe are best suited for teaching English to preteens and teenagers?

GRAMMATICAL ERRORS

Every teacher of English is aware that students' progress is marked by an abundance of grammatical errors. These errors have several sources.

Causes of Grammatical Errors

We can identify four sources of grammatical errors made by L2 learners.

Performance Errors

Some ungrammatical sentences produced by English learners may be caused by the same factors that contribute to errors made by native speakers of English. We call these *performance errors* to indicate that the error is not due to the speaker's ignorance of the grammatical rules. Instead, it is a processing mistake that occurs while a language learner or a native speaker is in the act of speaking or writing. A good example of this might be lack of subject-verb agreement in a sentence (e.g., the verb has a plural form even though the subject is singular) as in (7).

(7) *No matter where you live, the great taste of your favorite Lays flavors *are* just around the corner.

In sentence (7), the verb should be *is* (not *are*) to agree with the actual subject, *taste*. But the native speaker who produced this sentence, an advertisement writer, was apparently influenced by the immediately preceding noun, *flavors*, and thus incorrectly chose the plural form, *are*. Performance errors such as this one probably constitute the smallest percentage of all errors that English language learners make.

Imperfect Learning

Often English learners simply have not internalized a rule and/or the restrictions that apply to that rule. For example, a learner who produces a sentence such as (8) has probably not mastered the rules for forming English *yes/no* questions (questions that can be answered by *yes* or *no*).

(8) *Does he goes to school every day?

The question is almost grammatical. The learner has put the auxiliary verb *do* in front of the sentence and made the form of *do* agree with the subject. However, the learner has also used the form of the main verb that agrees with the subject (*goes*), and this is what makes the sentence ungrammatical. The learner has not learned that the main verb has to be in its bare infinitive form, *go*.

As we might expect, a large number of the recorded errors made by learners with elementary and intermediate proficiency are a reflection of imperfect learning. The imperfect learning error shown in (8) is a common error and, as we will see in more detail in Chapter 4, represents one stage of development in the gradual process that English language learners make as they attempt to produce grammatically correct English *yes/no* questions. Pienemann, Johnston, and Brindley (1988) claim that learners always progress through the sequence shown in (9).

(9) **Stage 1:** (fragments or single words with rising intonation)
　　　　　Speak English?
　　　　　Charles in house?
　　Stage 2: (subject-verb order with rising intonation)
　　　　　He speak English?
　　　　　Charles is in the house?
　　Stage 3: (Insertion of *do* at the beginning of the sentence)
　　　　　Does he speaks English?
　　　　　Does Charles is in the house?
　　Stage 4: (Base form in the main verb; inversion of subject and verb)
　　　　　Does he speak English?
　　　　　Is Charles in the house?

As you can see, the error in (8) marks the third stage that English learners progress through before reaching stage 4, grammatically correct *yes/no* questions. Some learners may remain stuck at stage 3, even though they may have a native-speaker command of other aspects of English grammar.

Evidence for developmental sequences has also been found for English negative sentences and tense forms (Pienemann, 1984, 1987, 1988, 2003; Clahsen, 1987; Bardovi-Harlig, 1999). Based on such data, Pienemann (1984) proposed his "teachability hypothesis," which states that no amount of instruction will move learners to another stage unless they are ready to move. In testing the hypothesis, Pienemann (1988, 1999) found that learners made the best progress when they received instruction that emphasized the next stage beyond their current stage. Two studies by Spada and Lightbown (1993) did not confirm this but did find that learners who made progress followed the sequence shown in (9). Pienemann (2003) now claims that his processability theory (described in Pienemann, 1998) explains the limitations of moving on from a given stage.

Currently, there seems to be a general acceptance of developmental sequences in L2 learning, although some researchers, for example, Wong (2005, p. 32) believe that instruction may speed up the process of moving to the next stage. Lightbown (2003) notes that since developmental sequences have been found for very few grammatical structures and in very few languages, it seems impractical to consider designing language teaching syllabuses around them. The existence of developmental sequences in learning does suggest that as teachers, we should be patient when students seem to be stuck at a specific stage and that instruction should be targeted at helping them move on to the next stage.

Nevertheless, it is important to recognize that not all grammatical errors reflect a stage in a developmental sequence. Two other causes of errors, to which we now turn, are *overgeneralization* and *L1 transfer*. The latter accounts for a large percentage of errors.

Overgeneralization

Overgeneralization occurs when a learner applies a grammar rule to forms that do not take it.[5] To see how this works, consider the large set of verbs that are followed by an object and an infinitive complement. Some examples are shown in (10).

	Verb	*Object*	*Infinitive Complement*
(10) Mom	advised ordered forced persuaded got caused	Bill	[to go to the party.]

The verbs in (10) have been called *influence*, or *manipulative*, verbs because they all describe a state of affairs where the object (*Bill*) is influenced, or manipulated, by the subject of the sentence (*Mom*) to carry out the action expressed in the complement (*go to the party*). It would not be surprising to find English language learners using the verb *make* to produce sentences such as (11) because *make* seems to have the same manipulative meaning as the verbs in (10).

(11) *Mom made Bill to go to the party.

The error in (11) is, in fact, very common for learners with many different L1s. The problem is that *make* is one of very few verbs, (*let* and *have* among them), that must be followed by a complement in the bare infinitive form, as shown in (12).

(**12**) a. Mom *made* Bill *go* to the party.
     b. Susan *let* her daughter *wear* the sweater she liked so much.
     c. Liz *had* the plumber *install* a new sink in the bathroom.

Influence of the Native Language

Many of the ungrammatical sentences that English language learners produce result from the transferring of grammar rules from their native language to English. These *L1 transfer errors* can take many forms. For instance, sometimes a grammatical property associated with certain L1 verbs is transferred when the student begins to learn English. In Spanish, for example, verbs that have meanings equivalent to English modal verbs (such as *can* and *should*) are always followed by infinitives. The Spanish verb *poder*, which is the closest equivalent to the English modal verb *can*, is followed by the infinitive form *ir* (*to go*), as shown in (13).

(**13**) *Podemos   ir   en taxi.*
     We can   to go   in taxi.
     "We can go by taxi."

Because of this pattern in their L1, Spanish speakers, particularly beginners, frequently put the verb that follows an English modal verb in the infinitive form. Thus, when attempting to express the meaning of (13) in English, they produce the error shown in (14).

(**14**) *We can *to go* by taxi.

There is a substantial body of SLA research literature that supports the claim that many errors are traceable to the grammar of the L1.[6] Over the past two decades, a large number of SLA researchers have been investigating the ability of adults to learn L2 grammatical rules that appear less frequently than others in the languages of the world. This research paradigm is referred to as the *UG* (*universal grammar*) or the *parameters model*, and it has produced a systematic explanation of why speakers of some languages make particular errors when learning English, such as omitting object pronouns or placing frequency adverbs in the wrong position in a sentence, as illustrated in (4).[7] Researchers working within this paradigm have also raised the question of whether such errors can be overcome with focused instruction that involves correction. Some of these errors are briefly described in the chapters of this book where the research is germane. The question of whether grammatical errors should be addressed in your teaching is also dealt with.

Addressing Grammatical Errors

What should we do about the grammatical errors students make? Should we focus on every error, or on just a few? To answer these questions, we must look at the development of *interlanguage* – something that has been studied extensively for the past two decades.

Interlanguage Development

Interlanguage (IL)[8] refers to the language system (the grammar) that evolves as a learner studies an L2. At any given point in the development of a learner's IL, some aspects of the IL grammar may be identical to L2 grammar, but other aspects will be different. The eventual result of instruction and years of practice speaking an L2 will produce an IL we can call the *end-state grammar* (White, 2002) or *stabilized grammar* (Long, 2003). This is the grammar that the learner will use for communicating with native speakers of the L2 from that point on. It will not change much, and it probably will not be identical to the grammar of a native speaker, but it may be very close to it. (There are of course exceptions. Some L2 learners can pass for native speakers.) Thus, according to this model, the process of learning English is a process by which a learner begins to develop an IL, and that IL continues to grow more and more similar to the English grammar of a native speaker until it stabilizes (or reaches its end state). We could illustrate this evolution in a diagram such as (15), which depicts the ILs of three students.

(**15**) Interlanguages of 3 ESL students

Speaker A: L1 _____ IL1 .... L2 (English)

Speaker B: L1 _____ IL2 .... L2 (English)

Speaker C: LI _____ IL3 .... L2 (English)

The diagram illustrates the fact that the ILs of different learners vary in their approximation to the grammar of the L2 that is being learned. However, these diagrams do not provide a detailed picture of the individual IL grammars. They do not, for instance, show us which features make IL1 different from IL2. Are some of the errors present in IL1 absent from IL2? Are transfer errors present at all in IL3? Or have they disappeared or been replaced by other kinds of errors as the student approaches grammatical competence in English?

Until recently, it was not possible to know with any certainty the role of transfer errors in the development of a learner's IL. The compilation of large corpora of learner errors allows us to better understand the contributions of learners' native languages to their evolving ILs. By applying corpus analysis tools to L2 learner corpora that represent a broad range of proficiencies, ranging from beginning- to advanced-level learners, we can determine which L1 transfer errors are highly persistent and which disappear at earlier stages of IL development.[9]

Large corpora show a number of interesting trends regarding the persistence of L1 transfer errors as learners' ILs develop. Taking errors made by Spanish-speaking students as an example (Cowan & Leeser, 2007), we see that some errors, such as the use of infinitives after a modal verb as in (14) and (16), often disappear early as a student's proficiency increases. This seems to occur regardless of how much or how little correction students receive from teachers.

(**16**) *I *must to talk* in English, and the most important thing is that I *must to pronounce* correct English.

Other errors, such as the omission of *it* at the beginning of a sentence like (17a), also seem to disappear on their own. However, the problem may continue to appear in subordinate clauses, as shown in (17b).

(**17**) a. *Is very hard to live without privacy.
b. *To answer that question, is important to make a clear distinction between . . .

Still other errors, such as the placing of the definite article *the* in front of names and titles, as shown in (18), often do not disappear and may become part of a learner's stabilized IL grammar.

(18) *The President Lyndon Johnson undertook this policy in 1964.

What are the implications of this information for teaching? First, it helps us to understand that some errors will require more work to correct than others. Although we can expect some transfer errors to disappear relatively early in the developmental process, others will continue to appear in students' speech and writing. The persistent errors will require more attention from teachers and more long-term practice. The less persistent errors, on the other hand, will require less attention. In fact, in some cases they may not be worth addressing at all.

Throughout this book, we will draw on corpus-based and other SLA research in order to describe specific kinds of grammatical errors that are good candidates for pedagogical intervention. By the same token, we will note when a common error may not be worth addressing because it is likely to disappear as the learner receives more input in English.

Correcting Grammatical Errors

The issue of whether to address grammatical errors has been debated for some time. Some like Schwartz and Gubala-Ryzak (1992) and Truscott (1996) have argued the futility of any error correction but there is a body of evidence supporting the effectiveness of error correction. This evidence comes from research that focused on the interaction between teachers and students and how feedback from teachers can encourage students to "notice" the grammatical errors that they are making.[10] This *interaction feedback research* is devoted to determining which kinds of feedback are most effective in producing a sudden moment of insight, when a student notices the difference between what he or she has said and what the grammatical rule dictates. Many researchers in this field feel that without such moments, very little progress will be made in improving the student's grammar. A major consideration is how a teacher can get the student to notice a grammatical error and correct it without interrupting the communication that is taking place.

One technique that has been used with some success is called *recasting*. In recasting, the teacher draws the student's attention to what he or she has just said, with the expectation that the student will self-correct. Recasting can take several forms. In (19), we see the teacher asking a question that calls for a correction.[11]

(19) Student: He goed out at 8 o'clock.
Teacher: I see.
Student: And then he . . .
Teacher: But, uhm, goed, goed, is that correct?
Student: No . . . uhm, went. He went out.

A variation on this is to repeat what the student says, emphasizing the forms that need to be changed to draw sufficient attention to the need to repair the utterance. If the student does not respond, the teacher supplies a correct form to invoke a response. In (20), a teacher attempts to get a student to notice that the main verb and the modal verb in the sentence he has just uttered need to be changed to express past action. The teacher does this by stressing these two words in her repetition of the student's utterance. The student does not respond, so the teacher models the correct form, and the student then incorporates it.[12]

(**20**) José: I think the worm will go under the soil.
Teacher: I *think* that the worm *will* go under the soil?
(no response)
Teacher: I *thought* that the worm *would* go under the soil.
José: I *thought* that the worm *would* go under the soil.

Although the overall effectiveness of recasting remains to be determined by future research,[13] this technique has been shown to increase learners' use of certain grammatical forms (Doughty & Varela, 1998). The advantages of getting students to notice errors and to repair them without seriously interrupting the flow of communication in the classroom cannot be underestimated. This suggests that recasting is a technique that should be part of every teacher's repertoire.

Preemptive Targeting of Errors

Another way of addressing persistent errors is through an adaptation of processing instruction. This procedure involves explicitly teaching a specific structure, then drawing attention to a frequent problem associated with that structure, and finally having students apply what they have learned by processing sentences. In this last stage, the students provide judgments about the grammaticality of sentences under the teacher's guidance. A greatly simplified example of the procedure is shown in (21). Here, the error is in the placement of adverbs that, as discussed earlier, is commonly made by French speakers.

(**21**) **Stage 1:** Description of the grammar point
The teacher describes frequency adverbs as including *always*, *continually*, *occasionally*, *often*, *regularly*, *sometimes*, and *usually* and as answering the question *How often does the action occur?* Then he or she provides examples.
She *often* comes in over an hour late.
John *always* takes the metro.
Sarah *usually* drives her father's car to work.
Stage 2: Caution regarding negative interference from L1
The teacher explains that frequency adverbs cannot come after the verb, as they do in French, coming instead between the subject and verb. He or she then provides examples of correct and incorrect placement and cautions students against making this error.
Correct: Bill often takes the metro.
Not correct: Bill takes often the metro.
Stage 3: Students' processing of structured input
A volunteer is asked to read a list of sentences that contain frequency adverbs. Some of these are grammatical (e.g., *Susan occasionally plays basketball*), but others violate the rule (e.g., **Tom takes frequently the shuttle*). Everyone is asked to indicate whether each sentence is grammatical or ungrammatical. The teacher does not offer a correction if some students declare an ungrammatical sentence to be grammatical. Instead, he or she relies on the other students to raise an objection and offer a reason for their disagreement.

This adaptation of PI can be followed by a productive writing activity or a speaking activity such as a dictogloss with a text containing multiple examples of the target structure. Used in this way, PI seems to be a good way of initially drawing students' attention to potentially persistent errors, and, as a periodic review, it may be effective in helping students to eradicate them. In this book, PI activities are suggested where the approach might be helpful.

MAKING YOUR TEACHING EFFECTIVE

Based on the information in the previous sections, we might ask this question: is there a single most effective approach for teaching ESL/EFL? The answer is no, or more precisely, it depends on who your students are.

Considerations for Teaching in K–12 Programs

If you are teaching ESL students in a K–6 program, you should draw heavily on the kinds of activities favored in communicative language teaching. Focusing on meaning is of primary importance with these students, since they are at an age where they will pick up English grammar with little or no explicit instruction. There are good grounds for believing that K–6 children respond well to language instruction that provides them with ample opportunities to use English within the context of games and activities, especially those involving music, art, and movement.

With middle and high school students, you – as well as regular classroom teachers – can integrate language learning with content from other subject areas (science, social studies, language arts, etc.) through an approach referred to as *content-based instruction*, on which there is fairly extensive literature.[14] It has become increasingly popular because of its practicality, especially with the current emphasis on standards-based curriculum and assessment. At these grades, you may choose to begin introducing more explicit grammar instruction. However, the tasks you design for the classroom should take into consideration the interests and needs of young people in general and your students in particular as well as the language standards that they will have to meet. In addition to trying to accelerate your students' abilities to speak and read English well enough to participate in classes with native speakers, your instruction should provide interactive opportunities that will help prepare them for conversing socially with their peers. Discourse markers (see Chapter 26), idioms, slang, and politeness formulas relevant to talking to adults, and teenage language would be an important part of your instruction. Use the first three steps of TBLT, particularly the needs analysis, to come up with ideas to help you design activities that will facilitate your students' abilities to communicate with their native-speaking peers.

Designing and Teaching ESP Courses

At some time, you may become involved in *English for Special Purposes* (ESP) instruction. ESP courses are specially designed for students who require English instruction for their work. So, for example, you might be asked to set up an ESP course for pilot trainees. Your instruction might focus on teaching students to comprehend and respond to the English they hear from air traffic controllers. Usually, ESP students have some proficiency in English. There are many books on how to design ESP courses, but you may also find the steps for task-based instruction described earlier useful since TBLT originated in the field of ESP. It is important to carry out a needs analysis (step 1) and to draw on the assistance of an expert in the profession of the students. This person will be able to explain what English skills are most important for your students, and this will enable you to determine which grammar structures need to be stressed. It is also important to remember that ESP courses are not general ESL/EFL courses. Designing ESP courses is somewhat daunting for most ESL/EFL teachers, since they feel they may display their ignorance of the students' profession. Nonetheless, with the assistance of a professional, you should be able to design tasks that mirror the situations in which students commonly need to use English, and you will find ESP instruction a very rewarding experience.

Evaluating Textbook Exercises

Many teachers who use this book will teach adults in ESL or EFL courses in a school setting. Most schools either adopt commercial English language teaching materials or design their own materials to use with their students, who are generally assigned (possibly by a test) to classes by levels of language proficiency. Whether produced commercially or by the school, textbooks and other materials contain some combination of the following three types of grammar exercises, which are often referred to, as here, by the classification developed by Paulston (1971).

1. Mechanical Exercises

Mechanical exercises limit the output of the students to one answer. A serious defect of this kind of exercise is that students can, in many cases, carry out the exercise successfully without understanding the sentences. A good example of a mechanical exercise is shown in (22). Here the student has to insert *got* + the past participle of the verb in parentheses to form the so-called *get* passive (see Chapter 17). Notice that we could change the noun and main verb in the sentence to nonsense words, as shown in item 2, and a student would still most likely be able to perform the exercise correctly. The exercise focuses on mechanically changing form with very little reference to meaning.

> (22) Exercise: Fill in the blanks with *get* + past participle of the verb in parentheses.
> *Example:* Who <u>got chosen</u> for the part of the movie?
> (choose)
> 1. Reagan _____ in 1980.
> (elect)
> 2. The gormish _____ last week.
> (snoodle)

Other mechanical exercises involve changing word order, verb forms, and so on, as shown in (23).

> (23) Exercise: Change the subject in each sentence to the gerund form.
> *Example:* It is a pleasure to watch children grow up.
> Watching children grow up is a pleasure.
> 1. It is difficult to learn a new language.
> 2. It is really fun to ride horses.

2. Meaningful Exercises

Meaningful exercises control student output, but more than one correct answer is possible. A sentence completion exercise, as shown in (24), would qualify as a meaningful exercise since the student cannot create meaningful sentences without knowing the rule that certain verbs, including those in the items shown, must be followed by a gerund complement. Even though possible answers are unlimited, the sentences are devoid of surrounding context and hence not really samples of language used in a conversational setting.

> (**24**) Exercise: Now make your own sentences. Complete each sentence using a gerund.
> *Example:* I really enjoy going for long walks in the country.
> 1. On the weekends, I enjoy _____.
> 2. I dislike _____.
> 3. I often regret _____.

3. Communicative Exercises

Communicative exercises involve using the rule that has been presented in a way that reflects normal communication. In such exercises, the communication should have some duration, and the student should be required to use the rule more than once. For example, if the purpose is to practice the comparative and superlative forms of adjectives (e.g., *happy / happier / happiest*), a communicative exercise might present pictures of people and have students compare them using various adjectives such as *tall, short, happy, young,* and *old.*

Another exercise might have students form and practice comparisons with *more, fewer, less, as much,* and *as many* based on the information in a table or a bar graph that shows the number of Americans who participate in a set of recreational activities as compared to the number of Canadians who participate in the same activities. Students would produce sentences such as *More Canadians watch DVDs than Americans do* or *Americans watch hockey as much as Canadians do.*

Most English language teaching textbooks contain a preponderance of the first two types of exercises, whose value is largely limited to introducing specific grammar points. Working on mechanical and meaningful exercises will not insure that students will make progress learning the grammar structures, however. Communicative exercises, which involve students in realistic communication, should promote learning. To enhance the impact of the instruction in your textbooks, you may need to create communicative activities and tasks that focus on form. It can be difficult to create communicative activities or tasks that focus on a particular grammar point, such as the comparison exercise described earlier – but there are teacher resources in books and educational Web sites that can be helpful. Throughout this book, in the Suggestions for Teaching sections, you will see examples of such activities, some of which were created by ESL teachers who have never written a textbook. These activities can serve as starting points on which you can build. They are directed at students who have different levels of proficiency in English and include writing as well as speaking activities.

An Eclectic Approach

You have no doubt noticed that the research studies on classroom instruction and, particularly, the competing theories of SLA do not always agree on what fosters learning. For example, processing instruction says that output plays no role in learning, whereas the output hypothesis says that output is crucial to developing speaking accuracy. How should teachers react to these conflicting claims? Should we choose one position and ignore the other?

The best answer may lie in the pragmatic philosophy of H. Douglas Brown, a continual contributor to the field of ESL and applied linguistics. Brown (1994) wisely points out that it may be best to strive for an "enlightened eclecticism" in language teaching rather than adopting one method of instruction exclusively. Much of the classroom research we have looked at has one serious fault: it does not test whether positive changes in grammar resulting from controlled studies have much permanence. As we saw in the Trahey and White study, initial gains may turn out to be temporary. For this reason, it is probably best not to accept a single theory of how learners acquire an L2 as definitive and adopt only the classroom applications of that theory. Each of the different approaches has different strengths. PI offers a good way to address predetermined errors, while pushed output may extend students' command of more complex grammar. Thus, Brown's philosophy makes good sense. In the context of the discussion in the previous sections, the following points should guide teachers in deciding what to incorporate in their classroom instruction.

- Collaborative language instruction in the form of pair and group activities is an established norm. However, teachers are now assuming a more active role in choosing instructional tasks and activities and guiding students to focus on forms. Explicit instruction by teachers produces greater impact than implicit instruction and is particularly useful in introducing new grammatical structures.
- Correction of errors can be effective in calling students' attention to grammatical forms. Isolated correction may have little effect, but adaptations of input processing and techniques that emphasize noticing can result in the restructuring of interlanguage grammars if they are used repeatedly. Correction through recasting is desirable because it allows communication to proceed and encourages persistence.
- Teaching should incorporate input processing as well as output practice. Learner input should be at a level that students can comprehend, but students must actively produce language to make gains in speaking and writing.
- We should recognize that grammar is important for improving skills in speaking and writing. Certain grammatical structures that are widely used in different registers, such as academic writing and journalism, need to be focused on in composition classes. A number of these are covered in greater detail in subsequent chapters.

New Developments to Consider

Finally, we should take note of two new developments that are assuming a larger role in the teaching of grammar. The first of these is *computer assisted language learning* (CALL), a vibrant if often overlooked field that specializes in the use of electronic technologies in the teaching of second languages. Emerging research shows that CALL programs can be used to improve learners' L2 grammar and their ability to edit their compositions. Furthermore, CALL research such as Cowan, Choo, and Lee (2005) shows that improvement in editing persistent errors is permanent. This has direct application to the teaching of writing. You can familiarize yourself with the work being done in this field by going to the Web site www.calico.org.

The second development is the application of corpus linguistics techniques to analyze L2 corpora. The resulting analysis of L2 learner corpora constructed by following the progress of learners through several levels of proficiency, as described in Cowan and Leeser (2007), reveal which grammatical errors disappear with increased proficiency and which remain in learners' end state grammars. We looked at this research earlier in the discussion of a learner's interlanguage. It is precisely these persistent errors that need to be addressed by pedagogical intervention. The penultimate section of each chapter, Problems That ESL/EFL Students Have . . . , is based on research studies and error corpora data that distinguish between the two kinds of errors.

CONCLUSION

In this chapter, we have looked at some of the current approaches to instruction that are being studied and incorporated in the teaching of grammar. Over the next ten years, some of these ideas will undoubtedly be shown to have marginal use in the classroom and will be largely rejected, much like past approaches such as total physical response, suggestopedia, and the use of Cuisenaire rods. This is the natural process of development in teaching English and other languages. The coverage of instructional techniques in this chapter has been limited to those that appear to be the most promising or the most commonly used. (Some methods have been included because, though perhaps less promising, they are nevertheless widely debated and, therefore, merit inclusion). The Suggestions for Teaching section in each chapter offers activities from the approaches presented here that are appropriate for the topic of grammar.

ENDNOTES

[1] Bley-Vroman refers to this as the Fundamental Difference Hypothesis.

[2] See also Gregg (1984) for an additional critique of Krashen's theory of SLA.

[3] See, for example, Skehan (1996 a, b).

[4] Savignon adapted this term for the context of L2 teaching and learning from Hymes's (1971) article, in which he proposed the concept of "communicative competence" as the capacity of using language in various contexts in society according to conventions of normal use. Communicative competence is thus a sociolinguistic concept that is distinct from grammatical competence discussed in Chapter 1.

[5] This was variously described by Selinker (1972) and Richards (1974).

[6] See Odlin (2003) for a comprehensive discussion of L1 transfer and the problems associated with determining whether errors are due to transfer.

[7] The validity of the parameter-setting model for explaining L2 acquisition is complicated by changing linguistic theory and by processing considerations such as those described in the Problems section of Chapter 13.

[8] The term was invented by Selinker (1972), a pioneer and major contributor to the study of L1 transfer and other mechanisms involved in SLA.

[9] In addition to the International Corpus of Learner English described in Granger (1998), there are new corpora of learner English in Europe and East Asia. These are emerging on a yearly basis and are organized in terms of features such as learner age, learning context, level, medium, genre, technicality, sex, L1, topic, and task setting.

[10] Studies of the effect of interaction feedback research include Doughty and Varela (1998); Iwashita (2003); Long, Inagaki, and Ortega (1998); Mackey and Philip (1998); Nassaji (1999); and Nassaji and Swain (2000). See also reviews of research in Gass, Mackey, and Pica (1998) and Gass (2003).

[11] Van den Branden (1997, 604).

[12] This example is from Doughty and Varela (1998), p. 124.

[13] See Gass (2003) for an overview.

[14] For a short review of the different types of instructional programs that fall under the rubric of *content-centered* or *content-based* instruction, see Crandall (1994).

REFERENCES

Allan, Q. (2000). Form-meaning connections and the French causative. *Studies in Second Language Acquisition*, *22*, 69–84.

Bardovi-Harlig, K. (1999). From morpheme studies to temporal semantics: Tense-aspect research in SLA. *Studies in Second Language Acquisition*, *21*, 341–381.

Beale, J. (2002). Is communicative language teaching a thing of the past? *Babel*, *37*(1), 12–16.

Bley-Vroman, R. (1989). What is the logical problem of foreign language learning? In J. Schachter & S. Gass (Eds.), *Linguistic Perspectives on Second Language Learning* (pp. 41–68). Cambridge, England: Cambridge University Press.

Brown, H. D. (1994). *Teaching by principles: An interactive approach to language pedagogy*. Englewood Cliffs, New Jersey: Prentice Hall.

Cadierno, T. (1995). Formal instruction from a processing perspective: An investigation of the Spanish past tense. *Modern Language Journal*, *79* (2), 179–193.

Carroll, S., & Swain, M. (1993). Explicit and implicit negative feedback: An empirical study of the learning of linguistic generalizations. *Studies in Second Language Acquisition*, *15*(3), 357–386.

Carter, R., Hughes, R., & McCarthy, M. (2000). *Exploring grammar in context: Grammar reference and practice*. Cambridge, England: Cambridge University Press.

Celce-Murcia, M., Dörnyei, Z., & Thurrell, S. (1997). Direct approaches in L2 instruction: A turning point in communicative language teaching? *TESOL Quarterly*, *31* (1), 141–152.

Clahsen, H. (1987). Connecting theories of language processing and (second) language acquisition. In C. Pfaff (Ed.), *First and second language acquisition processes* (pp. 103–116). Cambridge, MA: Newbury House.

Crandall, J. A. (1994, January). *Content-centered language learning*. Retrieved October 31, 2005, from www.cal.org/resources/digest/cranda01.html.

Cowan, R., Choo, J., & Lee, G. (2005). Investigating the effectiveness of a CALL program designed to improve editing. Paper presented at the 2005 *CALICO Symposium*.

Cowan, R., & Leeser, M. (2007). The structure of corpora in SLA research. In R. Facchinetti (Ed.), *Corpus linguistics 25 years on* (pp. 289–304). Amsterdam/New York: Rodopi.

DeKeyser, R. (1998). Beyond focus on form: Cognitive perspectives on learning and practicing second language grammar. In C. Doughty & J. Williams (Eds.), *Focus on form in classroom second language acquisition* (pp. 42–63). New York: Cambridge University Press.

DeKeyser, R. (2003). Implicit and explicit learning. In M. Long & C. Doughty (Eds.), *The handbook of second language acquisition* (pp. 313–348). New York: Blackwell.

DeKeyser R., & Sokalski, K. (2001). The differential role of comprehension and production practice. *Language Learning*, *46* (4), 613–642.

Doughty, C. (1991). Second language instruction does make a difference: Evidence from an empirical study of SL relativization. *Studies in Second Language Acquisition*, *13*, 431–469.

Doughty, C. (2003). Instructed SLA: Constraints, compensation, and enhancement. In M. Long and C. Doughty (Eds.), *The handbook of second language acquisition* (pp. 256–310). New York: Blackwell.

Doughty, C., & Varela, E. (1998). Communicative focus on form. In C. Doughty & J. Williams (Eds.), *Focus on form in classroom second language acquisition* (pp. 114–138). New York: Cambridge University Press.

Doughty, C., & Williams, J. (1998). *Focus on form in classroom second language acquisition*. New York: Cambridge University Press.

Ellis, N. C. (1995). Consciousness in second language acquisition: A review of field studies and laboratory experiments. *Language Awareness, 4*, 123–146.

Ellis, R. (1990). *Instructed second language acquisition: Learning in the classroom*. Oxford: Blackwell.

Ellis, R. (1994). *The study of second language acquisition*. Oxford: Oxford University Press.

Ellis, R. (1997). *SLA research and language teaching*. Oxford: Oxford University Press.

Ellis, R. (2001). Introduction: Investigating form-focused instruction. *Language Learning, 51*, 1–46.

Ellis, R. (2002). Does form-focused instruction affect the acquisition of implicit knowledge? *Studies in Second Language Acquisition, 24*, 223–236.

Ellis, R. (2003). *Task-based language learning and teaching*. Oxford: Oxford University Press.

Fotos, S. (1993). Consciousness-raising and noticing through focus on form: Grammar task performance vs. formal instruction. *Applied Linguistics, 14* (4), 299–323.

Fotos, S. (1994). Integrating grammar instruction and communicative language use through grammar consciousness-raising tasks. *TESOL Quarterly, 28* (2), 323–351.

Gass, S. (1997). *Input, interaction and the second language learner*. Mahwah, NJ: Lawrence Erlbaum.

Gass, S. (2003). Input and interaction. In M. Long & C. Doughty (Eds.), *The handbook of second language acquisition* (pp. 224–255). New York: Blackwell.

Gass, S. M., Mackey, A., & Pica, T. (1998). The role of input and interaction in second language acquisition. *Modern Language Journal, 2*(3), 299–307.

Gass, S. & Varonis, E. (1994). Input, interaction and second language production. *Studies in Second Language Acquisition Research, 16*, 283–302.

Granger, S. (1998). The computer learner corpus: A versatile new source of data for SLA research. In S. Granger (Ed.), *Learner English on computer* (pp. 3–18). London: Longman.

Gregg, K. (1984). Krashen's monitor and Occam's razor. *Applied Linguistics, 5*, 78–100.

Hammerly, H. (1987). The immersion program: Litmus test of second language acquisition through language communication. *The Modern Language Journal, 71*, 395–401.

Han, Z-H. (2000). Persistence of the implicit influence of the NL: The case of the pseudo passive. *Applied Linguistics, 21* (1), 55–82.

Harley, B. (1989). Functional grammar in French immersion: A classroom experiment. *Applied Linguistics, 10* (3), 331–359.

Harley, B. (1993). Instructional strategies and SLA in early French immersion. *Studies in Second Language Acquisition, 15*, 245–260.

Harley, B. & Swain, M. (1984). The interlanguage of immersion students and its implications for second language teaching. In A. Davies, C. Criper, & A. P. R. Howatt (Eds.), *Interlanguage* (pp. 291–311). Edinburgh, Scotland: Edinburgh University Press.

Hymes, D. (1971). Competence and performance in linguistic theory. In R. Huxley & E. Ingram (Eds.), *Language acquisition: Models and methods* (pp. 3–28). London: Academic Press.

Hymes, D. (1971). Communicative competence. In J. B. Pride & J. Holms (Eds.), *Sociolinguistics* (pp. 269–293). Harmondsworth, England: Penguin.

Iwashita, N. (2003). Negative evidence and positive feedback in task-based interaction. *Studies in Second Language Acquisition, 25, 1,* 1–36.

Izumi, S. (2002). Output, input enhancement and the noticing hypothesis: An experimental study on ESL relativization. *Studies in Second Language Acquisition, 24,* 1–36.

Kowal, M., & Swain, M. (1994). Using collaborative language production tasks to promote students' language awareness. *Language Awareness, 3,* 73–93.

Krashen, S. (1985). *The input hypothesis: Issues and implications.* London: Longman.

Krashen, S. (1989). We acquire vocabulary and spelling by reading: Additional evidence for the input hypothesis. *Modern Language Journal, 73,* 440–464.

Krashen, S. (1993). The effect of formal grammar teaching: Still peripheral. *TESOL Quarterly, 27,* 722–725.

Krashen, S., & Terrel, T. (1983). *The natural approach: Language acquisition in the classroom.* Hayward, CA: Alemany Press.

Kumaravadivelu, B. (1994). The post-method condition: Emerging strategies for second/foreign language teaching. *TESOL Quarterly, 28*(2), 27–48.

Lardiere, D. (1998a). Case and tense in the fossilized steady-state. *Second Language Research, 14,* 1–26.

Lardiere, D. (1998b). Disassociating syntax from morphology in a divergent L2 end-state grammar. *Second Language Research, 14,* 359–375.

Lardiere, D. (2000). Mapping features to forms in second language acquisition. In J. Archibald (Ed.), *Second language acquisition and linguistic theory.* New York: Blackwell.

Lapkin, S., Hart, D., & Swain, M. (1991). Early and middle French immersion programs: French language outcomes. *Canadian Modern Language Review, 48,* 11–40.

Larsen-Freeman, D., & Long, M. (1991). *An introduction to second language research.* New York: Longman.

Leaver, B. L., & Willis, J. R. (2004). *Task-based instruction in foreign language education.* Washington, D.C.: Georgetown University Press.

Leow, R. (2001). Attention, awareness, and foreign language behavior. *Language Learning, 51,* 113–155.

Lightbown, P. (1991). What have we here? Some observations on the influence of instruction on L2 learning. In R. Philipson, E. Kellerman, L. Selinker, M. Sharwood-Smith, & M. Swain (Eds.), *Foreign/Second language pedagogy research*: *A commemorative volume for Clause Faerch* (pp. 197–212). Clevedon, UK: Multilingual Matters.

Lightbown, P. (1992). Can they do it themselves? A comprehension-based learning ELS course for young children. In R. Courchene, J. S. John, & J. Glidden, (Eds.), *Comprehension-based second language teaching.* Ottawa, Canada: University of Ottawa Press.

Lightbown, P. (2003). SLA research in the classroom. *Language Teaching Journal, 28,* 4–13.

Lightbown, P., Halter, R., White, J., & Horst, M. (2002). Comprehension-based learning: The limits of "do it yourself." *Canadian Modern Language Review, 58,* 427–464.

Lightbown, P., & Spada, N. (1990). Focus on form and corrective feedback in communicative language teaching: Effects on second language learning. *Studies in Second Language Acquisition, 12,* 429–448.

Long, M. (1997). Focus on form in task-based language teaching. *Fourth Annual McGraw-Hill Satellite Teleconference.*

Long, M. (2003). Stabilization and fossilization in interlanguage development. In C. Doughty & M. Long (Eds.), *The handbook of second language acquisition* (pp. 487–536). Oxford: Blackwell.

Long, M., Inagaki, S., & Ortega, L. (1998). The role of implicit negative feedback in SLA: Models and recasts in Japanese and Spanish. *Modern Language Journal, 82* (3), 357–371.

Loschky, L., & Bley-Vroman, R. (1993). Grammar and task-based methodology. In G. Crookes & S. Gass (Eds.), *Tasks and language learning* (pp. 123–163). Clevedon, UK: Multilingual Matters.

Mackey, A. (1999). Input, interaction and second language development: An empirical study of question formation. *Studies in Second Language Acquisition, 21,* 557–587.

Mackey, A., & Philip, J. (1998). Conversational interaction and language development: Recasts, responses and red herrings? *Modern Language Journal, 82*(3), 338–356.

Master, P. (1994). The effect of systematic instruction on learning the English article system. In T. Odlin (Ed.), *Perspectives on pedagogical grammar* (pp. 229–252). Cambridge, England: Cambridge University Press.

McLaughlin, B. (1987). *Theories of second-language learning.* London: Edward Arnold.

Mitchell, R. (2000). Applied linguistics and evidence-based classroom practice: The case of foreign language grammar pedagogy. *Applied Linguistics, 21,* 281–303.

Nagata, N. (1998). Input vs. output practice in educational software for second language acquisition. *Language Learning and Technology Journal, 1, 2,* 23–40.

Nassaji, H. (1999). Towards integrating form-focused instruction and communicative interaction in the second language classroom: Some pedagogical possibilities. *The Canadian Modern Language Review, 55,* 385–402.

Nassaji, H. (2002). Schema theory and knowledge-based processes in second language reading comprehension: A need for alternative perspectives. *Language Learning 52*(2), 439–481.

Nassaji, H., & Swain, M. (2000). A Vygotskian perspective on corrective feedback: The effect of random versus negotiated help on the learning of English articles. *Language Awareness, 9,* 34–51.

Nobuyoshi, J., & Ellis, R. (1993) Focused communication tasks and second language acquisition. *ELT Journal, 47,* 113–128.

Norris, J., & Ortega, L. (2000). Effectiveness of L2 instruction: A research synthesis and quantitative meta-analysis. *Language Learning, 50,* 417–428.

Nunan, D. (1989). *Designing tasks for the communicative classroom.* Cambridge, England: Cambridge University Press.

Nunan, D. (1998). Teaching grammar in context. *ELT Journal, 52*(2), 101–109.

Odlin, T. (2003). Cross-linguistic Influence. In C. Doughty & M. Long (Eds.), *The handbook of second language acquisition* (pp. 436–486). Malden, MA: Blackwell.

Overstreet, M. (1998). Text enhancement and text familiarity: The focus of learner attention. *Spanish Applied Linguistics, 2,* 229–258.

Paulston, C. B. (1971). The sequencing of standard pattern drills. *TESOL Quarterly, 5,* 167–208.

Paulston, C. B. (1980). The sequencing of structural pattern drills. In K. Kroft (Ed.), *Readings on English as a second language* 2nd ed. (pp. 300–316). Cambridge, MA: Winthrop.

Pienemann, M. (1984). Psychological constraints on the teachability of languages. *Studies in Second Language Acquisition, 6*(2), 186–214.

Pienemann, M. (1987). Determining the effect of instruction on L2 speech processing. *Australian Review of Applied Linguistics, 10*(2), 83–113.

Pienemann, M. (1988). Determining the influence of instruction on L2 speech processing. *AILA Review, 5,* 40–72.

Pienemann, M. (1998). *Language processing and second language development: Processability theory.* Amsterdam: John Benjamins.

Pienemann, M. (1999). *Language processing and second language development: Processability theory*. Amsterdam: John Benjamins.

Pienemann, M. (2003). Language processing capacity. In C. Doughty & M. Long (Eds.), *The handbook of second language acquisition* (pp. 679–714). Malden, MA: Blackwell.

Pienemann, M., Johnston, M., & Brindley, G. (1988). Constructing an acquisition-based procedure for second language assessment. *Studies in Second Language Acquisition, 10*(2), 217–243.

Prabhu, N. S. (1987). *Second language pedagogy*. Oxford: Oxford University Press.

Richards, J. C. (1974). Error analysis and second language strategies. In J. H. Schumann & N. Stenson (Eds.), *New frontiers in second language learning* (pp. 32–53). Rowley, MA: Newbury House.

Robinson, P. (1996). Learning simple and complex second language rules under implicit, incidental, rule search, and instructed conditions. *Studies in Second Language Acquisition, 18*, 27–68.

Savignon, S. J. (1972). *Communicative competence: An experiment in foreign language teaching*. Philadelphia: Center for Curriculum Development.

Savignon, S. J. (1983). *Communicative competence: Theory and classroom practice; texts and contexts in second language learning*. Reading, MA: Addison-Wesley.

Savignon, S. J. (1991). Communicative Language Teaching: State of the art. *TESOL Quarterly, 25*, (2) 261–277.

Schwartz, B., & Gubala-Ryzak, M. (1992). Learnability and grammar reorganization in L2A: Against negative evidence causing the unlearning of verb movement. *Second Language Research, 8.1*, 1–38.

Selinker, L. (1972). Interlanguage. *International Review of Applied Linguistics, 10*, 209–231.

Skehan, P. (1996a). A framework for the implementation of task-based instruction. *Applied Linguistics 17*, (1) 38–62.

Skehan, P. (1996b). Second language acquisition and task-based instruction. In J. Willis & D. Willis (Eds.), *Challenge and change in language teaching* (pp. 17–30). Oxford: Heinemann.

Spada, N., & Lightbown, P. (1993). Instruction and the development of questions in L2 classrooms. *Studies in Second Language Acquisition, 15*, 205–224.

Stoller, F. L. (2004). Content-based instruction: Perspectives on curriculum planning. *Annual Review of Applied Linguistics, 24*, 261–283.

Swain, M. (1985). Communicative competence: Some roles of comprehensible input and comprehensible output in its development. In S. Gass & C. Madden (Eds.), *Input in second language acquisition* (pp. 235–253). Rowley, MA: Newbury House.

Swain, M. (1995). Three functions of output in second language learning. In G. Cook & B. Seidlhofer (Eds.), *Principle and practice in applied linguistics: Studies in honor of H. G. Widdowson* (pp. 125–144). New York: Oxford University Press.

Swain, M. (2000). The output hypothesis and beyond: Mediating acquisition through collaborative dialogue. In J. P. Lantof (Ed.), *Sociolinguistic theory and second language learning* (pp. 97–114). Oxford: Oxford University Press.

Swain, M. (2001). Integrating language content teaching through collaborative tasks. *Canadian Modern Language Review, 58*, 44–63.

Swain, M., & Lapkin S. (1989). Canadian immersion and adult second language teaching – What's the connection? *Modern Language Journal, 73*, 150–159.

Swain, M., & Lapkin, S. (1995). Problems in output and cognitive processes they generate: A step towards second language learning. *Applied Linguistics, 16*, 371–391.

Swain, M., & Lapkin S. (2001). Focus on form through collaborative dialogue: Exploring task effects. In M. Bygate, P. Skehan, & M. Swain (Eds.), *Researching pedagogic tasks*: *Second language learning, teaching* and *testing*. Harlow, UK: Longman.

Swain, M., & Lapkin, S. (2002). Talking it through: Two French immersion learners' response to reformulation. *International Journal of Educational Research*, *37*, 3–4, 285–304.

Trahey, M., & White, L. (1993). Positive evidence and preemption in the second language classroom. *Studies in Second Language Acquisition*, *15*, 181–204.

Truscott, J. (1996). The case against grammar correction in L2 writing classes. *Language Learning*, *46*, 327–369.

Van den Branden, K. (1997). Effects of negotiation on language learners' output. *Language Learning*, *47*(4), 589–636.

VanPatten, B. (1996). *Input processing and grammar instruction in second language acquisition*. Norwood, NJ: Ablex.

VanPatten, B., & Oikennon, S. (1996). Explanation vs. structured input in processing instruction. *Studies in Second Language Acquisition*, *18*, 495–510.

Wajnryb, R. (1990). *Grammar dictation*. Oxford, England: Oxford University Press.

White, J. (1998). Getting the learner's attention: A typographical input enhancement study. In C. Doughty & J. Williams (Eds.), *Focus on form in classroom second language acquisition* (pp. 85–113). Cambridge, England: Cambridge University Press.

White, L. (2002). Morphological variability in endstate L2 grammars: The question of L1 influence. In B. Skarabela, S. Fish, & A. H.-J. Dp (Eds.), *Proceedings of the 26th Annual Boston University Conference on Language Development*. Somerville, MA: Cascadilla Press.

Wong, W. (2005). *Input enhancement: From theory and research to the classroom*. Boston, MA: McGraw-Hill.

CHAPTER 4

Questions

INTRODUCTION

In this chapter we learn about the different ways to form questions in English, including spoken English. The cartoon below shows something basic about English questions – they have unique *intonation* patterns. *Intonation* is simply the rising and falling of pitch over a spoken sentence.

The girl in the cartoon, Zuma, is describing an event using statements, which normally end in a falling pitch. But she applies rising pitch to the end of her statements, which is typical of English *yes/no questions* (questions that can be answered by *yes* or *no*). This is what two boys notice and are whispering about in the last panel while poking fun at Zuma by mimicking her.[1]

Because intonation is so important in forming questions in English, some example questions in this chapter are accompanied by diagrams that show their intonation patterns. The diagram is a line that traces the pitch movement throughout the question. Speakers differ in the amount of up or down change they apply, thus the direction of the line is more important than the amount of change that occurs from one pitch level to another. The predominant intonation patterns for the questions in this chapter are also described using the terms *rise* and *fall* to indicate the pitch direction.[2] For example, the *yes/no* question intonation that Zuma uses is called *rising*. The pitch moves *up* on the last word and then continues to rise beyond the stressed syllable. The *rising intonation* pattern applied to what Zuma says in the first panel of the cartoon is shown in (1).

(1) So then?

Me and this guy?

We were sharing a hamburger?

And he got this blob of ketchup on his face?

It is important that students produce the different kinds of questions in this chapter with the appropriate intonation. Just learning the grammar rules for questions is not sufficient. The intonation pattern of every question type has to be covered in class.

Questions in English can be classified in terms of four basic types: *yes/no* questions, tag questions, *wh-* questions, and miscellaneous question forms that have features in common with the first three types.

YES/NO QUESTIONS

Yes/no questions may be answered with a simple *yes* or *no*. If a declarative sentence contains an auxiliary verb like *have* or *be*, a modal auxiliary such as *may* or *could*, or the copular[3] form of *be*, a *yes/no* question is created from the sentence by applying the rule of *subject–auxiliary* (or *subject–aux*) *inversion*. *Subject–aux inversion*[4] switches the position of the subject and the verbal element that follows it.

The sentences labeled (b) in (2) through (7) are *yes/no* questions that result from the application of subject–aux inversion to the declarative sentences labeled (a). Notice that in each case, the position of the subject and the position of the verbal element that follows it have been reversed to create a question. The labels on the right describe the verb in italics in each sentence.

(2) a. He *is* a policeman.
   b. *Is* he a policeman?
                                                copular be

(3) a. She *could do* it.
   b. *Could* she *do* it?
                                                modal could + *verb*

(4) a. She *is sleeping* right now.
   b. *Is* she *sleeping* right now?
                                                aux is + *verb (present participle)*

(5) a. The boss *has read* the report.
   b. *Has* the boss *read* the report?
                                                aux has + *verb (past participle)*

(6) a. He *should have read* the report.
                                                modal should + *aux* have + *verb*
                                                (past participle)
   b. *Should* he *have read* the report?

(7) a. She *could have been working* then.
                       modal could + *aux* have + *aux*
   b. *Could* she *have been working* then?   been + *verb (present participle)*

For declarative sentences that do not have an auxiliary verb, a modal, or copular *be*, the rule of subject–aux inversion is not applied to form a *yes/no* question. Instead, an appropriate form of the auxiliary verb *do* is placed at the beginning of the sentence. This process of adding *do* to a sentence is referred to as *do insertion* or *do support*. The auxiliary *do* allows the speaker to express tense differences, as (8a) and (8b) illustrate.

	Statement	*Yes/No Question*	
(**8**) a.	He runs every day.	*Does* he run every day?	*simple present tense*
b.	He ran every day.	*Did* he run every day?	*simple past tense*

In British English, sentences with the main verb *have* (not the auxiliary verb *have*) also undergo subject–aux inversion to form *yes/no* questions, as shown in (9b). But in American English, *do* insertion is used instead, as shown in (9c). This is an important difference that teachers of English should know.

(**9**) a. You have a pencil.
   b. Have you a pencil?   *subject–aux inversion*   *British English*
   c. Do you have a pencil?   do *insertion*   *American English*

Yes/no questions carry rising intonation.[5] The diagram in (10) shows that the pitch moves up on the last word of the question, which is stressed on the first syllable, and it continues to rise at the end, a pattern called *up-rise intonation*.[6]

(**10**) Would you like to go swimming?   *up-rise intonation pattern*

Positive and Negative *Yes/No* Questions

Yes/no questions are either *positive*, as in (11a), or *negative* (i.e., they contain *not*), as in (11b).

(**11**) a. Are you coming?
   b. Aren't you coming?

Negative *yes/no* questions are formed by contracting the verbal element at the beginning of the question (auxiliary verb, modal verb, or copular *be*) with *not*. This is illustrated in (12).

	Positive	*Negative*
(**12**) a.	*Have* you been here before?	*Haven't* you been here before?
b.	*Will* you agree to those terms?	*Won't* you agree to those terms?
c.	*Were* they feeling better?	*Weren't* they feeling better?

Positive *yes/no* questions usually do not imply any expectation about what the answer will be.[7] The person who asks (11a), for instance, does not necessarily have any idea whether the answer will be *yes* (*I am coming*) or *no* (*I am not coming*). Negative questions, on the other hand, are generally asked to confirm a specific expectation or assumption on the part of the asker, as in (13).

(**13**) Susan to Alice: Didn't John tell you that I was coming?

Susan may ask Alice the negative question in (13) because she assumes, initially, that John would have told Alice that she was coming, and she wants to confirm that John did, in fact, tell her.

If Susan notices that Alice seems surprised when she shows up, her initial assumption may change to something like *It looks like John didn't tell Alice that I was coming, after all*. She may still, however, ask the same negative question to find out if her new assumption is correct.

(**14**) Susan: Didn't John tell you that I was coming?
   Alice: No. He didn't.
   Susan: Well, if he forgot, I'm sorry. I was sure that you would be expecting me.

Thus, regardless of what Susan's expectations/assumptions are as she meets Alice, she asks a negative question in order to confirm those expectations/assumptions.

Negative *yes/no* questions can often express annoyance, as in (15a), or disappointment, as in (15b), when it seems that the asker's previous expectations or hopes have not been met.

(15) a. Can't you ever give me a simple answer?
        (Implication: I want a simple answer, but apparently you can't give me one.)
     b. Haven't you called him?
        (Implication: I really hoped that you had, but it appears that you haven't.)

Negative questions that contain *positive polarity items*, like *someone, somebody*, and *already*, are posed when the asker expects a positive answer. (See Chapter 5 for more on *negative* and *positive polarity items*.)

(16) a. Didn't *somebody* call me this afternoon?
        (Implication: I'll bet somebody did.)
     b. Hasn't he *already* done that?
        (Implication: I think he has OR I was sure that he had.)

A negative answer (*no*) to either a positive or a negative *yes/no* question in English has the same meaning. This is illustrated in (17).

(17) a. Joel: Can you come to the ceremony?
        Rich: No. (= I can't come.)

     b. Joel: Can't you come to the ceremony?
        Rich: No. (= I can't come.)

Notice that an answer of *no* to both the question in (17a) and the question in (17b) serves to indicate that the person responding will not be able to attend the ceremony. This is an important point for many English language learners because in some languages (e.g., Japanese, Korean, Hausa), a *no* answer to a negative question such as (17b) means *No, that is not correct. In fact, I can come*, and a *yes* answer means *Yes, that is correct – I can't come*. This issue is discussed in more detail at the end of this chapter in Problems ESL/EFL Students Have with Questions.

Reduced *Yes/No* Questions
Yes/no questions are often reduced (shortened) in informal conversation. Two ways in which this is done are by the formation of *elliptical yes/no questions* and by the formation of *declarative* (or *statement*) *yes/no questions*.

Elliptical *Yes/No* Questions
Native speakers sometimes reduce *yes/no* questions by omitting auxiliary verbs and copular *be* to form elliptical statements with up-rise intonation.

Yes/No *Question*	Elliptical Yes/No *Question*
(18) a. Has he been talking to you?	He been talking to you?
b. Are you coming?	You coming?
c. Do you want to talk to me about it?	You want to talk to me about it?
d. Is she taking her pills regularly?	She taking her pills regularly?
e. Are you hungry?	You hungry?

Declarative *Yes/No* Questions

Declarative, or *statement*, *yes/no questions* have the form of a statement but also contain question intonation. They are often difficult to distinguish from elliptical *yes/no* questions; notice that (19a) is identical to the corresponding elliptical *yes/no* question formed by omitting *do*, whereas (19b) is slightly different, the corresponding elliptical question being *You already talked to him?* The intonation in declarative questions will not always follow the up-rise pattern shown in (19a) exactly, rather it may rise slightly and be maintained over the rest of the utterance, as shown in (19b).[8]

Yes/No *Question*	Declarative *Question*
(**19**) a. Do you play hockey?	You play hockey?
b. Have you already talked to him?	You've already talked to him?

Declarative questions have at least three functions:[9]

1. to check some piece of information.

(**20**) Robert: He said he'd be here at 8:00.

    Jay: *You've already talked to him?*

2. to repeat all or part of something that has already been said for the purpose of questioning or confirming information (see also *echo questions* later in this chapter in Other Types of *Yes/No* and *Wh-* Questions).

(**21**) Alan: Hey, Bev! Where have you been? We were supposed to meet in front of the grocery store, remember?
Beverly: I was at the police station giving the cops some information about what happened to me. I was robbed out in the parking lot when I was getting out of my car.

    Alan: *You were robbed?*
Beverly: Yeah. It happened so fast, I couldn't believe it. A guy just grabbed my purse and ran off with it.

3. to show surprise, amazement, or annoyance at what was just said (see also *exclamatory questions* later in this chapter in Other Types of *Yes/No* and *Wh-* Questions).

(**22**) Fred: You know, I'm really sorry that I scratched the fender on your car the other day.

    Al: *You scratched the fender on my car?!* You never said anything about it last night at dinner!

Quite often declarative *yes/no* questions perform two and three functions simultaneously.

SUMMARY

YES/NO QUESTIONS

Yes/no questions can be answered with a *yes* or *no*, and they normally carry up-rise intonation.

> *Would you like to go swimming?*

For sentences with auxiliaries, modal verbs, or copular *be*, *yes/no* questions are formed by applying the **subject–auxiliary inversion**.

> *Would you do the same thing?*
> *Is he a hard worker?*

For sentences without auxiliaries, modal verbs, or copular *be*, apply **do insertion** to form a *yes/no* question.

> *Does he run every day?*

> *Did you remember your passport?*

Positive yes/no questions do not imply any expectation regarding whether the answer will be *yes* or *no*.

> *Do you like winter sports?*
> *Will you be joining us?*

Negative yes/no questions are generally asked to confirm an assumption or expectation.

> *Didn't he tell you about it?*
> (Implication: I thought he had OR I'm sure he did.)

They can also express annoyance or disappointment because a previous expectation has not been met.

> *Haven't you called him yet?*
> (Implication: You were supposed to call him.)

Reduced yes/no questions are shortened question forms sometimes used in informal conversation. There are two types:

a. Elliptical yes/no questions omit auxiliary verbs and copular *be*.

> *He been talking to you?*
> *They here yet?*

b. Declarative questions have the form of a statement. They are used to:

- check information
  > *A: The food there is great.*

  > *B: You've eaten there before?*

- repeat something someone has said in order to question or confirm it
  > *A: I lost my job yesterday.*

  > *B: You lost your job?*

- express surprise or amazement
  > *A: I can't believe we lost after being up by 10 points.*

  > *B: You lost the game?!*

EXERCISE 4.1

Indicate whether each question implies any expectation or assumption on the part of the asker. If the question implies an expectation or an assumption, state what that expectation or assumption might be.

Example: Do you watch much TV?

Answer: no expectation

1. Hasn't he already told her?
2. Is she a student?
3. Isn't Ann coming too?
4. Did anyone call while I was out?
5. Did someone call while I was out?

EXERCISE 4.2

Identify the function of each declarative question shown in italics.

Example: Steve: Well, we can expect John to pitch for our team in next Sunday's game.
Alex: *You know that for sure?*
Steve: Yeah. I talked to him yesterday.

Answer: to confirm information

1. Lisa: Where is everybody?
Bonnie: Down at the drugstore watching the fire.
Lisa: *The drugstore is on fire? Oh my gosh!*
2. Alan: Hey, Bill! You know that book you lent me? I'm really sorry, but it seems I've lost it.
Bill: *You lost that book?* Man! That was a present from my brother!
3. Nancy: Well, I guess we can count on Alice to join us for dinner on Saturday.
Bob: *You've talked to her recently?*
Nancy: Yes. I called her last night, and she said she was 90 percent sure that she could come.

TAG QUESTIONS

Tag questions consist of a *tag*, which is a short question form, attached to a *stem*, which is a statement. They are of two main types: *opposite polarity* and *same polarity tag questions*.

Opposite Polarity Tag Questions

Opposite polarity tag questions are shown in (23). Notice that the subject in the tag corresponds to the subject in the stem. The tag has the *opposite value* from the stem: if the stem is positive, then the tag is negative, as in (23a), (23b), and (23c); if the stem is negative, the tag is positive, as in (23d).

	Stem	*Tag Question*
(23) a.	You are going.	You are going, *aren't you*?
b.	They have done it.	They have done it, *haven't they*?
c.	Betty can come.	Betty can come, *can't she*?
d.	He isn't a vegetarian.	He isn't a vegetarian, *is he*?

The stems in (23a) and (23b) contain the auxiliary verbs *are* and *have*, respectively. In the corresponding tag questions, these same auxiliary verbs are located in the tags but in their negative forms (*aren't, haven't*). The stem in (23c) has a modal (*can*), which also appears in the tag but in its negative form (*can't*). In (23d), the stem is a negative form of the copular *be* (*isn't*), while the corresponding positive form *is* appears in the tag.

If the stem in a tag question does not contain an auxiliary verb, a modal, or copular *be*, then *do* appears in the tag.

Stem	*Tag Question*
(24) He likes her.	He likes her, *doesn't he*?

Four types of opposite polarity tag questions occur, depending upon whether the stem is positive or negative and whether the intonation on the tag is falling or rising. These four types are shown in (25).

(25) a. He likes to do that, doesn't he?   *positive stem, negative tag*

b. He doesn't like to do that, does he?   *negative stem, positive tag*

c. He likes to do that, doesn't he?   *positive stem, negative tag*

d. He doesn't like to do that, does he?   *negative stem, positive tag*

Tag questions such as (25a) and (25b), in which the tag starts out in the high pitch range and rises at the end, signal that the asker is not completely sure of the answer and is seeking information. In contrast, tag questions such as (25c) and (25d), in which the pitch on the tag starts high and then falls, assume that the person being asked will assess the situation the same way that the speaker would; that is, the asker expects the interlocutor to agree with the proposition in the stem. These tag questions often carry the force of a statement, as in (26), and speakers use them in contexts such as (27), in which they have no reason to expect an answer that disagrees with the proposition expressed in the stem.

(26) Al: You know, I was sure that Manchester United was going to beat Real Madrid last night.

Fred (looking downcast): Well, they didn't, did they? I watched the whole game.

(27) Amy: My caterpillar is waving its legs at you.

Sally (looking at caterpillar): Yes, it is, isn't it?

Questions with negative tags and *falling intonation* can be formed from sentences with complement clauses if the main verb of the stem indicates that there is good evidence that the complement is true. The complement clause in (28) is in brackets.

(28) Kim: It appears [that we are going to win,] doesn't it?

Su Jung: Yes. I can hardly believe it. We were behind 2 to 1.

Examples of verbs that the speaker uses to indicate the truth of the complements in sentences such as (28) are: *appear, believe, expect, guess, imagine, look like, see, seem,* and *suppose*.[10] Since the asker believes that what is asserted in the complement is probably true, and the person being asked is capable of judging this (and agreeing with the asker), the tag has high pitch that falls.

Same Polarity Tag Questions

Both the stem and the tag are positive in *same polarity tag questions*. One common type of same polarity tag question is shown in (29). It typically has a low pitch that jumps up on the tag. It is often preceded by *oh* or *so* and indicates that the speaker has inferred or reached a conclusion that is expressed in the stem. Same polarity tag questions are often perceived as sarcastic statements.

(29) So, that's your little game, is it? Well, you won't get away with it.

It is also possible to use a tag to form an emphatic imperative statement that conveys urgency, as in (30a). This same structure can serve as a polite request, as in (30b) and (30c), or a suggestion, as in (30d).

(30) a. Hurry up, *will you*!   *emphatic imperative denoting urgency*

    b. Get me a glass of water, *would you*?   *polite request*

    c. Turn out the light, *will you*?   *polite request*

    d. Let's talk about that later, *shall we*?   *suggestion*

All of the examples in (30) have the form of regular tag questions. The first element of each tag question, a modal, has a lower pitch that rises to the second element, the pronoun *you* or *we*.

Same polarity tag questions may have a verb in the tag that is different from the verb in the stem, as in (31a), (31b), and (31c). Typically, a verb like *know, remember, see,* or *understand* appears in the tag.[11]

(31) a. We were supposed to meet outside of
      the theater, *remember*?   *reminder*

    b. You're supposed to be here at 8 o'clock,
      you know?   *admonition/reminder*

    c. You hold it like this, *see*?   *instruction/request for feedback*

    d. You know what I'm talking about, *right*?   *request for feedback*

Notice that in (31a), (31b), and (31c), the tags themselves seem to be shortened forms of the tag questions *You remember that, don't you? You know that, don't you?* and *You see that, don't you?* respectively. Similarly, in (31d), in which the tag does not have a verb, *right* can be considered a shortened form of *That's right, isn't it?* Depending upon the tone the speaker uses and the context in which it is uttered, this kind of same polarity tag question functions as an *admonition*, a *reminder*, an *instruction*, or a *request for feedback* to ensure that the listener understands the speaker.

Tag Questions as Exclamations

Tag questions are sometimes used as exclamations. Here the tag seems almost unnecessary, but is added in hopes of eliciting agreement from the person(s) addressed. The intonation moves from high to low at the end, as shown in (32).

(32) Oh! That's a fantastic car, isn't it! (= What a fantastic car that is!)

A British English equivalent of the American exclamatory tag shown in (32) is *innit*. The speaker who says, *Bit old, this program, innit!* is making a statement that in his or her opinion *this program is a bit old*, and he or she assumes this should be obvious to the person addressed, so we have a pitch fall on *it*.[12]

A fairly recent variation on the tag question as exclamation in American English is the *or what* tag placed after a *yes/no* question, as shown in (33).[13] Sentences with *or what* tags do not ask for information, but instead demand agreement from the person to whom they are addressed. Thus the speaker who utters (33a) believes that *of course this is a great idea*. Here the pitch jumps up on *what* with little or no fall.

(33) a. Is this a great idea, or what!
b. Do you love it, or what!
c. Was that the best performance ever, or what!

SUMMARY

TAG QUESTIONS

Tag questions are made up of a stem (statement) and a tag (short question form).

In **opposite polarity tag questions**, the verb in the tag and the verb in the stem have opposite values.

Rising intonation on the tag indicates that the speaker is asking for information.

Rich will pay me back, won't he?

You weren't lying, were you?

Falling intonation on the tag indicates that the speaker expects the listener will agree with the information in the stem.

Sarah owns a car, doesn't she?

In **same polarity tag questions**, both the stem and the tag are positive. A low pitch that jumps up on the tag and then falls indicates the speaker has reached a conclusion, which is stated in the stem.

So, that's the reason you told him, is it?

Same polarity tag questions can also function as:

• an **urgent imperative**

Turn down the TV, will you!

• a **polite request**

Lend me your pen, would you?

• a **suggestion**

Let's stop for lunch, shall we?

continued

> • a **reminder/admonition**
>
> *You were supposed to pick me up at 5:00, remember?*
>
> • a **request for feedback**
>
> *You understand what I'm talking about, right?*

EXERCISE 4.3

Indicate whether each tag question (in italics) should carry rising or falling intonation. State why.

Example: Bill: You know, it might be more fun to go on this trip with another couple. Some people who like winter sports. Any idea who we might ask to join us?
Sally: *Well, Steve and Joan like to ski, don't they?*
Bill: I'm not sure.
Sally: I think I remember Steve mentioning that they do.

Answer: rising intonation (speaker is asking for information)

1. Alan: Darn. I was hoping that Paris would be chosen as the site of the 2012 Olympics!
Alice: *Well, it wasn't, was it?* Too bad.
2. Alan: I am going shopping now to get all the stuff we need for Andrea and Christine's party.
Nick: OK. As I remember, we decided on chicken for the main course.
Alan: Right. Hey, I just thought of something. *They aren't vegetarians by any chance, are they?*
3. Teresa: I hear your wife is sick.
Ron: Yeah. I'm spending most of my time looking after her.
Teresa: *So I guess you won't be coming to our meeting this week, will you?*
Ron: No. I don't see how I can.
4. *Oh, you're going to tell him all about it, are you?* Well, think again.
5. Hal: Too bad Arsenal lost to Leeds United last night.
Nick: Well, it's not all that surprising. *After all, they didn't have their star goalie, did they?*

EXERCISE 4.4

Identify the function of each tag question.

Example: Was that a great catch, or what!

Answer: exclamation

1. Susan: Bill will be joining us for dinner.
Alice: That's great. Joan's coming too, isn't she?
Susan: No, she has to work late.
2. Turn on the TV, will you?
3. Nobody can speak French on that trip, not even the teachers! That's so stupid, innit!
4. Let's talk about that over dinner, shall we?
5. So, you think you're some kind of genius, do you?
6. Is that a fantastic dress, or what!

WH- QUESTIONS

Wh- questions are formed with an interrogative word (*who, whom, whose, what, which, when, where, why, how*).

Forming *Wh-* Questions

Consider the declarative sentence. in (34).

(**34**) The boy lost his bicycle.

Notice that there are various constituents in (34) that could be questioned with a *wh-* question. For instance, we could pose a question about the subject NP (*the boy*), as in (35a), or we could ask about the object NP (*his bicycle*) with (35b).

(**35**) a. Who lost his bicycle?
   b. What did the boy lose?

Wh- Questions About an Object

When any object (i.e., direct object, indirect object, or object of a preposition) in a declarative sentence is questioned and the sentence contains an auxiliary verb, a modal verb, or copular *be*, two rules come into play: *wh- movement* and *subject–aux inversion*. For example, the *wh-* question in (36a) asks for information about the direct object in sentence (36b). The steps that are followed to produce (36a) are shown in (36c) and (36d).

(**36**) a. What are you watching?
   b. You are watching <u>something</u>.   *declarative sentence*
   c. What you are watching _____?   wh- *movement*
   d. What are you watching?   *subject–aux inversion*

First, the object, *something*, is converted into the appropriate *wh-* question word, *what*, and this is moved to the beginning of the sentence by the process of *wh- movement* (also referred to as *wh- fronting*). Subsequently, subject–aux inversion switches the positions of the subject, *you*, and the *auxiliary* verb, *are*.

If the underlying sentence does not contain an auxiliary verb, a modal verb, or copular *be*, then a slightly different process is applied to create a *wh-* question. This process is shown in (37).

(**37**) a. Who did you see?
   b. You saw <u>someone</u>.   *declarative sentence*
   c. Who you saw _____.   wh- *movement*
   d. Who did you see?   do *insertion,* saw *becomes* see

Wh- movement is applied in (37c), followed by *do* insertion and a change of the verb to its bare infinitive form, shown in (37d).

Wh- questions usually begin with a *wh-* word, but there are exceptions. For instance, when asking a question about the object of a preposition in a declarative sentence, as in (38), two possible question patterns may be used.

(**38**) a. You went to the concert with <u>someone</u>.   *declarative sentence*
  b. Who did you go to the concert with?
  c. With whom did you go to the concert?

In (38a), *someone* is the object of the preposition *with*. In (38b), we see that *someone* has been converted to the *wh-* question word *who*, which has been moved to the front of the sentence. However, in (38c) the preposition *with* has been moved to the front of the sentence along with the *wh-* word. The *wh-* word has been changed from *who* to *whom*. Both of these question forms are grammatically acceptable, but (38c) is considered by some to be more appropriate for formal or academic writing.

Wh- Questions About a Subject

When the subject of a declarative sentence is questioned, no fronting or inversion rules apply. The subject is simply converted into the appropriate *wh-* word. This is illustrated in (39).

(**39**) a. Who needs a lift?
  b. <u>Someone</u> needs a lift.   *declarative sentence*
  c. <u>Who</u> needs a lift?   *subject,* someone, *becomes* who

Wh- Questions with *How* + Adjective/Adverb

How combines with adjectives and adverbs to form questions beginning with *how many*, *how long*, *how often*, and so on, as shown in (40).

(**40**) a. How long did the press conference last?
  b. How many stamps did she take?

Embedded *Wh-* Questions

Wh- questions can be embedded inside a longer sentence, as in (41).

(**41**) I have no idea *how much this sandwich costs.*

Note that when a *wh-* question about an object is embedded in this way, it does not undergo subject–aux inversion or *do* insertion. Instead, only *wh-* movement is applied. Notice the difference between the regular *wh-* questions and their embedded versions in (42).

	Regular Wh- *Question*	*Embedded* Wh- *Question*
(**42**) a.	What was she doing?	I want to know *what she was doing.*
b.	Where is she going?	I want to know *where she is going.*
c.	How could he do it?	I want to know *how he could do it.*
d.	How much does it cost?	I want to know *how much it costs.*

Types of *Wh-* Questions

Wh- questions can be categorized according to the purpose they serve for an asker. Three types exist: *information* questions, *repeat please* questions, and *elaborate please* questions.

Wh- Information Questions

Information *wh-* questions are the basic type. They are used to request information that has not been previously mentioned, and they take the different forms considered thus far.

Unlike *yes/no* questions, *wh-* information questions always contain a presupposition. For instance, when we ask the question *What did John do?* we presume that John did in fact do something.

Question	Presumed Information
(43) a. *How* did they do it?	They did it *somehow*.
b. *Where* did John go?	John went *somewhere*.
c. *Whose* book was stolen?	*Someone's* book was stolen.
d. *What* has he done?	He has done *something*.
e. *Who* is doing it?	*Someone* is doing it.

Information *wh-* questions have *up-fall intonation*, as shown in (44a), (44b), and (44c) or *down-rise intonation*, as shown in (44d) and (44e).

(44) a. *How* can they do it?

b. What did she want?

c. How long did the meeting last?

d. Where did John go?

e. What has Julia done now?

Repeat Please Questions

Repeat please questions are often uttered when the asker either did not hear or understand the information she or he was given or is having difficulty accepting it. This type of *wh-* question frequently functions as a request for verification. *Repeat please questions* can have two word orders: question word order with the *wh-* word fronted, as in (45a), or normal declarative statement word order, shown in (45b). Both have rising intonation. A greater degree of stress on the *wh-* word and a higher rise in the intonation patterns signal a greater degree of surprise on the part of the asker.

(45) Fred: When did Susan come home this morning?
    Alice: At five o'clock.

    Fred: a. When did she get in?

        b. She got in when?

Elaborate Please Questions

Elaborate please questions are used when the asker has already been told something but needs more information regarding what was said. A question is then posed about someone, something, or somewhere mentioned by the speaker. In (46), Al is trying to sell his car, and Fred has found a prospective buyer. He tells Al that this person will come and look at the car tomorrow. Al wants more information about the time that has been arranged for the inspection. In (47), the police officer needs more precise information about the person before he or she can act.

(46) Fred: He'll come by tomorrow and have a look at the car.

    Al: When will he come by?

(**47**) Susan: Officer, that guy over there just stole my purse.

Police Officer: Which guy?

Elaborate please questions can either consist of a longer sentence such as (48a) or a shorter answer such as (48b). The *wh-* word is always stressed, and questions consisting of two or more words carry up-fall intonation.

(**48**) Sandra: We lived for over a year in France.

Joan: a. Where in France?

b. Where?

SUMMARY

WH- QUESTIONS

Wh- questions normally begin with an interrogative word (e.g., *who, whom, which, what, whose, where, how*).

How can they do that?

When did Roger leave?

Embedded *wh-* questions are embedded inside a larger sentence and do not undergo subject–auxiliary inversion or *do* insertion.
He wants to know how far it is to Boston.
I'm not sure what the professor's name is.

Wh- information questions are used to request information that has not been previously mentioned.
What time is it?
Excuse me, where is the Golden Gate Bridge?

Repeat please questions are usually uttered when the speaker wants someone to repeat part of something he or she said. They may have the normal *wh-* question structure, or they may have the structure of a declarative sentence.

A: She got in at five o'clock.

B: When did she get in? OR She got in when?

Elaborate please questions are asked to get someone to elaborate on an answer that has been given.
A: He'll come by tomorrow and look at it.
B: When?

A: Hey! That guy just picked my pocket!
B: Which guy?

EXERCISE 4.5

Identify each question as a *wh-* information question, *repeat please* question, or *elaborate please* question, and draw an appropriate intonation pattern for the question.

Example: A: John took your car.
　　　　 B: Who took my car?
Answer: repeat please question (Who took my car?)

1. How do you get to New Orleans from here?
2. A: We saw him in California.
   B: Where in California?
3. How much does this cost?
4. A: She left this afternoon.
   B: When?
5. A: Alice told me about it.
   B: Who told you about it?

OTHER TYPES OF *YES/NO* AND *WH-* QUESTIONS

All of the questions described in this section are types of either *yes/no* questions or *wh-* questions. Most of them have virtually the same intonation patterns as the *yes/no* and *wh-* questions presented earlier in this chapter. These question types are presented separately, however, because they serve specific functions that are different from the question types covered thus far. You will notice that the names given to these questions reflect their functions.

Alternative Questions

Alternative questions offer a choice between at least two alternative answers. Each of the alternatives in the question is stressed, as in (49).

　(**49**) a. Would you like eggs, pancakes, or waffles?

　　　 b. Are you coming or going?

Notice that the intonation pattern of an alternative question is the same as the pattern used when listing a series of options following a standard *wh-* question, as in (50).

　(**50**) a. Which flavor would you like? Chocolate, vanilla, or strawberry?

　　　 b. Which color do you like best? Yellow or orange?

Any positive *yes/no* question can be turned into an alternative question by adding *or* and a negative tag using an auxiliary or the appropriately tensed form of *do* as in (51a) and (51b). Shortened tags consisting of *not*, as in (51c) are common. These alternative questions with tags can carry a petulant or annoyed tone.

　(**51**) a. Are you coming or aren't you?

　　　 b. Do you like it or don't you?

　　　 c. Are you coming or not?

Echo Questions

Echo questions repeat all or part of what has just been said. The *repeat please* questions discussed earlier are, in fact, one type of echo question. As was mentioned earlier, these questions can have the function of confirming a previous utterance, as in (52a), or requesting clarification of a previous utterance, as in (52b).

(52) a. John: I'll fax it to Elizabeth right now.

   Bill: You'll fax it to her?

b. Sue: Take a look at this.

   Ann: (Take a look) at what?

Echo questions are also used to request that a previously posed question, or some part of a question, be repeated. In (53), Bill presumably did not hear what Al said or he is surprised that Al would ask the question.

(53) Al: Did you borrow my car keys?

   Bill: Did I borrow your car keys?

If the intonation pattern of an echo question rises and remains level throughout as in (54), this lends a pensive quality to the question. It is as if the speaker were pausing, seeking time to come up with an answer. The intonation in this case signals that the speaker does not expect a response. He or she is echoing the question aloud while thinking about how to answer it.

(54) Susan: And what do you think of this slogan?

   Alan: What do I think about it? Well, my initial reaction is . . .

Exclamatory Questions

Exclamatory questions, as shown in (55), are really exclamations that assert the belief of the speaker. They have the form of *yes/no* questions and normally carry falling intonation.

(55) a. Isn't he big!

   b. Am I ever starved!

Rhetorical Questions

Rhetorical yes/no questions express the asker's opinion. They are not intended to solicit a reply, as indicated by the second speaker in (56) and (57). Their intonation patterns often vary from one speaker to another.

(56) Diane: Have you heard the news about Alan?

   Bill: Who hasn't?

   (Implication: Everyone has heard.)

(57) A: Guess what? Andrew and Fergie split up.

   B: Who cares?

   (Implication: I don't care.)

Display Questions

Teachers often use question forms that do not begin with a *wh-* word. In (58a) and (58b), for instance, the *wh-* word comes at the end of the question. In (58c), the *wh-* word precedes a noun phrase at the end of the question. These questions are often referred to as *display questions* because the teacher is asking the student to display his or her knowledge about something. Display questions have *wh-* information intonation and stress on the *wh-* word.

(**58**) a. So this play is about what?

b. And these isotopes are formed how?

c. So this book deals with what important issue?

SUMMARY

OTHER TYPES OF *YES/NO* AND *WH-* QUESTIONS

Alternative questions offer at least two alternative answers.

Is your birthday in June or July?

Would you prefer coffee, tea, or milk?
Are you leaving or not?

Echo questions repeat all or part of what has been said.
A: Sarah will be leaving for China in May.
B: She'll be leaving for where?

A: Are you cold?

B: Am I cold?

Exclamatory questions are exclamations asserting the belief of the speaker.

Don't you look great!

Rhetorical questions are not intended to be answered, but instead, serve to state the opinion of the asker.
A: Have you heard the news about Alan?

B: Who hasn't?

Of course I enjoyed the dinner. Who wouldn't?

Display questions do not begin with a *wh-* word and are often used by teachers to request that students display their knowledge about something.

So this story is about what?

EXERCISE 4.6

Classify each question in italics as an alternative, echo, exclamatory, rhetorical, or display question, and draw the appropriate intonation pattern for each one.

Example: A: I certainly wouldn't want to be sued.
       B: *Who would?*

Answer: rhetorical question. Who would?

1. A: She always has lunch at Timponi's.
   B: *She always has lunch where?*
2. A: *Do you like the blue one or the red one?*
   B: I've gotta go with the blue.
3. A: Have you seen my glasses anywhere?
   B: *Have I seen your glasses?*
4. A: *So his essay discusses what?*
   B: Relationships between men and women.
5. A: *Isn't she a beauty!*
   B: Yeah. She must be a movie star.
6. A: Have you heard about the latest scandal?
   B: *Who hasn't?*

PROBLEMS THAT ESL/EFL STUDENTS HAVE WITH QUESTIONS

The problems that ESL/EFL students have formulating English questions appear in part to reflect the developmental stages hypothesis described in Chapter 3. However, some errors in question formation also appear to be due to the influence of L1 transfer (Chapter 3).

Positive *Yes/No* Questions (Portuguese and Arabic)

As we have seen, English forms *yes/no* questions in most cases through the processes of subject–aux inversion or *do* insertion. Many languages, French and German, for example, have rules similar to these. However, more often languages express questions by using only intonation or by using intonation plus a special question particle placed at the beginning of the sentence.

Portuguese is a good example of a language in which *yes/no* questions can be formed by intonation alone. Both (59a) and (59b) display a declarative sentence word order with rising intonation to indicate that the sentence is a *yes/no* question. Without the rising intonation, each sentence would be a declarative statement.

(59) a. *Você   mora   perto   daqui?*
        you   live   near   here
        "Do you live near here?"
     b. *Sally   é   uma   estudante   boa?*
        Sally   is   a   student   good
        "Is Sally a good student?"

Arabic is an example of a language in which a question marker is added to the beginning of a declarative sentence along with a change in intonation to form a *yes/no* question. This is shown in the comparison of the declarative sentence in (60a) with the *yes/no* question in (60b), where the question marker *hal* appears initially.[14]

(60) a. *juri:du　　an　jaku:na　ta:dziran*
　　　he wants　to　be a　　　merchant
　　　"He wants to be a merchant."
　　b. *hal　　　juri:du　　an　jaku:na　ta:dziran*
　　　(question　he wants　to　be a　　　merchant
　　　marker)
　　　"Does he want to be a merchant?"

Speakers of these languages sometimes follow the pattern of their L1 when forming English *yes/no* questions. Speakers of Portuguese, for instance, will often form English *yes/no* questions by applying intonation only, instead of applying subject–aux inversion or *do* insertion. This results in questions such as those in (61), which may carry the intonation pattern of an L1 question but have the form of a declarative sentence.

(61) a. It is your birthday?
　　b. The plane is arriving soon?
　　c. She likes coffee?

This is not a particularly serious problem, since (61a), (61b), and (61c) would most likely be understood as questions by a native speaker. They look and sound, however, like echo questions, which is not the speaker's intention.

Speakers of languages such as Arabic, on the other hand, tend to start *yes/no* questions with a form of *do* that agrees with the tense of the main verb. The word order remains the same and the verb maintains its tense inflection instead of taking on its bare infinitive form. This results in ungrammatical questions such as those in (62).

(62) a. *Does he wants to be a merchant?
　　b. *Did she had a large serving tray?
　　c. *Did he wanted to go?

The errors in (62) look very much like stage 3 in the developmental sequence that English language learners pass through when learning English *yes/no* questions. This sequence is discussed in Chapter 3.

We get a more precise picture of stage 3 development from a study by Mukattash (1980). He asked 600 first-year students at the University of Jordan, all of whom were speakers of either Modern Standard Arabic or Jordanian Arabic, to form *yes/no* questions from simple declarative statements. The error type exemplified in (63a), (63b), and (63c) constituted the highest percentage of the 1,237 erroneous questions that were produced.

(63) a. *Does the teacher has been looking at the notebooks?
　　b. *Did the girl knew many languages?
　　c. *Does her mother could have made a mistake?
　　d. *Is the weather was terrible?

In (63a), (63b), and (63c), students formed questions by simply inserting a form of *do* that agrees with the tensed form of the verb in the sentence. In (63d), a similar type of error is shown. Here a student formed a *yes/no* question by inserting a form of copular *be* (*is*) at the beginning of the sentence.

Mukattash hypothesized that these beginning college students had adopted a question formation strategy based on the native language pattern; that is, place a question marker at the beginning of the sentence (*be* for sentences which contain some form of copular *be*, and *do* for all other sentences). Today we would probably consider this data as evidence for the developmental acquisition of English questions. What seems to be going on here is that the students have reached a plateau at stage 3 and are not able to make the last step to stage 4.

Negative *Yes/No* Questions (Korean, Japanese, and Hausa)

Speakers of Korean, Japanese, and African languages like Hausa will often supply an answer to a negative *yes/no* question in English that is the opposite of what they intend. This is because in these languages the answers would have exactly the opposite meaning in English. The Korean example in (64) demonstrates this.

(64) A: *Ne   ol   swu-eps-ni?*
      You   come   can- neg-ques?
      "Can't you come?"
    B: *A-ni,   na   ka-l- swu   iss-e*
      No,   I   come-can   be- dec.
      "No, I can come."

While Speaker B's response is literally translated in English as *no*, it in fact carries the opposite meaning. By responding to A's negative question with a negative answer, Speaker B is contradicting the underlying proposition of the question and basically saying, *No, that is incorrect. In fact, I CAN come.* Speakers of Korean, Japanese, or Hausa will, therefore, often answer *no* to a negative question such as (64) when they mean, *Yes, I can* and respond *yes* when they mean, *No, I can't.* To supply a correct answer, students with these native languages must reconceptualize the question in terms of the underlying proposition (the statement version of the question), and it will take some time before the student does not instinctively provide an answer that carries the opposite of his or her intended meaning.

Tag Questions (Farsi, Arabic, and Turkish)

The problem previously described can also occur with tag questions that have a negative stem. Some languages like Farsi and Arabic attach a negative expression to a positive declarative sentence to form what is the closest equivalent to a tag question in English. For example, Farsi adds *intor nist* (*it isn't so*) with rising intonation to a declarative sentence, as shown in (65).

(65) *goftid   mirid   širaz,   intor   nist?*
    you said   you're going   Shiraz   so   it isn't
    "You said you're going to Shiraz, didn't you?"

Students who speak Farsi (or Arabic or Turkish) often follow the pattern of their native language by attaching *isn't it* to a declarative stem. This results in ungrammatical utterances like those shown in (66).

(66) a. *You said you are going to Shiraz, isn't it?
    b. *They live in New York, isn't it?

Wh- Information Questions (Romance Languages, Farsi)

Many languages, including the Romance languages and Farsi, form *wh-* information questions by placing a *wh-* word at the beginning of a declarative sentence (*wh-* movement) and inverting the subject and verb. In many of these languages, however, *do* insertion is not applied. An example of this from Portuguese is shown in (67) below.

(**67**) a. *O que   falou   a Nicole Kidman?*
       what   said   Nicole Kidman
       "What did Nicole Kidman say?"

Speakers of these languages are often heard making the errors shown in (68).

(**68**) a. *Why you said that?
       b. *What Nicole Kidman said?
       c. *Who he gave a book to?

The developmental sequence for the acquisition of English questions by L2 learners that we saw in Chapter 3 also includes *wh-* questions. At the third stage of this sequence, learners can apply *wh-* movement, but they are not yet able to apply *do* insertion. So, although it is possible that the errors in (68) are due to L1 transfer, there is also a possible developmental explanation for them. Although we would expect errors such as those shown in (68) to disappear with more input and use of English, surprisingly, we still find errors such as (69), which comes from a Spanish-speaking student, in the speech and writing of advanced-level students.

(**69**) *Why that happened so many times in a short period?

Embedded *Wh-* Questions

As just shown, *wh-* questions in Romance languages have the word order *wh-* word + verb + subject NP. This order is exemplified in the Portuguese example in (70a). The same order is used in an embedded question, as (70b) shows.

(**70**) a. *Quanto   custa   o almoço?*
       how much   costs   the lunch
       "How much does the lunch cost?"
       b. *Você   pode   me   dizer   quanto   custa   o   almoço?*
       You   can   (to) me   say   how much   costs   the   lunch
       "Can you tell me how much the lunch costs?"

The word order in the embedded question in (70b) shows the *wh-* word (*quanto*) and the verb (*custa*) before the subject (*almoço*). Transferring this word order pattern to English embedded questions results in errors like the one in (71), which comes from a composition by a Spanish-speaking undergraduate student at an American university.

(**71**) * . . . the question is *how can be imposed guidelines* to restrict this . . .

SUGGESTIONS FOR TEACHING QUESTIONS

Most English language teaching courses and textbooks begin dealing with the topic of questions by teaching *yes/no* questions and *wh-* questions before moving on to tag questions. This makes good sense, since these two types will be used with great frequency in the conversations in which elementary students participate. Many textbooks do a good job of teaching the grammar and use of the different question types. However, many textbooks do not include any references to the intonation patterns for questions other than to direct students to "listen carefully to your teacher."

You will have to include some instruction on the intonation patterns for the basic question types – *yes/no*, both types of tag questions, the three types of *wh-* questions, and at least alternative questions. This is necessary because a great many ESL students with L1s that have intonation patterns that differ from English (especially speakers of South East Asian and African languages) will master the form but not the correct intonation patterns of English questions. This is a persistent problem that has been verified on a yearly basis by production tests administered to graduate students admitted to the University of Illinois. When teaching the basic question types, it may be helpful to draw a simple diagram of a particular pattern like those shown in this book. Many workbooks on English pronunciation use diagrams, but sometimes students and teachers find these confusing. You may find it easier and more effective just to show the critical points where the pitch jumps up or moves down and to use simple labels like "rising" and "falling." Research shows that, whereas overall improvement in students' pronunciation of words and stress placement is fairly minimal, some progress in improving sentence intonation appears to be achievable.[15]

Addressing the kinds of mistakes that arise when a student has reached stage 3 in the learning of English questions (e.g., **Does he has a pencil? *Who he gave a book to? *What he gave to her?*) and moving the student on is worth some effort. Here the use of recasting techniques discussed in Chapter 3 may be helpful. Students whose native languages contain the conflicting meaning associated with answers to negative *yes/no* questions (e.g., Japanese and Korean), could benefit from activities designed to check whether they are aware of the potential for giving the inappropriate response. Arabic- and Farsi-speaking ESL students may also benefit from recasting activities designed to correct their incorrect negative tags. Some type of editing activity may be used for addressing the grammatical errors involving embedded *wh-* questions discussed earlier.

Most of the types of questions discussed in this chapter under Other Types of Yes/No and *Wh-* Questions will, it is hoped, be acquired as a result of exposure to dialogs and texts and television over time, and hence probably do not require any special focus. Still, you should know enough about these other types to be able to supply knowledgeable answers to anyone – a colleague or a student – who might ask you about them.

Yes/No Questions

The simplest and most effective way of practicing positive *yes/no* questions is through guessing games. Two of the most popular and widely used are described below. The games can be played as a class or in small groups.

Activity 1: Twenty Questions (High Beginning Through Low Intermediate)

One student says, "I'm thinking of something." The other students ask "Is it an animal? Is it a vegetable? Is it a mineral?" to establish the category. Once the category has been established, the students can ask up to 20 *yes/no* questions to discover the answer. The student who guesses the answer takes the place of the person who was answering *yes* or *no*. If no one guesses the answer, the student answering the questions wins.

A variation on this game involves bringing a number of objects to class and then concealing them behind a large piece of cardboard or in a box. The students try to identify the object by asking questions like "Is it round, soft, hard, square? Do you use it for washing? Do you wear it?"

Activity 2: What's My Line? (Intermediate Through Advanced)

This game has its origin in a popular TV show. The class suggests famous people well-known by all students. A student chooses one of them and pretends to be him or her without divulging the person's name. You may want to find out the student's identity and introduce him or her as today's guest in a way that will limit the guessing, such as "Our guest is living today" or "Our guest lived in the previous century." The class then asks the "guest" questions such as, "Are you a man or a woman?" "Are you in the movies?" Set a time limit for this. Again, if no one guesses the identity of the guest, he or she is the winner. This activity can be played as a competition between teams.

Activity 3: Making Excuses – Answering Negative *Yes/No* Questions (Intermediate)

This activity provides a natural context for students to practice responding to negative *yes/no* questions. On the board, list activities that are popular with students (e.g., *go to the movies*, *go to a party*, *study together*). Be sure that the activities are appropriate for all students to do socially together; in some countries not all of the above examples would be appropriate. Tell students that they must give full answers to the questions they answer. Point to an activity and say, "Su Jung, some of us are going to the movies tonight. Can't you come with us?" The student responds, "No, sorry, but I really can't come. I have to study" (or provides some other excuse). Another student then takes over the teacher's part and addresses another student in the class with a negative question.

Activity 4: Addressing Stage 3 Problems (High Beginning Through Intermediate)

This activity is designed for students who seem to be stuck at stage 3. It is a variation of VanPatten's processing instruction (PI) described in Chapter 3, which draws students' attention to the input – the question itself. Using either a picture of a famous person or someone in the class, say, "This is (person's name). I'm going to tell you about him." Describe the person in short, simple sentences (e.g., *He has two brothers. His father works for the government. He lives in Bordeaux*). Write the sentences on the board as you say them. Afterward say, "Now I'm going to ask some questions about him. If you think I asked the question correctly, say, 'Yes, it's okay.' If you think I asked the question incorrectly, say, 'No, it's not okay.'" Give two examples to make it clear that you are not interested in the answer to the question, but only in whether the question is formed correctly. Then point to a sentence and ask a question about it. Make some of your questions grammatically correct (e.g., *Does he have two brothers?*) and others with errors that reflect the kinds students make (e.g., **Does he lives in Bordeaux?*). Direct each question to a student. If the student says the sentence is okay when it is not, say, "Are you sure?" and repeat the question. Have the student correctly restate each incorrect question.

Activity 5: Role-Playing Using Alternative Questions (High Intermediate)

Role-playing in pairs is a good way to practice the intonation for alternative questions. Review the pattern with students first. Then hand out slips of paper describing situations that involve alternative choices, such as buying an airplane ticket through a travel agent, shopping in a department store for an item that comes in different colors, buying ice-cream cones at a fast-food restaurant that offers only three or four flavors, and ordering tickets for the opera, theater, or concerts. Write out a short dialog that fits the situation, as in (72).

> (**72**) Student A (customer): I want to fly to Washington next week.
> Student B (travel agent): When do you want to leave?
> Student A: Friday or Saturday.
> Student B: Good. We have cheap fares then. Would you like to fly on Friday or Saturday?
> Student A: Friday.
> Student B: Fine. Would you like to return on Monday, Tuesday, or Wednesday?

Have the students in pairs read the roles and practice acting them out. Monitor the exchanges. If a student is having trouble with the intonation pattern, demonstrate it for him or her again.

Wh- Questions
Activity 6: Forming *Wh-* Information Questions (Low Intermediate Through Intermediate)
Write various *wh-* words on the board (*what, when, where, why, what time, how many, how long*). Choose a context (e.g., leaving on a trip, going shopping, visiting a friend). Say, "I'm going on a trip. I want you to ask me some questions about my trip using these question words." Point to *where* and call on a student. Continue around the class, prompting students to form questions such as "*Where are you going? Why are you going there? How long will you stay in _____ ?*"

Activity 7: Quiz Show (Low Intermediate Through Advanced)
The popular quiz show *Jeopardy!* offers another way of practicing *wh-* information questions. Briefly explain the rules and have the students watch a taped segment of the show, if possible. In your adaptation, the quizmaster will read the answer to a question, and four contestants (students) will have 30 seconds to supply the appropriate question for that answer. A possible question/answer pair for the category Geography is shown in (73).

> (**73**) Quiz Master: Mount Everest.
> Contestant: What is the tallest mountain in the world?

Contestants receive points for each correct response. (Omit the rule of losing points for incorrect responses.) Set a time limit. The student who has the highest score at the end of each round goes on to play against three new contestants.

This can be a modified TBLT activity. Select questions for each category from among those created by the students. These are the questions which will be asked. A group of four contestants then competes against each other as one of the students plays the role of the quiz master and reads the answers. One student in the class who is not competing should keep time with a stopwatch. Another student should keep score, while two others judge whether or not the contestants' responses are close enough to be correct. The contestants' responses must always be framed in the form of a *wh-* question (e.g., "Who is . . . ?" "What is . . . ?" "Where is . . . ?"). There is a board game version of *Jeopardy!*, which you may want to purchase for use with your class.

Activity 8: Embedded *Wh-* Information Questions (High Intermediate Through Low Advanced)

As we saw in the previous section, the formation of grammatical embedded *wh-* information questions is a problem for many advanced students. This fact has been recognized in some of the better textbooks for teaching advanced writing, for example, Swales and Feak (2004). The authors draw attention to the fact that subject–aux inversion does not occur in English embedded questions, and they point out that these kinds of questions are used in academic writing for explaining the purpose of research and are likely to occur in problem-solution text format.

In the *Problems* section earlier in this chapter, we learned that a common error in the production of these questions can be due to English learners transferring the word order from their L1. A number of approaches can be combined to attack this problem. First, explain the difference between regular *wh-* information questions and the embedded version. (You may even show the embedded question pattern of the L1 if you know this well enough.) Next, try a PI activity in which you ask students to discriminate between grammatical and ungrammatical embedded questions. Then try small group or pair work. Have students decide on a context, for example, buying a car, and list the different kinds of *wh-* questions that they would need to ask, such as, "How much does it cost?" "How many people can it carry comfortably?" "What kind of gas mileage does it get?" "How expensive are the services that have to be done?" "How often does it have to be serviced?" "How large is the trunk (boot)?" "How much luggage will it hold?" After a brief explanation, give the students the task of making up questions about any object that they might purchase and then posing the questions in a role play. They are to frame them as embedded questions (e.g., "I would like to know how much this car costs?" "Could you tell me what the average gas mileage is?" "Could you give me an idea of how often it has to be serviced?") Follow this up later with an editing task in which students have to identify erroneous embedded questions in a short passage. The activities, particularly the last task, can be repeated later for further review.

ENDNOTES

[1] Zuma's tendency to apply rising intonation to statements appears to be quite common (currently) among young people. No one knows why some people talk like Zuma. It may be because they believe that applying question intonation to statements holds the listener's attention, or invokes empathy with what they are saying.

[2] Simple line diagrams similar to those in Dickerson (1989) and Hahn and Dickerson (1999) are used to describe the intonation patterns of questions treated in this chapter. These diagrams are easy to understand and are therefore useful for describing the intonation patterns of English questions to ESL/EFL teachers and students. Not everyone will agree with these patterns or be able to hear all of them. However, as Kelly (2000) notes, "the same thing can be said in different ways. There is also more flexibility when it comes to *yes/no* questions. However, . . . the teacher who applies these rules to their treatment of intonation in the classroom is unlikely to lead students astray; that is to say that in using these patterns, students will not go drastically wrong" (page 90).

[3] The "copular" form of *be* occurs in sentences which have predicate nominals, like *He is a doctor*, or predicate adjectives, like *She is tall*.

[4] Subject–auxiliary inversion is sometimes referred to as *subject–verb inversion*.

[5] This has apparently been disputed by Roach (2001), according to a personal communication cited in Jenkins (2004). However, the up-rise pattern is shown in pitch meter tracings in Levis (1996).

[6] In addition to the up-rise intonation pattern shown in (10), three other intonation patterns may occur with *yes/no* questions, and are shown as an up-fall pattern in (10a), a down-rise pattern in (10b), and a down-low-rise pattern in (10c). Not all native speakers hear the differences in all of these patterns, but they all hear and use the up-rise pattern in (10), so that is the one that should be taught to students.

(10) a. Would you like to go swimming?   *up-fall intonation pattern*

     b. Would you like to go swimming?   *down-rise intonation pattern*

     c. Would you like to go swimming? *down-low-rise intonation pattern*

[7] Positive *yes/no* questions can express bias when they contain words like *already*, *still*, and *definitely*. For example, the question *Has the train already left?* will be asked when the speaker is seeking to confirm the suspicion that the train has in fact already left. If the speaker is not seeking to confirm this suspicion, the question will take the neutral, unbiased form: *Has the train left yet?*

[8] The designation "declarative *yes/no* question" was proposed by Quirk et. al. (1972).

[9] The functions and examples (21) and (22) are from Larry Bouton, personal communication.

[10] Houk (1991), p. 33.

[11] These verbs may also be attached as tags to negative stems (e.g., *You're not supposed to do that, you know?*).

[12] See Biber et. al. (1999), p. 210.

[13] See Lightner (1998).

[14] Examples are Jordanian Arabic from Mukattash (1980).

[15] For a recent review of current trends in the teaching of pronunciation, see Jenkins (2004). For a more sobering appraisal of the limits of phonological learning, including the acquisition of intonation by L2 learners, see the research by Flege and his colleagues: Flege (1999), Flege, Yeni-Komshian, and Lui (1999).

REFERENCES

Biber, D., Johansson, S., Leech, G., Conrad, S., & Finegan, E. (1999). *Longman grammar of spoken and written English*. Essex: Pearson Education.

Dickerson, W. (1989). *Stress in the stream of speech: Teacher's manual*. Urbana: University of Illinois Press.

Flege, J. E. (1999). Age of learning and second-language speech. In D. Birdsong (Ed.), *Second-language acquisition and the critical period hypothesis* (pp. 101–131). Mahwah, NJ: Erlbaum.

Flege, J. E., Yeni-Komshian, G. H., & Lui, S. (1999). Age constraints on second-language acquistion. *Journal of Memory and Language, 41*, 78–104.

Hahn, L., & Dickerson, W. (1999). *Speech craft: Discourse pronunciation for advanced learners*. Ann Arbor: University of Michigan Press.

Houk, N. (1991). Tag questions: A necessary pragmatic context. In L. Bouton & Y. Kachru (Eds.), *Pragmatics and language learning: Monograph series vol. 2* (pp. 29–40), Division of English as an International Language, University of Illinois at Urbana-Champaign: Urbana, Illinois.

Jenkins, J. (2004). Research in teaching pronunciation and intonation. In M. McGroarty (Ed.), *Annual review of applied linguistics* 24 (pp. 109–125). Cambridge, England: Cambridge University Press.

Kelly, G. (2000). *How to teach pronunciation.* Essex: Longman.

Levis, J. (1996). An experimental study of two rising intonation patterns in American English, Ph.D. dissertation. University of Illinois.

Lightner, J. E. (1998). Say What? *Atlantic Monthly.*

Mukattash, L. (1980). Yes/no questions and the contrastive analysis hypothesis. *English Language Teaching Journal, 34* (2), 133–145.

Mukattash, L. (1981). *Wh-* questions in English: A problem for Arab students. *International Review of Applied Linguistics, 19* (4), 317–325.

Quirk, R., Greenbaum, S., Leech, G., & Svartvik, J. (1972). *A grammar of contemporary English.* London: Longman.

Roach, P. (2001). *Phonetics.* Oxford: Oxford University Press.

Swales, J. M., & Feak, C. A. (2005). *Academic writing for graduate students.* 2nd ed. Ann Arbor: University of Michigan Press.

CHAPTER 5

Negation

INTRODUCTION

The term *negation* refers to the process of forming negative sentences, as opposed to sentences that are affirmative (i.e., *She is not at the office* vs. *She is at the office*). Negative sentences can serve a variety of functions in English. For instance, a negative sentence can be used to make an assertion about something. An assertion that something will not happen is shown in (1).

(1) I won't be able to make the next meeting.

Negative sentences can also deny the truth of something that has been said. A typical example of this is shown in the cartoon below.

In the first panel, Cathy's mother repeatedly denies Cathy's statement that she had been rude to her in an earlier telephone conversation.[1] Their conversation is eventually reduced to the repetition of short, single-word, affirmative utterances (*was*) and denials (*weren't*) by the third panel.

A negative sentence can also function as a refusal. In (2), speaker B refuses speaker A's offer.[2]

(2) Speaker A: Would you like another cup of tea?
    Speaker B: No, thank you.

TWO FORMS OF NEGATION

There are two principal types of negation, *verbal* and *nonverbal*.[3] *Verbal negation* uses the negative element *not* with a verb to negate an affirmative statement, as in (3).

Affirmative Statement	*Negative Statement with* Not
(**3**) Lance is very happy.	Lance *isn't* very happy.

Nonverbal negation involves the use of words such as *nobody, nothing, no, none, neither/nor*, and *never* or the use of negative affixes such as *un-* and *non-*. The sentences in (4) illustrate nonverbal negation.

(**4**) a. He did *nothing*.
     b. There is *no* milk in the fridge.
     c. Luisa has *never* been there.

VERBAL NEGATION

Verbal negation can in turn be divided into two types, *primary* and *secondary verb negation*. They differ in the form of the verb with which *not* is used.

Primary Verb Negation

Primary verb negation refers to the use of *not* to negate a clause that contains a present or past tense verb.[4] In the negative column in (5), for instance, the affirmative *not* is used with the tensed verbs *are* and *lived* respectively.

Affirmative	*Negative*
(**5**) a. My cousins *are staying* with me.	My cousins *are not staying* with me.
b. We *lived* there for a long time.	We *did not live* there for a long time.

Primary verb negation takes the following forms:

1. Sentences with *Auxiliary Verbs*

If the affirmative form of a sentence has one or more auxiliary verbs or modal auxiliaries (such as *can* or *should*), *not* comes after the first auxiliary, as the examples in the second column in (6) demonstrate. The third column in (6) demonstrates that *not* contracts with auxiliary verbs and modals.

Affirmative	*Negative*	*Contracted* Not
(**6**) a. He *is* working.	He *is not* working.	He *isn't* working.
b. He *has* been trying.	He *has not* been trying.	He *hasn't* been trying.
c. He *can* read it later.	He *can not* read it later.	He *can't* read it later.

2. Statements with Copular *Be*

Negation for sentences with copular *be* operates just like negation for sentences with auxiliary verbs; that is, *not* is inserted following the verbal element as shown in (7). Note that *not* contracts with copular *be* as well, as illustrated in the third column of (7).

Affirmative	*Negative*	*Contracted* Not
(**7**) a. He *is* a doctor.	He *is not* a doctor.	He *isn't* a doctor.
b. There *is* some milk.	There *is not* any milk.	There *isn't* any milk.
c. They *were* in class.	They *were not* in class.	They *weren't* in class.

3. Statements with No Auxiliary Verb or Copular *Be*

If there is no auxiliary verb or copular *be* present in the affirmative version of a sentence, then an auxiliary must be added to make negation work properly. This is achieved by inserting the appropriate form of *do*, as shown in (8).

	Affirmative	*Negative*	*Contracted* Not
(**8**) a.	I liked the play.	I *did not* like the play.	I *didn't* like the play.
b.	She plays the piano.	She *does not* play the piano.	She *doesn't* play the piano.
c.	She has a car.	She *does not* have a car.	She *doesn't* have a car.

Note *not* comes after *do* and may contract with it. The main verb must be in its bare infinitive form while *do* carries the tense.

In American English, sentences with the main verb *have* (not the auxiliary verb *have*) are usually negated as shown in (8c); they take *do* + *not*. *Have* without *do*, as in (9), is slightly more common in British English.[5]

> (**9**) a. She hasn't a car.
> b. Roger hasn't time to talk right now.

Negative imperative sentences, shown in (10), also require the use of *do not* before the main verb. (See Chapter 6 for more on imperative sentences.)

	Affirmative	*Negative*	*Contracted* Not
(**10**) a.	Answer the phone.	*Do not* answer the phone.	*Don't* answer the phone.
b.	Pick me up at 8:00.	*Do not* pick me up at 8:00.	*Don't* pick me up at 8:00.

4. Yes/No Questions

In negative *yes/no* questions, the auxiliary verb, which has been moved to the beginning of the sentence by subject–aux inversion, contracts with *not*, as shown in (11a), (11b), and (11c). In *yes/no* questions with no auxiliary verb, *not* is contracted with *do*, as in (11d). (See Chapter 4 for more on *yes/no* questions.) Uncontracted forms such as *Is he not coming?* are occasionally heard.

	Affirmative	*Negative*
(**11**) a.	Is he coming?	*Isn't* he coming?
b.	Has the train arrived yet?	*Hasn't* the train arrived yet?
c.	Can you lift it?	*Can't* you lift it?
d.	Do you like opera?	*Don't* you like opera?

5. Tag Questions

Opposite polarity tag questions with positive stems always have contracted negative tags, as shown in the left-hand column in (12). (See Chapter 4 for more on tag questions.) Negating the stem of an opposite polarity tag question results in a positive tag, as shown in the right-hand column in (12).

	Affirmative	*Negative*
(**12**) a.	He likes football, doesn't he?	He *doesn't* like football, does he?
b.	She can come, can't she?	She *can't* come, can she?
c.	He is helping her, isn't he?	He *isn't* helping her, is he?
d.	She's a doctor, isn't she?	She *isn't* a doctor, is she?

6. *Wh-* Questions

In negative *wh-* questions, *not* can contract with auxiliaries after the initial *wh-* question word. When contraction occurs, the contracted form follows the *wh-* word. When contraction does not occur, *not* follows the subject.

Affirmative	*Negative*	
(**13**) a. What have you seen?	What *haven't* you seen?	*contracted* not
	What have you *not* seen?	*no contraction*
b. What do you like about it?	What *don't* you like about it?	*contracted* not
	What do you *not* like about it?	*no contraction*
c. Who do you want to invite?	Who *don't* you want to invite?	*contracted* not
	Who do you *not* want to invite?	*no contraction*

Negative/Positive Polarity Items and Verbal Negation

As shown previously in (7b), the affirmative sentence contains the noun phrase *some milk*, while the corresponding negative sentence reads *any milk*. This same shift from *some* to *any* is illustrated in (14).

Affirmative	*Negative*
(**14**) Ron brought *some* friends.	Ron didn't bring *any* friends.

Any is one of a set of words that can appear in negative statements but normally do not appear in affirmative statements. This restriction on the use of *any* can be seen if we remove *not* from a negative sentence such as (15a). The resulting positive statement in (15b) is ungrammatical.

(**15**) a. She doesn't have *any* money.
b. *She has *any* money.

Words such as *any*, which normally occur only in negative statements but are themselves not negative, are called *negative polarity items*.[6] The set of words and expressions formed with *any* (i.e., *anybody, anything, any longer, anymore, anyone, anywhere*) also belong to this group. Words such as *some*, on the other hand, normally occur only in positive statements and are therefore referred to as *positive polarity items*. Other members of this set are *somebody, someone, something, somewhere, somewhat*, and *somehow*. Examples are shown in (16).

(**16**) a. There are *some* crows roosting in that tree.
b. *There aren't *some* crows roosting in that tree.
c. There was *somebody* else in the car.
d. *There wasn't *somebody* else in the car.

The negative polarity items *anymore* and *any longer* have a corresponding positive polarity item, *still*. Notice that negating the verb in (17a) with *doesn't* produces (17b), which is ungrammatical. A corresponding negative version of (17a) can be formed by negating the verb and using the negative polarity items *anymore* or *any longer*, as shown in (17c).

(**17**) a. She *still* lives in that old house.
b. *She doesn't *still* live in that old house.
c. She doesn't live in that old house $\begin{Bmatrix} anymore \\ any\ longer \end{Bmatrix}$.

The negative polarity item *yet* has a corresponding positive polarity item, *already*, as shown in (18).[7]

(**18**) a. I have *already* read that report.
    b. I haven't read that report *yet*.

A list of other words that are typically used only in negative sentences are shown in (19). These negative polarity items do not have corresponding positive polarity items.

(**19**) *much*   I don't see her much.
    at all   She didn't like the play at all.
    a bit   Andy doesn't care for him a bit.
    bother   I wouldn't bother to have it repaired.
    faze   It didn't faze him.

Negative and positive polarity items also appear in corresponding ways in secondary verb negation, which will be discussed in the next section.

SUMMARY

VERBAL NEGATION: PRIMARY VERB NEGATION

Verbal negation uses *not* with a verb to negate an affirmative statement. There are two types of verbal negation: **primary verb negation** and **secondary verb negation**.

Primary verb negation uses *not* with a verb that is in the present or past tense (simple present/past, present/past progressive, etc.). The *not* appears after or is contracted with an auxiliary verb, a modal auxiliary, or a copular *be* in statements and questions.

> *She can come, can't she?*
> *She hasn't been here.*
> *She cannot come.*
> *Who isn't coming?*

Not appears after *do* or is contracted with *do* in statements, questions, and imperative sentences that do not have an auxiliary, a modal, or a copular *be*.

> *She does not like sports.*
> *Don't you want one?*
> *Don't touch that button!*

Negative polarity items such as *any, anyone, anything,* and *yet* almost always appear in negative statements.

> *There isn't any food in the fridge.*
> *He hasn't watched it yet.*

Positive polarity items such as *some, someone,* and *still* normally appear in positive statements.

> *There is some food in the fridge.*
> *He's still watching it.*

EXERCISE 5.1

Say whether each sentence is grammatical. If it is not grammatical, indicate what is wrong with it and supply the correction.

Example: He not always studies in the library.

Answer: ungrammatical (In primary negation, *not* combines with *do* to indicate the tense.)
        Correction: He doesn't always study in the library.

1. She visits her grandmother much.
2. He went to their house, didn't he?
3. I have read the newspaper yet.
4. Who isn't going to the mall?
5. There aren't some cherries in the bowl.

Secondary Verb Negation

Secondary verb negation refers to the use of the negative element *not* to negate a clause that has a verb in one of its *secondary forms* – that is, a verb in its infinitive, bare infinitive, present participle, or past participle form – and does not have a tensed verb.[8]

Clauses That Take Secondary Negation

Secondary verb negation is most commonly applied to subordinate clauses, in which verbs often take a secondary form. For example, the affirmative sentence in (20) includes an infinitive complement clause (in brackets), with a verb in its infinitive form.

Affirmative	*Negative*
(20) She promised him [*to come*].	She promised him [*not to come*].

By contrast, the column on the right in (20) shows what happens when *not* is placed before the infinitive. The meaning of the complement is changed from "*she would come*" to "*she would not come.*"

By comparing the affirmative column in (21) with the corresponding negative column, you can see the effect of negating a verb in an infinitive complement in (21a), a *that* complement with the verb in its bare infinitive form in (21b), and a *gerund* complement with its verb in its present participle form in (21c). Note that (21a) also illustrates that positive and negative polarity items occur in clauses taking secondary verb negation.

Affirmative	*Negative*
(21) a. It's important *to be seen by someone.*	It's important *not to be seen by anyone.*
b. She recommended *that we buy it.*	She recommended *that we not buy it.*
c. He hates *hearing the truth.*	He hates *not hearing the truth.*

In sentences with infinitive complements, such as (20) and (21a), many native speakers place *not* after *to*, as shown in (22).

(22) a. She promised him *to not* come.
      b. It's important *to not be* seen by anyone.

There is some debate about the acceptability of this alternative word order, since in secondary verb negation, *not* is supposed to premodify (precede) the verb phrase in the subordinate clause.[9] Many native speakers think that this alternative placement in (22) is ungrammatical, but for others it is "acceptable," that is, not quite as good as the position before the infinitive, but not ungrammatical either. You should be aware of this division of opinion because you might be asked about the acceptability of the alternative placement.

Negative Raising

In (23a), the negative *that* complement is shown in brackets. When we apply the rule of *negative raising* to (23a), we get (23b).

(**23**) a. I imagine [that he *won't want* to come].
      b. I *don't imagine* [that he will want to come].

Negative raising moves *not* up into the main clause of a sentence and combines it with an auxiliary or the appropriate form of *do*.[10] While the verb associated with *not* changes, the meaning of the sentence does not change.

As illustrated in (23), the negative raising rule can be applied to a sentence when the main verb expresses an opinion (i.e., *think, believe, anticipate, expect, imagine, suppose,* etc.) and the *that* clause contains a modal (*should, could, will,* etc.). Negative raising is also possible in sentences that have main verbs of appearance like *appear* and *seem*, as shown in (24) and (for some native speakers) sentences with *be* + an adjective of probability, such as *likely*, as shown in (25).[11]

(**24**) a. It appears [that we won't win after all].
      b. It doesn't appear [that we will win after all].

(**25**) a. It is likely [that John won't come].
      b. It isn't likely [that John will come].

Although both patterns – *not* in the main clause and *not* in the *that* clause – have basically the same meaning, there appears to be a preference for the former, especially with verbs such as *think*. Hence, native speakers may be more likely to say, *I don't think he's going* rather than *I think he's not going*.

Note that negative raising is not possible with sentences in which the main clause verb is not one of the types mentioned above.[12] With other types of main clause verbs, moving *not* from the complement into the main clause changes the meaning of the sentence, as shown in (26).

(**26**) a. We forgot that she doesn't like him.
      b. We didn't forget that she likes him.

Additional Facts about Verbal Negation

The form of negation can differ from what we have already seen and other factors can significantly change the meaning of a negated sentence.

Multiple Negation

Multiple negation occurs when a clause contains at least two negative forms. For example, in (27), *not* appears with the auxiliary verb *could* and the main verb *respond*. This is an example of independent multiple negation, in which two negatives make the statement positive.

(**27**) I couldn't not respond.

In (27), the speaker states that there was something that he or she could not do, and that was *not respond*. Thus, (27) implies that the speaker did respond. Sentences such as these occur in spoken English; even imperatives may have *not* twice, as (28) illustrates.

(**28**) Don't not go because of me. (= You shouldn't decide not to go because of me.)

In many cases, particularly if the first verb is a modal, the meaning could be expressed in a simpler fashion by an affirmative sentence such as those shown in parentheses in (29), (30), and (31).

(**29**) I didn't not pay attention. (= I paid attention.)

(**30**) She won't not tell the truth. (= She will tell the truth.)

(**31**) You can't not go with them. (= You must go with them.)

Scope of Negation

Linguists and grammarians often talk about the *scope of negation*. The term *scope* here simply refers to the part of the meaning of a sentence that is negated.[13] In an affirmative sentence with a single verb, such as (32a), the addition of *not* after the first auxiliary element changes the meaning of the whole sentence, so the scope of negation is the entire sentence, as shown in (32b).

(**32**) a. Tom knew my father.
     b. Tom did not know my father.

However, when the sentence contains a subordinate clause, the scope of negation can be all or part of the sentence. Examples (33) and (34) contain a subordinate clause (the *that* complement in brackets). The scope of negation in (33) is the entire sentence *Tom said that he knew my father*, because *not* combines with the verb clause *say*. However, the scope in (34) is limited to the subordinate clause, *that he knew my father*, because *not* combines with the verb *know* in this clause.

(**33**) Tom didn't say [that he knew my father].

(**34**) Tom said [that he didn't know my father].

Changes in the Relative Scope of Negation

In (35a), the scope of the negation is the entire sentence. This is because, as we saw in the previous examples, the *not* changes the meaning of its corresponding affirmative sentence in (35b).

(**35**) a. Tom did not destroy the evidence.
     b. Tom destroyed the evidence.

With adverbs like *deliberately, expressly, intentionally, knowingly, on purpose, purposely,* and *willfully,*[14] the scope of negation is different, depending on whether the adverb is before *not*, as in (36), or after it, as in (37). The position of the adverb causes (36) and (37) to have different meanings.

(**36**) Tom *deliberately* did not destroy the evidence.

(**37**) Tom didn't *deliberately* destroy the evidence.

The meaning of (36) is "*Tom acted deliberately in not destroying the evidence.*" Here, Tom did not destroy the evidence.

The meaning of (37) is "*Tom did not act deliberately in destroying the evidence.*" In this case, Tom did destroy the evidence, but not on purpose.

Stress Can Focus Negation

In negative sentences, heavy stress on a particular word implies that the stressed word is the focus of negation. In (38a), the scope of negation is the entire sentence. But by stressing *your*, as in (38b), we focus the negation on that word. The sentence then implies that there may be other children who hate school, but yours do not. Moving the stress to *children*, as in (38c), implies that someone else related to you may hate school (e.g., your parents, your husband), but your children do not. In (38d), placing the stress on the verb implies that your children don't actually hate school, but they might not like it. Heavy stress on *school*, as shown in (38e), implies that your children do not hate school, but they do hate something else, for example, homework.[15]

> (38) a. Your children don't hate school.
>   b. YOUR children don't hate school.
>   c. Your CHILDREN don't hate school.
>   d. Your children don't HATE school.
>   e. Your children don't hate SCHOOL.

SUMMARY

VERBAL NEGATION: SECONDARY VERB NEGATION

Secondary verb negation uses *not* with verbs in their bare infinitive, infinitive, past participle, and gerund forms, and it typically is applied in subordinate clauses.

Not appears before the verb, and *do* is never inserted.
> *It's important not to be nervous.*
> *I suggest that you not stand here.*
> *They walked away not knowing what the future held.*

Negative raising moves *not* out of a subordinate clause and into the main clause of a sentence and combines it with *do*.
> *I imagine* [*that he won't come.*] → *I don't imagine* [*that he will come.*]

Multiple negation refers to instances in which at least two negative forms occur in a clause.
> *I couldn't not respond.* (= *I had to respond.*)

EXERCISE 5.2

Indicate whether each sentence is grammatical. If it is not grammatical, indicate what is wrong with it and supply a correction.

Example: It's important to be not seen.

Answer: ungrammatical (*Not* should appear before the infinitive or before *be*.)
      Correction: *It's important not to be seen* OR *It's important to not be seen.*

1. We promised them to not call.
2. Lori expected her not to show up.
3. He suggested not buying it.
4. I sat on the bus thinking not about my destination.
5. You can't not take the test.

EXERCISE 5.3

Explain the difference in meaning between the pairs of sentences shown.

Example: a. She expressly did not withhold information from the police.
      b. She didn't expressly withhold information from the police.

Answer: Sentence (a) means that she didn't withhold information. Sentence (b) means she did withhold information, but this was not done on purpose.

1. a. Susan didn't deliberately delete all of her e-mail messages.
  b. Susan deliberately didn't delete all of her e-mail messages.
2. a. My sister doesn't dislike classical music.
  b. My sister doesn't dislike CLASSICAL music.
3. a. The winner of the "Employee of the Month" award intentionally did not take credit for important changes that she was not responsible for.
  b. The winner of the "Employee of the Month" award did not intentionally take credit for important changes that she was not responsible for.
4. a. My brother doesn't enjoy watching news programs on television.
  b. My BROTHER doesn't enjoy watching news programs on television.

EXERCISE 5.4

Explain whether each pair of sentences has the same meaning.

Example: a. It appears that he won't be successful.
      b. It doesn't appear that he will be successful.

Answer: same meaning (Negative raising has been applied to (a) to produce (b), with no change in meaning.)

1. a. We think that we will not have to postpone the conference.
  b. We don't think that we will have to postpone the conference.
2. a. I think he won't agree to our terms.
  b. I don't think that he will agree to our terms.
3. a. She understood that he didn't want to come.
  b. She didn't understand that he wanted to come.
4. a. We don't expect that they will automatically accept everything that the president proposes.
  b. We expect that they won't automatically accept everything that the president proposes.

NONVERBAL NEGATION

There are basically two forms of nonverbal negation. The first involves the use of certain negative words; the second involves the use of negative affixes.

Negative Words

The most grammatically complex method of nonverbal negation is through the use of a set of *negative words*,[16] some common examples of which are presented on the next page. Some negative words, such as *neither/nor*, are correlative conjunctions and have a connecting function that is discussed in Chapter 25. Others, such as *nowhere* and *no place*, are adverbs.

COMMON NEGATIVE WORDS				
no	nobody	nothing	no place	nor
none	no one	nowhere	neither	never

Sentences with these negative words can often be paraphrased using verbal negation as illustrated in (39). Note that in the sentences in the right-hand column, *not* has been added, and the negative word has been replaced by a negative polarity item (e.g., *any, anything, either,* and *ever*).

Nonverbal Negation　　　　　　　　　*Verbal Negation*

(**39**) a. He revealed *no* information.　　He *didn't* reveal *any* information.
　　　b. She chose *none* of them.　　　She *didn't* choose *any* of them.
　　　c. They did *nothing* to stop him.　They *didn't* do *anything* to stop him.
　　　d. We were going *nowhere*.　　　We *weren't* going *anywhere*.
　　　e. We knew *neither* of them.　　　We *didn't* know *either* of them.
　　　f. She had *never* done that before.　She *hadn't ever* done that before.
　　　g. There is *no* news.　　　　　　There *isn't any* news.

"Double Negatives" with Negative Words

In some dialects of British and American English, sentences with so-called double negatives are common.[17] A sentence is said to have a double negative when it either has more than one negative word, such as (40a), or it contains *not* plus one or more negative words, such as (40b) and (40c).

(**40**) a. You've never seen nothing like it.
　　　b. I can't get no satisfaction.
　　　c. I told her not to say nothing to nobody.[18]

Each item in (40) has a counterpart with verbal negation and *any*, as shown in (41).

(**41**) a. You've never seen anything like it.
　　　b. I can't get any satisfaction.
　　　c. I told her not to say anything to anybody.

Speakers of Standard English (the dialect of English commonly used in newspapers, textbooks, news programs, academic discourse, etc.) might label the sentences in (40) ungrammatical. However, it is important for teachers to understand that these sentences are perfectly acceptable in some English dialects. A common, erroneous assumption is that the sentences in (40) are somehow illogical because they contain two negatives, and two negatives make a positive. While this is true in logic, it is not true in grammar. In fact, many languages of the world use double negatives to express negation.[19]

If the opportunity arises to talk about double negative sentences with your students, point out that for speakers of dialects with double negatives, all of the sentences in (40) are grammatical. Furthermore, most speakers of Standard English would have no problem understanding these sentences to be negative statements. However, students should be aware that the disadvantage of using double negative sentences is they may be judged as speaking "uneducated" English by speakers of the standard dialect.

Negative/Positive Polarity Items Compared with Negative Words

In (14) through (19), we looked at negative and positive polarity items. The table below shows an important relationship between polarity items and negative words.[20]

POSITIVE POLARITY ITEMS	NEGATIVE POLARITY ITEMS	NEGATIVE WORDS
some	any	no
someone/somebody	anyone/anybody	no one/nobody
something	anything	nothing
somewhere/someplace	anywhere/any place	nowhere/no place
sometimes	ever	never
sometime, once	anytime, ever	never

This table may be useful for demonstrating that positive polarity items with *some* must be shifted to the corresponding negative polarity item with *any* in a sentence with verbal negation, and that such negative statements can also have corresponding sentences with nonverbal negation using a negative word. The relationship between positive polarity items, negative polarity items, and negative words is illustrated in (42).

(**42**) a. They found *someone* who had witnessed the accident.
     b. They *didn't* find *anyone* who had witnessed the accident.
     c. They found *no one* who had witnessed the accident.

Not in Nonverbal Negation

Not appears before words other than verbs – for example, quantifiers, adjectives, and adverbs – as a form of nonverbal negation. Different meanings are produced, depending upon the element that *not* precedes.

When *not* appears before the quantifiers *all*, *every*, *many*, and *much*, as in (43), the resulting implied meaning is "*some*" or "*a limited amount of.*"

(**43**) a. *Not* all of his suggestions were accepted.
       (*Implication:* Some of his suggestions were accepted.)
     b. *Not* every person is born rich.
       (*Implication:* Some people are born rich.)
     c. After the two boys had finished eating, *not much* was left for me.
       (*Implication:* Something was left for me.)

Not one before a noun can mean "*not any*," "*no*," or "*none*," as in (44a). The same meaning can be conveyed by *not a single*, as shown in (44b). Similarly, *not* preceding a number + *ago* can mean "*less than*" that number as shown in (44c).

(**44**) a. *Not one customer* has protested so far. (= no customers)
     b. *Not a single customer* has protested so far. (= no customers)
     c. I was on the phone with him *not 5 minutes ago*. (= less than 5 minutes ago)

When *not* precedes *a little* or *a few* and a noun, the resulting meaning is the opposite of *a little* or *a few*, as shown in (45).

(**45**) a. His remarks resulted in *not a little* confusion. (= a good deal, fair amount of confusion)
     b. *Not a few of the members* attending the meeting were upset by the chairman's remarks. (= Quite a few members were upset.)

When *not* precedes an adjective with a negative prefix, such as *un-* or *in-*, the meaning is "*somewhat*," or "*to a certain degree*."

(46) a. It is *not uncommon* for me to write multiple drafts. (= It is somewhat common.)
b. That behavior is *not uncharacteristic* of him. (= It is somewhat characteristic of him.)

Note that adjectives that can appear in the construction in (46) have to be gradable (i.e., be capable of taking comparative and superlative suffixes *-er* and *-est* or the comparative words *more* and *most*).

Not often is a negative adverbial phrase, similar to negative frequency adverbs *never*, *rarely*, *seldom*, and *only*. When any of these forms occurs at the beginning of a sentence, the rule of subject–aux inversion must apply, as shown in (47a) and (47b). Failure to apply subject–aux inversion will produce an ungrammatical result as in (47c) and (47d).

(47) a. Never in my entire life have I witnessed such bravery.
b. Not often have I witnessed such bravery.
c. *Never in my entire life I have witnessed such bravery.
d. *Not often I have witnessed such bravery.

Negative Affixes

Lexical items (words) can also undergo nonverbal negation, and this is done by attaching affixes to them. Negation by affixation is parallel to verbal negation, as in (48).

(48) a. That remark was not appropriate.   *verbal negation*
b. That remark was *in*appropriate.   *nonverbal negation (affixational)*

English has many prefixes. The common negative prefixes are *un-*, *in-*, *im-*, *il-*, *ir-*, *dis-*, *a-*, and *non-*. They may be attached to adjectives, adverbs, nouns, and in some cases verbs, as the examples in the following table show.

NEGATIVE PREFIXES			
Adjective	**Adverb**	**Noun**	**Verb**
*un*happy	*un*happily	*un*happiness	
*in*efficient	*in*efficiently	*in*efficiency	
*im*plausible	*im*plausibly	*im*plausibility	
*il*legal	*il*legally	*il*legality	
*ir*regular	*ir*regularly	*ir*regularity	
*dis*loyal	*dis*loyally	*dis*approval	*dis*like
*a*symmetrical	*a*symmetrically	*a*symmetry	
*non*violent	*non*violently	*non*violence	

Certain English adjectives derive from Latin, and lexical negation in Latin involved variations of the prefix *in-* that were conditioned by the first sound in the root word. Thus, the prefix *in-* became *im-* when it was attached to adjectives or nouns beginning with the bilabial consonants /b/, /p/, and /m/ (*imbalance*, *impossible*, *immobile*), and *il-* and *ir-* were attached to adjectives beginning with /l/ and /r/ (*illiterate*, *irreverent*). *In-* appeared before adjectives beginning with vowels (*inappropriate*). This prefix is now unproductive; that is, we cannot form any new words with the *in-/im-/il-/ir-* prefix; we are restricted to the words that have been handed down to us.

Today, the most productive negative prefix is *un-*. It appears before adjectives beginning with consonants and vowels (*unbeatable*, *uninhabitable*), and it is applied to words that begin with consonants that should theoretically take the prefixes *in-* and *im-* (*unbelievable*, *unproductive*, *undeserved*, *unmanageable*). One measure of the productivity of *un-* is that it is replacing *il-* with some adjectives. For instance, *illimitable* ("not capable of being limited; immeasurable") is usually rendered as *unlimitable*. The prefix *un-* also conflicts with *im-* for attachment to words having the same stem (e.g., the noun *imbalance* vs. the adjective *unbalanced*). In many cases, therefore, the sound of the root is of limited help in determining a correct negative prefix. You will often hear native speakers produce negative adjectives with *un-* that should actually have a different prefix, (e.g., *an *unhospitable environment*, *an *undefensible position*).

Note also that the prefix *un-* has another meaning, "to undo or reverse the action" when used with verbs such as *tie*, *wrap*, *seal*, and *fasten*. This use is often mentioned in ESL materials.

Non- is prefixed to adjectives and increasingly to nouns. We hear new creations, such as *nonstarter*, every day. It has been observed that some negative prefixes impart a pejorative or evaluative meaning when attached to stems, whereas others impart a purely descriptive meaning.[21] For example, *dysfunctional* implies criticism or fault, whereas *non-functional* is essentially a descriptive adjective that means "*not functioning*." Similarly, *unprofessional* describes conduct that deviates from normal professional standards, but *nonprofessional* simply implies that someone is not a professional in a particular field.

A number of other prefixes, such as *anti-*, *counter-*, *mal-*, and *mis-*, are sometimes cited as negative prefixes, but these meanings are usually not purely negative. For example, *antiwar* means "against war" and *counterintuitive* means "against intuition" or "the opposite of intuitive." *Maladroit* means more than "not adroit"; it also means "clumsy" or "awkward," and *malformed* means "abnormally formed." *Mis-* is applied to verbs and adjectives and nouns derived from verbs. In each case, the resulting meaning is "incorrect" (e.g., *misapply* means "incorrectly apply," *misleading* means "giving the incorrect impression"). Similarly, the suffix *-less* is often cited as a negative suffix, but its meaning is actually "without" (e.g., *limitless* means "without limit," *shameless* means "without shame").

SUMMARY

NONVERBAL NEGATION

Nonverbal negation can be accomplished through the use of negative words (e.g., *nobody*, *nothing*) or by negative affixes attached to words.

Negative words used in nonverbal negation include the following: *no*, *nobody*, *nothing*, *none*, *no one*, *no place*, *nowhere*, *never*, *neither*, and *nor*.
> *The police found no clues as to his whereabouts.*
> *We went nowhere on vacation this year.*
> *My older brother did nothing all day.*

continued

Positive polarity items with *some* must be shifted to corresponding negative polarity items with *any* in sentences with verbal negation. Negative statements with *any* can often be changed into sentences with a negative word.

He knows something. He doesn't know anything. (= He knows nothing.)
She has some money. She doesn't have any money. (= She has no money.)

Not appears before words including quantifiers, frequency adverbs such as *often*, numbers, and adjectives as a form of nonverbal negation.

Not all of the news was well received.
It's not often that you see something like that.
I was talking on the phone to him not five minutes ago.
It is not uncommon for me to write multiple drafts.

Negative affixes are attached to adjectives, adverbs, nouns, and verbs to negate them.

The most common negative prefixes are: *un-, in-, im-, il-, ir- dis-, a-* and *non-*.

Adjective	Adverb	Noun	Verb
*un*grateful	*un*gratefully	*un*gratefulness	
*in*decent	*in*decently	*in*decency	
*dis*dainful	*dis*dainfully	*dis*dain	*dis*dain

EXERCISE 5.5

For each sentence with verbal negation, provide an equivalent sentence with nonverbal negation using a negative word.

Example: He doesn't ever do any work.

Answer: He never does any work.

1. There wasn't anybody we knew at the party.
2. There aren't any more muffins left.
3. I didn't see anything suspicious.
4. She wasn't anywhere near the accident when it happened.
5. He didn't see John or Susan.
6. The people who usually attend these concerts didn't come this time.

EXERCISE 5.6

Indicate whether each sentence is ungrammatical. If a sentence is ungrammatical, explain what is wrong with it and supply a correction.

Example: There aren't some e-mail messages for me.

Answer: ungrammatical (*Some* is a positive polarity item and can't occur in a negative statement.)
Correction: *There aren't any e-mail messages for me.*

1. I've never seen nothing like that.
2. Not often you will have a streak of luck like that.
3. She phoned me not five minutes ago.
4. Many senators said that the president's position on taxes was undefensible.

5. I didn't do nothing wrong.
6. He took no prisoners.
7. The method that he was using was highly inefficient.

PROBLEMS THAT ESL/EFL STUDENTS HAVE WITH NEGATION

The errors that ESL/EFL students make when attempting to produce negative sentences in English reflect a developmental progression that is overlaid by influences from their native languages.

Primary Verb Negation

In Chapter 3, we noted evidence that English language learners pass through several developmental stages on their way to mastering certain structures in English. Evidence from several languages (e.g., Spanish, Swedish, Turkish) has been cited to support this. From the mid-1970s until recently, it was generally believed that developmental patterns for negation were similar across all L2 groups and had in fact something in common with the way that children acquire negation in their L1. Recent research suggests, however, that this may be inaccurate and that learners may in fact not all follow the same developmental pattern for the acquisition of negation. For example, in one study on the development of negation, Meisel (1997) argues that the "[negative] sentence structures [learners produce] are transferred from the L1" (pp. 257–58). He asserts, in other words, that L1 grammar plays a strong role in the decisions learners make about how to express negation in an L2.[22]

The widely accepted stages of L2 negation development are shown in (49).[23]

> **(49) Stage 1:** **No* that one. **No* you playing here.
> **Stage 2:** **I *no* have job. I *don't* have time.
> **Stage 3:** I *can't* play the guitar.
> **Stage 4:** She *doesn't* drink alcohol. They *weren't* working there. She *hasn't* finished it yet.

In stage 1, *no* is placed before a fragment of a phrase or sentence. In stage 2, *no*, *not*, and *don't* function as negation markers and are moved into preverbal position, producing both grammatical and ungrammatical sentences. In stage 3, the L2 learners begin to combine *not* correctly with modals and copular *be*, but they may still be inserting *no*, *not*, and *don't* before verbs that are not preceded by modals. In stage 4, *not* is moved into the full auxiliary system (i.e., *be*, *have*, and *do*).

Each of the recorded negation errors in (50) through (54) seems to match one of the stages outlined. The sentences were produced by Spanish speakers who were either university students or were in the highest-level class of an Intensive English Program (IEP) preparing for entry into universities in the United States.

Sentence (50) was produced by an IEP student. Note that the student appears to be at stage 2 or 3 since *not* is placed before the main verb.

> **(50)** *Finally, the society's customs and beliefs *not always* pass from one age group to another.

We cannot rule out L1 transfer as the source of the error in (50) since in Spanish, primary negation is accomplished by placing the negative word *no* in front of the verb, as shown in (51). Transferring the order of primary verb negation in the L1 to English would also produce the error in (50).

> (51) *Él   no   va   a   clase.*
> he (negative) go to class
> "He doesn't go to class."

The error in (52), which was made by another IEP student, seems to illustrate an example of someone who is stuck at stage 3. Although this student still makes a stage 2 error by placing *not* before the verb *talk*, he nevertheless correctly combines *not* with the modal verb *can*.

> (52) *I must to pronounce a correct English, because *if I not talk* and pronounce the words correctly, maybe many people *can't* understand me.

Finally, we have a number of errors made by students who have been admitted to a university and are enrolled in courses to improve their writing ability. Students exhibit stage 2 errors in subordinate clauses like the one shown in (53).

> (53) *Kevin's mother tells that she had a bad experience with her two other sons because they *don't had a* father.

Secondary Verb Negation

Errors with secondary verb negation can also be found in corpora of learners with advanced proficiency. One common error type is the use of *don't* when *not* is required. In fact, even after learners begin to use *do* + *not* correctly in main clauses, they may continue to make this error in complements in which secondary verb negation is required. Consider, for example, (54), which appeared in a composition by an undergraduate Spanish speaker. Here the student undoubtedly wanted to write something such as *campus installations can help foreign students not to become segregated*.

> (54) Nevertheless, the practice of sports along the campus installations can help foreign students *to don't become segregate*.

Double Negatives (Spanish, Portuguese)

Spanish and Portuguese allow double negative constructions. Therefore, Spanish- and Portuguese-speaking students can carry this over when formulating English sentences. The negation pattern in (55a) is most likely due to the fact that the L1 equivalent shown in (55b) has been transferred to English. This seems a more plausible explanation than supposing that (55a) is the result of the student's exposure to a dialect of English that allows double negatives.

> (55) a. *He doesn't know nothing about the activities of his wife.
>   b. *Él   no   sabe   nada   de   las actividades   de su esposa.*
>   he (negative) knows nothing of the activities   of his wife
>   "He doesn't know anything about the activities of his wife."

SUGGESTIONS FOR TEACHING NEGATION

In English language teaching textbooks, negation is usually introduced with copular *be*. This is then followed by a demonstration of negation with other verbs, often using the main verb *have* as a model for the combination of *not* with the *do* auxiliary. Thereafter, primary verb negation is usually included as a feature associated with each new structure that involves verbs. For instance, negation is dealt with when modals and the various tense/aspect combinations are taught.

Although this may seem to be the only way of teaching negation, the interface of negation with other structures also needs to be taken into consideration. For example, the teaching and practice of *nonreferential there is/are* structures requires an understanding of *some* and *any* as positive and negative polarity items as well as of nonverbal negation forms. If you are going to use an information gap task such as the one described in Activity 6, which is quite popular for practicing *there is/are* structures, you have to keep in mind that the students can respond to *yes/no* questions with primary verbal negation or nonverbal negation forms. For instance, the question "Are there any people in your picture?" can be answered "No, there aren't"; "No, there are no people in my picture"; or "No, there are none."

There is no way of knowing whether the way negation is taught in ESL/EFL textbooks – in bits and pieces – contributes to the halting acquisition on the part of the students. It is quite possible, however, that supplementing the way negation is taught in your textbook with the details of primary negation as they are presented at the beginning of this chapter will accelerate acquisition.

Some suggestions for teaching primary and secondary negation are presented below.

Contradiction/Denial Activities
Many activities designed to help students form negative statements consist of either asking a question or making a statement that will elicit a contradiction or a denial. Some of the more popular activities of this type are described here.

Activity 1: Places and Capitals (Beginning Through Intermediate)
In one column, write the name of different countries on the board. Write the capitals of those countries in another column. The students form two teams. A member of one team says something like "Riga is the capital of Finland, isn't it?" A student from the other team responds, "No, Riga isn't in Finland. It is the capital of Latvia." The teams continue taking turns in this way.

This activity can be introduced as a teacher-fronted activity in which you direct the questions to individual students who volunteer to answer, or it can be a small-group or pair activity. It can be converted into a discovery activity by asking students to first search out countries or states and their capitals on a map or globe. After each team has assembled a list, they give the lists to the teacher, who combines them for the activity. This activity can also be done with the countries that the students come from, provided you have a highly heterogeneous class. The teacher can say, for example, "Janos is from France," and a student responds, "No, he isn't from France. He's from Hungary." The activity can also be adapted so that students make statements about the languages that they speak (e.g., "Reiko speaks Chinese." "No, she doesn't. She speaks Japanese.").

Activity 2: Likes and Dislikes (High Beginning Through Intermediate)
The activity above can also be adapted to deal with students' likes and dislikes. Ask students what their favorite activities are. Write these on the board. Tell them that you

are going to identify the students who like to do various activities, and they should correct you whenever you make a mistake. Say, for instance, "Jinhee likes classical music." A student responds, "No, she doesn't like classical music. She likes rock and roll." You can also use students' abilities. This provides an opportunity to form negative sentences with the modal *can* (e.g., "Boris can play the piano." "No, he can't. But he can play the guitar.").

Activity 3: Descriptions (High Beginning Through Intermediate)

Pass out pictures of people who can be described with adjectives like *young, old, handsome, tall, short, happy, sad, fat, thin, beautiful, famous,* and so on. These can be taken from a newspaper or downloaded from the Internet. Make sure that there is a number under each picture to identify it. Supply students with a list of adjectives to use to describe the people. Make sure that everyone knows the meanings of the words. Put students in pairs. One partner says: "The woman in picture 5 is very old." The other responds, "No, she isn't old. She's young." Students then continue to take turns making and correcting statements about the people in the pictures.

Activity 4: Relating Facts (Low Intermediate Through Intermediate)

Show the class a short video of an incident, e.g., an argument between two people, or tell a complete story with accompanying pictures. Afterward, begin relating the account with intentional inaccuracies. Whenever someone spots an error in your account, he or she should raise a hand. When called on, the student should supply a correction (e.g., "The man didn't slap the woman, the woman slapped the man."). You can also have the students wait until the end of your account of the incident and then ask them to account for all of your errors.

Negative *Wh-* Information Questions

This topic is often barely touched on in many English language teaching textbooks. The following activity, in which students ask each other to evaluate things that they are all familiar with, such as a TV program, movie, or book, will get students to use both positive and negative *wh-* questions.

Activity 5: Negative Questions and Negative Answers (High Intermediate)

Tell the students to make a note of the things they liked and did not like about a particular TV show, movie, or book with which everyone is familiar. After they have made their notes, each student asks another student, "What did you like about _____?" and then, "What didn't you like about it?" Students should be encouraged to supply complete sentences in response (e.g., "I didn't like . . . "). This activity may also provide students with exposure to a type of sentence that will be discussed in Chapter 22 called a *cleft construction*, which is frequently used to express opinions (e.g., "What I didn't like about it was . . . ").

Contrasting Negative Polarity Items and Nonverbal Negation

A number of activities are commonly used to practice the use of negative polarity items in answers to questions. Some of these follow.

Activity 6: *Anybody/Anyone* and *Nobody/No One* (Intermediate Through Low Advanced)

Practicing the use of *anybody/anyone* and *nobody/no one/none* is often done through information gap tasks. Have students form pairs. Student A has one picture and Student B has more than one picture, one of which matches Student A's picture. The objective is for Student B to discover which of his or her pictures matches the one held by Student A.

In order to do this, Student B asks questions such as, "Is there a car in your picture?", to which Student A responds, for example, "Yes, there's a car in my picture." Student B may then ask, "Is there anyone in the car?", and Student A replies, "No, there is no one in the car," or "Yes, there is someone in the car."

The activity proceeds until Student B settles on one picture and asks, "Is this your picture?" If Student B has correctly identified the picture, then the roles are reversed. (Additional variations on this information gap activity can be found in Chapter 7.)

Activity 7: *Somebody* vs. *Nobody* (Low Intermediate Through Low Advanced)

Place an array of objects on a table. These can be things that you normally find in the class. One student, who is designated as the questioner, gets a good look at the objects and then leaves the room. Someone in the class moves one of the objects. (The move must be significant, across the room, for instance, not just a few centimeters away.) The questioner returns and, after looking at the table, asks a student, "Did somebody move the eraser?" The student addressed answers, for example, "No, nobody moved the eraser." The questioner gets three guesses to correctly identify the moved object. If the questioner correctly guesses which object was moved, he or she scores one point and gets another turn. If the questioner doesn't find it, the student who moved the object becomes the questioner. The student with the highest score wins.

Secondary Verb Negation

Secondary verb negation should probably be taught at the upper-intermediate level and revisited at the advanced level when students are developing proficiency with more complex sentence structures. You might begin with sentences that have infinitive complements (see Chapters 20 and 21) and use an activity such as the one following.

Activity 8: Negation in Infinitive Clauses (High Intermediate Through Advanced)

Take a situation such as a job interview and ask students to list things that are important to do if they want to make a good impression on the interviewer and get the job. Explain that students should use structures such as *It is important to . . .*, *Remember to . . .*, *It's a good idea to . . .*, and so on in their lists of dos and don'ts. Their lists might include statements such as "It's important not to be late," "It's a good idea not to speak too fast," and so on. Repeat this activity with other situations familiar to students.

You might also design similar activities to cover secondary negation in object complements beginning with *that* (see Chapter 21). Here, your activity could focus on negation after verbs such as *recommend* and *suggest*. You could pick a topic that involves advising a friend regarding what to do and what not to do on a first date, for example, or when visiting a foreign country for the first time.

ENDNOTES

[1] Here, the expression "I was short with you" means "I responded to you in an abrupt, inconsiderate manner."

[2] Refusal can be explicit, where there is a negative word *no*, or implicit, as shown in (1), in which the speaker's response does not contain any negative words but still conveys the same meaning (Tottie, 1991).

    (**1**) A: Would you like another cup of tea?
            B: I think I've had enough.

[3] The categories of negation here referred to as *verbal* and *nonverbal* are sometimes called *propositional negation* and *constituent negation*, respectively.

[4] These are sometimes referred to as the *primary forms* of a verb; hence the term *primary verb negation*, which is taken from Huddleston and Pullum (2002), p. 788.

[5] Biber et al. (1999), p. 162, point out that "the use of *have* without *do*-insertion in British fiction . . . appears to occur regularly in collocations like *haven't a clue, haven't (the) time, haven't the heart, haven't the foggiest idea*, etc."

[6] Negative polarity items can occur in affirmative questions (e.g., *Did you see any birds? Do you have any matches?*). There is also a *free choice* version of *any* that appears in affirmative sentences such as *Anyone can do that* and *She can have any car she likes.*

[7] *Yet* is also a contrastive conjunction; its meaning and use are discussed further in Chapter 25.

[8] The term *secondary verb negation* is also adapted from Huddleston and Pullum (2002), p. 788.

[9] See, for example, the discussion in Huddleston and Pullum (2002), pp. 805–806.

[10] *Negative raising* is sometimes referred to as *not transportation*.

[11] Negative raising also appears to be possible with some verbs that take infinitive complements. The examples in (2) and (3) with *want* illustrate this. For some native speakers, however, (2) sounds awkward, thus, (3) is most common.

    (**2**) They want us not to talk to the reporters.

    (**3**) They don't want us to talk to the reporters.

[12] The list and the descriptive categories, (i.e., verbs of "opinion," "advice," "wanting," and "perception" that take negative raising) is in Huddleston and Pullum (2002), p. 840.

[13] See Huddleston and Pullum (2002, p. 790).

[14] These words are also known as *volitional adverbs* or *act-related adjuncts*. The examples in (36) and (37) are modeled on Huddleston and Pullum (2002), p. 793.

[15] The examples in (38) come from Huddleston and Pullum (2002), p. 799.

[16] The term *negators* is also used; (e.g., Huddleston and Pullum, 2002).

[17] In Cockney and African-American English, for example.

[18] Examples (40a) and (40c) are recorded examples from Biber et al. (1999), p. 178.

[19] Some people who dabble in languages have said that double negatives are illogical, but, in addition to modern languages like Spanish, languages like classical Greek used them. Therefore, there is nothing illogical about a double negative.

[20] This insightful table comes from Huddleston and Pullum (2002), p. 831. They add that it has its limitations, since the relations between the positive and negative polarity items are not always identical.

[21] For a more complete discussion, see Horn (1989).

[22] Other researchers who have postulated acquisitional sequences for negation are Stauble (1984) and Hyltenstam (1977, 1978). Additionally, researchers like Milon (1974) and Wode (1981) have suggested that second language learners may be guided by some universal limitations, but L1 transfer nevertheless accounts for observed differences in the sequence of acquisition among learners.

[23] Larsen-Freeman and Long (1991), p. 94.

REFERENCES

Biber, D., Johansson, S., Leech, G., Conrad, S., & Finegan, E. (1999). *Longman grammar of spoken and written English*. Essex, England: Pearson Education.

Horn, L. (1989). *A natural history of negation*. Chicago: University of Chicago Press.

Huddleston, R., & Pullum, G. K. (2002). *The Cambridge grammar of the English language*. Cambridge: Cambridge University Press.

Hyltenstam, K. (1977). Implicational patterns in interlanguage syntax variation. *Language Learning*, *27*, 383–411.

Hyltenstam, K. (1978). A framework for the study of interlanguage continua. *Working Papers: Phonetics Laboratory/Department of Linguistics*, *16*. University of Lund.

Larsen-Freeman, D., & Long, M. (1991). *An introduction to second-language acquisition research*. London/New York: Longman.

Meisel, J. M. (1997). The acquisition of the syntax of negation in French and German: Contrasting first and second language development. *Second Language Research*, *13*(3), 227–263.

Milon, J. P. (1974). The development of negation in English by a second language learner. *TESOL Quarterly*, *8*, 137–143.

Schumman, J. H. (1979). The acquisition of English negation by speakers of Spanish: A review of the literature. In R. Anderson (Ed.), *The acquisition and use of Spanish and English as a first and second language* (pp. 3–32). Alexandria, VA: TESOL Publications.

Stauble, A. M. (1984). A comparison of a Spanish-English and a Japanese-English second language continuum: Negation and verb morphology. In R. W. Andersen (Ed.) *Second languages: A cross-linguistic perspective* (pp. 323–353). Rowley, MA: Newbury House.

Tottie, G. (1991). *Negation in English speech and writing: A study of variation*. San Diego: Academic Press.

Wode, H. (1981). *Learning a second language*. Tübingen: Gunter Narr.

CHAPTER 6

Imperative Sentences

INTRODUCTION

This chapter will explore how various types of English imperative sentences are formed and used. Imperatives are used to convey commands, orders, instructions, and requests. Several sentence structures fall within the general category of imperatives. Their grammar is not particularly complex, but choosing which imperative form to use in a given situation is often difficult for learners. Certain imperative forms are more appropriate than others, depending upon the meaning that the speaker wishes to convey. It is, therefore, important that English language learners understand how these different imperative structures will be interpreted by native speakers of English and that they learn to use the forms appropriately in different conversational contexts.

FORMS OF IMPERATIVES

Imperative sentences can be seen as variations of simple declarative sentences. They have the same intonation as declarative sentences, but they differ in three ways. First, imperative sentences do not need visible subjects, but declaratives do. The declarative sentences in (1) will always be interpreted as imperative commands if their subjects are removed.

	Declarative Sentence	*Imperative Sentence*
(**1**) a.	You look at me.	Look at me.
b.	You take her to dinner.	Take her to dinner.

Second, the main verb in an imperative is always in its bare infinitive form, whereas declarative sentences can have inflected verb forms, as shown in (2). Here, the verb *are* in the declarative sentence agrees in number with the subject pronoun *you*. But the corresponding imperative sentence has the bare infinitive form *be*.

	Declarative Sentence	*Imperative Sentence*
(**2**)	You are quiet.	Be quiet.

As shown in (3), it is possible to have an inflected verb after the copula *be* in an imperative sentence, but the verb must be in the progressive (*-ing*) form. The meaning of

(3) is similar to "You had better be working when I get back" or "I expect you to be working when I get back."

> (**3**) *Be working* when I get back.

The third major difference between imperative and declarative sentences lies in the ways they are negated. To negate a declarative sentence, as shown in (4), *do* is absent and *not* is contracted with the verb. In the corresponding imperative, the auxiliary *do* is combined with *not* and placed at the beginning of the sentence before the verb. (For more on negation, see Chapter 5.)

> *Declarative Sentence*   *Imperative Sentence*
> (**4**) You aren't lazy.   Don't be lazy.

As shown in (5), negative declarative sentences whose affirmative forms do not contain an auxiliary verb or copular *be* also take *do not* before the verb. Unlike their imperative counterparts, however, these negative declaratives must still have a visible subject.

> *Declarative Sentence*   *Imperative Sentence*
> (**5**) You don't use it.   Don't use it.

Another way to distinguish negative declaratives from negative imperatives is by using the *tag test*. Negative declaratives such as (5) can take a tag, like *do you*, to form a tag question, as in (6a). This is not possible with negative imperatives, as (6b) shows. Positive imperatives can, however, have tags with *will* or *would*. This is discussed later, in the section on imperatives with tags.

> (**6**) a. You don't use it, do you?
> b. *Don't use it, do you!

Emphatic Imperatives

Do occurs in front of so-called *emphatic imperatives* like the example shown in (7b). *Do* before the bare infinitive indicates that the speaker is adding a sense of urgency to the command being uttered.

> (**7**) a. Hurry up.   *basic imperative*
> b. Do hurry up!   *emphatic imperative*

Imperatives with Tags

Emphatic imperatives sound a bit stilted and archaic to some native speakers of American English, who would prefer to attach the tag *will you*, as shown in (8a), to add a sense of urgency to a command. Imperatives with *would you* tags, like (8b), do not carry the same sense of urgency as those with *will you*, and are usually interpreted as informal polite requests.

> (**8**) a. Hurry up, *will you*!
> b. Get my gloves out of the car, *would you*?

You may see these tagged imperatives written with exclamation marks after them, as in (8a). Some writers put a question mark after them, although they function more as a command or a request for compliance than as an actual question. The convention of putting a comma before the tag is usually followed with these imperatives.

Imperatives with Visible Subjects

For some time, it has been claimed that imperatives have an underlying subject, *you*.[1] In other words, while an imperative sentence may have no visible subject, the second-person singular or plural pronoun *you* is nevertheless understood to be the subject of the sentence. As support for this claim, we can point to the fact that subjectless imperatives such as those in (7) have variants such as those in (8) with a tag that contains *you*. We can also point to the fact that imperatives with reflexive pronouns, as in (9a), can only take the reflexive pronoun *yourself*. Other reflexive pronouns do not occur, as (9b) through (9e) demonstrate.[2]

> (**9**) a. Behave *yourself*!
> b. *Behave *myself*!
> c. *Behave *herself*!
> d. *Behave *ourselves*!
> e. *Behave *themselves*!

Additional support for the proposition that subjectless imperatives have an underlying *you* subject is the fact that, under certain circumstances (which are discussed in greater detail later in this chapter), imperatives include a visible pronoun subject *you*, as shown in (10a). Other pronouns, in contrast, are not permitted as subjects of imperatives, as (10b), (10c), and (10d) demonstrate.

> (**10**) a. You behave yourself!
> b. *She behave herself!
> c. *He behave himself!
> d. *They behave themselves!

There are special cases when other subjects can occur in imperatives, for instance, when the speaker is addressing a particular group of people, as in (11a). Also, the indefinite pronouns *someone*, *somebody*, and *nobody* often occur as subjects when the speaker is uttering a directive to everyone who may be present. Examples (11b) and (11c) illustrate such cases.

> (**11**) a. Passengers going to Dayton, form a line over here.
> b. Somebody please go find a doctor.
> c. Nobody move!

Vocative Imperatives

The term *vocative* refers to utterances that contain a noun phrase that is a proper name or some kind of address form, for example, *Ma'am*, *Sir*, *waiter*, *Dear*, or *you all*. Vocatives are used to call someone or to direct a person's attention to something. They are sometimes used as part of an imperative to direct a particular person or group to do something. The vocative noun phrase is usually separated from the rest of the utterance by a pause, which is represented in writing by a comma. Although vocatives usually appear in the first position in a sentence, as in (12a) and (12b), they can also occur at the end, as in (12c).

> (**12**) a. Ann, you go first.
> b. Dear, look what I found under the couch.
> c. Look what I found under the couch, dear.

Idiomatic *I Need You* Imperatives

A new kind of softened command imperative that begins with *I need you* has developed in American English. The three-word formula that begins this type of imperative is always followed by an infinitive complement that describes what the speaker wants the addressee to do. Such imperatives, as shown in (13), are very impersonal and are widely used by people in professions who deal with many strangers each day (receptionists, nurses, police officers, etc.).

(13) a. I need you to fill out this form.
   b. I need you to take off your clothes and put on this robe.
   c. I need you to step back from the car, sir.

Let's Imperatives

An imperative that begins with *let's*, such as (14a), proposes an action that includes the speaker and the listener.[3] The meaning of (14a), therefore, is shown in (14b).

(14) a. Let's eat breakfast.
   b. I propose that you and I eat breakfast.

Let's imperatives can also have a meaning that is closer to an order or an instruction. This is the meaning conveyed by the imperatives in (15a) through (15d).[4]

(15) a. Let us bow our heads in prayer.
   b. You all have something to do for Ms. Johnson. Let's do it, please.
   c. Let's have a look at your tongue.
   d. OK. It looks like we may have gone too far, so let's take the next exit and turn around.

The more formal *let us* used in (15a) announces that the speaker is about to bow his or her own head in prayer and expects all of those within hearing to do the same. In (15b), a teacher instructs a group of children to begin carrying out their assignments. The use of *let's* as a polite way of framing a command occurs in many different settings, such as the one in (15c), where a doctor is actually conveying an instruction, *Stick out your tongue*. In (15d), a passenger uses a *let's* imperative to politely tell the driver to exit the freeway and turn around.

Let's imperatives sometimes occur with tags that have rising intonation. The tag *shall we*, as in (16a), appears to be more common in British English, whereas American English tends to use the tag *OK*, shown in (16b).[5] Most writers insert a comma before the tag in these imperatives and end the imperative with a question mark, as if it were a tag question. *Let's* imperatives are negated by placing *not* after *let's*, as in (16c) and (16d).[6]

(16) a. OK, let's keep that on, shall we? (British English)
   b. Let's take turns, OK? (American English)
   c. Let's not talk about what happened anymore, please?
   d. Let's not discuss it anymore, shall we?

The following two structures begin with *let's* but are not true imperatives:

1. *Let's see* sentences. *Let's see* is an idiomatic expression that often precedes an utterance in conversation, as shown in (17). It seems to indicate that the speaker is thinking, searching for information, or trying to decide on something.[7]

(17) a. Let's see. Are you working now?
   b. Um, let's see, I'll have to give you some more.

2. Open *let* imperatives. The so-called *open let imperative* differs in meaning from the *let's* imperative. It is not an instruction to do something and is therefore not a true imperative. Instead, its meaning is best paraphrased using the modal *should*. Thus, (18a) means the same thing as (18b), and (18c) has the same meaning as (18d).

(**18**) a. If that is what he really intends to do, *let him say so.*
　　　b. If that is what he really intends to do, *then he should say so.*
　　　c. *Let that be* a lesson to you.
　　　d. *That should be* a lesson to you.

SUMMARY

FORMS OF IMPERATIVES

The basic form of imperatives has a bare infinitive and no visible subject. Negative imperatives have *do not/don't* before the verb.
　Be quiet!
　Don't touch that.

Emphatic imperatives, which express a sense of urgency, begin with *do*.
　Do hurry up!

Imperatives with tags have tags with the modal verb *will* or *would*.
　Hurry up, will you!
　Close the door, would you?

Imperatives with visible subjects may have the pronoun *you*, third-person subjects directed at particular groups, or indefinite pronoun subjects such as *everyone, nobody,* and *somebody* in the subject position.
　You behave yourself!
　Somebody please go find a doctor.

Vocative imperatives begin or end with an address form, which is separated from the rest of the sentence by a comma.
　Ann, you go first.
　Look what I found under the couch, dear.

Idiomatic *I need you* imperatives always begin with the formula *I need you* and are followed by an infinitive complement.
　I need you to fill out this form.

Let's imperatives begin with *let's* or *let us*. They either propose an action to be taken by the speaker and the person addressed, or they function as a command or instruction for the listener.
　Let's eat breakfast.
　Let's have a look at your tongue.

Two structures beginning with *let's* are not imperatives:

1. *Let's see* is an idiomatic expression that precedes an utterance and indicates that the speaker is thinking, searching for information, or trying to decide on something.
　Let's see. Are you working now?

2. The so-called *open let imperative* is not an instruction but has a meaning that is best paraphrased with the modal *should*.
　If that is what he really intends to do, let him say so. (= *he should say so*)

EXERCISE 6.1

Identify each imperative sentence as a basic imperative, emphatic imperative, imperative with visible subject, vocative imperative, *let's* imperative, open *let* imperative, or *I need you* imperative. Indicate whether the imperative is negated, and identify any structures that are not true imperatives.

Example: Don't breathe a word to your sister about this.

Answer: basic imperative (negated with *don't*)

1. Let's just keep this a secret between you and me, OK?
2. Everyone be back here by three o'clock.
3. Do be careful.
4. Do as you're told!
5. If she really believes her method is better than the one we are using, let her prove it.
6. Those with a bus to catch, feel free to leave.
7. Private Henderson, take the first watch.
8. I need you to fill out this form and give it to the nurse when she comes in for you.

THE MEANINGS OF IMPERATIVES

Imperatives are about speaker manipulation. They may be used as actual commands, such as those a military officer or a parent issues to a soldier or a child. They may also be used as more gentle directives or as quasidirectives, in which the speaker merely expects or envisions some behavior on the part of someone else and casts that expectation in terms of a directive, although not actually demanding anything.

Commands, Orders, and Demands

With imperatives that are intended as commands, orders, or demands as shown in (19a), (19b), and (19c), the speaker expects the persons addressed to do what he or she has said. If the persons addressed do not do what the speaker says, they can expect that some kind of retaliation may be taken against them. For example, the person to whom the command in (19a) is addressed may expect to be pushed aside if he or she does not comply. The imperative in (19d) is a highly stylized command that is used only in opening ceremonies.

> (**19**) a. Get out of my way!
>   b. Right face! Forward, march!
>   c. Keep off the grass.
>   d. Let the games begin![8]

Requests

Requests, as in (20), have the same subjectless form as command imperatives. The person addressed is not necessarily expected to comply with the request, and since the speaker is asking for help, this type of imperative is often accompanied by *please* or a *will you/would you* tag, as seen in (20a) and (20b).

> (**20**) a. Please help me finish this.
>   b. Shut the window, will you?
>   c. Kindly lower your voices.

Advice, Recommendations, and Warnings

Here, the speaker is directing the attention of the person addressed to do something that is for his or her benefit, not the speaker's. It is up to the person who receives the advice, recommendation, or warning to decide whether to follow it.

(21) a. Keep your options open.
   b. Remember, always buy low and sell high.
   c. Watch your head. That doorjamb is a little low.

Instructions and Expository Directives

The purpose of instructions is to enable the person addressed to accomplish some goal, as illustrated in (22a), (22b), and (22c). The *expository directives*[9] in (22d) and (22e), are often used in expository prose and are framed in a manner that attempts to get the reader to actively participate in the discussion or argument at hand.

(22) a. Remove all the tape and the packing material from the printer.
   b. For full details of performances, talks, workshops, contact the Third Eye Center.[10]
   c. Take a left at the first stop light.
   d. Compare example (4a) with (4b).
   e. Take the airline industry, for example.

Invitations

An imperative may function as an invitation to the person addressed. The invitation may have benefit for both the speaker and the person addressed, or it may benefit only one of them. The speaker does not necessarily expect the person addressed to comply, that is, to accept the invitation.

(23) a. Drop by after work, and we'll discuss it in more detail.
   b. Have another piece of cake.
   c. Feel free to call me any time.

Permission

Speakers may also use a subjectless imperative when granting permission to carry out an action. The granting of permission may not be something that the speaker is happy with; it only signals that he or she has the power to grant it.

(24) a. OK. Go ahead and do it.
   b. Take as much time as you feel you need.
   c. Come in.

Acceptance

Utterances such as (25a) and (25b) express the speaker's acceptance of something that he or she may not necessarily want but nevertheless is powerless to prevent.

(25) a. Since you feel so strongly about it, go ahead and tell him.
   b. Hey, it's your money. Invest it any way you want.

Wishes

Wishes sometimes take the form of imperatives. Some wishes include modals such as *may*, as in the proverb in (26a). Wishes such as (26b) through (26e) extend a blessing to the person addressed, usually as he or she is leaving or when the speaker is terminating a conversation. The wish in (26e) has become somewhat impersonal by overuse.[11]

(**26**) a. May the wind be always at your back.
     b. Have a safe journey.
     c. OK. See ya. Have a good time at the game.
     d. Enjoy yourself! Enjoy!
     e. Have a nice day.

Structures with Imperative Form but Conditional Meaning

Sentences (27a) and (27b) look like imperatives, but they have the meaning of a conditional sentence (i.e., "If you do *X*, then *Y* will happen.").

(**27**) a. Do that and you're fired! (= If you do that, you will be fired.)
     b. Touch that knob and the telly goes wrong.[12]
        (= If you touch that knob, the telly will go/goes wrong.)

SUMMARY
THE MEANINGS OF IMPERATIVES

Imperatives are used by speakers to manipulate the behavior of the person who is addressed. As these attempts may be more direct or less direct, imperatives have the following specific functions:

- **Commands, orders, and demands.** The speaker expects the persons addressed to do what he or she has said. Failure to comply can have unpleasant consequences.
  Get out of my way!

- **Requests.** The person addressed is not necessarily expected to comply. Requests are often accompanied by *please* or a *will you/would you* tag.
  Please help me finish this.
  Shut the window, will you?

- **Advice, recommendations, and warnings.** The speaker directs the attention of the person addressed to something that is for his or her benefit.
  Keep your options open.
  Watch your head. That doorjamb is a little low.

- **Instructions and expository directives.** Instructions are meant to enable the person addressed to accomplish some goal. Expository directives attempt to influence the listener in order to make a point or state evidence for an argument.
  Remove all the tape and the packing material from the printer.
  Take the airline industry, for example.

- **Invitations.** The speaker invites the person addressed to do something.
  Drop by after work, and we'll discuss it in more detail.

- **Permission.** The speaker grants permission to the listener to carry out an action.
  OK. Go ahead and do it.

continued

- **Acceptance.** The speaker expresses acceptance of something that he or she may not necessarily want.
  Hey, it's your money. Invest it any way you want.

- **Wishes.** Wishes are in effect a stylized form of imperative that occurs with *have*, the modal *may*, or *let*. They often extend a blessing and are used to terminate a conversation when the speaker or the listener is leaving.
  Have a nice day.

In certain conditions, the speaker uses what appears to be an imperative to state a condition and the result that can occur. This type of sentence is, however, not a true imperative.
Do that and you're fired! (= *If you do that, you will be fired.*)

EXERCISE 6.2

Identify the meaning of each imperative. Explain your choice of meaning by describing the circumstances under which the sentence might be said.

Example: By all means, borrow it any time you need it.

Answer: permission (lending something to your neighbor or a friend)

1. OK, buy it. I wouldn't, but it's all a matter of taste.
2. Wait until the price is right.
3. Bring your girlfriend along, too.
4. Release the prisoners!
5. Insert the disc with the label side facing up.
6. Have a good day, sir.
7. But there are plenty of counterexamples. Take, for example, the last president.

IMPERATIVES WITH A VISIBLE *YOU* SUBJECT

Imperatives with a visible *you* subject are quite common.[13] They have two basic purposes, depending on whether the *you* is contrastive.

Contrastive *You*

You can be used to mark a contrast when two or more roles are being assigned to different agents. In (28), we see examples in which the speaker singles out two people who are supposed to carry out two distinct tasks or roles.

(28) a. You be Butch Cassidy, and I'll be the Sundance Kid.
   b. You take the high road, and I'll take the low road.

Noncontrastive *You*

Imperatives with *you* subjects that are noncontrastive are used when the speaker feels he or she is in a position to claim some authority over the person who is being addressed. The use of a *you* subject can convey several different emotional tones, which depend upon the circumstances in which the imperative is uttered.

Impatience or Irritation

The presence of *you* may indicate that the speaker is irritated or impatient with the person being addressed. In this case, the *you* subject imperative can have an "aggressive, hectoring effect,"[14] as in (29).

(**29**) "Now, now, can't you take a little joke, my friend?" Santiago slowly raised his head. "*Don't you call me your friend.* The only friend you have is yourself."

Comfort or Encouragement

The use of a *you* subject can also convey a tone of friendly encouragement as in (30a), in which the cheers from the stands are meant to comfort and encourage the person at whom they are directed. Again, in (30b) and (30c), the *you* subject imperatives clearly have the function of comforting and reassuring.

(**30**) a. Chrissie shed bitter tears in private, but she walked out in the summer sunshine with her head held high. Most of her acquaintances shunned her, but not everyone condemned her. The bleachers, who were embarked on a bitter strike against their employer, cheered as she passed the empty bleach fields. "Good for you, lass! *You show 'em!*" someone shouted.
b. He ran out into the downpour, sped across the yard into the buggy room. "*Don't you be afraid,*" he said. He would save her.
c. Clayton looped the reins in a knot over the veranda post and patted the warm flesh of his neck. "*You take it easy, boy,*" Clayton whispered.

Admonishment, Threat, or Advice

A speaker may use a *you* subject imperative to admonish someone to do something or to threaten or advise someone. The *you* subject adds an extra element of emotion to the imperative.

(**31**) He led her to the door. "*And don't you ever forget what we swore to do.*" Insulted by his authoritarian tone, Heather lifted her chin. As if she would ever forget the importance of what they'd just promised.

In (31), the *you* subject makes the imperative sound more like a command than if the speaker had used a simple subjectless imperative such as *Don't ever forget what we swore to do.* As the last sentence demonstrates, this extra emotional tone is interpreted negatively by the person who is addressed. It offends her.

A *you* subject imperative can have several other interpretations. The sentence in (32) is an emphatic directive. Again, it has more emotional impact than it would without the visible *you* subject. The same can be said for (33), which is a threat, and (34), which conveys friendly advice.[15]

(**32**) More importantly, *don't you ever forget to check the oil before you start the engine.* Remember, this is the only engine we have, and I've seen too many engines burn out because of oil starvation.

(**33**) *Don't you ever address me in that tone again*, or I will see that you never get a job in this town.

(**34**) She smiled at me and I heard her say, "Well, Becky, *you be careful at night* with the burglaries around your neighborhood."

SUMMARY

IMPERATIVES WITH A VISIBLE *YOU* SUBJECT

Imperatives with a *you* subject are common. There are two types:

Contrastive *you* marks a contrast when two or more roles are being assigned to different agents.
> *You be Butch Cassidy, and I'll be the Sundance Kid.*

Noncontrastive *you* is used when the speaker feels he or she is in a position to claim some authority over the person addressed. The use of noncontrastive *you* subject imperatives can convey:

- **impatience or irritation**
  Don't you call me your friend.

- **comfort or encouragement**
  "Good for you, lass! You show 'em!" someone shouted.

- **admonishment, threat, or advice**
  And don't you ever forget what we swore to do.
  Don't you ever address me in that tone again.
  Well, Becky, you be careful at night.

EXERCISE 6.3

Identify each *you* subject imperative as contrastive or noncontrastive. Indicate the emotional tone that each noncontrastive *you* subject imperative conveys.

Example: Don't you tell me to go away! I've been here since you were born. I'll teach you to tell me to go away.[16]

Answer: noncontrastive imperative (irritation or anger)

1. "Don't you worry, young lady," said the cab driver. "I'll get you there in plenty of time."
2. You sign up for that event, and I'll sign up for this one. That way we will have a greater chance at winning something.
3. He raised the pistol and pointed it at him. "Now, you tell him to get back here," he said menacingly.
4. You be sure to rub that horse down and water him. He's had a hard workout.
5. A: Quiet down over there. We'll have no arguing in this restaurant.
   B: You mind your own business! This is a private argument.

PROBLEMS THAT ESL/EFL STUDENTS HAVE WITH IMPERATIVES

Problems that ESL/EFL students have with imperatives may involve grammatical form but also appropriateness of use.

Grammatical Form

Not a great deal is known about the grammatical errors English learners make with imperatives. One anecdotal report, Walter (2001), suggests possible L1 transfer with one type of directive. Walter claims that the future tense is often used in French for giving directions, and that English language learners who speak French may adopt the corresponding tense in English for this purpose, resulting in odd-sounding sequences such as *You will go straight until the light, and then you will turn left*[17] instead of *Go straight until the light, and then turn left*. We have no data to confirm whether this is a common problem, but if it is, it indicates that teachers should pay attention to the forms students use when they are engaged in task-based activities such as giving directions.

Some ungrammatical imperatives might be the result of other phenomena. For example, if we encountered imperatives such as **Give him* or **Give it*, this might simply be a reflection of the fact that, in the learner's native language, object pronouns that have been mentioned in discourse can be omitted, and that this has been carried over into English and the forming of English imperatives (Yuan, 1997). However, until we have more data about ungrammatical imperatives produced by English learners, any discussion about them and whether they need to be addressed is largely speculative.

Using Appropriate Imperatives

A concern that ESL teachers may have is that their students' use of imperatives could be perceived by native speakers as rude or too abrupt. A study by Carrell and Konneker (1981) showed that native and nonnative speakers of English display a good deal of agreement about ranking declarative, interrogative, and imperative sentences in terms of a scale of perceived politeness. Reports of students' inappropriate use of imperatives, though largely anecdotal, warrant teachers' attention. Imperatives present a unique problem for teaching since they are used very frequently in many different conversational settings. Furthermore, appropriate use of imperatives requires the speaker to accurately assess certain dimensions in the conversation, such as the status of the speaker and the person to whom the imperative is addressed and the degree of formality and politeness implied by different imperative forms.

SUGGESTIONS FOR TEACHING IMPERATIVES

English language teaching textbooks pay varying degrees of attention to the issue of which imperative form is appropriate in a given setting. Some simply present the basic subjectless imperative and explain that *please* may be added to create a more polite form. Others attempt to show how the relationship between the speaker and addressee may make a form that does not contain *please* more appropriate. Some textbooks actually attempt short explanations of some of the imperative meanings shown in the Summary Box on page 120. The basic form of imperatives and the more polite form with *please* will normally be introduced early in textbooks and syllabi. To practice these basic forms, you can supplement the exercises in your textbook with the activities below. Activities 1 through 3 are commonly used to practice the basic forms of imperatives with beginning- and low-intermediate level students. For intermediate- and advanced-level students, it is important to revisit the topic of imperatives. With these higher level students, you may want to focus on issues of appropriateness. That is, students must consider the settings in which they are likely to use imperatives and learn to choose the most appropriate forms, given factors like register (e.g., conversation vs. academic writing) and the relative status of the speaker and the listener.

Giving Instructions and Expository Directions

Activity 1: Following Directions (Beginning Through Low Intermediate)

Have students follow directions that you give them. A series of simple commands, some of which incorporate vocatives, may be used, as in (35).

> (35) Roberto, stand up, please. Come here. Erase the blackboard. Write your name on the blackboard. Go back to your seat. Sit down, please.

Next, find some objects that students can use to practice giving and following directions in pairs. Simple props can be used to incorporate negative imperatives like those in (36).

> (36) Don't put the book in the small box; put it in the big box.

Activity 2: Assembling and Troubleshooting (Beginning Through Low Intermediate)

Find or write simple directions for assembling something or troubleshooting a piece of equipment (e.g., unjamming a printer or programming a DVD player). It is important to find a task that will provide the students with a sense of satisfaction when they have followed the instructions successfully. Have students work in pairs, in which Student A recites the directions to Student B. Student A must be coached to correct Student B with negative imperatives whenever appropriate (e.g., "No, don't put the disc in yet. First turn the DVD player on.").

It is not necessary to use machines with this activity. Simple assembly tasks also work very well. If you are going to assemble something reasonably complex, you will need a picture of the fully assembled object.

Activity 3: Giving Directions (Beginning Through Low Intermediate)

Giving directions to a place is an obvious choice for practicing imperatives. Here is one type of direction-giving classroom activity.

Have students work in pairs. Give each pair of students two maps. Student A gets a map with the names of buildings, streets, and landmarks on it. Student B gets an identical map that only has street names on it. Student A says, "I'm going to tell you how to get to _____ from the corner of _____ and _____." Student B marks the starting point on his or her map and then follows Student A's directions until he or she is finished. Student B then marks the final destination and shows it to Student A. If the destination has been correctly identified, Student B labels the destination. Students then exchange maps, and Student B now gives directions from the previous destination to another point on the map.

It is important for both teachers and students to pay attention to form while they are doing this activity, particularly if students show a propensity for the type of L1 transfer problem mentioned in the previous section.

Wishes
Activity 4: Leave-Taking Expressions (Intermediate Through Advanced)

Collect common expressions for leave taking, like those in (37), and write them on the board. Point out that they have the basic form of a command and are expressions commonly used when the speaker or the listener is leaving.

(37) a. Take care!
     b. You take care now!
     c. Take it easy!
     d. Don't work too hard!
     e. Have a good one!
     f. Have a nice day.
     g. Be good!

Take the first expression and supply an example situation where you might use it (e.g., "I have been talking to a friend I met on the street, and I have to leave."). As you move to each new expression, supply a situation in which it might be used. Indicate that all of these expressions are fairly informal and would not be used with certain people. For example, you would not want to use (37d) with your boss unless you were close friends with him or her. Point out variations as in (37e) and (37f) and that certain expressions (e.g., *Have a nice day*) are usable in a wider range of situations (e.g., *Be good!*). Next, present (either orally or using an overhead projector) a written description such as the one in (38). Ask the students to select the best expression for this situation.

(38) You are standing at the checkout counter in the supermarket. You have just bought some groceries. The cashier hands you the sales slip and some change and says, "Thank you. Have a nice day."[18]

What should you say in return?
A: Take care.
B: Don't work too hard!
C: Thanks. Same to you.

After the students have chosen what they feel to be the best expression for the situation, discuss reasons for rejecting A and B. Point out that A is a little too familiar to be used with someone you have never met before. Response B, on the other hand, could be misconstrued, for example, if the clerk is tired, he or she may understand your response to be critical or mocking. Then discuss why answer C is the most appropriate response. You may explain that it is a neutral parting wish that responds to what the cashier has said and does not assume or imply any measure of familiarity between the customer and the cashier.

Next, provide descriptions of the other situations, have the students select an appropriate response, and then discuss their choices.

Requests
Activity 5: Requests and the Degree of Urgency (Intermediate Through Advanced)

Students need to be able to produce requests for help that fit the different situations that they are likely to encounter. Some situations are more urgent than others, and requests for help must be made in a way that gives the speaker the best chance of receiving the assistance he or she needs. In some cases, a particular type of imperative will be appropriate. In other, less urgent cases, no imperative may be appropriate, and another form of request should be used instead. The purpose of the following activity is to heighten students' understanding that different types of requests imply different degrees of urgency.

Write the two columns of sentences shown in (39) on the board.

(**39**) a. Help! Somebody help me!   I have been waiting to see the doctor for over an hour.

b. Help me, would you?   This box is too heavy for me to lift.
c. Could you please help me?   Somebody stole my purse.
d. Excuse me. Could you help me?   I am looking for this address.

Point out, first of all, that some of the expressions in the first column contain imperatives while others do not (*Could you please help me?* and *Could you help me?* are not imperatives). Then explain that (39a) would be appropriate only in an emergency. For instance, if you are in serious trouble, you would use expression (39a). Ask the students which of the utterances in the second column describes a serious situation for which (39a) would be the best choice. Once a correct answer is received (and perhaps discussed), proceed to (39b) and explain that this is more appropriate when you need help with something that is not very serious, and you are in the position to request assistance from a friend. Once again, ask which situation in the second column fits that description. Proceed through (39c) and (39d) in this way. Some of the expressions are appropriate in more than one of the situations listed, and your students should be made aware of this.

Next, hand out slips of paper with situations similar to the previous ones, and have small groups or pairs decide which situation is the right match for each request. These situations can be made up fairly easily. Use (40) as a guide.

(**40**) a. Somebody help me!   I am looking for City Hall.
b. Help me, would you?   This bag is so heavy. I can't carry it any longer.

c. Could you please help me?   My husband is hurt. He's bleeding!
d. Excuse me. Could you help me?   I'm lost.

In each case, you need to be sure that one of the utterances clearly reflects an urgent situation and that one or two of the other utterances require imperatives that have the form of a polite request. You do not need to argue whether (40c) or (40d) is more appropriate in a given situation, since they are both polite requests.

Activity 6: Requests and Politeness (Intermediate Through Advanced)
Requests imply varying degrees of politeness. Students are often taught to make polite requests by either adding *please* to an imperative (e.g., *Please pass me that wrench*), or by using a statement beginning with a modal like, *would, could, may, will,* or *can,* plus *please* (e.g., *Would you please pass me that wrench?*). Some ESL/EFL textbooks present request forms like these as part of a politeness continuum such as the one in (41). Expressions beginning with modals are at the high end of the politeness continuum, while basic imperatives are presented as the least polite option.

(41) a. Would you please pass me that wrench? *Very polite*
    b. Could you pass me that wrench?
    c. Pass me that wrench, would you?
    d. Let me have that wrench.
    e. Give me that wrench. *Not polite*

After several examples similar to (41) have been modeled and explained, present students with a few situations that require a polite request form (e.g., taking a phone message, asking someone not to smoke, asking to borrow something). Then have students choose the most appropriate request form from one of a number of options written on the board.

This same process may be followed again, but this time, do not supply students with the possible options for request forms. Instead, have them make up their own requests based on the situations with which they are presented.

Imperatives and English for Specific Purposes

A good understanding of the variables that go into selecting an appropriate imperative for a given situation is extremely relevant for a course in English for Specific Purposes (ESP). Students will have varying degrees of familiarity with others in the workplace, and the dynamics of these different relationships should help to shape the imperatives they use.

The ESP classroom is a good setting for focusing on imperatives that serve as requests, directions, and invitations. Examples of imperatives collected from real-world workplace situations – tape recordings or videos, when this is permitted – are obviously most useful, since they provide the necessary element of authenticity. Such examples enable the teacher to explain implications drawn from the intonation pattern the person employs. These examples can also be developed into realistic dialogs and role-plays for classroom activities. You can focus on comprehending the true meaning of an imperative as well as matching the imperative to the situation.

Activity 7: Giving Instructions in the Workplace (Intermediate Through Advanced)

Design an activity around the way one employee might show another employee how to perform a particular job-related task. The activity should focus on developing a sensitivity to the degrees of politeness or consideration implied by imperative forms that one might use for instructing. The person giving the instructions has to bear in mind that the person trying to learn will be insulted or annoyed if the instructions are perceived as conveying an attitude of impatience or frustration, or if the instructions are presented in an abrupt or inconsiderate tone. Some different attitudes that may be conveyed by job-related instruction are shown in (42).

(42) a. Try doing it slower.
    b. No. Don't do it like that! Do it like this, see?
    c. Let's try it again.
    d. Look, just take it like this, and put it in the vice.
    e. Look, it's simple! Put it in the vice like this.
    f. Now take it like this. Turn it over . . . place it in the vice . . . and you've got it.

Activity 8: Expressions of Willingness/Accessibility (Intermediate Through Advanced)

Students need to develop a sense of how willing an employer or supervisor is to discuss problems that they, as employees, may encounter. You can address this need by presenting a possible range of expressions, as in (43), that students might encounter from a boss when this type of topic arises. Discuss possible interpretations for each of these imperative expressions, giving special attention to the intonation that the boss may use.

(43) a. Well then, give me a ring/send me an e-mail.
b. Let's talk about that another time.
c. Don't hesitate to contact me.
d. Let me know if you need any help.
e. Well, if you have any trouble, tell Stevens about it.

Activity 9: Caretaker Situations (Intermediate Through Advanced)

Students may get a job in which they have to enforce certain regulations. This type of situation requires considerable sensitivity regarding the choice of imperatives that signal prohibition. An imperative such as *Stop! Don't do that!* may evoke the wrong type of response. It might be useful to ask students how they should respond in given situations and then role-play various scenarios in which the student attempts to deal forcefully, but as politely as possible, with someone who attempts to violate a prohibition (e.g., entering a prohibited area without proper security ID). These may be some of the most stressful situations that a nonnative speaker has to deal with, and they are not often treated in ESL courses.[19]

Imperatives in Written English

Imperatives occur in a range of contexts in written English. You can simultaneously make students aware of the fact and exploit it for materials for classroom activities.

Activity 10: Academic English (Intermediate Through Advanced)

Swales and Feak (2005) point out that directives with verbs such as *notice*, *consider*, *imagine*, *refer*, *compare*, *recall*, and *observe* appear often in the style of writing referred to as academic English. These directives are typically found in research reports, a genre of writing for which many ESL writing teachers need to prepare their students, especially those students who have been admitted to universities' undergraduate and graduate programs. One technique that may be beneficial for improving students' command of imperatives is to find authentic examples of imperatives that contain these particular verbs in research reports, discuss them in class, and then encourage students to incorporate the structures into short writing assignments.

Activity 11: Examining Imperatives in Advertising (Intermediate)

Looking at authentic samples of language can be helpful for promoting comprehension in intermediate level students. Have your students bring in examples of advertisements for various products and sales that are going on in local stores. They are likely to find ads that contain statements such as *Save up to 50%! Get a 10% reward! Clip this coupon for extra savings! Buy one now, get one free! Call for this week's hottest deals! To order or for information call 1-800 . . .*, and so on. Discuss the intended meanings of the ads. This type of activity is fun as well as practical since the discussion will sometimes reveal that the full implication of the ad is often not understood. On the practical side, the students may not understand the basic meaning of the imperative (e.g., *Clip this coupon . . .*). More abstract slogans, (e.g., *Discover a new digital age!*) also present opportunities for the teacher to probe for comprehension.

ENDNOTES

[1] The *you* as understood subject for imperatives has been discussed by many linguists, for example, Lees (1964), Hasegawa (1965), Schmerling (1975), Levenston (1969), and McCawley (1988).

[2] A somewhat weaker piece of evidence that supports the existence of an underlying *you* subject in command imperatives is that emphatic imperatives can be rephrased with command intonation as a question that contains this pronoun (i.e., *Be quiet! = Will you be quiet?!*). A nice summary of some of the arguments for an underlying *you*, along with many crucial examples, is found in Stockwell, Schachter, and Partee (1973).

[3] *Let's* imperatives are sometimes called *first-person inclusive imperatives*, because the *let's* is a shortened form of *let us* (*you and I*).

[4] Examples (b) and (c) are from Biber et al. (1999), p. 1117. Example (b) is altered by inserting a fictitious name.

[5] Examples (16a) and (16b) are taken from Biber et al. (1999), p. 1117.

[6] Biber et al. found *don't let's* as a variant of *let's not* in their corpus, but they point out that this is very rare and is not likely to be considered acceptable by many native speakers. Their example (p. 1117) is: *Oh, well, then don't let's put a five-hundred-dollar stipend in.*

[7] Examples (17a) and (17b) are taken from Biber et al. (1999), p. 1118.

[8] This is sometimes referred to as a *third-person imperative*.

[9] See Huddleston and Pullum (2002).

[10] This sentence is taken from Biber et al. (1999), p. 222.

[11] Historically, wishes beginning with *may* quite possibly predate wishes with *have*. Some wishes like the single-word *Enjoy* are fairly recent innovations which have longer forms such as *Enjoy yourself* and *Enjoy it*.

[12] This example is modeled on a sentence in Biber et al. (1999), p. 220.

[13] Imperatives with *you* as a subject have been widely studied; see for example Davies (1986), Quirk et. al. (1985), Huddleston and Pullum (2002), Jespersen (1961, p. 222), Levenston (1969), Schmerling (1975, 1982), Stefanowitsch (2003), and Flagg (2001). The pragmatic explanation of when and why native speakers use noncontrastive imperatives with *you* subjects has been adopted in this book because it appears to cover all cases, including the recent explanations by Stefanowitsch and Flagg. This pragmatic position is argued for in De Clerck (2004). All examples in this section, which are actual spoken sentences drawn from different corpora, appear in De Clerck (2004).

[14] Huddleston and Pullum (2002), p. 926.

[15] *You* subject imperatives cannot be used with certain verbs (e.g., *know, love, own, inspire*), as shown in (1), (2), and (3). An advertising slogan is demonstrated in (1), a general exhortation in (2), and a proverb in (3). In each case, the (b) version with the *you* subject is ungrammatical as an imperative.

> **(1)** a. Own it on video and Disney DVD!
>
> b. *You own it on video and Disney DVD.

(**2**) a. Know your rights and responsibilities.

  b. *You know your rights and responsibilities.

(**3**) a. Love thy neighbor.

  b. *You love thy neighbor.

[16] This and other examples in this exercise are taken from De Clerck (2004).

[17] See Walter (2001), p. 67.

[18] This activity is modeled on the "conversation maze" exercise in McClure (1996), p. 152. Although many of the activities in that book may not necessarily improve ESL students' grammatical accuracy, this one seems to be very well suited for raising ESL students' sensitivity to the pragmatic dimensions that affect the use of different kinds of imperatives.

[19] Mitra Cowan, personal communication.

REFERENCES

Biber, D., Johansson, S., Leech, G., Conrad, S., & Finegan, E. (1999). *Longman grammar of spoken and written English*. Essex: Pearson Education.

Carrell, P., & Konneker, B. (1981). Politeness: Comparing native and nonnative judgements. *Language Learning*, *31* (1), 17–30.

Davies, E. E. (1986). *The English imperative*. London: Croom Helm.

De Clerck, B. (2004). Imperative subjects in English: A pragmatic corpus-based analysis of explicit *you*-subjects. Paper presented at the *25th Conference of the International Computer Archive of Modern and Medieval English*. May 19–23. Verona, Italy.

Flagg, E. (2001). "You" can't say that: Restrictions on overt subjects in the English imperative. In M. Andronis, C. Ball, H. Elston, & S. Neuvel, (Eds.), *Papers from the 37th meeting of the Chicago Linguistic Society*. Chicago: Chicago Linguistic Society.

Hasegawa, K. (1965). English imperatives. In *Festschrift for Professor Nakajima* (pp. 20–28). Kenkyusha: Tokyo.

Huddleston, R. D. (1984). *Introduction to the grammar of English*. Cambridge, England: Cambridge University Press.

Huddleston, R. D., & Pullum, G. K. (2002). *The Cambridge grammar of the English language*. Cambridge, England: Cambridge University Press.

Jespersen, O. (1961). *A modern English grammar on historical principles*. Copenhagen: Munksgaard.

Leech, G. (1999). The distribution and function of vocatives in American and British English conversation. In H. Hasselgård, & S. Oksefjell, (Eds.), *Out of corpora: Studies in honour of Stig Johansson* (pp. 107–118). Amsterdam: Rodopi.

Lees, R. B. (1964). On passives and imperatives in English. *Gengo Kenkyu*, *46*, 28–41.

Levenston, E. A. (1969). Imperative structures in English. *Linguistics*, *50*, 38–43.

McCawley, J. (1988). *The syntactic phenomena of English*. Chicago: University of Chicago Press.

McClure, K. (1996). *Putting it together: A conversation management text*. Upper Saddle River, NJ: Prentice Hall Regents.

Quirk, R., Greenbaum, S., Leech, G., & Svartvik, J. (1985). *A comprehensive grammar of the English language*. London: Longman.

Schmerling, S. F. (1975). Imperative subject deletion and some related matters. *Linguistic Inquiry*, *6*, 501–511.

Schmerling, S. (1982). How imperatives are special and how they aren't. In R. Schneider, K. Tutte, & R. Chamentzky, (Eds.). *Papers from the parasession on nondeclaratives* (pp. 202–218). Chicago: Chicago Linguistics Society.

Stefanowitsch, A. (2003). The English imperative: a construction-based approach. Paper presented at the *DGfS Jahrestagung 2003* in Munich.

Stockwell, R., Schachter, P., & Partee, B. (1973). *The major syntactic structures of English*. New York: Holt, Rinehart and Winston.

Swales, J. M., & Feak, C. B. (2005). *Academic writing for graduate students: A course for nonnative speakers of English*. Ann Arbor: University of Michigan Press.

Walter, C. (2001). French speakers. In M. Swan, & B. Smith, (Eds.), *Learner English: A teacher's guide to interference and other problems*. 2nd ed. (pp. 52–72). Cambridge, England: Cambridge University Press.

Yuan, B. (1997). Asymmetry of null subjects and null objects in Chinese speakers' L2 English. *Studies in Second Language Acquisition, 19*, 467–497.

CHAPTER 7

Nonreferential
It and *There*

INTRODUCTION

The words *it* and *there* commonly function as pronouns; that is, they refer to some other element in the same sentence or in the preceding discourse. As we will see, however, each of these forms fills a different function as well, that of a *nonreferential* subject. Sentences beginning with nonreferential *it* and *there* occur frequently in all registers of spoken and written English, and it is therefore important that English language learners master this simple yet sometimes problematic feature of English grammar.

NONREFERENTIAL *IT*

The word *it* in (1) is a pronoun that refers to the noun phrase *a flat stone*. This is an example of *referential it*.

(**1**) He picked up *a flat stone* and skipped *it* across the surface of the water.

In (2), *it* is *nonreferential*; that is, it does not refer to anything. Here, *it* has no particular meaning by itself; it simply fills the subject position of the sentence.[1]

(**2**) *It*'s raining pretty hard.

We know that *it* fills the subject position in (2) because, like all subjects, *it* undergoes subject–aux inversion in *yes/no* questions, as shown in (3a). *It* also reappears in the tag of a tag question, as shown in (3b), and contracts with *has* and copular *be*, as (3c) and (3d) illustrate. Notice also that like other subjects, nonreferential *it* must agree with the verb in a sentence, which is why (3e) is ungrammatical.

(**3**) a. Is it raining?
   b. It was raining earlier, wasn't it?
   c. It's been raining all day.
   d. It's a rainy day.
   e. *It are raining.

Uses of Sentences with Nonreferential *It*

Sentences with nonreferential *it* are used to talk about a number of things, as shown in (4).

(4) a. It's sunny today.	*weather*
b. It's raining.	*weather*
c. It's 20 degrees below zero out there.	*temperature*
d. What time is it?	*time*
e. It's 4:30.	*time*
f. I'm not even sure what day of the week it is.	*days*
g. It's Tuesday, October 29.	*dates*
h. It's Halloween.	*holidays*
i. It's only 2 weeks until we go on vacation.[2]	*elapsed time*
j. It's a good 250 miles from here to Washington, D.C.	*distances*
k. It's so noisy in this restaurant that I can hardly hear myself think.	*environment*
l. Can you open a window? It's hot in here.	*environment*

Special Constructions with Nonreferential *It*

It fills the subject position in various special constructions.

Cleft Sentences

Nonreferential *it* appears in so-called cleft sentences as in (5) and (6). Cleft sentences are discussed in greater detail in Chapter 22.

(5) It's my brother who got married, not me.

(6) It was 6 months ago that he got his promotion.

Extraposed Subject Clauses

Nonreferential *it* also commonly appears in constructions with certain adjectives such as *amazing*, *interesting*, *remarkable*, and *unusual*, as shown in (7), and with certain transitive verbs such as *annoy*, *astound*, *depress*, *disturb*, and *upset*, as shown in (8). In order for nonreferential *it* to be used in this way, the sentence must contain an extraposed subject clause – a subject clause that has been moved to the end of the sentence (*extraposed*), as discussed in Chapter 20.

(7) a. It is interesting [that you believe that].
   b. It's unusual [to find such wisdom in someone so young].

(8) a. It annoys me [that he is always late].
   b. It upsets her [to see her daughter behave that way].

In (7) and (8), the sentences can be converted into a structure that begins with *what*. For example, (7a) means the same thing as (9a), and (8a) means the same thing as (9b).

(9) a. What is interesting is that you believe that.
   b. What annoys me is that he is always late.

SUMMARY

NONREFERENTIAL *IT*

Nonreferential *it* fills the subject position in a sentence.

Sentences with nonreferential *it* are used to talk about the weather, temperature, time, days of the week and holidays, distances, and the environment.

> *It's Tuesday, the twenty-fourth of June.*
> *I don't know what time it is.*
> *It's five o'clock.*
> *It's really noisy in here.*

Special constructions with nonreferential *it* include:

- **cleft sentences**
   It's my brother who got married, not my sister.
   It was two years ago that she started her own business.

- **extraposed subject clauses**
   It would be wonderful if we could meet for lunch sometime.
   It's unusual that this would happen twice.
   It upset him that she wants to see you.
   It annoys me when you do that.

EXERCISE 7.1

Identify the use of *it* in each sentence as referential or nonreferential.

Example: It's been snowing all day.

Answer: nonreferential

1. It was so smoky in that room that my eyes were watering.
2. The lost and found department called. They think they found your watch, but you will have to go and identify it.
3. Speaker A: Are you going out?
   Speaker B: Are you kidding?! It's freezing out there.
4. He is so disorganized that he doesn't even know what day it is.
5. He found a good solid stock and invested all his money in it.
6. It's so great to be here with you.
7. It's strange that this door would be open.

NONREFERENTIAL *THERE*

The word *there* in (10a) refers to the word *Paris* in the preceding sentence and thus has the referential function of a pronoun. *There* in (10b) is also referential because it indicates a place that the speaker can point to.

> (**10**) a. I was in Paris in 1926. It was *there* that I met Ernest Hemingway and Ford Maddox Ford.
> b. Put the boxes over *there*.

The word *there* is often called *nonreferential*, or *existential, there*.[3] As shown in (11), *there* fills the subject position and does not refer to anything previously mentioned.

    (11) *There* is a unicorn in the garden. (= A unicorn is in the garden.)

Note that *there* is followed by a form of the copular *be* and by an NP (noun phrase) that would be the subject if the sentence did not include *there*. Nonreferential *there* can be distinguished from referential *there* by the fact that it fills the subject position in a clause. Referential *there*, in contrast, can occur in many positions in a sentence. Nonreferential *there* passes the three tests of subjecthood we saw earlier in (3): It undergoes subject–aux inversion, as shown in (12a); it reappears in tags, as in (12b); and it contracts with copular *be* in speech and informal writing, as in (12c).

    (12) a. Are there any cookies left?
        b. There was another road, wasn't there?
        c. There's something we need to talk about.

Contractions and Their Occurrences

There contracts with *is* before a singular NP, as shown in (13a), and with *are* before a plural NP, as shown in (13b). The contracted form *there're* is heard as a lengthening of the *r* sound. In fast speech, this may be shortened, resulting in the impression that the verb *are* has been omitted.

    (13) a. There's a hole in my tire.
        b. There're lots of deer out in the field.

Uncontracted forms are used in positive answers to *yes/no* questions, as (14) shows.

    (14) a. Is there any milk left in the fridge? Yes, there is.
                                     *Yes, there's.
        b. Are there any apples left?   Yes, there are.
                                       *Yes, there're.

However, contracted forms with *be* and *not* tend to be used in negative answers to *yes/no* questions. For many native speakers, the use of the uncontracted form, as shown in (15), sounds more formal and emphatic.

    (15) A: Are there any good beaches on this side of the island?
        B: No, there aren't.
           No, there are not.

Modal verbs may appear before copular *be* in sentences with nonreferential *there*, as (16) illustrates.

    (16) a. There must be another solution to this problem.
        b. There would be at least three other people who could tell you.
        c. There might be more than one solution.

Contractions occur with the modals *will* and *would*, and the different forms of the auxiliary verb *have* (*have/has/had*). These contractions are not normally written.

    (17) a. There'll be over 3,000 people at the concert.   *will*
        b. There'd be at least three other people who could tell you. *would*
        c. There's been some criticism of his book.   *has*
        d. There've been several objections to that plan.   *have*
        e. There'd been a lot of talk about his resignation.   *had*

Subject–Verb Agreement

In sentences with nonreferential *there*, the form of the verb *be* agrees in number with the following NP. In (18a), the NP that follows copular *be* is plural (*two beds*), so *be* is in its plural form (*are*).

(**18**) a. There are two beds in my room.
b. *There is two beds in my room.

In some cases, however, agreement depends on how the subject NP following *be* is interpreted.[4] The speaker in (19) refers to *king prawns cooked in chili, salt, and pepper* as a single dish, and therefore uses a singular form of *be* (*was*).

(**19**) He served a number of delicious dishes. There was king prawns cooked in chili, salt, and pepper, which is a big favorite of mine.

There are also some other exceptions to the general agreement rule. For example, (20a), (20b), and (20c) show that plural units of measurement (e.g., *pounds*, *dollars*) and time (e.g., *minutes*, *hours*) may take a singular form of *be*.[5] However, with the expression *a number of*, as shown in (20d) and (20e), *be* must agree with the noun that follows (*issues*) rather than with *a number*.[6]

(**20**) a. There was 20 pounds of cocaine hidden in the trunk of the car.
b. There's 30 dollars in his wallet.
c. There's only five minutes left.
d. There were a number of issues that he wanted to discuss.[7]
e. *There was a number of issues that he wanted to discuss.

A commonly heard violation of the agreement rule is the use of *there's* before an NP that has a plural count noun as its head. Such an error is exemplified in the cartoon.

The correct sentence is in (21), in which the plural *are* agrees with the noun *things*.

(**21**) It seems that every summer, *there are* more of these things around.

Recent research shows that this kind of error has to do with the planning of speech before it is uttered.[8] Subject–verb agreement violations in *there* nonreferential sentences such as the one in the cartoon probably result from the fact that speakers have to commit to one or the other form – *there is* or *there are* – when they convert the mental proposition that they have formulated into words. If there are more words between *there* + *be* and the head noun that determines the number of the verb, the chance of an incorrect choice may be increased. Interestingly, in cases such as this, speakers choose to use *there is* more frequently than *there are*, and this may be

THE FAR SIDE® BY GARY LARSON

"Crimony! ... It seems like every summer there's more and more of these things around!"

because it covers two out of the three possibilities that could follow – a noncount noun or a singular count noun. As we saw in (19) and (20), *there is* also works with some plural nouns. All these factors may combine to bias the speaker's choice in favor of *there is* when there is a long separation between the verb and the NP that should determine the number of the verb. Regardless of whether this explanation is a correct account of why this particular agreement error occurs in nonreferential *there* sentences, it might be helpful to point out to students that it does often arise in spoken English but is less frequent in writing.

SUMMARY

NONREFERENTIAL *THERE*

Nonreferential *there* fills the subject position in a clause. It is usually followed by a form of copular *be* and an NP that has been displaced from the subject position.
> *There is a fly in my soup.*
> *There were many people in the room.*

There contracts with *be* before a singular or plural NP.
> *There's a hole in my tire.*
> *There're lots of deer.*

The uncontracted form of *there* is used in positive answers to *yes/no* questions.
> *Are there any apples? Yes, there are.*

There contracts with modals (e.g., *will*, *would*) and the forms of auxiliary verb *have*. These contractions are normally not written.
> *There'll be over 3,000 people there.*
> *There'd been a lot of talk.*
> *There's been some criticism of his book.*

The verb that follows *there* should agree in number with the NP after it.
> *There is a crack in the ceiling.*
> *There are cracks in the ceiling.*

However, *there is* occurs, for example:

- **when a plural NP is viewed as a single unit.**
  > *There was king prawns cooked in chili, salt, and pepper, which is a big favorite of mine.*

- **with some units of measurement, currency, and time.**
  > *There's 100 tons of water behind that dam.*
  > *There was 20 dollars in his pocket.*
  > *There's 10 minutes on the clock, and Erving has the ball.*

In conversation, many native speakers often violate agreement by starting a sentence with *there is* when the following NP is plural, particularly when more than one word intervenes between the verb and the NP which determines number.
> **There's almost never two games on the same Monday night.*

EXERCISE 7.2

Identify the use of *there* in each sentence as referential or nonreferential.

Example: He climbed to the top of the hill. From there he could see the entire valley.

Answer: referential (*There* refers to *the top of the hill*.)

1. I don't think there are any more ties like that one.
2. When he arrived in San Diego, he went straight to the hotel. There he met his brother.
3. Are you telling me that there are only three cookies left?
4. There was a time when we couldn't afford a new car.
5. You're going to the Caspian Sea? Well, you certainly won't see any whales there. But you might catch a few sturgeon.

EXERCISE 7.3

Indicate whether each sentence is grammatical. If it is ungrammatical, explain what is wrong with it.

Example: There's quite a lot of students who want to see the chancellor about the new tuition increase.

Answer: ungrammatical (the verb *is* doesn't agree in number with *students*)

1. Is there any gas in that can over there? No, there isn't.
2. There's quite a lot of really strange looking characters hanging around in the supermarket parking lot.
3. There's a number of ways to do that!
4. My guess is that there was over 40 pounds of powdered sugar in the bag.
5. She told me that there was a dozen place mats in that drawer.

NONREFERENTIAL *THERE* IN DISCOURSE

The basic function of sentences with nonreferential *there* is to present information. This presentational function is shown below.

Introducing New Information

Sentences with nonreferential *there* can introduce new information into an ongoing conversation or written discourse. The new information may begin a topic that is subsequently expanded on, as in the case of the lady from Niger in the limerick by Cosmo Monkhouse in (22) and the case of the sheriff in Dodge City in (23).

(22) There was a young lady from Niger
   Who smiled as she rode on a tiger;
   They returned from the ride
   With the lady inside,
   And the smile on the face of the tiger.[9]

(23) There's a new sheriff in town.
   He used to work in Dodge City.

Responding to Questions

Nonreferential *there* constructions are also often used to respond to questions about the existence of something. In (24), speaker B is responding to speaker A's question about the location of a video store by providing the new information that was requested. Since new information is being introduced here (in the form of a response), this function of *there* may be considered a subclass of the function described above.

(24) A: I'm looking for a video store. D'ya know where I can find one?
  B: Yeah. Go down the street to the first stoplight. Turn left and go down that street about four . . . no, three blocks, and you'll see a mall. There's a video store on the far side of that mall.

Shifting the Focus of a Discussion

Sentences with nonreferential *there* can also be used to shift the focus of a discussion to a new but related topic. Journalists, for instance, frequently use *there* to introduce new paragraphs, as in the second paragraph in (25).

(25) The general has embarked on what amounts to a one-candidate election campaign, since both of his main opponents are in exile and have been banned from voting. Public skepticism about the election next week is evident, and the turnout at political rallies has been low, consisting largely of civil servants and soldiers in civilian clothes, all loyal to the general.

  There are no reliable polls to suggest how the vote may go, but few doubt that the general will prevail. Officials of the Human Rights Commission note that the computing apparatus for vote counting is in the hands of the current government.[10]

The first paragraph in (25) develops the general background information concerning an upcoming election. The second paragraph begins with a nonreferential *there* sentence that shifts the focus of the discussion to the possible outcome of the election. The writer includes a reference to *the vote* in the nonreferential *there* structure, thereby maintaining a connection with the topic discussed in the first paragraph.

Calling Something to Mind

Nonreferential *there* sentences with the definite article *the* or the demonstrative determiner *that* are often used by a speaker to remind a listener of some information that is known to both of them. In (26), Speaker B reminds Speaker A of something he has forgotten – a comprehensive exam that Speaker B must pass before he can graduate.

(26) A: Well, you're taking your final classes this semester. You'll graduate in June and be off to your cushy job overseas. I'll bet you haven't got a care in the world.
  B: Actually, I am not all that carefree yet. *There's still the comprehensive exam.* I've got to pass that before I graduate.

SUMMARY

NONREFERENTIAL *THERE* IN DISCOURSE

Sentences with **nonreferential *there*** serve several basic functions:

- **introducing new information**
  There's a new sheriff in town. And he's going to clean up all the corruption.

- **responding to questions about the existence of something**
  A: *Where can I get some gas?*
  B: *There's a gas station two blocks up this street.*

- **shifting the focus of a discussion**
  Public skepticism about the election next week is evident, and the turnout at political rallies has been low.
  There are no reliable polls to suggest how the vote may go, but few doubt that the general will prevail.

- **calling something to mind**
  A: *I can't decide where to take Debbie for lunch.*
  B: *Well, there's that Thai restaurant we ate at last month.*

EXERCISE 7.4

Indicate how nonreferential *there* is being used in the discourses below (shift focus, introduce new information, respond to question regarding the existence of something, call something to mind).

Example: There's trouble on the other side of the chain-link fences surrounding the state government's Foothills Wildlife Research Facility. The dusty pastures are ground zero for a deer-killing plague that is frighteningly similar to mad cow disease.

Answer: to introduce new information

1. The workers have expressed a desire to negotiate a new five-year contract with management. They believe that they hold most of the cards in such a negotiation, since the company recently signed a contract to produce a jet fighter for the government. The workers reason that the company will not be able to produce the fighter on time unless the company acquiesces to most of their demands.
   At present, there is no indication of whether the management of the company is disposed to negotiate with the workers. All attempts to discover what management thoughts are regarding negotiation have come up with nothing.

2. A: So why don't you buy that car? You have enough money to meet the price that the dealer is asking.
   B: *Well, there's still the sales tax and the luxury tax.* I don't think I can afford it when those extra costs are added on.

3. A: Can you tell me where the nearest post office is?
   B: Yeah. *There's one on 17th Street.*

4. *There is a lot of evidence that heredity is an important factor in health.* People who have a family history of diseases like cancer, diabetes, and Alzheimer's are much more likely to contract these conditions than people whose family history shows no record of them.

ADDITIONAL FACTS ABOUT NONREFERENTIAL *THERE*

The information about sentences with nonreferential *there* presented in this section may be more useful for answering students' and colleagues' questions than for organizing your teaching. It may also be helpful for judging the treatment of nonreferential *there* sentences in published ESL/EFL teaching materials.

Nonreferential *There* Sentences and Their Counterparts

Some sentences with nonreferential *there* can be rewritten as sentences with indefinite subjects (i.e., a subject composed of the indefinite article *a/an* or *some* and a noun). For instance, (27a), which begins with *there*, may be rewritten as (27b). Likewise, (28a) has the counterpart shown in (28b).

> (**27**) a. There is a man standing under that tree.
> b. A man is standing under that tree.

> (**28**) a. There are some very expensive cars in front of your house.
> b. Some very expensive cars are in front of your house.

Based on these examples, we might assume that there are rules that convert sentences with indefinite subjects like (27b) and (28b) into sentences with nonreferential *there*. For example, we might propose a rule that moves the subject in (27b), (*a man*), to the position following the auxiliary verb *is*. Then another rule would insert *there* in the empty position left by movement of the subject.

Unfortunately, such rules would not always work. In some cases we would have to derive nonreferential *there* sentences from ungrammatical sentences. Consider (29).

> (**29**) a. There was an accident on the freeway last night.
> b. *An accident was on the freeway last night.

When the NP after *be* in a sentence with nonreferential *there* describes an event or an occurrence, as illustrated in (29), it does not have a grammatical counterpart sentence with an indefinite subject.

The same problem occurs with nonreferential *there* sentences that have relative clauses modifying the noun phrase after the verb *be*, as in (30a).

> *Indefinite NP*   *Relative Clause*
> (**30**) a. There are [[several possibilities] [that we haven't considered]].
> b. *Several possibilities are that we haven't considered.

As (30) illustrates, nonreferential *there* sentences with a relative clause cannot be derived from sentences with an indefinite subject.[11] If we want to apply the two rules described above to derive the sentence in (30a), we would have to apply them to the ungrammatical sentence in (30b).

In the past, some ESL/EFL textbooks have suggested that sentences beginning with *there* + *be* always have corresponding sentences with indefinite subjects. This is shown to be inaccurate in (29) and (30). For this reason, teaching English language learners rules that convert one sentence type to the other and engaging in pattern practice with these rules is probably not a good idea. In fact, it could cause your students to begin producing ungrammatical sentences. Teach *there is/are* sentences without any comparison to sentences with indefinite subjects, and use plenty of appropriate contexts to show their meaning.

Nonreferential *There* with Verbs Other Than *Be*

Although nonreferential *there* is usually followed by a form of copular *be*, there are cases in which it is followed by other verbs, as shown in (31).

(31) a. In 1963, *there occurred* a tragic event in the history of the United States.
b. Deep within his breast *there smoldered* an unquenchable desire.
c. *There comes* a time in everyone's life when you need to take a stand.

Verbs other than *be* that occur in sentences with nonreferential *there* include (1) verbs that describe existence or position (*dwell, exist, live, remain, stand*); (2) verbs of motion or direction (*approach, come, fly, gallop, go, run, walk*); and (3) verbs of happening or materializing (*appear, arise, begin, develop, emerge, ensue, happen, occur, seem*).[12]

These verbs occur much less frequently with *there* than *be* does,[13] and they tend to sound much better when *there* is preceded by a phrase or an adverbial clause. Notice that (32a), in which *there* is not preceded by an adverbial clause, does not sound quite as good as sentence (32b).

(32) a. There appeared a strange face in the window.
b. *Just as she lit the old candle*, there appeared a strange face in the window.

Likewise, (33b), which begins with an adverbial phrase (*on the far side of the forest*), sounds much better than (33a), which has the same adverbial phrase at the end.

(33) a. There dwelled an ancient woodsman *on the far side of the forest*.
b. *On the far side of the forest*, there dwelled an ancient woodsman.

Sentences such as (32b) and (33b) are more typical of written English than of spoken English. In fact, to most native speakers, they would probably sound odd and unnatural in conversation but would seem fine as part of a written story or fairy tale. A particular pattern commonly found in fairy tales and legends has a *there* construction preceded by the fixed phrase *once upon a time*. This common pattern is illustrated in (34).

(34) *Once upon a time*, there lived an ancient mariner.

Academic prose often contains nonreferential *there* sentences with verbs such as *remain*, as in (35), and infinitive clauses after verbs such as *appear* and *seem*, as in (36).[14]

(35) There remain only two more issues to be dealt with.

(36) There $\begin{Bmatrix} seem \\ appear \end{Bmatrix}$ to be several possible solutions to the problem.

A number of ergative verbs like *break, change, decrease, die, disappear*, and *increase* do not appear in nonreferential *there* sentences, as (37) illustrates. (See Chapters 2 and 17 for discussion of ergative verbs.)

(37) a. *Over the past 10 years, there have died a number of famous authors.
b. *Soon afterward, there broke a large stained glass window in the cathedral.
c. *One day there disappeared a workman in the stockyard.

Idioms with Nonreferential *There*

Nonreferential *there* appears in a number of idiomatic expressions that have the pattern *there's* + *no* + present participle verb form.[15] This pattern is illustrated in (38), (39), and (40).

(**38**) *There's no telling* what he will do.

(**39**) *There's no getting out* of it.

(**40**) *There's no sidestepping* the central issue of this campaign.

These expressions may be shortened versions of the expression *there's no way of* + present participle verb form. They always express the idea that something is impossible.

PROBLEMS THAT ESL/EFL STUDENTS HAVE WITH NONREFERENTIAL *IT* AND *THERE*

Although sentences with nonreferential *it* and *there* occur frequently in both spoken and written English, many English language learners face a good deal of difficulty in mastering these forms. Some of the more common L1-related difficulties experienced by learners are described here.

The Absence of Nonreferential *It* (Chinese, Spanish, Italian)

Many languages do not use nonreferential subjects, and this L1 feature appears to cause initial difficulty for some students. Languages such as Chinese, Spanish, and Italian, for instance, do not have sentences with nonreferential *it* subjects. As a result, Chinese speakers might translate directly from their L1 and end up producing (41a) in an attempt to express the meaning in (41b).

(**41**) a. *Today very hot.
      b. It's very hot today.

A Spanish- or Italian-speaker might render the sentence in (41b) as **Is very hot today*, also omitting the necessary nonreferential *it*. These errors are quite often made by beginning level students, but they are also characteristic of the stabilized grammars of learners who have had little or no formal English language instruction. There is no evidence that it cannot be corrected through appropriate contextualized practice.

Missing Relative Pronouns in Nonreferential *There Is/Are* Sentences (Chinese)

A well-documented error that occurs in the compositions of Chinese speakers is the omission of relative pronouns in sentences beginning with nonreferential *there is* and *there are*. Some examples from Schachter and Rutherford (1979) and Yip (1995) are shown in (42).

(**42**) a. *There are many varieties of cancer exist.
      b. *There was a tire hanging from the roof served as their playground.

These sentences would be grammatical if relative pronouns were inserted after the NP that comes after *there + be*. If we insert *that* after *many varieties of cancer* in (42a) and *a tire hanging from the roof* in (42b), we get the grammatical sentences in (43).

(**43**) a. There are many varieties of cancer *that* exist.
      b. There was a tire hanging from the roof *that* served as a playground.

The cause of this persistent error was not well understood until recently. It will be explained in Chapter 18, which deals with relative clauses. For now we should note that this is a persistent error for Chinese speakers that needs to be addressed in teaching.

Incorrect Use of Polarity Items with Nonreferential *There* (Korean)

The errors shown in (44) were found in a review written by a Korean graduate student. The student clearly is having difficulty producing negative sentences with nonreferential *there*.

(44) a. *There's *no any* questions which check students' reading comprehension.
    b. *There's *no particular* difficulties in understanding cultural background.
    c. *Nevertheless, there is *no any* vocabulary or idiom lists, and *no any* grammatical explanation or exercises.

Korean uses a verb (*sup-ni*)[16] to express the equivalent of English *there is/are*. To express negation with this verb, Korean uses a negative marker (*eps*), as shown in (45), which means the same thing as (46).

(45) *chayk* *eynun* *dane* *list* *ka*   *eps-sup-ni-ta*
    book   in   word list (nom.) (neg.) exist

(46) a. There aren't any word lists in the book.
    b. There are no word lists in the book.

Notice that there is no Korean equivalent to the English negative polarity item *any* in (45), which is obligatory in the corresponding English sentence in (46a). All three errors in (44) contain *there is no*, and they all have a singular verb form (*is*), which does not agree with the NPs *questions* and *difficulties*. These two facts suggest that this Korean student may be equating *there is* with *sup-ni* and is simply placing the English negative word *no* after it (see stage 2 of negation development in Chapter 5). Sentences (44b) and (44c) suggest that the student is learning the environment in which the negative polarity item *any* must occur. However, it is not clear whether the student has grasped the fact that there are two possible ways of making negative sentences with nonreferential *there + be* (i.e., the primary negation option illustrated in [46a] and the nonverbal negation option shown in [46b] with the negative word *no*). Since the data in (44) comes from the written English of only one student, we cannot determine whether this error is a case of L1 transfer or a failure to master nonverbal negation. Nevertheless, it argues the desirability of dealing with both types of negation when teaching nonreferential *there* sentences.

SUGGESTIONS FOR TEACHING NONREFERENTIAL *IT* AND *THERE*

English language teaching textbooks typically do a reasonably good job of presenting and practicing nonreferential *it* and *there*. Both are introduced at the beginning or low-intermediate level. Nonreferential *it* structures are fairly easy to teach because they occur in such limited contexts. Nonreferential *there* is often taught in conjunction with positive and negative polarity items, but negative words that can also be answers to questions are not always included. In addition to these topics, subject–verb agreement is often treated, which means that students must already have covered the difference between count and noncount nouns before they come to learn about this aspect of nonreferential *there* constructions. Some quantifiers (see Chapter 10), such as *a lot* and *a little*, are also commonly introduced along with *it* and *there* as well as the formation questions that include nonreferential *there* (e.g., *How many supermarkets are there in your town?*).

Good examples of the kinds of activities that are used to teach nonreferential *it* and *there* sentences can be found in *Student Book 1* of the *New Interchange* series (Richards et. al., 1997). All of these activities are well chosen and easily adaptable to different teaching environments.

Activities 1 through 5, which follow, are commonly used to practice the use of *it* and *there* with students at a low level of proficiency. However, even at higher levels, you should revisit nonreferential *there* constructions, for example, in composition classes, to demonstrate the conditions under which they are most effectively deployed in discourse. An example of how this might be done with more advanced students is shown in Activity 6.

Nonreferential *It*
Activity 1: Weather Report (Beginning)
A popular way to practice *it* constructions is to role-play a weather report. A flannel board with cut outs of the symbols for rain, snow, sunny weather, clouds, and so on, is often recommended as necessary equipment for this activity.[17] However, it may be possible to role-play a report modeled on an actual video recording of the local weather. The teacher can play the tape as a demonstration and then recap what the students have just watched using examples of nonreferential *it* constructions such as those in (47).

> (47) a. It's raining in the northern part of the state.
>   b. Tomorrow it's going to be sunny and cold.
>   c. It's been a cold winter.

Nonreferential *There*
Activity 2: Map Work (Beginning Through Low Intermediate)
Perhaps the most widely used activities found in commercial textbooks are the map activities designed to encourage the production of sentences with *there is/are*. In pairs, one student asks another student who has the same map what is located at a certain point (e.g., "*What is across from the movie theater?*"). The other student answers with a nonreferential *there* structure (e.g., "*There's a school across from the movie theater.*") Students take turns asking and answering. You can make up your own maps or find a map on the Internet and enhance it with real or imaginary buildings.

Activity 3: Information Gap (Low Intermediate)
Questions and answers with nonreferential *there* sentences are automatically produced in the classic "information gap" activity with two pictures that differ slightly. This is popular with teachers who like to do paired work, and it involves discovering the similarities and differences in the pictures. Often pictures of a room with furniture and other objects will be sufficient.

Begin by asking the students whether single objects are present (e.g., "*Is there a lamp in the room?*" Answer: "*No, there isn't.*"). Write the responses on the board and then proceed to elicit several more examples. Then switch to questions about more than one item (e.g., "*Are there any pictures on the walls?*" Answer: "*No, there aren't any pictures on the wall.*"). Demonstrate the other option for expressing the same meaning with *no* (e.g., "*There are no pictures on the wall.*"). Proceed in this manner until it is clear that the students are grasping the two alternatives. Then have the students pair off and ask similar questions using another set of pictures.

Activity 4: Asking About a Familiar Environment (Intermediate)

This activity reflects the kind of conversations that frequently occur when people meet for the first time. Begin by having your students ask each other questions about their hometown, country, or neighborhood in which they currently live. Give them some help by providing a list of nouns that relate to the environment. For example, if the topic is the neighborhood or city, you might suggest things such as crime, shops, cinemas, pollution, transportation, and so on. This allows them to ask questions with count and noncount nouns and quantifiers (e.g., *"Is there much crime in that part of the city?"* *"Are there any supermarkets in your neighborhood?"* *"How many are there?"*).

Activity 5: Writing Follow-Up (Beginning Through Low Intermediate)

Writing can be a good follow-up activity for a listening or reading comprehension activity with low-level students. Have them either listen to or read a short passage about a city in another country. Then have them list some of the good and bad points regarding the city they have learned about and compare these with their own town or city. After they have written down a series of pros and cons about their own city or town, which in each case will involve nonreferential *there* sentences, have them write a short composition about their hometown that incorporates these sentences.

Activity 6: Analyzing the Use of Nonreferential *There* in Discourse (High Intermediate Through Low Advanced)

In high-intermediate and low-advanced level composition classes, it is important to give students an idea of when nonreferential *there* sentences are used in written discourse. Probably the most direct way of doing this is to collect examples from texts such as articles in newspapers and magazines. You will find abundant examples of the two uses of nonreferential *there* structures listed earlier – introducing new information and shifting the focus of a discussion – and these should be the focus of your instruction. Begin by showing two or three examples of how *there* is used in a topic sentence. The topic sentence in (48) is taken from Exercise 7.4 on page 138.

> (**48**) *There is a lot of evidence that heredity is an important factor in health.* People who have a family history of diseases such as cancer, diabetes, and Alzheimer's are much more likely to contract these conditions than people whose family history shows no record of them.

Explain that *there* structures are often used to present new information or a topic that will be expanded on in the sentences that follow.

Next, present the students with several examples of topic sentences such as the ones in (49), which do not use *there*.

> (**49**) a. We know that heredity is an important factor in health because we have a lot of evidence of this.
> b. That heredity is an important factor in health is supported by a lot of evidence.

Ask the students to rewrite these topic sentences using nonreferential *there*. Then discuss why the rewrite is better, pointing out that the nonreferential *there* sentence keeps the new information at the end of the sentence, which is the most common way of presenting new information.

Next, show how nonreferential *there* sentences can be used to shift focus to new but related topics. Consider (50), taken from a review of a book on the life and work of the famed English photographer Roger Fenton.[18]

> **(50)** Fenton's rivals in the field were not other photographers . . . they were the illustrators and artists, and it is clear from Fenton's letters that he was alive to their shortcomings, as rivals are. The artists had the advantage over the photographer: they could do what they liked with their images, but he could in no way manipulate his. He was at the mercy of his lens, and of the long exposure time required for each shot.
>
> *There were several different kinds of artists and illustrators around.* A painting by J. D. Luard called *The Welcome Arrival* gives us a kind of genre scene missing from Fenton's photographs.

Point out that the nonreferential *there* sentence in the second paragraph is connected to the topic introduced and developed in the first paragraph, but that the new information presented in it constitutes a shift from the original topic to a description of the illustrators who were Fenton's rivals. Then repeat the writing procedure described above. This time, the alternative topic sentences you provide can have an indefinite NP subject (e.g., *Several different kinds of artists and illustrators were around*).

You can present more dramatic shifts of topic and discuss them. Eventually, this activity should culminate in a writing assignment in which the students produce a short passage that contains appropriate examples of both uses of nonreferential *there*.

ENDNOTES

[1] In this case, *it* is often referred to as *dummy it*. Nonreferential *it* has also been called a *pleonastic pronoun*, an *expletive subject*, and *prop it*.

[2] This is equivalent to the sentence *Only two weeks remain until we go on vacation*. Similarly, *It's only two weeks since he left* means "Only two weeks have elapsed since he left."

[3] The term *existential there* is preferred in most textbooks because these sentences talk about the existence of something.

[4] This is referred to as *notional concord* by Biber et al. (1999), p. 187.

[5] This observation is from Biber et al. (1999), p. 187.

[6] However, when modifiers precede *number*, e.g., *a finite number of*, then for many native speakers, the singular form of *be* seems more appropriate, that is, *There is a finite number of words in any language*.

[7] For most native speakers, this agreement *does not* hold for other qualifying expressions, (e.g., *a group of*, *a platoon of*, *a flock of*, etc.). For example, *There was a group of men standing around outside that main entrance* is grammatical. But it does apply to other numerical qualifiers like *a dozen* (e.g., *There were a dozen eggs on the plate*, not **There was a dozen eggs on the plate*).

[8] The investigation of why subject–verb agreement errors occur is being pursued by Bock and her colleagues. The evidence from her studies, in particular, Bock and Cooper Cutting (1992), suggests that "verb number is specified at some point prior to that at which the verb is actually spoken or put into place in the word string" (p. 119). For a different explanation involving ease of articulation, see Celce-Murcia and Larsen-Freeman (1999), p. 448. An explanation that merges both of these views is offered by Breivik (1981). Biber et al. (1999) offer a "processing" explanation for this phenomenon, but this seems unlikely, since the phenomenon under investigation has to do with the assembly of speech for production, not perception of uttered speech.

[9] *The Norton Book of Light Verse*, Baker, (1986), p. 360.

[10] These two paragraphs have been adapted from Ahmed Jahid's article: "In Pakistan, an Election Slate of One," *Wall Street Journal*, April 11, 2002. A16.

[11] For a more extensive discussion of this topic, see Huddleston and Pullum (2002), pp. 1392–1401.

[12] From Celce-Murcia and Larsen-Freeman (1999) and Huddleston and Pullum (2002), p. 995. See also other verbs in Biber et al. (1999), p. 945.

[13] See Biber et al. (1999), p. 945.

[14] See more verbs and examples in Huddleston and Pullum (2002), p. 1402.

[15] See Rando & Napoli (1978) for examples of nonreferential *there* sentences with definite articles.

[16] This is similar to the Chinese *you*, which means "exist" (Yip, 1995).

[17] See, for example, Celce-Murcia and Larsen-Freeman (1999), p. 445.

[18] James Fenton (2004), *The Photograph Man*. Review of *All the Mighty World: The Photographs of Roger Fenton, 1852–1860*. *New York Review of Books*, Vol. LVII, No. 1, p. 34.

REFERENCES

Baker, R. (1986). *The Norton book of light verse*. London/New York: W. W. Norton.

Biber, D., Johansson, S., Leech, G., Conrad, S., & Finegan, E. (1999). *Longman grammar of spoken and written English*. Essex, England: Pearson Education.

Bock, B., & Cooper Cutting, J. (1992). Regulating mental energy: Performance units in language production. *Journal of Memory and Language, 31*, 99–127.

Breivik, L. (1981). On the interpretation of existential "there." *Language, 57* (1), 1–25.

Celce-Murcia, M., & Larsen-Freeman, D. (1999). *The grammar book: An ESL/EFL teacher's course*. 2nd ed. Rowley, MA: Newbury House.

Celce-Murcia, M., & Hudson, J. K. (1981). What "there" is to subject-verb agreement. Paper presented at the *Annual TESOL Conference*, Detroit, March 5, 1981.

Fenton, J. (2004). *The photograph man*. Review of *All the mighty world: The photographs of Roger Fenton, 1852–1860*. *New York Review of Books*, Vol. LVII, No. 1.

Huddleston, R., & Pullum, G. K. (2002). *The Cambridge grammar of the English language*. Cambridge, England: Cambridge University Press.

Rando, E., & Napoli, D. J. (1978). Definites in "*there*" sentences. *Language, 54* (2), 300–313.

Richards, J. C., Hull, J., & Procter, S. (1997). *New Interchange Workbook 1*. New York: Cambridge University Press.

Schachter, J., & Rutherford, W. (1979). Discourse function and language transfer. *Working Papers in Bilingualism, 19*, 1–12.

Yip, V. (1995). *Interlanguage and learnability: From Chinese to English*. Amsterdam/Philadelphia, PA: John Benjamins.

CHAPTER 8

Prepositions

INTRODUCTION

In this chapter, we look at the grammar and meaning of English prepositions. Mastering the use of prepositions is one of the most challenging learning tasks English language learners face. Research and simple observation indicate that prepositions are a problem for learners at every level of proficiency. We will examine typical preposition errors that come from ESL student compositions and suggest strategies for minimizing them. We will also examine some of the approaches used for teaching prepositions.

POSITIONS OF OCCURRENCE

The position of occurrence for English prepositions typically described in grammar and ESL/EFL textbooks is at the head of a *prepositional phrase* (PP), which is before the head noun of a noun phrase (NP). Typical examples of prepositional phrases made up of a preposition and an object NP are bracketed in (1) and (2).

             Prep   *NP*
(**1**) I was reading [[in] [the garden]].   *prepositional phrase*

             Prep   *NP*
(**2**) The cat hid [[under] [a bench]].   *prepositional phrase*

Here, the prepositions *in* and *under* precede an NP composed of a definite article (*the*) or indefinite article (*a*) and the nouns *garden* and *bench*, respectively. The preposition is viewed as the head of the prepositional phrase, and the NP is viewed as the object of the preposition. While (1) and (2) illustrate the most typical position for prepositions, prepositions also occur in other environments that are not phrases. Some of these environments are the source of continuing problems for English learners. Examples of these environments are discussed in the next section.

Prepositional Verbs

Prepositions can occur as part of a *prepositional verb*, a two-word unit made up of a transitive verb and a preposition. Typical examples of prepositional verbs are: *apply for* something, *comment on* something, *tamper with* something, and *worry about* something or someone. The verb and preposition usually have the meaning of a single-word verb; for example, *decide on* means "choose" and *stand for* means "represent." In (3), we have two identical sentences with the verb *decide* followed by the preposition *on*. How do we decide whether the sequence *decide on* + NP is to be interpreted as a prepositional verb, as in (3a), or as a verb followed by a prepositional phrase, as in (3b)?

VP

(3) a. They finally [decided on] [the boat].   *prepositional verb*

V   PP

    b. They finally [decided] [on the boat].   *verb + PP*

Different syntactic tests can be used to determine which of these two possibilities is intended. One test involves using *wh-* questions – specifically, seeing what types of *wh-* questions are possible. If the sentence has a prepositional verb, it is possible to form *who(m)* or *what* questions about the object of that verb. These questions often have two forms: one with the preposition next to the verb, as in (4a), and the other with the preposition before the *wh-* word, as in (4b). Notice that the answers are an NP. In contrast, if the sentence has a verb followed by a PP of location, only *where* questions can be formed about the prepositional phrase, and the answer is a prepositional phrase.

(4) a. What did you finally decide on?   Answer: The boat.
    b. On what did you finally decide?   Answer: The boat.

    c. Where did you finally decide?   Answer: $\begin{cases} \textit{On the boat.} \\ \textit{The boat.} \end{cases}$

A second test to determine whether a verb + preposition + noun phrase sequence has the structure of (3a) or the structure of (3b) involves movement. A prepositional phrase, because it is a unit, can be moved to the beginning of a sentence. For example, the prepositional phrase *over the plains* in (5a) can be moved to create the sentence in (5b).

(5) a. They galloped over the plains.
    b. Over the plains they galloped.

However, a preposition that is part of a prepositional verb cannot be moved along with a following object. Thus, we cannot change sentence (6a), understood as having the prepositional verb, to (6b) without changing the intended meaning.

(6) a. They finally decided on the boat.
    b. On the boat, they finally decided.

Sentence (6b) is grammatical only if *on the boat* is understood to be a prepositional phrase that describes where they decided, that is, if the meaning is that of (3b) rather than of (3a). Other syntactic tests that are useful for distinguishing prepositional verbs are described in greater detail in Chapter 9.

Adjective + Preposition Combinations

Prepositions also occur in adjective + preposition combinations. That is, some adjectives can be followed by certain prepositions, as shown in (7b) and (8b). Note in (8b) that the object NP can be a gerund.

Adj
(**7**) a. The manager was very [*sorry*].

                  Adj   Prep   NP
b. The manager was very [*sorry*] [*for*] [the inconvenience].

              Adj
(**8**) a. She is [*afraid*].

             Adj   Prep   NP
b. She is [*afraid*] [*of*] [frightening the child].

In (7b), the adjective *sorry* is followed by the preposition *for*. In (8b), the adjective *afraid* is followed by the preposition *of*. Some other adjectives that take certain prepositions are *angry* (*about/at/with*), *capable* (*of*), *dependent* (*on*), *disappointed* (*about/at/with*), *excited* (*about*), *furious* (*about/at/with*), and *mad* (*about/at*).

Idiomatic Constructions with Two Prepositions

Prepositions also occur in pairs as part of idiomatic constructions that also include nouns, such as those shown below.

in case of	on account of	at the behest of
in compliance with	in comparison with	for want of
at odds with	in/with respect to	under the auspices of
in view of	at the hands of	by dint of
with regard to	in contact with	in accordance with

There are no rules for predicting which prepositions will occur before or after a particular noun in idioms such as those listed. We can observe, however, that the initial prepositions come from a larger set (*at, by, for, in, on, under,* or *with*) than the prepositions that occur after the noun (*of, to,* or *with*).

These constructions are followed by an NP, which may be simply a head noun, as in (9a), or a head noun with one or more modifiers, as in (9b), (9c), and (9d).

(**9**) a. *In case of fire*, break glass.
    b. *For want of a horse*, the battle was lost.
    c. Your house is not *in compliance with the building code*.
    d. Their government's policy is *at odds with several important provisions in the accord*.

All of these idiomatic structures still involve a basic prepositional phrase structure. At least two analyses of these structures are possible. We will adopt the one shown in (10), in which *in case of* is considered to be a complex preposition composed of more than one word, followed by the object NP, in this case, the noun *fire*.[1]

       Prep   NP
(**10**) [in case of] [fire]

Constructions with Prepositions That Are Followed by *That* Clauses

Constructions such as *in the event, on the basis, on the grounds, on (the) condition, to the effect* may be followed by *that* clauses. The prepositional constructions and their clauses have been bracketed in (11).

$$
\quad\quad\quad\quad\quad\quad\quad\quad\quad\quad\textit{Prep}\quad\quad\quad\quad\quad\quad\quad\quad\quad\quad\textit{Clause}
$$

(**11**) a. You should notify my wife [in the event] [that something happens to me].

$$
\quad\quad\quad\quad\quad\quad\quad\quad\quad\quad\quad\quad\quad\quad\quad\quad\textit{Prep}
$$

b. The lawyer asked for a reduced sentence [on the grounds] [that the crime he

$$
\quad\quad\quad\textit{Clause}
$$

had committed was his first offense.]

The *that* clauses in (11) are closely connected to the nouns that follow the prepositions (i.e., *event* and *grounds*). Evidence of this is shown in the rephrased versions in (12), in which the bracketed prepositional phrases with the demonstrative determiners *that* and *those* clearly refer back to the clauses that begin the sentences.

(**12**) a. *Something might happen to me*, and [in that event] you should notify my wife.
  b. *The crime her client had committed was not serious and it was his first offence*, and [on those grounds] the lawyer asked for a reduced sentence.

As with (10), we can argue that *in the event* and *on the grounds* are complex prepositions. Thus, we still have a basic prepositional phrase structure in which the clause functions as the object of the preposition, as shown in (13).[2]

$$
\quad\quad\quad\quad\quad\quad\textit{Prep}\quad\quad\quad\quad\quad\quad\quad\quad\textit{Clause}
$$

(**13**) a. [in the event] [that something happens to me]

$$
\quad\quad\quad\quad\quad\quad\textit{Prep}\quad\quad\quad\quad\quad\quad\quad\quad\textit{Clause}
$$

b. [on the grounds] [that the crime was not serious]

In Order + Infinitive Clauses

The preposition + noun construction *in order* introduces an infinitive clause. *In order* is often deleted, leaving *to*, as shown in (14b).

$$
\quad\quad\quad\quad\quad\quad\quad\quad\textit{Prep}\quad\quad\quad\quad\quad\quad\textit{Clause}
$$

(**14**) a. He did it [*in order*] [to impress his girlfriend].
  b. He did it to impress his girlfriend.

Infinitive clauses that are introduced by *in order* are referred to as *purpose clauses* because they answer the question *why*, as shown in (15). Purpose clauses, a type of adverbial subordinate clause, are further discussed in Chapter 23.

(**15**) a. Why did he do it? *In order* to impress his girlfriend.
  b. Why did they stop at the grocery store? *In order* to buy some eggs.

Preposition + Preposition Combinations

Sequences made up of two prepositions, such as *from behind* and *down to*, occur frequently, as illustrated in (16). The first preposition can often be followed by a number of others. For example, *from* occurs freely with prepositions such as *behind, inside*, and *beside*, whereas *down* occurs freely with prepositions such as *beside, around*, and *by*.

(**16**) a. He took the package [*from* $\left\{ \begin{array}{l} behind \\ inside \\ beside \end{array} \right\}$ *the box*] and gave it to her.

b. She wandered [*down* $\left\{ \begin{array}{l} beside \\ around \\ by \end{array} \right\}$ *the river*].

These sequences of two adjacent prepositions followed by an NP function as single prepositional phrases and can therefore be moved to the beginning of the sentence, as demonstrated in (17), and as we saw earlier with (5b).

(**17**) a. A strange vehicle suddenly emerged *from behind the house.*
b. *From behind the house*, a strange vehicle suddenly emerged.

Preposition + Adjective Combinations

Constructions such as *in brief, at first, in full, in private, for certain, in short, in vain*, and *for sure*, composed of a preposition followed by an adjective, also occur frequently in English. As demonstrated in (18), they can occur in different positions in a sentence. These constructions often have meanings similar to adverbs (e.g., *in private = privately, in vain = vainly, in full = fully, of late = lately*).

                  Prep   Adj
(**18**) a. Can I talk to you [in] [private]?
b. I tried *in vain* to get him to change his mind.
c. We can't tell *for certain.*
d. Tell her what happened *in full.*
e. *Of late* he has been quite depressed.

SUMMARY

POSITIONS OF OCCURRENCE

Prepositions typically appear as the head of a prepositional phrase (PP), followed by an object NP.
The book was lying on the table.
The car is in the garage.

However, prepositions occur in a range of other constructions as well:

- **Prepositional verbs.** These are verb + prepositional phrases in which the verb + preposition has the same meaning as a single-word verb.
  My daughter still hasn't decided on a college.
  This recipe calls for two cups of sugar.

- **Adjective + preposition combinations.** These constructions are followed either by a standard NP or a gerund.
  Why are you afraid of the dark?
  He isn't capable of doing something like that.

- **Idiomatic constructions with two prepositions.** These idiomatic expressions, in which a preposition is followed by an NP that is followed by another preposition, can be analyzed as complex (multiword) prepositions.
  He will receive justice at the hands of his fellow countrymen.
  Your house is not in compliance with the building code.

continued

- **Constructions with prepositions that are followed by *that* clauses.** These prepositional phrases are composed of a complex (multiword) preposition, followed by a *that* clause which functions as the object of the preposition.
  The suspect was released on the condition that he return to court in a week.
  Call me in the event that there is a problem.

- ***In order* + infinitive clause.** Prepositional phrases consisting of the preposition *in* and the noun *order* are followed by an infinitive complement or purpose clause. *In order* is often deleted.
  He did it in order to impress her.
  He did it to impress her.

- **Preposition + preposition combinations.** Some prepositions (e.g., *from*, *down*) may be immediately followed by another preposition.
  They emerged from behind the cottage.
  The sound seemed to be coming from inside the chest.

- **Preposition + adjective combinations.** These constructions often have meanings similar to adverbs (e.g., *in private* = *privately*, *in vain* = *vainly*, *in full* = *fully*, *of late* = *lately*).
  I'd like to speak to the senator in private.
  She tried in vain to arrange a meeting with the senator.

EXERCISE 8.1

Indicate whether each preposition in the sentences functions as part of a prepositional verb or heads a prepositional phrase with a locative meaning. Justify your choices.

Example: He drove down the street.

Answer: down the street = prepositional phrase (A *where* question can be formed and answered with a prepositional phrase: *Where did he drive? Down the street*.)

1. She depended on her neighbors.
2. They drove across the river.
3. The admissions committee looked at the new applications.
4. *UAE* stands for *United Arab Emirates*.
5. My keys are on the table.
6. We walked around the plaza and stopped beside the monument.

EXERCISE 8.2

Identify each of the italicized structures with prepositions (Adj + Prep combination, Prep + Adj combination, Prep + NP + Prep, Prep followed by a *that* clause combination, Prep + Prep combination) in the sentences.

Example: They found it *down beside the river.*

Answer: down beside the river = Prep + Prep combination

1. I can assure you that he will be paid *in full*.
2. When she heard what he had done, she was *furious with* him.
3. The senator voted for the president's bill *in return for* a favor.

4. The extension to the museum is not *in compliance with* the city building code.
5. He agreed to drop his lawsuit *on the condition* that our company would apologize.
6. *From inside* the house came a cry for help.
7. *In brief*, the performance was a success.

THE MEANINGS OF PREPOSITIONS

In the previous section, we saw that certain verbs and adjectives commonly occur with particular prepositions. For instance, the verb *depend* commonly occurs with *on*, and the adjective *afraid* commonly occurs with *of*. It is often difficult to decide why these verbs or adjectives take the particular prepositions they do. For example, the verb *believe* takes the preposition *in*; however, we sense that this is not the prototypical use of the preposition *in*. Instead, our intuitions tell us that the basic meaning of *in* has to do with *physical location*. In fact, when we look at some other languages – for example, German – we discover that native speakers "believe on" something rather than "in" it. This confirms our intuition that there is much in preposition use that is idiomatic. In this section, we will examine less idiomatic, more prototypical uses of English prepositions.

Thematic Roles

Over the past 30 years, linguists have developed the notion of *thematic roles*,[3] a concept which, as we will see, helps us to understand the meanings of prepositions when they appear in different environments.[4] Thematic roles indicate the semantic (i.e., meaning) relationship between the NP and the verb in a sentence. In other words, they tell us what "role" the NP plays in the action described by the verb in a sentence. The concept will, no doubt, become clearer as we consider several examples of thematic roles. Once we have considered these examples, we will see how the concept of thematic roles relates to the topic of prepositions. Some of the different thematic roles that seem to hold in many, if not all, languages are shown in (19) through (24). The NP that illustrates each thematic role is in italics.

- An *agent*, or *actor*, is the thing that causes, or instigates, the action in a sentence. The agent acts by volition, or free will. In sentences that are in the passive voice, the agent is often preceded by the preposition *by*, as in (19b).

  (**19**) a. *The goalie* caught the ball.
      b. The ball was caught by *the goalie*.

- The *patient*, or *theme*, is the thing affected by an action or the thing that undergoes a change, as illustrated in (20).

  (**20**) a. The basketball player bounced *the ball*.
      b. *The ball* was bounced by the basketball player.
      c. *The ball* bounced several times before rolling under the bench, where it came to a stop.

- An *instrument*, or a *means*, is the thing, usually some tool, that is used to carry out an action. The instrument is usually, but not always, inanimate and does not act but is acted upon, as seen in (21).

  (**21**) a. He sliced the salami with *a knife*.
      b. The scarf was knitted by *hand*.

- *Source* designates the place from which, or person from whom, an action originated, as shown in (22).

  (**22**) a. I took the book from *the library.*
     b. He got the book off *the shelf.*
     c. *Fire* gives off heat.

- *Goal*, or *recipient*, is the place toward which, or the person toward whom, an action is directed. It includes indirect objects, adverbs, and objects of a preposition, as shown in (23).

  (**23**) a. He sent a birthday card to *his wife.*
     b. He went *upstairs.*
     c. We finally reached *the coast.*

- *Location* designates the place at or in which an action takes place. This thematic role often includes *temporal* relationships (i.e., times at which actions occur), as shown in (24).

  (**24**) a. The wallet was under *the bed.*
     b. Your application is next to *those papers.*
     c. He came at *ten o'clock.*
     d. He left on *Wednesday.*

Prepositions and Thematic Roles

Notice that the italicized NP is the object of a preposition in (19b), (21a) and (21b), (22a) and (22b), (23a), and (24a) through (24d). These sentences illustrate that the relationships indicated by thematic roles can often be captured by prepositions. For instance, in (22a) *the library* fills the thematic role of *source*; that is, it is the source from which *the book* is taken. We know it is the source because of the preposition used before it, *from.* If we were to change the preposition to *to,* the role of the library would change from source to goal. This tells us that the meanings of *from* and *to* may be understood in terms of the thematic roles of source and goal, respectively. It also illustrates that the meaning of a preposition can often be understood in terms of the thematic roles with which it is associated.

We will now take a closer look at the complexity of spatial and temporal relationships and how these are expressed by prepositions.

Roles Concerned with Spatial Relations

A primary function of prepositions in English, and in other languages, is to locate things in space. In this role, prepositions are classified according to whether they describe a *static location* or a *change of location*. Prepositions in the latter category can be further divided into those that indicate movement away from a source and those that indicate movement toward a goal. In the tables on the following page, you will see that some prepositions fall squarely into a certain category, while others occupy more than one category. For example, many prepositions that are used for static location – *at, behind, between, beyond,* and so on – can also show movement toward a goal when they appear after verbs of motion (e.g., *The dog ran at him*). Similarly, certain prepositions that indicate a source, such as *off,* can be used to describe static location (e.g., *The house is just off the main road*). *Away* is another example; it can indicate movement from a source (e.g., *She walked away from me*) but can also describe a static situation (e.g., *He is away from the office right now*).

PREPOSITIONS INDICATING STATIC LOCATION	
Preposition	**Example**
across	My classroom is across the hall.
against	He's standing against the wall.
among	He stood among the trees.
around	He spent two hours walking around the park.
at	She's been at the library for hours.
away (from)	She's away from her desk right now.
before	I can remember standing before that judge.
behind	We waited behind the building.
below	I can feel something just below the surface.
beneath	There's a door just beneath the stairs.
beside	She sat beside the pool.
between	I found a quarter between the cushions.
beyond	The bridge is just beyond that tollbooth.
by	I love reading by the pool.
in	The letter is still in the envelope.
inside	It's inside the box.
off	Our favorite restaurant is just off the road.
on	The dictionary is on the shelf.
opposite	The school is opposite a large park.
over	This painting will look great over the fireplace.
under	My keys were under the dresser.

PREPOSITIONS INDICATING A SOURCE	
Preposition	**Example**
away (from)	The horse galloped away from its owner.
from	I got a call from my son today.
out (of)	I walked out of the house at 6:00.
off	The stampeding cattle ran right off the cliff.

PREPOSITIONS INDICATING A GOAL	
Preposition	**Example**
against	The boy was tossing a ball against the wall.
at	I shot at the target.
behind	I dropped my wallet behind the dresser.
beneath	The ship quickly disappeared beneath the surface.
between	It felt great to slip between the warm sheets.
beyond	We traveled just beyond the border.
in	Can't you put your dirty laundry in the hamper?
inside	I ran inside the house and answered the phone.
into	He walked into the room and slammed the door.
on	Please don't throw things on my desk.
onto	The entire team ran onto the court.
to	From Paris he flew to Berlin.
toward	The troops marched toward the village.
under	The puppy crept under the chair.

STATIC LOCATION

Different prepositions are used to indicate a static location with increasing specificity. *In* is used before countries, regions, states, and cities, but *at* is used to designate a more a precise landmark within any of these larger locations, as (25) illustrates. This distinction is taught in some ESL/EFL textbooks.

> (25) a. I met her *in* the United States/the Midwest/Illinois/Chicago.
> b. I met her *in* Chicago *at* the Lyric Opera.

Static location can also be conceptualized either as an object's fixed position or as its position in terms of a path that must be taken to reach it. The latter is referred to as *endpoint location.*[5] This distinction is illustrated in (26) with the preposition *over.*

> (26) a. The portrait of their mother hangs *over* the fireplace.   *fixed static location*
> b. The house lies just *over* that hill.   *endpoint location*

CHANGE OF LOCATION: INTERMEDIATE LOCATION

A change in location involves movement from a source and toward (or to) a goal, as shown in (27).

> (27) a. We went *from* Chicago *to* Zurich.
> b. The ball fell *off* the table, *onto* the floor, and rolled *under* the bed.

With verbs of motion that do not have a fixed duration (*drive, walk, run, roll,* etc.), prepositions such as *across, by, over, past, through,* and *under* can express the idea of an intermediate, temporary location on a path toward an endpoint location. In (28a), *through* indicates a location that is temporary and transitory but is bounded ultimately by the edge of the forest. In (28b), *through* indicates an intermediate position, *Kassel*, between the origin location, *Frankfurt*, and the endpoint location, *Hanover*.

(28) a. When he awoke they were driving *through* the forest.
　　b. We drove from Frankfurt *through* Kassel to Hanover.

Extended Meanings of Spatial Prepositions

The meanings of many prepositions that express a spatial relationship may be extended to express other meanings. For example, the preposition *from*, which has the basic meaning of marking a source location (e.g., *She drove from New York to Boston*), also has the extended *causal* meaning, as illustrated in sentences such as *He died from pneumonia*. However, this use of *from* is restricted to diseases or other physical conditions or problems (exhaustion, back pains, etc.). Thus, we cannot say **The barn was destroyed from a tornado.*[6]

From can also be used with the verbs *hear* and *learn* to express the communication of information, as shown in (29). In instances like this, *from* can emphasize the source of the information that is received.

(29) a. I heard it *from* her.
　　b. We learned a lot *from* Professor Kearns.

From can also be used with a fairly large number of verbs of persuasion and abstention, such as *ban, block, delay, discourage, dissuade, distract, divert, exclude, exempt, prevent*, and *prohibit*. With these verbs, as illustrated in (30), the preposition has been extended from its role as an indicator of the source of some action to an indicator of an action (described in a following gerund) that is held back or prevented.[7]

(30) a. He dissuaded her *from reporting him to the director.*
　　b. They prevented her *from leaving the meeting.*
　　c. She abstained *from casting a vote of no confidence.*

The spatial location meaning of many prepositions can also be extended to the domain of time. For example, the spatial location meaning of *at* in (31a) also marks a *fixed point in time*, as illustrated in (31b).

(31) a. A compass is useless *at the North Pole.*
　　b. He said he was coming *at four o'clock.*

Similarly, *by* has a basic locative meaning of proximity, as in (32a), which is extended to *motion past something* in (32b), and can also be extended to temporal contexts like that in (32c).

(32) a. She was standing *by the window.*
　　b. The troops marched *by the stand where the general and guests were seated.*
　　c. Time is passing *by.*

Other temporal meanings conveyed by prepositions we have looked at are shown in the table below. There are only two prepositions in the table – *during* and *for* – that do not also occur in prepositional phrases that describe spatial relations.

PREPOSITIONS INDICATING TEMPORAL RELATIONSHIPS		
Preposition	**Meaning**	**Example**
about	approximately	It was about 3:00 when we stopped.
around	approximately	We stopped around 3:30.
at	fixed point	We are meeting at 8:00 p.m.
before	prior to/earlier than	I can see you before 3:00.
between	in this interval	She's coming between 2:00 and 3:00.
by	not later than	I'll be there by 4:00.
during	fixed duration	He works during the day.
for	duration	They worked for three hours.
from	starting point of fixed duration	You will work from 8:00 to noon every day.
in	point in fixed period	He came here in 2003.
over	spanning a period	Over the years, he became wiser.
through	in the course of/ for a period	Through the years, she became more proficient. They worked through the night.
to	end point in a time period	He worked from 3:00 to 4:00.
toward	sometime close to	Toward morning, he fell asleep.
under	less than	She completed the assignment in under an hour.

Instrumental Thematic Role

As we saw earlier in this chapter, another basic thematic role is that of instrument. The most common prepositions for instrumental meaning are *by* and *with*, as illustrated in (33). Instrumental prepositional phrases answer the question "How?" or "By what means?"

(33) a. They communicate *by sign language.*
b. The information was obtained *by subterfuge.*
c. She opened the door *with a master key.*
d. They ate *with chopsticks.*

The instrumental meaning of *by* has been extended to indicate a mode of transportation (e.g., *by train*), a route or way of access (e.g., *by a window*), and a cause (e.g., *by accident*) as illustrated in (34).

(34) a. He opened the jar *by* unscrewing the lid.   *instrumental*
b. They came *by* train.   *mode of transportation*
c. The thief came in *by* the window.   *route/access*
d. It was sent to the wrong destination *by* accident.   *causal*

In addition to the locative and instrumental meanings and their extensions, the NP following *by* can have a number of specialized meanings, some of which are illustrated in (35). In (35a), *by* is used to indicate the size of a gap or a difference; in (35b), it indicates a time deadline; in (35c), it is used to describe the measurement of an area; and in (35d), it is used to indicate the unit of measurement by which something is divided and sold.

> (**35**) a. The Bolivians won *by* two goals.   *size of a gap or difference*
> b. The boss wants it on his desk *by* two o'clock.   *time deadline*
> c. The living room is 25 feet long *by* 14 feet wide.   *measurement of an area*
> d. It's sold *by* the kilo.   *unit of measurement*

By is also part of a number of idiomatic phrases, some of which have an adverbial function, as shown in (36).

> (**36**) a. They walked down the aisle *side by side*.
> b. I like doing things *by myself*.
> c. They came ashore *by night*.
> d. *Day by day* he sat in the library, taking notes for his book.

This property of prepositions, that a single form such as *by* can have many different meanings, is known as *polysemy*, and it is frequently cited as one of the reasons that the meanings of prepositions are so difficult to teach.

Comitative Thematic Role

In the previous section, we saw that *with* is one of the two prepositions that express an instrumental role. However, another basic meaning expressed by prepositional phrases headed by *with* is the notion of accompaniment, as illustrated in (37).

> (**37**) Alicia went to the ball *with her old boyfriend, Bill*.

This *comitative* role of *with* has been extended to other contexts, some of which are illustrated in (38). These include *location*, as shown in (38a); *properties* of NPs, as in (38b) and (38c); *manner*, as in (38d); and *agreement*, as in (38e).

> (**38**) a. I left the keys to my house *with my neighbor*.   *location*
> b. He works for a young Iranian *with long black hair*.   *properties/characteristics*
> c. John always had a weakness for fast cars
>   *with powerful engines*.   *properties/characteristics*
> d. She wrote about her cause *with great passion*.   *manner*
> e. I'm *with you* on this.[8]   *agreement*

Synonymous Prepositions

Just as a single preposition can have a range of meanings, certain meanings can be expressed by more than one preposition. For example, the proximity meaning of *by* can also be expressed by *near*. *She lives by the railroad station* means essentially the same thing as *She lives near the railroad station*. Other examples of this overlap are shown in (39).

(39) a. She lives $\begin{Bmatrix} next\ to \\ beside \end{Bmatrix}$ the school yard.

    b. I found it $\begin{Bmatrix} behind \\ in\ back\ of \end{Bmatrix}$ the house.

    c. The family portrait was hanging $\begin{Bmatrix} above \\ over \end{Bmatrix}$ the fireplace.

    d. We drove $\begin{Bmatrix} by \\ past \end{Bmatrix}$ the old house we used to live in.

    e. He finally found it $\begin{Bmatrix} under \\ underneath \\ beneath \end{Bmatrix}$ the sink.

    f. Right $\begin{Bmatrix} below \\ under \end{Bmatrix}$ the painting was a metal plaque that identified the artist.

    g. He pointed $\begin{Bmatrix} at \\ to \\ toward \end{Bmatrix}$ the man and said, "That's him."

    h. She said she would be here at a quarter $\begin{Bmatrix} to \\ of \end{Bmatrix}$ four.

    i. They always take a trip to Europe $\begin{Bmatrix} during \\ in \end{Bmatrix}$ the summer.

Sentences (39a) through (39g) all relate to location in space, whereas (39h) and (39i) relate to time. Note that native speakers do not always agree that sentences with these alternate prepositions necessarily have identical meanings. For example, in (39g), *at the man* indicates a precise goal, whereas, for some native speakers, *toward* would mean "in the general direction of."

SUMMARY

THE MEANINGS OF PREPOSITIONS

Thematic roles such as source, goal, and location are used to describe the NPs in a sentence in terms of their relationship to a verb in the sentence. The meanings of many English prepositions can be understood in terms of the thematic roles occupied by their object NPs.

Location prepositions are classified according to whether they describe a static location, a source, or a goal:

- **Static location.** Prepositions such as *in*, *on*, *under*, and *beside* can be used to describe a place where something is located.
  The book is at my apartment.
  I live in Seoul.

- **Source.** Prepositions such as *from* and *off* can be used to describe an action's point of origin, or source.
  She fell off the ladder.
  We just arrived from Los Angeles.

- **Goal.** Prepositions such as *to*, *into*, and *onto* can be used to describe an action's point of termination, or goal.
  He fell onto the floor.
  I took the Eurostar to Rome.

- **Instrumental.** The prepositions *with* and *by* can be used to indicate the thing, usually some tool or instrument, that is used to carry out an action.
  She sliced the rope with a knife.
  The scarf was knitted by hand.

- **Comitative.** *With* also expresses the notion of accompaniment.
  Lee is at the movies with his wife.
  I had an interesting conversation with Laura.

The prototypical meanings of many prepositions are often extended into different domains. Some prepositions of location, for instance, can be used to refer to time.
  He said he was coming at four o'clock.
  I need to get home by 6:30.
  Alice's class runs from noon to 1:30.

Just as a single preposition can have a range of meanings, certain meanings can be expressed by more than one preposition.

She lives $\begin{Bmatrix} next\ to \\ beside \\ by \end{Bmatrix}$ *the schoolyard.*

The family portrait was hanging $\begin{Bmatrix} above \\ over \end{Bmatrix}$ *the fireplace.*

EXERCISE 8.3

Name the thematic role (endpoint static location, fixed static location, source, goal, intermediate location, instrumental, comitative) indicated by each italicized preposition in the following sentences.

Example: From where we are standing right now, his house is just *over* that hill.

Answer: over = endpoint static location

1. He opened the bottle *with* a corkscrew.
2. She fired her gun directly *at* him.
3. The panther leapt *off* the rock *onto* the horse.
4. She put her ring *in* the jewelry box.
5. He was standing *by* the water fountain.
6. On the way *to* the lodge, they had to drive *through* a tunnel.
7. He went to the movies *with* his wife.
8. He computed the total cost *with* an abacus.

EXERCISE 8.4

Explain the meaning of each preposition in italics.

Example: I am meeting him *at* nine o'clock.

Answer: at = fixed point in time

1. His condition deteriorated hour *by* hour.
2. *Over* the years, he has mellowed.
3. He wants to leave *by* three o'clock.
4. He left his car *with* his brother.
5. Our team won *by* 15 points.
6. He finished the exam in just *under* an hour.
7. Fabric is sold *by* the yard.

PROBLEMS THAT ESL/EFL STUDENTS HAVE WITH PREPOSITIONS

Many languages, such as English, express thematic roles by means of prepositions. Some languages, however, use *postpositions* (i.e., morphemes that express the same thematic roles but come after head nouns). Languages that use postpositions in this way include Korean and Japanese. For example, in Korean, the postposition -*e*, which corresponds to the goal-directed English preposition *to*, comes after the NP goal. This contrast between the English preposition and the Korean postposition is shown in (40).

> **(40)** a. *mikuk   e   Korean*
>   U.S.   to
>   b. "to the U.S."   *English*

Other languages, such as Finnish, express most of the thematic relationships that English uses prepositions for by means of inflectional morphemes that are attached to a noun. Thus, just as English adds the morpheme -*s* to a noun to express the idea of plurality, Finnish adds different morphemes to nouns to express the meanings that would be expressed by English prepositions. A partial list of these meanings is shown in (41).

> **(41)** *kauppa*   shop
>   *kauppa-ssa*   in the shop
>   *kauppa-sta*   from (inside) the shop
>   *kauppa-an*   into the shop
>   *kauppa-lla*   at the shop
>   *kauppa-lta*   from the shop

Do the different ways of expressing thematic relationships in a student's L1 make a difference in learning to use English prepositions? The answer appears to be yes. An interesting study by Jarvis and Odlin (2000) demonstrated conclusively that the presence or absence of English prepositions in narratives produced by two groups of English learners – speakers of Finnish and speakers of Swedish – was directly related to their respective L1s. In a production task, Finnish speakers omitted static locative prepositions such as *in* and *on* before nouns that indicated place (e.g., *in the water*, *on the table*); Swedish speakers, in contrast, never omitted these prepositions. Jarvis and Odlin point out that the most plausible reason for this is that Swedish uses prepositions much like English does, but Finnish has a larger number of options for expressing spatial relations, predominantly the use of the inflectional morphemes shown in (41).

For those students who have prepositions or postpositions in their native language, English prepositions are still a source of difficulty, and they remain so even as students' levels of proficiency increase. One reason for this is the problem of polysemy. In learning a second language, students attempt to draw correspondences between their L1 prepositions and prepositions in the L2. Perfect one-to-one correspondences would facilitate learning, but, given polysemy, finding these is virtually impossible. Nevertheless, L2 learners will not abandon the search for correspondences as a learning strategy. Spanish speakers will conclude fairly quickly that the Spanish preposition *en* is roughly equivalent to the English prepositions *in* and *on*. The basis of this conclusion is not only the orthographic (spelling) similarity of *en* to *in* and *on*; it is also the fact that these two prepositions appear in the same grammatical contexts that *en* does for indicating static location in Spanish, as (42) illustrates.

(**42**) a. *Está   en   la   mesa.*
     "It is   on   the   table."
   b. *Está   en   el   cuarto.*
     "It is   in   the   room."

To correctly use *in* and *on*, Spanish speakers must learn that *in* implies that the NP object is enclosed or encompassed, whereas *on* implies physical contact with the object. This learning problem is compounded as the students face new extended uses of these two prepositions. In public transportation, for instance, the choice of *in* or *on* seems to be due to the relative mobility of the passenger inside the vehicle or to the size of the vehicle. Hence, you ride *in* a taxi or *in* a small airplane, but you ride *on* a bus and *on* an airliner.[9]

Another source of the difficulty that ESL/EFL students have learning prepositions may be L1 transfer. However, it is not always easy to determine the basis for what appears to be a case of L1 transfer when a student produces an English sentence with the wrong preposition such as in (43).

(**43**) * . . . the knowledge that a student has *in* any level of his education . . .

The student who incorrectly used *in* instead of *at* in (43) might be aware that Spanish *en* also corresponds to English *at* in sentences like *Está en la casa* (which means "It's at the house"). However, why did the student choose *in* instead of *at* or *on*? This may be the result of an incorrect guess, or it may be that the student conceptualizes *in* as the best English option for capturing the meaning of *en* in this environment.

One type of L1 transfer that is the source of many errors made by Spanish speakers has nothing to do with the confusion of prepositional meanings or with their extensions to other contexts. It is a clear case of transferring grammatical form. A number of Spanish prepositions (*a*, *en*, *de*, *con*, *por*, and *para*) appear before verb complements in which the verb has the infinitive form. In (44), the complement *hacer* + *lo* (which means "do it") follows the preposition *de*.[10]

(**44**) *una   manera   de   hacerlo*
    a   way   (prep)   to do it
   "a way of doing it"

When attempting to produce English sentences that would be rendered with *de* and a following verb in their L1, Spanish speakers will often render the corresponding English verb as an infinitive. However, the corresponding English sentence usually has the preposition *of* followed by the verb in the present participle (*-ing*) form. When the Spanish configuration (NP + *de* + infinitive) is carried over into English, this creates errors such as those shown in (45a) in which the infinitive *to define* should be replaced by *of defining*.[11]

> (45) a. *I consider that the expression . . . is *a precise method to define* a fundamental characteristic of the American culture.

Preposition-related errors such as the one in (45) were some of the most frequent and persistent found in the compositions of Spanish speakers with advanced English proficiency at an American university. They were matched in number only by problems related to prepositional verbs. (Prepositional verb errors are discussed in Chapter 9.)

SUGGESTIONS FOR TEACHING PREPOSITIONS

The treatment of prepositions in English language teaching textbooks is sometimes not comprehensive. In lower-level textbooks, the usual approach is to introduce a limited number of locative and directional prepositions and illustrate their meanings with simple diagrams. Practice using them usually comes in the form of single isolated sentences with an illustration beside each one depicting spatial relationships between people and objects. For example, next to an illustration of a cat jumping off a table there will be a sentence such as *The cat jumped _____ the table*. The student fills in the blank with the appropriate preposition.

Another favorite textbook activity is to have a street map on a page with a dialog underneath in which one person asks for directions and another responds using prepositions. The sentences in such a conversation have blanks indicating missing prepositions. Textbooks beyond the beginning level often do not contain many activities for teaching and practicing the use of prepositions, although you can occasionally find some limited coverage of adjective + prepositional phrase combinations. This sparse treatment of prepositions in grammar textbooks may have led to the production of a number of specialty ESL/EFL textbooks that are devoted solely to teaching this topic. Two such textbooks are Yates (1999), and Lindstromberg (1997). The former is clearly intended as a self-study book for ESL/EFL students, whereas the latter seems to be designed for teachers.

Whether or not these specialty books are effective, they at least enable teachers to widen their coverage of prepositions. One possible weakness of books like Yates's concerns the types of exercises they contain. More evidence is emerging that shows students will not gain real competence in certain areas of grammar by filling in blanks in written sentences. (See Chapter 3 for more on this issue, as well as Chapter 16.) In light of this growing body of evidence, it is a good idea to have your students practice the use of prepositions with activities that require active production of the desired forms. The activities that follow are designed to do this.

You should continue to teach prepositions to students even as their level of proficiency increases. Their ability to use prepositions correctly in different contexts will improve if they are periodically presented with new meanings for prepositions and asked to create original sentences that reflect these meanings.

Activity 1: Teaching Prepositions of Location and Movement (Beginning)

The static location, source, and goal meanings of prepositions are often introduced using classroom objects, as illustrated in (46). Begin by moving an object and describing its movement and location. Then ask students to give the object's location.

(46) Teacher: I am putting the eraser *on* the desk. Where is the eraser?
　　　Student: It's *on* the desk.
　　　Teacher: Good. It's *on* the desk. Now I am going to put my pen *in* my pocket. Where is my pen?
　　　Student: It's *in* your pocket.

After several exchanges like these, you may choose to use a chart like the one following with simple line drawings using circles, squares, and horizontal lines to illustrate the prototypical meanings of several prepositions. Notice that all three thematic relations – static location, source, and goal – are shown. Lines with arrows illustrate movement.

As you demonstrate each meaning, point to its corresponding diagram on the chart. You may also ask students to demonstrate the meaning after you. Next, give students directions such as the ones in (47). As you give each direction, point once again to its corresponding diagram as a visual reference for the students.

(**47**) a. Su Jung, please put your book *on my book.*
b. Mario, please walk *around Su Jung's desk.*

The purpose of an activity like this one is simply to teach the meanings of as many prepositions as possible. Activities that solidify students' knowledge of these and extend the prototypical meanings to other contexts should follow.

Activity 2: Solidifying Meaning with TBLT Activities (Intermediate)

After the prototypical meanings of spatial prepositions have been taught, TBLT (see Chapter 3 for a discussion of TBLT) can be helpful for solidifying their knowledge. Alosh (2004) suggests using picture tasks because they can be used with all levels of proficiency. Collect pictures of scenes that students are familiar with (e.g., people at a restaurant, wedding, hotel, airport, etc.). Have the students split up into pairs or small groups and describe various objects in the pictures using locative prepositions.

As indicated earlier, maps are quite useful for practicing prepositions that describe static location, source-to-goal movement, and movement past an object or location. Take an enlarged map and demonstrate the following prepositions: *from, to, down to, past, over,* and *next to.* Then tell students, "I want to get from the bank to the library. How do I do that? I'll show you on this map." Describe the route to your students, emphasizing the prepositions.

After you have done this, quickly review the meanings of the prepositions by writing them on the board. Add more prepositions that describe static location as well as motion past (*behind/in back of, under/underneath,* etc.). Have students work in pairs or small groups. Hand out the same map with several possible routes indicated in color (draw them with a marker). Tell students to take turns describing how to get from the beginning to the end of each of these predetermined routes. Emphasize that the person describing the route must use landmarks throughout the description.

Activity 3: Contrasting *In, On,* and *At* (Low Intermediate Through Intermediate)

Some textbooks give special treatment to the static position meanings of *in, on,* and *at.* However, they sometimes miss the major generalization that *in* is typically used for describing locations that have large areas, such as countries, states, and cities (e.g., *in* Japan, *in* Ontario, *in* Buenos Aires); whereas *on* is used to indicate smaller, more specific locations (e.g., *on* Main Street, *on the corner of* Main Street and Washington Avenue, *on the south side of* town), and *at* is used with even smaller, more specific locations (e.g., *at* the train station, *at* the library, *at* the doctor's office).

You might introduce this general guideline by writing examples on the board or on a chart, as in (48).

(**48**) You live *in* a country, state, city.   in the United States, in California, in Albany
on a street.   on State Street, on Hamilton Boulevard
at a specific place.   at 2305 Anderson Street, at the library

This approach allows you to point out special idioms such as *at home*, *at work*, *at college*, and *at the university* (in American English vs. *at university* in British English).

After the examples have been presented and the general principle explained, play a game in which students ask one another where they live. The asker has to keep pressing for more details (e.g., "Where do you live in Canada? What province? What city? What street in ____? What's the address?") Students have to respond using sentences with the prepositions *in*, *on*, and *at*.

You can also contrast the meanings of *in*, *on*, and *at* by directing students to set up meetings with each other at particular locations in the city where they are studying English (e.g., "Let's meet in Chinatown, on the corner of Canal and Broadway.")

Activity 4: Teaching Prepositions of Time (Low Intermediate)

Using the situation described in Activity 3 (arranging a meeting) provides a means of illustrating how some prepositions are used to talk about time. Demonstrate the meanings of the prepositions *at*, *about*, *around*, and *before* with ____ o'clock in the context of meeting someone. Next, show how you might use *by* to stipulate a time that cannot be exceeded. Then show how the expressions *between* ____ *and* ____ and *from* ____ *to* ____ define intervals of time. Finally, work with the students as a class to write a role play that depicts the process of setting up a teacher–student meeting, as illustrated in (49).

> **(49)** Teacher: OK, Claire. What time shall we meet for coffee tomorrow?
> Claire: Could we meet before 3:00? I am busy at 3:00.
> Teacher: I'm free between 1:00 and 3:00. Should we meet at 1:30?
> Claire: All right. I'll have to leave by 2:30, but that should give us enough time. Where should we meet?
> Teacher: How about Espresso Royale? That coffee shop on Green Street.
> Claire: That sounds good. I'll see you at 1:30.

After you act out the role play with several of the students, have the class divide into pairs, and have each pair write and practice a new role play to be performed for the class. Write the time prepositions on the board as a quick reference for students as they develop their role plays.

Activity 5: Teaching Extended Meanings (Intermediate Through Advanced)

Once your students understand the prototypical meanings of several prepositions, you can engage in an activity that teaches the extended meanings. Here is an example with *by*.

Begin by showing a picture of someone standing next to a window. Ask the class, "Where is she?" If a student responds with something such as, "She is by the window" or "She's standing by the window," acknowledge the answer as correct. If no answers are supplied or if students use *next to* or *beside* in their answers, explain that *by* can mean the same thing as those prepositions. Next, show a picture that illustrates the use of *by* to indicate motion past something. You might, for instance, use a picture of a car driving by a billboard.

Once students understand this spatial meaning of *by*, ask them, "What are some other ways we can use *by*?" Show some pictures that illustrate the instrumental meaning of *by* (e.g., people communicating *by* phone, *by* e-mail, etc.). After showing these examples of the instrumental meaning, use photographs and pictures to illustrate the extended meanings of the preposition: mode of transportation (*by car*), route (*by the front door*), and causal (*by accident*).

In order to practice these meanings, you can give students a short passage in which the meanings of *by* are expressed in other ways. The passage may include sentences such as *She walked past the building*, *They stood next to each other*, *He entered through the side door*, *They often talked to each other on the phone*, and so on. Direct the students to find every instance in the passage where *by* can be used to express the same meaning, and change those sentences accordingly.

You can make this activity less or more challenging by choosing either to indicate the items that should be changed, or to let the students find them without any clues. Follow up with a quick exercise in which the students have to write down sentences you dictate, replacing part of your sentence with an appropriate *by* expression. For example, you read "He drove past the apartment several times," and they write "He drove by the apartment several times."

ENDNOTES

                   Prep   N   Prep   N

[1] A second possible analysis is: [in] [case] [of] [fire].

[2] Some linguists, such as Quirk et al. (1972), might claim that these prepositional constructions (*in the event*, *on the grounds*, etc.) are a kind of compound subordinator. Quirk et al. list *in order to* and *in order that* as examples (p. 727).

[3] These are sometimes referred to as *theta roles*.

[4] The concept of thematic roles was developed initially by Fillmore (1967, 1977). There have been some changes in the definitions of some of the thematic roles over time. A list of the more commonly recognized roles with easy-to-understand definitions can be found in Brinton (2000). Some of the definitions and comments in this chapter have been modeled on those.

[5] See Huddleston and Pullum (2002), p. 649.

[6] This example and observation is from Huddleston and Pullum (2002), p. 656.

[7] See Huddleston and Pullum (2002), p. 657.

[8] Observations and examples modeled on Huddleston and Pullum (2002), p. 661.

[9] The Spanish examples in (42) as well as the argument is from Stockwell, Bowen, and Martin (1965), pp. 207–208, one of the great pioneering works in contrastive linguistics.

[10] These prepositions are also referred to as "relaters," in Stockwell, Bowen, and Martin (1965).

[11] Example (45) is from Cowan and Leeser (2007).

REFERENCES

Alosh, M. (2004). Learning Arabic: From language functions to tasks in a diglossic context. In B. L. Leaver & J. R. Willis (Eds.), *Task-based instruction in foreign language education: Practices and programs*. Washington D.C.: Georgetown University Press.

Brinton, L. J. (2000). *The structure of modern English*: *A linguistic introduction*. Amsterdam/ Philadelphia: John Benjamins.

Cowan, R., & Leeser M. (2007). The structure of corpora in SLA research. In R. Facchinetti (Ed.), *Corpus linguistics 25 years on* (pp. 289–304). Amsterdam/New York: Rodopi.

Fillmore, C. J. (1967). The case for case. In E. Bach & T. Harms (Eds.), *Universals in linguistic theory* (pp. 1–80). New York: Holt, Rinehart & Winston.

Fillmore, C. J. (1977). The case for case reopened. In P. Cole & J. M. Sadock (Eds.), *Syntax and semantics vol. 8*: *Grammatical relations* (pp. 59–81). New York: Academic Press.

Huddleston, R., & Pullum, G. K. (2002). *The Cambridge grammar of the English language*. Cambridge: Cambridge University Press.

Jarvis, S., & Odlin, T. (2000). Morphological type, spatial reference and language transfer. *Studies in Second Language Acquisition, 22*, 535–556.

Lindstromberg, S. (1997). *English prepositions explained*. Amsterdam/Philadelphia: John Benjamins.

Quirk, R., Greenbaum, S., Leech, G., & Svartvik, J. (1972). *A grammar of contemporary English*. London: Longman.

Stockwell, R. P., Bowen, D. J., & Martin, J. W. (1965). *The grammatical structures of English and Spanish: An analysis of structural differences between the two languages*. Chicago: The University of Chicago Press.

Yates, J. (1999). *The ins and outs of prepositions*: *A guidebook for ESL students*. Hauppage, NY: Barrons.

CHAPTER 9

Multiword Verbs

INTRODUCTION

English has a large number of *multiword verbs*, which consist of a combination of a verb and one or two other elements. The discussion in this chapter recognizes three main categories of multiword verbs – *phrasal verbs, prepositional verbs*, and *phrasal prepositional verbs* – and each category is described in terms of both syntactic and semantic characteristics. The relatively simple treatment that these verbs receive here accords with their treatment in the syntax literature on this topic and is intended to make the topic easier for both teachers and students to grasp.

A clearer understanding of the different types of multiword verbs can provide a basis for explaining some of the documented difficulties that English language learners have with them. It should also enable teachers to better organize the teaching of these special verbs, which sometimes receive an inaccurate and incomplete presentation in textbooks.

PHRASAL VERBS

Phrasal verbs are made up of a verb and a following particle. The term *particle* is used to refer to words that function as prepositions or adverbs in other contexts (e.g., *up, down, away, around*) but do not function as prepositions or adverbs when part of a phrasal verb. Examples of phrasal verbs are presented in (1).

(1) a. Tony *set up* all the chairs before class began.
b. Daniela *handed in* her homework early.
c. Don't *give up*!

The meaning of a phrasal verb cannot always be predicted from the meanings of its individual elements. For example, the meaning of *rule out* ("eliminate") cannot be determined by simply understanding what *rule* means and combining that meaning with the meaning of *out*. This is one reason that phrasal verbs present a challenge to English language learners.[1]

Phrasal verbs fall into two major categories: *transitive phrasal verbs*, as in (2a), and *intransitive phrasal verbs*, as in (2b).

$$\overset{V}{} \qquad \overset{NP}{}$$

(**2**) a. Maggie [*looked up*] [the address].

$$\overset{V}{}$$

b. Maggie [*sat up*].

Transitive Phrasal Verbs

Transitive phrasal verbs fall into three categories, depending on where the object NP can occur in relation to the verb and the particle.

Separable Transitive Phrasal Verbs

In (2a), we see the transitive phrasal verb *looked up* followed by the direct object NP *the address*. This sentence could, however, be rewritten as in (3).

(**3**) Maggie *looked* the address *up.*

Sentence (3) illustrates that *look up* is a *separable transitive phrasal verb*. It is classi- fied as such because its parts may be "separated" by an object; that is, the direct object may appear between the verb *looked* and the particle *up.*

Separable transitive phrasal verbs occur frequently in conversation, fiction, and news reports.[2] They appear less frequently in academic writing. Examples of separable tran- sitive phrasal verbs that occur with high frequency are *get back, pick up, put on, look up, make up, take off, take on,* and *turn off.* A more complete list of these verbs is in Appendix A.

PARTICLE MOVEMENT

The separation of the phrasal verb is the result of applying the *particle movement rule*, which moves the particle to the position following the object. This is shown in (4b).

(**4**) a. Maggie looked up the address.
 b. Maggie looked __ the address up.

Most transitive phrasal verbs take the particle movement rule. As long as the direct object of a separable phrasal verb is not a pronoun, the particle movement rule is op- tional (i.e., you can apply it or not). If, however, the direct object is a personal pronoun (*him, her, it, them,* etc.) or a demonstrative pronoun (*this/that, these/those*), the particle movement rule must be applied. Thus, if we change the direct object in (5a), *the tele- phone number,* to the pronoun *it,* we must apply the particle movement rule, as shown in (5b). Otherwise, an ungrammatical sentence results, as shown in (5c).

(**5**) a. John looked up the telephone number.
 b. John looked it up.
 c. *John looked up it.

The particle movement rule is optional if the direct object is an indefinite pronoun, such as *some* and *other,* or a quantifier, such as *a few* and *several,* as (6a) and (6b) illustrate.

(**6**) a. I picked up $\left\{\begin{matrix} some \\ a\,few \end{matrix}\right\}$ this morning.

 b. I picked $\left\{\begin{matrix} some \\ a\,few \end{matrix}\right\}$ up this morning.

BLOCKING PARTICLE MOVEMENT: END WEIGHT

Although the particle movement rule is optional except in cases such as the one shown in (5c), native speakers will not apply it if a transitive phrasal verb is followed by a long object noun phrase, as illustrated in (7).

(**7**) John looked up *some information about an early religion in which forces of nature such as fire were worshipped.*

One reason for not applying the particle movement rule in this case is to avoid creating a sentence such as (8).

(**8**) John looked *some information about an early religion in which forces of nature such as fire were worshipped* up.

Although (8) is grammatical, it sounds clumsy because the particle is so far away from the verb. The sentence violates the principle of end weight, a general tendency in English that can be formulated as follows: put long, "heavy" elements such as complex NPs at the end of a clause or sentence, rather than in the middle. Failure to follow the principle of end weight with phrasal verbs that have long object NPs makes a sentence harder to process or understand.[3]

Inseparable Transitive Phrasal Verbs

A small group of transitive phrasal verbs do not permit the particle to move over the direct object even if it is a pronoun, as (9) and (10) illustrate. Particle movement is not possible with these *inseparable phrasal verbs*.

(**9**) a. Don't pick on my brother.
    b. Don't pick on him.
    c. *Don't pick him on.

(**10**) a. Look after my sister, will you?
     b. Look after her, will you?
     c. *Look her after, will you?

As with separable transitive phrasal verbs, the meanings of inseparable transitive phrasal verbs usually cannot be deduced from the sum of their parts. For example, the meaning "annoy, pester" is not obvious from the verb + particle combination *pick on* in (9). This small group of verbs includes *come by* ("acquire"), *look into* ("investigate"), and *run into* ("encounter"); see also Appendix A.

Permanently Separated Transitive Phrasal Verbs

A very small group of transitive phrasal verbs require that the direct object occur between the verb and the particle. These verbs are therefore referred to as *permanently separated transitive phrasal verbs*. The particle cannot appear directly after the verb, as (11) and (12) illustrate.[4]

(**11**) a. That job is getting Janice down.
     b. That job is getting her down.
     c. *That job is getting down Janice.

(**12**) a. The judge let the thief off with a light sentence.
     b. The judge let him off with a light sentence.
     c. *The judge let off the thief with a light sentence.

In addition to *get* (someone) *down* and *let* (someone) *off*, this group of verbs includes *ask* (someone) *out*, *do* (something) *over*, and *see* (something) *through*; see also Appendix A.

There are a few idioms that appear to be permanently separated transitive phrasal verbs. However, in contrast to permanently separated verbs, these verbs are highly restricted to certain nouns for their objects. It is therefore more appropriate to view the structures as idioms that have the same form as permanently separated transitive phrasal verbs. The idioms in (13a) and (13b) mean "cry profusely," and "laugh uproariously," respectively.

(**13**) a. He cried his eyes out.
b. She laughed her head off.

Intransitive Phrasal Verbs

We can distinguish two types of intransitive phrasal verbs: *pure intransitive phrasal verbs* and *ergative phrasal verbs*. As with other phrasal verbs, the meaning of an intransitive phrasal verb usually cannot be arrived at by simply combining the meanings of its individual parts.

Pure Intransitive Phrasal Verbs

The pure intransitive phrasal verbs *took off* and *sat down* are shown in (14) and (15), respectively. As (14b) and (15b) illustrate, the verb part of an intransitive phrasal verb usually cannot be separated from the following particle by an adverb.

(**14**) a. The plane took off quickly and climbed to cruising altitude.
b. *The plane took *quickly* off and climbed to cruising altitude.

(**15**) a. She sat down very slowly and began to cry.
b. *She sat *very slowly* down and began to cry.

Pure intransitive phrasal verbs, common examples of which include *come over* ("visit"), *get together* ("meet"), and *line up* (see Appendix A for others), are used primarily in conversation and fiction. They are used less frequently than transitive phrasal verbs in news reports and much less frequently in academic prose.

Like single-word intransitive verbs, intransitive phrasal verbs may be followed by prepositional phrases. These often describe thematic relations that we saw in Chapter 8. For example, *the next item* in the PP headed by *on* in (16b) has the thematic role of goal. It is what we are moving on toward. Similarly, *the hotel* in the PP headed by *of* in (17b) has the thematic role of the source of the action expressed by *checked out*. Sentences (17c) and (17d) show that prepositional phrases of location (*in Nice*) and time (*on Tuesday*) may follow thematic relations of goal or source.

(**16**) a. We are going to move on.

         PP
b. We are now going to move on [to the next item].

(**17**) a. He checked out.

     PP
b. He checked out [of the hotel].
c. He checked out *of the hotel on Tuesday*.
d. He checked out *of a hotel in Nice on Tuesday*.

It is important for teachers to recognize that prepositional phrases of goal and source are not part of the preceding intransitive phrasal verbs. Failure to do this can result in teaching students that there are two different verbs that they have to learn – *check out* and *check out of.* This error, which occurs in some textbooks, can lead students to believe that the task of learning phrasal verbs is far more daunting than it actually is.[5]

Ergative Phrasal Verbs

Some phrasal verbs are ergative; that is, they describe an action that is experienced by the subject. Typical examples are *die down*, *taper off*, and *crop up*, as shown in (18); see Appendix A for others.

(**18**) a. After about an hour, the storm began to *die down.*
　　 b. At the end of December, sales of consumer goods usually *taper off.*
　　 c. Over the past two weeks, a number of problems *have cropped up.*

Some ergative phrasal verbs have transitive counterparts, which take the particle movement rule. Examples of these *paired ergative phrasal verbs* and their transitive counterparts are shown in (19) and (20). (The verbs in [18], in contrast, can be termed *unpaired ergative phrasal verbs*).

(**19**) a. The ship blew up.　　　　　 *ergative*
　　 b. The terrorists blew up the ship.　 *transitive counterpart*
　　 c. The terrorists blew the ship up.　 *transitive counterpart*

(**20**) a. Her shoes wore out.　　　　　　　 *ergative*
　　 b. She wore out her shoes walking to work.　 *transitive counterpart*
　　 c. She wore her shoes out walking to work.　 *transitive counterpart*

SUMMARY
PHRASAL VERBS

Phrasal verbs consist of a verb and particle, which together have the meaning of a single verb. There are two types: transitive and intransitive.
　He picked up some milk at the supermarket.
　Wake up! It's late.

Transitive phrasal verbs may be separable, inseparable, or permanently separated:

- **Separable transitive phrasal verbs** have parts that can be separated by the direct object of the phrasal verb through application of the **particle movement rule**.
　He looked up the number.
　He looked the number up.

- **Inseparable transitive phrasal verbs** cannot take particle movement.
　He ran across a picture of his father in a photo album.
　*He ran a picture of his father across in a photo album.

- **Permanently separated transitive phrasal verbs** have parts that must be separated by the direct object.
　The coach's attitude is getting the team down.
　*The coach's attitude is getting down the team.

> **Intransitive phrasal verbs** can be divided into two categories:
>
> • **pure intransitive phrasal verbs**
> *The plane took off and climbed to cruising altitude.*
> *She sat down very slowly.*
>
> • **ergative phrasal verbs**
> *Bit by bit the intensity of the storm tapered off.*
> *All of a sudden several problems cropped up.*
>
> Some phrasal verbs, called **paired ergative phrasal verbs**, have transitive counterparts.
> *The sun came out, and the water dried up.*   ergative
> *The hot sun dried up the pools of water on the pavement.*   transitive

EXERCISE 9.1

Identify each phrasal verb in italics as separable transitive, inseparable transitive, permanently separated transitive, pure intransitive, ergative, or paired ergative.

Example: On his way home, Alec stopped at the supermarket to *pick up* some milk.

Answer: pick up = separable transitive phrasal verb

1. Under the intense heat of the sun, the water hole gradually began to *dry up*.
2. As he was walking through the woods he *came upon* a freshly killed deer.
3. He didn't know the answer, so he *made* one *up*.
4. Would you please *hand out* these brochures to the other members of the committee?
5. The police thought they had the thief cornered, but he *got away*.
6. *NE* stands for "never exceed" speed. If you fly the plane over the NE speed, it may *break up* and start to shed parts.
7. She believes that he loves her, but I think he is *stringing* her *along*.
8. We're *getting together* this weekend with some friends from college.

PREPOSITIONAL VERBS

Prepositional verbs consist of a verb and a following prepositional phrase, as already discussed in Chapter 8. Typical examples are *decide on, stare at, care for, stand for, depend on*, and *apply for*. (See Appendix A for others.) Like many phrasal verbs, prepositional verbs are transitive. However, their second element is a preposition and so their two parts cannot be separated by the object, in contrast to separable transitive phrasal verbs, to which particle movement can apply. An attempt to separate the verb and preposition will produce an ungrammatical sentence, as (21b) and (22b) illustrate.

(**21**) a. He applied for the job.
　　　b. *He applied the job for.

(**22**) a. Alice depends on her mother.
　　　b. *Alice depends her mother on.

Also, in contrast to phrasal verbs, with most prepositional verbs meaning can usually be deduced from the verb alone. However, some have meanings that are not obvious from the verb alone or from the two parts together. Examples of these prepositional verbs include *stand for*, which means "represent," and *call on*, which means "visit."

Tests for Distinguishing Between Phrasal and Prepositional Verbs

It is sometimes difficult to determine whether a sentence contains a phrasal verb or a prepositional verb. One test that can sometimes help with this determination is that phrasal verbs have meanings that are not the sum of their parts, whereas the meanings of prepositional verbs are usually revealed in the verb that precedes the preposition. But using this *semantic test* alone will not be sufficient to decide many cases. A number of *syntactic tests*, one of which we have already touched on in Chapter 8, provide evidence that allows us to determine whether we have a phrasal or prepositional verb.

The Particle Movement Test

Only separable phrasal verbs can take particle movement. Thus, if the element after the verb can be moved over a following direct object, as (23) and (24) illustrate, we know that we have a separable phrasal verb.

(**23**) In an argument, Sam will always *back up* his buddies.

(**24**) Bill won the argument because Sam *backed* him *up*.

The Adverb Insertion Test

Earlier, we saw that intransitive phrasal verbs usually do not permit the insertion of an adverb between the verb and the particle, and the same is true of transitive phrasal verbs, as (25a) and (25b) show. In contrast, prepositional verbs do permit adverb insertion because the preposition is part of a PP.

(**25**) a. *He *turned* quickly *out* the light.   *separable phrasal verb*
　　　 b. *He *ran* unexpectedly *into* his cousin.   *inseparable phrasal verb*
　　　 c. He *stared* intently *at* the target.   *prepositional verb*

The Relative Clause Test

Relative clauses in which the relative pronoun is the object of a preposition permit the two patterns shown in (26).

(**26**) a. The man [*that* they were waiting *for*] was late.
　　　 b. The man [*for whom* they were waiting] was late.

In (26a), the preposition *for* is at the end of the relative clause enclosed by square brackets, but (26b) shows that this preposition can also occur at the beginning of the clause before the relative pronoun *whom*. The pattern in (26b) is possible only with prepositional verbs, and not with phrasal verbs. The preposition in a prepositional verb can appear with the relative pronoun; the particle in a phrasal verb cannot. Thus, if we take a phrasal verb such as *put on* and a prepositional verb such as *depend on* and put them in relative clauses, we find that only the sentence with the prepositional verb is grammatical if the element following the verb is moved in front of the relative pronoun, as in the pattern in (26b). This comparison is illustrated in (27b) and (28b).

(**27**) a. The dress, *which she tried on*, didn't fit her.   *phrasal verb*
　　　 b. *The dress *on which she tried* didn't fit her.

(**28**) a. The person *who he depends on the most* is his brother.   *prepositional verb*
　　　 b. The person *on whom he depends the most* is his brother.

The *Wh-* Question Test

Wh- questions with prepositional verbs can have two forms. In the first, shown in (29a), the preposition remains at the end of the question. In the second, shown in (29b), the preposition occurs at the beginning of the question.

> (**29**) a. Who were you shouting at?
> b. At whom were you shouting?

Phrasal verbs cannot have the pattern shown in (29b), as (30b) illustrates.

> (**30**) a. What are you looking up?
> b. *Up what are you looking?

Thus, the *wh-* question test is similar to the relative clause test, and together these four tests permit us to distinguish between phrasal verbs and prepositional verbs, both of which appear to have the same external structure – verb + element. Particle movement is possible only with separable transitive phrasal verbs; adverb insertion and the two patterns for relative clauses and for *wh-* questions are possible only with prepositional verbs.

These tests provide a justification for proposing the small class of inseparable transitive phrasal verbs. These verbs, unlike other phrasal verbs but like prepositional verbs, do not take particle movement, so why put them with phrasal verbs rather than prepositional verbs? The reason is that they do not pattern with prepositional verbs on the other syntactic tests. This is shown in (31) with the verb *run across*, which means "encounter" or "discover."

> (**31**) a. He ran across an old manuscript in the library. *inseparable phrasal verb*
> b. *He ran unexpectedly across an old manuscript in the library. *adverb insertion*
> c. *The manuscript across which he ran was quite valuable. *relative clause*
> d. *Across what did you run in the library? *wh- question*

In addition to failing the adverb insertion, relative clause, and *wh-* question tests for prepositional verbs, *run across* passes the semantic test that most phrasal verbs do: its meaning is not readily determined from the sum of its parts or primarily from the verb, as is the case with most prepositional verbs. The combination of these syntactic and semantic factors justifies categorizing verbs such as *run across*, *fall for* ("become attracted to"), *look into* ("investigate"), *look after* ("care for"), and *pick on* ("molest, mistreat") as inseparable transitive phrasal verbs. More examples can be found in Appendix A.

Constructions That Look Like Prepositional Verbs

There are two constructions that have a superficial similarity to prepositional verbs. A closer look reveals the clear differences.

Verb + Noun Phrase + Adjective

Verbs such *cut*, *set*, and *wash* can be followed by adjectives to create a meaning that differs from that of the verb when it stands alone. For instance, *cut short* means "curtail," and *set free* means "liberate." These combinations seem to have meanings that are a literal product of their components, rather like prepositional verbs. However, these combinations differ from prepositional verbs in that the element following the verb is an adjective; and although the combinations are transitive, its two elements are usually separated, as shown in (32) and (33). There are some exceptions to the latter point, for example, *cut short*, as shown by (34b), in which the adjective appears directly after the verb.

(32) a. The gamekeepers *set* the young lion *free*.
   b. *The gamekeepers *set free* the young lion.

(33) a. After a few minutes she was able to *work* the ropes *loose*.
   b. *After a few minutes she was able to *work loose* the ropes.

(34) a. Robert had to *cut* his vacation *short* and fly home the next day.
   b. Robert had to *cut short* his vacation and fly home the next day.

Be + Adjective + Preposition

The verb *be* combines with various adjectives and specific prepositions (primarily *of* and *to*) to form predicates that have the same meaning as simple verbs. For instance, *be able to* and *can* have the same meaning, as do *be afraid of* and *fear*, *be fond of* and *like*, and *be aware of* and *know*. These combinations clearly differ from prepositional verbs in their inclusion of an adjective. They are discussed in greater detail in Chapter 12.

(35) a. I'm *aware of* your objections to the plan.
   b. He *is* not *fond of* my brother-in-law.

SUMMARY

PREPOSITIONAL VERBS

Prepositional verbs consist of a transitive verb followed by a preposition with which it is closely associated.
   He stared at the girl.
   She finally decided on the blue car.

Prepositional verbs do not take the particle movement rule. The verb and the following preposition can be separated by an adverb, and the preposition can precede a relative pronoun and appear at the beginning of a *wh-* question.
   He stared intently at the girl.
   The girl at whom he was staring was strikingly beautiful.
   At whom was he staring?

In addition to being distinguished from phrasal verbs, prepositional verbs can be distinguished from two constructions that they superficially look like: verb + noun phrase + adjective sequences and *be* + adjective + preposition sequences.
   They set the captive animals free.
   He is very fond of my sister.

EXERCISE 9.2

Identify each verb + element combination as a phrasal or prepositional verb and use the syntactic tests (particle movement, adverb insertion, relative clause, *wh-* question) to support your choice.

Example: He *shouted at* the girl.

Answer: prepositional verb (It doesn't take particle movement: **He shouted the girl at.* It takes adverb insertion: *He shouted angrily at the girl.* The preposition can occur at the beginning of a relative clause, *The girl at whom he shouted ran away*; or a *wh-* question, *At whom was he shouting?*)

1. He finally *figured out* the answer.
2. The chairman *didn't comment on* the proposal.
3. He *is* just *getting over* a bad case of the flu.
4. This new fad *is catching on* all over the country.
5. All of the stress that was associated with the job *was getting John down*.

EXERCISE 9.3

Answer each question about phrasal and prepositional verbs.

1. Which of these two classes of multiword verbs has intransitive forms?
2. How many subclasses of phrasal verbs are there? Provide an example of each one.

PHRASAL PREPOSITIONAL VERBS

The final category of multiword verbs, *phrasal prepositional verbs*, consists of verbs that are followed by two elements. The verb and the first element, a preposition, is followed by a prepositional phrase. All phrasal prepositional verbs are followed by objects, and hence are transitive. Some common examples of verbs in this category are *do away with (something)*, *look up to (someone)*, *put up with (something)*, *run up against (something)*, and *look forward to (something)*. See Appendix A for other examples.

Most of these verbs have one-word equivalents. For example, *do away with* is equivalent to "exterminate" or "abolish"; *look up to* to "admire"; *put up with* to "endure" or "tolerate"; *run up against* to "encounter"; *look forward to* to "anticipate"; *come up with* to "produce"; *come down with* to "develop (an illness)"; and *look down on* to "despise." The final element of these verbs cannot be omitted before the object without changing the intended meaning, as (36), (37), and (38) illustrate.[6]

(**36**) a. I guess I will have to *put up with* his bad behavior.
　　　b. *I guess I will have to *put up* his bad behavior.

(**37**) a. Joan really *looks up to* her father. She almost worships him.
　　　b. *Joan really *looks up* her father. She almost worships him.

(**38**) a. You will have to *come up with* a better excuse than that.
　　　b. *You will have to *come up* a better excuse than that.

An object may follow some of these verbs, for example, *He let her in on a secret* and *They put his grouchiness down to overwork*. Some verbs in this category may take objects other than nouns and pronouns. For example, the phrasal prepositional verbs in (39a) and (40a) are followed by gerund complements, which is true for other types of multiword verbs.

(**39**) a. We are looking forward to *seeing you at the party*.
　　　b. We are looking forward to the party.

(**40**) a. He got away with *telling a terrible lie*.
　　　b. He got away with murder.

SUMMARY

PHRASAL PREPOSITIONAL VERBS

Phrasal prepositional verbs consist of a verb followed by two elements: a particle and a preposition. They are transitive.

Joan really looks up to her father.
He'll have to come up with a better excuse.

EXERCISE 9.4

Indicate whether each sentence contains a phrasal prepositional verb, an intransitive phrasal verb followed by a prepositional phrase, a prepositional verb, or a construction that simply looks like a prepositional verb.

Example: He came up with a great idea.

Answer: came up with = phrasal prepositional verb

1. I wasn't aware of that.
2. She listened intently to what the speaker was saying.
3. It took her over 15 minutes to scrub the pot clean.
4. The new boss said that he planned to do away with some procedures that he felt were inefficient and costly.
5. They broke out of prison and fled across the border.
6. She thinks that her boss looks down on her, but he doesn't.

THE USE OF MULTIWORD VERBS

Some scholars claim that English multiword verbs are used more frequently in informal, colloquial speech than in formal speech and writing.[7] The *Longman Spoken and Written English Corpus* (the LSWE corpus) shows that this is not exactly true. Overall, both phrasal and prepositional verbs are used most frequently in speech and fiction, less frequently in news reports, and much less frequently in academic English. However, even this distribution does not tell the entire story. Some prepositional verbs (e.g., *refer to*, *live on*) are used with greater frequency in academic English than in conversation. Other prepositional verbs of a type referred to as "causative" (e.g., *lead to*, *result in*, *contribute to*, *allow for*) actually occur more than twice as frequently in academic English as in news reports or fiction and much more frequently than in conversation. Thus, it appears that the frequency of usage of multiword verbs depends as much on the verb as on the register of English.

Given the widespread use of multiword verbs in different registers, it seems that a good policy for teachers might be to avoid any statements about preferences for using the verbs in certain contexts. Instead, teachers can tell their students that multiword verbs are on a par with single-word verbs and that, as with single-word verbs, their meanings and grammar have to be individually learned.

PROBLEMS THAT ESL/EFL STUDENTS HAVE WITH MULTIWORD VERBS

Three studies (Dagut & Laufer, 1985; Hulstijn & Marchena, 1989; Laufer & Eliasson, 1993) examined learners' avoidance of phrasal verbs in favor of their single-word synonyms. All three studies found that ESL students whose L1s do not contain phrasal verbs – for example, Hebrew – tend to prefer single-word English verb equivalents to phrasal verbs, whereas students whose L1s have phrasal verbs tend to use English phrasal verbs. A study by Sjöholm (1995) indicates that results in learning English phrasal verbs are related in part to their presence or absence in the learner's native language. Thus, it appears that experience with phrasal verbs in the L1 is an important factor influencing whether students will be receptive to learning and using them.

Two types of errors were found in our corpus of written errors made by Spanish and Korean ESL students. The errors in our corpora all involve prepositional verbs. Their specific details and possible causes are discussed next.

Omitting Prepositions from Prepositional Verbs (Spanish, Korean)

When an English prepositional verb has a meaning equivalent to a verb in the student's L1 that lacks a preposition, the learner may omit the appropriate English preposition. Spanish speakers' compositions provide examples of this. The equivalent of the English prepositional verb *listen to* is *escuchar* in Spanish. Similarly, *look at* corresponds to the Spanish *mirar* or *ver*, and *cope with* is equivalent to the Spanish *aguantar*. The errors in (41) are the result of omitting the necessary prepositions from the English verbs. The Spanish equivalents are shown below the errors.

(**41**) a. *Every day I listen the radio and I hear . . .
      Todos los días escucho la radio . . .
    b. *If I look a picture I can learn very well . . .
      Si miro una foto . . .
    c. *They are coping this situation with calm . . .
      Están aguantando esta situación . . .

This problem occurs in other languages as well. The example in (42) is from a Korean student's composition. The Korean equivalent of the English prepositional verb *major in* has no preposition before a direct object.

(**42**) *There are many careers which students majoring psychology can choose.

Inserting Unnecessary Prepositions After a Verb (Korean)

An English single-word verb may have an L1 equivalent that takes a specific preposition. In this case, the English language learner may insert an English preposition that matches the required L1 preposition. The Korean equivalent of English *enter* requires a directional postposition *-e* ("to") following its object (as discussed in Chapter 8, Korean uses postpositions instead of prepositions). This inclusion is carried over to English in (43), where the preposition *to* is included before the object, *the United States*.

(**43**) *There are hundreds of other ways for terrorists to enter to the United States.

These errors are quite common in the Korean corpus. They can also result from the fact that transitive verbs in Korean may be preceded by more than one case particles. For example, the Korean verb '*taytap-hata*' (*answer-do*) can take either the dative case particle ~*ey*/~*ekey* by itself or ~*ey*/~*ekey* plus the accusative particle (*l*)–*ul*/*ey* and *tayhayse* (*on* or *about*). Korean learners of English may assume that the dative particle ~*ey*/~*ekey*, which appears in both options, corresponds to the English preposition *to*. Furthermore, they may be unaware of the restrictions on the English verb *answer*. Hence when they use the verb *answer* they may insert their English equivalent of ~*ey*/~*eykey* after it, thereby producing ungrammatical sentences like the one in (44).

(44) *All students are answering to the questions at their own speed.

Incorrect Choice of Verb

Some errors that we have found, such as the one in (45), seem to be due to imperfect learning, not L1 transfer. They occur in the writing of students from a variety of L1 backgrounds. In (45), a Korean ESL student appears to have chosen the prepositional verb *look for* ("seek") instead of the appropriate phrasal *look after* ("care for, tend").

(45) *They [women] can accept changes like spending most of their time looking for babies happily and willingly.

SUGGESTIONS FOR TEACHING MULTIWORD VERBS

Multiword verbs are often given limited coverage in English language teaching textbooks. A number of specialty textbooks are devoted solely to teaching the meanings of multiword verbs, but the coverage and presentation in these is often haphazard.[8] The particle movement rule may be indirectly conveyed by modeling both patterns, but often transitive phrasal verbs are lumped together with verbs that are neither phrasal nor prepositional. Little or no attempt at showing the structure of multiword verbs is made, beyond stating that some verbs are separable and others are not. As a result, students can see no system to multiword verbs in these presentations, and the erroneous descriptions that are sometimes provided give the impression that learning multiword verbs requires more effort than it actually does.

Since you will frequently encounter incorrect information or virtually no information about multiword verbs in commercial textbooks, it will be helpful to you and your students if you become familiar with the different categories of these verbs presented in this chapter. This will allow you to correct errors in commercial texts and prepare your own teaching materials and tests on this subject. Your goal should be to teach all of the categories of multiword verbs covered in this chapter. Of course, you do not have to teach these categories in a particular time span or consecutively as part of a series of connected lessons. It is probably better to stagger your presentation and provide review sessions to see whether your students have grasped the grammar as well as the meaning of previously taught items. You may then want to use Processing Instruction (PI) techniques to examine how well the students have mastered both aspects (syntax and semantics) of the verbs they have learned. The research cited previously suggests that English learners may have more trouble learning phrasal verbs that have a figurative meaning – that is, verbs for which a corresponding one-word synonym cannot easily be deduced from the component parts, such as *play up* ("emphasize"), *back up* ("support"), *face down* ("not yield to"), and *bring off* ("execute successfully") – thus, you might want to spend a little more time on these.

You should demonstrate the basic grammatical facts of verbs in each category described in this chapter. You can find plenty of examples in Appendix A, and you can add to these, using the syntactic tests to help you decide which category the verbs belong in. In teaching and organizing your presentation of multiword verbs, you do not have to use the category labels that were used in this chapter. Other labels are fine, provided they are consistent and unambiguous.

It is important to introduce and practice multiword verbs within a context. For instance, you might select examples of the types of verbs you want to teach and then prepare extended discourse modeling the use of these verbs. It is very helpful to find actual prose or oral discourse that uses the items you want to introduce your students to, but this may not always be possible. The best alternative is to write a prose passage or dialog that uses several multiword verbs. It is possible to start out with phrasal verbs and then move on to prepositional verbs, but you do not have to follow the order of presentation in this chapter rigidly. For example, if you are working on a lesson that deals with intransitive phrasal verbs and a particular prepositional phrasal verb seems to fit in nicely, then include it. Just be sure that you show your students the grammatical structure of this new verb category before practicing it. You can expand your coverage of these verbs in a later lesson or in a review.

Finally, you should address any persistent errors that your students make with multiword verbs using recasting, PI, and editing activities as illustrated in Activity 4.

Activity 1: Introducing Transitive and Intransitive Phrasal Verbs (Beginning)

To introduce transitive and intransitive phrasal verbs to beginning-level students, select a set of these verbs that can be demonstrated through actions alone, in the case of intransitives (e.g., *stand up*, *sit down*, *speak up*, *turn around*), or through actions with classroom objects in the case of transitives (e.g., *pick up*, *put down*, *hand out*, *hand in*, *write down*, *cross out*). Have the students act out the phrasal verbs with you. For the separable phrasal verbs, illustrate the particle movement rule with a diagram on the board, using one of the sentences that the students act out. Another good activity for practicing phrasal and prepositional verbs is to present them with a series of illustrations that are used as cues for telling a story.

Activity 2: Rewriting Dialogs with Phrasal Verbs (Intermediate)

Write some short dialogs that contain phrasal verbs that you want to practice. Then replace the phrasal verbs with single-word verbs that have the same meaning. In class, write on the board the phrasal verbs that are no longer in the passage you prepared and teach their meanings. Erase the items on the board and hand out to groups of students the versions of the dialogs that do not contain the phrasal verbs. Each group is expected to work on recognizing the points in the dialog where the phrasal verbs are more appropriate. After the groups have finished, have them act out their dialog for the entire class. If the purpose of the activity is to review phrasal verbs that the class has covered, simply give them the dialogs and tell them to find appropriate phrasal verbs to substitute for verbs in their dialog.

Activity 3: Multiword Verb Card Games (Intermediate)

This activity is a variation of an idea suggested by Sansome (2000). Divide your class into two teams. Give one team a set of cards that have written on each one a multiword verb. The set of cards should include several multiword verbs with the same first element (e.g., *put on*, *put off*, and *put out*). Give the other team a set of cards that separately list the meanings of the multiword verbs.

The team with the meanings selects a card and shows it to the other team. That team has to select the appropriate multiword verb. If the correct word is selected, the team with the definitions then has to make up a sentence in which the verb is used correctly. Each team gets one point – one team for choosing the correct multiword verb, the other for making a sentence in which the multiword verb is used correctly.

An alternative game, which is perhaps even more useful, is to give several small groups a set of cards with multiword verbs written on them. All of the groups are allotted an amount of time in which to write a story that uses all of the verbs on the cards. When the time is up, each group presents its story to the class. Points are awarded for using the multiword verbs correctly. Members of other teams can challenge the usage of any verb by an opposing team, but if the challenge is incorrect, the challenging team loses a point. The teacher is the final authority in deciding whether challenges are valid.

Activity 4: Focusing on Errors with Prepositional Verbs (Intermediate)

A very useful activity is to collect samples of errors that your students make using prepositional verbs. Compositions are the best source of these. As context, use the paragraph within which an error is embedded. Correct any other errors in the paragraph. Put several paragraphs together on a handout. Do not reveal the writers' identities. Ask the class to read through the paragraphs and see if they can find any errors. When someone finds an error, have him or her correct it. Write down the corrected error on the board and ask various students to produce other sentences using the multiword verb. The passage in (46) is from a composition written by a Spanish-speaking ESL student in a high-intermediate level class. The passage has been altered slightly to remove errors that were not related to multiword verbs.

> (46) For me it is easier to learn a foreign language when I see what I am learning. One advantage of seeing the language is that I can learn the correct spelling of words. *When I look a picture or a graph*, I remember what I saw. That is why I prefer a visual style of learning.

In order to present several errors at once, you may have to include several short paragraphs from different compositions. Although this activity requires some work, it has one big advantage – it addresses attested errors. This is far better than making up paragraphs that contain errors that may never occur. As more corpora of errors made by English learners with different L1s are amassed, our understanding of what real errors involving multiword verbs look like and how persistent they are will help us develop instruction that can effectively address them.

ENDNOTES

[1] Radford (1988), p. 94, notes that phrasal verbs have an "idiosyncratic," or idiomatic, meaning. Nevertheless, there may be some gradation of transparency within phrasal verbs, as Laufer and Eliasson (1993) suggest. The meanings of so-called literal phrasal verbs such as *hand out* ("distribute") and *take away* ("remove") are transparently predictable. The meanings of *semitransparent* phrasal verbs such as *clear up* ("solve") and *lay aside* ("save") are less obvious. And the largest group of phrasal verbs are said to be *figurative*, in which a corresponding one-word synonym is not so easily deduced from the parts.

[2] See Biber et al. (1999), pp. 409–411.

[3] Arnold et al. (2000) point out that another reason for following the principle of end weight is to facilitate the planning and production of sentences. By postponing the production of long, complex NPs, the speaker has time to formulate them.

[4] As with irregular verbs, where, for example, the past tense of irregular *dive* has become regularized to *dived*, some items in this class will inevitably migrate into the separable verb

category. This can happen under pressure from *end weight*. As an example, *The judge let the robber off* sounds better than **The judge let off the robber*, but *The judge let off the poor old woman with three small children* sounds marginally acceptable to some native speakers. Verbs such as *ask out*, *do over*, and *see through* are good candidates for this migration.

[5] See Hart (1999), p. 59, for an example of this practice.

[6] There are some exceptions to this. For some native speakers, the preposition can be deleted when the object is indefinite. Thus, some native speakers will say "Can't we all just get along?" Other native speakers prefer an indefinite pronoun object. This requires a preposition: "Can't we all just get along with each other?"

[7] Celce-Murcia and Larsen-Freeman (1999, p. 434) suggest that native speakers of English may prefer a two-word verb like *put off* as opposed to its Latinate counterpart, *postpone*, because the former is considered less formal, although they cite evidence from Cornell (1985) that two-word verbs are "not absent from formal discourse." It is not clear that this preference for phrasal verbs in informal discourse can be documented. Data from Biber et al. (1999) suggest that the reasons for preferring certain phrasal and prepositional verbs may be more complex than whether some single word verbs appear to be more formal.

[8] See for example Acklam (1992), Britten (1991), and Hart (1999).

REFERENCES

Acklam, R. (1992). *Help with phrasal verbs*. Oxford: Heinemann.

Arnold, J. E., Wasow, T., Losongo, A., & Ginstrom, R. (2000). Heaviness vs. newness: The effects of structural complexity and discourse status on constituent ordering. *Language*, *76* (1), 28–55.

Biber, D., Johansson, S., Leech, G., Conrad, S., & Finegan, E. (1999). *Longman grammar of spoken and written English*. Essex: Pearson Education.

Britten, D., & Dellar, G. (1991). *Using phrasal verbs*. London: Prentice Hall.

Celce-Murcia, M., & Larsen-Freeman, D. (1999). *The grammar book: An ESL/EFL teacher's course*. 2nd ed. Boston: Heinle & Heinle.

Cornell, A. (1985). Realistic goals in teaching and learning phrasal verbs. *International Review of Applied Linguistics in Language Teaching*, *23* (4), 269–280.

Dagut, M., & Laufer, B. (1985). Avoidance of phrasal verbs: A case for contrastive analysis. *Studies in Second Language Acquisition*, *7*, 73–79.

Hart, C. R. (1999). *The ultimate phrasal verb book*. Hauppage, NY: Barron's Educational Series.

Hulstijn, J. H., & Marchena, E. (1989). Avoidance: Grammatical or semantic causes? *Studies in Second Language Acquisition*, *11*, 241–255.

Laufer, B., & Eliasson, S. (1993). What causes avoidance in L2 Learning: L1-L2 difference, L1-L2 similarity, or complexity? *Studies in Second Language Acquisition*, *15*, 35–48.

Radford, A. (1988). *Transformational grammar: A first course*. Cambridge: Cambridge University Press.

Sansome, R. (2000). Applying lexical research to the teaching of phrasal verbs. *International Review of Applied Linguistics*, *38*, 59–69.

Sjöholm, K. (1995). *The influence of crosslinguistic, semantic, and input factors on the acquisition of English phrasal verbs*. Turku: Abo Adedemi University Press.

CHAPTER 10

Determiners

INTRODUCTION

In this chapter, we look at some of the kinds of words that come before head nouns in noun phrases. The *prenominal modifiers* discussed in this chapter are often referred to as *determiners*. Our discussion will be confined to those types of determiners that appear most frequently in ESL/EFL textbooks and those that have been shown to cause problems for English language learners with different native languages. One important kind of determiner – the *article* – will not be discussed here because it is treated in the next chapter.

Although *adjectives* are also prenominal modifiers, they are not classified as determiners since they differ from determiners in their meaning and in their form. Determiners indicate important characteristics about head nouns, such as definiteness vs. indefiniteness, possession, and quantity. Adjectives do not do this; instead, they describe properties of head nouns such as color, height, weight, size, and so on. Adjectives can appear one after another (e.g., *tall*, *dark*, *handsome man*), whereas determiners cannot do this as readily. Individual determiners tend to be restricted to modifying nouns that have specific properties related to countability and number, but adjectives are not restricted in this way. For instance, the demonstrative determiner *this* has to precede a singular noun, while *those* has to precede a plural noun. The adjective *beautiful*, in contrast, can come before singular and plural nouns. Adjectives can often have comparative and superlative forms with *-er* and *-est*, but determiners cannot. These are just some of the reasons that justify excluding adjectives from the category of determiners. Adjectives will be discussed in detail in Chapter 12.

DETERMINERS AND THEIR ORDER OF APPEARANCE

Grammarians recognize several kinds of determiners. Many of these are listed in (1) through (10) along with some examples.

- **Articles** (*a/an*, *the*)

> (**1**) a. He met *a* woman.
> b. *The* woman got out of *a* car.

- **Demonstrative determiners** (*this/that, these/those*)

    (**2**) a. I want *that* book not *this* one.
      b. *These* sweaters are more expensive than *those* sweaters over there.

- **Possessive determiners** (*my, his/her, our, your, its, their*)

    (**3**) That's *her* book. This is *my* book over here.

- **Nouns as possessive determiners** (*John's, Bill's*)

    (**4**) *Anne's* car is older than *Jessica's* car.

- **Quantifiers** (*all, any, few, many*)

    (**5**) a. She has *all* the money.
      b. There are *many* ways to do it.

- **Partitives** (*glass of, loaf of, bit of, acre of*)

    (**6**) He bought a *loaf of* bread.

- **Cardinal numbers** (*one, two, three*)

    (**7**) She bought *three* hats.

- **Ordinal numbers** (*first, second, next, last*)

    (**8**) That is the *second* time he has done that.

- **Multipliers** (*double, twice, three times*)

    (**9**) She bought *double* the amount we need.

- **Fractions** (*three-fourths, two-fifths*)

    (**10**) *Three-fourths* of the audience was made up of young people.

It is possible to identify a relative order of occurrence for these different types of determiners within a noun phrase by looking at them in terms of the general categories listed in the table below: *predeterminers*, *central determiners*, and *postdeterminers*.

ORDER OF DETERMINERS IN NOUN PHRASES		
Predeterminers[1]	**Central Determiners**[2]	**Postdeterminers**
quantifiers (*all, both, each*)	quantifiers (*any, every, some*)	quantifiers (*many, much, few, little, less, least, more, most*)
multipliers (*double, twice, five times*)	articles (*a/an, the*)	
	possessive determiners (*my, our, your*)	cardinal numbers (*one, two*)
fractions (*three-fourths, two-fifths*)	nouns as possessive determiners (*John's, Anne's*)	ordinal numbers (*first, second, another, next, last*)
	demonstrative determiners (*this/that*)	partitives (*glass/bottle/jar of*)

The order shown in the table represents a general tendency that applies to a sequence of prenominal modifiers. Note that different types of quantifiers can occupy different positions and are categorized accordingly; for example, *all* is a predeterminer, *every* is a central determiner, and *many* is a postdeterminer. The other determiner types (multipliers, articles, partitives, etc.) each occupy just one category. A head noun can be directly preceded by a member of any category, but if determiners from different categories are used, switching the order – *predeterminer*, *central determiner*, *postdeterminer* – results in ungrammaticality, as (11d) and (11h) demonstrate.

(11) a. Both sisters wanted to go.   *quantifier, noun*

b. The sisters wanted to go.   *article, noun*

c. Both the sisters wanted to go.   *quantifier, article, noun*

d. *The both sisters wanted to go.   *article, quantifier, noun*

e. Those children are coming.   *demonstrative determiner, noun*

f. Two children are coming.   *cardinal number, noun*

g. Those two children are coming.   *demonstrative determiner, cardinal number, noun*

h. *Two those children are coming.   *cardinal number, demonstrative determiner, noun*

SUMMARY

DETERMINERS AND THEIR ORDER OF APPEARANCE

Determiners are words that precede head nouns in a noun phrase. There are different types of determiners, including the following:

- **articles** (*a/an, the*)

- **cardinal numbers** (*one, two, 25*)

- **ordinal numbers** (*first, second, 70th, last, next*)

- **multipliers** (*triple, twice, 10 times*)

- **fractions** (*one-half, one-tenth*)

- **demonstrative determiners** (*this/that, these/those*)

- **possessive determiners** (*my, your, their*)

- **nouns as possessive determiners** (*Sarah's, president's, supervisor's*)

- **quantifiers** (*both, any, many, much, few*)

- **partitives** (*slice of, bottle of, glass of*)

Determiners fall into three groups that describe their relative order of appearance before head nouns: **predeterminers**, **central determiners**, and **postdeterminers**.

EXERCISE 10.1

Identify each determiner in the bracketed NPs using the correct term (article, cardinal number, ordinal number, multiplier, fraction, demonstrative determiner, possessive determiner, noun as possessive determiner, quantifier, partitive). If any NP has an incorrect order, explain how the order is wrong, and then correct it.

Example: They didn't have blueberries, so he bought [a fifth of a quart of raspberries].

Answer: a = article; *fifth* = fraction; *quart of* = partitive

1. [The first two runners] crossed the finish line two hours after the start of the race.
2. [His both sisters] are in the army.
3. [One-third of her last salary check] went to paying off her debt.
4. I have to attend [that party]. It's a party for [my brother's twentieth anniversary].
5. A: How many [bags of ice] did they order for the party?
   B: [Twice the number] that we ordered for [your party].
6. While at the supermarket, he bought [a bunch of grapes] and [a loaf of bread].

TYPES OF DETERMINERS

Following our review of determiners and their order of appearance, we now focus on the individual types of determiners.

Numbers, Fractions, and Multipliers

English cardinal numbers (*one, two, three*, etc.) and fractions (*half, one-third, a fifth*, etc.) are usually not difficult for English language learners to grasp. Learners will, of course, already be familiar with the concepts of whole numbers and fractions and, therefore, will have words or phrases in their L1 to express them.

The cardinal number *one* is used before singular count nouns, as in (12a). The other cardinal numbers (*two, three, ninety-nine*, etc.) are used with plural count nouns, as illustrated in (12b) and (12c).

(**12**) a. There's only *one seat* left on the whole bus.
b. Bill's *three granddaughters* are visiting from Australia.
c. Meteorologists are predicting the worst storm in *fifty years*.

Fractions can occur with singular and plural count nouns, as shown in (13a) and (13b), as well as noncount nouns, as shown in (13c).

(**13**) a. *Half* the *team* is injured.
b. *Two-thirds* of the *players* were late for practice.
c. I've finished about *one-third* of my *homework*.

The examples in (13) and (14) illustrate an important fact about fractions: They normally do not appear immediately before a head noun. They are usually followed by an article, a possessive determiner, or *of*.

(**14**) a. I'm willing to pay *half* the *amount*.
b. *I'm willing to pay *half amount*.
c. He's *half* your *age*.

Multipliers, such as *double, triple*, and *four times*, occur with singular and plural count nouns, as in (15a) and (15b), as well as with noncount nouns, as in (15c).

(**15**) a. He's *twice* the *man* you are!
b. For some reason, she's earning *three times* our *salaries*.
c. The price you are paying is *five times* the *cost* of production.

Multipliers must always be followed by some other determiner, as illustrated in (16).

> (**16**) a. He received an offer that was *double the* amount that she got.
>   b. *He received an offer that was *double* amount that she got.

The ordinal numbers generally have a one-to-one relation to the cardinal numbers; that is, the ordinal *first* corresponds to the cardinal *one*, *second* corresponds to *two*, and so on. Ordinal numbers occur before singular and plural count nouns, as illustrated in (17a) and (17b). They are preceded by another determiner, often the definite article. The determiners *next*, *last*, *other*, and *another*[3] are included in the category of ordinal numbers because they often have the same function as these numerical ordinals; that is, they designate a place in an ordered sequence (e.g., *first*, *second*, *next*, *last*), as illustrated in (17c) and (17d). As (17d) shows, *another* can sometimes mean the same thing as *an additional* when it appears before the ordinal *one*.

> (**17**) a. The tickets will go to the *tenth* caller.
>   b. My parents just celebrated their *50th* anniversary.
>   c. The *next* step will be to conduct a physical checkup.
>   d. I already have *two* bicycles, but I have to buy *another one* so that my son can go cycling with us.

Demonstrative Determiners

This and *that*, and their plural forms, *these* and *those*, are determiners when they premodify a head noun. *This* and *that* modify singular count nouns and noncount nouns, as demonstrated in (18a) and (18b), respectively. *These* and *those* modify only plural count nouns, as shown in (18c), and cannot be used to modify noncount nouns as illustrated in (18d) and (18e). Note that *this/that* and *these/those* can also function as pronouns. This pronoun function will be discussed in Chapter 13.

> (**18**) a. $\begin{Bmatrix} This \\ That \end{Bmatrix}$ novel is completely captivating.
>
>   b. Does anyone enjoy $\begin{Bmatrix} this \\ that \end{Bmatrix}$ music?
>
>   c. $\begin{Bmatrix} These \\ Those \end{Bmatrix}$ people have been waiting for over an hour.
>
>   d. *These* furniture have to be moved.
>   e. *Be sure to verify *those* information.

Meaning of Demonstrative Determiners

The meaning distinction between *this/these* and *that/those* applies to four dimensions. The first of these is *physical distance*. *This/these* refer to something close to the speaker, and *that/those* refer to something more distant. This distinction is commonly taught in English language courses using sentences such as (19), where it is clear that *this* indicates a lamp that is close by and *that* indicates another lamp that is more distant from the speaker.

> (**19**) No. I want *this lamp. That one* over there is OK, but it needs a halogen bulb. And they're so expensive.

An extension of this distinction can be made to the *dimension of time*. In (20), the two sets of demonstrative determiners refer to *more distant in time* vs. *more immediate in time*. *That/those* refer to something that happened farther back in the past; *this/these* refers to something that happened more recently. The speaker in (20a) is referring to the previous summer, but in (20b), the speaker is referring to a summer in the more distant past.

(**20**) a. We bought a house *this summer.*
　　　b. We bought a house *that summer.*

A third dimension in which the two sets of determiners have a meaning distinction is *information packaging.* Noun phrases with *this/these* often introduce new information, particularly in nonreferential/existential *there* constructions, as illustrated in (21).[4] This third dimension is discussed in Chapter 7.

(**21**) a. *There is this pub* in Dublin that has my family's name on the sign over the door. I was told that artists hang out there a lot.
　　　b. *There was this really good-looking girl* on the other side of the room, and she kept giving him the eye, so he decided to walk over and chat her up.

The use of *this/these* to introduce new information is not limited to nonreferential *there* structures, as illustrated in (22), where it is clear that the speaker's intention is to convey something new to the listener.[5]

(**22**) So they stuck us in *this crazy motel*, which turned out to be a stop for all the truckers that passed through West Virginia. And the walls of the rooms were as thin as paper, so you would hear *this loud music* all night long.

NPs with *that/those* constitute information that the speaker presumes is familiar to the listener. The speaker in (23) uses *those* because he or she believes the listener knows what "knock-knock" jokes are and that Carl is in the habit of telling them.

(**23**) Carl was telling *those stupid "knock-knock" jokes* again.

The two sets of demonstrative determiners also divide on a dimension of *relevance: high relevance/low relevance.*[6] *This/that* precede head nouns that have high relevance for the speaker. In (24a), *this* and an intensifying adjective, *terrible*, precede the head noun *crime*, signaling that it has particular relevance for the speaker. In (24b), there is no particular reason to assign special focus to the head noun *crime*, and this is signaled by the use of *that*. Alternatively, the speaker could have used the pronoun *it* to indicate a lack of focus, as in example (24c). The examples in (24a) and (24b) show *this* and *that* being used anaphorically, that is, the NPs they appear in refer back to something mentioned previously.[7]

(**24**) a. Who has the right to try a man for a crime like genocide? Why, certainly it must be the courts of the nation in which *this terrible crime* was committed.
　　　b. Who has the right to try a man for a crime? Why, certainly it must be the courts of the nation where *that crime* was committed.
　　　c. Who has the right to try a man for a crime? Why, certainly it must be the courts of the nation where *it* was committed.

The adjectives and degree adverbs that occur with *this* tend to be attention-getting exaggerations (*really, wild, strange, gigantic*) that are designed to "summon the attention" of the reader to the head noun.[8] Conversely, the kinds of modifiers that occur with *that* (*specific, classic, traditional*) tend to be much more neutral in emotional content. This contrast is shown in (25).

(**25**) a. He turned around and saw *this really strange light* coming from under the closed door.
　　　b. Aeschylus wrote plays in *that classical style* developed by the Greeks in the 5th century BC.

That/Those for Defining a Concept

That/those are often used before a head noun in academic prose and in newspaper writing to define a concept or specify a class of people or things for the reader. This is a special stylistic use of *that/those*, in which a relative clause following the head noun supplies the definition or characterization of the concept or class. In (26a), we have a typical academic definition, whereas in (26b), the editor of the *Manchester Guardian* uses *those* to designate a specific group of readers who did not receive the paper. In both sentences, the relative clause is enclosed in brackets. Note also that in each case *that/those* could be replaced by a definite article.[9]

(**26**) a. The unit of heat was defined as *that quantity* [*which would raise the temperature of unit mass of water*,] at standard atmospheric pressure, through one degree on some temperature scale.

   b. We apologize to *those readers* [*who did not receive the* Guardian *on Saturday*, . . .]

SUMMARY

TYPES OF DETERMINERS: NUMBERS, FRACTIONS, MULTIPLIERS, AND DEMONSTRATIVE DETERMINERS

Cardinal numbers indicate quantity in numerical terms and occur with singular and plural count nouns.
> *I bought three ties and one shirt.*
> *We've lived here for 20 years.*

Fractions also indicate quantity, and can occur with count and noncount nouns.
> *You left half your peas on the plate.*
> *Two-thirds of the audience left before the show was over.*

Ordinal numbers designate a place in an ordered sequence and immediately precede countable nouns.
> *That's the third bus that passed by without stopping.*
> *The last band to perform was definitely the best.*

Multipliers occur with count and noncount nouns.
> *He's twice the size of his brother.*
> *She makes double the amount that he does.*

Demonstrative determiners *this* and *that* modify singular count nouns and noncount nouns. Their plural equivalents, *these* and *those*, modify plural count nouns.
> *This information is very useful.*
> *These cars over here are more expensive.*

This/these can designate head nouns as being **physically closer to** the speaker; *that/those* can designate head nouns as **farther away**.
> *No, I want this lamp. That one over there is OK, but it needs a halogen bulb.*

This/these can designate a head noun as **closer in time** (more recent), and *that/those* can designate it as **farther away in time**.
> *This winter was unusually warm.*
> *That winter was brutal.*

This/these + head noun can be used to introduce **new information**; *that/those* + head noun specifies **old, familiar information**.

> *There's this guy in my class who gets As on all his tests.*
> *Can you make those chocolate chip cookies again?*

This/these precede nouns of **high relevance** to the speaker; *that/those* precede nouns of **low relevance**.

> *Who has the right to try a man for a crime like genocide? Why certainly it must be the courts of the nation in which this terrible crime was committed. Who has the right to try a man for a crime? Why certainly it must be the courts of the nation where that crime was committed.*

NPs with *that/those* + head noun are often followed by a relative clause that **defines or characterizes** the head noun.

> *The unit of heat was defined as that quantity which would raise the temperature of unit mass of water.*

EXERCISE 10.2

Indicate whether the italicized determiner in each sentence is grammatical or not. Explain the source of any error.

Example: I love *those* music.

Answer: those = ungrammatical (The plural demonstrative determiner *those* cannot appear before a noncount noun such as *music*. The correct word is *that*.)

1. He is *tenth* student who signed up for this course.
2. *This* orange juice tastes sour.
3. There is *one* more luggage in the baggage compartment of the plane.
4. The small statue is *half* size of the big one.
5. We only have to move *two* furniture to rearrange the room.

EXERCISE 10.3

State the function of each demonstrative determiner in the sentences.

Example: A: Do you like *this* sofa?
        B: Not very much, but I really like *that* one over there.

Answer: This indicates something closer to the two speakers, and *that* indicates something farther away.

1. There was *this guy* standing at the counter. And he sort of looked at me as if he knew me. So I smiled at him.
2. *That summer* we traveled all over the place. *This summer* we have no plans to go anywhere.
3. You have to read *this wonderful book*!
4. The center of gravity is *that theoretical point* where the entire weight of the airplane is considered to be concentrated.
5. A: Anything happen while I was on vacation?
     B: Well, sort of. Your secretary told the boss about *those mistakes* in the report that you told me about before you left.

Quantifiers

Quantifiers are a set of determiners that indicate an amount or number of something. The most common quantifiers are shown below according to the kind of nouns they occur with.

Singular Count Nouns

any	*Any* computer will do.
each	*Each* book was by a different author.
every	*Every* computer in the school was replaced.

Plural Count Nouns

any	*Any* of those computers can process that much data.
both	*Both* shows were canceled after one season.
(a) few	*A few* cell phones don't have this feature.
many	*Many* voters are still waiting at the polls.
several	Brian lived in that apartment for *several* years.
all	*All* students must take the placement exam.
most	*Most* travelers use the Internet to plan trips.
more	Would you like *more* vegetables?
some	*Some* birds cannot fly.

Noncount Nouns

(a) little	I think I'll have *a little* soup.
less	He gave us *less* homework than he usually does.
much	We don't have *much* time.
all	Vanessa loves getting *all* the attention.
most	*Most* of the furniture is in good shape.
more	That recipe requires *more* milk than you have.
some	*Some* of the information was not accurate.

Notice that while some quantifiers occur with only one type of noun, *all*, *most*, *more*, and *some* can be used with both plural count nouns and noncount nouns.

It is customary to teach that *much* can only occur before noncount nouns, and examples such as those in (27) are often cited as evidence that it can only appear with a negative element such as *not* or *never* or in questions.[10] (A question mark before a sentence indicates that it is marginally grammatical for many native speakers.)

(27) a. I don't have *much* money.   *declarative sentence negative* not
b. ?I have *much* money.   *declarative sentence without a negative element*
c. Do you have *much* money?   *question*

To most native speakers, (27b) would seem odd, as they would prefer a sentence with *a lot of* (i.e., *I have a lot of money*). Still, there are examples of *much* occurring in declarative sentences without a negative element, such as those in (28).[11]

(28) a. Psychologists have given these matters *much* consideration.
b. The dining room was the scene of *much* confusion.

Why is this? It may be because the sentences in (28) appear to be in a more formal style, as in literary writing. In fiction, sentences such as these would seem quite acceptable.

Quantifiers can introduce noun phrases with nouns that have no other modifiers, as shown in (29), or they can precede articles and demonstrative and possessive determiners, as shown in (30). In the latter case, they are always followed by *of*. *All* is an exception to this rule, as shown in (30c) and (30d); it can optionally appear without *of*. For some native speakers, *both* can also appear with or without *of*.

(**29**) a. *All* men are created equal.
　　　 b. *Some* boys like sports.

(**30**) a. *Some of* the women in this room like tall men.
　　　 b. *Many of* his friends are Republicans.
　　　 c. *All* (of) the men are married.
　　　 d. *Both* (of) these cars are brand new.

Quantifier Floating

The quantifiers *all*, *both*, and *each* can occur in more than one position in a sentence. The rule that states the alternative positions that quantifiers can have is called *quantifier floating*. The possible positions if the verb is *be* are shown in (31). We can see that the quantifier *all*, which is part of the subject NP *all of my relatives* in (31a), can move to a position after the noun when *of* is deleted, as in (31b), or after the verb, as shown in (31c). In (31d), *all* is part of the NP *all of my friends*, which is the subject of the complement in square brackets. Notice that here *all* can move to a position where it splits the *nonfinite (infinitive)* form *to be*, as in (31f), but it cannot move over the infinitive, as shown in (31g).

(**31**) a. *All* of my relatives are farmers.
　　　 b. My relatives *all* are farmers.
　　　 c. My relatives are *all* farmers.
　　　 d. I want [*all* of my friends to be at the airport].
　　　 e. I want my friends *all* to be at the airport.
　　　 f. I want my friends to *all* be at the airport.
　　　 g. *I want my friends to be *all* at the airport.

In sentences with other verbs, the quantifier cannot move over the verb, as (32c) demonstrates. The restriction against moving across nonfinite verb forms holds for all verbs, as (32e) shows.

(**32**) a. All of the boys waved at the girls.
　　　 b. The boys *all* waved at the girls.
　　　 c. *The boys waved *all* at the girls.
　　　 d. Your mother wants [*all* of her sons to go to college].
　　　 e. *Your mother wants [her sons to go *all* to college].

The quantifier *each* can also be floated rightward.[12] When it appears after the subject NP, as in (33b), the verb agrees in number with the subject rather than with *each*, as in (33a).

(**33**) a. $\begin{Bmatrix} Each\ of\ the\ boys \\ Each\ boy \end{Bmatrix}$ owns a motorcycle.
　　　 b. The boys *each* own a motorcycle.

With *each*, but not *all* and *both*, quantifier floating can apply to NPs other than subject NPs. In (34a), *each* is part of an indirect object NP, whose head noun is *children*. Quantifier floating can move *each* to follow this NP, as in (34b), or to follow the direct object, *a dollar*, as in (34c).

(**34**) a. Uncle Harold gave *each* of the children a dollar.

b. Uncle Harold gave the children *each* a dollar.

c. Uncle Harold gave the children a dollar *each*.

Each can be moved from a subject NP to a position behind an NP that expresses quantity after stative verbs such as *cost*, *measure*, and *weigh*, particularly as shown in (35c).

(**35**) a. *Each* of the new wide-body jets will cost $2 million.

b. The new wide-body jets will *each* cost $2 million.

c. The new wide-body jets will cost $2 million *each*.

Quantifiers other than *all*, *both*, and *each* cannot be moved by quantifier floating, as (36) illustrates.

(**36**) a. *Some* of the guests made speeches.

b. **The guests *some* made speeches.

c. *Most* of the guests are diplomats.

d. **The guests are *most* diplomats.

Quantifier–Pronoun Flip

When *all*, *both*, and *each* appear in an NP whose head is a pronoun, they must be followed by *of*, and the pronoun is therefore in the object form, as shown in (37).

(**37**) a. *All (of)* his books got good reviews.

b. *All of them* got good reviews.

c. *Both of them* got good reviews.

d. *Each of them* got a good review.

e. **All them* got good reviews.

The quantifier and the pronoun can optionally switch positions through a rule called *quantifier–pronoun flip*.[13] As (38) shows, when this happens, the pronoun, which no longer follows *of*, has the subject form.

(**38**) a. *All of them* got good reviews.

b. *They all* got good reviews.   *quantifier–pronoun flip*

Quantifier-pronoun flip also applies to pronouns that are not sentence subjects, as (39) shows. In (39b), the NP to which the flip applies is the object of the verb *unpacked*, so the flipped pronoun in (39c) remains in the object form.

(**39**) a. John unpacked *all (of)* his books.

b. John unpacked *all of them*.

c. John unpacked *them all*.

For some native speakers, quantifier–pronoun flip with *each* can apply only to subject NPs. Applying it to object NPs, as in (40b), produces a questionable sequence as in (40c).

(**40**) a. John reviewed each of the books.

b. John reviewed each of them.

c. ?John reviewed them each.

Reducing Quantifier + *Of* + Pronoun Constructions

The sequence quantifier + *of* + pronoun can be reduced by dropping *of* and the pronoun. The quantifier then functions like a pronoun (see Chapter 13) that must have an antecedent in an earlier part of the discourse. Both the quantifier + *of* + pronoun constructions in (41a) and reduced forms *some* and *most* in (41b) refer to the antecedent, *the candidate that you interviewed*, in the question.

(**41**) Tom: What did you think of the candidates that you interviewed?
    Susan: a. *Some of them* were pretty good, but *most of them* weren't.
             b. *Some* were pretty good, but *most* weren't.

Meanings of Quantifiers

Quantifiers can be classified in terms of their meaning. Some quantifiers have a meaning of *inclusiveness*.[14] That is, they refer to an entire group. *Both* refers to two members of a group of two, *few* to a subgroup of the entire group, and *all* to the totality of members of a group of unspecified size. *Every* and *each* refer to single members of a group. The difference between *all*, *a few*, and *both* on the one hand and *each* and *every*, is reflected in subject–verb agreement, as shown in (42).

(**42**)

Quantifier	Meaning	
all	whole group	*All* (of) the recruits are over 18 years old.
any	single member	$\left\{\begin{array}{l} Any \text{ of these cell phones} \\ Any \text{ cell phone} \end{array}\right\}$ fits your requirements.
both	two members	*Both* (of the) recruits are over 18 years old.
each	single members	$\left\{\begin{array}{l} Each \text{ of the recruits} \\ Each \text{ recruit} \end{array}\right\}$ is over 18 years old.
every	single members	$\left\{\begin{array}{l} Every \text{ one of the recruits} \\ Every \text{ recruit} \end{array}\right\}$ is over 18 years old.
few	small group	$\left\{\begin{array}{l} A\ few \text{ of the recruits} \\ Few \text{ recruits} \end{array}\right\}$ are over 18 years old.

Other quantifiers are noninclusive and have a meaning related to size or quantity. These quantifiers can be classified by the relative size they indicate. For example, *many* and *much* refer to large quantities, *some* to a moderate quantity, and *little* and *few* to small quantities, as illustrated in (43).

(**43**) a. He has *many* friends.   *large quantity*
       b. He has *some* friends.   *moderate quantity*
       c. He has *few* friends.   *small quantity*

The difference in meaning between the quantifier + head noun pattern in (43) and the patterns shown in (44) can be understood in terms of the dimensions of inclusiveness and size. The meaning in (44a) is understood as "from the population comprising all scientists in the world" there are few that deny global warming is occurring. The meaning of (44b) is understood as "there is a specific group of scientists, and this group comprises just a few people" who deny the reality of global warming.[15]

(**44**) a. *Few scientists* would argue that global warming   *scientists in general*
         is not occurring.
       b. *A few scientists* would argue that global warming   *a specific group of scientists*
         is not occurring.

This distinction is also used in many in English language teaching textbooks to explain the differences in meaning between particular quantifiers.

Partitives

Partitives are multiword expressions containing a count noun + *of* (e.g., *loaf of, piece of, cup of, liter of*). The count noun in a partitive expression (e.g., *loaf, piece, cup, liter*) denotes a unit by which a following head noun can be counted. We may therefore consider partitives to be a kind of quantifier.

Partitives are listed in the postdeterminer column on page 187 because they are always preceded by another determiner, which can come from any column, as shown in (45a) through (45d). Partitives are sometime also followed by another determiner or an adjective, as shown in (45e). Note that partitives appear before noncount nouns, as in (45a), (45b), and (45e), as well as count nouns, as in (45c) and (45d).

> (**45**) a. I'll have *a glass of* water.
> b. I'll have *a loaf of* bread.
> c. I'll have *two pieces of* pie.
> d. I'll have *that slice of* cake.
> e. I'll have *a bowl of* your new soup.

Some partitives, such as *gallon/ liter of*, can be applied to any head noun that is a liquid, and partitives such as *ton/gram/pound of* can be used to quantify anything that is appropriately measured by weight. Similarly, partitives such as *bottle of* can be applied to different types of liquids that come in this container (e.g., beer, wine, catsup, milk). In contrast, partitives used to quantify food are more restricted. Portions of baked goods such as cake, pie, pizza, and bread are measured by *slices*, and only bread is quantified by the partitive count noun *loaf.* Certain types of vegetables (e.g., cauliflower, cabbage, lettuce) are quantified by *head.* Textbooks usually do a pretty good job of introducing the general partitive expressions that apply to noncount nouns (e.g., *glass of, cup of, bottle of*, etc.).[16]

Nouns are also used in a partitive sense to describe groups of humans and animals. As with the examples in the previous paragraph, some of these nouns can have a broader application, for example, *a band of* can describe robbers, roving minstrels, and gypsies and *a bunch of* can describe ruffians, teenagers, and sailors. Other nouns used in this sense are applied to occupations. Thus, *squad* and *platoon* usually define units of soldiers (e.g., a platoon of infantrymen). The same range of general to more restricted application is found with nouns that group animals. A *herd* can be used with most large four-footed animals (e.g., *a herd of* antelope/cattle/elephants), *flock* is used for birds, and *school* is applied only to fish. However, subgroupings of these nouns are species specific. Thus, a group of lions is called a *pride*, a group of whales is a *pod*, and a group of quail is a *covey.*[17]

Other Ways of Expressing Quantity

Any noun that can be visualized as a quantity can be used to create a new quantifier construction. For example, we have expressions such as *a mountain of work*, which is a quantifier of size, since it is another way of saying *a huge amount of work.* Expressions such as *a lot of, loads of, oodles of, plenty of, a smidgen/tad of*, and so on, seem to have the same function as partitives, so we might want to consider including them in this category. But here we run into a problem: partitives are postdeterminers and these expressions don't behave like other postdeterminers, because they can't be preceded by pre- and core determiners. You can't say **double a lot of marbles, *my plenty of marbles.* Perhaps they should be another type of quantifier. However, unlike the regular quantifiers we have looked at, these are also more idiomatic and vary from one dialect of English to another, giving rise to new creations; for example *lashings of,* is a British English equivalent of American English *a great deal of.* Furthermore, unlike regular quantifiers, these expressions display varying degrees of formality from very informal (*a smidgen of*) to decidedly formal (*a good/great deal of*).[18] Thus, it is best to simply view them as idiomatic expressions of quantity that mean the same thing as regular quantifiers. The process by which they are created is quite productive, and new ones may appear in the future. It is not important that we give them a special name; however, we should recognize that they should be taught in ESL/EFL classes, and that the best way of doing this is to treat them as new vocabulary that has to be related to the quantifiers already taught.

SUMMARY

QUANTIFIERS, PARTITIVES, AND OTHER WAYS OF EXPRESSING QUANTITY

Quantifiers are a set of determiners that indicate the quantity or number of something. They include *all, any, both, every, each,* (*a*) *few, less,* (*a*) *little, many, most, much,* and *several.*

Quantifier floating optionally moves the quantifiers *all, both,* and *each* rightward from a position in a subject NP to a position immediately preceding the main verb or, if the verb is a finite form of *be,* after it. If the verb is nonfinite, the quantifier may precede *to* or split the infinitive.

> *All the boys waved at the girls.*   OR   *The boys all waved at the girls.*
> *All my relatives are farmers.*   OR   *My relatives are all farmers.*

As a result of **quantifier–pronoun flip**, the quantifiers *all, both,* and *each* may appear either before a pronoun (with *of*) or after a pronoun.

> *Lori Sims played all of them.*
> *Lori Sims played them both.*
> *Tell each of them to come.*
> *Tell them each to come.*

A quantifier + *of* + pronoun construction can be reduced by dropping *of* and the pronoun.

> *Many of them arrived late.*   OR   *Many arrived late.*

Partitives are expressions containing a count noun + *of* (e.g., *loaf of, piece of, cup of, liter of*) that denote a unit by which a following head noun can be counted.

> *I already had a piece of cake.*
> *We're going to need two tons of concrete.*

Other ways of expressing quantification include idiomatic paraphrases of regular quantifiers such as *a lot of, lots of, a great deal of, loads of, oodles of, plenty of, a smidgen of,* and *a tad of.*

State why each of the following sentences is incorrect and supply a correction.

Example: Delegates many opposed the resolution.

Answer: Quantifier floating cannot apply to the quantifier *many*.
        Correction: Many of the delegates opposed the resolution.

1. They wanted each to go to the same college in the United Kingdom.
2. She liked every sweater they showed her, so she bought all them.
3. Those T-shirts cost each fifteen dollars.
4. I want you to both write me 500 words on why you should be hired.
5. Students most are accomplished musicians.

Apply quantifier floating or quantifier–pronoun flip to each of the following sentences.

Example: Both of his sisters are married to lawyers.

Answer: His sisters are both married to lawyers.

1. He said that all of us should come to his party.
2. Both of my colleagues received raises, but I didn't.
3. Their mother hoped that each of the girls would marry a rich man.
4. He had only one day to visit his relatives in Montreal, but he managed to visit all of them.
5. Each of the candidates must study very hard if they want to get a scholarship.

POSSESSIVE DETERMINERS

Possessive determiners provide one way of indicating possession in English. A full list of these determiners is shown below. Also listed is a set of words that English language learners often confuse with possessive determiners: *possessive pronouns.*

Possessive Determiners		*Possessive Pronouns*	
singular	*plural*	*singular*	*plural*
my	our	mine	ours
your	your	yours	yours
his/her/its	their	his/hers	theirs

Although possessive determiners and possessive pronouns are very similar in appearance, they are classified as two different syntactic categories on the basis of the environments in which they can occur. The determiners occur only in NPs preceding head nouns, while the pronouns occur only by themselves to mark things that have already been mentioned, as shown in (46). (See Chapter 13 for more on pronouns.)

(46) a. He told my father.
    b. *He told mine father.
    c. That coat is Lisa's and this one is mine.
    d. *That coat is Lisa's and this one is my.

Sentence (46b) is ungrammatical because a possessive pronoun (*mine*) is being used to modify a head noun (*father*), for which the equivalent determiner is necessary, as (46a) demonstrates. The sentence in (46d) is ungrammatical because a possessive determiner is being used where a possessive pronoun is required. Substituting the pronoun form results in the grammatical sentence shown in (46c).

Nouns as Possessive Determiners

Another way to indicate possession in English is by inflecting a noun to turn it into a possessive determiner. Most nouns are made possessive by adding an apostrophe + *s* (e.g., *Bill's, the woman's*), while nouns ending in *s* are inflected by adding just an apostrophe. These possessive constructions express the idea that the head noun belongs to or is associated with the noun that has the -*'s* ending. Most grammarians prefer to call this a *genitive* construction. Like the possessive determiner, it is entered under the central determiner column in the table on page 187 because although it frequently occurs directly before the head noun of an NP, it can be followed by one or more postdeterminers as (47b) and (47c) illustrate.

(**47**) a. Susan's coat
    b. Bill's five brothers
    c. John's last five attempts

The meaning of these inflected nouns can also be expressed by an *of-* phrase. The two constructions in (48) mean the same thing. Given this synonymy, the question arises: Are there any reasons for preferring one over the other?

(**48**) a. the committee's decision
    b. the decision of the committee

In fact, several factors influence native speakers' choice of one or the other construction. In one case only an *of-* phrase can be selected. In other cases, both constructions are possible, but certain factors inherent to the noun phrase tend to bias the choice toward one of the two possibilities.

Noun phrases that refer to humans and, to a lesser extent, animals tend to appear in the inflected noun form, as in (49) and (50). The choice is not always automatic, but there is a definite bias toward this form with these types of NPs.[19]

(**49**) a. Felicia's shiny black hair   *preferred*
    b. the shiny black hair of Felicia   *not preferred*

(**50**) a. the tiger's paw   *preferred*
    b. the paw of the tiger   *not preferred*

With NPs that refer to months and geographical locations, there seems to be little or no bias toward one possessive form over the other, as illustrated in (51) and (52).

(**51**) a. December's storms
    b. the storms of December

(**52**) a. London's pubs
    b. the pubs of London

Noun phrases that refer to inanimate entities or objects will usually appear in an *of-* phrase construction, as illustrated in (53) and (54). Again, this is not a fixed rule regarding these NPs, but it reflects a clear tendency among native speakers.

(53) a. the roof of the house   *preferred*
    b. the house's roof   *not preferred*

(54) a. the hem of your skirt   *preferred*
    b. your skirt's hem   *not preferred or ungrammatical*

A noun phrase with a possessive determiner that refers to a human (e.g., *his coat, your arm*) usually cannot be replaced with an *of* + pronoun pattern, as illustrated in (55).

(55) a. his nose   *preferred*
    b. the nose of him   *not preferred*

There are, however, some instances in which the *of* + pronoun pattern will be preferred, as in (56). If the speaker or writer wants *her* in the bracketed NP to be understood as the subject of the portrait, then (56a) will be selected. Although (56b) is grammatical, it is also ambiguous in this regard. *Her* could refer to either the artist or the subject of the portrait.

(56) a. [The only portrait of her] is in the National Gallery.   *preferred*
    b. [Her only portrait] is in the National Gallery.   *not preferred*

Finally, there appears to be a tendency for relatively short noun phrases to have the inflected noun form, as in (57a) and relatively long noun phrases to have the *of-* phrase form, as in (57b).[20] The latter choice seems to reflect the information-structuring principle referred to as *end weight*, which states that long phrases should be put at the end of a phrase, clause, or sentence, (in this case after a head noun). Apparently, native speakers feel that longer, more complex modifiers should appear after the head noun rather than before it.

(57) a. [The designer's creations] were on display.
    b. [The creations of a relatively young designer from Italy]
      were on display.   *preferred*
    c. [A relatively young designer from Italy's creations]
      were on display.   *not preferred*

SUMMARY

POSSESSIVE DETERMINERS AND NOUNS AS POSSESSIVE DETERMINERS

Possessive determiners (*my, your, his, her, its, our, their*) appear before head nouns and indicate possession.
    Remember to take your passport.
    Someone stole all their money.

Nouns as possessive determiners have been inflected with an apostrophe + *s* (*Michael's*) or an apostrophe (*Mrs. Jones'*) to indicate possession.
    Remember Michael's passport.
    Someone stole all Mrs. Jones' money.

Constructions with an *of-* phrase are also used to show possession.
    The members of the panel refused to discuss that topic.
    I'm reading a book on the history of England.

The choice between an inflected noun and an *of-* phrase is heavily influenced by several factors:

- NPs referring to humans and, to a lesser extent, to animals, tend to appear in the inflected noun pattern.
  Felicia's shiny black hair   RATHER THAN   *the shiny black hair of Felicia*
  the tiger's paw   RATHER THAN   *the paw of the tiger*

- NPs referring to months and geographical places will often take either form.
  December's storms   OR   *the storms of December*
  London's pubs   OR   *the pubs of London*

- NPs referring to inanimate entities usually appear in the *of-*phrase construction.
  the hood of the car   RATHER THAN   *the car's hood*

- NPs with a possessive determiner that refers to a human usually cannot be replaced by an *of* + pronoun pattern.
  her arm   RATHER THAN   **the arm of her*

- Relatively long NPs are more likely to occur in the *of-*phrase construction.
  the thoughts of a brilliant philosopher at Harvard
              RATHER THAN
  a brilliant philosopher at Harvard's thoughts

EXERCISE 10.6

Indicate whether the italicized NP pattern in each sentence is preferable or not preferable. If not, explain why.

Example: What happened to *Jen's hand*?

Answer: preferable (The NP refers to a human.)

1. She ran her fingers through *the shiny red fur of the dog*.
2. I have a passion for *Chicago's jazz clubs*.
3. There was a deep cut over *the left eye of the player*.
4. It was only later that I saw him standing in *the corner of the room*.
5. The house is *a successful young architect from Milan's latest design*.

PROBLEMS THAT ESL/EFL STUDENTS HAVE WITH DETERMINERS

As more error corpora become available, we will be able to develop a more comprehensive picture of the problems that ESL/EFL students have with determiners and of the errors that are the most persistent. The available corpora permit documentation and description only of the errors described in this section. Other types of errors (e.g., a preference for the *of* + noun pattern over the possessive determiner + noun pattern, overuse of *much*) have only been described anecdotally. Therefore, they are not discussed here.

Demonstrative Determiners (Korean)

Korean has a single form, *-i*, that corresponds to both the singular and plural English demonstrative determiners *this* and *these* and a single form, *ce*, that corresponds to the demonstrative determiners *that* and *those*. This is illustrated in (58), in which the morpheme *-tul* indicates plural.

(58) *i salam*   this person
     i salam-tul   these persons
     ce salam   that person
     ce salam-tul   those persons

The singular–plural distinction for the equivalent of English demonstrative determiners is collapsed in Korean. This results in agreement errors when Korean speakers produce sentences containing NPs with these determiners, as illustrated in the examples in (59), which come from our Korean corpus. The fact that in speech Koreans often do not use the plural morpheme *-tul*, relying instead on the listener's ability to infer number from the context of the discourse no doubt exacerbates the problem.

(59) a. *We admit that *those argument* is not wrong in some sense that the financial status can make an effect on the quality of medical service.
     b. *Children taking *these kind of education* will lose their chances to develop their creativity.
     c. *This processes* are referred to socialization.
     d. *They became already adults who can manage their life even if *that choices and behaviors* are not right because everyone have a right of freedom.

Other and *Another* (Spanish)

A problem similar to the one previously discussed occurs when Spanish speakers use the English postdeterminers *other* and *another* (meaning "additional" and "an additional," respectively). A single form in Spanish, *otro*, encompasses these two English forms. As a result, Spanish speakers often put the wrong form in front of a head noun, as shown in (60).

(60) a. *The virtual reality is *other important item* about the research labs.
     b. *Another professionals* in the civil engineering programs are trying to . . .

The relative infrequency of these kinds of errors suggests that they will eventually disappear with increased input and use of English. Notice, nevertheless, that (60a) also contains an article transfer error (the inclusion of a definite article before technical terms) that persists for some time in the speech and writing of Spanish speakers (see Chapter 11).

Other Quantifiers (Korean)

In Korean, the genitive morpheme *-uy* is used following some quantifiers. Examples (61a) and (61b) illustrate how this morpheme is used with the Korean equivalents of *most* and *some*, respectively.

(61) a. *taypwupwun*   *-uy*   *mikwukin*   *-tul*
        most   (genitive   American   plural
                      marker)
        "most Americans"
     b. *ilpwu*   *-uy*   *haksayng*   *-tul*
        some   (genitive   student   plural
                  marker)
        "some students"

Korean speakers sometimes perceive the genitive morpheme *-uy* in their L1 as having the same meaning and function that *of* has in English NPs containing quantifiers. Note also that Korean does not have morphemes that correspond to English definite and indefinite articles. These factors appear to conspire to produce a fairly common error pattern in which the quantifiers *most* and *some* are combined with *of* and a head noun, as shown in (62).

(**62**) a. She donated one million dollars to UIUC when she died. *Most of money was used to build a library.
b. *The power of daily television programs is so enormous that *some of audiences* are easily influenced.

Quantifier errors like these have also been found in writing samples of students with other L1s that are typologically different from Korean. Granger (personal communication) has recorded similar errors found in the International Corpus of Learner English (ICLE).[21] Those errors, which include phrases such as "many of students," were made by French-speaking university students. These might also be transfer errors, since French uses quantifiers with *de* (which may be translated as *of*). For instance, *beaucoup d'étudiants* means "many students."

On the other hand, additional data may show that this error type is typical of a general stage that learners pass through as they learn to use English quantifiers. In a study conducted at an American university,[22] Korean graduate students showed significant improvement in their use of these forms after being exposed to computer-administered focus-on-form instruction designed to enhance their ability to recognize and correct writing errors with English quantifiers like those in (62). They were even able to absorb and utilize the meaning distinction between the quantifier + head noun pattern (*most scientists*) and the quantifier + *of* + *the* + head noun pattern (*most of the scientists*), and they retained this ability on a post test given five months after the instruction.

SUGGESTIONS FOR TEACHING DETERMINERS

Determiners are usually taught in first-year English language courses, and textbooks cover them with varying degrees of comprehensiveness. Terms such as *partitive* are rarely used in these books. Instead, partitives are usually called *quantifiers* and are included in whatever activities are devoted to that larger topic, which is probably a good idea.

With regard to demonstrative determiners, most textbooks teach the concept that *this/ these* and *that/those* are used to indicate different degrees of proximity. This is frequently practiced in dialogs in which students use the demonstratives to refer to items that are either near or far away. It is also a good idea to teach the other meaning distinctions between *this/these* vs. *that/those* that are covered in this chapter. Begin with concepts of physical proximity, time, and given vs. new information. Then introduce the concept of relevance with high-intermediate and advanced-level students.

Your coverage of quantifiers should include at least the following points:

• Which quantifiers precede count nouns and which precede noncount nouns. (This presupposes that students already have a knowledge of the distinction between the two noun types.)

- The meanings of the more frequent quantifiers and the restrictions on use of certain quantifiers such as *much*.

- The distinction between general statements with a quantifier + a noun (*most students*) and statements that refer to specific groups with a quantifier + *of* + det + noun (*most of the students*).

All of these points are typically covered in English language teaching textbooks.

Possessive determiners (called *possessive adjectives* in many textbooks) are fairly easy to teach and are covered in all professionally produced materials. Guidelines for the use of the inflected noun versus *of*-phrase constructions are usually confined to the human/animate versus inanimate criterion, which is somewhat of an oversimplification. Your students would certainly be helped by learning the other factors that influence the choice between one construction and the other.

Demonstrative Determiners

Activity 1: Using Demonstratives to Shop (Beginners)

Bring to class several items that you might buy in a department store. Make sure you have at least two examples of each item and try to make them as similar as possible in color and shape. Arrange the items in different positions on a desk in front of you. Have the students role-play a shopping trip. They cannot pick up an item or touch it. Instead, they have to indicate the objects they want by using a sentence such as, "I'd like that T-shirt, please." Depending upon how far the salesperson is from any of the items, she or he responds, "Do you mean this T-shirt right here or that T-shirt over there?" Students take turns being shoppers and salespeople.

Activity 2: Guessing Game with Possessive Determiners (Beginners)

A nice guessing game activity suggested by Pavlik (2004) can be played in pairs or in groups. One student thinks of three sentences that describe another student in the class. These all involve a possessive determiner (e.g., *Her hair is black*, *Her eyes are brown*, *Her hair is short*.) Other students ask *yes/no* questions before guessing who is being described. They might ask, for instance, *Is her sweater red? Is she tall?* The game does not have to be limited to students in the class. Famous people could be included. However, the description should always involve characteristics that require possessive determiners.

Activity 3: Indicating Given and New Information (Intermediate Through Advanced)

To illustrate how *this/these* introduces new information and *that/those* relates given information, tell a story. The sample in (63) shows *this* and *these* being used repeatedly to present new information along with a few examples of *that* before nouns that are old information.

(**63**) I won this prize. It was a three-day trip to Hollywood. So I flew out there on this big plane. I think it was a 747. When we got to Los Angeles, there was this man waiting for me. He had a small sign with my name on it. He told me that he was a chauffeur, and he was going to drive me to my hotel. So I got in this big, long limousine, and we drove down the freeway. I noticed that there was this sort of yellow-brown haze in the air. So I asked the driver what that was. And he said, "Smog." Of course, I knew what that was, but I didn't realize you could see it. But the driver told me it was really smoggy that day. So after awhile we pulled up in front of this fantastic hotel in Beverly Hills. I went inside and they had this fantastic room reserved for me. It was so huge. And it had a Jacuzzi in the bathroom. The room was on the 12th floor, so I had a good view of Los Angeles. I couldn't see too far, though, because the smog made everything in the distance hard to see. So the first thing I did was try out that Jacuzzi, and it was great. Then I got a telephone call from this guy from the company that takes care of all the prize winners. He told me about all the things they had arranged for me to see on my trip. The next day I visited Century City and a movie studio and I watched them filming this movie. I also went out to dinner at this famous restaurant. I can't remember the name. It began with "*S*." Anyway, I had dinner with this nice young actor, and afterwards he took me to this club on the Sunset Strip – that's a street where they have a lot of clubs where actors and actresses hang out. And he knew all these people at that club. I had a great time. You know, I think that trip to Hollywood was the best thing I've ever won. Actually, it's the only thing I've ever won."

You can use a variation of the dicto-comp activity (see Chapter 3) to practice this point. After you have read the story twice, hand out a short outline with sentence fragments that supply the main events of the story, (e.g., *Won prize. Took trip to Hollywood. Flew out on a big plane. Got into limo. Drove down freeway. Noticed brown-yellow haze.*) Have the students pair off and use this outline to retell the story as accurately as possible. While they are doing this, move around the room monitoring the retelling. After each student has finished, point out where *this*/*these* or *that*/*those* could have been inserted or where one of the determiners was incorrectly used. After all students have had an opportunity to tell the story, direct them to write the entire story down, inserting the appropriate demonstrative determiners throughout. At a later time, give them the story as a cloze test, where they must fill in all of the blanks with the appropriate demonstrative determiners. Do this several times during the semester with different stories.

Activity 4: Addressing Demonstrative Determiner Issues in Korean (Intermediate Through Advanced)

This is intended as practice for composition classes. Take examples from student compositions and reproduce these for editing practice. Errors made by several students on a single topic can be combined to make a more challenging passage. Use (63) to highlight the problem. Then hand out the passage you prepared and ask them to find and correct the errors. Give them about 10 minutes and then go over their corrections in class. This approach could also be applied to the *another*/*other* confusions made by Spanish speakers as shown in (60).

Quantifiers
Activity 5: Using Partitives to Make a Shopping List (Beginning)

Role plays involving buying food in a market are a good way to practice partitives (*a head of lettuce*, *a loaf of bread*, *a quart of milk*, etc). Have students work in pairs to make a list of groceries using partitives. You may want to bring in flyers from grocery stores for students to use for this activity and review partitives that are used for common grocery items before students begin. As students work, ask them to use the partitives in their conversations with each other. Model the activity first with a student so that they understand the task, for example, you say, "We need some bread." Your partner asks, "How many loaves?" You say, "We should also get some soup."' Your partner replies, "Yeah. I like tomato soup. Let's get three cans of tomato soup and two cans of mushroom soup for you." This should be followed by an actual TBLT activity in which students take their shopping lists to the store and purchase the items or simply find out how much each item costs. They must then report what each item costs using partitive expressions, for example, "A head of cauliflower costs $2 in this supermarket."

Activity 6: Using Quantifiers (Beginning)

In this activity, you will ask students questions that will require them to use quantifiers. First, explain that *much* and *a little* can be used only with noncount nouns (and that *a few* and *many* can be used with count nouns). Write a list of count and noncount nouns on the board that you will use in your questions, for example, *homework*, *quizzes*, and *rain*. Then write *Large Amount* and *Small Amount* on the board in two columns. Tell the class, "I am going to ask you a question that has a large amount (point to *Large Amount*) or a small amount (point to *Small Amount*). I want you to give me an answer that uses *many* or *much* or *a few* or *a little* in it." Then ask the question: "Nasrine, how much homework did I give the class yesterday?" You point to *Small Amount*. She replies with a sentence using *not . . . much*, or *a little* (e.g., "You gave us a little homework" or "You didn't give us much homework"). Continue asking questions for the words in your list.

Activity 7: Making General and Specific Statements (Intermediate)

Intermediate level students should be taught the meaning contrast between general statements such as *All dogs like to play* and statements that are restricted to a specific context such as *All of the dogs like to play*. Explain the difference using examples. Then write a set of adjectives such as *amusing*, *beautiful*, *funny*, *handsome*, *intelligent*, *poor*, *rich*, *stingy*, or *stupid* on the board. Explain the meaning of any adjectives that your students are unfamiliar with.

Ask the students to form sentences about what men and women like, using the quantifiers *all*, *some*, *many*, *most*, and *few*. Model a couple of sentences for them, such as, "All men are attracted to beautiful women," and "Most women are attracted to handsome men." At this point, the activity can continue in this fashion or the students can pair off and form sentences together. The activity can also be converted into a team competition in which members of each team try to come up with the largest number of sentences that use all of the quantifiers.

After the students have finished doing this, write a sentence that refers to a specific group. Here you need to prime the activity with sentences that describe preferences of more specific groups. You could demonstrate this with a poll that has been taken about elections, where you compare demographic groups – university students, foreign students, housewives, retirees, young working people, etc. Teams are supplied with the breakdown of the poll results in the form of percentages and report them with sentences such as "Most of the housewives polled said they preferred candidate X," "Very few of the workers like candidate Y," "Many of the university students said they were going to switch to candidate X," etc. The members of each team now have to write a sentence that shows the specific use of each of the quantifiers on the board. Again, the team that comes up with good examples for all of the quantifiers first, wins.

Possession
Activity 8: Choosing Between Inflected Nouns and *Of-* Phrase Constructions (Beginning)

To contrast these two patterns, bring some pictures that contain people, animals, and inanimate objects. Review the factors that bias the choice between the inflected noun and *of-* noun constructions. Then point to features in the pictures and ask, "What's this?" Elicit responses such as, "That is the horse's tail," "That is the girl's shoe," "That is the leg of the table," and "That is the roof of the house." Draw students' attention to their errors by recasting or asking students to self-correct.

Activity 9: Indicating Possession with Long and Short NPs (Advanced)

The concepts of short and long NPs can be quantified in some approximate way to help students. For instance, a "short" NP can be described as "a noun with just one or two modifiers." The cloze format is often recommended for practicing the two possessive noun patterns, but for demonstrating factors that override the two rules above, a side-by-side comparison like the one in (57) seems justified. Present pairs of sentences similar to those in (57) and ask your students which sentence is better and why. Then ask students to create their own sentences using long and short NPs.

ENDNOTES

[1] Predeterminers are mutually exclusive, that is, they cannot occur together (e.g., *I ate all half of the cake).

[2] Celce-Murcia & Larsen-Freeman (1999) refer to these as *core determiners*. The term *central determiner* is being used here because it describes the position of these determiners with respect to other determiners. Biber et al. (1999) also use this designation.

[3] *Other* and *another* carry the meaning of "additional" and "an additional," respectively. However, these determiners can also mean "different" as in *That rose looks kind of wilted. Give me another one.*

[4] The examples in (21) are modeled on Biber et al. (1999), p. 274.

[5] Example (22) is modeled on Strauss (1993), p. 407.

[6] These observations are due to Strauss (1993). She refers to this as *focus*. By this she means that the demonstrative determiner *this* has high importance for the speaker and that its use should draw the listener's attention to the NP it modifies. I have taken the liberty of calling this *relevance* rather than *focus*.

[7] The examples in (24) are modeled on Strauss (1993), p. 408.

[8] Strauss (1993), p. 415, notes that this claim is supported by her data.

[9] Examples (25a) and (26) are from Biber et al. (1999), p. 273.

[10] This claim is essentially made by Huddleston and Pullum (2002) pp. 826–827. *Much* is a negative polarity item when it appears in a sentence such as *She doesn't write me much*. (See Chapter 5 for negative polarity items.)

[11] *Much* can also occur without a negative element when it is modified by a degree adverb such as *so* or *too* (e.g., *She makes so much trouble*; *We have too much money tied up in stocks right now*).

[12] See McCawley (1988), pp. 88–89. The description of quantifier floating provided here, while accurate and suitable for English language teachers, is quite different in minimalist linguistic theory. For those interested in this treatment, see Radford (1997).

[13] This description of quantifier–pronoun flip is based on McCawley (1988), p. 93.

[14] Biber et al. (1999), pp. 275–276.

[15] The same distinction applies to *little* preceded by the indefinite article *a*. The sentence *Little gasoline was available in the 1970s* refers to all the gasoline that existed in the larger universe of the world or a specific country. *A little gasoline was available at one or two gasoline stations* refers to a smaller universe such as the amount of gasoline in a particular town.

[16] More complete lists of partitives can be found in Biber et al. (1999), pp. 250–255.

[17] The idiomatic nature of terms that denote animal groups has spawned a game played by some English teachers whereby the players try to invent new terms for specific species. The best I have ever heard was a *flourish of baboons*, by A. R. Evans.

[18] These are referred to as "phrasal partitives" by other authors, like Celce-Murcia and Larsen Freeman (1999), p. 335. I don't agree with this classification for the reasons stated above plus the fact that they have the syntactic structure of a prepositional phrase, and this makes it difficult to distinguish them as a separate class from prepositional phrases. However, I do agree with the authors about the need to teach these paraphrases of regular quantifiers to ESL/EFL students.

[19] These examples are from Huddleston and Pullum (2002), p. 477.

[20] Biber et al. (1999), p. 304, found that one-word dependent phrases occur in the inflected noun construction. If the phrase is longer than one word, the *of*-phrase construction is used.

[21] More information about the International Corpus of Learner English can be found at the following Web site: http://cecl.fltr.ucl.ac.be/Cecl-Projects/Icle/icle.htm.

[22] As reported in Cowan, Choo, and Lee (2004). See also Ferris (2002), pp. 85–97, for a detailed approach to error correction in teaching writing.

REFERENCES

Biber, D., Johansson, S., Leech, G., Conrad, S., & Finegan, E. (1999). *Longman grammar of spoken and written English*. Essex: Pearson Education.

Celce-Murcia, M., & Larsen-Freeman, D. (1999). *The grammar book: An ESL/EFL teacher's course*. 2nd ed. Boston: Heinle & Heinle.

Cowan, R., Choo, J. H., & Lee, G. (2004). Designing effective assessment measures for CALL research. *Conference on Technology for SLL*. Ames, Iowa.

Ferris, D. R. (2002). *The treatment of error in second language student writing*. Ann Arbor: The University of Michigan.

Granger, S. (1998). The computer learner corpus: A versatile new source of data for SLA research. In S. Granger (Ed.), *Learner English on computer* (pp. 3–18). London: Longman.

Huddleston, R., & Pullum, G. K. (2002). *The Cambridge grammar of the English language*. Cambridge: Cambridge University Press.

Maling, J. (1976). Notes on quantifier postposting. *Linguistic Inquiry*, *7*, 708–18.

McCawley, J. (1988). *The syntactic phenomena of English: Volume 1*. Chicago: University of Chicago Press.

Pavlik, C. (2004). *Grammar sense 1*. Oxford: Oxford University Press.

Radford, A. (1997). *Syntax: A minimalist introduction*. Cambridge: Cambridge University Press.

Strauss, S. (1993). Why 'this' and 'that' are not complete without 'it'. In K. Beals., G. Cooke, D. Kathman, S. Kita, K. McCulloch, & D. Testen (Eds.), *Papers from the 29th regional meeting of the Chicago linguistic society* (pp. 403–417). Chicago: Chicago Linguistics Society.

CHAPTER 11

Articles

INTRODUCTION

As mentioned in Chapter 10, articles are members of the larger class of prenominal modifiers known as determiners. They are generally recognized as one of the most difficult and intractable problems that adult ESL/EFL learners have with English grammar. Many learners attain near–native-speaker competence in English but still feel insecure about correctly using articles. This problem is nicely depicted in Richard Lourie's humorous account of a Russian cultural attaché's continual frustration at not being able to figure out a system for using the English definite article, *the*, and the indefinite article, *a*.[1]

> Busy though he was, Poplavsky usually found ten minutes each morning for the reading of intelligently written articles from the American press. He was determined to win a final victory in his eleven-year struggle with his linguistic arch enemies, the definite and indefinite articles. The conflict first erupted in his class at the special school at Gatchina where students were taught not only in classrooms but in a full-scale replica of an American town – supermarkets crammed with toilet paper, dog food, and chicken parts; gas stations with Coke machines and Chevies with hand-lettered, cardboard FOR SALE signs on their windshields; and a McDonald's run by perky teenagers. "I want **a** box. I want **the** box. Why not simply – "GIVE ME BOX"' Poplavsky had roared at his instructor who was running the checkout counter at the supermarket that day. Tearfully, she explained that not even the Soviet Academy of Syntax had been able to come up with a concrete rule that worked in all cases. "Then I'll figure one out myself!" Poplavsky had vowed with all the bravado of the youngish lieutenant he was then; but now, as a middle-aged full colonel, he continued to struggle with those bedeviling linguistic will-o'-the-wisps.

> "I don't think you want the 'the' here; I think you want an 'a'," an American had once remarked to Poplavsky after reading a Soviet-Embassy cultural press release.

> "I don't want **a** 'the', I want **the** 'a'?" Poplavsky had replied, frowning in consternation that was bordering on rage.

"That's right, a 'the' is not **the** right choice."

"But an 'a' is **the** right choice?" asked Poplavsky.

"Yes, an 'a' is **the** right choice."

"How can an '**a**' be **the** right choice?" asked Poplavsky.

"A 'the' is right. The 'a' is wrong."

"Stop it, stop it!" said Poplavsky in a voice that managed to beg and threaten at the same time. *Zero Gravity*, pp. 7–8.

Readers who are familiar with Russian grammar will understand and sympathize with Poplavsky's problem. Russian does not have anything like English definite and indefinite articles. However, as we shall see, the issue of whether something corresponding to English articles exists in the learner's L1 is only part of a larger problem that English learners have with these forms.

TYPES OF ARTICLES

There are basically two types of articles in English – *definite* (*the*) and *indefinite* (*a*/*an*). *The*, *a*, and *an* are usually unstressed in connected speech and are pronounced with the short vowel /ə/. The form *a* appears before words that begin with a consonant sound; *an* appears only before words beginning with a vowel sound. We will refer to certain cases where a noun is not preceded by an article as instances of the *zero article*. These cases will be justified and explained in greater detail later.

The terms *definite* and *indefinite* designate meanings associated with the noun that an article precedes. *Definite* implies that a noun is "specifically identifiable." The use of the definite article, *the*, therefore, presupposes that the speaker and the listener can identify the noun that follows it.[2] For example, in (1), we can presume that the speaker is referring to a particular noise that the person addressed can also hear.

(**1**) Can you do something about *the noise*?

Indefinite means "identifiable in general." The indefinite article, *a*/*an*, occurs when the listener is not expected to be able to identify the object specifically. The listener may know the concept represented by the noun, but that is all. The contrast between indefinite and definite articles in (2) illustrates this distinction.

(**2**) a. Bring me *a screwdriver.*   *indefinite article*
　　 b. Bring me *the screwdriver.*   *definite article*

In (2a), the speaker assumes that the person addressed knows what a screwdriver is. The request is for any object within the category "screwdriver" – a Phillips screwdriver, a flathead screwdriver, or any other screwdriver. However, in (2b), the speaker assumes that the listener has knowledge of a specific screwdriver, which they both can identify, and it is this particular screwdriver that is requested.

The indefinite article, *a*/*an*, can express at least two kinds of indefiniteness. It can express the idea of "one," as in (3a), in which *a new dress* means "one new dress," and it can also indicate membership in a particular group or set, as in (3b), in which a *veterinarian* means "a member of the class of doctors who care for animals."

(3) a. Susan bought *a new dress.*
   b. My brother is *a veterinarian.*

THE OCCURRENCE OF ARTICLES

The grammar of articles is fairly straightforward. It involves understanding the distinction between count nouns such as *lamp, pen,* or *child,* which have plural forms (*several lamps, two pens, many children*), and noncount nouns, such as *stuff, furniture,* or *information,* which do not have plural forms (**three stuffs, *several furnitures, *many informations*).

The Definite Article

The definite article may appear before singular and plural count nouns, as shown in (4), and before noncount nouns, as in (5).

(4) a. Give him *the key.*   singular count noun
   b. Give him *the keys.*   plural count noun

(5) I gave him *the information* that he wanted.   noncount noun

The definite article does not normally occur before people's names, as (6a) and (6b) illustrate. In many languages, however, it is common practice to use a definite article with a person's name or with a person's title and name, which can lead learners to errors of a sort discussed later in this chapter.

(6) a. I would like to meet Donald.
   b. *I would like to meet the Donald.

There are, however, cases in which it is appropriate to use *the* with a person's name. For example, the definite article is used before a person's name if the speaker wishes to single out a particular person who might be confused with someone else, as in (7a); this use involves a modifier that specifies the noun, a context for the use of definite articles discussed later. In (7b), *the* is stressed because the speaker wants to emphasize the special (celebrity) status of the person mentioned; *the Brad Pitt,* in this case, has roughly the same meaning as *the one and only Brad Pitt. The* is also used with plural proper names to indicate a particular family. In (7c), the speaker is most likely referring to a Mr. and Mrs. Smith (and perhaps their children). In (7d), the speaker is referring to the Medici family, or "clan."

(7) a. Oh, the Harry Kilgore you are referring to clearly isn't the Harry Kilgore I know.
   b. I actually met THE Brad Pitt. You know, the movie star.
   c. You remember that we are having dinner with the Smiths on Friday, right?
   d. The Medicis held power for a long time.

The Indefinite Article

The indefinite article, *a/an,* can appear before singular count nouns, as in (8), but not normally before noncount nouns, as (9) shows (although there are exceptions, as discussed later). In many languages, the distinction between English count and noncount nouns isn't paralleled, at least not precisely; thus, English learners often make errors such as in (9) and (10) with abstract noncount nouns, as we shall see later in this chapter.

(**8**) She has a brother who lives in Seattle.   *singular count noun*

(**9**) *He gave me a water because I was so thirsty. I drank all of it.   *noncount noun*

(**10**) *Rachel gave me an information about it.   *noncount noun*

As we saw in Chapter 10, partitives are used to measure the quantity of noncount nouns. The partitive is often preceded by *a*, as shown in (11):

	Article	Partitive	Noncount Noun
(**11**) a.	a	slice of	pizza
b.	a	piece of	cake
c.	a	loaf of	bread
d.	a	bowl of	oatmeal

With some noncount nouns, such as *coffee*, *tea*, or *hot chocolate*, the partitive is sometimes omitted in everyday speech. It is therefore possible to hear both (12a) and (12b).

(**12**) a. Would you like to go somewhere and have *a cup of coffee*?
b. Would you like to go somewhere and have *a coffee*?

With these and other noncount nouns, the partitive can also be omitted when the speaker wishes to indicate the idea "a type of." Thus, for example, (13a) means a particular type of cheese and (13b) means a particular type of tea.

(**13**) a. After dinner, he offered us *a cheese* from southern Italy.
b. She served *a tea* that she had found in a gourmet tea shop in Chicago.

Some as an Indefinite Article

Unstressed *some* can be considered as the plural form of the indefinite article *a/an* when it appears before count nouns.[3] Thus, *some* in sentences like (14) indicates an indefinite quantity of at least two.

(**14**) There were *some books* in the box.   *plural count noun*

Unstressed *some* also functions as an indefinite article before noncount nouns, as shown in (15). Here it is interpreted as "a certain/indefinite amount" of something.

(**15**) Tom provided *some information* about it.   *noncount noun*

In front of singular count nouns, *some* can also designate a particular person or thing whose identity is not determinable or important. Thus, (16a) with *some* means virtually the same thing as (16b) with the indefinite article *a*. The example with *some . . . or other* in (16c) also has roughly the same meaning. While such uses of *some* are common in conversational English, it is important to note that sentences like (16a) and (16c) can carry a flippant or slightly disparaging tone.

(**16**) a. *Some guy* came by and left this package for you.
b. *A guy* came by and left this package for you.
c. *Some student or other* is waiting to see you.

Additional Facts About *Some*

In addition to the functions shown in (16), the basic meaning of *some* ("an unspecified amount") takes on an extra added value in certain contexts. In these other contexts, however, *some* is not functioning as an article, but as another type of prenominal modifier.

In (17a) and (17b), *some time* is interpreted as "a considerable amount of time." In (17c), *some* defines a quantity that is relative to a larger set or group – *some* people left, but *not all or most* of the audience. And when *some* has contrastive stress, as in a sentence such as (17d), it indicates a strong emotional response (which can be favorable or unfavorable) to something exceptional that the speaker has experienced.[4]

> (**17**) a. We talked about it for *some time.*
>   b. It was *some time* before I saw her again.
>   c. *Some* of the audience members left after the intermission, but quite a few stayed for the last act.
>   d. Boy, that was SOME party! I've never had such a great time.

Zero Article

Those instances in which count and noncount nouns have no preceding article (or any other modifier) may be referred to as instances of *zero article* (symbolized as ø). Nouns with zero article often denote meanings that could be represented using either an indefinite or definite article. For example, the noncount noun *milk* in (18a) denotes an unspecified quantity of milk and corresponds to the indefinite *some milk* in (18b).

> (**18**) a. There's ø *milk* in the fridge, if you are thirsty.
>   b. There's *some milk* in the fridge, if you are thirsty.

In (19a) and (19b), plural count nouns *bullets* and *leaves* with zero article, like the noncount noun *milk* in (18a), denote an indefinite amount of these entities. In (19c) and (19d), the plural count nouns with zero article are examples of *generic reference*. The plural count noun *teachers* denotes teachers generally, or as a group, and *tigers* denotes members of that species generally. Other possibilities for expressing generic reference with articles are discussed later in this chapter.

> (**19**) a. ø *Bullets* were flying everywhere.
>   b. The street was covered with ø *leaves.*
>   c. ø *Teachers* want good materials.
>   d. ø *Tigers* are dangerous.

Abstract Nouns

Nouns preceded by zero article can denote a particular meaning that contrasts with that denoted by nouns preceded by definite and indefinite articles. With abstract noncount nouns such as *education, beauty, intelligence,* and *consciousness,* zero article plus noun denotes the general concept, state, or field expressed by the noun, as in (20a), (21a), and (22a). In such cases, zero article contrasts with the definite article, which means "specifically identifiable," as in (20b), (21b), and (22b); and with the indefinite article, which usually means "type/kind of," as in (20c), (21c), and (22c).

(20) a. Is ø intelligence hereditary?   *zero article*
　　 b. *The* intelligence we saw was remarkable for one so young.   *definite article*
　　 c. Apes display *an* intelligence similar but not identical
　　　　to that found in humans.   *indefinite article*

(21) a. ø Education is becoming more specialized these days.   *zero article*
　　 b. *The* education I received at my alma mater prepared
　　　　me for life.   *definite article*
　　 c. He received *a* good, old-fashioned, liberal arts education. *indefinite article*

(22) a. ø Beauty is ephemeral, but character is definable and
　　　　recognizable.   *zero article*
　　 b. The beauty of her smile was legendary.   *definite article*
　　 c. She has a beauty that I find elusive but nevertheless
　　　　compelling.   *indefinite article*

Names

Names of people, places, and many professional titles usually appear with zero article, as in (23), although we will see that this is not the case for many names of institutions and geographical entities.

(23) a. ø Mary is a successful interior decorator.   *personal name*
　　 b. I would like you to meet ø Dr. Phillips.   *professional title*
　　 c. She went to ø Harvard University.   *institutional name*
　　 d. John lives in ø Melbourne.   *city name*
　　 e. They have a large house on ø Lake Michigan.   *geographical name*

Nouns Designating Customs or Institutions

Zero article often precedes nouns that are being used to designate a custom or an institution. For example, in (24a), *breakfast* preceded by the zero article refers to the custom of eating the first meal of the day. By contrast, in (24b), *breakfast* preceded by the definite article refers to a particular morning meal that has been eaten, and in (24c) *breakfast* preceded by the indefinite article refers to the particular kind of morning meals the restaurant serves. In (24b) and (24c), the placement of definite and indefinite articles before the noun *breakfast* particularizes it.

(24) a. He always eats ø *breakfast* in
　　　　the kitchen.   *a custom*
　　 b. *The breakfast* was delicious!   *a particular meal known to the listener*
　　 c. They serve *a fantastic breakfast* at
　　　　that restaurant.   *particular kind of meal served*

The distinction illustrated in (24) is paralleled in (25) with two nouns that designate institutions, *church* and *jail*.

(25) a. He's in ø *church* right now.   *an institution*
　　 b. They held the ceremony in *the church*. *a particular place known to the listener*
　　 c. They were both sent to ø *jail*.   *an institution*
　　 d. *The jail* houses over 300 inmates. *a particular place known to the listener*

In addition to the nouns in (25), zero article is also used with *school, college, class, prison*, and *camp* when these are used in their "institutional" sense. The use of zero article with institutions is, however, somewhat unpredictable, in that some institutions do not take zero article. For instance, we can say *They go to ø church every week*, but we don't say **They go to ø mosque every week*. We must use an article with that particular institution (*They go to a/the mosque every week*). Moreover, certain nouns that are never used with zero article in American English do occur with zero article in British English when used in their institutional sense. For example, these two dialects diverge with respect to the nouns *hospital, university,* and *government,* as illustrated in (26). This is an important point that ESL teachers should be aware of, since they may have occasion to teach students who have received instruction from native speakers of British English. Teachers who are not familiar with this divergence in article use may mistakenly view a zero article in these contexts as an error.

(26) a. Lucy is in ø hospital. She had a bad automobile accident.   *British English*
 b. Lucy is in the hospital. She had a bad automobile accident.   *American English*
 c. We were at the university together.   *American English*
 d. We were at ø university together.   *British English*

Additional Facts About Zero Article
In addition to the situations previously illustrated, zero article also frequently occurs with other types of count nouns.[5] These uses are almost always idiomatic, and often definite or indefinite articles could be used in these or similar contexts.

DAYS, MONTHS, AND SEASONS
With seasons, there is considerable variation between use of zero article and of the definite article, especially when the season follows a preposition. For example, *In winter we go to Florida* means the same thing as *In the winter we go to Florida*. However, days and months generally take only zero article, as shown in (27a), (27b), and (27c). The definite article with other noun modifiers, as in (27d) and (27e), can be used in designating particular months or days.[6] The indefinite article is commonly used with days when a specific day is not intended, as in (27f). Notice that (27c) could also take the indefinite article (*He always visits his mother on a Tuesday*).

(27) a. May is the most pleasant month.
 b. She usually goes skiing in December.
 c. He always visits his mother on Tuesday.
 d. That was the December when it snowed over 30 inches in two days.
 e. She always visits her mother on the second Tuesday of each month.
 f. Let's schedule our next meeting on a Monday.

MODES OF TRANSPORTATION AND COMMUNICATION
Nouns that denote modes of transportation, such as *bus, car, taxi,* and *train,* take zero article when they are preceded by the preposition *by*, as in (28a). This is also true for nouns that denote modes of communication, such as *telephone, mail, e-mail,* and *fax*, as in (28b), (28c), and (28d).

(28) a. They went *by plane*, but we prefer to travel *by train*.
 b. You can contact him *by phone*.
 c. I'll send it *by express mail*.
 d. You can always get in touch with me *by e-mail*.

Note, however, that if the mode of transportation or communication is not preceded by the preposition *by*, a definite or indefinite article is required, as (29) indicates.

> (**29**) a. He got off *the train* at Penn Station.
>   b. She took *a plane* to Toledo.
>   c. It is not a good idea to send money through *the mail*.
>   d. We spoke briefly over *the phone*.

PARALLEL STRUCTURES

In expressions where two identical or semantically related count nouns are joined by a preposition or a coordinating conjunction, both nouns may take zero article, as shown in (30).

> (**30**) a. They went from *place to place*.
>   b. It's an agreement between *father and son*.
>   c. That is privileged information between *lawyer and client*.
>   d. She quickly made the transition from *backup musician to superstar*.

PREDICATE NOMINALS THAT ARE UNIQUE TITLES

Predicate nominals that are unique titles, in the sense of positions being held by one person, can take zero article or a definite article, as shown in (31a) and (31b). Certain "naming" verbs such as *name*, *elect*, and *appoint* take an object with zero article, as shown in (31c). (See Chapter 21 for more on "naming" verbs and their complements.)

> (**31**) a. John is managing editor of the *St. Louis Post-Dispatch*.
>   b. John is the managing editor of the *St. Louis Post-Dispatch*.
>   c. She was elected president of her stock club.

HEADLINES AND SIGNS

Articles are commonly omitted from signs and headlines of newspapers to save space since the nouns with zero article retain enough information for the reader to interpret them. Readers understand that the headline in (32a) means (32b) and that the road sign in (32c) has the same meaning as (32d).

> (**32**) a. FIRE DESTROYS DOWNTOWN OFFICE BUILDING
>   b. A fire destroyed a downtown office building.
>   c. Slippery When Wet!
>   d. The road surface is slippery when it is wet.

SUMMARY

TYPES OF ARTICLES AND THEIR OCCURRENCE

Articles are a type of determiner and can be classified as definite or indefinite.

The **definite article (*the*)** appears before singular and plural count nouns as well as noncount nouns.

Count Noun	Noncount Noun
the lamp	*the furniture*
the lamps	*the juice*
the ocean	*the water*

The **indefinite article (*a/an*)** appears before singular count nouns. It is used with noncount nouns only when it precedes a partitive.

Count Noun	*Noncount Noun*
a lamp	*a piece of furniture*
*a lamps	*a glass of juice*
an ocean	*an ounce of water*

Some is often considered to be the plural form of the indefinite article *a/an*. It is used with plural count nouns as well as noncount nouns.

Count Noun	*Noncount Noun*
some lamps	*some furniture*
some islands	*some juice*
	some water

Zero article (ø) refers to the absence of a definite or an indefinite article before a noun. In addition to occurring in contexts where it is interchangeable with a definite or indefinite article, zero article occurs before:

• abstract nouns such as *beauty, intelligence,* and *education* to denote a concept, state, or field.
  ø Beauty is ephemeral, but ø character is definable and recognizable.
  Is ø intelligence hereditary?
  ø Education is becoming more specialized these days.

• names and professional titles.
  I would like you to meet ø Dr. Jane Phillips and her husband, ø George.
  She went to ø Harvard University.
  John lives in ø Melbourne.
  They have a large house on ø Lake Michigan.

• nouns that refer to a custom or an institution.
  He enjoys ø breakfast.
  She talks a lot in ø class.

EXERCISE 11.1

Identify any article-related errors in each sentence and explain why the error has occurred.

Example: The subject of his lecture was the human intelligence.

Answer: error: *the human intelligence* (Here *intelligence* refers to the concept of intelligence, so it should be preceded by zero article.)

1. Have you met the Professor Granger yet?
2. I met him at university.
3. She gave me an information about it that I can use in my report.
4. A: Can I help you with the project?
   B: I don't need help – I need data.
5. Let's go get a coffee and talk this over.
6. I called Phil the other day, and his brother answered the phone. He told me that Phil is in hospital with a broken leg.

7. I don't like him very much because he always talks in a class.
8. Some girl just called you.
9. We sent the package by the express mail.
10. The teacher gave us a homework that looks really difficult.

USING ARTICLES

Corpus-based research into the ways that native speakers of English use articles has revealed that the semantic and grammatical descriptions presented earlier are not sufficient for helping English language learners understand all of the conditions that may affect the choice of a particular article in a given situation.[7] A more comprehensive list of conditions that affect article usage is presented here.

Definite Articles in Discourse

The conditions that affect article choice are best phrased in terms of the use of definite articles.[8] They require taking the discourse context into account.

First Versus Second Mention of a Noun

Definite articles are used when we want to refer to something that has already been mentioned. This is sometimes referred to as the *anaphoric*, or *second-mention*, function of *the*. In (33), *a brother* and *a sister* are mentioned in the first sentence. When they are mentioned again in the second and third sentences, they are preceded by *the* to indicate that these are the same people referred to earlier.

(**33**) She has *a brother* and *a sister*. *The brother* is a university student. *The sister* is still in high school.

In (34), the first sentence is the same as in (33), however, in the two following sentences, the nouns *brother* and *sister* are modified by the indefinite article *a*. It is immediately clear that the *brother* and *sister* do not refer back to these same nouns in the first sentence. The nouns are not anaphoric; rather, they denote brothers and sisters in general.

(**34**) She has *a brother* and *a sister*. *A brother* can either be a good friend to *a younger sister* or make her life miserable. The same can be said for *a sister*.

Nouns Designating Objects in the Immediate Environment

When a speaker wants to refer to something specific that is present or visible in the immediate environment, a definite article is used. In (35), the object being referred to is visible to the speaker and the listener.

(**35**) Pass *the butter*, please.

We can use *the* even if we have not seen the thing we are referring to if we know that it is present in the immediate environment and can readily be identified by the hearer. For example, at a zoo, a sign might read *DO NOT FEED THE BEARS*. We may not see the bears referred to in the sign, but the use of *the* is appropriate since we know that bears are present.

Nouns Designating Objects Present in a Larger Context

Definite articles are also used when the speaker assumes that because the listener belongs to the same community, he or she shares specific knowledge of their surroundings. For example, if two people who work in the same place are discussing where to meet for lunch, one of them might say something like the first sentence in (36).

> (36) Rebecca: Let's meet at *the cafeteria* at 12:15.
>   Paul: Okay, I'll see you then.

Here, the definite article is used because both speakers are part of the same work community; the cafeteria is part of their shared knowledge.

Knowledge of Relationships Between Things

Definite articles are used in situations where the speaker can assume that the listener knows about the relationships that exist between certain objects and things usually associated with them. This is referred to as the *associative anaphoric* use of definite articles. In (37), the speaker assumes that the listener knows that automobiles must have drivers and that they frequently have passengers. Thus, a definite article comes before both *driver* and *passengers*, even though this is the first time they are mentioned. Notice that the definite article in front of *freeway* is an example of the effect of assumptions related to larger context. The speaker assumes that the listener knows what specific freeway is intended.

> (37) An SUV was involved in an accident on the freeway last night. *The driver* and *the passengers* were injured.

Generic Reference

As discussed earlier, when a noun refers generally to members of a species or class (e.g., *cats*, *dogs*, *teachers*), this is called *generic reference*. Generic reference can be expressed three ways in English: by a plural noun preceded by zero article, as discussed earlier and as shown in (38a); by a singular noun preceded by an indefinite article, as in (38b); and by a singular noun preceded by a definite article, as in (38c).

> (38) a. *Tigers* are dangerous animals.   *zero article*
>   b. *A tiger* is a dangerous animal.   *indefinite article*
>   c. *The tiger* is a dangerous animal.   *definite article*

The use of the definite article before a singular count noun for generic reference is very rare in conversation. It is more typical, however, in academic prose and seems to work better with complex NPs like *the howler monkey, the red-breasted merganser, the white-eyed vireo*, and so on.

Grammatical Structures That Require the Use of the Definite Article

In many cases, the grammatical forms and structures surrounding a noun make the use of a definite article necessary since they make the noun specific.

Relative Clauses That Specify a Noun

Nouns modified by a relative clause are usually preceded by *the*. Although they can be preceded by either an indefinite or a definite article, there is a tendency for the article to be definite. This is because relative clauses are often used to define or specify something, making it specifically identifiable and hence definite.[9] This defining function is shown in (39), in which the relative clause in brackets after *woman* establishes the identity of this woman. This is important, because the context that this sentence appears in consists of only two previous sentences, neither of which contains any mention of a woman.

(**39**) A: What happened to Bill? He looks so depressed.
        B: Oh, *the woman* [he went out with last night] was nasty to him.

Without the relative clause, the reply in (39) sounds odd, as (40) illustrates. Again, this is because the two previous sentences do not help establish the identity of the woman, so the reader has no way of knowing who the woman is that is being referred to.

(**40**) A: What happened to Bill? He looks so depressed.
        B: Oh, *the woman* was nasty to him.

Prepositional Phrases That Specify a Noun

Like relative clauses, prepositional phrases can perform this specifying or defining function. Thus, in (41), *op-ed page* is preceded by the definite article because it is made definite by the prepositional phrase *of* the *New York Times*.

(**41**) Her letter appeared on *the op-ed page* [of the *New York Times*].

That Clauses That Specify a Noun

Nouns followed by clauses beginning with *that* also take definite articles. In (42a) and (42b), the nouns *fact* and *suggestion* precede clauses introduced by *that*. In both cases, the clause further defines the noun. (These clauses are discussed in greater detail in Chapter 21.)

(**42**) a. *The fact* [that he refused their offer] surprised me.
        b. *The suggestion* [that she might have lied] was rejected by the jury.

Nouns Modified by Superlative Adjectives

Nouns preceded by superlative adjective forms usually take definite articles, regardless of whether the superlative is formed with *the most* or an *-est* ending, as shown in (43).

(**43**) a. His teacher said he was *the most intelligent student* in the class.
        b. When she won the lottery, she believed that she was *the luckiest person* in the world.

Nouns Modified by Ordinals

Nouns preceded by ordinal numbers (including *next* and *last*) usually take definite articles, as shown in (44).

(**44**) a. I ran all the way to the station and just caught *the last train*.
        b. She was *the first student* to finish the exam.

ADDITIONAL FACTS ABOUT THE DEFINITE ARTICLE

A number of English idioms and names take a definite article. Some of the more common groups of these are presented here.

Idioms

A fair number of idioms take definite articles before a noun. Structurally, these idioms fall into several groups. The first group consists of an NP followed by a prepositional phrase in which the object NP contains *the*, as shown in (45).

(**45**) a. The positive feedback on his writing was *a shot in the arm* for him. He worked harder after that.
b. Everybody said she acted just like her mother. She was *a chip off the old block*.
c. *The fly in the ointment* was my brother. He was the only one who didn't like the idea.
d. She was no longer angry about what happened. It was all *water under the bridge*.

The second group, shown in (46), consists of a transitive verb followed by an object NP that contains *the*.

(**46**) a. Their car was very old. They knew it would *bite the dust* soon.
b. Someone tell those slow people in front of us to *get the lead out* and walk faster.
c. If you want to stay at this school, you have to work hard to *cut the mustard*.
d. They were going to New York to *paint the town red* once they graduated.
e. We need someone who knows what he's doing to *lead the way*.

The third group consists of a verb followed by an NP referring to a person and then a prepositional phrase in which the object NP contains *the*, shown in (47).

(**47**) a. Sitting all day at work *drives her up the wall*. She prefers to be active.
b. He told no one of his decision beforehand. He wanted to *keep everyone in the dark*.

Names That Take Definite Articles

As we saw earlier, the general rule is that names take zero article, but there are quite a few exceptions to this rule. Many names of things take definite articles. Two notable examples are the recently created names *the Internet* and *the Web*. Some classes of names that take definite articles are listed below.

Geographical Place Names

Geographical entities whose names take definite articles include the following:

• Certain countries, including those viewed as unions and federations: *the United Kingdom, the United Arab Emirates, the United States, the Democratic Republic of Congo*.
• Lakes that form a complex: *the Great Lakes, the Finger Lakes*. The names of single lakes usually begin with *Lake* and zero article: *Lake Victoria, Lake Erie*.
• Mountain ranges: *the Himalayas, the Alps, the Andes, the Alburz Mountains*. The names of single mountains usually begin with *Mount* and zero article: *Mount Kilimanjaro, Mount Rainier, Mount Everest*. There are exceptions, e.g., *the Matterhorn* and *K2*.
• Island chains: *the Philippines, the Canary Islands, the Solomon Islands, the Antilles*.
• Oceans, seas, and gulfs: *the Atlantic Ocean, the Pacific Ocean, the Caribbean Sea, the Caspian Sea, the Gulf of Guinea, the Persian Gulf*. Although one of the largest bays in the world is *the Bay of Bengal*, there are more bays with zero article: *Hudson Bay, Baffin Bay, San Francisco Bay*.
• Straits: *the Bering Strait, the Formosa Strait, the Strait of Gibraltar*.

- Deserts, plains, plateaus, and peninsulas: *the Gobi Desert, the Sahara Desert, the Central Siberian Plain, the Atlantic Coastal Plain, the Great Plains, the Plateau of Tibet, the Mongolian Plateau, the Iberian Peninsula, the Korean Peninsula,* but *Kamchatka Peninsula.*
- Rivers and canals: *the Amazon River, the Yangtze, the Rhein, the Panama Canal, the Suez Canal, the Grand Canal.*
- Terms of longitude and latitude: *the Tropic of Cancer, the Tropic of Capricorn, the Equator, the International Dateline, the Prime Meridian.*
- Celestial bodies: *the sun, the moon,* and (optionally) *the earth.* However, all planets other than the earth get zero article: *Venus, Saturn, Mercury.*

Names of Newspapers

Many newspaper titles, full or abbreviated, are preceded by *the*: *the* Manchester Guardian (*the* Guardian), *the* New York Times (*the* Times), *the* Wall Street Journal (*the* Journal), *the* Washington Post (*the* Post).

Names of Governmental Bodies and Titles of Officials

Government departments and other bodies are preceded by *the*: *the Department of Commerce, the Treasury Department, the Federal Bureau of Investigation* (*the FBI*), *the Central Intelligence Agency* (*the CIA*). The titles by which government officials are referred to also include *the*: *the President, the Prime Minister, the Vice President.*

Names for Parts of the Body

The names for parts of the body are preceded by *the, a/an,* or zero article, as shown in (48).

(48) a. He was shot in the arm.
   b. He lost an arm in an automobile accident.
   c. It is a strange kind of lizard that doesn't have legs.

However, parts of the body are also preceded by possessive determiners such as *my, your, his,* and *her* in sentences such as (49), and this usage restriction results in problems for many learners. The nature of the problem will be explained in the next section.

(49) a. He injured his hand.
   b. Close your eyes and go to sleep.

SUMMARY

USING ARTICLES

Many factors can influence the choice a speaker or writer makes to use a definite article, an indefinite article, or zero article. Most can be stated in terms of definite article use.

In the **anaphoric**, or **second-mention**, use of the definite article, second mention of a noun usually requires the use of the definite article.
They have a German shepherd and a beagle. The beagle is two years old.

The **immediate presence** of the thing denoted by a noun often calls for the use of the definite article.
Pass the salt, please.
Can you please answer the phone?

If the thing denoted by a noun is **part of a larger context** in which a conversation is taking place, and is therefore familiar to both the speaker and the hearer, then the definite article is used.

I saw you at the car wash yesterday.
I'll meet you in the lobby.

In the **associative anaphoric use** of the definite article, the speaker assumes that the hearer is aware of a basic relationship between a given object and some other object that has already been mentioned.

I'm having problems with my computer. The hard drive is malfunctioning and the monitor won't turn on.

Generic reference to a species or class can be made with a definite article, an indefinite article, or zero article.

The orchid requires a good deal of water and sunlight to survive.
An orchid requires a good deal of water and sunlight to survive.
Orchids require a good deal of water and sunlight to survive.

Various grammatical forms related to a noun make use of the definite article usual or necessary:

- relative clauses that specify a noun
  The car [I just bought] is great on gas.
  Did I tell you about the guy [who I met at the library]?

- prepositional phrases that specify a noun
  You plan to climb to the top [of that mountain]?
  What's the topic [of the discussion]?

- clauses beginning with *that* that specify a noun
  The fact [that I wasn't there] proves my innocence.
  Their constitution states the concept [that all people are equal].

- nouns modified by superlative adjectives
  This is the least expensive car on the market.
  They hired the best lawyers they could find.

- nouns modified by ordinals
  I was on the last flight out of Washington.
  The first time is always the hardest.

EXERCISE 11.2

Indicate why the definite article (*the*) is used in each of the following italicized instances (second mention, immediate presence, part of larger context, relative clause defining a noun, associative anaphoric use, generic reference, ordinal, *that* clause).

Example: A man and a woman entered the restaurant. *The couple* was led to a table by the headwaiter.

Answer: second mention (*The couple* refers to *a man* and *a woman* in the first sentence.)

1. Be careful! You are going to knock *the vase* over.
2. As he was standing on the corner, one of those large diesel-powered buses drove by. *The exhaust fumes* were so overpowering that he began to cough.

3. Alan was typing up a report on his laptop. All of a sudden *the screen* went blank.
4. Mary flew to Paris. *The journey* lasted six and a half hours.
5. A: What's up with Sara? She seems really irritable today.
   B: Oh, *the woman* who she works for has been giving her a hard time.
6. The meeting is in *the conference room*.
7. *The first person* to sail to America was an Icelander.
8. He was amazed by *the fact* that there is so much life on earth.

PROBLEMS THAT ESL/EFL STUDENTS HAVE WITH ARTICLES

While not all languages have forms like English articles, they all have some way of accomplishing the functions of English articles. Therefore, concepts that these articles express, such as definiteness and indefiniteness, will not be new to students. Nevertheless, the kinds of forms and constructions used for expressing definiteness and indefiniteness vary widely in the languages of the world, and this makes learning the English article system challenging and problems with articles persistent. Many students who have lexical items in their L1 that correspond to English articles deploy these items in environments not permitted in English. Following are some typical cases from our corpus and elsewhere as noted where L1 rules regarding article use are transferred to English, resulting in ungrammatical sentences.

Using Articles Instead of Possessive Determiners (Spanish, French, Italian, German)

In some languages, definite articles are used in contexts where English normally uses a possessive determiner (*your, his, her*, etc.). In Spanish, French, Italian, and German, this is true when parts of the body are referred to, as illustrated by the German and Spanish examples in (50) and (51), respectively.

(**50**) *Er   schloss   die   Augen   und   schlief   sofort   ein.*
he   closed   the   eyes   and   fell   immediately   asleep
"He closed his eyes and fell asleep immediately."

(**51**) *Saque   la   lengua.*
stick out   the   tongue
"Stick out your tongue."

There are also other sorts of nouns, such as the piece of clothing in the Spanish example in (52), which in the L1 require a definite article instead of the possessive determiner that is required in English, as Stockwell, Bowen, and Martin (1966) pointed out over 40 years ago.

(**52**) *Quítese   la   camisa.*
take off   the   shirt
"Take off your shirt."

Students with these L1s may sometimes use *the* in a context where a possessive determiner is preferred or required in English, as in (53) and (54).

(**53**) *The ambulance attendant asked the injured man to open *the eyes*.

(**54**) *The doctor told to him to take off *the shirt* so he could examine him.

Using Articles with Professional Titles (Spanish)

In some languages, including Spanish, professional titles are preceded by definite articles. This use of articles before professional titles seems to transfer often, resulting in errors such as those in (55) and (56).

(55) *In Tanya Schevitz's chronicle, *the Professor David Presti*, who teaches at University of California, Berkeley, caught some of his students with plagiarized papers.

(56) **The President Lyndon Johnson* undertook this policy in 1964 in order to protect the civil rights of the blacks.

Our corpus has shown that these errors still occur when students have attained a fairly high level of competence.

Using Definite Articles Rather than Zero Article with Abstract Count and Noncount Nouns (Spanish, French, Hungarian)

Count nouns used in an abstract sense (e.g., *life*, *love*, *time*) and abstract noncount nouns that refer to a general phenomenon such as a quality or process (e.g., *beauty*, *education*, *globalization*) take zero article in English, but in some languages they take the definite article, as (57a) illustrates for Spanish, and (57b) for French.

(57) a. *La   belleza   es   un   don   del   cielo.*
      the   beauty   is   a   gift   from   heavens
      "Beauty is a gift from heaven."
   b. *La   vie   est   belle!*
      the   life   is   beautiful
      "Life is beautiful!"

Spanish and French speakers will often place a definite article before these types of nouns in English, when zero article is required. Typical examples from Spanish speakers are shown in (58a) and (58b); the examples in (58c) and (58d) are from French speakers. In each case, zero article is required before the italicized noun.[10]

(58) a. *He says *the self-esteem* is the most important thing in *the life* for cope with success.
   b. *They develop several kinds of positions that can be improved with *the time*.
   c. * Is *the alcohol* a problem in our society?
   d. *This will not favor *the equality* among people.

Researchers have documented similar errors by Hungarian-speaking EFL students. Hungarian has a definite article (*a/az*), corresponding to *the*, and for count nouns used in an abstract sense, especially in subject position, the definite article is obligatory, as shown in (59).

(59) a. *Az   idő   repül.*
      the   time   flies
      "Time flies."
   b. *Az   idő   pénz.*
      the   time   (is)   money
      "Time is money."

In his early study of Hungarian speakers, Stephanides (1974) found that about 9 percent of the errors involving articles were caused by use of the definite article with nouns like those in (59).

Using Indefinite Articles Rather than Zero Articles with Certain Nouns (Spanish, Korean)

In Spanish, indefinite articles appear before adjectives that modify nouns. However, they cannot in sentences like (60). Here, as in English, there should be no article before *buen*.

> (60) a. ***Él   habla   un   buen   inglés.*
>   he   speaks   a   good   English
>   "He speaks good English."

But we do find errors such as those in (61), which were made by intermediate level students in an English language institute that prepares ESL students for admission to American universities. The source of the error is not clear; it may be overgeneralization.

> (61) a. *The most important thing is that I must pronounce *a correct English*.
>   b. *But I think learning in the United States give me the opportunity to learn *a good English* and faster than in my country.

In Korean, many noncount nouns, such as *evidence, stuff, homework, information, news, research,* and *equipment*, are countable. Korean speakers may transfer this feature to English, resulting in the addition of plural *-s* to the equivalent English nouns (**evidences, *informations, *researches,* etc.). They have also been found to use these noncount nouns with indefinite articles rather than with zero article, as shown in (62).

> (62) a. *However, it must have been easy for him to develop and incorporate *a prior information* into his new research.
>   b. *HL with *a technical equipment* can reduce the children's access to the reality.[11]

Omitting Articles (Korean)

ESL/EFL students with L1s that do not have forms corresponding to English articles often omit articles in English NPs where they are obligatory. As shown in the introduction to this chapter, Russian is one such language. Korean is another. The written English of Korean speakers also offers abundant examples of article omission. It is not always clear whether an omission is due to uncertainty regarding which article to use or to L1 transfer, but the tendency is pervasive. Both indefinite and definite articles are dropped. Omission of indefinite articles is often consistent throughout a sentence, as shown in (63a) and (63b). Omission of definite articles tends to be more sporadic, as (63c) and (63d) illustrate.

> (63) a. *Sustainable architecture could be *ø alternative way* to build *ø better living environment* for both human . . .
>   b. *Hence it is better to empower women through *ø systematic program* . . . moreover, women's role is now being changed from *ø passive position* to *ø active position*.
>   c. *Many countries in the world don't recognize the serious effect of destroying *ø environment* . . .
>   d. *The average debt rate of *ø 30 largest countries* at the end of '96 was 386.5 percentages.

SUGGESTIONS FOR TEACHING ARTICLES

Given the many facts that ESL/EFL students must master in order to use articles correctly, and the complications that can arise from L1 transfer, it is not surprising that articles are especially difficult for them. There are reports indicating that students' learning of English articles does not seem to be affected by instruction (Pica, 1985; White, 1992). However, there have been some notable successes, such as Master's (1994) nine-week instruction experiment at UCLA and a 14-week replication at Cal State–Fresno.

Since most of the article errors discussed in the previous section were produced by advanced ESL students in or preparing for entrance into an American university, it would appear that articles are a persistent problem that cannot be eradicated through coverage in English language courses. However, this may be due, at least in part, to the fact that the opportunities for article practice provided by most textbooks are limited largely to fill-in-the-blank exercises.

Acquiring English articles will no doubt be a slow and gradual process. You will have to continue to focus on aspects of article usage as your students move through different levels of proficiency, especially in EFL instructional settings. Nevertheless, there is reason to expect improvement as your students are exposed to correct examples of article usage and are given opportunities to use articles in real communication.

All of the major points covered in this chapter should be covered in the ESL classroom. If you are teaching classes in an EFL setting or if most or all of your students share the same L1, then you should attempt to address some of the particular L1 transfer problems that may exist.

The discussion of teaching points and activities that follow has been divided into two sections. The first section covers specific teaching points to be covered at different stages in a curriculum. No particular order is advocated, although the count/noncount distinction is usually the starting point for dealing with articles. The second section contains suggestions for addressing some of the problems that students with different L1s are likely to have.

Suggested Activities for Specific Teaching Points
Activity 1: Using Indefinite Articles with Count Nouns (Beginning)
List a set of count nouns that are found in the classroom (*eraser, chair, exercise, dollar, student, book,* etc.) and a set of noncount nouns (*money, homework, chalk, furniture,* etc.) in two columns under the labels *Count* and *Can't Count.* If the count/noncount distinction has not already been taught, explain that the count nouns have plural forms and can have numbers and quantifiers such as *several, a few,* and *many* in front of them but the nouns in the other column do not have plural forms and cannot take numbers and quantifiers. Explain that only the nouns in the *Count* column can have the indefinite article, *a* or *an,* in front of them. Ask the students to make up sentences such as *I want _____* or *Please give me _____* using the nouns on the board. If anyone creates a sentence such as **"I want a chalk,"* ask, "Can you say that? Is that a good sentence?" Point out that you can use *some* in front of both count and noncount nouns. If noncount nouns have not been covered earlier, you will have to show the specific partitive expressions that can be used before noncount nouns.

You can extend this activity by showing the students a picture of an advertisement for an electronics store. Ask them, "What are three things you can buy in this store?" As they provide answers, model that item in a sentence, for example, "That's right. You can buy a cell phone/cell phones." Now have the students break into small groups and ask them to make the following lists:

- three things you would find in a drugstore
- three things you would find in a bookstore
- three things you would find in a hardware store
- three things you would like to see in a large city (use an actual city name)
- three things you would put on the table before eating dinner
- three things you would take on a short trip

Walk around the classroom and help any group that has trouble coming up with items. After they have finished, pose questions out loud to members of different groups (e.g., "What are three things you can buy in a hardware store?"). The student's answer must contain either *a/an*, *some*, or zero article. Answers can be short or can take the form of complete sentences, provided the appropriate article is included.

Activity 2: Articles with First and Second Mention (Beginning Through Low Intermediate)

Explain that when something is mentioned for the first time we use *a* or *an* in front of the noun, and when it is mentioned again we use *the*. You could use (33) in this chapter as an example. Have students pair off and give each pair a list of types of programs that are regularly broadcast on television (e.g., a movie, a reality show, a game show, a sitcom, a football game). Student A asks, "What did you watch on TV last night?" and Student B responds with at least two programs. Student B might say, for instance, "I watched a football game on Channel 7 and a sitcom on Channel 2." Student A then asks, "How were they? or "Were they any good?" Student B must then respond with a comment that includes both programs and the appropriate use of articles ("The football game was good; the sitcom was kind of boring.") The students take turns asking and answering questions.

Activity 3: Using Zero Article with Names (Low Intermediate)

Explain that people's names, names with titles (e.g., *Governor Johnson*, *Professor Carter*), geographical names (e.g., *Nigeria*, *Tokyo*), names of many universities, and a variety of other proper nouns do not take articles. Have the students make a list of examples like these and keep expanding it to include exceptions in some categories. They might come up with exceptions like *the Ivory Coast* or *the University of Michigan*.

Ask your students how they would address people with various titles if they spoke with them or had to introduce them to a friend. Then explain that titles do take definite articles when they are being used to describe who a person is. These two uses of titles are contrasted in (64).

> (64) a. I would like you to meet Senator Richard Durbin.
> b. Richard Durbin is *the* Majority Whip of the U.S. Senate.

Have your students suggest the names of famous politicians and demonstrate how they would introduce them to someone and describe what their positions are.

Activity 4: Using Zero Article with Noncount Nouns (Intermediate)

Briefly review the limitation on using *a/an* in front of noncount nouns. Explain that you cannot use *a/an* with a noncount noun as in (65a) but that *a/an* is used with partitives (call them *quantity words*) followed by a noncount noun, as in (65b).

(**65**) a. *I drank a milk.
  b. I drank a glass of milk.

Then review the use of either *some* or no article with noncount nouns. Use a sentence such as *There is juice/some juice in the fridge* to illustrate this. Point out that you can use indefinite articles with these noncount nouns when you mean a particular kind of that noun, as in (66).

(**66**) I bought a cheese from Italy.

Ask the students to provide other examples with nouns such as *bread*, *cheese*, *coffee*, and *tea*.

Activity 5: Using Zero Article with Noncount Nouns (High Intermediate Through Advanced)

Explain that with nouns that describe academic fields, such as *education*, *philosophy*, and *psychology*, you do not use articles. Ask your students to make up sentences using nouns like these and write them on the board. With advanced students, use the sentences in (67) to explain that nouns that describe abstract qualities, such as *beauty*, *intelligence*, and *consciousness*, do not take articles either.

(**67**) a. Intelligence is difficult to measure.
  b. Education is becoming more specialized.
  c. Beauty is difficult to describe.

Contrast the use of the nouns in (67) with the use of the nouns in (68) that are preceded by *a/an* to indicate a particular type of the abstract quality.

(**68**) a. She had a special kind of beauty that came from within.
  b. Their child is receiving an excellent education.

Have students write sentences like those in (67) and (68) and then read and discuss them in small groups.

Activity 6: Using the Definite Article (High Intermediate Through Advanced)

After you have established that your students know the general rule about using definite and indefinite articles with count and noncount nouns, and that they understand the first mention–second mention rule, present them with other cases in which definite articles normally occur.

The following is actually a series of five teaching points and four corresponding activities that may be used over several classes. The bulleted explanations and example sentences are meant to communicate important information about definite articles in student-friendly language. Once you have explained a bulleted teaching point, use the corresponding activity to practice the point.

- When a noun refers to an object that is present and that you and your listener can see, use *the*. If you are sitting at a table and you want some salt, you say:

(**69**) Pass *the* salt, please.

Even if you can't see something, if you and your listener know it is there, use *the* in referring to it. For example, if you go to the zoo, you might see this sign even if you are not standing in front of and looking at animals:

(**70**) Please don't feed *the* animals!

Now ask the students to create signs like the one in (70) for public places such as museums, parks, banks, amusement parks, and so on. The signs could warn people against picking flowers in a park, walking on the grass in a garden, touching pictures in an art gallery, putting their hands through bars of a cage in a zoo, and so on. Afterwards, have students present their signs to each other.

- When a noun refers to something you and your listener know about because you live, work, study, and so on, in the same place, and your listener will know what thing you are referring to, use *the* when referring to it. For example, if you live in a university town where there is a building where students go to eat and study, and this building is called the student union, you might say to a friend:

  (**71**) Let's meet at *the* student union for lunch.

Now ask the students to think of other places and things in the community and have them create other suggestions as to where to meet each other as in (71).

- When a noun refers to something that you know is often or always connected to something else that was already mentioned, use *the*. For example, a news report about a car accident might read as in (72).

  (**72**) A car went off Interstate 74 yesterday at around 2 o'clock in the morning. *The* driver and *the* passengers were injured.

  You know that cars have drivers and that they often have passengers. In the first sentence, the indefinite article, *a*, is used with *car* because it is the first time that the noun is mentioned. In the second sentence, *the* is used before the noun *driver*, which refers to a specific driver, even though *driver* hasn't been mentioned before. Why? Because the writer and the reader know that cars have drivers. For this same reason, *the* is used in front of *passengers* even though this is the first mention of passengers.

Now ask the students to find examples of this article usage pattern in newspapers and bring them to class for discussion. This kind of discussion activity can also be useful for reviewing other conditions that force the choice of definite articles, which you have already covered. After the discussion, have students practice choosing correct articles with some short cloze exercises that involve this use of *the*.

- When a noun is followed by a relative clause that specifies the noun – that is, makes it refer to someone or something specific – use *the*, as in (73).

  (**73**) Jack is a wealthy man. *The* woman that he married has a lot of money.

  The noun *woman* by itself is not specific, but the relative clause *that he married* specifies the noun, so we use *the* in front of *woman*.

- When a noun is followed by a prepositional phrase that specifies the noun, use *the*. In (74), *the* comes before *editorial page* because the prepositional phrase *of the New York Times* tells us which editorial page.

  (**74**) His short article appeared on *the* editorial page of the *New York Times*.

Now, for the preceding two teaching points, ask the students to write a description of a famous person (e.g., an athlete, a movie star, a politician, a rock musician) and work in examples of these uses of *the* at least three times, as in (75), which is based on a newspaper article.[12]

> (**75**) Melinda Gates is the wife of the founder of Microsoft Corporation, Bill Gates. After the birth of her first child, a decade ago, she left her job at the software giant. Now that her third child is nearing school age, the 42-year-old Mrs. Gates is stepping forward to take a leading role in directing the philanthropic foundation, which she and her husband founded, the Bill and Melinda Gates Foundation. One of the projects the foundation will be giving 83 million dollars to is the development of new vaccines for the treatment of malaria. Malaria is a mosquito-borne disease that kills one million people a year, most of whom are children.

Have the students bring these to class. Present some of the best examples.

Activity 7: Making Generic References (Intermediate Through Advanced)

Write (76) on the board. Explain that in this sentence members of the group "teachers" are continually looking for good textbooks. "Teachers" does not mean a particular group of teachers, but teachers in general. Then write (77) on the board.

> (**76**) *Teachers* are always looking for good textbooks.

> (**77**) *A teacher* is always looking for good textbooks.

Point out that "A teacher" in this sentence means any member of the group "teachers," not a particular teacher. The meanings of (76) and (77), therefore, are essentially the same. Ask the students to produce more examples of generic reference with *a/an* and zero article, and write them on the board.

Next, tell students that when we want to refer to a particular group or kind of animal or plant – to all its members generally – the best way to do this is either with no article or with *the*. Write (78) on the board.

> (**78**) a. *Lions* are the largest members of the cat family.
> b. *The lion* is the largest member of the cat family.

Point out that *the lion* in the second sentence is another way of saying *lions* in the first sentence. Both refer to lions as a group within the larger family of *cat*. Provide another example. Say that birds form a single family of animals that fly. Within that family there are many smaller subgroups – for example, wrens, hawks, or ducks. If we want to talk about, for example, marsh wrens, we can say either *wrens* or *the wren*, either *marsh wrens* or *the marsh wren*. Add that in speaking, we usually use the plural without an article (zero article) but in academic prose, *the* is used more frequently.

Next, hand out a passage like the one in (79) and ask them to change the articles + nouns that refer to groups in general so that they all fit one of the patterns that students have just seen. Point out that they may have to change the verbs from singular to plural or vice versa to agree with the choices they make. The target words are underlined here for easy identification; they would, of course, not be underlined in the passage you give to the students.

(79) Birds are members of a class of animals called Aves. They have three features that, in combination, distinguish them from other animals – feathers, wings, and beaks. Birds' wings can vary in size and shape, and this can affect flight. <u>Ruffed grouse</u> has short, broad wings. In order to fly, it must flap its wings quickly and maintain a high airspeed. <u>Hawk</u> has larger wings that are longer and narrower than those of <u>ruffed grouse</u>. Because of this wing shape, <u>hawk</u> can fly more slowly without flapping its wings so frequently. <u>Albatross</u> has even longer, narrower wings, which make <u>albatross</u> a very good glider.[13]

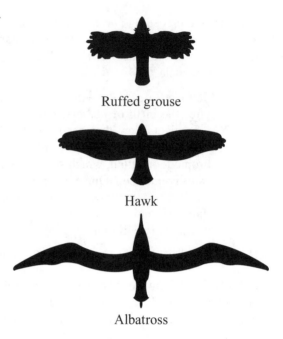

Ruffed grouse

Hawk

Albatross

This activity lets you avoid using the technical term *generic*; however, you may feel that it should be introduced. Since article proficiency is only acquired gradually, teachers will find it beneficial to repeat this kind of activity frequently.

Addressing Specific Article-Related Problems
Activity 8: Difficulties with *The* and Possessive Determiners (High Beginning Through Low Intermediate)

This activity is intended for an EFL or linguistically homogenous ESL classroom with students whose L1 (e.g., Spanish, Italian, French, or German) uses a definite article in contexts that in English would use a possessive determiner. Collect examples of such uses of the definite article. Take one or two of these examples and show how the sentences would be correctly rendered in English.

Explain that in English we use a possessive word (*your*, *my*, *his*, etc.) with sentences that refer to body parts and articles of clothing, as shown in (80).

(80) a. Please lift your arms.
b. I just twisted my ankle.
c. I tied my shoes and ran out the door.
d. May I take your jacket?

Further illustrate this with some other comparison sentences from those that you have collected. Follow this with an exercise that contains contexts where the students are likely to transfer the native language usage convention. Make this a continuous discourse like the passage in (81), which is designed for Spanish speakers. If you are not a native speaker of the L1, you should check your passage with a native speaker to make sure that you have some blanks that would require definite articles in the L1.

(**81**) Cecilio wasn't feeling very good. His teacher told him that he should go to the doctor, so he did. When he got to _____ doctor's office, he had to wait for about 40 minutes before the nurse told him to go in. The doctor said, "So, Cecilio, what seems to be the matter?" Cecilio replied, "I don't feel so good doctor. _____ whole body aches." The doctor said, "Stick out _____ tongue." Cecilio stuck out _____ tongue and the doctor looked down _____ throat. Then the doctor said, "OK, now take off _____ shirt, please." Cecilio took off _____ shirt and the doctor looked at _____ body. Then he asked Cecilio, "Where did you get all those bruises? That's why _____ body aches so much." Cecilio told the doctor that he had fallen off his bicycle the other day. Then the doctor wrote out a prescription for some medicine. He told Cecilio to take _____ prescription to the drugstore and to take _____ pills that the druggist would give him every four hours. Cecilio did this and he felt better. It was about five days before he could stop taking _____ pills.

Activity 9: Difficulties with Abstract Nouns (Intermediate Through Advanced)

This activity extends Activity 5, targeting a particular problem. As we have seen, speakers of Spanish, Korean, Hungarian, and doubtlessly students with other L1s tend to mistakenly use *the* with abstract nouns. This is, therefore, a problem worth emphasizing as part of the general treatment of articles, regardless of the language background of your students. Make a list of abstract nouns like *life*, *youth*, *old age*, *beauty*, *honor*, *intelligence*, and so on, and nouns that refer to concepts or subjects like *education*, *globalization*, *culture shock*, *anthropology*, *philosophy*, and so on. Explain that these nouns have no articles when they refer to an idea or concept. Provide some examples of this, as illustrated in (82).

(**82**) a. Youth fades quickly into middle age.
　　　　b. Life is difficult.
　　　　c. Reality is often hard to accept.

Discuss the meanings of these nouns as they appear in the example sentences. Have your students make up their own sentences with these nouns and discuss what they mean. Collect examples of sentences that you have found in your students' compositions where these nouns are intended to mean a concept or subject but are preceded by *the*. Present these sentences along with some sentences where the abstract nouns are correctly used without articles and ask your students to identify the grammatically correct ones.

Activity 10: The Omission of Indefinite and Definite Articles (Advanced)

When teaching students whose L1s do not have anything comparable to English articles, such as Korean, Polish, or Russian, it is a good idea to collect short passages and convert them into cloze passages by deleting all the articles. A variety of passages taken from different sources – magazine articles, newspaper articles and academic articles – will help familiarize your students with article use in different registers and provide them with the widest range of article use.

After the students fill in the articles, discuss any disparities and indicate cases where more than one type of article would be possible. Discuss any differences you may find in the occurrence of different articles across various written registers.

ENDNOTES

[1] Lourie's novel is set during the Cold War era, and Poplovsky is a KGB colonel masquerading as a cultural attaché.

[2] This is the criterion of *identifiability* referred to in Huddleston and Pullum (2002), p. 37.

[3] For this treatment, see, for example, Celce-Murcia and Larsen-Freeman (1999), p. 272.

[4] Huddleston and Pullum (2002), pp. 380–381.

[5] Biber et al. (1999), pp. 261–263.

[6] In (27d), *December* is followed by a relative clause (*when it snowed over 30 inches in two days*). Definite articles typically precede nouns that are followed by relative clauses. This is discussed later in this chapter.

[7] Poesion & Vieira (1998).

[8] Most of the usage conditions that are described in this section are derived from the third chapter in Hawkins (1978), where he expands on the original scholarship in this area by Christopherson (1939). I have also drawn on the excellent summary of article usage in Kachru (2003). Some of the examples in this section are hers or are modeled on hers.

[9] Postmodification guarantees that an article must precede the modified noun, but it does not guarantee what kind of article will be chosen. Relative clauses as well as prepositional phrases are examples of postmodification.

[10] The errors made by Spanish-speaking students are from our Spanish error corpus. The errors made by French speakers are from the *International Corpus of English Learners* (*ICLE*) of over 2 million words of EFL writing from learners with 11 different languages. These are from higher intermediate and advanced learners. See Granger (2002) and Granger, Dagneaux, and Meunier (in press) for more information on the ICLE corpus.

[11] We have seen that the insertion of definite articles before these kinds of nouns may be due to transfer with languages like Spanish. But since Korean has no morphemic representation of definite articles, it is possible that this is due to imperfect learning.

[12] Melinda Gates, Unbound. *Wall Street Journal*, B1, December 11, 2006.

[13] This description is modeled on Sibley, (2001), p. 23.

REFERENCES

Biber, D., Johansson, S., Leech, G., Conrad, S., & Finegan, E. (1999). *Longman grammar of spoken and written English*. Essex: Pearson Education.

Celce-Murcia, M., & Larsen-Freeman, D. (1999). *The grammar book: An ESL/EFL teacher's course*. 2nd ed. Boston: Heinle & Heinle.

Christopherson, P. (1939). *The articles: A study of their theory and use in English*. Copenhagen: Einar Munksgaard.

Cowan, R., Choi H-Y., & Kim, D-H. (2003). Four questions for error diagnosis and correction in CALL. *CALICO Journal*, *20* (3), 451–463.

Granger, S. (2002). A bird's-eye view of learner corpus research. In S. Granger, J. Hungard, & S. Petch-Tyson (Eds.), *Computer learner corpora, second language acquisition and foreign language teaching* (pp. 3–36). Amsterdam/Philadelphia: John Benjamins.

Granger, S., Dagneaux, F., & Meunier, F. (in press). *International corpus of learner English*. CD-ROM & Handbook. Louvaine-la-Neuve: Presses universitaires de Louvain.

Hawkins, J. A. (1978). *Definiteness and indefiniteness*. London: Croom Heim.

Heim, I. (1982). *The semantics of definite and indefinite noun phrases*. Unpublished dissertation, University of Massachusetts at Amherst.

Huddleston, R., & Pullum, G. K. (2002). *The Cambridge grammar of the English language*. Cambridge: Cambridge University Press.

Kachru, Y. (2003). On definite reference in world Englishes. *World Englishes*, *22*(4), 497–510.

Löbner, S. (1985). Definites. *Jounal of Semantics*, 4, 279–326.

Lourie, R. (1987). *Zero gravity*. New York: Harcourt Brace Jovanovitch.

Master, P. (1994). Effect of instruction on learning the English article system. In T. Odlin (Ed.), *Perspectives on pedagogical grammar* (pp. 229–252). New York: Cambridge University Press.

Pica, T. (1985). The selective impact of classroom instruction on second language acquisition. *Language Learning*, *33*(4), 465–497.

Poesion, M., & Vieira, R. (1998). A corpus-based investigation of definite description use. *Computational Linguistics 24*(2), 183–216.

Sibley, D. A. (2001). *The Sibley guide to bird life & behavior*. New York: Knopf.

Stephanides, É. (1974). *A contrastive study of the English and Hungarian article*. Budapest: Linguistics Institute of the Hungarian Academy of Sciences and Center for Applied Linguistics.

Stockwell, R. P., Bowen, J. D., & Martin, J. W. (1966). *The grammatical structures of English and Spanish*. Chicago: University of Chicago Press.

White, L. (1992). On triggering data in L2 acquisition: A reply to Schwartz and Gubala-Ryzak. *Second Language Research*, *8*, 120–137.

CHAPTER 12

Adjectives and Adverbs

INTRODUCTION

In this chapter, we consider two classes of words that have descriptive functions – adjectives and adverbs. Adjectives describe characteristics or properties of nouns.[1] Adverbs perform a similar function in modifying verbs, adjectives, and other adverbs. They also provide supplementary information about the content of clauses.

CHARACTERISTICS OF ADJECTIVES

Adjectives describe the properties of an entity that a noun represents. An adjective may describe inherent properties of the entity – for example, its color (*green*, *blue*), size (*big*, *tiny*), weight (*light*, *heavy*), age (*young*, *old*), or quality (*good*, *awful*). An adjective may also describe properties that classify or define the entity in relation to others – for example, *environmental* in *environmental factors* defines the factors as related to the environment.

Stacking of Adjectives

Unlike determiners, adjectives can occur one after another. This is referred to as "stacking." However, stacks of more than three adjectives rarely occur, and the adjectives tend to occur in a preferred order, such as the order shown in (1). Here an adjective sequence begins with an adjective of subjective judgment or evaluation (*ugly*). Then it is followed by an adjective of measurement (*old*), an adjective of color (*yellow*), and finally, a noun acting as an adjective that describes the material (*tin*) out of which the head noun (*bucket*) is made.

(**1**) An *ugly, old, yellow tin* bucket stood beside the stove.

Changing this order of the different types of adjectives, as shown in (2), produces phrases that native English speakers are uncomfortable with to a greater or lesser degree.

(**2**) a. ?an old, ugly, yellow tin bucket
    b. ?an ugly, yellow, old tin bucket
    c. ?an ugly, old, tin yellow bucket

Gradability of Adjectives

Most adjectives are gradable; that is, they can indicate degrees of a property. As shown in the table below, some gradable adjectives have comparative (*-er*) and superlative (*-est*) forms, while others use the adverbs *more* and *most* to express varying degrees. Many adjectives (e.g., *lively*) take the *-er/-est* inflections as well as *more* and *most*.[2] A great many more (e.g., *private*) take only *more/most*, while a few (e.g., *good*) allow only the *-er/-est* endings to express gradability. The facts that determine whether an adjective takes inflections or degree adverbs to form its comparative and superlative versions are discussed in Chapter 24.

ADJECTIVE	INFLECTIONS		*MORE/MOST*	
	comparative	superlative	comparative	superlative
lively	livelier	liveliest	more lively	most lively
private	*privater	*privatest	more private	most private
good	better	best	*more good	*most good

Negative gradability (i.e., describing diminishing degrees of a property) is indicated by placing *less* and *least* before adjectives to create the comparative and superlative forms, as shown in (3a) and (3b), respectively.

(**3**) a. The result was *less successful* than anticipated.
   b. His third campaign was the *least successful* of all his attempts.

Gradability of Absolute Adjectives

A number of adjectives, such as *absolute, complete, correct, essential, impossible, perfect, pregnant, ultimate,* and *unique,* have been called *absolute adjectives* because their meaning is supposedly not gradable as they express a quality that cannot be increased or decreased.[3] For example, *unique* means "one of a kind"; hence it seems both illogical and incorrect to say, for example, *That painting is very/somewhat unique.* How could something that is unique be particularly or partially unique? And yet native English speakers tend to write and say sentences like those in (4).

(**4**) a. He has the *most complete* game of the top 10 pros.
   b. After the first four months they found it *somewhat impossible* to control the outbreaks of sporadic violence.
   c. It's the *most perfect* copier ever invented.

Gradability of Participial Adjectives

Adjectives are frequently formed from present or past participles. For example, the adjective in (5a) is formed from the present participle of the verb *interest,* and the adjective in (5b) is formed from the past participle of the verb *bore.* These are referred to as *participial adjectives.*

(**5**) a. That was really an *interesting* lecture.
   b. He was standing around with a *bored* expression on his face.

Some of the more frequently used adjectives formed from present participles include *amazing, boring, corresponding, encouraging, exciting, existing, following, increasing, interesting, leading, missing, outstanding, promising, remaining, threatening, underlying, willing,* and *working.*

Frequently used adjectives formed from past participles include *advanced, alleged, armed, bored, complicated, confused, depressed, determined, disabled, disappointed, educated, excited, exhausted, frightened, interested, pleased, surprised, tired, unemployed, unexpected,* and *worried*.[4]

Participial adjectives have comparative and superlative forms only with *more* and *most* and with *less* and *least*. They cannot add *-er* and *-est*, as is illustrated by (6b) and (6d).

(6) a. That was the *most amazing* performance I've ever witnessed.
    b. *That was the *amazingest* performance I've ever witnessed.
    c. When she heard that the plane was overdue she became even *more* worried.
    d. *When she heard that the plane was overdue she became even *worrieder*.
    e. I couldn't be *less concerned*.
    f. Of the many solutions to this problem, his is the *least promising*.

There are a few exceptions to this. For example, native speakers of English might sometimes use the comparative form *tireder* instead of *more tired*.

Modification of Adjectives

A final characteristic of adjectives is that they can be modified by adverbs, as shown in (7).

            Adv   *Adj*
(7) a. These shrimp are [unusually] [large].

                 Adv   *Adj*
    b. They appear to be [remarkably] [happy].

SUMMARY

CHARACTERISTICS OF ADJECTIVES

Adjectives modify nouns by describing the inherent properties of an entity.
    Please hand me that black hat, will you?
    That old man had many nice things to say.

Adjectives can occur in a string, usually of no more than three, and in a preferred order.
    They're planning to buy a beautiful, old, brick house.
    She's wearing a big, red leather jacket.

Most adjectives are **gradable** and have comparative and superlative forms, *-er/-est* and/or *more/most*, as well as *less/least* for negative gradability. Native speakers treat even **absolute adjectives** (e.g., *absolute, unique*) as gradable.
    I thought you were taller.
    He's the happiest groom I have ever seen.
    He was the least successful of all.

> **Participial adjectives** are formed from present and past participles. They have comparative and superlative forms only with *more/most* and *less/least*.
> *That performance was amazing.*
> *She had a bored expression.*
> *She become even more worried.*
>
> Adjectives can be modified by adverbs.
> *This meeting is incredibly boring.*
> *The program proved extremely informative.*

EXERCISE 12.1

Indicate whether the comparative or superlative form of each adjective in these sentences is grammatical or ungrammatical. If a form is ungrammatical, explain why.

Example: That was the interestingest lecture that I have heard in a long time.

Answer: ungrammatical (Participial adjectives form their superlative versions with *most*, not with an *-est* ending.)

1. The test they used to measure the students' proficiency is less reliable than the one that is usually used.
2. This is the most unique example of iconography that I have ever seen.
3. She supplied a less convincing alibi than the other suspect.
4. As it got darker, the two children became worrieder and worrieder.
5. That puppy over there is a lot more lively than the others.

POSITIONS OF ADJECTIVES

Adjectives can be classified according to where they occur in sentences. *Attributive adjectives* modify the head noun in an NP and occur before that head noun, as in (8a) and (8b).

    (8) a. That *big* car is his.   *attributive*
         b. They chose a *young* man for the job.   *attributive*

Predicative adjectives, in contrast, appear after a verb and not in an NP; they may describe the subject, as in (9a), or an object, as in (9b) and (9c).

    (9) a. She is *insane.*   *predicative*
         b. You have got your priorities *wrong.*   *predicative*
         c. She found him dreadfully *dull.*   *predicative*

The vast majority of adjectives, including participial adjectives, can appear in both attributive and predicative positions, as shown in (10).

    (10) a. That elephant has a really *big* trunk.   *attributive*
          b. That elephant's trunk is really *big.*   *predicative*
          c. He gave an *interesting* talk.   *attributive*
          d. His talk was *interesting.*   *predicative*

The occurrence of participial adjectives in predicative positions following *be*, as in (10d), means English language teachers need to be able to recognize and explain the difference between participial adjectives and verb participles. A test that can often be used to distinguish between them involves degree adverbs such as *very* or *too*. Only adjectives can be modified by these two words, as indicated by (11).

(**11**) a. Her story was *very frightening*.   *present participial adjective*
b. *John was *very frightening her*.   *verb participle*
c. John was *too startled* to move.   *past participial adjective*
d. *John was *too startled* by his boss.   *verb participle*

Particular difficulties can arise with past participial adjectives. Occasionally, a form used in a sentence is ambiguous; that is, you cannot tell whether it is functioning as a past participial adjective or as a verb past participle, as illustrated in (12).

(**12**) The shop is closed at five o'clock.

Past participial adjectives describe a state (e.g., *The vase is broken*, with the past participial adjective *broken*, means the vase is in the state of being broken). If *closed*, in (12), is functioning as a participial adjective, then the sentence can be restated as *At five o'clock, the shop is no longer open* (i.e., is in the state of being closed). However, if *closed* is a past participle in a sentence in the passive voice, then the sentence can be restated as *At five o'clock someone closed the shop*. Certain past participles such as *assembled*, *broken*, and *smashed* are often ambiguous; they can be interpreted either as adjectives indicating a state or as participles expressing the passive voice. The context will usually indicate which meaning is intended, as will be discussed in greater detail in Chapter 17.

Attributive-Only Adjectives

A number of adjectives, including *drunken*, *erstwhile*, *eventual*, *future*, *mere*, *principal*, and *utter*, can appear only as modifiers of head nouns; that is, they can appear only in the attributive position, as shown in (13).

(**13**) a. At last night's party, he saw one of his *former* wives.
b. *At last night's party, he saw one of his wives who is *former*.
c. She thought that he was an *utter* fool.
d. *In terms of being a fool, he was *utter*.

Some major types of attributive-only adjectives can be established on the basis of meaning. Several of these types follow.[5] In some cases, the adjectives are attributive-only just in contexts where they are *not* expressing a property that is inherent to the referent of the head noun. For example, with *new*, we can say *his new friend* but not **His friend is new*; and yet we can say both *his new jacket* and *His jacket is new*. The reason is that *new* expresses a property that is an inherent characteristic of the jacket but not of the person.

Adjectives of Degree

Adjectives of degree describe the degree of the property expressed by the head noun. For instance, in the sentence *The show was an utter disaster*, the adjective *utter* describes the degree of the disaster. The degree expressed by such an adjective is usually absolute, as shown in (14).

(**14**) a. an *absolute* hero
b. a *complete* ballplayer
c. a *total* moron
d. *sheer* nonsense

Quantifying Adjectives

Quantifying adjectives indicate the amount, quantity, or frequency of the head noun, as illustrated in (15).

(15) a. the *only* way
     b. the *entire* crew
     c. an *occasional* cloud
     d. the *usual* suspects

Adjectives of Time and Location

Adjectives of time and location place a head noun within a particular time frame or location, as shown in (16).

(16) a. a *future* appointment
     b. an *old* friend
     c. his *former* girlfriend
     d. a *previous* version
     e. her *left* arm
     f. the *northeastern* provinces

Associative Adjectives

Associative adjectives do not express literal properties of a head noun but instead describe it in terms of some entity that is associated with it. For instance, the phrase *nuclear physicist* certainly does not imply that the physicist is somehow nuclear. Instead, the adjective describes the area of science in which the physicist works. Similarly, in the phrase *criminal attorney*, the adjective does not express a property of the attorney but instead describes an entity with which the attorney is associated. More examples of associative adjectives are shown in (17).

(17) a. a *mathematical* journal
     b. *urban* planning
     c. a *gothic* novelist
     d. a *public* official
     e. a *moral* dilemma

Adjective Compounds

English has a large number of *adjective compounds*, which function as adjectives. Many of these compounds combine an adjective and a word from any of various parts of speech, as exemplified in (18).

(18) a. grayish-blue   *adjective + adjective*
     b. big-name   *adjective + noun*
     c. street-smart   *noun + adjective*

Adjective compounds are also formed with past participles (*clean-shaven*) and present participles (*best-selling*). The process of compounding two nouns (*glass-bottom*) and a noun + participle (*world-renowned*, *community-planning*) is highly productive and is used particularly in fiction and in news reports.

All of these adjective compounds function as attributive adjectives, as illustrated in (19).[6]

(**19**) a. He was driving a *grayish-blue* foreign sports car.
b. There were a number of *big-name* Hollywood producers at the party.
c. Mr. Stenson turned out to be a *clean-shaven* young man dressed in a white flannel suit.
d. He has just produced his fifth *best-selling* novel and is on tour promoting it.
e. They went for a short ride in a *glass-bottom* boat to a coral reef, where they saw differently colored coral and thousands of multicolored fish.
f. He is a *world-renowned* physicist.

Some of these adjective compounds are attributive-only adjectives, although others can also be used predicatively, in which case they are written as two words. The sentences in (20) exemplify the two types; only the compounds in (20a) and (20d) can be used predicatively.

(**20**) a. His foreign sports car is *grayish blue*.
b. *The Hollywood producers were *big name*.
c. *That boat is *glass bottom*.
d. The physicist is *world renowned*.

Predicative-Only Adjectives

Predicative-only adjectives can occur only in the predicative position. They are divided into three groups.

Adjectives Beginning with the Prefix *A-*

The first group of predicate-only adjectives is formed with the prefix *a-* and includes adjectives such as *afloat, afraid, aghast, alive, asleep,* and *awake.* These cannot occur attributively, as (21b) and (21d) illustrate.

(**21**) a. The young girl was *asleep*, so she did not hear the storm outside.
b. *The *asleep* girl did not hear the storm outside.
c. The rescue squad finally discovered a man who was still *alive*.
d. *The rescue squad was happy to discover an *alive* man.

Adjectives That Take Complements

The second group of predicative-only adjectives is made up of adjectives that take complements that are either infinitives (e.g., *able to run, liable to sue*) or prepositional phrases (e.g., *devoid of fear, fraught with tension*), as shown in (22).

(**22**) a. She is *liable to make a scene*.   infinitive
b. *The *liable person* has to pay.
c. He is *devoid of any humor*.   prepositional phrase
d. *He was a *devoid comic*.

Adjectives Referring to Medical Conditions or Health

Finally, there is a small group of adjectives that refer to medical conditions or health (i.e., *faint, ill, poorly, unwell, well,* etc.) that can appear only in the predicative position, as shown in (23). The adjective *ill* can appear attributively if it is modified (e.g., *a mentally ill patient*).

(23) a. He feels *faint.*
     b. *They revived the *faint* patient.
     c. My mother is *ill.*
     d. *They took the *ill* woman to the hospital.

SUMMARY

POSITIONS OF ADJECTIVES

Adjectives can be classified as **attributive** (occurring in an NP) or **predicative** (occurring after a verb). Many adjectives can occur in both positions.

They chose a young man for the job.	attributive
The man they chose is very young.	predicative
He gave an interesting talk.	attributive
His talk was very interesting.	predicative

Attributive-only adjectives fall into the following categories (examples are in parentheses):

- **adjectives of degree** (*absolute, sheer, total, utter*)
  Ms. Johnson is an absolute asset to the department.
  At the time, we were total strangers.

- **quantifying adjectives** (*entire, occasional, only*)
  The entire team arrived late.
  You're the only person who understands me.

- **adjectives of time and location** (*future, previous, left, northern*)
  I'll keep that in mind for future projects.
  Jane is originally from northern California.

- **associative adjectives** (*economic, moral, public*)
  Voters are calling for major economic reform.
  We're facing a difficult moral dilemma.

- certain **adjective compounds** (*big-name, best-selling*)
  Steve is expecting some big-name producers to show up at this party.
  She wrote a best-selling novel.

Predicative-only adjectives include the following:

- **adjectives with the prefix a-** (*asleep, awake*)
  How long have you been awake?
  I can't believe he's still asleep!

- **adjectives taking infinitive or prepositional phrase complements** (*devoid, liable*)
  How can you be devoid of sympathy?
  This is liable to cause a problem.

- **adjectives describing medical conditions or health** (*faint, ill*)
  I'm feeling faint.
  I didn't realize you were ill.

EXERCISE 12.2

Indicate whether each sentence below is grammatical or ungrammatical. If a sentence is ungrammatical, explain why.

Example: The alive man was taken to the hospital.

Answer: ungrammatical (*Alive* is an adjective with the prefix *a-* and occurs only predicatively.)

1. Susan turned out to be the eventual winner.
2. The fireman picked up the afraid child and carried him out of the blazing building.
3. The audience was aghast when the president admitted that he was wrong.
4. The nurse helped the ill woman to a chair and called the doctor on duty.
5. He has a full-time job now.

ADJECTIVE PHRASES

Adjective phrases can consist of just an adjective, as in (24a), of an adjective with a preceding adverb, as in (24b), with a following prepositional phrase, as in (24c), or with both an adverb and prepositional phrase, as in (24d).

$$\qquad\qquad\qquad Adj$$
(24) a. The customers were [angry].

$$\qquad\qquad Adv \qquad Adj$$
b. He was [[extremely] [upset]].

$$\qquad\qquad Adj \qquad\qquad PP$$
c. He was [[upset] [about the poor service]].

$$\qquad\qquad Adv \qquad Adj \qquad\qquad PP$$
d. He was [[extremely] [upset] [about the poor service]] .

Many adjectives are normally followed by a particular preposition. For instance, when *upset* occurs in predicative position, it is often followed by the preposition *about*, as in (24c) and (24d). The prepositions *at*, *by*, and *with* are also common with *upset*. Other adjectives take different prepositions. For example, *grateful* normally takes a prepositional phrase headed by *for*, as (25) illustrates.

(25) My father was *grateful for* the police officer's intervention.

Since English language learners sometimes choose the wrong preposition when attempting to speak or write sentences such as (24c) and (25), and teachers are not always aware of the reason why such sentences are ungrammatical, adjectives that take prepositional phrase complements are presented below, grouped by the preposition they commonly occur with. Each group is illustrated by an example sentence.[7] A more complete list of adjectives like these can be found in Appendix B.

Adjective + *about*

Adjectives followed by prepositional phrases beginning with *about* include *angry, annoyed, concerned, delighted, glad, happy, mad, pleased,* and *upset*, as shown in (26). In many cases, *at* can also occur with these adjectives (e.g., *They were delighted about/at the response*).

(26) They were *concerned about* the possibility that he might refuse.

Adjective + *at*

Adjectives that are often followed by prepositional phrases beginning with *at* include *adept, aghast, alarmed, amazed, angry, awful, clever, disgusted, gifted, great, hopeless, indignant, mad, pleased, skilled, talented,* and *terrible.* This group can be divided into two subgroups based on meaning. One subgroup consists of adjectives like *amazed* and *indignant,* which convey a psychological reaction, as shown in (27a). The other subgroup consists of adjectives that describe an ability or lack of ability with regard to some activity, displayed in (27b).[8]

> (**27**) a. The author was *amazed at* the reaction he received from the critics.
> b. I am really *terrible at* sports.

Adjective + *for*

This group includes the adjectives *answerable, anxious, bad, difficult, eager, easy, good, grateful, greedy, necessary, prepared, responsible,* and *sorry.*

> (**28**) a. Everyone knows that smoking is not *good for* you.
> b. We are very *sorry for* the inconvenience.

Adjective + *with*

This is a fairly large group, which includes *angry, bored, busy, cautious, careful, conversant, cross, disappointed, enchanted, familiar, fed up, fraught, furious, happy, impatient, pleased, obsessed, riddled, satisfied, strict,* and *tinged.* An example is shown in (29).

> (**29**) Yes, I am *familiar with* that term.

SUMMARY

ADJECTIVE PHRASES

Adjective phrases can consist of just an adjective or can also include a preceding adverb and/or a following prepositional phrase.

> *My brother was angry.*
> *He was extremely angry.*
> *He was angry about the service he received at that restaurant.*

Some adjectives often appear with a particular preposition (examples are in parentheses):

- **Adj + *about*** (*angry, annoyed, pleased, delighted*)
  Kyle is still upset about his test results.

- **Adj + *at*** (*adept, angry, great, talented, terrible*)
  The author was amazed at the reaction of the press.

- **Adj + *for*** (*bad, difficult, easy, good, responsible*)
  We are very sorry for the inconvenience.

- **Adj + *with*** (*bored, busy, fed up, impatient*)
  Jason is completely obsessed with her.

Indicate whether each sentence below is grammatical or ungrammatical. If a sentence is ungrammatical, supply an appropriate correction.

Example: We were amazed with his reaction to our suggestion.

Answer: ungrammatical
       correction: at his reaction

1. Linda is terribly worried at this situation.
2. He was afraid about the possibility that his remarks might have been misunderstood.
3. Yes, I'm familiar with the program.
4. He's responsible with this mission, so he'll have to come up with a solution.
5. We were glad at the response we received.

CHARACTERISTICS OF ADVERBS

The traditional schoolbook definition of an adverb – a word that supplies information about *how*, *where*, *when*, *why*, and *to what extent* some action occurs – makes intuitive sense. As you will see, our classification of adverb meanings still largely reflects this definition. With regard to function, adverbs can modify adjectives, adverbs, verbs, and clauses, as illustrated in (30). More than any other part of speech, adverbs are fluid in terms of their position in a sentence. They often can be moved to various positions in a sentence without altering its meaning, and in many cases their placement may therefore depend on stylistic considerations.

(**30**) a. She had a *surprisingly high* score.   *modifying an adjective*
       b. He comes *relatively* often.   *modifying an adverb*
       c. He behaved *abominably*.   *modifying a verb*
       d. *Surprisingly*, she had a high score.   *modifying a clause*
       e. She had a high score, *surprisingly*.   *modifying a clause*

-ly and Other Adverbs

The majority of adverbs are formed by adding *-ly* to an adjective, as shown in (31).

	Adjective	*Adverb*
(**31**) a.	quick	quickly
b.	fine	finely
c.	accurate	accurately
d.	dangerous	dangerously

There are, however, some adjectives, such as *fast*, *hard*, *high*, *late*, and *low*, that have identical adverb forms. In (32a), we see *fast* as an adjective modifying the noun *worker*, but in (32b), *fast* is an adverb modifying the verb *work*.

(**32**) a. He is a *fast* worker.
       b. He works *fast*.

Adverbs formed by adding *-ly* to adjectives can have the same basic meaning as the adjectives from which they are formed, as in (33a) and (33b), but adverbs that have the same form as their corresponding adjectives often do not. In (34a), for instance, the meaning of the adjective *dead* is "deceased," but the adverb *dead* in (34b) means "completely" or "absolutely."

(33) a. He tried on the suit and found that it was a *tight* fit.
    b. He gripped the dog's collar *tightly*.

(34) a. She cried when she saw the *dead* dog.
    b. You're *dead* right.

Types of Adverbs

Adverbs fall into several types, based on the meaning they express. The most commonly recognized types are shown below, with example sentences.[9]

Manner Adverbs

Manner adverbs describe *how* the action expressed by the verb is carried out. Examples of manner adverbs include *erratically, hesitatingly, loudly, methodically, quickly, quietly,* and *slowly.*

(35) He walked *quickly* across the plaza.

Degree Adverbs

Degree adverbs describe *how much* or the *degree to which* the verbal action is carried out. These adverbs include *awfully, barely, completely, dreadfully, enormously, extremely, greatly, hugely, infinitely, minutely, really, relatively, slightly, somewhat,* and *thoroughly.*[10] Degree adverbs that modify only adjectives and other adverbs include *rather* and *very.*

(36) a. The price of stocks has increased *enormously.*
    b. I agree *completely* with everything that has been said.

Duration Adverbs

Duration adverbs answer the question *How long does the action go on?* These adverbs include *briefly, momentarily, permanently,* and *temporarily.*

(37) He's *temporarily* staying with his cousin until he finds a new place.

Frequency Adverbs

Frequency adverbs, like *always, constantly, continually, never, occasionally, often, regularly, sometimes,* and *usually,* answer the question *How often does the action occur?*

(38) She *often* comes in over an hour late.

Time Adverbs

Time adverbs, like *already, earlier, later, now, subsequently,* and *then,* answer the question *When did the action occur?*

(39) He has *already* spoken to her about it.

Instrumental Adverbs

Instrumental adverbs answer the question *By what means was this done?* They are formed by adding *-ly* to a corresponding adjective (e.g., *mechanical, mechanically; hydraulic, hydraulically*).

(40) It has been *mathematically* proven to be correct.

Place Adverbs

Place adverbs answer the question *Where did the action occur?* They are a diverse set, consisting of forms created by adding -*ly* to an adjective (e.g., *local, locally*) and of others such as *abroad, inside, here, outside,* and *there.*

> (**41**) a. The grapes are grown *locally.*
>   b. The owner of the restaurant told them to take their argument *outside.*

Additive and Restrictive Adverbs

Additive adverbs show that something additional was done or something was added to something else, as shown in (42a) and (42b). They include *also, as well, even,* and *too. Exclusively, just, merely, only, purely,* and *solely* are referred to as *restrictive* or *restrictive focus adverbs* because they restrict the meaning of an action or proposition.[11]

> (**42**) a. The thief *also* took the VCR.   *additive adverb*
>   b. The thief took the VCR *too.*   *additive adverb*
>   c. You can *only* get off at this stop.   *restrictive adverb*

Act-Related Adverbs

Act-related adverbs provide background or motive for the action expressed by the verb. They include *deliberately, expressly, knowingly, voluntarily,* and *willfully.*

> (**43**) She *deliberately* left the gas on.

Stance Adverbs

Stance adverbs constitute a special category of act-related adverbs. They express the speaker or writer's attitude or judgment about the content of a clause. In the examples in (44), the stance adverbs *foolishly* and *regrettably* indicate the speaker or writer's attitude about the actions described in these sentences.

> (**44**) a. Alice *foolishly* tried to have John fired.
>   b. He *regrettably* chose to ignore my advice.

Stance adverbs can indicate a degree of certainty, as in (45a), or doubt, as in (45b), that the speaker or writer has about the content of a clause.

> (**45**) a. He will *undoubtedly* experience some feelings of remorse when he hears the
>   bad news about his old friend.
>   b. It is *probably* not as luxurious as the car he owned.

Other stance adverbs of certainty are *arguably, assuredly, decidedly, definitely, incontestably,* and *incontrovertibly.* Additional examples of adverbs that express a degree of doubt include *conceivably, imaginably, maybe, perhaps,* and *possibly.*

Stance adverbs like *allegedly, apparently, purportedly,* and *reportedly* are used in academic reports and in journalism to indicate that something is supported by evidence while at the same time taking an objective stance toward that evidence or declining to reveal its source, as illustrated in (46).

> (**46**) a. The king *reportedly* refused to eat his asparagus.
>   b. The request for discretionary spending by the president will *apparently* exceed what Congress had anticipated.

Stance adverbs such as *generally/in general*, *largely*, *mainly/in the main*, and *typically* limit the generality of a proposition. Examples are shown in (47).

(47) a. Young children *typically* utter their first words near their first birthday.
b. New assistant professors *generally* have a teaching load of two courses per semester.

A small number of stance adverbs, such as *in fact*, *for a fact*, *really*, and *truly*, express the idea that a proposition reflects reality, as illustrated in (48).

(48) *In fact*, there is no scientific evidence that any one race is superior to any other.

Phrases such as *in our opinion*, *in our view*, and *from our perspective*, illustrated in (49), are considered stance adverbs because they indicate that a proposition is true or accurate in the opinion of the speaker or writer.

(49) *In our view*, his proposal is a step in the wrong direction.

Stance adverbs such as *sort of*, *kind of*, and *roughly* are referred to as *hedges* because they express a degree of imprecision and allow the speaker to avoid making a definitive statement. The hedge in (50) comes from a conversation; the hedge in (51) comes from an academic text.[12]

(50) I ain't seen this series. I just *sort of* remember from the last series.

(51) The ratio of clerks to total employees in the same manufacturing industries *roughly* averages 9 percent.

Connective Adverbs

Adverbs that link sentences to other sentences, such as *additionally*, *alternatively*, *moreover*, and *therefore*, are often referred to as *connective* or *linking adverbs*, or *discourse connectors*. They express a wide range of meanings, including addition, as in (52a); concession, as in (52b); contrast; summation; result; and transition. These adverbs will be covered in detail in Chapter 26.

(52) a. The use of hydrogen would reduce the price of fuel for vehicles. *Additionally*, it would be good for the environment.
b. It has been reported that the company has received several new orders from Asian countries. *However*, company officials would not confirm this.

SUMMARY

CHARACTERISTICS OF ADVERBS

Adverbs can modify adjectives, other adverbs, verbs, and clauses.
The meeting was enormously successful.
Sam and Chris travel relatively often.
They quickly climbed the stairs to the apartment.
Regrettably, he ignored our advice.

continued

A majority of adverbs are formed by adding *-ly* to adjectives; others have the same form as adjectives.

He drives dangerously.
He works fast.

Adverbs can be divided into the following categories (examples are in parentheses):

- **manner adverbs** (*loudly, quietly, slowly*)
  He tiptoed quietly across the plaza.
  Janet plays her guitar loudly every evening.

- **degree adverbs** (*awfully, enormously, thoroughly*)
  The price of stocks has increased enormously.

- **duration adverbs** (*briefly, momentarily, temporarily*)
  Helen paused briefly to catch her breath.

- **frequency adverbs** (*always, continually, constantly, often*)
  She often comes in over an hour late.

- **time adverbs** (*already, earlier, later, now, subsequently, then*)
  He then decided to change his plans and go back to New York.

- **instrumental adverbs** (*arithmetically, hydraulically, mathematically*)
  The plane is hydraulically lifted off the floor of the hangar.

- **place adverbs** (*abroad, nationally, regionally,* and *locally*)
  The grapes that this juice was made from are grown locally.

- **additive adverbs** (*too* and *also*) and **restrictive adverbs** (*just, only, merely, purely*)
  The thief took our VCR too.

- **act-related adverbs** (*deliberately, expressly, knowingly*)
  She deliberately suppressed valuable information.

- **stance adverbs** a category of act-related adverbs (*foolishly, rudely, wisely, regrettably*), as well as **hedges** (*kind of, sort of, roughly*)
  Regrettably, she chose to ignore my advice.
  I sort of remember what happened.

- **connective adverbs** (*additionally, alternatively, moreover, therefore*)
  Additionally, it would be good for the environment.

EXERCISE 12.4

In each sentence that follows, identify the adverb by its type (manner, degree, time, instrumental, place, additive, act-related, stance, connective).

Example: She often spends hours in front of her computer.

Answer: Often = frequency adverb

1. Investments in technology stocks have decreased sharply.
2. I kind of think that he said something derogatory about her.
3. He rarely comes in on Friday.

4. She wisely decided to talk to her husband before accepting their offer.
5. Assistant professors are typically expected to produce one article per year.
6. She backed slowly away from the snake, which was coiled and ready to strike.
7. He deliberately sabotaged our efforts.
8. She now lives in a small apartment.
9. He only goes there on Friday.

POSITIONS OF ADVERBS

In this section, we will look at the positions that adverbs can occupy in a sentence. This varies depending on what constituent the adverb modifies.

Modifying Adjectives and Adverbs

Adverbs precede the adjectives and other adverbs they modify, as shown in (53). Since adverbs can modify adverbs, stacking is of course permitted, as shown in (53b). Nonetheless, as a general rule, stacking that exceeds two adverbs before an adjective, as in (53c), sounds clumsy and will probably be avoided in writing, although such sentences might be uttered by an excited speaker.[13]

(53) a. It was a really beautiful ceremony.   *adverb adjective*
    b. He gave her a really incredibly beautiful ring.   *adverb adverb adjective*
    c. *He got her a really, fantastically, incredibly beautiful ring.

Modifying Verbs

Adverbs that modify verbs can occur in several positions in a sentence but never between a verb and its object, as the comparisons in (54) show.

(54) a. He *often* takes the metro.
    b. *He takes *often* the metro.
    c. She *sometimes* reads detective novels.
    d. *She reads *sometimes* detective novels.

The possible positions that an adverb that modifies a verb can occupy are the following: sentence initial, before a main verb (including between an auxiliary or modal and a main verb), between the main verb and a following element such as a PP, and sentence final.

Adverbs from all of the types discussed earlier can appear before a main verb. This is the favored position for verb modification. Some types are shown in (55).

(55) a. He *quickly* slipped the key into his pocket.   *manner*
    b. He *really* enjoyed the concert.   *degree*
    c. He *briefly* considered the proposal before he rejected it.   *duration*
    d. She *often* takes the bus to work.   *frequency*
    e. They have *already* seen it.   *time*
    f. It was *arithmetically* confirmed.   *instrumental*
    g. They *expressly* asked him to do it.   *act-related*

Sentences (56a) through (56d) show the placement of adverbs after a verb and before another constituent that is not an object NP; as (56e) and (56f) illustrate, frequency and stance adverbs generally do not seem very acceptable in this position.

(56) a. He tiptoed *quietly* out of the room.   manner
    b. The price of stocks rose *enormously* in the late 1990s.   degree
    c. He's staying *temporarily* with his parents.   duration
    d. He's standing *outside* in the rain.   place
    e. ?She works *always* in the afternoon.   frequency
    f. ?He will come *conceivably* on Tuesday.   stance

Sentences (57a) through (57f) show adverbs of various types in sentence-final position; (57g) shows that stance adverbs sometimes are not acceptable sentence finally.

(57) a. He left the room *quickly*.   manner
    b. She enjoyed the party *tremendously*.   degree
    c. He lost his balance *momentarily*.   duration
    d. He comes in late *sometimes*.   frequency
    e. She's done that *already*.   time
    f. Today navigation is done *electronically*. instrumental
    g. *She will leave *definitely*.   stance

Fewer types of adverbs are acceptable in sentence-initial position. Prominent among them are time adverbs, as in (58a), and certain frequency adverbs (e.g., *occasionally*, *sometimes*, and *usually*), as in (58b). But others, such as *always*, cannot appear in initial position, as shown by (58c). Manner adverbs also seem marginal or ungrammatical in sentence-initial position, as (58d) illustrates.

(58) a. *Earlier* he told us a different story.
    b. *Sometimes* she comes in over an hour late.
    c. **Always* she speaks English to her mother.
    d. ?*Contentedly* they would watch TV for hours.

Adverbs of a given type may differ considerably in the positions in which they can occur. For example, although many degree adverbs occur in sentence-final position, as in (57b), others, such as *almost* and *nearly*, cannot occur sentence finally, as shown in (59a) and (59b). This variation is especially evident with frequency adverbs. As shown in (57d) and (58b), *sometimes* can occur in sentence finally and sentence initially. In contrast, *always* cannot appear in initial position, as shown by (58c), except in imperative sentences, as in (59c), and sounds odd in sentence-final position, as in (59d).

(59) a. *He fainted *almost*.
    b. *She caught up *nearly*.
    c. *Always* remember to call your mother once a week.
    d. ?She speaks English to her mother *always*.

Particularly worth mentioning in this context are negative frequency adverbs (e.g., *never*, *scarcely ever*, *hardly ever*, *seldom*, *rarely*). As we saw in Chapter 4, when a frequency adverb appears sentence initially, the rule of subject–aux inversion must be applied, as in (60a) and (60b) with *do*. Otherwise, the sentence is ungrammatical, as (60c) and (60d) show.

(60) a. *Never have I* seen anything as brilliant as that.   subject–aux inversion
    b. *Seldom does John* forget to do his taxes on time.   subject–aux inversion
    c. **Never I have* seen anything as brilliant as that.
    d. **Seldom John forgets* to do his taxes on time.

Modifying Clauses

Adverbs can also modify clauses. Compare the two sentences in (61).

(**61**) a. He answered the question *foolishly*.
b. *Foolishly*, he answered the question.

In (61a), *foolishly* is a manner adverbial. It describes *how* he answered the question, that is, he gave a foolish answer. However, in (61b) *foolishly* is not a manner adverb. It is an evaluation of what he did. Answering the question was a foolish act. We do not know why it was foolish to do this, but the speaker feels that it was. Adverbs that make a comment about the entire sentence are called *adjuncts*. They are not internal to the sentence; rather, they are supplements to it and in this sense can be said to modify an entire clause. Adverb adjuncts have a comma after them. The comma represents a slight pause and falling intonation. Many stance adverbs function as adjuncts, and they may also appear at the end of the sentence or internally, set off by a comma or commas, as the examples in (62) illustrate.

(**62**) a. *Regrettably*, he had a previous engagement.
b. He is not available just now, *unfortunately*.
c. There is, *in fact*, no basis whatsoever to his claim.
d. *Reportedly*, he will announce his candidacy sometime next week.

In Embedded Clauses

Adverbs can also modify verbs in *that* clauses and infinitive clauses, called *complements*. (Complements are discussed in Chapter 21.) Example (63a) shows a possible position for the adverb *eventually* modifying the verb *have* in a *that* clause, as does (63b) for the same adverb in an infinitive clause.

That *Clause*
(**63**) a. John hopes [that he will *eventually* have his own business].

Infinitive Clause
b. John hopes [to *eventually* have his own business].

The infinitive clause could, of course, be rewritten with the adverb before the *to*, as in (64).

(**64**) John hopes *eventually* to have his own business.

When the adverb is in the position shown in (63b), the result is referred to as a *split infinitive*, a violation of a prescriptive rule, in existence since the second half of the eighteenth century, to the effect that a writer should never insert an adverb between the *to* and the verb in an infinitive. Exactly why this is bad practice was never explained. Today, infinitives are regularly split in writing and in speech, especially by adverbs like *actually*, *even*, *further*, *really*, and *utterly*. The examples in (65) are typical.

(**65**) a. It's possible to *actually* reduce the image to the size of a pinhead.
b. They had intended to *even* add a third section to the study.
c. She doesn't want to *further* exacerbate the problem.

Splitting an infinitive usually does not affect the meaning of a sentence. For example, the sentences in (63b) and (64) mean the same thing. Sometimes, however, the position of the adverb can produce two different meanings, as shown in (66).

(**66**) a. The city council voted to *immediately* approve raising the sales tax.
    b. The city council voted *immediately* to approve raising the sales tax.

In (66a), where the adverb *immediately* splits the infinitive, it is seen as modifying *approve* (i.e., the approval was immediate). But in (66b), where the adverb precedes the infinitive, it is seen as modifying the preceding verb, *voted* (i.e., the vote was immediate).[14]

ADDITIONAL INFORMATION ABOUT ADVERBS

Modifying Adjectives and Other Adverbs

Some words that are manner adverbs when they are used to modify verbs become degree adverbs when they modify adjectives. This change in meaning is illustrated in (67).

(**67**) a. After the engine had been overhauled, the
      car performed *perfectly*.   *manner*
    b. I wouldn't worry, John is *perfectly capable*. *degree*
    c. She played so *unbelievably*.   *manner*
    d. It was an *unbelievably awkward* moment. *degree*

Some degree adverbs that do not end in *-ly* are used primarily with adjectives. These adverbs, exemplified in the sentences in (68), include *darn*, *mighty*, *pretty*, *quite*, and *real*.

(**68**) a. He was *real* generous to us.
    b. We were *darn* lucky to be there.
    c. That's a *pretty* good cup of coffee.

These adverbs can also be used to modify other adverbs (e.g., *He behaved quite generously*). Another mixed set of adverbs, including *even*, *far*, *way*, and *still*, frequently modify *less*, *better*, and *more* used before an adjective, again by expressing degree, as shown in (69).

(**69**) a. That's *far more* interesting.
    b. His explanation is *way more* convincing than yours.
    c. The news was *even less* comforting than we had expected.

In Adverb Phrases

Like adjectives, adverbs can take complements consisting of prepositional phrases. However, the possibilities for such complements are considerably more limited than they are with adjectives. The structure of adverb phrases is shown in (70), in which the adverbs *independently* and *similarly* take prepositional phrase complements.[15]

                    Adv   *PP*
(**70**) a. A duel resolves disputes [*independently*] [*of the law*].
                   Adv   *PP*
    b. These purchases were handled [*similarly*] [*to all state purchases*].

Adverbs can take prepositional phrases headed by *from*, *of*, *to*, and *with*, as shown in (71).

(**71**) a. This branch operates *separately from* the rest of the company.
    b. He made his decision *independently of* the other members of the board.
    c. It is done almost *identically to* the method that is currently preferred.
    d. The information was released *simultaneously with* a description of the new plan.

SUMMARY

POSITIONS OF ADVERBS

Adverbs modifying adjectives and adverbs appear before the words. A limited amount of stacking can occur.

> *He gave her a really incredibly beautiful ring.*

Adverbs modifying verbs do not appear between a verb and an object.

> *She often takes the metro to work.*
> **She takes often the metro to work.*

These adverbs may occur:

- before a main verb (the preferred position).
> *He really enjoyed the concert.*
> *She has often taken the bus to work.*

- between the main verb and a following constituent that is not an object NP.
> *He tiptoed quietly out of the room.*
> *The price of stocks rose enormously in the late 1990s.*

- in sentence-final position.
> *She enjoyed the party tremendously.*
> *He lost his balance momentarily.*

- in sentence-initial position (time adverbials and some frequency adverbs).
> *Earlier he told us a different story.*
> *Sometimes he comes in over an hour late.*

Adverbs modifying clauses are often stance adverbs that are in sentence-initial position, followed by a comma. Set off by one or more commas, they can also appear at the end of or within sentences. These **adverbial adjuncts** are a comment on the entire sentence.

> *Frankly, I don't think he should have told her.*
> *He neglected to tell her, unfortunately.*
> *There is, in fact, no basis to his claim.*

EXERCISE 12.5

Indicate whether each sentence is grammatical. If a sentence is ungrammatical, explain why.

Example: Never we have witnessed such a daring rescue.

Answer: ungrammatical (When *never* appears in initial position, subject–aux inversion must occur.)

1. I was so dizzy that I fell down almost.
2. She gently set the baby in the crib and ran into the next room to answer the phone.
3. Seldom I have seen a performance as good as that one.
4. John doesn't drive to work every day. He takes sometimes the bus.
5. Always he has to take out the trash.

PROBLEMS THAT ESL/EFL STUDENTS HAVE WITH ADJECTIVES AND ADVERBS

A number of problems that ESL/EFL students have with adjectives and adverbs may have nothing to do with L1 transfer. For example, when Arabic-speaking ESL/EFL students frequently say, *"He drives very dangerous" instead of "He drives very dangerously" (Smith, 2001, p. 206), it is not absolutely clear that this is attributable to the fact that Arabic does not have single-word expressions equivalent to English adverbs. *Dangerously* is an adverb that is derived from the adjective form, as we saw in (31). Thus, perhaps the student simply hasn't mastered the use of the *-ly* form in this context. We would need many examples like this from a corpus of Arabic-speaking students' errors to determine the frequency of occurrence, and, more importantly, if this error is a persistent problem that warrants targeting in the classroom.

With other problems, the L1 clearly seems to be implicated. One of these is the use of a present participle adjective in contexts in which a past participle is required (e.g., *I am very boring* for *I am very bored*). This problem is actually more complex than it seems, and is discussed in greater detail in Chapter 21. Other attested errors that appear to be due to L1 transfer follow.

Ungrammatical Adjective + *to* Constructions (Spanish)

In Chapter 8, we saw that Spanish speakers often produce errors such as *a precise method to define a characteristic* instead of *a precise method of defining a characteristic*. This happens because the students follow their L1 pattern of NP *de* + infinitive. The same error occurs with adjectives. Spanish adjectives are also followed by *de* and a verb in the infinitive form. The corresponding English adjective usually is followed by the preposition *of* and a verb in the present participle form. When a Spanish speaker follows the L1 pattern with an adjective like *capaz* ("capable"), an error like the one in (72) occurs.

(72) *The student, who failed a test in the past and now he *is capable to pass* the test after some preparation, knows that he is not a fool.

Positions of Adverbs (Spanish, French)

The position of adverbs in other languages differs from English, and this results in speakers of these languages producing ungrammatical English sentences. The sentence in (73) was written by an intermediate level student whose L1 is Spanish. As noted earlier, the frequency adverb *always* cannot appear sentence initially; the equivalent in Spanish, *siempre*, can.

(73) *Always* the teachers talk in English.

French permits the occurrence of frequency adverbs between verbs and objects, as shown in (74a). English does not, as shown in (74c). Notice also, in (74d), that the common position for English frequency adverbs is not permitted in French.

(74) a. *Jean   regarde   souvent   la   télévision.*
        John   watches   often   the   television
     b. John often watches television.
     c. *John watches often television.
     d. *Jean souvent regarde la télévision.*

French speakers often place frequency adverbs in the position illustrated in (74c), producing an ungrammatical sentence. Learning to adopt the position that is correct for English appears to be particularly difficult. White (1991) conducted an experiment in which 25 French Canadian students received three months of form-focused instruction that incorporated information about the correct and incorrect positions of English frequency adverbs. The instruction was initially successful. The students demonstrated that they had learned that these adverbs should not occur in the position shown in (74c). But a year later, when a subgroup of these students was retested, it was found that they accepted this incorrect position as possible in English.[16] Apparently, the instruction had only a temporary effect. In a later study, Trahey and White (1993) exposed French Canadian speakers to many examples (via input flood) of English sentences with correct adverb placement. The learners eventually began to use and recognize English sentences with the correct placement of adverbs, but they still accepted and used the sentences with the French order.

The results of these two studies suggest that French speakers persistently put English adverbs between verbs and objects, because they follow the position of occurrence in the L1. We should note, however, that the English learners in both studies were high school students. Since we have no data showing that adult language learners cannot overcome this problem with the assistance of periodic focus-on-form activities, it seems worthwhile to address it in the classroom.

Negative Frequency Adverbs in Initial Position (Romance Languages)

In Romance languages (e.g., Portuguese, Spanish, Italian), sentences that begin with negative adverbs like *never*, *seldom*, *rarely*, and *hardly* do not undergo subject–aux inversion, as the Portuguese example in (75) illustrates.

> (**75**) *Raremente   o   Jorge   esquece   de   fazer   o   seu   dever de casa.*
>   rarely   Jorge   forgets   to   do   his   work of home
>   "Rarely does Jorge forget to do his homework."

Following this L1 pattern, Portuguese English learners will often neglect to apply subject–aux inversion to English sentences with initial negative adverbs, producing ungrammatical sentences like (76), where *does* should appear before the subject.

> (**76**) *Rarely Jorge forgets to do his homework.

This error is apparently fairly persistent, perhaps because initial negative adverbs do not occur very often; students have little occasion to write such sentences.

SUGGESTIONS FOR TEACHING ADJECTIVES AND ADVERBS

The teaching of adjectives normally begins at the beginning level. ESL/EFL students are typically taught the basic position of high-frequency adjectives of color, size, weight, and so on. For beginners, some work on the relative order of adjectives may be helpful; activities 1 and 2 show how this topic might be introduced.

Teaching Adjectives

Activity 1: Forming Sentences with Adjectives (Beginning Through Low Intermediate)

Try a communicative activity that encourages the use of adjectives through role play. The context of the role play is a lost-and-found situation. Divide the class into pairs of students. Student A plays the role of someone who has lost something, and Student B is in charge of the Lost and Found Office. Prepare a list of adjectives of size, color, and age, some of which can be compound adjectives (e.g., *medium-sized*, *sky-blue*), and a list of things that are typically lost (luggage, rings, watches, etc.). It is preferable to have visuals to explain the meanings of the adjectives and items. Give these lists to Student A, who then uses them to inquire about something he or she has lost. Student B can ask Student A for more descriptive adjectives by requesting a more detailed description of the item (e.g., "Well, we have a lot of brown suitcases, can you describe it a little more?"). Student A should then expand the description (e.g., "Well, it's also old and scratched"). If you wish to extend this activity to practice the relative order of adjectives (see Activity 2), Student B would then repeat this added information by putting it into a noun phrase with the adjectives in the proper order (e.g., "OK, so it's an old, brown, scratched suitcase").

Activity 2: Relative Order of Adjectives (Beginning Through Low Intermediate)

Create two tables like those shown below.[17] You may choose to have students look up the meanings of any adjectives and nouns that they do not know, or you can define the words in class, using pictures and objects. This is a TBLT (Task-Based Language Teaching) task, and in the pretask stage, the students take the tables home to study the first table and to practice making sentences using the adjectives and nouns in the second table. In order to help them construct NPs that have more than one adjective before the noun, go over the order shown in the first table. Mention that sequences of more than three adjectives rarely occur and that the more common sequences are size + shape + color (*big, round, green vase*) and shape + color (*long, black car*).

	ADJECTIVES							HEAD NOUN
Article or Number	**Opinion**	**Size**	**Shape**	**Condition**	**Age**	**Color**	**Origin/ Material**	
three	nice	little	oval		antique		Spanish	dressers
the					old	black		chair
a		huge	round		modern		plastic	table
some					new	blue	linen	sheets
an	ugly			cracked				mirror
a	beautiful				old	reddish-brown	cherry	desk

Next, ask the students to take the tables home and make sentences about the items in the second table using sequences of adjectives like those shown in the first.

ITEMS AROUND THE HOUSE		
Items	**Size/Height/Shape**	**Color**
stove, jar, microwave, coffeemaker, refrigerator, toaster, knife	small, large, big, long, tall, wide, sharp	black, tan, white, ivory, blue
mattress, bed, bedspread, sheets, pillow, blanket, dresser, mirror, table	king-size, queen-size, single, linen, cotton, mahogany, circular, oval, small, large, long, wide	blue, white, beige, gray-green, pink, red, yellow
couch, sofa, rug, chair, nightstand, coffee table	long, wide, narrow, large, small, leather, rectangular, square, oval, low, thick	beige, cream, green, blue, black, red, brown, yellow
desk, lamp, telephone, paper	rectangular, large, small, tall, metal, wood, thick, thin, letter-size	beige, black, white, colored
goldfish, bird, tropical fish, cat, dog	small, large, big	orange, blue-green, red, black, yellow, brown, white

In class the next day, the students pair off, with one taking the role of the shopper and the other the role of the salesperson. The student who is the shopper chooses the kind of shop (pet store, department store, hardware store, furniture store, etc.). Then the pair begin the role play, which is similar to that in Activity 1. The salesperson should be given some options to use in responding to the requests of the shopper in order to keep the conversation going (e.g., "I'm not sure that we have a mahogany table, but we have a nice cherry table. We have a long sofa in that color. I have a narrow couch in that color. Would you like to see it?"). After the students have role-played the shopping task, if appropriate, send them out to look for items in a store. In this way, they can have the experience of using adjectives in describing items to a real salesperson.

Activity 3: Participial Adjectives (Intermediate)

You can focus on the contrast in meaning between present participial adjectives and past participial adjectives by selecting common pairs and using them in related sentences. Write *interested* and *interesting* on the board, and below the words write sentences using the words, such as "I am very interested in that subject" and "That was a very interesting lecture." Explain the notion of being *interested* in something ("Interested describes how the person feels about the subject") versus that of being *interesting* ("Interesting describes the lecture"). Then hand out slips of papers with pairs of sentences like the ones shown in (77), and have the students work with a partner to decide which participles are appropriate for the blanks. You may want students to draw an arrow from each participle to the noun it modifies. Use the common participial adjectives listed on pages 239–240 to create other pairs of sentences.

(77) encouraged/encouraging
We got some _____ results from the last two experiments.
We were _____ by the results of the last two experiments.

bored/boring
He thought that it was a very _____ lecture.
He was definitely _____ by the lecture.

confused/confusing
He gave a rather _____ answer. I didn't really understand it.
I was _____ by the answer he gave. I didn't really understand it.

Activity 4: Adjective + Preposition Collocations (Intermediate Through Advanced)

This activity is essentially vocabulary building that also has syntactic value. Select some of the high-frequency adjectives from the adjective phrase categories listed in Appendix B, for example, the adjective + *of* NP category (e.g., *afraid*, *aware*, *certain*, *convinced*). On the board, write one of these adjectives with which your students are familiar, for example, *afraid of*. Ask students to tell you what they are *afraid of*. Have them respond in full sentences and write the sentences on the board. Next, write the rest of the adjectives on the board. Ask the class questions with these adjectives (e.g., *Who are you proud of? What are you fond of?*). Point out that in all of these expressions, the adjective is followed by *of*. Divide the class into small groups and have them write down as many sentences as they can think of using these adjective + *of* combinations. Move around the room and check the sentences. When the students have finished, have them write down a conversation that uses them all. Then have each group present its dialog to the class.

Use this approach to systematically work through other adjectives that are followed by prepositional phrases. Do this from time to time over different semesters – a comprehensive treatment of adjective + preposition collocations will take quite a while. Treat this as a special form of vocabulary expansion that is spread across levels, including the advanced level. Test your students periodically using cloze passages.

If you teach students with Romance L1s, collect examples of transfer errors involving adjectives and following clauses. Using PI activities and editing activities like the one in Activity 6, you should help eradicate these errors.

Teaching Adverbs

A good way to integrate adverbs into the ESL/EFL syllabus is to use situations in which certain types have to be used for a classroom activity that focuses on meaning and form. For example, talking about concerts, movies, books, and TV shows that students have seen or current events that they have read about is a good vehicle for practicing degree adverbs modifying adjectives. Students can describe these as *awfully dull*, *really exciting*, *slightly boring*, *thoroughly engrossing*, and so on. Activity 5 shows how this might be done with frequency adverbs modifying verbs.

Activity 5: Frequency Adverbs (Low Intermediate)

On the board, write the positive frequency adverbs *sometimes*, *often*, *always*, *occasionally*, and *usually* in one column and the negative frequency adverbs *never*, *rarely*, *scarcely ever*, *hardly ever*, and *seldom* in another. As you write each adverb, ask the students its meaning. Next, write the names of four activities. Examples are listed below. Choose activities that you think students might do with varying degrees of frequency (usually, probably, seldom, never).

ACTIVITIES

watch television	go dancing	go to a rock concert
eat at the student union	have coffee with friends	go to a football game
go to the movies	rent a movie	phone your parents
go out on Saturday night	take the bus to campus	go mountain climbing
	go shopping	go skiing
study in the library	go swimming	go biking

Then say, "I am going to ask you some questions about these activities, and I want you to give me an answer with a complete sentence that has one of these adverbs in it." Demonstrate this with a student by asking, "How often do you [the activity]?" Remind the student to respond in a complete sentence. Then ask the students to give you more examples of activities that they engage in with varying degrees of frequency. Add these to the items on the board. Have students pair off and give each pair two copies of a longer list that you have prepared. Students take turns asking their partner about the activities in the list and giving full sentence replies.

Activity 6: Focusing on Correct Position (Intermediate Through Advanced)
The teaching of adverbs should include focusing on the insertion of adverbs between verbs and NP objects.

To focus students' attention on the correct position, try a discovery approach like that shown in Carter, Hughes, and McCarthy (2000). Present your students with examples of frequency (and other) adverbs used in real texts and then ask them to figure out (with careful prompting) the rules describing where they usually occur. You may also want to introduce the issue of adverb position in this way.

To address the problem that French speakers have, present the students with written sentences that have the correct subject + adverb + verb + object pattern and the incorrect (L1) subject + verb + adverb + object pattern. Ask whether each sentence is correct. When students identify the SVAO examples as not correct, ask them why. Let them provide correct examples. Repeat this with another set of sentences presented orally.

Next, hand out a short piece of writing (e.g., a paragraph from a story, an e-mail message) that contains examples of the issue. Have students work in pairs. One person reads the passage sentence by sentence, and the other stops the reader when he or she hears a sentence that may have an adverb in the wrong position. The two students then decide whether there is an error. If it is determined that there is an error, the two students decide together how to correct it. Walk around the class and monitor the activities but do not provide definitive answers. When all of the pairs have finished the passage, go over it as a class. For each sentence, call on a pair, asking a member of the pair to read it and to state whether it has an error. When a student says yes, ask the student to identify the error and to give a correction. Affirm the correction or prompt the student by referring to the rule for adverb placement.

Repeat this process over several semesters and include examples of other errors like those shown in (56), (58), and (73). An example of a passage for editing that includes several types of adverb placement errors is shown in (78).

(**78**) Hi, Alicia!

> I am sending you this e-mail to tell you how things are going for me this summer in Vancouver. I didn't write sooner because I couldn't get an Internet connection. But now I have one. I am taking English classes, and I am having a good time in this beautiful city. Vancouver is really pretty and is right on the water. My classes are good. Always my teachers speak English, so I get lots of practice. I live pretty close to the school, so I take often the bus from my apartment to my classes. There are a lot of students from my school in the building where I live. So I never am alone, and I don't get too homesick. Sometimes on the weekend I take a short trip with my friends outside the city. The weather has been good. Hardly ever we get a lot of rain. I think maybe it rained only once. Talk to you soon.

ENDNOTES

[1] Adjectives exist in all languages. They are either premodifiers of nouns, as in English (i.e., [adjective] [noun]), or postmodifiers of nouns, as in French (i.e., [noun] [adjective]).

[2] *More* and *most* have other grammatical functions. The use of *more . . . than* to link clauses of comparison is discussed in Chapter 24. As shown in Chapter 10, *more* and *most* also function as quantifiers.

[3] See Huddleston and Pullum (2002), pp. 531–532, for a more detailed account.

[4] Biber et al. (1999), p. 530.

[5] The semantic types listed here are identified and exemplified in greater detail in Huddleston and Pullum (2002), pp. 555–559.

[6] Some of these adjective compounds can appear in the predicate position when they are used as separate words (i.e., without a hyphen). For example, we can say, "The color of the car was grayish blue."

[7] All examples in the text discussion and in Appendix B are drawn from Huddleston and Pullum (2002). Many of these can take phrases beginning with other prepositions.

[8] Huddleston and Pullum (2002), p. 543.

[9] The terms *manner*, *degree*, *duration*, and *frequency adverb* are fairly conventional. The category *act-related adverb* comes from Huddleston and Pullum (2002). Other linguists refer to these as *stance adverbs*. For a more complete list of semantic adverb types, see Huddleston and Pullum (2002), p. 576.

[10] Biber et al. (1999), pp. 554–555. Subdivide these into two subcategories, *intensifiers* and *diminishers*.

[11] See Biber et al. (1999), p. 556, and Huddleston and Pullum (2002), pp. 586–595.

[12] Examples (50) and (51) are from Biber et al. (1999), p. 557.

[13] Huddleston and Pullum (2002), p. 573.

[14] The examples are modeled on Huddleston and Pullum (2002), p. 582.

[15] These examples are modeled on Huddleston and Pullum (2002), p. 571.

[16] Working within the UG principles or parameters paradigm of L2 acquisition, (Chapter 3, page 45), White (1991) argued that the different positions that adverbs can assume in French and English can be explained by a *verb movement parameter*. French and English have different parameter values. White claimed that the results of her experiment showed that the use of negative evidence (teaching that incorporates correction or showing L2 learners what is not grammatically possible in the L2) is necessary to get them to reset parameter values and restructure their interlanguage grammars. Schwartz and Gubala-Ryzak (1992) disputed this and concluded that negative evidence will produce only short-term results that do not constitute

restructuring. The view that the L1 influences L2 acquisition is widely acknowledged in the parameter setting model, but the question of how it interacts with UG is still under investigation. (See Montrul, [2000] for empirical evidence and a discussion of the interaction factors.) The issue of whether negative evidence can cause L2 learners to change their interlanguage is still debated. Studies like Slabakova (2002) suggest that negative evidence in the classroom can lead to higher grammatical accuracy.

[17] This is a variation on a TBLT activity suggested by Macias (2005). I have expanded her table somewhat as well as the directions of how it might be used. Ur (1998) also has some inventive activities that use tables of adjectives for classroom teaching.

REFERENCES

Biber, D., Johansson, S., Leech, G., Conrad, S., & Finegan, E. (1999). *Longman grammar of spoken and written English*. Essex: Pearson Education Limited.

Carter, R., Hughes, R., & McCarthy, M. (2000). *Exploring grammar in context*: *Grammar reference and practice*. Cambridge: Cambridge University Press.

Huddleston, R., & Pullum, G. K. (2002). *The Cambridge grammar of the English language*. Cambridge: Cambridge University Press.

Macias, C. (2005). Task-based instruction for teaching Spanish to professionals. In B. L. Leaver, & J. R. Willis (Eds.), *Task-based instruction in foreign language education* (pp. 142–160). Washington, D.C.: Georgetown University Press.

Montrul, S. (2000). Transitivity alternations in L2 acquisition: Toward a modular view of transfer. *Studies in Second Language Acquisition, 22*(2), 229–273.

Schwartz, B., & Gubala-Ryzak, M. (1992). Learnability and grammar reorganization in L2A: Against negative evidence causing the unlearning of verb movement. *Second Language Research 8*(1), 1–38.

Slabakova, R. (2002). The compounding parameter in second language acquisition. *Studies in Second Language Acquisition 24*, 507–540.

Smith, B. (2001). Arabic speakers. In M. Swan & B. Smith (Eds.), *Learner English: A Teacher's Guide to Interference and Other Problems*. 2nd ed. (pp. 195–213). Cambridge: Cambridge University Press.

Trahey, M., & White, L. (1993). Positive evidence and preemption in the second language classroom. *Studies in Second Language Acquisition. 15*, 181–204.

Ur, P. (1998). *Grammar practice activities*. Cambridge: Cambridge University Press.

White, L. (1991). Adverb placement in second language acquisition: Some effects of positive and negative evidence in the classroom. *Second Language Research*, 7, 133–61.

CHAPTER 13

Pronouns

INTRODUCTION

Pronouns are grammatical forms that substitute in some way for an NP or for an entire clause. In this chapter, we look at the different kinds of pronouns that exist in English and the learning problems they pose for English language learners. We also examine certain conventions of pronoun use that learners must be sensitive to when writing in English. Relative pronouns, which introduce relative clauses, will be discussed in Chapter 18.

ANAPHORA AND PERSONAL PRONOUNS

In (1), the pronouns *she* and *it* in the second sentence substitute for *Alan's wife* and *your plan* in the preceding sentence. The element that the pronoun substitutes for is called the *antecedent*[1] of that pronoun.

> (1) Don't mention your plan to Alan's wife. *She* might not approve of *it*.

The connection between pronouns and their antecedents is called *anaphora*. The anaphora can be *intersentential* (across sentences), as in (1), or it can be *intrasentential* (within a sentence), as in (2), in which the pronoun *it* refers to an NP in the same sentence, *the briefcase*.

> (2) He set *the briefcase* down on the table before he opened *it*.

In English sentences, pronouns usually occur after their antecedents, as in (1) and (2). This is called *forward anaphora*.[2] However, it is also possible for pronouns to precede their antecedents, as in (3), in which the two instances of *they* and the following pronoun *them* refer to NPs that come later in the sentence (*the boys* and *pancakes*). This order is called *backward anaphora*.

> (3) Because *they* discovered that *they* really didn't like *them*, *the boys* decided not to order *pancakes* for breakfast anymore.

Although English has both backward and forward anaphora, forward anaphora predominates. Some languages, like Japanese, have predominantly backward anaphora.

Personal Pronouns

English has two sets of *personal pronouns*; one is used in subject position in sentences, the other as objects of verbs or prepositions.

	SUBJECT PRONOUNS		OBJECT PRONOUNS	
	Singular	**Plural**	**Singular**	**Plural**
1st person	I	we	me	us
2nd person	you	you	you	you
3rd person	he/she/it	they	him/her/it	them

The pronoun *one* is used as an alternative to *you*, in the sense of "a person," as is illustrated in (4b). It conveys a more formal, less personal tone and appears more often in written than in spoken English.[3]

> (4) a. *You* can't be too careful with money.   *informal*
> b. *One* can't be too careful with money.   *formal*

Variability of Personal Pronouns

In certain structures, native speakers' use of subject and object pronouns is more variable than the previous definitions suggest.

Predicate Nominals

According to the prescriptivist rule, subject personal pronouns should always be used when the pronoun is a predicate nominal following *be*, as illustrated in the responses in (5a) and (5c). This sounds too formal to many native speakers, however. Thus, you will often hear the object pronoun used instead, as shown in (5b) and (5d).[4]

> (5) a. Who's there? It is *I*.
> b. Who's there? It's *me*.
> c. Which one is the movie star? That is *she* over there.
> d. Which one is the movie star? That's *her* over there.

Comparisons

In *inequality comparisons*, one thing is described as greater than or less than another. In *equality comparisons*, two things are described as equal in some respect. The former kind of comparison is shown in (6), and the latter in (7). (See Chapter 24 for more on equality and inequality comparisons.)

> (6) a. He is a lot faster than *I am*.   *regular comparison*
> b. He is a lot faster than *I*.   *shortened comparison*
> c. He's a lot faster than *me*.   *shortened comparison with object pronoun*

> (7) a. She's just as strong as *I am*.   *regular comparison*
> b. She's just as strong as *I*.   *shortened comparison*
> c. She's just as strong as *me*.   *shortened comparison with object pronoun*

In (6a) and (7a), a subject pronoun and a form of the verb *be* occur after the comparison words *than* and *as*, respectively. The verb *be* may be elided to form the shortened versions in (6b) and (7b). This ellipsis leaves the subject pronoun *I* at the end of both sentences. Although subject pronouns are considered the prescriptively correct pronoun forms for shortened comparisons, native speakers will often use an object pronoun, as shown in (6c) and (7c).

Object pronouns are particularly common in shortened comparisons involving *more*, *less*, *better*, or *worse*, as illustrated in (8).

(**8**) a. He's less sophisticated than *she is.*
     b. He's less sophisticated than *her.*
     c. They were better prepared than *she was.*
     d. They were better prepared than *her.*

Why native speakers commonly select the object pronoun form over the subject form is not known. It may be that speakers view the comparison words *as* and *than* as prepositions and feel that they should therefore be followed by object forms.

In addition, native speakers sometimes use reflexive pronouns after comparison words, as shown in (9).[5] It may be that they are using the reflexive pronoun as a default strategy that allows them to avoid choosing between a subject and an object pronoun.

(**9**) a. He judged her to be a year or so younger than *himself.*
     b. She was slightly taller than *himself.*

Conjoined Personal Pronouns

Native speakers frequently do not use appropriate forms in sentences when two pronouns are conjoined by *and*. Confusion over which pronoun form to use often results in sentences like (10).

(**10**) *Just between *you* and *I*, Bill's not going to be promoted.

Here the speaker has added the subject pronoun *I* after *and*. But the pair of pronouns should be *you* and *me*, since both pronouns are functioning as objects of the preposition *between*.[6]

The following cartoon illustrates a similar instance of confusion.

While the man's echo appears to correct him, it seems that in this case either a subject or an object pronoun form would be acceptable. This is because the pronouns are operating as predicate nominals (NPs following the verb *be*), not as objects of a preposition.

The same confusion over pronoun forms is common when a pronoun is conjoined to a noun, as in (11). Here the appropriate pronoun would be *me* (not *I*) since it is the object of the preposition *by*. Some native speakers would avoid the problem by using a reflexive pronoun as in (11b).

(11) a. *The research proposal was prepared by Dr. Carver and *I*.
  b. The research proposal was prepared by Dr. Carver and *myself*.

Incorrect pronouns are also used when two pronouns or a pronoun and a noun are conjoined in subject position, as shown in the sentences in (12), spoken by a college student.

(12) a. *There's another project that is being supervised by a graduate student, and *him* and *I* are working on it.
  b. *Me* and Julie are going shopping.

Although you should teach students to use the appropriate pronouns in sentences like those in (10), (11), and (12), especially in writing, you should also tell them not to be surprised when they hear native speakers say sentences that don't follow the rules they have learned in ESL/EFL classrooms.[7]

Additional Information About Personal Pronouns

In conversation, native speakers often attach to the beginning of a sentence a noun phrase followed by a pause (represented by a comma), as shown in (13). This *peripheral noun phrase* designates a topic for the sentence. As (13d) shows, the peripheral noun phrase can also be attached to the end of a sentence. If the noun phrase contains pronouns, they will usually be object pronouns, as shown in (13a) and (13b). Another possibility is a noun and a reflexive pronoun, as in (13d).

(13) a. *You and me*, we're two of a kind.
  b. *Me and my friend Bob*, we'd been to the game.
  c. He thinks Philadelphia is going to win. *Me*, I'm betting on the Lakers.
  d. "By the way," he says, "we'll be over to see you soon, *Elsie and myself*."[8]

Like the errors in (10), (11), and (12), the peripheral noun phrases with pronouns in (13) are a feature of spoken English that English language teachers should be aware of. Your students may ask questions about them. If you are taking a grammar-in-context approach, you can show students contexts in which these peripheral NPs could be used.

SUMMARY

ANAPHORA AND PERSONAL PRONOUNS

Anaphora is the connection between a pronoun and its antecedent.

In **forward anaphora**, the antecedent precedes the pronoun.
  Jason took Emily to the library and picked her up an hour later.

In **backward anaphora**, the pronoun precedes the antecedent.
  Since they were being so noisy, I asked the boys to leave the room.

continued

In **intersentential anaphora**, the pronoun and its antecedent are in separate sentences.
The manager of the hotel had told Susan that there were lots of deer in the forest. After breakfast, she took a long walk and saw a doe with two fawns.

In **intrasentential anaphora**, the pronoun and its antecedent are in the same sentence.
I bought an apple and ate it while I strolled to the park.

Personal pronouns fall into one of two categories:

- **subject personal pronouns**

I	*we*
you	*you*
he/she/it/one	*they*

- **object personal pronouns**

me	*us*
you	*you*
him/her/it	*them*

According to the prescriptive rule, subject pronouns should be used in the predicate nominal position. However, native speakers often use object pronouns instead.
It is he!
It's him!

Similarly, despite the prescriptivist rule, object pronouns as well as subject pronouns, are used in shortened comparisons.
He's taller than I.
He's taller than me.

Conjoining two personal pronouns, or a noun and a pronoun, often causes confusion concerning which pronoun form should be used.
*He was at the reception with Joan and I.
*Me and Julie are heading out to lunch.

EXERCISE 13.1

In the following sentences, identify the antecedent of each pronoun in italics. Then identify the anaphora as intrasentential or intersentential and as forward or backward.

Example: Before she went out shopping, Beatrice told Benny to take out the trash. When she got back, she saw that he still hadn't taken *it* out.

Answer: trash = intersentential anaphora, forward

1. Joan was sure that *she* would like John, and *she* was surprised to discover that *she* didn't.
2. Crows are among the smartest birds in the animal kingdom. *They* have a sixth sense that protects *them* from the craftiest hunters.
3. Because they find *them* boring, many elementary-school-aged boys don't like to play with girls.
4. The new bicycle I bought last week was stolen from my garage. Fortunately, the police found *it* near the bus station.
5. No matter how hard *they* tried, the boys simply could not push the car out of the ditch.

EXERCISE 13.2

In each sentence that follows, indicate whether the italicized pronoun is "appropriate" according to the prescriptivist rule. For each pronoun that isn't, indicate what the appropriate pronoun would be and why.

Example: So John and *me* were standing there, freezing cold and wondering what we could do to get warm.

Answer: not appropriate (should be *I*, since the conjoined noun and pronoun are in subject position)

1. Alice went with Bill and Fred, and Joan came along with John and *I* a little bit later.
2. Somehow *me* and this other bloke managed to get out of the car before it blew up.
3. Actually, the final design was submitted by Joan and *myself*.
4. *Me* and Susan are living over on the west side of San Francisco.
5. Between you and *me*, I don't think she is going to come.

REFLEXIVE PRONOUNS

The set of English reflexive pronouns is shown in the following table.

REFLEXIVE PRONOUNS

	Singular	Plural
1st person	myself	ourselves
2nd person	yourself	yourselves
3rd person	himself/herself/itself/oneself[9]	themselves

Reflexive pronouns are said to have a nonemphatic function and an emphatic function. The sections that follow look at each in turn.

Nonemphatic Function

The *nonemphatic function* of pronouns – that is, their use other than for emphasis – in fact, comprises two basic functions: lexical and anaphoric. In the first function, reflexive pronouns occur as part of a reflexive verb; in the second, they refer to a preceding NP.

After Reflexive Verbs

As is the case in many languages, some verbs can only take a reflexive pronoun as an object. These so-called *reflexive verbs* include *pride oneself, commit oneself, apply oneself,* and *acquit oneself.* They often combine with a particular preposition, which follows the reflexive pronoun – *on* in the case of *pride,* as illustrated by (14).

(**14**) Fred *prides himself on* his knowledge of basketball.

Some reflexive verbs, such as *adjust oneself, behave oneself, shave oneself,* and *wash oneself* may optionally appear without the reflexive pronoun with no change in meaning. Thus, (15a) and (15b) mean the same thing.

(**15**) a. He *shaved himself* with a rusty razor.
　　　 b. He *shaved* with a rusty razor.

Referring to Preceding NPs

Most commonly, a reflexive pronoun is used not because the sentence has a reflexive verb, as in (14) and (15a), but simply because the entity to which the pronoun refers has been mentioned in the sentence. Typically, this antecedent is the subject, as in (16a), in which *herself* refers to *Alice*. In (16b), the antecedent of the object personal pronoun, *her*, cannot be *Alice*; rather, *her* must refer to some other person, probably a person mentioned prior to this sentence.

> (**16**) a. Alice recognized *herself* in the picture.
> b. Alice recognized *her* in the picture.

Restrictions on Reflexive Pronouns

A reflexive pronoun must be in the same clause as its antecedent. This restriction can help to make clear which NP is the antecedent of a reflexive pronoun, particularly in complex sentences.

In Simple Sentences

In simple sentences (i.e., sentences that consist of only one clause), the antecedent of a reflexive pronoun is usually obvious, as in (17), in which it is the subject, *Alice*. Here the gender of the reflexive pronoun makes it clear which of the two nouns is the antecedent.

> (**17**) Alice told John all about herself.

However, sometimes more than one noun can agree in gender and number with the reflexive pronoun, as in (18), in which the antecedent of *herself* could be *Mary* or *Cathy*.

> (**18**) Mary told Cathy all about herself.

We tend to assume that the subject (*Mary*) is the antecedent. However, Mary could conceivably tell Cathy all about Cathy, if, for instance, she knows a lot about Cathy and wants to prove it. In cases like this, how can we definitively establish which NP is intended as the antecedent? The best way is to examine the context of the sentence, which usually makes clear the correct choice.

This potential ambiguity is not an issue in some languages. In Japanese and Korean, for instance, only the subject NP can be the antecedent in such sentences. Thus, native speakers of these languages who have not learned the restrictions that apply to English reflexive pronouns would likely select *Mary* as the only possible antecedent in (18).

In Complex Sentences

In complex sentences (i.e., sentences that have a main, or independent, clause and one or more subordinate clauses), the task of determining the antecedent of a reflexive pronoun does not become more difficult, because, as noted, the antecedent and the pronoun are always in the same clause. Thus, in a sentence such as (19), *himself* can only refer to *Tom*, which is the only other noun in the same clause.[10] *Bill* and *Al* are not possible antecedents because, as (19b) shows, they are not in the same clause as the pronoun.

> (**19**) a. Bill knew that Al thought that Tom was fond of himself.
> b. Bill knew [that Al thought [that *Tom* was fond of *himself*]].

In Place of Personal Pronouns

Earlier we saw reflexive pronouns used in place of personal pronouns after comparison words. Thus, in addition to their basic nonemphatic uses, reflexive pronouns can take the place of personal pronouns in certain grammatical contexts. Particularly in spoken English, reflexive pronouns are often substituted for personal pronouns after the words *as*, *like*, *but*, *besides*, and *other than*, as illustrated in (20). They are also used after *and* when it conjoins two personal pronouns or an NP and a personal pronoun, as shown in (21).

(**20**) a. This must really be a big thrill for someone like $\begin{Bmatrix} you \\ yourself \end{Bmatrix}$.

b. Assume that someone other than $\begin{Bmatrix} you \\ yourself \end{Bmatrix}$ will be directing the project.

(**21**) a. There was barely enough room in the cabin for *her* and $\begin{Bmatrix} me \\ myself \end{Bmatrix}$.

b. Please respond to *Sue* and $\begin{Bmatrix} me \\ myself \end{Bmatrix}$ by e-mail.

As we speculated earlier about reflexive pronouns following comparison words, the choice of a reflexive pronoun in these conjoined structures may be a default strategy to avoid choosing between subject and object pronouns. For example, a speaker who is not confident about which pronoun is conjoined with *Dr. Carver* in (22) may avoid the problem in (22b) by inserting a reflexive pronoun, producing a sentence such as (22c), which has become an acceptable alternative.[11]

(**22**) a. The research proposal was prepared by Dr. Carver and *me*.
b. *The research proposal was prepared by Dr. Carver and *I*.
c. The research proposal was prepared by Dr. Carver and *myself*.

Emphatic Function

In their emphatic function, reflexive pronouns supplement a noun (or pronoun), rather than occurring in its place.

Emphasis in Conversation

Particularly in conversation, a reflexive pronoun is often used to emphasize and distinguish a noun or pronoun with which it occurs. In such cases, the reflexive pronoun often has heavy stress, and first person and third person forms are especially common. The reflexive pronoun can appear in any of several positions, as shown in (23b), (23c), and (23d).[12] Here the speaker is using a reflexive pronoun to distinguish himself or herself from someone else.

(**23**) a. Of course, I would never do anything like that.
b. Of course, I *myself* would never do anything like that.
c. Of course, *myself*, I would never do anything like that.
d. Of course, I would never do anything like that *myself*.

Emphatic Contrast Across Clauses in Writing

Particularly in academic prose and other writing, reflexive pronouns are used to emphasize a contrast between two NPs, which are often in different clauses. In such cases, the typical position for the reflexive pronoun is immediately after the NP it is used with.[13] This is shown in (24a) and (24b).

(**24**) a. If the symptoms of the disease are difficult to recognize, *the disease itself* is even harder to treat.

b. Even though the factors contributing to the current recession are readily identifiable, *the recession itself* may not be susceptible to traditional economic cures.

In both examples, the reflexive pronoun emphasizes the NP it is used with, thereby shifting attention from an NP mentioned earlier and heightening the distinction between the two. Therefore, in (24a), the attention is switched from the *symptoms* to the *disease*, and in (24b), it is switched from the *factors* contributing to the current recession back to the *recession*.

RECIPROCAL PRONOUNS

The reciprocal pronouns are *each other* and *one another*. The meaning of (25a), which contains the reflexive pronoun *themselves*, differs in meaning from (25b), which contains the reciprocal pronoun *each other*.

(**25**) a. Alice and Joan admired *themselves*.
b. Alice and Joan admired *each other*.

The meaning of (25b) is that Alice admired Joan, and Joan admired Alice. That is, the action in the sentence is reciprocal, and this is captured through the use of a *reciprocal pronoun*.

Although the two reciprocal pronouns have the same meaning, *one another* is used especially in expressing a reciprocal relationship among more than two individuals or among many people. In (26), it refers to a relationship between all members of humanity.

(**26**) It is only in teaching respect for *one another* that the different races can live peacefully together.[14]

One another appears fairly frequently in fiction and in academic prose, but it is not common in spoken English, where *each other* tends to be used instead.[15]

SUMMARY

REFLEXIVE PRONOUNS AND RECIPROCAL PRONOUNS

The **reflexive pronouns** are as follows:

myself	*ourselves*
yourself	*yourselves*
himself, herself,	*themselves*
itself, oneself	

Reflexive pronouns have emphatic and nonemphatic functions.

In their **nonemphatic function**, reflexive pronouns occur:

- **after reflexive verbs** and verbs that are optionally reflexive.
She prides herself on her knowledge of history.
You'd better behave yourself today!   OR   *You'd better behave today!*

• **when they refer to preceding NPs.**
Tom told Maria a lot about himself.
John knew that Tom believed [*that Alan had injured himself*].

In their **emphatic function**, reflexive pronouns are used with a noun or pronoun in order to emphasize it. The reflexive pronoun can appear in several different positions.
Myself, I would never do anything like that.
I, myself, would never do anything like that.
I would never do anything like that myself.

Reflexive pronouns can take the place of personal pronouns after the words *as*, *like*, *but*, *besides* and *other than*.
This must be a really big thrill for someone like yourself.

The reciprocal pronouns, *each other* and *one another*, are used to indicate that an action is being performed by two or more individuals, each on the others.
Fred and Bill criticized each other.
We must all learn to get along with one another.

EXERCISE 13.3

In each sentence, identify all the nouns that could be the antecedent of the reflexive pronoun.

Example: Su Jung told Hannah that Mary bought it for herself.

Answer: Mary

1. Ted asked Alan whether Bruce had defended himself.
2. Cathy showed Emily an old picture of herself.
3. Frank knew that Paul was referring to himself when he said that.
4. Susan told Barbara an anecdote about herself.
5. Sam warned Mary that Alice had introduced herself to Archie.

EXERCISE 13.4

Indicate whether the sentences in each pair that follow have the same meaning. Explain any differences in meaning.

Example: a. John saw him reflected in the mirrorlike surface of the pond.
 b. John saw himself reflected in the mirrorlike surface of the pond.

Answer: not the same meaning (Sentence (a) means John saw someone else; sentence (b) means John saw John.)

1. a. She told the boys to behave themselves.
 b. She told the boys to behave.
2. a. Francine told Alice all about her.
 b. Francine told Alice all about herself.
3. a. After their sister had left, Fred and Bill blamed themselves for the fiasco.
 b. After their sister had left, Fred and Bill blamed each other for the fiasco.
4. a. Alice showed Francine a picture of herself.
 b. Alice showed Francine a picture of her.
5. a. He might very well have told her, but I would never have.
 b. He might very well have told her, but, I myself would never have.

POSSESSIVE PRONOUNS

English possessive pronouns replace NPs that indicate possession. For example, the possessive pronoun *hers* in (27b) can replace *Alice's car* in (27a).

(**27**) a. You take the big car, and I'll drive *Alice's car*.
      b. You take the big car, and I'll drive *hers*.

POSSESSIVE PRONOUNS

	Singular	Plural
1st person	mine	ours
2nd person	yours	yours
3rd person	his, hers, its	theirs

Possessive pronouns can be used in a possessive construction in which they are preceded by a determiner + noun + *of*, which can, as in (28), refer to someone or something that the speaker cannot or does not want to identify more precisely.

(**28**) A *teacher of yours* mentioned that you weren't in school today.

The determiner in this construction may be an indefinite article, as in (28); a zero article, as in (29a); a demonstrative determiner, as in (29b); or a quantifier, as in (29c). It generally may not, however, be a definite article, as in (29d).

(**29**) a. They're *friends of hers*.
      b. *This friend of mine* told me that you won some money recently.
      c. *Some friends of mine* are throwing a big farewell party for her.
      d. *He introduced me to *the friend of his*.[16]

This construction with the possessive pronoun differs from the alternative of possessive determiner + noun (e.g., *my friend*) mainly in that it is more indefinite. The sentences in (30) below illustrate this point.

(**30**) a. You know John? *A friend of his* told me that the food served at that restaurant is awful.
      b. You know John? *His friend* told me the food served at that restaurant is awful.

The construction with the possessive pronoun, in (30a), can be used if the speaker hasn't specified and doesn't need to specify the identity of the friend. In contrast, the construction with the possessive determiner, in (30b), implies that the speaker and listener both know what friend is intended.

INDEFINITE PRONOUNS

Certain pronouns in English refer to indefinite or unspecified entities. These are called *indefinite pronouns*, and they are formed by combining *some*, *any*, *every*, and *no* with the endings *-one*, *-body* and *-thing*, as shown in the following table. With the exception of *no one*, these indefinite pronouns are written as one word.

POSITIVE INDEFINITE PRONOUNS

	some +	*any* +	*every* +
-one	someone	anyone	everyone
-body	somebody	anybody	everybody
-thing	something	anything	everything

NEGATIVE INDEFINITE PRONOUNS

	no +
-one	no one
-body	nobody
-thing	nothing

The positive indefinite pronouns that end in *-body* are largely interchangeable with those that end in *-one*, although corpus research indicates that, at least in American English, the *-body* pronouns tend to be used more frequently.[17]

As is explained in Chapter 4, *someone*, *somebody*, and *something* are positive polarity items, in that, normally, statements in which they are used are affirmative, whereas *anyone*, *anybody*, and *anything* are *negative polarity items* (see Chapter 5), in that normally statements in which they are used are negative.

As was also discussed in Chapter 5, a statement in which a negative indefinite pronoun – *no one*, *nobody*, *nothing* – follows the verb can often be rewritten as a negative statement with an indefinite pronoun that is a negative polarity item – *anyone*, *anybody*, or *anything* – as illustrated in (31).

> (**31**) a. I saw *no one*. (= I didn't see *anyone*.)
> b. We brought *nothing*. (= We didn't bring *anything*.)

Indefinite Pronouns and Agreement

When an indefinite pronoun is the subject of a sentence, the verb should be in the singular form, as shown in (32).

> (**32**) a. I hope everyone arrives on time.
> b. *I hope everyone arrive on time.

While this subject–verb agreement rule treats indefinite pronouns as singular subjects, it is nevertheless common to hear native speakers vacillate between singular and plural pronouns or possessive determiners to refer back to indefinite pronouns, as shown in (33).

> (**33**) a. When it comes to food, *everybody* knows what *he* does and doesn't like.
> b. When it comes to food, *everybody* knows what *they* do and don't like.
> c. Did *someone* leave *her* scarf at my house on Friday night?
> d. Did *someone* leave *their* scarf at my house on Friday night?

The use of plural pronouns and possessive determiners to refer to indefinite pronouns is discussed in greater detail in the section on writing that follows.

Expectation with *Somebody*, *Someone*, and *Something*

As mentioned in Chapter 4, *somebody*, *someone*, and *something* express an expectation when used in questions instead of *anybody*, *anyone*, and *anything*. For example, the speaker who utters the question in (34a) is probably expecting a call. In contrast, the question in (34b) does not imply this expectation. The speaker is simply asking if a call came in at any time during his or her absence.

(**34**) a. Did *somebody* call while I was out?
b. Did *anyone* call while I was out?

SUMMARY

POSSESSIVE PRONOUNS AND INDEFINITE PRONOUNS

The **possessive pronouns** are as follows:

mine	*ours*
yours	*yours*
his, hers, its	*theirs*

Possessive pronouns can replace NPs that indicate possession.
Is that her purse? Yes, of course it's hers.

Possessive pronouns can be used in determiner + noun + *of* + possessive pronoun constructions.
A teacher of yours mentioned that you weren't in school today.
This friend of mine told me that you won some money recently.

The **indefinite pronouns** are as follows:

someone	*anyone*	*everyone*	*no one*
somebody	*anybody*	*everybody*	*nobody*
something	*anything*	*everything*	*nothing*

Indefinite pronouns take a singular form of the verb. However, native speakers refer back to indefinite pronouns with both singular and plural pronouns and possessive determiners.
Everyone has his own preferences.
Everyone has their own preferences.

Someone, somebody, and *something* express an expectation when used in questions.
Did someone call while I was out? (I was expecting a call.)
Did anyone call while I was out? (I wasn't necessarily expecting a call.)

EXERCISE 13.5

Indicate whether the sentences in each pair that follow have any differences in meaning or implication. If there is a difference, explain it.

Example: a. Did somebody talk to him?
b. Did anybody talk to him?

Answer: Sentence (a) implies an expectation that somebody talked to him; sentence (b) doesn't imply this expectation.

1. a. Your neighbor told me you were moving.
   b. A neighbor of yours told me you were moving.
2. a. Did someone remove something from this desk?
   b. Did anyone remove anything from this desk?

3. a. Everyone has his own special way of dealing with difficult matters.
   b. Everyone has their own special way of dealing with difficult matters.
4. a. Susan told no one about the accident.
   b. Susan did not tell anybody about the accident.

PRONOUNS AND AGREEMENT

This section examines several problems related to pronouns and agreement. The first concerns pronoun use with a small set of nouns and is a problem mainly for English language learners. The other two are problems for native speakers as well and are particularly relevant to writing.

Nouns That Refer to Single Items but Are Plural in Number

English has a number of nouns – such as *scissors, shears, tweezers, glasses, goggles, pants, trousers,* and *shorts* – that refer to single items but have plural number. Because these nouns have plural number, pronouns that refer to them must be plural forms, as illustrated in (35).

> (35) a. He took his *glasses* off, and then he put *them* on again.
>   b. *He took his *glasses* off, and then he put *it* on again.

Collective Nouns

English has a large number of collective nouns – such as *army, audience, band, committee, crowd, family, parliament, team,* and *town* – that designate a group of individuals.[18] The prescriptive rule states that if a speaker is focusing on the group as a whole, the following verb and any pronouns that refer to the collective noun are singular, as in (36a), whereas if the speaker is focusing on the individuals that make up the group, then the verb and any pronouns are plural, as in (36b).

> (36) a. The noisy crowd, which *has* up until now been engaged in cheering *its* team, *is* finally *settling* down.
>   b. The noisy crowd, which *have* up until now been engaged in cheering *their* team, *are* finally *settling* down.

British English tends more than American English to have plural agreement with collective nouns. Thus, (37a) is more likely in British English, and (37b) is more likely in American English.

> (37) a. The Admissions Committee *are* holding *their* meeting in the conference room today.
>   b. The Admissions Committee *is* holding *its* meeting in the conference room today.

In discourse, it is not uncommon with collective nouns to find lack of agreement between the following verb and pronouns that appear later. For instance, in American English, the verb form that follows a collective noun might be singular, the norm with collective nouns, but a pronoun appearing later might be plural. This lack of agreement becomes more likely when pronouns become more distant from the collective noun, as illustrated in (38a) and (38b).

> (38) a. The Ways and Means Committee *has* from the very beginning of this session of Congress misused *their* rights in failing to consider the evidence submitted to *them* by the Speaker of the House.
>   b. The platoon *was* called together at the last minute before the attack, given special instructions, and sent out to take up *their* positions.

This switch from singular to plural often goes unnoticed in spoken English, but it is one of the so-called errors of written English that writing teachers seek to eradicate. Because of the general principle of consistency – here, that the writer should maintain either singular or plural number – writing teachers will consider a sentence such as (39) unacceptable.

(**39**) Every Sunday the entire congregation *marches* into the church, *seats itself* on the uncomfortable hard wooden benches, and then listens stoically for a good two hours, while an aged pastor preaches to *them* of *their* wicked and sinful lives.

In (39), the forms used with *congregation* initially are singular (*marches, seats itself*) but later in the sentence are plural (*them, their*). There is a good reason for the writer's shift here – it avoids the incongruous, even nonsensical, *an aged pastor preaches to it of its wicked and sinful life*. The writer has moved from the congregation as a group to the congregation as individuals, who, according to the pastor, lead wicked and sinful lives.

These kinds of shifts in sentences with collective noun subjects are understandable, but they can be avoided in writing. For (39), one correction might be to change the number of the subject to plural (e.g., "Every Sunday all of the members of the congregation. . . .").

Gender-Free Language

Traditionally, the third person masculine pronouns and possessive determiners have been used when agreement requires singular forms and the intent is to refer to both males and females. Thus, in (40), the masculine pronoun *his* is used with the indefinite pronoun *everyone*.

(**40**) *Everyone* should pick up *his* check in the office.

In recent decades, there has been a shift to what has been termed *gender-free language*. This entails, for example, using gender-neutral nouns when referring to both genders (e.g., *salespeople* rather than *salesmen*) and avoiding masculine forms with antecedents that refer to both genders, whether indefinite pronouns or nouns like *a person*. This shift means that writers need to rework sentences such as those in (40) and (41).

(**41**) a. If *a person* masters these techniques, *he* can defend *himself* in all situations.
b. *Anyone* who has spent part of *his* life abroad can see *his* own country in a different light.
c. In this country, *everybody* over 65 believes that the world owes *him* a living.

One way to do this is to recast sentences such as those in (41) with plural subjects, as in (42).

(**42**) a. *People* who master these techniques, can defend *themselves* in all situations.
b. *People/Individuals* who have spent *their* lives abroad can see *their* own country in a different light.
c. In this country, *everybody* over 65 believes that the world owes *them* a living.

In (42a), the subject is made plural and a plural pronoun is used. Similarly, in (42b), the indefinite pronoun *anyone* is replaced with a plural noun and possessive determiners are used. In (42c), the indefinite pronoun *everybody* is retained, but a plural pronoun is used with it. As mentioned earlier, using plural forms with indefinite pronouns is very common in speech; however, this is viewed by some as unacceptable, especially in writing.

Another alternative is to replace third person singular masculine pronouns with pronoun pairs such as *his or her, her or his*, and *him/her*, as in (43).

(**43**) a. If *a person* masters these techniques, *he or she* can defend *him- or herself* in all situations.
 b. *Anyone* who has spent part of *his* or *her* life abroad can see *his* or *her* country in a different light.
 c. In this country, *everybody* over 65 believes that the world owes *her/him* a living.

The alternatives shown in (43) can prove awkward, especially if such pairs accumulate within a passage. Almost all writer's guides recommend using the plural alternatives shown in (42a) and (42b) as the best approach.

The issue of gender-free writing is an important one and should be discussed with students. For example, many journals require that articles submitted display gender-free language. You should point out the various possibilities, including recasting sentences that have indefinite pronouns, and discuss potential problems.

SUMMARY
PRONOUNS AND AGREEMENT

Nouns that refer to single items but are plural in number, such as *glasses*, *scissors*, and *pants*, require pronouns in the plural form.
 My pants are dirty. Can you drop them off at the dry cleaner?

Collective nouns may be treated as singular or plural depending on whether the writer wishes to focus on the group as a whole or on its individual members.
 He stared out at the audience. It was bigger than he expected.
 He stared out at the audience. They were all staring back silently.

Gender-free writing with pronouns refers to the practice of not using third person singular masculine pronouns with antecedents that are indefinite pronouns or nouns referring to both genders.
 Everyone has his or her own way of dealing with problems.
 People who have lived abroad see their countries in a different light.

EXERCISE 13.6

In each of the sentences, indicate whether there is a problem related to pronoun-antecedent agreement. If there is a problem, identify it and suggest a correction. (There may be more than one correct answer.)

Example: Every citizen should cast his vote at the nearest polling station.

Answer: problem: The masculine pronoun *his* referring to *Every citizen* is not gender-free writing.
 correction: *All citizens should cast their votes at the nearest polling station.*

1. The audience in Boston was great. They all loved the play.
2. I left the tweezers on this counter, and now it's gone.
3. Every weekend the team drives to a baseball diamond in a quaint little park on the other side of town. There they practice diligently for two hours while their coach watches and critiques their performance.

4. The committee has been putting in all the time it can and has been working diligently to get their report out by July.
5. Anyone who graduates in the top 10 percent of his class expects to get a good job.

DEMONSTRATIVE PRONOUNS

As we saw in Chapter 10, *this* and *that*, and their plural forms, *these* and *those*, are demonstrative determiners when they modify nouns. However, when *this/these* and *that/those* appear by themselves in discourse, as in (44) and (45), they have an anaphoric function and are called *demonstrative pronouns*.

(**44**) Here are some application forms. You will need to fill *these* out and return them before the deadline.

(**45**) This book isn't bad. But I read her first book, and *that* was more interesting.

In (44), *these* refers back to the NP *some application forms* in the previous sentence. In (45), *that* refers back to *her first book*.

As (44) and (45) suggest, with demonstrative pronouns, as with demonstrative determiners, *this* and *these* are used in referring to things that are relatively close, *that* and *those* in referring to things that are more distant.

The antecedent of *this* or *that* can be an NP, as shown in (44) and (45), or it can be one or more clauses.

(**46**) Hayden's wife cut up some of his musical scores to make hair curlers. *This* infuriated him, but he could do nothing about it.

(**47**) Bernard Herrmann, who created the scores for *Psycho* and *North by Northwest* and some of Hitchcock's other masterpieces, said that there were only "a handful of directors like Hitchcock who really know the score and fully realize the importance of its relationship to the film." But it was more than *that*. For Hitchcock, the score was more than an accompaniment. It was a focus.[19]

In (46) and (47), *this* and *that* refer to multiple clauses, with (46) referring to the entire sentence, and (47) to the content of the quote. We can call cases like (46) and (47), where a pronoun refers to one or more clauses, *sentence anaphora*. If the speaker or writer views the antecedent as old information or low-relevance information, the pronoun used is likely to be *that*. In contrast, if the speaker or writer views the antecedent as information that is new or of high relevance and wishes to place it in focus, the pronoun is likely to be *this*.

A common stylistic device in journalism is to begin an article with a single sentence that states the general topic that the writer is going to discuss, and then start a new paragraph that initiates the discussion of that topic. A writer using this device will often link the new paragraph to the topic in the first sentence with anaphoric *this*, as is illustrated in (48).

(**48**) A growing body of research suggests that there is no such thing as a compatible couple.

This may come as no surprise to all those who have endured years of thermostat wars, objectionable spending habits, and maddening tendencies at the wheel. But it flies in the face of Hollywood, Shakespeare, most people's core fantasies, and all those dating Web sites touting scientific screening to find a perfect match.[20]

SUMMARY

DEMONSTRATIVE PRONOUNS

The English **demonstrative pronouns** are *this* and *these* and their plural counterparts, *that* and *those*.

Demonstrative pronouns can have as their antecedent a noun phrase or, in what is known as **sentence anaphora**, can have an entire clause or a series of clauses.

Here are application forms. You need to fill these out.
The number of divorces has leveled off. This is shown by recent statistics.

EXERCISE 13.7

In each sentence that follows, identify the antecedent of the italicized pronoun.

Example: Our flight was delayed due to mechanical problems. Because of *that*, when we arrived in Hong Kong, we missed our connection to Phnom Penh.

Answer: entire preceding sentence

1. The opening battle of what became known as the Hundred Years' War took place on August 26, 1346, near the village of Crécy in northern France. *This* is where King Phillip VI's French bore down on a much smaller English force commanded by Edward III.
2. He continues to speak about controversial issues in all of his campaign speeches. *This* has gained him a lot of supporters over the past month.
3. She really likes the campus atmosphere at this university. *That's* why she came here.
4. Alice is trying to decide between these gloves and those gloves, and I think *those* are more stylish.
5. "Time to reflect on the results." *That* was what the incumbent said he was giving his opponent yesterday.

PROBLEMS THAT ESL/EFL STUDENTS HAVE WITH PRONOUNS

Current research indicates that the problems that ESL/EFL students have with learning English pronouns result from the differences and similarities between the pronoun system of the learner's native language and that of English. The errors students make are: (1) selecting incorrect pronouns; (2) inserting unnecessary pronouns; (3) misidentifying antecedents; and (4) omitting obligatory pronouns.

Selecting the Wrong Personal Pronoun (Farsi)

In students with L1s that do not have separate forms for subject, object, and possessive pronouns, the use of pronouns in spoken English can be mixed up. In Farsi, for example, subject pronouns are optional, since verb inflections indicate number and person. Thus, either (49a) or (49b) can be used to express the sentence *She/He/It left*, and the norm is to use (49b). Notice that when a pronoun is used, it does not carry any information about gender.

(49) a. *u*   *ræft*
         (He/She/It)   left.
     b.   *ræft*
         (He/She/It)   left.

Native speakers of Farsi learning English may select pronouns of the wrong gender, saying, for example, *I saw him yesterday*, in referring to a woman. This confusion has been noted as an end-state feature in the grammar of some Farsi speakers who, in most other areas of English grammar, are very proficient.

Transfer of Reflexive Verbs (French, German, Spanish)

Students with L1s that contain a great many more reflexive verbs than English does (e.g., French, German, Spanish) commonly insert reflexive pronouns after English verbs that do not need them. This occurs when the English verb has a meaning similar to an L1 verb that takes a reflexive pronoun. This sort of language transfer accounts for the errors in (50a) and (50b), which were made by francophone Canadian English-language students (Adjemian, 1983).

(**50**) a. *At sixty-five years old they must retire *themselves* because this is a rule of society.
   b. *They want to fight *themselves* against this.

Here the French speakers have established a correspondence between the English verbs *retire* and *fight* and the French verbs *se retirer* and *se battre*, which are reflexive, as shown in (51).

(**51**) a. *A soixante-cinq ans   ils   doivent se   retirer.*[21]
      at sixty-five   years they   must   themselves retire
   b. *Ils   veulent se   battre contre cette hausse.*
      they   want   themselves   fight   against this   rise (in tuition)

Sentence (51b) shows that the student who made the error in (50b) also transferred the preposition that must follow *se battre* (*contre*) into the English rendition as *against*.

Misidentifying Antecedents of Reflexive Pronouns (Korean, Japanese, Chinese)

As we saw earlier, in a sentence such as (52), which has a *that* clause, there is only one possible antecedent for the reflexive pronoun *himself*, and that antecedent is *Mike*.

(**52**) Tom thinks that Mike likes *himself*.

However, in a Korean translation of the sentence above, both *Mike* and *Tom* are possible antecedents of the reflexive pronoun *casin*.

(**53**) *Tom-un   Mike-ka   casin-ul   coahanta-ko   sayngkak-hanta.*
     Tom   Mike   himself   likes   thinks

Korean has two sets of reflexive pronouns – the simple forms and the complex forms – either of which could be used in a sentence such as (54). The reflexive pronoun, *casin*, is a simple form. Languages such as Japanese and Chinese also have simple and complex forms of reflexive pronouns. It appears that in all of these languages, when the simple forms are selected, their antecedents can be beyond the boundaries of a single clause, as we see in the Korean example. If the complex forms are used, their antecedents must occur within a single clause, just as in English.

A number of studies seemed to indicate that Japanese and Korean speakers with low levels of English proficiency associate English reflexive pronouns with the simple forms in their respective L1, and only later do they begin to associate them with the complex L1 forms.[22] However, subsequent research by Jung (1999) has shed more light on this. Jung asked Korean speakers who fell into three proficiency groups (beginner, intermediate, advanced) and a control group of 30 native speakers of English to indicate the antecedents of reflexive pronouns in sentences such as those in (54). The sentences in (54) test the students' ability to correctly identify the antecedent of a reflexive pronoun in which the sentence has more than one clause. Square brackets have been placed around the subordinate clause complements.

(54) a. Tom believes [that Mike hurt himself].
    b. Mike expected [Alan to protect himself].

Jung found that only the beginning students had difficulty with (54a), but that all the Korean students had difficulty with (54b), proving significantly poorer at recognizing the correct antecedent than the English-speaking control group. Apparently (54a) is easier because the complementizer *that* marks the clause boundary. Jung also asked the Korean students which L1 form – simple or complex – they thought was the correct equivalent of the English reflexive pronouns. She found no relationship between the choice of form in Korean and the accuracy of the subjects' choice in English. This suggests that for Korean speakers, interpreting antecedents of English reflexive pronouns is more than just associating simple and complex L1 forms with English forms. Since Korean speakers have more problems recognizing antecedents in sentences with an infinitive complement such as (54b), this might be worth targeting in your instruction.

Substitution of *it* for *this* and *that* in Sentence Anaphora (Korean)

There seem to be cases in which L2 learners equate a particular form in their language with a particular form in English and then use the English form in contexts in which other English forms are appropriate. Korean uses *ku* ("that") followed by *kes* ("thing") to refer to sentences in previous discourse, a context in which English uses *this* or *that*.[23] Korean speakers often equate *ku* + *kes* with English *it*, and therefore use *it* in contexts in which *this* or *that* would be appropriate.

Errors that result from this kind of transfer are shown in (55). Since this type of error is still prevalent in the writing of students with advanced proficiency, additional instruction on this topic appears to be warranted. Note that the use of *it* in (55b) may be acceptable to some native speakers, even though *this* would be more appropriate.

(55) a. He took care of people who were poor and sick. *I admire *it*.
    b. At the end of the century the so-called genome theory underwent changes.
     **It* was due to the discovery of prions.

Omission of Subject Pronouns (Spanish, Italian)

Languages such as Spanish and Italian permit sentences without subject pronouns. For example, the Spanish sentence in (56) has no subject pronoun. The third person plural verb form *son* with which it begins is enough to indicate that the subject must be *they*.

(56) *Son mis amigos.*
    are   my   friends
    "They are my friends."

Because these languages do not require a subject pronoun, they have been called *pro-drop* or *null-subject* languages.[24] In one small-scale study by Phinney (1987) at the University of Puerto Rico, compositions by ESL/EFL students who had received 12 years of English in school were found to include sentences that lacked subject pronouns (e.g., **Is my brother* instead of *He is my brother*). In two studies by White (1985, 1986), adult intermediate-level ESL students were asked to make grammaticality judgments regarding sentences with missing subjects. Both studies found that Spanish speakers tended to accept subjectless English sentences more than French speakers. (French is not a pro-drop language.) These results and evidence from other studies indicate that the preference for missing pronouns is carried over when speakers of pro-drop languages learn English.

The omission of subject pronouns tends to decrease markedly as the overall proficiency of the student increases, so many teachers believe that the problem will take care of itself. This seems to be accurate; however, I have found some examples of missing subjects in the English compositions of Spanish speakers enrolled in advanced-level intensive English language classes.

Discourse-Related Pronoun Omission (Chinese)

Research by Huang (1984, 1989) has shown that a rule called *topic NP deletion* operates in Chinese to delete "the topic of a sentence" when it is identical to the topic of a preceding sentence. Huang (1984) calls this a "topic chain." For example, (57a)[25] has the topic *zheixie hua* ("these flowers") and the following subject pronoun *tamen* ("they"). Both of these are omitted (as indicated by ø) by the topic NP deletion rule to produce the version in (57b).

(**57**) a. *Wo   zai   huayuan   li   zhong-le   yixie   hua   zheixie   hua*
I   at   garden   in   plant   some   flower   these   flower
tamen zhang de   hen   hao.
they   grow   very   well
"I have planted some flowers in the garden. They grow very well."

b. *Wo   zai   huayuan   li   zhong-le   yixie   hua   ø*
I   at   garden   in   plant   some   flower   (these flower)
ø   zhang de   hen   hao.
(they) grow   very   well

In (58), the object pronoun *ta* ("it") has been deleted at the end of the sentence since it refers to the topic, *xin jisuanji* ("a new computer"), of the previous clause.

(**58**) *Zhangsan mai le yi tai xin   jisuanji   dan ta   bu   zhidao zenmo young   ø*
Zhangsan buy   one   new   computer but he   not   know   how   use   (it)
"Zhangsan has bought a new computer, but he does not know how to use it."

As (57) and (58) make clear, the topic NP deleted can be the subject or object. The latter deletion is more typical. Third person singular pronouns are always deleted if they refer to inanimate entities. Not surprisingly, Chinese speakers often omit both subject and object pronouns in English. Examples are plentiful. Yip (1995) cites the sentences shown in (59), from compositions by Chinese intermediate- and advanced-level students. Sentence (59a) was written by an intermediate-level student, and (59b) by an advanced-level student. (The deleted elements are indicated by ø.)

(59) a. *The previous paragraphs describe a bit history of Hong Kong. If you want to know more details, please go to the library and find ø.
    b. *He told me, "You will get culture shock," and yes, I indeed get ø.

Similarly, Fuller and Gundel (1987) cite the omission of subject and object pronouns in the speech of Chinese speakers, as shown in (60).

(60) a. *Every time I concentrate to speak out, ø don't know why ø always had Chinese in my mind.
    b. *He win a golden fish – he is very happy and (great). He take ø and he put ø in a glass bowl.

In an interesting study that looked at the grammar judgments of Chinese-speaking students, Yuan (1997) found that 159 of them were able to recognize English sentences with missing subject pronouns as ungrammatical, but they could not do this very well with missing object pronouns. Taken together, the evidence from these studies suggests that the dropping of object pronouns by Chinese speakers should be targeted for pedagogical intervention.

SUGGESTIONS FOR TEACHING PRONOUNS

For many years, authors of intermediate- and advanced-level English language textbooks designed to improve reading skills have viewed anaphora as a potential problem in reading comprehension. As a result, they have developed exercises to provide students with practice in locating correct antecedents. However, research (Boudeguer-Yerkovic, 1991) has demonstrated that making the connection between pronouns and their antecedents in discourse is not a serious problem for intermediate- through advanced-level ESL/EFL students. They may, however, have trouble processing sentences that involve backward anaphora, such as in (61), in which *it* refers to the entire clause *they might see a lion*.

(61) They hoped that they might see a lion, but the guide told them *it* was unlikely.

Boudeguer-Yerkovic's research indicates that exercises in ESL reading textbooks that ask students to identify antecedents of pronouns in paragraphs and short texts are probably a waste of time (even though they are quite popular with students and teachers), since students can already establish most anaphoric connections by the time they reach intermediate-level proficiency. Thus, teachers might better spend their energy on other activities that promote reading comprehension. The following activities address some of the problems mentioned in the previous section and foster the production of pronouns in discourse.

Activity 1: Practicing Subject and Object Personal Pronouns (High Beginning Through Low Intermediate)

Strip stories provide a simple but engaging way of getting students used to the idea that NPs that have been mentioned in running discourse need to be referred to by an appropriate pronoun. A strip story is a set of individual sentences written on strips of paper or written out as numbered sentences on the board. Each sentence contains no pronouns. The students first order the sentences so that they make a coherent story. Then they look at each sentence and use pronouns to replace NPs that have already been mentioned in a previous sentence.

Activity 2: Introducing Possessive Pronouns (Beginning)

If students are already familiar with possessive determiners, these forms can be contrasted with possessive pronouns by using objects in the classroom. Set the stage by modeling a sentence with a possessive determiner and then drawing the contrast (e.g., *Your sweater is brown. Mine is red. His book bag is black. Yours is orange.*). Next, move to other objects and body parts (eyes, hair, etc.). Be careful to avoid any contrast that could in some way offend students. Then have pairs of students first say and then write similar statements.

Activity 3: Introducing and Practicing Reflexive Pronouns (Low Intermediate)

Reflexive pronouns can be introduced through a brief story such as the one shown in (62). The story can be accompanied by pictures that illustrate the content of each sentence.

> **(62)** Hamid's bike was broken. He took it to a bicycle repair shop. The man at the shop wanted too much money. So Hamid fixed it *himself.*

Ask a student, "Did the people at the repair shop fix Hamid's bike?" When the student says "no," ask who fixed it. The student should respond, "He fixed it himself." Next, begin asking students about various things you know they have done without help. When they have difficulty with the proper form, prompt them. Possible questions to ask are: "Did someone do your homework for you?" "Did someone tie her shoes for her?" "Did someone take the test for him/her?" "Will someone read the story for you?"

Next, have the students work in pairs to write down things that someone does for them every day at home and other things that they do themselves.

Activity 4: Recognizing Antecedents of Reflexive Pronouns (Intermediate)

This activity is intended for those teaching in an EFL environment, or in some other setting where all the students share an L1. Jung (1999) suggests an inductive approach to address the problem that Korean speakers have with finding the appropriate antecedent in sentences such as *Bill wanted Fred to protect himself.*

Begin by reviewing that in a single-clause sentence such as *Mark is always talking to himself*, the reflexive pronoun refers to the subject, *Mark*. Further, if the sentence is written with a nonreflexive pronoun (*Mark is always talking to him*), that pronoun refers to someone other than *Mark*. Then show students the use of reflexive pronouns in a pair of single-clause sentences such as *Mark is talking to Paul about himself* and *Mark is talking to Paul about him*. Explain that in the first sentence *himself* can refer either to Mark or to Paul, and that in the second sentence *him* refers to someone other than Mark or Paul.

Then write sentence (63) on the board and ask the students who *herself* refers to.

> **(63)** Mary thinks that Jane likes herself.

If they say *Mary*, explain that in a sentence such as this, *herself* can only refer to *Jane*. Then write sentence (64) on the board and again ask the students who *herself* refers to (*Jane*).

> **(64)** Mary expects Jane to talk about herself.

Now ask the students to formulate a rule for finding the antecedent of *herself* in sentences such as (63) and (64). Once they have arrived at a rule (with your help), present students with several examples such as those in (65), and ask them to choose the pronoun that makes the best sense in each case.

(65) a. Most parents think that their children should obey (them/themselves).
b. The judge expected the suspect to defend (him/himself).
c. John told his father to stop telling (him/himself) what to do. He insisted he could make his own decisions and that he knew what was best for (him/himself).
d. Susan expects her sister to call (her/herself).

Students can work in pairs or small groups and report their answers to the class. Always ask the students, "Why is that the best choice? What does the sentence mean if you choose the other word?"

Activity 5: Introducing Sentence Anaphora with Demonstrative Pronouns (High Intermediate)

The use of sentence-initial *that* and *this* to refer back to one or more preceding clauses is an important grammatical device in the development of coherent paragraphs. Use an example such as (66) to show how *this* and *that* frequently refer to an entire preceding sentence.

(66) Over 50 percent of all marriages in America end in divorce. *This* certainly says something about relationships between men and women in American society.

Ask what *this* in the second sentence refers to. Then show an example in which *that* is used, such as in (67).

(67) No matter what politicians may say publicly, after they lose an election, they feel depressed and demoralized. *That* makes it difficult for them to turn to relatives after a loss, since the relatives are often even more depressed.

Ask what *that* refers to in the second sentence. Indicate that the most likely antecedent is the clause *they feel depressed and demoralized* in the previous sentence. You may want to point out that if the writer had wanted to add extra emphasis, he or she could have used *this*.

Then have students write two sentences in which the second sentence uses *this* or *that* to refer to the entire previous sentence or to a clause within it.

Activity 6: Addressing Discourse-Related Pronoun Deletion (Intermediate)

One way to raise the consciousness of Chinese speakers in identifying topic NP deletion in their compositions is to present them with a passage that has deleted pronouns and ask them to insert the appropriate pronouns wherever necessary. Before you begin, review the use of pronouns by presenting a few sentences such as in (68) on an overhead projector.

(68) Adam found a vase and put the flower in. Was really beautiful, he said to himself. But was not sure where to put.

Correct the text by adding pronouns as shown in (69).

(69) Adam found a vase and put the flower in *it*. *It* was really beautiful, he said to himself. But he was not sure where to put *it*.

Next, have the students work in pairs to correct the passage you have prepared by inserting the appropriate pronouns.

ENDNOTES

[1] Also called the *referent* of the pronoun.

[2] Another term for forward anaphora is *cataphora*.

[3] Biber et al. (1999), p. 331, note that *one* is "virtually restricted to written registers and is perceived as a 'non-casual' choice."

[4] This is confirmed in the data of Biber et al. (1999), p. 335.

[5] Examples (9a) and (9b) are from Biber et al. (1999), p. 337.

[6] Linguists have traditionally explained these errors as "hypercorrections" (i.e., the use of a form that appears to the speaker to be the "prestige" dialect and hence more correct).

[7] Additional examples of these error types can be found in Biber et al. (1999), p. 337.

[8] The term *peripheral noun phrases* and examples (13a), (13b), and (13d) are from Biber et al. (1999), p. 339.

[9] Biber et al. (1999), p. 343, note that there is a "specialized form," *ourself*, which is used to refer to people in general (e.g., *We find ourself examining the way we speak to, inform, and educate one another about health*). Here the use of *ourself* is a rhetorical device for including the audience he or she is writing for – and by implication people in general – as the group that should examine the way we speak to inform others about health.

[10] The subordinate clauses in (19) are *that* clauses.

[11] This observation is also suggested by Staczek (1988a, 1988b). It appears that in some cases reflexive pronouns have become established in formulaic phrases, so that they replace object personal pronouns. An example is the expression *on behalf of X and Y*. For example, *on behalf of the entire committee and myself* sounds much more appropriate than *on behalf of the entire committee and me*.

[12] See Quirk et al. (1972), p. 213.

[13] See Biber et al. (1999), p. 346.

[14] This example is taken from Biber et al. (1999), p. 346.

[15] See Biber et al. (1999), pp. 346–347.

[16] It might be argued that there are some contexts where a definite article is permissible, e.g., *The friend of his that I was referring to is standing over there*. But in most of these cases native speakers would use a demonstrative determiner: *That friend of his that I was referring to is standing over there*.

[17] See Biber et al. (1999), p. 353.

[18] Quirk et al. (1972) point out that these can be subclassified into three categories: (1) common collective nouns such as *class*, *team*, and *gang*; (2) unique collectives such as *the Vatican*, *Parliament*, *the Kremlin*, and *Congress*; (3) generic collectives such as *the aristocracy*, *the bourgeoisie*, *the clergy*, and *the intelligentsia*.

[19] R. Rothstein. *Hitchcock, Thrilling the Ears as Well as the Eyes*. New York Times, p. B1, January 8, 2007.

[20] H. Stout. *The Key to Lasting Marriage: Combat*. Wall Street Journal, p. D1, Nov. 1, 2004.

[21] The examples from Adjemian (1983), p. 259 have been shortened slightly.

[22] For example, Finer and Broselow (1986), Thomas (1989), Broselow and Finer (1991), Finer (1991), Hirakawa (1990), Eckman (1994), and Lakshmanan and Teranishi (1994). In the UG principles and parameters paradigm, within which all of these researchers work, the anaphoric relationships between reflexive pronouns and their antecedents in different languages are constrained by a Governing Category Parameter which has multiple values, depending on what kinds of clauses are involved. A nice summary of some of the early research on how this parameter affects L2 acquisition can be found in Eckman (1994). See also White (1989, 157–169).

²³ *Ku* is one of three determiners in Korean according to Kim (2001).

²⁴ In the principles and parameters paradigm, a pro-drop parameter is part of the universal grammar that children use to acquire their native languages (L1s). Children learning Spanish choose a setting of [+ pro-drop] on the basis of the input they hear as they grow up. Speakers of English choose a setting of [− pro-drop] based on the spoken language they hear. The issue for L2 acquisition is whether adult L2 learners can change their L1 setting to that of the L2. When they apply (transfer) their L1 setting when speaking the L2, ungrammatical utterances occur (e.g., when Spanish speakers drop subject pronouns in English).

²⁵ Examples (57) and (58) are taken from Yuan (1997).

REFERENCES

Adjemian, C. (1983). The transferability of lexical properties. In S. Gass & L. Selinker (Eds.), *Language transfer in language learning* (pp. 250–268). Rowley, MA: Newbury House.

Biber, D., Johansson, S., Leech, G., Conrad, S., & Finegan, E. (1999). *Longman grammar of spoken and written English*. Essex: Pearson Education.

Boudeguer-Yerkovic, M. (1991). An investigation of second language learners' ability to resolve anaphora in texts. *M.A. thesis at the University of Illinois at Urbana-Champaign.*

Broselow, E., & Finer, D. (1991). Parameter setting in second language phonology and syntax. *Second Language Research, 7,* 35–59.

Eckman, F. (1994). Local and long-distance anaphora in second language acquisition. In E. Tarone, S. M. Gass, & A. D. Cohen (Eds.), *Research methodology in second language acquisition* (pp. 207–226). Hillsdale, NJ: Lawrence Erlbaum.

Finer, D. (1991). Binding parameters in second language acquisition. In L. Eubank (Ed.), *Point counterpoint: Universal grammar in the second language* (pp. 351–371). Amsterdam: John Benjamins.

Finer, D., & Broselow, E. (1986). Second language acquisition of reflexive binding. *NELS, 16,* 154–168.

Fuller, J. W., & Gundel, J. K. (1987). Topic prominence in interlanguage. *Language Learning, 37*(1), 1–18.

Hirakawa, M. (1990). A study of the L2 acquisition of English reflexives. *Second Language Research, 6,* 60–85.

Huang, C-T. J. (1984). On the distribution and reference of empty pronouns. *Linguistic Inquiry, 15,* 531–574.

Huang, C-T. J. (1989). Pro-drop in Chinese: A generalized control theory. In O. Jaeggli & K. Safir (Eds.), *Parameter setting* (pp. 1–22). Dordrecht: Reidel.

Jung, E. (1999). Universal parameter-setting model revisited: Korean learners' acquisition of English anaphora. *Ph.D. dissertation, University of Illinois: Urbana, Illinois.*

Kim, H-Y. (2001). Factors in the choice of referential forms in Korean discourse: Salience, thematic importance, and empathy. Paper presented at Georgetown University Round Table in Languages and Linguistics. Georgetown University, March 8–10, 2001.

Lakshmanan, U., & Teranishi, K. (1994). Preferences versus grammatical judgments: Some methodological issues concerning the governing category parameter in second language acquisition. In E. Tarone, S. Gass, & A. Cohen (Eds.), *Research methodology in second-language acquisition* (pp. 185–206). Hillsdale, NJ: Lawrence Erlbaum.

Phinney, M. (1987). The pro-drop parameter in second language acquisition. In T. Roeper & E. Williams (Eds.), *Parameter setting*. Dordrecht: Reidel.

Quirk, R., Greenbaum, S., Leech, J., & Svartvik, J. (1972). *A grammar of contemporary English*. London: Longman.

Staczek, J. (1988a). Sentential and discourse reflexives in English: A matter of variation. *Studia Anglica Posnaniensia, 20*, 115–121.

Staczek, J. (1988b). Variation in plural reflexive in spoken English. *SECOL Review, 12*, 25–35.

Thomas, M. (1989). The interpretation of English reflexive pronouns by nonnative speakers. *Studies in Second Language Acquisition, 11*, 281–303.

White, L. (1985). The pro-drop parameter in adult second language acquisition. *Language Learning, 35*, 47–61.

White, L. (1986). Implications of parametric variation for second language acquisition: An investigation of the pro-drop parameter. In V. Cook (Ed.), *Experimental approaches to second language acquisition*. Oxford: Pergamon Press.

White, L. (1989). *Universal grammar and second language acquisition*. Amsterdam/Philadelphia: John Benjamins.

Yip, V. (1995). *Interlanguage and learnability: From Chinese to English*. Amsterdam/Philadelphia: John Benjamins.

Yuan, B. (1997). Asymmetry of null subject and null objects in Chinese speakers' L2 English. *Studies in Second Language Acquisition, 19*, 467–497.

CHAPTER 14

Modal Verbs

INTRODUCTION

In this chapter, we learn about *modal verbs*, or *modals* for short.[1] Modals express special meanings such as ability, necessity, and permission. The cartoon below illustrates an important fact about modals: they can have more than one meaning.

The husband in the cartoon insists that his wife use a modal of polite request, *may*, instead of making a more informal request with *can*. However, his wife points out that her use of *can* was intended to indicate the meaning of possibility.

Because English learners need to be able to express the various meanings of modals as soon as possible in their communication with others, modals are among the first grammar topics taught in most English language courses. In this chapter, you will find detailed coverage of the meanings that modals have. Even though you may not teach all of these meanings, you will find that having this knowledge can be useful in answering questions about these verbs.

CHARACTERISTICS OF MODALS

Modals (MOD) are one kind of *auxiliary verb* (AUX). In declarative sentences, auxiliary verbs come before the main verb (V). As we saw in Chapter 2 and Chapter 4, *be* and *have* can be auxiliaries as well as main verbs. Examples (1a) and (1b) show the verbs as auxiliaries preceding a main verb. When they appear together as auxiliaries, some form of *have* always precedes *been*, as shown in (1c).

              AUX   *V*
(1) a. He [is] [waiting].

            AUX   *V*
    b. She [has] [waited] for a long time.

           AUX   *AUX*   *V*
    c. They [have] [been] [waiting] for over three hours.

Modals appear either directly before a main verb, as in (2a), or before the auxiliary verbs *be* and *have*, as shown in (2b), (2c), and (2d). Note that a verb following a modal is always in its basic (bare infinitive) form.

           MOD   *V*
(2) a. He [must] [work] very hard to earn that much money.

          MOD AUX   *V*
    b. He [must] [be] [working] very hard to earn all that money.

          MOD   *AUX*   *V*
    c. He [must] [have] [worked] very hard to earn all that money.

          MOD   *AUX*   *AUX*   *V*
    d. He [must] [have] [been] [working] very hard to earn all that money.

Modals, like other auxiliary verbs, have some characteristics that distinguish them from main verbs. First of all, as shown in (3), modals can contract with *not*, whereas main verbs cannot.

(3) a. He *shouldn't* see her.
    b. *He *worksn't* with her.

There are, however, two modals that do not form contractions with *not*. *May* does not contract, as (4b) shows.[2] *Shan't* exists as a contraction of *shall not* only in British English and is restricted largely to use with a first person pronoun, as in (4c) (*won't* is used in American English instead).

(4) a. He *may not* come.
    b. *He *mayn't* come.
    c. We *shan't* be very long.   *British English*
    d. We *won't* be very long.   *American English*

Second, modals undergo subject–aux inversion in *yes/no* questions, as shown in (5a), and in statements with an introductory negative word such as *never*, *rarely*, or *not often*, as in (5b). (For more on modals and subject–aux inversion, see Chapter 4 and Chapter 5.)

(5) a. *Should I* finish that book?
    b. *Rarely*, if ever, *will you* see a performance as good as that.

Third, in retorts, modals are repeated with primary stress, indicated in (6) with capital letters.[3]

(6) You think he *can't* do it? Well, he *CAN*!

This repetition also occurs in tag questions, in which a modal verb in the stem reappears in the tag. (For tag questions, see Chapter 4.)

(**7**) He *can* come, *can't* he?

Finally, modals do not take the present tense -*s* ending or the past tense -*ed* ending, as illustrated for *can* in (8a). Some modals, however, have what can be seen as a corresponding irregular past tense form, for example, *could* in the case of *can*, as (8b) indicates.[4]

(**8**) a. *He *canned* run a mile in almost four minutes when he was younger.
   b. He *could* run a mile in almost four minutes when he was younger.

TYPES OF MODALS

Modals can be classified according to form and according to meaning. In this section, we classify modals both ways; these classifications then organize the rest of the discussion of modals.

The Forms of Modals

Modals can be classified into three categories according to their form. The first category, *pure modals*, is comprised of verbs such as *can*, *could*, and *may*. With the one exception shown in (4b), pure modals display all four of the characteristics mentioned above – contraction, inversion, repetition in retorts and tags, and invariant form. Pure modals do not appear together, except in some dialects of American English where you sometimes hear sequences such as *might could* and *might should*.[5]

The second category, *marginal modals*, has only three members – *dare*, *need*, and *ought to*. They are classified as marginal because they display only two of the syntactic characteristics of pure modals – contraction with *not* and subject–aux inversion – and do so very rarely, for the most part just in British English.[6]

The modals in the third category, *semimodals*, are fixed idiomatic expressions beginning with *have*, *had*, or *be* – for example, *have to*, *had better*, and *be going to*. With most of the semimodals, the words *have*, *had*, and *be* contract with *not*, are involved in subject–aux inversion, and occur in tags. Unlike the pure modals, the semimodals are not invariant, since *be* and *have* both change form (e.g., *has to*, *were going to*). *Have*, *had*, and *be* often contract with preceding pronouns (e.g., *you'd better*, *I'm going to*).

The following table lists the modal verbs in each category. Example sentences using modals from each category are shown in (9).

MODALS		
Pure Modals	**Marginal Modals**	**Semimodals**
can	dare	be going to
could	need	be supposed to
may	ought to	had better
might		had best
must		have got to
shall		have to
should		
will		
would		

(9) a. She *must* turn in that report tomorrow.   *pure modal*
    b. You *should* see a doctor.   *pure modal*
    c. She *needn't* turn in that report tomorrow. *marginal modal*
    d. You *ought to* see a doctor.   *marginal modal*
    e. I *have got to* turn in that report tomorrow. *semimodal*
    f. You *had better* see a doctor.   *semimodal*

In addition to the modals listed in the table, there are several multiword expressions, such as *be able to*, *be obliged to*, and *be willing to*, that have meanings similar to those of modals. For example, *be able to* indicates ability like *can*, and *be obliged to* indicates necessity like *must*. Unlike the corresponding modals, however, these expressions have only one meaning. For example, *be able to* is restricted to this ability meaning, whereas *can* also has other meanings, which are shown in (12) and (13). For this reason, these expressions are not considered semimodals, and they will not be discussed here, even though they are often used in ESL/EFL textbooks to explain the meanings of different modals.

The Meanings of Modals

As we have seen, modals can be categorized into three groups according to form: pure, marginal, and semimodals. All of these modals can also be grouped according to the meanings they express. Many modals have meanings in addition to basic meanings related to these groupings.[7]

Basic Meanings of Modals

Modals can be categorized into three groups according to meaning:[8]

- **Modals of ability, permission, and possibility.** This group includes the modals *can*, *could*, *may*, and *might*.
- **Modals of advice and necessity.** This group includes *must*, *should*, *dare*, *need*, *have to*, *had better*, *had best*, *have got to*, *ought to*, and *be supposed to*.
- **Modals for expressing future time.** This group of modals includes *shall*, *will*, *would*, and *be going to*.

Extended Meanings of Modals

Modals can take on extended meanings depending on the contexts in which they appear. For example, the modal *can* has three basic meanings – of ability (*I can't swim*), of permission (*You can leave now*), and of possibility (*The temperature can fall below 60 degrees Fahrenheit at the South Pole*). However, in certain contexts, such as in (10), the meaning of *can* is extended to express something else.

(10) What? He lost the race? That *can't* be! I was so sure he'd win!

In (10), the modal *can* is used to express disbelief on the part of the speaker. The sentence *That can't be!* is not a literal comment on the possibility of the race result, but is instead a comment on its unexpectedness. The speaker is really saying, "It's hard to believe that this could have happened." Thus, while the use of *can't* here does not mean that the results are, in a literal sense, impossible, it expresses an extension of the modal's meaning of possibility.

Disbelief is not one of the basic meanings that *can* normally conveys, and interpreting *can* in this way depends on having a particular context. The extended meanings of a modal, such as the meaning of *can* illustrated in (10), are determined by the context, which includes the real world situation in which the modal is used.

In the following sections, the basic and extended meanings of various modals are presented. Some meanings are specifically for the modal followed by *not* and/or by *have*. For some modals, when we add these extended meanings to the basic meanings, we get a long list of possible meanings. Don't be overwhelmed by this. Keep in mind that all of the extended meanings need not be taught. As stated in the opening of this chapter, some of this material is best thought of as extra knowledge that may be useful in answering questions about particular modals.

PURE MODALS OF ABILITY, PERMISSION, AND POSSIBILITY

The modals of ability, permission, and possibility are all pure modals. They are *can*, *could*, *may*, and *might*.

Can

Can expresses all three basic meanings of this set.

Ability

Can means "be able to do something," as in (11a), or "know how to do something," as in (11b).

   (**11**) a. I *can* lift over 200 pounds.
        b. I *can* fly an airplane.

Permission

Can is used to request permission to do something, as in (12a). In (12b), *can* is used to grant permission. *Can* is considered to be more informal than *could* or *may* in such requests – the basis for the husband's comment in the cartoon at the beginning of this chapter.

   (**12**) a. *Can* I make a quick telephone call?
        b. You *can* go outside after you finish your homework.

Possibility

Can also expresses possibility. In the opening cartoon, for instance, the wife's reply to her husband's comment refers to the possibility of being able to clean the husband's glasses given that they are so dirty. In (13), the speaker is talking about the possibility of strong winds during a storm.

   (**13**) The wind *can* easily gust up to 60 miles per hour in a bad storm.

Extended Meanings

In addition to its basic meanings, *can* has several extended meanings:

   • **Admonition**. In American English, *can't* is sometimes used to admonish someone not to do something. In (14), the meaning of *can't* is very close to "must not." The sentence might be paraphrased as "Under no circumstances should you tell her."

   (**14**) You *can't* tell her! The shock would kill her.

- **Speculation**. *Can* also appears in questions such as (15a) and (15b), which refer to some unexpected or unexplained occurrence or event. Such questions ask the listener or reader to speculate about a possible explanation. In (16b), we see that speaker B offers a speculative answer to speaker A's question.

(15) a. (hearing the telephone ring at 1:00 A.M.) Now, who *can* be calling at this hour?
b. A: (hearing a loud noise) What *can* that be?
   B: I don't know, but it sounded kind of like an explosion.

- **Disbelief**. As we saw earlier, *can't* is used in conversation to express disbelief. The speaker draws a conclusion that surprises him or her, derived from certain facts or from other external circumstances. This meaning is exemplified by (10) as well as by (16).

(16) He didn't get the promotion? That *can't* be possible! He's the most qualified person we have in the department.

Could

Could, as mentioned earlier, corresponds to *can*, and it, too, expresses all three basic meanings of the set.

Ability

Could expresses past ability, as shown in (17).

(17) a. I *could* run a mile in four and a half minutes when I was 19 years old. I can't run that fast anymore.
b. When he was a child, he *could* speak several languages.

Permission

Could imparts a politer and more deferential tone to requests for permission than *can*, as illustrated in (18). It is not used in responses.

(18) a. *Could* I be excused?   *more polite*
b. *Can* I be excused?   *informal*

Possibility

Could expresses possibility, and in this use, as illustrated in (19), it is often interchangeable with *might* or *may*.

(19) (looking at large black clouds overhead)   It $\begin{Bmatrix} could \\ might \\ may \end{Bmatrix}$ rain today.

Extended Meanings

Could has the following extended meanings:

- **Speculation or regret**. *Could* and *could have* can express speculation about hypothetical possibilities in the present and past, respectively, as in (20a) and (20b). In (20c), in which *could have* appears in a hypothetical conditional sentence, it expresses regret about an opportunity that was missed (see Chapter 19, Conditional Sentences). (*Could have* is contracted to *coulda* or *could of* in conversation and is sometimes written as *could've*.)

(**20**) a. Who *could* be calling at this hour?
   b. She *could have* gone to the movies, but I'm not sure if she did.
   c. You know, I *could have* won a million dollars if I had played the numbers that I usually do. But I forgot to buy a ticket this week.

- **Disbelief**. *Couldn't have* expresses disbelief about a past event or action. In this case, it means "It is not possible that this happened" or "I don't believe that this happened." In (21a), the reason for the speaker's disbelief appears in the following sentence.

(**21**) No, you are wrong! John *couldn't have* stolen your watch. He's the most honest and trustworthy person I've ever met.

- **Suggestion or implied criticism**. *Could* and *could have* are used to advise someone to do something. In (22a), the speaker is advising someone to seek help from the teacher. In (22b), the speaker is showing criticism of a person's behavior.

(**22**) a. You know, if you don't understand the assignment, you *could* always ask your teacher to explain it. I'm sure that he would be glad to.
   b. Did you see that? She just burst into the room unannounced and interrupted the meeting. I've never seen such rude behavior! At the very least, she *could have* knocked before she came in.

In (22b), the projected tone is one of irritation, but this does not have to be the case. In (23), *could* is used in a suggestion that is intended to be ironic.

(**23**) A: How do you address an angry six-foot, seven-inch football player who weighs 295 pounds?
   B: Well, you *could* try, "Sir."

May

May expresses possibility and permission. *May have*, like *could have* and *might have* (discussed later), has the extended meaning of speculation, although the other forms are more commonly used to express this meaning.

Possibility

May is used to express possibility. In (24), for instance, the speaker expresses the possibility that the person referred to is telling the truth.

(**24**) He *may* be telling the truth.

Permission

May is also used to request and grant permission. In these uses, *may* is considered more formal than *can* in American English, as illustrated in (25).

(**25**) a. *May* I leave now?   *formal*
   b. *Can* I leave now?   *less formal*
   c. You *may* go in now.   *formal*
   d. You *can* go in now.   *less formal*

In statements, *may not*, which denies permission, imparts a formal tone, emphasizing prohibition, as shown in (26).

(**26**) You *may not* leave this room at any time during the examination.

Might

Might has only the basic meaning of possibility and several extended meanings.

Possibility

Might indicates possibility – often more tentative and remote than possibility indicated by *may*, as illustrated in (27).

(**27**) He *might* come, and then again, he *might not*.

Extended Meanings

Might has the following extended meanings:

- **Speculation**. *Might have* implies a high degree of speculation about the possibility that an event took place, as shown in (28).

  (**28**) He *might have* met her in Boston, but I'm not so sure he's ever been to Boston.

- **Suggestion**. *Might* can have the force of a neutral suggestion, as shown in (29).

  (**29**) No, I don't know what's wrong. But you *might* try flipping that switch and see what happens.

- **Implied criticism**. *Might* and *might have* can imply criticism. The tone of an utterance can be one of annoyance or surprise due to something that the person addressed has done or has failed to do. In (30a) and (30b), respectively, the speaker is annoyed because the person addressed acted selfishly, and upset because the person was irresponsible; in (30c), the speaker is surprised that the person did not take advantage of an opportunity. (In spoken English *might have* contracts to *mighta*, or what sounds like *might of*. These forms are never written unless the writer is attempting to imitate speech, and then you will usually see the contraction *might've*.)

  (**30**) a. You ate the rest of the pie?!! I can't believe you did that! Next time you *might* ask whether anyone else wants some.
  b. How could you let him go mountain climbing? You know how dangerous that is. You *might have* at least called me before he left! I could have stopped him.
  c. You mean to tell me that you were standing next to Steven Spielberg at that party, and you never even spoke to him?! What's the matter with you? You're an actor and he's the most powerful man in Hollywood. You *might have* at least introduced yourself to him.

- **Permission in formal requests**. *Might* is used in very formal requests with first person pronouns. This is perhaps more common in British English, as illustrated in (31).

  (**31**) *Might* I have a look at this masterpiece you have purchased?

SUMMARY

PURE MODALS OF ABILITY, PERMISSION, AND POSSIBILITY

Modals can be classified into three categories according to their form: **pure modals, marginal modals**, and **semimodals**.

They can be classified into three categories according to their basic meanings: **modals of ability, permission, and possibility; modals of advice and necessity**, and **modals for expressing future time**.

The modals of ability, permission, and possibility are all pure modals. They are **can, could, may**, and **might**. Their basic and extended meanings are as follows:

Can

- **ability**
  I can lift 200 pounds over my head.

- **permission**
  You can talk to him now.

- **possibility**
  In the summer, the temperature can reach 100 degrees Fahrenheit.

- **extended meanings**

  - **admonition**
    You can't tell her yet! The shock would be too much.

  - **speculation**
    Now who can that be at the door?

  - **disbelief**
    You can't be serious.

Could

- **ability**
  When I was 18, I could run faster and longer.

- **permission**
  Could I talk to you for a moment?

- **possibility**
  It could snow up to ten inches today.

- **extended meanings**

  - **speculation or regret**
    She could be at Linda's house, but I'm not sure.
    I could have been a contender.

  - **disbelief**
    It couldn't have been Jim! He'd never do something like that.

continued

- **suggestion or implied criticism**
  You know, you could knock before you barge in here like that.

May

- **possibility**
  He may be the man we're looking for, but I'm not sure yet.

- **permission**
  You may leave whenever you're ready.

Might

- **possibility**
  He might show up later than planned.

- **extended meanings**

  - **speculation**
    In 2000, they might have already been living in Florida – I'm not sure.

  - **suggestion**
    You might try stepping on the gas a few times before turning the key.

  - **criticism**
    She might have at least let me know ahead of time.

  - **permission in formal requests**
    Might I borrow that calculator?

EXERCISE 14.1

Indicate the meaning expressed by each modal verb in italics. Some modals express a basic meaning and others express an extended meaning.

Example: She's your sister, you know. You *might* try being a little more friendly when she's around.

Answer: might = implied criticism

1. You *can't* let on that you know about the party. Your parents have worked so hard planning this surprise. They would be terribly disappointed.
2. They *couldn't have* told him about the party. Catherine and I were the only people who knew about it, and we didn't tell anyone else.
3. You *may not* speak until you are spoken to.
4. You mean you had a chance to meet the president, and you turned it down? You *can't* be serious!
5. I really don't know much about repairing car engines, but you *might* try connecting that wire down there and seeing if it starts up.
6. He *could* do 35 chin-ups when he was 16 years old.
7. They *can* get as much as 60 inches of rain in a year in Seattle.
8. You *might have* told me that you were bringing someone home for dinner! All I ask for is a little advance notice so that we have enough food.
9. I *could* be a big star if I just practice enough.

PURE MODALS OF ADVICE AND NECESSITY

The pure modal of advice is *should*. It is interchangeable with the marginal modal *ought to* for expressing the basic meaning of advice – that which the speaker considers to be "right," in the sense of either morally called for or most practical or expedient. *Must* is the pure modal of necessity and is interchangeable with the semimodal *have to*. Necessity can be internal; that is, it may spring from an internal need, as in (32a), in which the subject, Fred, feels compelled to do something. Necessity can also be external, as in (32b), in which external circumstances create the compulsion.

(32) a. Fred is one of those people who *must* clear his desk of all papers before he leaves the office.
　　 b. Alice lost her job, so she *must* budget all her expenses very carefully until she finds a steady source of income.

Should

In addition to its root meaning of advice, *should* has two important extended meanings.

Advice

In (33), *should* is used to express advice. These are recommendations based on the speaker's subjective judgment.

(33) a. You *should* get some health insurance right away.
　　 b. The oil in this car *should* be changed every 1,500 miles if you want to keep it running.

Extended Meanings

Should has the following extended meanings:

- **Inferred probability**. *Should* can express probability based on evidence present at the moment of speaking. In (34), Tom, knowing the location of Bald Mountain in relation to where he is standing, expresses the likelihood that it can be seen.

(34) Susan: Boy, we really have climbed way up, haven't we?
　　 Tom: Yeah. We *should* be able to see Bald Mountain from here.

Similarly, in (35), in which the speaker has just finished tightening a leaky faucet, *should* in the first sentence expresses the idea that this action has probably stopped the leak, and *shouldn't* in the second sentence expresses unlikelihood.

(35) That *should* do it. You *shouldn't* get any more water dripping out of that faucet.

Should have can express surprise that an event that had high probability did not occur. The contrast between the use of *should* to express probability and the use of *should have* to express a measure of surprise is illustrated in (36).

(36) a. It's 12:18; the bus *should* come by any minute now.
　　 b. The bus *should have* been here 10 minutes ago. I wonder what's holding it up.

In (36a), the speaker uses *should* to indicate probability because he knows that the bus is scheduled to come at 20 minutes after the hour and the time is 12:18. In (36b), the speaker uses *should have* to express surprise that the bus did not come on schedule.

• **Reproach or reprimand**. *Should have* can express a reproach or reprimand about actions taken or not taken. In (37a), the tone is one of a reproach, in which the person being spoken to has not honored his obligation. In (37b), the tone is a reprimand, in which the person addressed has broken a law. *Should have* is often pronounced *shoulda* in fast speech, as is illustrated in (37a).

(37) a. You *shoulda* taken care of me a little bit. I coulda been a contender![9]
b. You *shouldn't* have run that red light. That's a $50 fine in this state.

Must

Must expresses necessity and obligation; followed by *not*, it expresses prohibition but not, as discussed here, absence of obligation.

Necessity or Obligation

Must expresses necessity or obligation. Necessity can be external or internal. In (38a) and (38b), external circumstances create an obligation. In (38a), the threat of prosecution is meant to compel the listener; in (38b), it is the law that compels the speaker to act. In (38c), however, the necessity expressed by *must* is internally motivated: the speaker simply feels obligated to carry through with a particular course of action.

(38) a. You *must* fulfill the terms of your contract or else we will take you to court.
b. In pursuance of article 54, I *must* regrettably issue a warrant for your arrest.
c. I have decided not to pursue a career in law. I feel very strongly that I will be happier as a teacher. This is my destiny, and I *must* pursue it.

As is discussed later in this section, obligation or necessity in the past tense is expressed by *had to*, a form of the semimodal *have to*. This correspondence between *must* and *had to* is illustrated in (39).

(39) a. If I want to be selected for the Olympic team, I *must* win this race.
b. In order to be selected for the Olympic team, I *had to* win this race.

In (39a), the speaker mentions the condition that she must fulfill to become a member of the Olympic team. In (39b), having won the race, she talks about that same condition using *had to*.

The necessity or obligation meaning of a sentence with *must not* is that the speaker is obligated *not* to do whatever is in the following proposition. Sentences with *must not*, therefore, enjoin, or admonish, someone not to do something. For example, (40) is a warning not to forget to turn off the gas.

(40) You *must not* forget to turn off the gas before you leave the house.

Prohibition

Must not can also be a statement of prohibition. In (41), the judge means that the listener is not allowed to contact former associates and criminals. If the paroled criminal violates this order, there will be serious consequences.

(41) Judge: You *must not* have any further contact with any of your former associates or any criminals. If you do, I will have to revoke your parole.

Although used in expressing prohibition, *must* is not used in expressing the meaning "it is not necessary." This meaning is usually expressed by either *need not* or *don't have to*, as is discussed in their respective sections. *Need not* is more typical of British English; speakers of American English prefer *don't have to*, as illustrated in (42).

(42) a. You *need not* answer every question on the exam.   *British English*
b. You *don't have to* answer every question on the exam.   *American English*
c. You *must not* answer every question on the exam.

It is important for students to realize that *must not* cannot be used to express the absence of necessity or obligation. A common mistake made by many English learners is to say sentences like (42c) when they want to express the absence of obligation meaning shown in (42a) and (42b). The reason for this is discussed in the Problems section of this chapter.

Minimal Requirement or Condition
Must is also used to indicate a minimal requirement or condition for something, as shown in (43). The minimal requirement meaning "at least" is not inherently a meaning of *must* and generally comes from the real-world context. A person hearing the sentence in (43) would assume a Ph.D. in microbiology would not be a disqualifying factor.

(43) You *must* have an M.A. in microbiology if you want to be considered for the job.

Extended Meanings
Must has the following extended meanings:

• **Inferred probability**. *Must* expresses inferred probability or supposition. In (44a), the speaker draws a conclusion on the basis of something the other person just said, and in (44b), the speaker guesses a man's age based on his appearance.

(44) a. Wow, you pronounced that perfectly! You *must* be French.
b. Well, judging from his appearance, he *must* be about 40.

Must have always signals inferred probability. In (45a), the speaker uses personal knowledge to infer when a past event took place, and in (45b), speaker B makes an inference about something that has just happened in order to answer speaker A's question.

(45) a. She said that they have been married for as long as she's known my brother.
Well, that means they *must have* gotten married about 20 years ago.
b. A: Look! There he is in front of us. How could he have passed us without our having seen him?
B: He *must have* taken a shortcut.

• **Polite insistence**. *Must* is used to express polite insistence in invitations and apologies. Particularly when the modal is stressed, as in (46a) and (46b), the speaker intends to convey the meaning "I insist that." In these contexts, the obligation meaning of *must* is extended by the speaker to urge the listener to do something. This use of *must* is more common in British than in American English.

(46) a. You *MUST* come to dinner on Friday! George Clooney is going to be there.
b. You *MUST* forgive me! I'm so sorry I spilled that on you. I'll pay for the cleaning bill, of course.

SUMMARY

PURE MODALS OF ADVICE AND NECESSITY

Pure modals of advice and necessity are as follows:

Should

- **advice**
  That's a very deep wound. You should see a doctor immediately.

- **extended meanings**

  - **probability**
    We replaced the alternator, so it shouldn't give you any more problems.

  - **reproach or reprimand**
    Mr. Blake should have been more careful, but he was driving recklessly, as usual.

Must

- **necessity or obligation**
  She must report to the office no later than Tuesday, or they will send someone out to bring her in.
  You must not be late.

- **prohibition**
  You must not leave the country, or your parole will be revoked.

- **minimal requirement or condition**
  You must have three years' experience to be considered for the position.

- **extended meanings**

  - **inferred probability**
    Joel must be in great shape. He runs six miles every day.

  - **polite insistence**
    You MUST visit us this weekend. I insist on it.

EXERCISE 14.2

Indicate the meaning expressed by each modal verb in italics. Some of the modals express a basic meaning, and others express an extended meaning.

Example: Judge: You *must* not drive your car for three months. If you do, you will be arrested and subject to a heavy fine.

Answer: must = prohibition

1. She *must* get a B on this exam if she wants to pass the class.
2. (hearing the telephone ring) That *should* be Mom.
3. Plumber to customer: That *should* take care of your hot water problem.
4. You *should* get some rest. You look beat.
5. Wife: You *mustn't* forget to take out the trash on Sunday evening.

6. We *should* be able to see Venus on a clear night like this. Look, there it is!

7. You really *should have* lent him the money. He's your best friend, you know.

8. We *must* contact him today before he leaves for Thailand.

MARGINAL MODALS AND SEMIMODALS OF ADVICE AND NECESSITY

With one exception (*be going to*), the marginal modals and semimodals discussed in this chapter all have meanings related to necessity and advice. We start with the three marginal modals (*dare*, *need*, *ought to*) and then turn to semimodals.

Dare

The marginal modal *dare* is rare and is more typical of British than American English.[10] *Dare* is sometimes referred to as a *nonassertive modal* because it appears only in questions and negative statements.[11] These two contexts are associated, respectively, with the modal's basic meaning of advice and with its extended meanings.

Advice

When it appears in questions, as in (47a), *dare* asks for advice. In American English, the question in (47a) would more likely be expressed using a pure modal such as *should* or *would*, as shown in (47b) and (47c).

(**47**) a. *Dare* I tell her?
    b. *Should* I tell her?
    c. *Would* it be OK to tell her?

Extended Meanings

In negative statements, *dare* has two extended meanings:

- **Admonition**. Statements with *dare not* that directly address someone are equivalent to admonitions with *must not* or *can't*. In (48), the speaker is admonishing someone not to tell the speaker's mother about something.

(**48**) You $\left\{ \begin{array}{l} dare\ not \\ must\ not \end{array} \right\}$ tell my mother about this. It would really upset her.

- **Impossibility**. In statements that are not intended as admonitions, *dare not* has an *impossibility* meaning (i.e., "it's not possible"), which can also be expressed with *can't*, as illustrated in (49).

(**49**) a. I *dare not* tell my mother about this. It would really upset her.
    b. I *can't* tell my mother about this. It would really upset her.

In these various uses, the modal *dare* must be distinguished from the intransitive verb *dare*, meaning "to have the courage/nerve to do something," shown in (50a), and the transitive verb *dare*, meaning "to challenge someone to do something," shown in (50b).

(**50**) a. He doesn't *dare* (to) jump off the bridge. He knows it's too high.
    b. I double *dare* you to try it!

Need

The marginal modal *need* has the basic meaning of necessity and an extended meaning related to advice.

Necessity

The marginal modal *need* expresses necessity. When directly followed by a verb, *need*, like *dare*, appears especially in British English in questions and negative statements. The former is shown in (51a); the latter – *needn't* to express that it is not necessary to do something – is shown in (51b). Speakers of American English will usually use *don't have to* instead of *needn't*, as shown in (51c).[12]

> (**51**) a. *Need* I remind you that what you are proposing is exactly
> what got us into this mess? (Is it necessary for me to
> remind you that what you are proposing is exactly what got
> us into this mess?)   *British English*
> b. You *needn't* tell her. (It isn't necessary to tell her.)   *British English*
> c. You *don't have to* tell her. (It isn't necessary to tell her.)   *American English*

Need is often followed by an infinitival complement, as in (52). In this case, it is considered to be a regular verb that has the same meaning of necessity.

> (**52**) We *need* to speak with him right now.

Extended Meaning (Advice)

The meaning of *need* can also be extended to express advice. For example, in (53a), the speaker is making a suggestion that could also be expressed with the advice modal *should*, as in (53b).

> (**53**) a. You look tired. You *need* to lie down and get some rest.
> b. You really *should* lie down and get some rest.

Ought To

Ought to is a marginal modal that conveys the same meanings as *should* and is interchangeable with it in almost all contexts, except that *ought to* is confined largely to affirmative statements. As shown in (55) and (56), its use in questions and negatives is more common in British than in American English. (In speech, *ought to* generally contracts to *oughta*.)

Advice

In (54), *ought to* is interchangeable with *should* in giving advice.

> (**54**) a. That's a bad cough. You $\begin{Bmatrix} ought\ to \\ should \end{Bmatrix}$ see a doctor.
>
> b. You $\begin{Bmatrix} ought\ to \\ should \end{Bmatrix}$ tell her about that.

Infrequently in British English, subject–aux inversion is applied to sentences with *ought to* to create *yes/no* questions, as shown in (55a). These questions sound somewhat clumsy and overly formal to speakers of American English, who tend to use *should* instead, as shown in (55b).

> (**55**) a. *Ought* we *to* tell him about it?   *British English*
> b. *Should* we tell him about it?   *American English*

Ought to with *not*, used very infrequently, can either be contracted, as in (56a), or be in an uncontracted form, as in (56b).[13] It occurs mainly in British English, with speakers of American English preferring *shouldn't*.

(56) a. You *oughtn't* (to) let him get away with that.   *British English*
     b. You *ought not* to let him get away with that.   *British English*

Extended Meanings

The extended meanings of *ought to* are the same as for *should*:

- **Inferred probability**. This meaning is illustrated in (57).

(57) a. We $\begin{Bmatrix} ought\ to \\ should \end{Bmatrix}$ be able to see the Eiffel Tower from here.

   b. That $\begin{Bmatrix} ought\ to \\ should \end{Bmatrix}$ do it.

   c. His flight $\begin{Bmatrix} ought\ to \\ should \end{Bmatrix}$ have arrived by now.

- **Reproach or reprimand**. *Ought to have* can express a reproach or reprimand about something that was not done. In (58), the speaker reproaches someone for failing to help his or her sister.

(58) You $\begin{Bmatrix} ought\ to \\ should \end{Bmatrix}$ have helped her. After all, she's your sister.

Had Better and *Had Best*

Had better and *had best* are the two semimodals used to give advice. *Had better* is more common, and for some speakers it has a wider range of meaning.

Had Better for Advice

Had better is a semimodal verb that expresses advice to someone, much as *should* does. The contracted form of *you had better* (*you'd better*) is often heard in spoken English, as in (59a); at times the subject pronoun and *had* are simply deleted, as in (59b).

(59) a. *You'd better* see a doctor about that cough. (I recommend that you see a doctor about that cough.)
     b. *Better* see a doctor about that cough.

Had better is often used to warn the listener of something, especially when the consequences of not heeding the warning may be severe, as in (60a) and (60b). *Had better* may also be used with a threat, as in (60c).

(60) a. *You had better* be careful – it's pretty icy out there.
     b. *You'd better* not go down there. You might never come back in one piece.
     c. *You'd better* keep your mouth shut about this, or I'll see to it that you're fired.

Had Best for Advice

Had best also expresses advice. This semimodal is often considered to be a dialectical variant of *had better*, but for some native speakers, *had best* is not used as frequently in the context of a warning. For these speakers, it would not be interchangeable with *had better* in a sentence such as (60b), which carries the warning of dire consequences. Both *had better* and *had best* are used in precautionary recommendations that do not carry such warnings, as shown in (61).

(**61**) *You'd best* take your raincoat. It looks like a big storm is sweeping in.

In (61), *you'd best* is used to express the idea that under the circumstances the best course of action would be for you to take your raincoat. In conversation, contractions are common and so are deletions of the subject pronoun and *had*, as shown in (62).

(**62**) *Best* take your raincoat.

Have To

Have to is a semimodal that expresses the same basic and extended meanings as *must*. Differences in the contexts in which the two appear, discussed later, relate to the fact that *must* is a pure modal, whereas *have to* is a semimodal. *Have to* is more common in American English than British English.[14] In spoken English, it is contracted to sound like *hafta* (a form not acceptable in written English).

Necessity or Obligation

The examples in (63) show the interchangeability of *have to* and *must* in expressing necessity or obligation. Earlier we saw that in American English, lack of obligation or necessity is typically expressed with *not + have to*, as illustrated in (63b).

(**63**) a. You $\begin{Bmatrix} have\ to \\ must \end{Bmatrix}$ notify the police right away.
   b. You *don't have to* notify the police right away.

As we also saw earlier, *had to* functions as the past tense of *must*, as illustrated in (64).

(**64**) He was so sick that we *had to* take him to the hospital yesterday.

Questions about necessity with *have to* require the use of *do* insertion, as demonstrated in (65a), whereas subject–aux inversion occurs with *must*, as in (65b).

(**65**) a. *Do* we *have to* invite all of your relatives to dinner?
   b. *Must* we invite all of your relatives to the wedding?

Have to can be preceded by the modal *will* to indicate future necessity or obligation, as shown in (66a). When preceded by a modal of possibility such as *may* or *might*, as in (66b), the meaning is that of possible future necessity.

(**66**) a. You *will have to* get that headlight replaced, or you will get a ticket.
   b. You *may have to* see a doctor if that wound doesn't heal soon.

Extended Meanings

Have to has the same extended meanings as *must*:

• **Inferred probability**. In (67), the second sentence supplies the grounds for the speaker's conjecture in the first sentence.

(**67**) He $\begin{Bmatrix} has\ to \\ must \end{Bmatrix}$ be over 70 years old. Look at those deep lines in his face!

• **Polite insistence**. In (68), *have to* is used like *must* in an apology.

(**68**) You $\begin{Bmatrix} have\ to \\ must \end{Bmatrix}$ forgive me. I'm afraid that I've forgotten your name.

Have Got To

Have got to and *have to* have the same meaning. *Have got to* is often reduced in spoken American English. *Got to* may be reduced to *gotta* (a form not acceptable in written English) as shown in (69). In addition, the *-'ve* contraction is often deleted, as shown in (69c) and (69d).[15]

(**69**) a. *I've gotta* work a lot harder.
   b. *John's gotta* be home early.
   c. I *gotta* read this article for the meeting tomorrow.
   d. I'm telling you, you *gotta* see this movie! It's fantastic!

Necessity or Obligation

Like *must* and *have to*, *have got to* can express necessity or obligation, as shown in (70).

(**70**) She $\begin{Bmatrix} has\ got\ to \\ has\ to \\ must \end{Bmatrix}$ return the book to the library tomorrow. It's overdue!

Although *have got to* and *have to* have the same meaning, *have got to* cannot be substituted in all contexts for *have to*. As (71) shows, only *had to* can be used as the past tense of *must*.[16]

(**71**) a. I was so sick that I *had to* go to the hospital.
   b. *I was so sick that I *had got to* go to the hospital.

Furthermore, unlike *have to*, *have got to* cannot be preceded by other modals like *may*, *might*, or *will*, as (72) shows.

(**72**) a. He's very sick. He *will have to* go to the hospital.
   b. He's very sick. *He *will have got to* go to the hospital.

Extended Meanings

The extended meanings of *have got to* are as for *must* and *have to*:

• **Inferred probability**, as in (73).

(**73**) Look at that bruise on her cheek. Boy, that $\begin{Bmatrix} has\ got\ to \\ has\ to \\ must \end{Bmatrix}$ hurt!

• **Polite insistence**, as in (74).

(**74**) You simply *have to* come with me to George's party. I can't possibly go alone.

Be Supposed To (Obligation)

Be supposed to is a semimodal that expresses obligation determined by some plan or preconceived view, as shown in (75).

(**75**) a. Whenever an emergency like that arises, you're *supposed to* notify your supervisor right away.
   b. A true scientist *is supposed to* view the phenomena with total objectivity and ignore any other factors such as emotional attachment to particular theories.

In (75a), the speaker uses *be supposed to* to express an obligation to follow established procedures. In (75b), the speaker uses the semimodal to express an obligation to follow a point of view dictated by a group.

SUMMARY

MARGINAL MODALS AND SEMIMODALS OF ADVICE AND NECESSITY

Marginal modals and **semimodals** all have meanings related to necessity and advice.

Marginal modals are as follows:

Dare

- **advice**

  Dare I bring this up in the meeting?   British English

- **extended meanings**

  - **admonition**

    You dare not tell her.   British English

  - **impossibility**

    I dare not tell my mother about this.   British English

Need

- **necessity**

  You needn't tell her.

- **extended meanings**

  - **advice**

    You really need to discuss this with your son. Otherwise, things will never change.

Ought to

- **advice**

  You ought to be more careful with your money.

- **extended meanings**

  - **inferred probability**

    His flight ought to have arrived by now.

  - **reproach or reprimand**

    Hey! That was a stop sign. You ought to have stopped.

Semimodals are as follows:

Had better and had best

- **advice**

  You'd better get down from that tree. You're going to fall and get hurt.
  You'd best take your raincoat. It looks like it's going to rain.

Have to

- **necessity or obligation**

  Ricardo has to finish his project by this evening.
  Erica had to be rushed to the hospital yesterday.

• **extended meanings**

  ▪ **inferred probability**
  Those kids have to be tired. They've been running around all afternoon.

  ▪ **polite insistence**
  We'd love to see you. You have to come visit.

Have got to

• **necessity or obligation**
  I've got to pay that phone bill today.

• **extended meanings**

  ▪ **inferred probability**
  Those kids have got to be tired. They've been running around all afternoon.

  ▪ **polite insistence**
  What a great cake! You've got to give me the recipe!

Be supposed to

• **obligation**
  You're supposed to call the doctor's office if you can't keep your appointment.

EXERCISE 14.3

Indicate the meaning expressed by each modal verb in italics. Some of the modals express a basic meaning, and others express an extended meaning.

Example: You *needn't* go into great detail. Just give us a summary of what happened.

Answer: needn't = lack of necessity

1. Wow, is it ever hot! *It's gotta* be at least 100 degrees in the shade.
2. We *oughta* tell him what happened.
3. He has a driver's license, so he *has to* be at least 18. I'd guess he's somewhere between 18 and 21.
4. You'*d better* take something to drink. It's going to be a hot day.
5. We'*ve gotta* find a way to increase our sales of tennis shoes.
6. I *need* to get ahold of him right now. It's an emergency.
7. You *have to* notify the police whenever something like this happens.
8. *Dare* I tell him?
9. We *ought to* be able drive there, have lunch, and get back in time for dinner.
10. *Isn't* he *supposed to* be helping her?
11. You'*d best* bundle up. It's cold outside.

PURE MODALS AND SEMIMODAL FOR EXPRESSING FUTURE TIME

Future time can be expressed with three pure modals – *will, shall,* and *would* – and the semimodal *be going to.* (For more on expressing future time with and without modals, see Chapter 16.)

Will

Will expresses future time, including predictions about the future, and has several extended meanings.

Future Time; Prediction

Will followed by a main verb is used to talk about future time, as in (76a). Sometimes this takes the form of making a prediction, as in the case of (76b) and perhaps also in (76c). *Will* is often contracted with a preceding pronoun, as in (76b) and (76c).

> (76) a. Sarah *will* retire in one or two years.
> b. *They'll* go on to win the championship.
> c. By this time tomorrow, *we'll* be in Cleveland.

Extended Meanings

In addition to generally expressing future time and to its predictive meaning, *will* has the following meanings:

- **Volition**. Some English language teaching textbooks and grammars explain that *shall* indicates *volition*, or strong intent, on the part of the speaker while *will* expresses a prediction. But this contrast does not always hold up well, especially in American English, in which *shall* is seldom used. The fact is that *will* can also be used to express volition.

  Volition springs from an internal desire of the speaker, and the decision to assign volition to a particular instance of a modal depends on the context. In (77a), for instance, *will* seems to express a prediction, or simply a future action, not volition. However, in (77b), the phrase *no matter what you want me to do* indicates that the speaker is expressing volition with *will*. A speaker's internal intent to do something may also be signaled by stress, as illustrated in (77c). Since it depends so heavily on context, volition is largely a pragmatically determined meaning.

> (77) a. I *will* probably leave tomorrow.   *future action/*
>   *prediction*
>
> b. I *will* leave tomorrow no matter what you want me to do.   *volition*
> c. I *WILL* leave tomorrow!   *volition*

- **Inferred probability**. *Will* can be used to express inferred probability, particularly about the immediate future. In (78), the speaker makes an informed guess based on the knowledge of certain facts and particular circumstances.

> (78) That'*ll* be the 5:15 train.

  If the speaker knows that a particular train is scheduled to arrive at 5:15 every day and, while standing on the station platform at 5:14, hears a train whistle in the distance, he or she may well utter the sentence above. The use of *will* implies more certainty than *should* in this context. Here *will* is similar to *must*. *Must* could substitute for *will* in (78) with no change in meaning – *That must be the 5:15 train*.

- **Requests (polite alternatives to commands)**. *Will* is used to change what would otherwise be a command into a request. Thus, (79b) is a slightly more polite version of the command in (79a).

(79) a. Step into my office for a second.
     b. *Will* you step into my office for a second?

Shall

Shall is the least used of all the pure modals, but it is clearly used more frequently in British English than in American English.[17] Like *will*, it expresses future time, including prediction, and has extended meanings.

Future Time

In (80a), *shall* is being used to express a prediction about the future. This same meaning is most commonly expressed in American English with *will*, as in (80b).

(80) a. According to the most recent polls, I *shall* win in November.　*British English*
     b. According to the most recent polls, *I'll* win in November.　*American English*

It is probably accurate to say that *shall* is becoming archaic, at least in American English, and is used primarily in polite requests, discussed next. However, *shall* can still be heard in sentences that express future time. Furthermore, in British English *shall* can impart a tone of legal and quasilegal insistence and formality, as it does in (81).[18] Here, again, American English favors *will*.

(81) We *shall* inform you of our decision within ten days.

The negative contraction *shan't* appears only in British English. Speakers of American English use *won't*.

Extended Meanings

Shall has the following extended meanings:

- **Volition**. In statements, *shall* can be used to express strong volition. However, this meaning usually occurs in a context like a speech or public statement that is designed to express commitment and to arouse public emotion for the particular cause, as shown in (82).

(82) a. We *shall* overcome these difficulties and go on to win!
     b. The person who committed this terrible crime *shall* be punished!

- **Suggestions and requests for advice**. *Shall* is used with first person pronouns in questions. Frequently this is a request for advice, as in (83a), but it may also be a suggestion, as in (83b) and (83c). In American English, *shall* occurs more frequently in tag questions such as (83c).

(83) a. *Shall* I tell him now or later?
     b. The weather is beautiful today. *Shall* we go for a stroll?
     c. Let's discuss that at our next meeting, *shall* we?

Would

Would can be seen as the past equivalent of *will*. This correspondence is reflected in some of its meanings.

Prediction in the Past; Future in the Past

Would is used to talk about future predictions made in the past and in statements about the past that correspond to statements about the present with *will*, as illustrated in (84).

(84) a. I think it *will* rain any minute.
b. I thought it *would* rain any minute.

More generally, *would* is used in talking about the future from the perspective of some point in the past. This is illustrated in (85), which involves events at various points in the past. *Would* is used in mentioning the events (the meetings) that occurred after the time of the event (the dinner) mentioned in the prepositional phrase.

(85) After dinner that evening, we *would* meet just three more times.

Extended Meanings

Would has the following extended meanings:

- **Regular action in the past**. *Would* is used to describe a regularly occurring action in the past. In (86), the speaker describes something that happened on a regular basis.

(86) He *would* come in here nearly every day to buy a newspaper.

- **Hypothetical results**. *Would* is the modal that indicates hypothetical results in conditional sentences. This is discussed in detail in Chapter 19. An example of a hypothetical conditional is shown in (87).

(87) If you went to Chicago, you *would* see some beautiful, modern buildings.

- **Inferred probability**. Like *will*, *would* can be used to express inferred probability, as in (88), where the speaker has been expecting a friend named Fred and guesses that he has arrived when there is a knock at the door.

(88) That *would* be Fred. (That's probably Fred.)

- **Polite requests**. *Would* is often used in polite requests. The request with *would* in (89a) is more polite than the one with *will* in (89b).

(89) a. *Would* you please stop talking so loudly? We're trying to study.
b. *Will* you please stop talking so loudly? We're trying to study.

Be Going To

The semimodal *be going to* is the modal in addition to *will* that is often used to talk about the future. As discussed later, the two are not often used interchangeably.

Future Time: Planned Action

Be going to indicates planned future action, as shown in (90).

(90) I'*m going to* leave a little after seven o'clock. (= I plan to leave a little after seven o'clock.)

In this sense of "plan to," *be going to* is similar to the modal *will* used to express future action, predictions, and volition. Nonetheless, *will* and *be going to* are not used interchangeably in sentences like these, and this fact is worth teaching to students. *Be going to* tends to be used when the speaker wants to talk about something that is a fairly fixed plan. When speakers refer to future actions that are still not firm or depend on conditions that are unknown or beyond their control, they tend to use *will* (with *probably*, *maybe*, *I think*, etc.) instead of *be going to*, as shown in (91). The first sentence contains *be going to* because the speaker is talking about a fixed, planned event. The following sentences use *will* because the future activities described are uncertain.

(91) Speaker: I'*m going* to visit Siena in October. I *will probably* spend some time in the Tuscan countryside around San Gimignano. And then *I think I'll go* on to Florence.

The tendency to use *be going to* for planned future action and *will* for future action that is less certain or less controllable is just that – a tendency. Thus, you may hear native speakers use *be going to* in the second and third sentences in (91). It is often claimed that *be going to* is less formal than *will* when used to speak of future events or actions, but this is hard to prove. While it is true that *will* is used more often in writing than *be going to*, the fact is that *will* is used more frequently in speaking as well.[19]

Future Time: Immediately Imminent Action

Be going to is used when speaking about an action that appears to be immediately imminent or has already started. If, for example, a passenger sees that the car she is riding in is about to crash into another car, she will utter (92a) rather than (92b), because the latter does not carry this sense of imminent occurrence. (The # indicates that this sentence does not fit its context – the preceding *Look out!*)

(92) a. Look out! We'*re going to* hit that car!
　　 b. Look out! #We'*ll* hit that car.

SUMMARY

PURE MODALS AND SEMIMODALS FOR EXPRESSING FUTURE TIME

The **pure modals** and **semimodal** for expressing future time are as follows:

Will

- **future time; prediction**
  She'll retire in one or two years.
  He'll lose in straight sets.

- **extended meanings**

  - **volition**
    I promise you that we will go on to victory!

  - **inferred probability**
    That will be Jorge. He always arrives promptly at 3:00.

  - **requests (polite alternatives to commands)**
    Will you move your car a bit to the left?

Shall

- **future time; prediction**
  It appears that his play shall be a great success.　　*British English*

- **extended meanings**

  - **volition**
    We SHALL beat them this year!

continued

- **suggestions and requests for advice**
  Let's get started, shall we?
  Shall I reschedule the meeting for next week?

Would

- **prediction in the past; future in the past**
  I thought our game would get rained out.
  I tried to convince the dean, but she wouldn't listen.

- **extended meanings**

  - **regular action in the past**
    Milo would always stop by to say hello before heading to school.

  - **hypothetical results**
    If you listened more carefully, you would get better grades.

  - **inferred probability**
    That would be Fred. He calls every day at 7 o'clock sharp.

  - **polite requests**
    Would you please refrain from smoking in here?

Be going to (semimodal)

- **future time: Planned action**
  I'm going to visit my grandmother next weekend.

- **future time: Immediately imminent action**
  Slow down! We're going to miss the exit!

EXERCISE 14.4

Indicate the meaning expressed by each modal verb in italics. Some of the modals express a basic meaning, and others express an extended meaning.

Example: They shall not pass!

Answer: volition

1. Back when she was just a little kid, she *would* talk your ear off.
2. We *shall* severely punish the people who committed this heinous crime.
3. He *would* come in here every day and tell me how to run my business.
4. If I didn't have so much work to do, I *would* go to a movie tonight.
5. That'*d* be Alice; she said she was coming over to drop something off after dinner.
6. *Shall* we have tea outside on the veranda? It's such a lovely evening.
7. I'*m going to* take a vacation in June. I'*ll* probably go out to California and visit my cousin.
8. My father waved good-bye as I got into the taxi. I did not realize that I *would* never see him again.

PROBLEMS THAT ESL/EFL STUDENTS HAVE WITH MODALS

ESL/EFL students have two documented problems with learning English modal verbs. The first is a syntactic problem. Students typically seek meaning correspondences between English modal verbs and verbs in their own L1. When a close correspondence is found, they will often transfer the L1 grammar associated with that L1 verb to the corresponding English modal. This can lead to grammatical errors like those described next for Spanish. The second problem involves choosing a modal that does not express the meaning that the student wishes to convey. This kind of complex, pragmatics-related problem is discussed later and is illustrated for German and Korean speakers.

Following Modals with Infinitives (Spanish)

Spanish does not have a set of modals comparable to English modals. Verbs such as *deber*, *poder*, and *tener que* have roughly the same meanings as *should/ought to*, *can/could*, and *must/have to*, but they do not share their grammatical characteristics. *Deber* carries a meaning roughly equivalent to the advice or recommendation meaning of *should* in (93a), and *poder* carries a meaning similar to the request for permission meaning of *can* in (93b). Notice that in (93a) *debes*, the second person singular of *deber*, is followed by an infinitive form, *ir* ("to go"), as is *puedo*, the first person singular of *poder* in (93b). Stockwell, Bowen, and Martin (1966) noted long ago that these Spanish verbs inflect for number and are followed by other verbs in the infinitive form.

(93) a. *Debes   ir   al cine   dos   veces   a   la   semana.*
            you should   to go to the cinema two   times   in   the   week
            "You should go to the movies two times a week."
        b. *¿Puedo   ir?*
            I can   to go
            "Can I go?"

When learning to use English modals, Spanish speakers will frequently use an infinitive after the modal. The result is errors such as the one in (94).

(94) *My daughter told me, "I *can't to believe* that you aged so quickly."

The speaker who uttered (94) is otherwise quite fluent. Examples of this kind of error have also been observed in the compositions of Spanish speakers who have been admitted to an American university. Two examples, taken from different compositions, are shown in (95).

(95) a. *In all situations I hear English and I *must to talk* English, and the most important thing is the I *must to pronounce* a correct English.
        b. *. . . he did not think or had in mind that provide economic support for his family is one thing he *must to do*.

This error type (95), which is pervasive with Spanish speakers who have beginning or low-intermediate proficiency, may not always disappear, even when these students become more proficient and hear correct use of English modals. You will therefore have to decide whether to use particular focus-on-form activities to show students that they should not use infinitives after modals.

Incorrect Use of *Must Not* (German)

Some ESL/EFL students incorrectly use *must not* to indicate that something is not necessary. The German modal verb *müssen* has the same necessity meaning as *must*. But *müssen* is also used to express the absence of necessity with *nicht* ("not") in German; in English we use *don't have to* to express the absence of necessity. In (96), *müssen* is used to express this absence of necessity meaning.

(96) *Aber wir müssen nicht unbedingt zu Fuß gehen.*
But we must not absolutely on foot go
"But we don't really have to walk (go on foot)."

German speakers who are beginners, and perhaps at the intermediate level, frequently make errors like those in (97), taken from a composition by an undergraduate at an American university.

(97) New technology has made my life much easier. I *must not* go to work by foot, I take the car instead. When I come home I *must not* warm up the room because the heating has done it automatically.

While the sentences in (97) are perfectly grammatical, they do not express the meaning intended by the writer.

Selecting an Appropriate Modal (Korean)

Korean speakers may often choose a modal that does not seem appropriate for a given context. Exactly why this happens is not clear. Sometimes it may relate to the fact that in certain cases a single form in Korean corresponds to meanings expressed by several English modals. For example, Korean has one form, *~hay-ya-man-hata*, that may be equivalent to the English modals *should* and *ought to* as well as *must* and *have to*. As we have seen, native English speakers would likely interpret a sentence such as *You should do that* as advice but a sentence like *You must do that* as an expression of strong obligation.

The context of the composition from which the sentence in (98) is taken indicates that the Korean speaker who wrote it intended to express advice, so one would expect the writer to use *should* or *ought to*. Instead, the modal that was selected, *must*, expresses obligation.

(98) In conclusion, shopping *must* be short and simple.

This problem requires more research. Since sentences like (98) are grammatical, it is hard to suggest a solution, and it is often difficult to tell if the modal used does not, in fact, express exactly what the writer or speaker intended.

A more blatant example of inappropriate choice is shown in (99), which was written by a Korean graduate student at an American university.

(99) In conclusion, the nativeness/nonnativeness *could not* be the absolute criterion in hiring English teachers if they are similar in proficiency.

From the context of the essay from which this sentence was taken, it appears that the writer's intent was to state that it is not advisable to use the stated criterion for hiring English teachers. A native speaker would naturally have written *should not* to express this meaning. The choice of *couldn't* is confusing, because it does not convey the idea of inadvisability, but instead seems to convey impossibility. More data from error corpora produced by English language learners with other L1s would allow us to determine how prevalent this type of error is in the writing of students with other L1s. You may want to keep an eye out for this type of error, and if you encounter it, take some corrective action through PI techniques.

SUGGESTIONS FOR TEACHING MODALS

The coverage of modals in English language teaching textbooks is improving, and you may come across fairly inventive lessons in books at various levels. Many textbooks do a reasonably good job of teaching basic meanings, in particular. Some of these books teach modals by grouping them in a way similar to the presentation in this chapter. There is certainly some intuitive value to this organization, since it is clearly important that students learn to recognize various important continua of the type that Celce-Murcia and Larsen-Freeman (1999) and Master (1996) have proposed (e.g., a continuum of politeness in the choice of modals in requests). However, native speakers do not always agree on the gradations within a particular continuum and the gradations proposed may be so nuanced that they are not easily taught. Groupings of modals may also be slightly misleading, since modals have more than one meaning. Moreover, textbooks may omit many of the extended meanings of modals. You should therefore look carefully at the ways modals are grouped in any textbook that you plan to use and decide whether you agree with the author's formulation.

It is a good idea to skip very low frequency modals and, if you are teaching American English, modals used mainly in British English. For example, you might skip *dare* or even *shall*. In addition, you may choose to delay teaching modal meanings that relate to grammatical constructions that you will be covering later in greater detail. For instance, if the use of *would* in conditional sentences will receive in-depth coverage at a later point in the syllabus, along with other forms used in conditional sentences, then you may choose to skip this use of *would* when dealing with modals in general.

Activity 1: Introducing Ability with *Can* and *Could* (Beginning)

You can introduce the meaning of ability with *can* by writing a number of professions on the board (e.g., pilot, photographer, bus driver, artist, writer, engineer) and then asking the question, "What can a(n) _____ do?" Go around the class and ask each student to supply a sentence such as *A pilot can fly an airplane*. Then ask, "Can you do that too?" Help students answer in short answers. Choose professions that the students are familiar with and that allow the formation of fairly easy answers. If possible, use pictures of the professions to avoid any confusion.

To introduce the use of *could* as the past tense version of *can*, begin with a pair of sentences that contrasts the two modals, such as in (100a) and (100b).

(**100**) a. When I was younger, I *could* swim 500 meters without stopping.
　　　　b. Now I *can* only swim 100 meters without stopping.

Think of other activities similar to the one in (100) that all students can relate to (e.g., hiking a certain distance, running a course at some speed, working for so many hours, partying until some late hour, dancing for some length of time). Write these on the board. Have the students suggest more activities. Then have the students pair off and write sentences like those in (100) with the activities. Encourage them to come up with outrageous and amusing exaggerations of how much more they can do now than they could in the past. Then call on students to present pairs of sentences to the class.

Activity 2: Practicing Modals of Possibility (Intermediate)

This game provides practice with modals of possibility (*might*, *may*, and *could*). It was inspired by an activity by Rutherford (1974) that used "droodles," conceptual drawings conceived by Roger Price, and by the "complete cloze" exercise by Rinvolucri (1984). (The Rutherford activity using "droodles" is shown in Chapter 18, Activity 5, page 444.) The game can be done as a group activity or with the entire class led by the teacher. It can be found in some English language textbooks. For this activity, you will need images (101) through (104). You can find these pictures and others like them on the Internet by searching for "optical illusions." Many sites allow you to download these pictures.

Project an enlarged version of the drawing in (101) using an overhead projector, or provide students with copies of the drawing. Then ask "What do you think this picture might be?" Call on one of the students, who will probably say something like "It looks like a vase" or "It looks like a cup." Respond by explaining that it might be a vase or cup but that, if you look carefully, you can see that it might be two people. Point out the noses, lips, and chins of the two people facing each other in the picture.

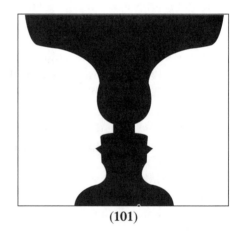

(101)

Next, hand out a sheet of paper with pictures (101), (102), and (103) on it. Tell the students that each of these drawings also has two possible interpretations. Ask them to guess what these *might*, *may*, or *could* be. Have students work in pairs and come up with their own interpretations and write them down (e.g., *The first picture might be a(n) _____, but it could also be a(n) _____*).

(102)

(103)

(104)

Possible interpretations are: (102), a duck or rabbit; (103), a man playing a horn or a woman looking at you; (104), the head of a man or the back of a person standing.

Richards (1999, p. 87), suggests an excellent variation on this activity. Divide the class into pairs, and give each pair a set of pictures demonstrating various gestures ("hello," "be quiet," "come here," "we won," etc.). Encourage them to guess what each gesture means. Afterwards, the students form groups and each member takes a turn acting out a sentence using gestures of his or her own creation (e.g., "I'm hungry," "I'm scared," "pay attention," "please"). The rest of the group members make guesses about the meanings of the gestures, using various modals (e.g., "He might be saying, 'I'm hungry' or he could be telling us to pay attention").

Activity 3: Contrasting *Will* with *Be Going To* (Intermediate)

One way to help your students distinguish the use of *will* (to talk about future actions and make predictions) from the use of *be going to* (to talk about planned activities) is to describe a sightseeing trip that you intend to take. For this, you might bring in a map that shows the cities and the area you intend to visit as well as pictures of the various attractions there.

If you choose to use the vacation to the Tuscany region of Italy described in (105), you might give the students a map of Tuscany with the cities you plan to visit. You can make an enlarged photocopy of a section of a map that shows Siena, Lucca, Pisa, and Florence. Next, find small pictures of the Plaza del Campo e Palazzo Comunale in Siena, the leaning tower of Pisa, the towers of Lucca, and attractions in Florence such as the Uffizi gallery, the statue of David, and the Ponte Vecchio. These pictures can most likely be obtained from a tourist agency free of charge. Cut out the pictures, make a collage on one sheet of paper, label each attraction, and make photocopies.

To prepare students for the activity, illustrate the difference in meaning between *be going to* and *will*, asking a question such as "What are you going to do after class (tomorrow at this time, etc.)?" Help students answer with *going to* and write their answers on the board. Point out that we use *going to* when we state definite plans. Then ask, "What are you going to do next week?" Help students who give indefinite plans to answer using *will* and write their responses on the board. Point out that we use *will* with words such as *probably*, *maybe*, and *I think* to talk about plans we are not sure of.

Now begin describing your planned trip, as shown in (105), as the students listen and follow along with their handouts and maps.

(105) "In June (next month/next summer), I'm going to take a trip to Tuscany. First, I'm going to go to Florence. There are so many things to see in Florence that I probably won't be able to see them all. I'll probably walk across the Ponte Vecchio, and I am sure that I will see the statue of David, but I don't know if I will be able to visit the Uffizi gallery. It's so crowded that it's hard to get in there."

As you mention each possible sightseeing attraction, hold up your handout and point to the picture of it. (The activity is even more effective with slides.)

After you finish describing the things you might see in Florence, go on to say, for example, "Next, I'm going to go to Siena," and proceed in the same manner.

Finally, assign your students the task of describing a trip that they are going to take. Ask them to write out their itinerary of the places and attractions they plan to and might visit. They must find pictures of some of these sights and locations and then come back to class and describe their trip to the other students using *be going to* and *will*.

Activity 4: Practicing Modals of Necessity (Intermediate)

Any kind of fixed procedure that involves several steps is useful for practicing the necessity modals and their negative forms. For example, you might use the procedure for registering at the university or the procedure for obtaining a driver's license. Try to think of procedures that the students have already gone through or may have to go through in the future.

Start with a procedure that the students are unfamiliar with, and describe it to them using modals and semimodals of necessity, as in (106).

> (**106**) First, you*'ve got to* pick up this form at the department office. Then you *have to* go see your advisor. She *must* sign your course list. Then you *have to* go back to the department office. . . .

You can write on the board an abbreviated sequence of the things to be done (pick up registration form, see advisor, advisor signs form, go back to department office, etc.) and point to these as you describe the routine. Try to include at least one instruction that uses a modal of necessity in its negative form (e.g., "You don't have to . . . "). Then the students pair up and have one student advise the other regarding the procedure.

Provide the students with several routines like this. Give them the assignment of preparing an explanation of a procedure they are familiar with to share with the class.

Activity 5: Focusing on Continua of Meanings (Intermediate)

One of the approaches that is used to teach continua of meaning (e.g., degrees of politeness or possibility) involves giving students sentences that can be restated with modals. For example, in what is sometimes called "the weatherman activity," one student supplies a cue such as "There is a 30 percent chance of snow on Wednesday," and another student restates the sentence using *might*, for example, "It might snow on Wednesday." These kinds of activities are useful and are included in some English language teaching materials.

The process can be reversed to draw students' attention to the appropriateness of modals in different contexts. Howard Williams (personal communication), at Teachers College, Columbia University, describes a simple but effective activity that gets students to focus on how important pragmatic factors are in the choice of some modals. He gives students a single sentence frame, like the one in (107), and changes the modal within it. Then he refers to each modal, asking the students if it is appropriate, and if not, why not.

$$
(107) \text{ You} \begin{Bmatrix} should \\ had\ better \\ must \\ need\ to \end{Bmatrix} \text{try one of these breath mints.}
$$

Students will not have much trouble in seeing that, in this sort of sentence frame, *should* is appropriate as an invitation. The choice of *had better* is likely to require some thought, however, and, in looking at *must*, you may want to point out that, while this modal has a polite insistence meaning appropriate to this context, its necessity meaning renders it inappropriate.

Although this activity is intended primarily as a review, it could be used to focus on the meanings of new modals through contrasts with modals that have already been taught. The activity is also useful for looking at the meaning changes that occur when a modal is substituted for others, all of which are appropriate in the context. You will have to give some thought to creating contexts in which some modals are more or less acceptable than others, but the payoff is worth it.

Activity 6: Practicing the Inferred Probability Meaning of *Must* (Intermediate)

Bowen and McCreary (1977) describe several activities that can be used to teach the different meanings conveyed by *must have* + past participle. It is a tribute to the ingenuity of these two teachers that their ideas are as fresh and as useful today as when they proposed them. Begin by telling students that we sometimes make guesses about things that happened, for example, "If I see my neighbor climbing into his window instead of using the front door, I might guess, 'He must have forgotten his key.'" Then ask students to guess what happened in each of the situations described in (108). This exercise can be done in groups or as a class.

(108)
Situation 1:
John's lawn is always very tall. But the other day, when I drove by, the grass was nice and short. ("He must have cut the grass.")

Situation 2:
Mary always takes the bus to work. But the other day she drove to work in a brand new car. She came to work in the same car today. ("She must have bought a car.")

Situation 3:
Mustafa said that he would not have time to go visit his mother in Minneapolis this weekend. But, when I called him several times on Saturday and Sunday, there was no one there. ("He must have changed his mind. He must have decided to visit his mother after all.")

Situation 4:
Ann and John have been together for the past three years. But last week I saw her three times and she was always with another guy. She looked very happy, too. ("She must have broken up with John.")

Situation 5:
Susan left her bike outside the post office when she went to mail a letter. She was in a hurry, so she didn't lock it. When she came out, the bike was gone. ("Somebody must have taken/stolen her bike.")

Activity 7: More Practice with Inferred Probability (High Intermediate Through Advanced)

Even better than the short contexts in Activity 6 are longer stretches of connected discourse, which provide reading practice and stimulate the use of modals. The mystery story is an excellent vehicle for getting students to use modals that express inferred probability. Present the class with a short mystery story involving some crime. An example is shown in (109).

Have the students work in small groups to examine the statements taken by the detective. Students must decide who could not and who must have stolen Mrs. Groot's necklace, according to the statements. Tell them to examine the people's statements and eliminate all those who they think could not have committed the crime. For each of these people, they will say, for example, "X couldn't have stolen the necklace because . . . ," and supply the reason. When students have eliminated all other suspects, they will be able to conclude who must have taken it ("X must have stolen the jewels / must be the thief because . . . "). Finally, have students come together as a class and present their conclusions about who must have committed the crime. (The identity of the thief can be found in the Answer Key, on page 655.)

(**109**) Kies Groot is the president of a small company in Holland. He often travels to other countries on business. Last year he took his wife with him on a business trip to London. While they were staying at a famous hotel near Hyde Park, Mrs. Groot's valuable pearl necklace was stolen. A detective from Scotland Yard questioned Mr. and Mrs. Groot about the robbery and then interviewed all of the people who might know something about it. From the statements of the following people, the detective was able to discover who the thief was. Who was the thief?

Mrs. Groot:
I kept the necklace in my jewelry case in the bedroom when I wasn't wearing it. I wore it all day Tuesday and put it back in the case that evening before I went to bed. On Wednesday morning, I took it out of the case to put it on, but before I could, I had to go down to the lobby of the hotel to see an old friend of mine. That was about 9:30. I left the necklace lying on the dresser. When I got back at 10:15, it was gone. The maid was making the bed.

Mr. Groot:
On Wednesday morning, I had breakfast with my wife in our room. The waiter brought in breakfast at about 8:15, I believe. Then Lady L., the wife of a business associate, came to pick up my wife to go shopping with her. We were there chatting until Mr. Zylex came to pick me up. I left with him to go look at his new factory at about 10:00 A.M. I got back to the hotel at about 5:00. That's when I heard about the theft.

Maid:
I always make the rooms up between 9:00 and 11:30. I don't remember exactly when I made up the suite that the Groots were staying in. I think it was a little after 10:00. I remember that I had just barely started to make the bed when Mrs. Groot came in. She went right into the dressing room. Then she came out and asked me if I had seen a necklace on the dressing table. When I said no, she phoned the front desk. I was really upset. I think she believes I took the necklace. But I didn't! I hadn't even gone into the other room yet.

Room Service Waiter:
I brought their breakfast up at 8:10 and took the dishes away at 10:00. I remember the time exactly because one of the maids in the hall asked me what time it was, and I looked at my watch. I just went in and rolled out the table with the dishes on it. There was some other woman – not Mrs. Groot – in the room at the time. She let me in when I knocked at the door. I didn't see anyone else in the room.

Mr. Zylex:
I went up to Mr. Groot's room at about 9:45. He introduced me to Lady L. and we talked briefly before Mr. Groot and I left to go to my factory, where we stayed until almost 5:00. I do remember that the room had not been made up when we left.

Lady L.:
I went up to pick up Mrs. Groot about 9:15. We talked about where we would go shopping. Mr. Groot was there too. At about 9:30, Mrs. Groot excused herself and went down to the lobby to see an old friend. She said she would be back in a few minutes, but she hadn't come back by the time Mr. Groot's friend arrived, a Mr. Zylex, or something. They both left at about 10:00, when the waiter came in to take away the dishes. I waited a few more minutes until Mrs. Groot phoned up from the lobby and said that she would be delayed. She told me to go on to Selfridges, where she would meet me at 11:00. I remember the maid was just about to move on to this room when I closed the door and went down to the hall elevator. It's really surprising that things like this happen in good hotels, isn't it?

As the groups work, walk around the room, answering any questions about vocabulary and addressing any problems that arise. When it appears that all groups have reached a solution, mention a character (not the real culprit) and ask a spokesperson for a group to state and justify the group's decision about that character. Make sure that the student uses some modals of inferred probability. Then ask another group about another character, keeping the real culprit until last. The other groups may comment during each spokesperson's presentation.

ENDNOTES

[1] Modal verbs are also referred to as *modal auxiliaries.*

[2] Example is supported by Biber et al. (1999), p. 166.

[3] This observation is made by McCawley (1988), p. 248.

[4] An additional difference between modals and main verbs is that modals are not deleted in the reduction of sentences conjoined by *and*. This is discussed in more detail in Chapter 25.

[5] This observation is made by Biber et al. (1999), p. 483. The three-way classification of modals presented here follows Biber et al. (1999) but includes additional syntactic criteria in McCawley (1988).

[6] Biber et al. (1999), p. 484.

[7] The different meanings that modals can have are often labeled as either *root* or *epistemic*. A root meaning involves actions or events over which humans have some degree of control. For example, obligation, permission, and volition are said to be root meanings. An epistemic

meaning involves the logical status or likelihood of actions, events, or states. Possibility, prediction, and necessity, for example, are epistemic meanings. The term *deontic* is also used instead of *root*. You may also hear *root* and *epistemic* referred to as *intrinsic* and *extrinsic*, respectively.

[8] This grouping follows the one suggested by Biber et al. (1999), p. 485.

[9] From the film *On the Waterfront*, spoken by Marlon Brando.

[10] See Biber et al. (1999), p. 484.

[11] See Quirk et al. (1972), p. 83.

[12] Huddleston and Pullum (2002), p. 206, point out that sentences with *needn't* and *don't have to* can have different meaning when referring to past time. *He needn't have told her* conveys the meaning that he told her. *He didn't have to tell her* does not.

[13] See Biber et al. (1999), p. 165.

[14] See Biber et al. (1999), p. 488.

[15] As a result, you may hear some native speakers use *do* and *don't* with *gotta* in questions (e.g., *"Do we gotta read three chapters by Friday?"). Sentences like these are considered ungrammatical in educated English usage.

[16] There is no theoretical reason that *have got to* could not develop a past tense form "*had got to*." Many irregular verbs develop two forms that compete for some time before one of them predominates. A good example is the verb *dive* and its past tense form *dove*, which has been all but eliminated in favor of *dived*, the form with the regular past tense ending *-ed*. But the history of modal verbs in English shows that each modal permits only one way of expressing past modality. *Had to* has existed as the single past tense form for *must* for hundreds of years. So it seems unlikely that a form like *had got to* would arise and compete with the established *had to*.

[17] See Biber et al. (1999), p. 483.

[18] See Quirk et al. (1972), p. 99.

[19] See Biber et al. (1999), p. 495.

REFERENCES

Biber, D., Johansson, S., Leech, G., Conrad, S., & Finegan, E. (1999). *Longman grammar of spoken and written English*. Essex: Pearson Education Limited.

Bowen, J. D., & McCreary, C. F. (1977). Teaching the English modal perfects. *TESOL Quarterly*, *11*, 283–301.

Celce-Murcia, M., & Larsen-Freeman, D. (1999). *The grammar book: An ESL/EFL teacher's course*. 2nd ed. Boston, MA: Heinle & Heinle.

Huddleston, R., & Pullum, G. (2002). *The Cambridge grammar of the English language*. Cambridge: Cambridge University Press.

Master, P. (1996). *Systems in English grammar*. Englewood Cliffs, NJ: Prentice Hall.

McCawley, J. D. (1988). *The Syntactic phenomena of English*. Chicago and London: the University of Chicago Press.

Quirk, R., & Greenbaum, S. (1985). *A concise grammar of contemporary English*. Harcourt Brace Jovanovich: New York.

Quirk, R., Greenbaum, S., Leech, J., & Svartvik, J. (1972). *A grammar of contemporary English*. London, Longman.

Richards, J. (1999). *New interchange: English for international communication*. Cambridge: Cambridge University Press.

Rinvolucri, M. (1984). *Grammar games: Cognitive, affective and drama activities for EFL students*. Cambridge: Cambridge University Press.

Rutherford, W. (1974). Pragmatic syntax in the classroom. *TESOL Quarterly*, *24*, 205–214.

Stockwell, R. P., Bowen, J. D., & Martin, J. W. (1966). *The grammatical structures of English and Spanish*. Chicago: University of Chicago Press.

CHAPTER 15

Indirect Objects

INTRODUCTION

In this chapter, we look at how to teach English language learners to form sentences that contain an indirect object (IO). Many English verbs may be followed by two NPs – a direct object (DO) and an indirect object.[1] Direct and indirect objects in sentences may follow one of two patterns, or orders. English language learners often choose the wrong pattern for a particular verb.

SENTENCES WITH INDIRECT OBJECTS: TWO PATTERNS

The two patterns for sentences with indirect objects are the prepositional pattern and the dative movement pattern. Depending primarily on the verb, both patterns or only one pattern may be possible.

The Prepositional and Dative Movement Patterns

In the prepositional pattern, the indirect object occurs after the direct object and is preceded by a preposition. In the dative movement pattern, the indirect object occurs before the direct object.

Prepositional Pattern

In the *prepositional pattern*, shown in (1), the direct object comes before the indirect object, which is preceded by the preposition *to*. In sentences such as (1), the direct object is the thing that undergoes the action and the indirect object is the person or other animate being toward whom the action is directed. To use terms introduced in Chapter 8, the direct object is the *theme* and the indirect object is the *goal*.

           DO   *IO*
(1) I gave [a book] *to* [John].

A large number of verbs, such as *bring*, *give*, *send*, *tell*, and *throw*, take indirect objects preceded by *to*. They are usually called *to dative verbs*.

Other verbs, such as *bake*, *build*, *buy*, *cook*, *do*, and *make*, take indirect objects preceded by the preposition *for*, as shown in (2). Since the indirect object with these *for dative verbs* benefits from the action performed on the theme, it is referred to as a *benefactive*.

           DO   *IO*
(**2**) I bought [a book] *for* [John].

Sentences with *for* dative verbs can also have a second meaning – the subject performs the action indicated by the verb as a proxy for the indirect object. Thus, in (2), someone might buy a book for John because John cannot go to the bookstore and buy it himself, not because the person wants to give it to him.

In addition to these two main classes of verbs, there are a few verbs such as *ask* and *require* that can have the preposition *of* before the indirect object, as shown in (3) and (4). This pattern sounds somewhat archaic to many native speakers.

             DO   *IO*
(**3**) We asked [a question] *of* [the child].

               DO   *IO*
(**4**) They require [an explanation] *of* [your Majesty].

Dative Movement Pattern

Indirect objects can also occur between a verb and its direct object, as in (5) and (6). In this pattern, called the *dative movement pattern*, the indirect object has no preposition before it.

         IO   *DO*
(**5**) I gave [John] [a book].

         IO   *DO*
(**6**) I bought [John] [a book].

A rule called *dative movement*[2] expresses the relationship between the prepositional pattern in (1) and (2) and the dative movement pattern in (5) and (6). The dative movement rule takes the indirect object in the prepositional pattern and moves it to the position between the verb and the direct object, while also deleting the preposition. This process, illustrated in (7), results in the dative movement pattern, as in (7b).

              DO   *IO*
(**7**) a. He gave [a beautiful ring] to [his fiancée].   *prepositional pattern*

                IO   *DO*
      b. He gave [his fiancée] [a beautiful ring] t̸o̸ _____.   *dative movement pattern*

The dative movement rule also applies to many *for* dative verbs, as shown in (8).

              DO   *IO*
(**8**) a. John bought [a present] for [his sister].   *prepositional pattern*

              IO   *DO*
      b. John bought [his sister] [a present] f̸o̸r̸ _____. *dative movement pattern*

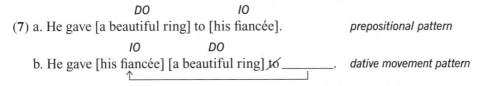

Factors That Restrict the Possible Patterns

Sometimes sentences with indirect objects can have only the prepositional pattern or only the dative movement pattern. In what follows, we look in turn at several factors that can restrict sentences to one pattern.

Animacy of Subject and Indirect Object

As a general rule, both the subject and the indirect object must be animate for both patterns to work. If this is not the case, sentences can generally take only one pattern, as shown in (9) and (10).

(9) a. The rain brought disaster to the farmers.
    b. *The rain brought the farmers disaster.

(10) a. *The bloodstains told a tale of terror to us.
     b. The bloodstains told us a tale of terror.

However, it is possible to find sentences with both patterns in which the indirect object is inanimate, as in (11), or the subject is inanimate, as in (12).[3]

(11) a. The justices often give a literal interpretation to the Constitution.
     b. The justices often give the Constitution a literal interpretation.

(12) a. The document gave enough clues to the cryptographers to enable them to crack the code.
     b. The document gave the cryptographers enough clues to enable them to crack the code.

Notice that, for example, in (12a) and (12b), the subject (*the document*) is not really performing an action that the indirect object (*the cryptographers*) receives. The meaning of *gave* in the sentences in (12) can be paraphrased as *provided* or *contained*, as shown in (13).

(13) a. The document provided the cryptographers with enough clues to enable them to crack the code.
     b. The document contained enough clues to enable the cryptographers to crack the code.

These examples demonstrate that, when both patterns are possible despite an inanimate subject and/or an inanimate indirect object, the verb, *give* in this case, has a meaning other than the action meaning it typically has when used with animate subjects and indirect objects. This contrast is reflected in the difference between the sentences in (11) and (12), on the one hand, and the pair in (1) and (5), on the other.

The Effect of Verb Meaning

Verbs that ordinarily take two patterns may in some cases be possible only with one pattern. Consider the verb *owe*. For most native speakers, this verb in its most common meaning, "to have an outstanding debt," takes the dative movement rule and can appear in both patterns, as shown in (14).

(14) a. I owe five bucks to Larry.   *prepositional pattern*
     b. I owe Larry five bucks.   *dative movement pattern*

However, when *owe* is used to express a sense of gratitude and acknowledgment, as in shown in (15), it is restricted to the prepositional pattern.

    (**15**) a. I owe this example to Georgia Green.   *prepositional pattern*
          b. I owe my success to my parents.   *prepositional pattern*

Sentence (15a) means "I acknowledge that Georgia Green gave me this example," and (15b) means "My parents are responsible for my success." Both sentences express the idea of gratitude. If we try to apply dative movement to these sentences, as in (16), the resulting sentences do not express this idea. Sentence (16a) expresses the idea of an outstanding debt, like the sentences in (14), while (16b) makes little or no sense at all.

    (**16**) a. I owe Georgia Green this example.   *dative movement pattern*
          b. *I owe my parents my success.   *dative movement pattern*

Verbs That Are Restricted to One Pattern

With some verbs, sentences with indirect objects may occur in only the dative movement pattern or, more commonly, only the prepositional pattern.

VERBS THAT ONLY OR USUALLY APPEAR IN THE DATIVE MOVEMENT PATTERN
Some verbs, including *allow*, *bet*, *begrudge*, *envy*, *fine*, *forgive*, *pardon*, *spare*, and *wager*, can appear only in the dative movement pattern, not in the prepositional pattern, as shown in (17), (18), and (19).

    (**17**) a. No one envies you that task.
          b. *No one envies that task to you.

    (**18**) a. We allowed Richard one more chance.
          b. *We allowed one more chance to Richard.

    (**19**) a. Alan doesn't begrudge Mary her success.
          b. *Alan doesn't begrudge her success to Mary.

Other verbs, including *bill*, *charge*, *cost*, and *wish*, usually occur in the dative movement pattern, as shown in (20), (21), and (22).

    (**20**) a. They charged me 50 bucks.
          b. *They charged 50 bucks to me.

    (**21**) a. It cost me 50 bucks.
          b. *It cost 50 bucks to me.

    (**22**) a. He wished Bill a happy birthday.
          b. *He wished a happy birthday to Bill.

However, in some contexts, the prepositional pattern may be possible with these verbs. In fact, with *bill* and *charge* the prepositional pattern is required when the indirect object is inanimate, as in (23) and (24), and even with an animate indirect object it is sometimes preferred, as in (25) and (26).[4]

    (**23**) a. I charged the hotel bill to my credit card.
          b. *I charged my credit card the hotel bill.

    (**24**) a. Please bill that call to my office phone number.
          b. *Please bill my office phone that call.

    (**25**) a. I charged the expense to my father.
          b. ?I charged my father the expense.

(26) a. I billed that plane ticket to my boss.
   b. ?I billed my boss that plane ticket.

VERBS THAT APPEAR ONLY IN THE PREPOSITIONAL PATTERN

Not all *to* dative verbs and *for* dative verbs can take the dative movement rule. Those that do not are restricted to the prepositional pattern. As we will discuss later, learning which members of each class of verbs can take the rule and which cannot is a distinct problem for English language learners.

Common verbs that appear only in the prepositional pattern include:

- ***To* dative verbs:** *administer, admit, confess, contribute, declare, deliver, demonstrate, describe, donate, explain, introduce, mention, repeat, report, return, reveal,* and *transfer,* among many others. Examples are shown in (27), (28), and (29). A more complete list of these verbs may be found in Appendix C, along with a list of *to* dative verbs that also occur in the dative movement pattern.

(27) a. John described the list to Joan.
   b. *John described Joan the list.

(28) a. We donated $10 to UNICEF.
   b. *We donated UNICEF $10.

(29) a. She transferred some stock to her husband.
   b. *She transferred her husband some stock.

- ***For* dative verbs:** *answer, cash, capture, collate, correct, create, eat, fix, pronounce, repeat,* and *select,* among others. Examples are shown in (30) and (31). See Appendix C for a more complete list of *for* dative verbs that only occur in the prepositional pattern, as well as for a list of *for* verbs that take both patterns.

(30) a. I pronounced the words for the teacher.
   b. *I pronounced the teacher the words.

(31) a. He fixed the leaky faucet for her.
   b. *He fixed her the leaky faucet.

Pronominal Direct Objects

Both direct and indirect objects can be pronouns, as (32) illustrates.

      DO   IO
(32) a. Give [the book] to [John].

     DO   IO
   b. Give [it] to [John].   *direct object as pronoun*

     IO   DO
   c. Give [him] [the book].   *indirect object as pronoun*

If the direct object is a pronoun used in place of an NP with a definite article, the sentence cannot occur in the dative movement pattern, as shown in (34) and (36). Note that this restriction holds for both *to* dative verbs and *for* dative verbs.

(33) a. They gave $\begin{Bmatrix} \text{the book} \\ \text{the books} \end{Bmatrix}$ to John.   *prepositional pattern*

   b. They gave $\begin{Bmatrix} \text{it} \\ \text{them} \end{Bmatrix}$ to John.

(34) a. They gave John $\begin{Bmatrix} the\ book \\ the\ books \end{Bmatrix}$.   *dative movement pattern*

b. *They gave John $\begin{Bmatrix} it \\ them \end{Bmatrix}$.

(35) a. We bought $\begin{Bmatrix} the\ book \\ the\ books \end{Bmatrix}$ for Helen.   *prepositional pattern*

b. We bought $\begin{Bmatrix} it \\ them \end{Bmatrix}$ for Helen.

(36) a. We bought Helen $\begin{Bmatrix} the\ book \\ the\ books \end{Bmatrix}$.   *dative movement pattern*

b. *We bought Helen $\begin{Bmatrix} it \\ them \end{Bmatrix}$.

This restriction does not hold if the direct object NP is a pronoun, such as *one* or *some*, used in place of an NP with an indefinite article, as the sentences in (37) show.

(37) a. We gave him $\begin{Bmatrix} a\ book \\ some\ books \end{Bmatrix}$.   *dative movement pattern*

b. We gave him $\begin{Bmatrix} one \\ some \end{Bmatrix}$.

It also does not hold if the direct object NP is a demonstrative pronoun (*this/that* or *these/those*), used in place of an NP with a demonstrative determiner, as in (38) and (39).

(38) a. Fred gave her $\begin{Bmatrix} this\ book \\ that\ book \end{Bmatrix}$.   *dative movement pattern*

b Fred gave her $\begin{Bmatrix} this \\ that \end{Bmatrix}$.

(39) a. John bought her $\begin{Bmatrix} these\ books \\ those\ books \end{Bmatrix}$.   *dative movement pattern*

b. John bought her $\begin{Bmatrix} these \\ those \end{Bmatrix}$.

SUMMARY

SENTENCES WITH INDIRECT OBJECTS: TWO PATTERNS

Sentences with an **indirect object (IO)** have either the prepositional pattern or the dative movement pattern.

In the **prepositional pattern**, the indirect object appears after the direct object and a preposition. Verbs are **to dative verbs** or **for dative verbs**, depending on which preposition occurs before the indirect object.

Joyce gave a book to Susan.
He bought a ticket for me.

continued

In the **dative movement pattern**, the indirect object appears between the verb and its direct object.

Joyce gave Susan a book.
He bought me a ticket.

The **dative movement** rule moves an indirect object to a position between the verb and its direct object and deletes the preposition.

Joyce gave a book to Susan. → Joyce gave Susan a book.

Restrictions on the patterns possible for sentences with indirect objects include the following:

- With some verbs, such as *allow*, *beg*, *forgive*, and *spare*, only the dative movement pattern is possible.
  No one envies you that task.

- With many verbs, such as *admit*, *contribute*, *explain*, and *return*, only the prepositional pattern is possible.
  John described the list to Joan.
  I pronounced the word for the teacher.

Direct object pronouns that replace NPs modified by definite articles (*the book/ books*) cannot occur in the dative movement pattern.

She gave John the books.
*She gave him them.
We bought my sister the blue scarf.
*We bought my sister it.

EXERCISE 15.1

For each sentence, decide whether the dative movement rule can apply.

Example: John donated a lot of money to his favorite charity.

Answer: no

1. Fred drew a map of how to get to the house for me.
2. The critic inadvertently revealed the ending of the movie to his readers.
3. He passed the bottle of milk to her.
4. She contributed some money to her favorite charity.
5. She suggested another course of action to Ralph.
6. The little girl recited a poem for her mother.
7. The city council granted an extension to the construction firm.

EXERCISE 15.2

For each sentence, decide what pronoun corresponds to the NP in italics and indicate whether that pronoun could replace the NP.

Example: I finally lent him *the money*.

Answer: *it*; no

1. He loaned her *a watch*.
2. She handed him *the flowers*.

3. He lent her *some gloves*.
4. Alice passed him *the salt*.
5. I gave her *those pictures*.

SENTENCES WITH INDIRECT OBJECTS IN DISCOURSE

Sentences with indirect objects occur frequently in everyday conversation, and are therefore introduced fairly early in most ESL/EFL courses. As we have seen, with some verbs these sentences must follow the dative movement or, more often, the prepositional pattern. English language teaching textbooks usually give the impression that, with verbs that allow both patterns, native speakers always have the option to choose either pattern and that neither choice is necessarily better or more appropriate. However, this is not always true, which is an important point for teachers to be aware of. In actual discourse, the choice between the patterns in a particular sentence, far from being totally arbitrary, is often determined by two information-structuring principles.

The Given–New Contract and Indirect Objects

The first of these information-structuring principles is the *given–new contract*. This principle, introduced in Chapter 1, states that "given," or "old" (previously mentioned), information in an ongoing discourse should appear in a sentence before "new" (not yet mentioned) information.

If a direct object was mentioned in a previous sentence, it qualifies as old information. In such a case, native speakers will tend to select the prepositional pattern, which places this old information before the new information, the indirect object. Example (40) indicates how this works.

> (**40**) I have two pistols here, a Colt .45 and a German Luger. Here are the rules of the duel.
> a. *I'm going to give the Colt to Fred and the Luger to Alex*. They will then walk in opposite directions for 20 paces, turn, and wait for my command to fire.
> b. *I'm going to give Fred the Colt and Alex the Luger*. They will then walk in opposite directions for 20 paces, turn, and wait for my command to fire.

The first sentence mentions two pistols, *a Colt .45* and *a German Luger*. This makes them old information, so most native speakers will choose the prepositional pattern in (40a) instead of the dative movement pattern in (40b) to continue the discourse. The option in (40a) is preferred because it puts *Fred* and *Alex* (new information) after the old information.

However, if the indirect object was mentioned in a previous sentence, the speaker will then choose the dative movement pattern, because this puts the old information (the indirect object) before the new information contained in the direct object, as illustrated in (41).

> (**41**) Susan: You know, I can't figure out what to get John for his birthday. Any ideas?
> Ann: a. *Give him a CD*. You know how much he likes music.
> b. *Give a CD to him*. You know how much he likes music.

In (41), Susan mentions *John*, so this makes him old information. Ann's answer would most likely be (41a), in which the indirect object pronoun *him* comes before the new information – the direct object, *a CD*. Option (41b) puts the old information after the new information, so it will not be chosen.

Experiments have shown that the given–new contract exercises a strong influence on a speaker's choice between the two indirect object patterns.[5] Notice, too, that the restriction on the prepositional pattern of sentences with a direct object that is an object pronoun is in keeping with the given–new contract: Pronouns are usually old information, and the prepositional pattern puts the direct object pronoun first whereas the dative movement pattern would put it last.

End Weight

The second information-structuring principle that can influence choice of pattern is known as *end weight*. According to this principle, which was introduced in Chapter 9, a long, complex ("heavy") NP should appear at the end of a clause. Such an NP should not, in particular, appear in the middle of a clause, a position that makes the information it contains harder to hold in short-term memory. A writer may, therefore, place a long NP at the end of a sentence to make the sentence easier to process (comprehend). Of the two sentences shown in (42), native speakers will most likely prefer the former.[6]

(**42**) a. Abby gave the kids foot-long frankfurters that had been roasted over an open hickory fire.
  b. Abby gave foot-long frankfurters that had been roasted over an open hickory fire to the kids.

The dative movement pattern in (42a) puts the long, heavy direct object NP at the end of the sentence. Sentence (42b), in the prepositional pattern, puts the heavy NP in the middle of the sentence. As a result, (42b) sounds awkward and almost ungrammatical.

End Weight and Avoidance of Ambiguity

The end weight principle can coincide with another motive for moving a long direct object NP to the end of a sentence: that of eliminating ambiguity. Notice that there is no reason to choose either (43a) or (43b) other than the personal preference of the speaker or the given–new contract.

(**43**) a. The man bought a rocking chair for his mother.
  b. The man bought his mother a rocking chair.

However, when (43a) is changed by lengthening the direct object NP as in (44), the sentence becomes ambiguous.

(**44**) The man bought a lovely old rocking chair that Frank had spent all summer restoring for his mother.

In (44), we are not sure whether the prepositional phrase, *for his mother*, is part of the relative clause, *that Frank had spent all summer restoring*, or whether it is an indirect object of the verb *bought*. In other words, did Frank restore the chair for his mother, or did the man buy the chair for his mother? If the writer intends to express the latter meaning, this can be done by simply applying the dative movement rule to (44), resulting in (45), which is much clearer.[7]

(**45**) The man bought his mother a lovely old rocking chair that Frank had spent all summer restoring.

End Weight and Verbs That Do Not Take Dative Movement

Notice that the dative movement rule cannot be applied to (46a) because the verb *demonstrate* does not take dative movement. Applying the rule would result in the ungrammatical (46b).

(**46**) a. John demonstrated the procedure to Alan.
b. *John demonstrated Alan the procedure.

However, what if a writer wants to use the verb *demonstrate* in a sentence such as (47), which has a long, complex direct object NP (*the method for fixing a carburetor that Harry's father had recently taught him*)?

(**47**) ?John demonstrated the method for fixing a carburetor that Harry's father had recently taught him to Alan.

This sentence, with its prepositional pattern, is difficult to process, yet the verb *demonstrate* rules out the application of the dative movement rule. How, then, can we solve the processing problem? Many writers might simply choose to move the long direct object NP to the end of the sentence, as shown in (48).

(**48**) John demonstrated to Alan *the method for fixing a carburetor that Harry's father had recently taught him.*

Sentence (48) follows not the prepositional pattern (DO + Prep + IO) or the dative movement pattern (IO + DO) but, rather, a third pattern: Prep + IO + DO. While this pattern is, strictly speaking, ungrammatical (e.g., *John demonstrated to Alan the procedure*), most native speakers would consider it a perfectly acceptable way to treat a sentence with an especially long indirect object NP and a verb that does not take dative movement. To most native speakers, (48) sounds much better and is more readily understandable than (47).[8] Sentences like (48) can be found in various genres of writing, including newspaper articles and fiction.

SUMMARY

SENTENCES WITH INDIRECT OBJECTS IN DISCOURSE

Two information-structuring principles help determine the choice of pattern in sentences with an indirect object:

- According to the **given–new contract**, information that has been mentioned in the previous context and is therefore given, or old, generally comes before new information in a sentence. Thus, in sentences with an indirect object:

  - If the indirect object is given information, the dative movement pattern is preferred.
    Susan: You know, I can't figure out what to get John for his birthday. Any ideas?
    Ann: Give him a CD. You know how much he likes music.

  - If the direct object is given information, the prepositional pattern is preferred.
    I have two pistols here, a Colt .45 and a German Luger. Here are the rules of the duel. I'm going to give the Colt to Fred and the Luger to Alex. . . .

continued

> • According to the **end weight** principle, a long, complex ("heavy") noun phrase can be moved to the end of the clause to increase comprehension and avoid ambiguity. This can be done by applying the dative movement rule.
> *Abby gave foot-long frankfurters that had been roasted over an open hickory fire to the kids.*   BECOMES   *Abby gave the kids foot-long frankfurters that had been roasted over an open hickory fire.*

EXERCISE 15.3

For each discourse, choose (a) or (b) as a completion and explain your choice.

Example: A: Who did you finally decide to hire?
        B: The last person we interviewed, Mrs. Choi.
          a. I sent an e-mail to her today. She accepted.
          b. I sent her an e-mail today. She accepted.

Answer: b (It puts the old information [*her*] before the new information [an *e-mail*].)

1. Fred wanted to make a good impression on his first date with Catherine, so he decided to
   a. bring her some flowers.
   b. bring some flowers to her.
2. I really wish I knew what to get Tom for his birthday. He's so hard to shop for!
   a. Why don't you get a gift certificate for him?
   b. Why don't you get him a gift certificate?
3. There were two more items on the table, a package and a letter. Do you remember who you sent them to?
   a. We sent a Mr. Green the package and a Mrs. Harrison the letter.
   b. We sent the package to a Mr. Green and the letter to a Mrs. Harrison.
4. When Alice arrived at the auditorium, she saw that hall was packed. But she wasn't worried about finding somewhere to sit because she was sure that
   a. John had saved her a seat.
   b. John had saved a seat for her.

EXERCISE 15.4

For each sentence, indicate whether it is easy to process. If a sentence is not easy to process, indicate what you could do to rewrite it and then rewrite the sentence.

Example: Without warning, John announced his decision to give up his job as a stockbroker on Wall Street and move to the northern Sahara Desert to work for Greenpeace to his wife.

Answer: no (Move the heavy direct object NP to the end of the sentence. Dative movement isn't possible with *announced*.)
        Rewrite: John announced to his wife his decision to give up his job as a stockbroker on Wall Street and move to the northern Sahara Desert to work for Greenpeace.

1. John reported the theft of his new sky-blue BMW convertible with the heated leather seats and the yellow fog lights to the police.
2. The mediator recommended an alternative solution for eliminating the barriers to a negotiated settlement of the dispute to the strikers.
3. Alan found a very comfortable little apartment near a supermarket that was within walking distance of a lovely little park for his grandmother.

PROBLEMS THAT ESL/EFL STUDENTS HAVE WITH INDIRECT OBJECTS

ESL/EFL students will most likely have a clear understanding of indirect and direct objects, based on their L1s. However, the patterns that are possible for verbs in students' L1s may not be the same as for the English verbs that correspond to them. In this section, we look at the types of problems that may result from transfer of L1 patterns and then more specifically at problems with the verbs *tell* and *say*.

Patterns for *To* Dative Verbs (Spanish, Korean)

As an example of patterns in other L1s, consider Spanish patterns for verbs equivalent to English *to* dative verbs. Spanish has a prepositional pattern for such verbs, as shown in (49a) for *mandar*, the equivalent of *send*.[9] It does not have a dative movement pattern for them, as (49b) illustrates. However, it does have a second prepositional pattern, in which the indirect object precedes the direct object, as shown in (49c).

(**49**) a. *Pablo   mandó   una   carta   a   la   niña.*
      Pablo   sent   a   letter   to   the   girl.

   b. **Pablo   mandó   la   niña   una   carta.*
      Pablo   sent   the   girl   a   letter.

   c. *Pablo   mandó   a   la   niña   una   carta.*
      Pablo   sent   to   the   girl   a   letter.

We might anticipate that Spanish speakers will have no problem producing the prepositional pattern with English *to* dative verbs. However, if these learners transfer the L1 pattern in (49c), they will produce ungrammatical English sentences such as **Pablo sent to the girl a letter*. Our Spanish corpus does not show any examples of this L1 transfer, but such transfer seems quite possible, since a study by Perpiñán and Montrul (2006) showed that English speakers learning Spanish tended to accept the dative movement pattern in (49b) as grammatical for Spanish.

Two studies indicate that English learners prefer the syntactic order of direct and indirect objects in their L1s when learning English. In both studies, the learners were presented with a context that cued the use of sentences containing indirect objects and then asked to judge which English pattern was most acceptable.[10] Bley-Vroman and Yoshinaga (1992) found that 85 adult Japanese speakers could not judge whether some English verbs were grammatical in the dative movement pattern when presented with examples of them in the prepositional pattern. Inagaki (1997) examined Japanese and Chinese undergraduate and graduate students' ability to judge English verbs as taking the prepositional or the dative movement pattern. Speakers of both languages tended to follow the "equivalent structures" in their L1 when making judgments.

L1 patterns seem to guide the performance of Korean students' production of English sentences with *to* dative verbs. Korean uses not prepositions but postposition case markers to indicate which words in a sentence are the indirect object, the direct object, and the subject. Sentences with verbs equivalent to English *to* datives have two possible patterns: DO + IO + V, as shown in (50a), and IO + DO + V, as shown in (50b). The case marker *-ekey* indicates the IO, *-ul* indicates the DO, and *-un* indicates the subject.

(**50**) a. *John-un   sacin-ul   Susan-eykey   poyecwuessta*
　　　John (Subject)　picture (DO)　Susan (IO)　showed
　　　"John showed a picture to Susan."

　　　b. *John-un   Susan-eykey   sacin-ul   poyecwuessta*
　　　John (subject)　Susan (IO)　picture (DO)　showed
　　　"John showed Susan a picture."

Korean students make two attested types of errors in producing English sentences containing *to* dative verbs that take dative movement: omitting a required preposition, as in (51a), and inserting the preposition in the wrong English pattern, as in (51b). Notice that (51a) follows the L1 prepositionless pattern shown in (50a), that is, DO + IO.

(**51**) a. *Technical journal and proceedings of symposia and conferences are cited to review previous works and to *give a hint readers* about New York.
　　　b. *This article *gives to us* the information.

The fact that these examples were taken from compositions written by high-level students admitted to an American university suggests that this problem may persist for some students.

English verbs that do not take dative movement, such as *report*, have Korean equivalents (*pokohata*) that do take both of the patterns shown in (50). Thus, in Korean, *John reported the accident to the police* and *John reported the police the accident* (*John–un kyengchal-eykey sako-lul pokohayssta*) would both be grammatical.[11]

This discussion of patterns in Spanish and Korean points out the typical kinds of errors students make in speaking and writing. They may sometimes use an L1 pattern that is not permitted in English. Many of their errors, however, will be attributable to uncertainty about which indirect object pattern may be used with a particular English verb. Moreover, it is not clear how persistent these problems are. Some studies indicate that they occur primarily at the intermediate level.

Tell and *Say* (German)

In many English language teaching textbooks, the verbs *tell* and *say* are covered in lessons on *to* dative verbs, since *tell* takes both patterns while *say* takes only the prepositional pattern. In addition, ESL/EFL students often use *say* in contexts in which *tell* is appropriate and vice versa. This confusion is probably due to the fact that, in the students' L1s, two or more different verbs are used in contexts in which English uses *tell*. In English, *tell* can mean "relate" (*He told her a story*), "inform" (*He told me he wasn't coming*), and "instruct" or "order" (*He told me to do it right away*).

For example, German uses the verb *sagen* (*say*) not only for the quotative sense of *say* (e.g., *He said,"I'll be away next week"*) but also for the inform and instruct/order senses of *tell*. (German uses the verb *erzählen* for the "relate" sense of English *tell*.) There are obviously many situations in which German speakers might equate the verb *sagen* with English *say* and then use *say* in contexts in which *tell* is the appropriate verb. Errors such as those in (52) can result.

(**52**) a. *He said me her name.
　　　b. *He said to her she should come.
　　　c. *He told to Judith, " I am coming."

However, the problem of confusing the English verbs *say* and *tell* is only peripherally related to indirect objects and therefore does not necessarily have to be addressed in conjunction with teaching indirect objects. Explanations regarding the usage of *say* and *tell* accompanied by focused practice may not always eradicate the problem right away. However, students may be helped by activities that involve posing questions with both verbs (e.g., *What did he tell the police?* and *What did he say to the police?*). Question pairs such as these can also help them learn that, whereas *tell* allows both patterns, *say* allows only the prepositional pattern.

SUGGESTIONS FOR TEACHING INDIRECT OBJECTS

ESL teachers have long assumed that students must learn which verbs permit both patterns and which verbs are restricted to one pattern. Linguists have used various criteria to subcategorize the verbs that can take the dative movement rule (see, e.g., Green, 1974; Grimshaw, 1985; Gropen et al., 1989; Mazurkewich & White, 1984; Oehrle, 1976; Pinker, 1989), but these categories are probably not very useful for organizing the teaching of indirect objects to English language learners.

The best way to teach indirect objects may be to take a traditional approach, in which instruction begins by focusing on high-frequency *to* dative verbs that take the dative movement rule and proceed to *to* dative verbs that appear only in the prepositional pattern. Most textbooks follow this approach and then repeat the sequence with *for* dative verbs.

One fairly large study by Carroll and Swain (1993), which compared four methods of teaching the two patterns associated with English indirect objects, found that giving students feedback about their errors by referring explicitly to the dative movement rule worked better than just correcting students, supplying only positive examples, or providing indirect clues, such as asking students if they were "sure" their answer was correct. These results suggest that, when you teach the dative movement rule, your students can benefit from grammatical explanations and focus-on-form instruction. They also suggest that, for classes made up of students who share the same L1 and have a particular problem with a pattern, providing activities that use techniques for correcting errors may be helpful.

Instruction on forming correct sentences with indirect objects should focus on:

- high-frequency *to* dative and *for* dative verbs, as mentioned earlier – those that take dative movement and those that do not.
- the restriction on pronouns occurring in the dative movement pattern.
- the influence of the given–new contract on the choice of pattern.[12]

Suggested Activities

The greatest challenge in teaching indirect objects is to come up with original contextualized activities that incorporate all of the disparate *to* dative and *for* dative verbs in a single context. Most ESL/EFL textbooks contain many fill-in-the-blank exercises or sentence completion tasks that focus on different verbs. However, it is far from clear that these activities are as effective as those that get the students to use the verbs in conversation. Your best option is to put a set of verbs together and to think of some situation that could serve as the basis for a conversation, as offered in the following activities.

Activity 1: Introducing Dative Movement Verbs (Beginning)

A favorite approach for introducing the patterns in which indirect objects occur involves choosing objects in the classroom to demonstrate *to* dative verbs that the students are already familiar with (*give*, *show*, *take*, etc.). The lesson might open as in (53):

(53) Teacher:	Here's a magazine. I'm going to give this magazine to Su Jung. What am I going to do, Serena?
Serena:	You're going to give that magazine to Su Jung.
Teacher:	That's right. [The teacher walks over to the designated student and hands the magazine to him.] OK. I gave the magazine to Su Jung. What did I do, Tina?
Tina:	You gave the magazine to Su Jung.
Teacher:	Good! Seichi, please show the magazine to Kazu. What's Seichi going to do, Yokiko?
Yokiko:	He's going to show the magazine to Kazu.
Teacher:	Right! [after Seichi shows the magazine to Kazu] Good. What did Seichi do with the magazine, Masahiro?
Masahiro:	He showed it to Kazu.

Write the answers you receive on the board. Next, choose another object and repeat the process with the other pattern. You can begin by showing the students several objects and asking questions such as "What shall I give Yokiko? Shall I give her the pen, the pencil, or this eraser?" These questions will elicit the dative movement pattern. After the students have answered several questions using this pattern and you have written their answers on the board, write a sentence with the prepositional pattern and point out the difference. Practice can continue with additional objects in groups of three: One student directs another student to perform an activity with verbs such as *bring*, *hand*, and *take*, and the third student describes it.

Activity 2: Drawing Attention to Verb Patterns (Intermediate Through Advanced)

This activity is a modification of a consciousness-raising task developed by Fotos and Ellis (1991). It can be used periodically to focus on the patterns of *to* and *for* dative verbs in Appendix C.

Give pairs of students a task card consisting of sentences in two patterns, such as those shown in (54). Each sentence pair should feature a different verb, and a card should contain at least 10 sentence pairs. Some of the verbs should take the dative movement pattern, and others should not. It is not necessary to have an equal number of verbs that do and don't. For demonstration purposes, we will only use six verbs here.

(54) a. Correct:	Susan sent an e-mail to her boyfriend.
Correct:	Susan sent her boyfriend an e-mail.
b. Correct:	UPS delivered a package to Mrs. Karzai.
Incorrect:	UPS delivered Mrs. Karzai a package.
c. Correct:	Masume described the accident to her teacher.
Incorrect:	Masume described her teacher the accident.
d. Correct:	Alan returned the book to the library.
Incorrect:	Alan returned the library the book.
e. Correct:	The teacher assigned some homework to the students.
Correct:	The teacher assigned the students some homework

f. Correct: Thomas suggested a solution to his boss.
   Incorrect: Thomas suggested his boss a solution.

If the students are acquainted with both patterns, tell them, "These sentences illustrate something that we talked about concerning verbs and indirect objects. Work with your partner to see what the correct and incorrect sentences tell you about the position of indirect objects with these verbs. When you have figured out the answers, write them down." To help students write the answers, provide the sentences in (55).

(55) 1. For these verbs – _____ – the position of the
         indirect object is _____.
      2. For these verbs – _____ – the position of the
         indirect object is _____.

Next, hand out the passage in (56) and have the students, again working in pairs, find any sentences that have the indirect object in the wrong position and correct them.

(56) The Valentine's Day Gift
      Mr. Smith wanted to give his wife a nice present for Valentine's Day because he would be away in San Francisco at that time. The day before Valentine's Day he spent a long time looking for a nice gift. In one of the stores he went to, a saleslady suggested Mr. Smith an electric back massager. Mr. Smith thought this would be a great present because his wife was always complaining about back pains. He asked the saleslady if the store could send the back massager to his home address. The saleslady said that they would do it right away, so Mr. Smith paid for the present and left. The saleslady assigned a clerk named Eddy the job of sending the back massager. Eddy wrapped the present and gave it to the UPS driver that afternoon. UPS delivered Mrs. Smith the package on Valentine's Day. She was happy when she saw what was in it, but when she tried out the back massager, it didn't work. Mrs. Smith was really upset. She decided to return the store the back massager. First she filled out a return form. On it she described the store the gift and explained why she wanted to return it. Mrs. Smith put the return form and the back massager into a box and mailed it back to the store. Mr. Smith wasn't very happy when he heard what had happened.

You can modify this activity if you wish to introduce your students to the dative movement rule. In this case, begin by writing an example of the dative movement pattern on the board. Help students identify the direct and indirect object. Then ask the students to look at the sentences on the task cards in (54) and notice which ones have objects in the same order as the sentence on the board and which have a different order. This will lead to a discussion in which you help them discover the rule and the fact that not all verbs take it. This activity can also be used to call attention to the restrictions on pronouns described in the section Pronominal Direct Objects. Repeat this activity periodically so that you cover all of the verbs in Appendix C.

Activity 3: Contextualized Production Activities (Intermediate)

This activity is designed to get students to produce sentences with verbs that have indirect objects. Choose a set of verbs that can be used for a particular situation. Have the students, in pairs, use the verbs to talk about things they are going to do. For example, you might give students the following activity:

(57) A friend of yours is going to come to the university where you are studying. She is going to need to know about registering and attending classes and about studying and living at the university. Tell someone what you are going to do to help your friend. Use these verbs: *describe, explain, introduce, recommend, show, tell.* Here are some suggestions about places and things that your friend will need to know about.

PLACES AND PEOPLE
the campus, the town
the campus bookstore
your friends
faculty advisor
the gym and other athletic
   facilities
the football stadium
good places to eat

THINGS TO DO
register for classes online
choose a major
find out about policy on class
   attendance, grades, etc.

It is somewhat challenging to find contexts that will naturally require your students to produce spoken discourse with indirect objects, but it is undoubtedly worth the effort.

Activity 4: Review with Processing Instruction (High Intermediate)

It is a good idea to periodically review the grammar of *to* and *for* dative verbs. One quick way to do this is by means of modified processing instruction tasks. Tell the students that you are going to read some sentences aloud. They are to write down each sentence's number and next to it put a "G" if the sentence is good or a "B" if the sentence is bad. Then read 10 or 15 sentences like those in (58). Include examples of grammatical and ungrammatical sentences with *to* and *for* dative verbs.

(58) a. He reported the police the accident.
    b. The postman delivered the package to her.
    c. She explained him the problem.
    d. She read her a story from the book.
    e. The students answered her the question.

Read each sentence again and ask, "Was that one OK?" When someone says no, ask why. The student should say something like "Because you can only say 'He reported the accident to the police'." Ask the rest of the class if they agree. Write on the board sentences about which there is disagreement, and help the students decide on the correct pattern. Intervene in the process only if the entire class comes up with the wrong answer. Do not linger over sentences that everyone correctly identifies as grammatical or ungrammatical. However, you can go back and check if students know whether some verbs that appeared in a correct pattern are restricted to that pattern, by repeating that sentence, for example, (58b), and asking about the other pattern (e.g., "Is it OK to say, 'The postman delivered her that package'?").

This activity could be done with pencil and paper and in pairs, but it is more challenging, and probably promotes greater learning, when students make judgments about orally presented sentences. Keep the activity brief.

Activity 5: Practicing the Effect of the Given–New Contract (Intermediate)

This activity allows students to practice using the given–new contract to guide their choice of indirect object pattern. Begin by saying, for example, "Our friend Farhad is going to have a birthday next Tuesday, and we are going to give him a present. I can say this two ways, can't I?" Then write the sentences in (59) on the board.

(59) a. We are going to give a nice present to him.
   b. We are going to give him a nice present.

Point out the differences between the patterns (59a) and (59b), and remind the students of how the given–new contract would affect which pattern a speaker chooses. Of course, you should not use the term "given–new contract"; rather, you need to point out that when the indirect object, *Farhad*, has already been mentioned, we tend to use the sentence in (59b).

Introduce more examples of short discourses like those shown previously in (40) and (41) to reinforce the point. Next, hand out a story like the one in (60), in which the two indirect object patterns appear several times. Have students read through the story and cross out and replace the inappropriate patterns as shown in (60). When they have finished, go through the passage with them, asking them to justify their choices. This exercise could also be done on an overhead projector with the entire class or as a small group activity in which the teacher moves around and monitors the groups' choices. It is also a good candidate for computer assisted language learning (CALL) exercises that supplement in-class grammar instruction.

(60) Jane's birthday was on Tuesday. Her two young sons, Billy and Jimmy, wanted to buy her a nice present but they didn't have much money. "I know what we can do," said Billy. "We can make our own special present." "Good idea," replied Jimmy. "But what should we make?" Billy thought for a moment and said, "Well, ~~I guess we could bake a cake for her~~ *"I guess we could bake her a cake."*" "OK," agreed Jimmy. "That should be fun. Just make sure it's chocolate. She really likes chocolate." Billy knew that chocolate was Jimmy's favorite flavor, but he didn't say anything.

The next afternoon, the two boys tried to bake the cake while their mother was out shopping. But they left it in the oven too long, and it burned. ~~They couldn't even feed their dog the cake~~ *They couldn't even feed the cake to their dog,* and their dog usually ate anything! When Jane came home she found a big mess in the kitchen and two small boys with sad faces. She asked them what they had been doing and they told her their plan and why it had failed. Jane was very happy. She kissed Billy and Jimmy and thanked them for the nice birthday present. Just then the boys' father came in. "Don't worry, guys," he said. "We're taking your Mom out to dinner tonight for her birthday. I've reserved a table at that restaurant she likes so much, and ~~I bought a nice present for her~~ *I bought her a nice present* from all of us. Now let's wish her a happy birthday and go out and eat!"

ENDNOTES

[1] These verbs are also referred to as *ditransitive verbs*.

[2] This rule is also referred to as *dative alteration* and *dative shift*.

[3] This observation and the examples are from Green (1974).

[4] Perhaps *my father* and *my boss* in (25) and (26) are perceived as substitutes for the inanimate NPs *my father's account* and *my boss's account*.

[5] See Cowan (1995).

[6] Biber et al. (1999), p. 928, state that the LGSWE corpus clearly shows a length effect in the dative movement pattern, with the indirect objects in sentences of this pattern tending to be short. This could be interpreted as support for the end weight principle of placing the long NP at the end of the sentence to facilitate processing.

[7] Arnold, Wasow, Losongco, and Ginstrom (2000) indicate that avoiding ambiguity is probably at least a "relatively weak determinant" (p. 33) in choosing a particular pattern. See also Gundel (1988) for universal ordering principles.

[8] Another example taken from Biber et al. (1999), p. 929, illustrates a similarly motivated use of this third pattern. In (1), the direct object, *a humor she herself did not possess*, is moved around the preposition and the indirect object, *to Anastasia's face*, to the end of the sentence. The resulting sentence is easier to understand and is deemed acceptable. Notice, in contrast, that a comparable sentence with a short direct object (e.g., **Her features gave to Anastasia's face a humor*) would be deemed ungrammatical.

> (1) The irregularity in her features was not grotesque, but charming, and gave to Anastasia's face a humor she herself did not possess.

[9] These examples are from Perpiñán and Montrul (2006).

[10] English learners were either presented with a series of pictures or a story that cued the use of a sentence with an indirect object. Bley-Vroman and Yoshinaga (1992) asked their subjects to judge if dative movement pattern sentences could be formed from prepositional pattern sentences that contained real and nonce verbs. (A nonce verb is one made up to fit a particular circumstance and meaning.)

[11] For a study of Japanese and Korean children's acquisition of dative structures, see Whong-Barr and Schwartz (2002). They conclude that L1 initially influences the learning of *to* datives. Mazurkewich (1988a, b) are typical adult SLA studies of indirect objects.

[12] Badalamenti and Henner-Stanchina (2000), pp. 208–210, contains a unit on the effect of the given–new contract on the choice of indirect object pattern.

REFERENCES

Arnold, J. E., Wasow, T., Losongco, A., & Ginstrom, R. (2000). Heaviness vs. newness: The effects of structural complexity and discourse status on constituent ordering. *Language*, *76*(1), 28–55.

Badalamenti, V., & Henner-Stanchina, C. (2000). *Grammar Dimensions 1*. Boston: Heinle & Heinle.

Biber, D., Johansson, S., Leech, J., Conrad, S., & Finegan, E. (1999). *Longman grammar of spoken and written English*. Essex: Pearson Education, Limited.

Bley-Vroman, R., & Yoshinaga, N. (1992). Broad and narrow constraints on the English dative alternation: Some fundamental differences between native speakers and foreign language learners. *University of Hawai'i Working Papers in ESL*, *11*, 157–159.

Carroll, S., & Swain, M. (1993). Explicit and implicit negative feedback: An empirical study of the learning of linguistic generalizations. *Studies in Second Language Acquisition*, *15*, 357–386.

Cowan, R. (1995). What are discourse principles made of? In P. Downing & M. Noonan (Eds.), *Word order and discourse* (pp. 29–50). Amsterdam/Philidelphia: John Benjamins.

Fotos, S., & Ellis, R. (1991). Communicating about grammar: A task-based approach, *TESOL Quarterly*, *25*(4), 605–628.

Green, G. M. (1974). *Semantics and syntactic irregularity*. Bloomington, IN: Indiana University Press.

Grimshaw, J. (1985). Remarks on dative verbs and universal grammar. Paper presented at the 10th Annual Boston University on Language Development (October, 1985).

Gropen, J., Pinker, S., Hollander, M., Goldberg. R., & Wilson, R. (1989). The learnability and acquisition of the dative alternation in English, *Language*, *65*(22), 203–257.

Gundel, J. K. (1988). Universals of topic-comment structure. In M. Hammond, E. Moravcsik, & J. Wirth (Eds.), *Studies in syntactic typology* (pp. 209–239). Amsterdam: John Benjamins.

Inagaki, S. (1997). Japanese and Chinese learners' acquisition of the narrow-range rules for the dative alternation in English. *Language Learning*, *47*(4), 637–669.

Mazurkewich, I. (1984a). The acquisition of the dative alternation by second language learners and linguistic theory. *Language Learning*, *34*(1), 92–109.

Mazurkewich, I. (1984b). Dative questions and markedness. In F. R. Eckman, L. H. Bell, & D. Nelson (Eds.), *Universals of second language acquisition* (pp. 119–131). Rowley, MA: Newbury House.

Mazurkewich, I. & White (1984). The acquisition of dative alternation: Unlearning overgeneralizations. *Cognition*, *16*, 261–283.

Oehrle, R. T. (1976). The grammatical status of the dative alternation in English. Ph.D. dissertation, MIT.

Perpiñán S., & Montrul, S. (2006). On binding asymmetries in dative alternation in Spanish. In C. A. Klee & T. I. Face (Eds.), *Selected proceedings of the 7th Conference of Spanish and Portuguese as first and second languages* (pp. 135–148). Somerville, MA: Cascadilla Proceedings Project.

Pinker, S. (1989). *Learnability and Cognition*. Cambridge, MA: MIT Press.

Whong-Barr, M., & Schwartz, B. (2002). Morphological and syntactic transfer in child L2 acquisition of the English dative alternation. *Studies in Second Language Acquisition*, 24, 579–616.

CHAPTER 16

Tense and Aspect

INTRODUCTION

Use of verb forms is one of the two or three most difficult areas for English language learners to master. New research indicates that several factors are responsible for the difficulties in learning to use appropriate verb forms. In order to understand the difficulties and how to deal with them, we first have to examine basic concepts of tense and aspect underlying these forms and their uses.

BASIC CONCEPTS: TENSE AND ASPECT

Verb forms – main verbs and combinations of auxiliary verbs and main verbs – indicate both the time of the action expressed by the verb and the speaker's view of that action in time, for example, as completed or ongoing, habitual or repeated. Two concepts are used to describe time and action in verbs – *tense* and *aspect*. In what follows, we look at each in turn.

Tense

Tense in verbs expresses the time that an action occurs in relation to the moment of speaking. It has three dimensions – present, past, and future. These can be represented as in the diagram in (1), some form of which is often used in English language teaching textbooks.

(1)

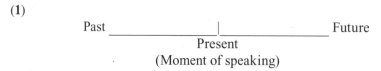

Past _____|_____ Future

Present

(Moment of speaking)

In fact, however, of the three times shown in (1), only two are expressed in English by inflections on the verb – present and past. Thus, present time, for third person singular, is indicated by adding -*s* to a regular verb, as in (2a), and past time is indicated by adding -*ed* to a regular verb, as in (2b), or changing the form of an irregular verb such as *go*, as in (2c). Many languages also express future time by changing the form of a verb, but English generally expresses future time with the modal auxiliary verb *will*, shown in (2d), or the semimodal *be going to*, in (2e).

(**2**) a. He *helps* her.   *present tense*
    b. He *helped* her.   *past tense regular verb*
    c. He *went* to the game.   *past tense irregular verb*
    d. He *will* help her.   *future time*
    e. He *is going to* help her.   *future time*

In addition to verb form, time is also signaled by time adverbs, such as *yesterday, today, tomorrow, at noon,* and *three o'clock,* and by prepositional phrases, such as *for three years* and *since two o'clock.*

Aspect

Aspect expresses how the speaker views the action of the verb. For example, an action that is seen as bounded and complete is *perfect* in aspect. If the action is seen as incomplete, it is *imperfect* in aspect; if seen as repeated, it is *iterative*; if seen as occurring regularly, it is *habitual*.[1] All of these aspects are represented in the verbs of different languages.

In English, two aspects are expressed through auxiliary verbs and the form of main verbs: a *progressive*, or *continuous*, aspect represents ongoing action, and a *perfect* aspect represents action that is complete. The progressive aspect is indicated with *be* + present participle (*-ing*), and the perfect aspect is indicated with *have* + past participle (*-ed*). As we will see, these two forms in English encompass a range of aspectual meanings that in other languages may be expressed by distinct forms. For example, an action that occurs repeatedly (e.g., *The shutter was banging against the wall*) would have an iterative aspect marker attached to a verb in a language like Hausa,[2] but in English this meaning is encompassed within the progressive aspect.

Tense/time and aspect intersect in English. The examples in (3) illustrate how the progressive aspect describes ongoing action that happens at the time of speaking, in the past, and in the future.

	Tense/Time	Aspect
(**3**) a. She *is running* right now.	present	progressive
b. She *was running* an hour ago.	past	progressive
c. She *will be running* in about an hour.	future	progressive

More than one aspect may combine with tense/time. To signify a point in the future when a period of ongoing action will be complete requires both the perfect and progressive aspects along with the future time indicator *will*, as shown in (4).

	Time	Aspect
(**4**) She *will have been working.*	future	perfect, progressive

The intersection of tense/time and aspect explains much about verb forms but leaves us with questions. For example, why do native speakers interpret the act in a sentence like (5a) as complete but that in (5b), which has the same verb form (*have* + past participle), as extending to the present? To answer this, we need to look at one other concept – *lexical aspect*.

(**5**) a. John has written only one novel since 1998.
    b. John has owned only one car since 1998.

Lexical Aspect

Verbs can be classified by the type of act they denote. That is, a verb can be classified based on answers to questions such as the following: Does the act have duration? Does it have an end point? Does it involve change? The resulting properties, called *semantic features*, make up the *lexical aspect* of verbs. The basic categories of English verbs from this standpoint of lexical aspect are *stative* and *dynamic*.[3]

Stative Verbs

Verbs such as *contain*, *hope*, *know*, *need*, *own*, *resemble*, and *understand* express states or situations rather than actions. These *stative verbs* can signify cognitive, emotional, and physical states. They have the following characteristics, which can serve as tests for stative verbs:

- The states expressed are continuous and unchanging while they last, which usually is for a long or indefinite time.
- They do not have an end point. Verbs expressing something that has no end point are referred to as *atelic verbs*.
- Thus, stative verbs occur with *start* and *stop* but not with *finish* (*He stopped loving Susan* but not **He finished loving Susan*).
- It is possible to ask the question *How long have/has . . . ?* (e.g., *How long have you known/needed/owned . . . ?*)
- They do not normally occur in progressive aspect forms (**She is having a car*).
- They cannot occur with most manner adverbs (**She understood methodically*).
- They usually cannot occur in pseudocleft sentences (e.g., **What Bill did was resemble his brother*; for more on pseudoclefts, see Chapter 22).

For convenience, in this chapter we refer to "the action" expressed by verbs rather than to "the action or state." The context clarifies whether states and statives are included.

Dynamic Verbs

Stative verbs contrast with *dynamic verbs* – verbs that require some input of action by the subject. Dynamic verbs can be further classified in terms of their lexical aspect features into three subcategories, each with its characteristics, or tests.

ACTIVITY VERBS

Activity verbs, which include *develop*, *grow*, *sit*, and *work*, are dynamic verbs with the following characteristics:

- The actions they express can go on for an indefinite period of time.
- Like stative verbs, they are *atelic*, lacking an end point. The actions expressed either are continuous – as is the case with, for example, *observe*, *pull*, *run*, *sit*, *stare*, *swim*, *walk*, and *work* – or changing – as, for example, with *decline*, *develop*, and *grow*.
- It is possible to ask the question *How long did . . . ?* (e.g., *How long did you work/ stare at the wall? How long did it grow?*).
- Activity verbs can occur in the progressive aspect.

ACHIEVEMENT VERBS

Achievement verbs describe actions that occur instantaneously (e.g., *He solved the problem*, *She turned on the light*, *He spotted the airplane*). These verbs fall into two classes. Achievement verbs that are *punctual*, including *bounce*, *faint*, *hit*, and *kick*, express an action that is instantaneous, ending as soon as it begins. Achievement verbs that are *change of state*, like *find* (*a solution*) and *cross* (*the finish line*), involve a preliminary activity that culminates in the act denoted by the verb. Thus, a person searches before finding the solution, and runs toward the finish line before crossing it. Other characteristics of achievement verbs include the following:

- Achievement verbs are *telic* verbs. In contrast to stative and activity verbs, they do have an end point. This is obviously true whether the verbs are instantaneous or change of state.
- They usually cannot occur with *stop* or *start* (e.g., **He stopped recognizing the thief, *He started catching the kitten*).
- With these verbs, it is possible to ask the question *At what time did . . . ?* (e.g., *At what time did he faint?*) or *How long did it take to . . . ?* (e.g., *How long did it take to find a solution?*).

With punctual verbs, progressive aspect form is understood as meaning repeated (rather than ongoing) action (e.g., *He is kicking the tires*). With change of state verbs, progressive aspect may or may not be possible, depending on whether the activity leading up to the achievement is treated as being the same activity – for example, *His train is arriving at noon*, but not **She is recognizing the thief.*

ACCOMPLISHMENT VERBS

Accomplishment verbs terminate in an end point that is logical in terms of their action. Thus, in the sentence *He wrote a best seller*, the action has a logical end point when the writing of the best seller is completed. Examples of accomplishment verbs include *attend*, *build*, *draw*, *make*, *paint*, *recover* (*from an illness*), *solve*, and *write*. Accomplishment verbs are telic verbs. Other characteristics of accomplishment verbs include:

- Since their action goes on for a certain amount of time and ends with completion, with accomplishment verbs it is possible to ask the question *How long did it take to . . . ?* (e.g., *How long did it take him to write the best seller?*).
- The activity expressed by an accomplishment verb can occur with *start*, *stop*, and *finish*. However, with these verbs, stopping and finishing are different, and if the action is stopped, the accomplishment does not occur. For example, if a person stops painting a picture, then, of course it isn't finished, and the action has therefore not been accomplished.
- With accomplishment verbs, the subject performs the action of the verb *in* a certain amount of time, not *for* a certain amount of time (*They built the stadium in less than a year*, not **They built the stadium for less than a year*).

Expressing More Than One Type of Action

It is possible for some verbs to express more than one type of meaning. There are two reasons for this. First, some verbs can be seen as belonging to two semantic classes. For example, *know*, *see*, and *understand*, are basically stative verbs, since they denote conditions that do not change – for example, *I see poorly = I have poor vision*. However, they can also express a dynamic event that occurs instantaneously – for example, *I see a parking spot over there*. In this case, they are achievement verbs.

Second, certain verbs will express a different meaning when constituents are added to the sentence they appear in. Activity verbs, for example, can express accomplishments. Thus, *run* is an activity verb in the sentence *He ran*, but if the prepositional phrase *to the post office* is added (i.e., *He ran to the post office*), it expresses an accomplishment. Only some prepositional phrases will have this effect. The sentence *He ran through/in the post office* is still an activity. The addition of an object NP after an activity verb like *sing* creates the context for an accomplishment. *He sang* is an activity, but *He sang a song* is an accomplishment. The grammatical features of the noun – count or noncount, singular or plural – can also play a role. With noncount nouns and plural count nouns (e.g., *They sang folk music/ songs*), we are dealing with an activity. With singular or plural count nouns preceded by articles or numbers (e.g., *They sang a song/two songs*), we have an accomplishment.

Effects of Lexical Aspect

An understanding of lexical aspect enables us to answer the question posed at the end of the section on aspect: Why do native speakers get different interpretations for the actions in the two sentences there, repeated here as (6a) and (6b)? Both sentences have the same verb form – *have* + past participle, or "present perfect tense" – so why is the action in (6a) interpreted as complete, but that in (6b) as continuing?

> (6) a. John has written only one novel since 1998.
>   b. John has owned only one car since 1998.

The answer lies in the lexical aspect of the verbs *write* and *own*. *Write*, as it appears in sentence (6a), describes an accomplishment. Hence, it expresses a completed activity. *Own* is a stative verb. Stative verbs have indefinite duration, so we infer that John still has that car.

Understanding how lexical aspect affects the interpretation of verb action will help teachers to explain why we can get different interpretations of verbs that have the same form, as illustrated in (6). ESL/EFL courses and materials often ignore lexical aspect and its effects. With an understanding of how lexical aspect factors into the learning of tense, teachers can address these shortcomings in textbooks, answer students' questions fully, and design materials that enhance students' ability to use verb forms accurately.

SUMMARY

BASIC CONCEPTS: TENSE AND ASPECT

Tense in verbs expresses time. It is referenced to the moment of speaking.

Past _____|_____ Future
                  Present
              (Moment of speaking)

English marks only past and present time by inflections on verbs.

Aspect expresses how the speaker views the action of the verb – for example, as complete (perfect aspect), incomplete (imperfect aspect), ongoing (progressive aspect), repetitive (iterative aspect), or regular (habitual aspect). English expresses **progressive aspect** by *be* + present participle and **perfect aspect** by *have* + past participle. These aspects combine with tense/time.

He is writing a letter.	*progressive aspect, present*
He was writing a letter.	*progressive aspect, past*
He will be writing the letter.	*progressive aspect, future*

He has read the book.	perfect aspect, present
He had read the book.	perfect aspect, past
He will have read the book.	perfect aspect, future

Lexical aspect refers to semantic properties of verbs, for example, whether or not an action is characterized by duration, an end point, or change. Thus, aspectual concepts are also conveyed through lexical aspect. Verbs fall into four categories in terms of lexical aspect – **stative verbs** and three types of **dynamic verbs**:

- **Stative verbs** describe states or situations rather than actions. States are continuous and unchanging and can be emotional, physical, or cognitive.
  He owns a large blue car.
  She hates her boss.

- **Activity verbs** express actions that go on for a potentially indefinite period of time. The actions are constant (e.g., *run*, *swim*, *walk*) or involve an inherent change (e.g., *decline*, *develop*, *grow*).
  He is walking around the park.
  This plant is really growing fast.

- **Achievement verbs** describe an action that occurs instantaneously – either *punctually* (e.g., *bounce*, *hit*, *kick*) or as a *change of state* (e.g., *find*). Change of state actions involve a preliminary activity that is terminated by the achievement verb.
He bounced the ball several times.	punctual
She crossed the finish line.	change of state

- **Accomplishment verbs** have a termination that is logical in terms of their action, as is the case, for example, with *build* (*a house*) or *paint* (*a picture*).
  He wrote a book about language teaching.
  She made a model of the house.

A verb may fall into more than one category.
He ran in the hall.	activity verb
He ran to the post office.	accomplishment verb

EXERCISE 16.1

Identify the tense/time and aspect of each verb in the following sentences.

Example: He had been studying for three hours.

Answer: past; perfect, progressive

1. He will be working on that project tomorrow.
2. They have locked up the store.
3. He will have finished it by then.
4. Tom was writing the introduction to the report.
5. They had cleaned the rooms.

EXERCISE 16.2

Identify each of the following sentences as expressing a state, an activity, an achievement, or an accomplishment.

Example: He reached the summit of the mountain around three o'clock.

Answer: achievement

1. He observed the bacteria under the microscope.
2. Olivia hated her boss with a passion.
3. John eventually recovered from a bad case of pneumonia.
4. She suddenly spotted the horse at the end of the pasture.
5. He did the crossword puzzle in less than an hour.
6. He hit the ball against the backboard.
7. At the party he recited poetry.
8. At the party he recited a poem.

TENSES IN ENGLISH LANGUAGE TEACHING

Explanations in English language teaching textbooks are, and traditionally have been, in terms of the unified phenomenon of "verb tenses." Thus, aspect is not discussed with much clarity, and lexical aspect is rarely mentioned at all. Instead, the aspect terms *progressive*, or *continuous*, and *perfect* are combined with the three times – past, present, and future – to produce, along with each time on its own, the 12 so-called tenses of English, shown in (7).

(7)	a. simple present	She *works.*
	b. simple past	She *worked.*
	c. future	She *will work.*
	d. present progressive	She *is working.*
	e. past progressive	She *was working.*
	f. future progressive	She *will be working.*
	g. present perfect	She *has worked.*
	h. past perfect	She *had worked.*
	i. future perfect	She *will have worked.*
	j. present perfect progressive	She *has been working.*
	k. past perfect progressive	She *had been working.*
	l. future perfect progressive	She *will have been working.*

Because English language instruction on verb forms is in terms of these twelve tenses, the rest of this explanation is devoted to presenting each tense and its meanings, basic and otherwise. We will use the tense designations in (7). At times, we will refer to the concepts of tense, aspect, and lexical aspect discussed earlier, and it may be useful to keep these in mind.

THE SIMPLE TENSES

In the simple present and simple past tenses, verbs are inflected for tense. These two tenses are called "simple" because they do not involve aspect. We look at each in turn.

Simple Present

As noted earlier, the simple present tense is represented by the third person singular *-s* inflection on verbs. It has a range of meanings, some much more common than others.

Basic Meanings

The *simple present* tense expresses *states*, as exemplified in (8), and *habitual action*, as in (9). Notice that the verbs in (8) are stative verbs. The habitual action meaning of the simple present, the most commonly targeted one in textbooks, generally requires the presence of time expressions (e.g., *every Friday, regularly, always* + time), as illustrated in (9).

> (8) a. The lake *looks* like it's frozen.   *states*
>   b. He *seems* to be confused.
>   c. She *owns* three rare Chinese vases.

> (9) a. He *eats* steak and kidney pie *every Sunday*.   *habitual actions*
>   b. They *always go* to the mosque *on Friday*.

In a third meaning usually included in textbooks, the simple present expresses what are often referred to as *general statements of fact* or *scientific truths*. This meaning, exemplified in (10), is actually a variation of the first meaning mentioned, since these statements of fact and scientific truths are usually expressed either with stative verbs such as *be, exist, equal, thrive*, and so on, or with ergative verbs that carry an inherent change of state meaning such as *boil, cool, dissolve, expand, freeze, grow, harden, rise*, and so on. Unfortunately, not many textbooks explain this or list the verbs that these sentences typically contain.

> (10) a. Salt crystals *dissolve* in water.
>   b. Water *boils* at 100 degrees centigrade, the equivalent to 212 degrees Fahrenheit.
>   c. The square root of 81 *is* 9.
>   d. Warm air *rises*.

Another meaning of the simple present tense that is also common and included in textbooks is that of *future action*. In this meaning, exemplified in (11), the simple present tense is accompanied by time expressions such as *at eight o'clock, at dawn*, or *tomorrow*.

> (11) a. The bus *leaves at 8:00 p.m.*
>   b. The game *starts at 2:30*.

Additional Uses of the Simple Present

The simple present tense also appears in particular contexts or genres of conversation or writing, some of which are not included in ESL/EFL textbooks.

INSTANTANEOUS PRESENT

The simple present occurs in the running commentary produced by a speaker to provide an ongoing account of what he or she is watching. For example, in (12) a sportscaster is describing a football game as it unfolds in front of his eyes. This is referred to as the *instantaneous present*.

> (12) Esiason *lets* fly and . . . Emory *has* the ball. He *shakes* one, . . . two tackles, and . . . he*'s* in for the touchdown!

CONVERSATIONAL HISTORICAL PRESENT

The simple present can also express something that happened in the past. As such, it occurs largely in conversation in which it gives a sense of immediacy to a past event; this meaning is therefore sometimes referred to as the *conversational historical present*.[4] The example in (13) is a description of a robbery, given by a witness.

(13) So I was standing there buying some groceries, right? And all of a sudden this guy *comes* in the door. He *pulls* out this gun, see. It's one of those, like . . . sawed-off shotguns. And he *points* it at the cashier, and *tells* him to *hand over* all the money. So, of course, everybody in the store *freaks out*!

NARRATIVE PRESENT

Another restricted use is that of the *narrative present*. Here the simple present narrates the plot of a movie, play, or novel that the speaker has seen or read, regardless of the time in which the plot is set. This is sometimes referred to as the *narrative*, or *historical*, present.[5] It is exemplified in (14), the first paragraph of a book review.

(14) The story *opens* in 1989 on All Souls' Day, the day of the dead, when people carry flowers to the cemeteries. Like Grass [the author], the hero, Alexander Reshcki, *is* an exile from Gdansk living in West Germany. A widower in his sixties, he *is* a professor of art history at the University of Bochum. The Polish widow Alexandra *is* a restorer and gilder by profession. She *is* not quite sixty when Alexander *meets* her in the market.[6]

STAGE PLAY AND SCREENPLAY DIRECTIONS

The simple present is used in directions for actors in plays, as in (15). Directions about exiting or entering the stage usually begin with the verb (e.g., *Enter the crowd*, rather than *The crowd enters*).

(15) They *fight*. Tybalt *falls*.

Directions for action and camera placement in screenplays for films are predominantly in the simple present tense, although the progressive is used when it is necessary to specify motion in progress, as at the beginning of the close shot in the scene in (16).[7]

(16) CLOSE SHOT   THE TOP OF THE DESK
Visser is pushing the fish away from his side of the desk with the eraser end of a pencil.
MARTY: What did you . . . ?
BACK TO MARTY
Still looking at the picture. He traces the outline of the desk with the eraser end of the pencil.

WITH COMMUNICATION VERBS

The simple present can occur with some *communication verbs* – for example, *inform*, *say*, *suggest*, *tell*, and *write*[8] – to refer to a past communication, as in (17).

(17) Mary *tells* me you have been to China. How fascinating!

Simple Past

As discussed earlier, the *simple past* tense is represented by the *-ed* inflection on regular verbs and by other changes in the case of irregular verbs.

Basic Meaning

The simple past expresses action carried out prior to the time of speaking as shown in (18).

(**18**) Last night we ate dinner in that Italian restaurant you like so much.

The simple past tense frequently occurs with expressions that indicate a specific point in time when the action was carried out, such as *yesterday*, *a week ago*, *last Monday*, *at four o'clock*, *in the morning*, *on Tuesday*, and so on. The sentences in (19), with verbs from each category, show this use of time expressions. Since states have unlimited duration, the presence of a time adverb such as *then* with a stative, as in (19a), leaves open the possibility that the state still exists. Since telic verbs (i.e., achievement and accomplishment verbs) have inherent end points, they commonly occur with an adverb that specifies the time of this end point, as in (19c) and (19d).

(**19**) a. I *loved* her *then*.   *stative verb*
    b. I *ran* three miles *yesterday*.   *activity verb*
    c. They *built* that house *a long time ago*.   *accomplishment verb*
    d. We *reached* the summit *just before noon*. *achievement verb*

Additional Uses of the Simple Past

The simple past is used instead of the simple present in some contexts that require a shift of tense – reported speech and unreal conditionals – or that are determined by pragmatic factors such as politeness. In general, past tenses often replace the corresponding present tenses in such contexts.

REPORTED SPEECH

In keeping with the sequence of tense requirement of *reported speech*, when speech is reported, the simple present is *backshifted* to the simple past. Thus, in (20), simple present *am* becomes simple past *was*. This requirement for reported speech is followed especially in writing. (For more on reported speech, see Sequence of Tense Rules in this chapter.)

(**20**) a. John said, "I am a doctor."   *quoted speech*
    b. John said that he *was* a doctor.   *reported speech*

UNREAL CONDITIONALS

In clauses introduced by *if*, the simple past expresses an unreal condition, as illustrated in (21). (*Unreal conditionals* are discussed further in Chapter 19.)

(**21**) If I *made* a mistake like that, my wife would never let me hear the end of it.

POLITE REQUESTS AND QUESTIONS

Particularly with requests and questions, the simple past is often used instead of the simple present to express a more deferential, polite tone. Thus, (22b) and (22d), with simple past verbs, are more polite than the corresponding (22a) and (22c).

(**22**) a. I want to ask you a favor.
    b. I *wanted* to ask you a favor.   *more polite*
    c. Do you want to see me now?
    d. *Did* you want to see me now?   *more polite*

SUMMARY

THE SIMPLE TENSES

The **simple present tense** is represented by the third person singular -*s* inflection on regular verbs.

Its most common meanings are:

- **states**
  The lake looks like it's frozen.
  He seems to be confused.

- **habitual action**
  He watches TV every night after dinner.

- **general statements of fact**
  Water boils at 100 degrees centigrade, the equivalent of 212 degrees Fahrenheit.
  The square root of 81 is 9.

- **future action** with time expressions
  Your plane leaves at noon.
  We arrive on Friday.

Additional uses of the simple present tense include:

- the **conversational historical present** (describing action in the past)
  He comes in and starts shouting at the hotel clerk. He's really angry, you know. So the manger calls the cops.

- the **narrative present** (for plot synopses)
  The second act of Verdi's opera Otello takes place in the castle. Iago urges Cassio to ask Desdemona to plead with her husband, Otello, to restore his rank, and watches him go in search of Desdemona.

- **stage and screen play directions**
  They fight. Tybalt falls.

- with **communication verbs** (*tell, say*, etc.)
  Alan tells me that you are a talented artist.

The **simple past tense** is represented by the -*ed* inflection on regular verbs. Its basic meaning is to express **action prior to the time of speaking**.
  We ate dinner in that Italian restaurant you like so much.

Additional uses of the simple past include:

- **reported speech**
  John said, "I'm a doctor."   quoted speech
  John said that he was a doctor.   reported speech

- **unreal conditionals**
  If I ever said something like that, she would kill me.

- **polite requests and questions**
  Did you want to speak with him now?

EXERCISE 16. 3

Identify the meanings of the simple present or past tense forms in each of the following sentences.

Example: If water is heated to 212 degrees Fahrenheit, it boils.

Answer: scientific truth (present tense)

1. A: What happened?
   B: It was the same old story. She comes in and starts chewing me out about the sale I lost. So, I don't like that, right? So, I tell her that I don't have to take that sort of talk from her. And, you know what? She says I'm right. I don't, because I don't work there anymore. I'm fired.
2. If I were John, I would accept her offer.
3. Did you want to pay for that now or later?
4. He listens to that program on NPR every Sunday night.
5. In this darkly comic short story collection, Sherman Alexie, a Spokane/Coeur d'Alene Indian, weaves memory, fantasy, and stark realism to paint a complex, grimly ironic portrait of life in and around the Spokane Indian Reservation. The author introduces us to characters raised on humiliation and government cheese, like Thomas Builds-the-Fire, who tells his stories long after people stop listening.
6. He seems to be perfectly healthy.

EXPRESSING FUTURE TIME

Action that will occur at some time in the future can be expressed a number of ways in English, but the two most common are with the modal *will* and the semimodal *be going to*.

Will and Be Going To

In (23a), future action is indicated by *will*, and in (23b), it is indicated by *be going to* in the same sentence.

> (**23**) a. He *will go* to the ball.
>   b. He *is going to go* to the ball.

The choice between *will* and *be going to* depends largely upon whether the speaker is expressing just probable occurrence or planned activity. *Will* tends to be used for the former, *be going to* for the latter. Sentence (24a), with *be going to*, is preferable to (24b), with *will*, because the visit is a planned activity. (For further discussion, see Chapter 14).

> (**24**) a. I'm going to go to Paris next week. I have business there.
>   b. I'll go to Paris next week. I have business there.

Simple Present

As we have already seen, the simple present tense used with a time expression can also indicate future action, as illustrated in (25).

> (**25**) He *arrives* here *on Thursday. On Saturday* he *flies* back to Lima.

Present Progressive

Actions planned for the near future are often indicated by the present progressive tense (i.e., *is/are* + verb + *-ing*). The near future has to be contextualized by adverbs and other time expressions, as in (26).

(26) a. *He's moving* to Phoenix *this summer.*
 b. Susan's plane *is leaving in five minutes.*

Be About To

Actions that are going to occur in the very near future – that is, momentarily – are indicated by *be about to* + the verb, as in (27).

(27) He'*s about to get* into the car and leave for the airport.

Be To

Actions in the future can be expressed by *be to* + verb. This form is relatively rare and is limited largely to contexts like commands, as in (28).

(28) You *are to stay* here and *guard* this prisoner until you are relieved by Private Jones.

PROGRESSIVE ASPECT

The *progressive aspect* is formed with *be* and the present participle (verb + *-ing*). It combines with present, past, and future for forms that express ongoing action at different times. These combinations are treated in English language instruction as the *present*, *past*, and *future progressive*, or *continuous*, tenses.

Present Progressive

The *present progressive* (*present continuous*) tense is formed with a present form of *be* (i.e., *am*, *is*, or *are*) and the present participle of the main verb.

Basic Meaning

The basic meaning of the present progressive, taught in every English language teaching textbook, is *ongoing action at the time of speaking*. Time adverbs such as *right now* emphasize the immediacy of the ongoing action, as in (29a), which has an activity verb, and (29b), which has an achievement verb. Ongoing action can be transpiring over a longer period, as the time expression in (29c) illustrates.

(29) a. They'*re studying* for a midterm *right now.*
 b. Her plane *is landing right now.*
 c. They'*re putting* the plan into effect *in the course of this semester.*

Punctual achievement verbs such as *bang*, *bounce*, *hit*, and *kick* take on an iterative meaning in the present progressive, as illustrated in (30).

(30) a. That window shutter *is banging* against the wall. You'd better secure it.
 b. He'*s bouncing* the tennis ball off the backboard.

Additional Meanings

In addition to expressing ongoing action, the present progressive can express a number of other meanings. As we have seen, one of these is a future event that is planned, as illustrated in (31). A time expression that indicates when the activity will occur is necessary for this interpretation.

(31) a. The New Art Theater *is showing* the film classic *Eraserhead next week.*
    b. Tom *is taking* tennis lessons *this summer.*
    c. We*'re climbing* Pikes Peak *tomorrow.*

HABITUAL ACTIONS

In sentences with adverbs such as *always* and *forever*, the present progressive can express *habitual action*. Frequently, in addition to emphasizing the repetitive nature of the activity, a negative attitude toward it is conveyed. In (32a), the speaker expresses irritation at the habitual action, and in (32b) the speaker expresses disapproval.

(32) a. *He's always calling* me *up* at the oddest hours to ask some silly question.
    b. *He's always teasing* his sister. I wish he wouldn't do that.

STATIVE PROGRESSIVES

Earlier we noted that stative verbs rarely appear in the progressive aspect. However, there are exceptions to this. For a number of reasons, a native speaker may use stative verbs in the present progressive. Some of the reasons for using these *stative progressives*, as they are sometimes called, are as follows:[9]

- **Giving statements more emotional strength and intensity.** The action becomes more emotional, intense, and vivid if a stative verb appears in the present progressive instead of the simple present. Thus, (33a), with the present progressive, expresses much more emotion than the more usual (33b), with the simple present. The presence of modifiers such as *really*, *always*, *constantly*, and *dreadfully*, common in these constructions, contributes to the effect.

(33) a. This operation *is really costing* a lot of money.
    b. This operation costs a lot of money.

- **Focusing on behavior as a change from the norm.** Progressive statives sometimes occur with a following predicative adjective – that is, in sentences of the type NP + *is/are* verb + *-ing* + adjective. This use of stative progressives expresses the idea that the behavior of the subject is not his or her usual behavior. Compare (34a) to (34b), its equivalent in the simple present; only (34a) conveys the notion of a change from the norm.

(34) a. You*'re being* very stubborn!
    (Implication: What's the matter with you? You don't usually behave this way.)
    b. You're very stubborn!
    (Implication: No one can get along with you.)

The notion of a change can be strengthened through the use of time adverbs like *today* and *this week*, for example, with stative verbs of sensory perception such as *feel*, *hear*, *smell*, and *taste*. Thus, (35a), with *today*, and (35b), with *this week*, both suggest a change from some other time.

(35) a. The river is smelling particularly bad *today.*
    b. She's looking much stronger *this week.*

If the sentences in (35) were in the simple present instead, they would still, because of the adverbs, suggest change. However, they would not suggest a process of change – of a changing extent of bad smells or changing degree of health and strength. Placing the stative verb in the progressive aspect allows us to conceptualize the two verbs as processes rather than states. Processes carry an inherent sense of change and evolution, but states do not.

- **Focusing on evolving change.** Stative *appearance verbs* such as *appear*, *resemble*, and *seem*, and stative *cognitive verbs* such as *believe*, *know*, *mean*, and *understand* occur in the progressive aspect when the speaker wishes to express the idea of evolving process, mentioned earlier. Sentences (36a), (36b), and (36c) have stative appearance verbs, and (36d) has a stative cognitive verb. Here the direction of the process is often indicated by expressions such as *more and more*, *worse and worse*, *faster and faster*, and so on.

(36) a. The baby *is resembling* his father *more and more every day.*
    b. He's *looking worse and worse by the minute.*
    c. That example *is sounding less and less acceptable with each repetition.*
    d. I'm *understanding more and more* about the English tense-aspect system.

- **Providing an informal, polite tone.** The present progressive seems less binding than the simple present, which, as we have seen, has a general truths meaning.[10] Thus, use of progressive statives instead of the simple present in expressing requests and wishes can give these a more informal and polite – milder – tone. Contrast, for example, the present progressive and simple present versions in (37a) and (37b), respectively. A similar effect can be achieved by using modals, as discussed in Chapter 14, or past tense forms, as discussed in this chapter (e.g., either *I would like . . .* or *I wanted . . .* is more polite than *I want . . .*).

(37) a. We *are hoping* you can explain this mess.
    b. We *hope* you can explain this mess.

- **Hedging or softening a definitive opinion.** Cognitive stative verbs, such as *doubt*, *remember*, and *think*, in the progressive aspect allow the speaker to hedge, or soften, what would otherwise seem a more definitive stance. In (38a), the speaker uses a progressive stative in an effort to avoid offending the person addressed while still expressing a degree of skepticism about what she has heard. In (38b), a speaker feeling pressured by a somewhat aggressive shoe salesperson wanted to politely reject his suggestion that she choose the pair of shoes that she had just tried on.[11]

(38) a. Mind you, I'm not *doubting* your word, but I did get a different version of what happened from Peter.
    b. No, I'm sort of *thinking* that I'd like to try a bit higher level heel, anyway.

Past Progressive

The *past progressive*, or *past continuous*, tense is formed with a past form of *be* (*was* or *were*) and a present participle. Its basic meaning is ongoing action in the past.

Often the action expressed with the past progressive was ongoing at the time another action occurred. In such cases, the action that occurred is expressed with the simple past, and the sentence generally includes a subordinate clause that begins with *when* or *while*. With *when*, the past progressive action can be in the main clause, as in (39a), or in the subordinate clause, as in (39b). With *while*, it is in the subordinate clause, as in (39b).

(39) a. He *was studying* for his exam when I saw him this afternoon.
    b. She accidentally cut her hand while/when she *was chopping* vegetables for a salad.

Although most textbooks stress the use of the past progressive in sentences like those in (39), quite frequently the past progressive is used in sentences like (40), in which two ongoing actions in the past were occurring simultaneously.

(**40**) She *was studying* in the library when I *was talking* to Tom.

The past progressive also frequently occurs with time expressions that indicate a point in time when the action was ongoing, as in (41a), the point when it was terminated, as in (41b), or the period during which it was ongoing, as in (41c). In that last case, the time expression has the form *from* (*time 1*) *to* (*time 2*).

(**41**) a. He *was watching* television *at eight o'clock.*
b. From what I could hear from the next room, he *was working* on those shelves *until midnight.*
c. I *was studying* in the library yesterday *from three to five o'clock.*

As we saw earlier with present progressive, the past progressive can impart an iterative sense to the actions expressed by the verbs, as seen in (42).

(**42**) She *was tossing* and *turning* in her sleep all night.

Future Progressive

The *future progressive* tense consists of *will* followed by *be* and a present participle. Its basic meaning is an action that will be ongoing in the (often near) future. As (43) illustrates, the time expressions that occur with the future progressive can indicate the time when the action begins, a time at which it is ongoing, or the length of time it is scheduled for.

(**43**) The president *will be meeting* with his staff $\begin{Bmatrix} \textit{at ten o'clock} \\ \textit{all morning} \end{Bmatrix}$ *tomorrow.*

Although the action in (43) takes place over a short period, the future progressive can also be used to talk about an action that will continue in the future for quite a long time. In this case, often the action is expressed by an activity verb, and its estimated duration is expressed in a time expression with *for*, as in (44).

(**44**) They*'ll be debating* the wisdom of letting the president wage a negative campaign against his opponent for a long time.

SUMMARY

EXPRESSING FUTURE TIME; PROGRESSIVE ASPECT

Future action can be expressed by:

- *will* + **verb** (especially to express probable actions).
  He will get on the plane tomorrow at around two o'clock.

- *be going to* + **verb** (especially to express planned actions).
  He's going to leave tomorrow at about two o'clock.

- the **simple present** with a time expression.
  The bus leaves at 8:30.

continued

- the **present progressive** (for planned future actions)
  That film you like so much is playing at the New Art Theater next week

- *be about to* + **verb** (for actions in the very near future)
  He is about to leave.

- *be to* + **verb** (especially for actions in commands)
  You are to stay until ten o'clock.

Progressive aspect, formed with *be* + the present participle, combines with present, past, and future to express ongoing action at different times.

The **present progressive** expresses **ongoing action at the time of speaking**.
  She's working on the report right now.

Additional meanings include:

- expressing **planned future events**
  She's flying to Paris tomorrow.

- expressing **habitual actions** (with adverbs such as *always* and *forever*)
  She's always calling me up late at night to complain about her boss.

- and with **stative verbs (stative progressives)**

  - **conveying emotional intensity**
    This is costing me a lot of money.

  - **focusing on change from the norm**
    You're being very difficult today.

  - **focusing on evolving change**
    He's looking worse every minute.

  - **providing an informal, polite tone**
    We're hoping you can solve this problem for us.

  - **hedging, or softening, a definitive opinion**
    I'm thinking that I should pass on that.

The **past progressive** expresses **ongoing action in the past**, including in relation to another action.
  She was working on the report when I saw her this afternoon.
  He was shopping while I was making dinner.
  At eight o'clock the game was just starting.
  She was tossing and turning all night long.

The **future progressive** expresses **ongoing action in the (often near) future.**
  The secretary of state will be meeting with the president at seven o'clock this evening to discuss the crisis.
  That was such an unexpected upset that all true sports fans will be discussing it for years.

EXERCISE 16.4

Indicate whether each of the following sentences is grammatical or ungrammatical. If a sentence is ungrammatical, explain why.

Example: He is going into town every day.

Answer: ungrammatical (The time expression *every day* indicates habitual action, so the simple present tense is required.)

1. I'll be discussing those issues with him at our meeting on Friday.
2. She was working on her paper since noon.
3. When a gas is heated, it is expanding.
4. He's always complaining about the service everywhere we go.
5. Jae Eun takes a statistics course next fall.

EXERCISE 16.5

The sentences in each pair differ at least slightly in how they would be used. For each pair, explain the difference.

Example: a. She always kids her brother.
       b. She's always kidding her brother.

Answer: Sentence (a) expresses habitual action; (b) emphasizes the repetitive nature of the activity and implies a complaint.

1. a. Your sister is about to get on the plane.
   b. Your sister is going to get on the plane.
2. a. The plane is landing at La Guardia Airport.
   b. The plane will land at La Guardia Airport.
3. a. He snored and talked in his sleep all night long.
   b. He was snoring and talking in his sleep all night long.
4. a. You are very rude.
   b. You are being very rude.
5. a. They will argue the wisdom of the president's tax cut for the next three years.
   b. They will be arguing the wisdom of the president's tax cut for the next three years.

PERFECT ASPECT

Perfect aspect, formed with *have* and the past participle (verb + *-ed*), expresses completed action. The three tenses formed by the combination of time and perfect aspect are the *present*, *past*, and *future perfect*. Of these, the present perfect tense is the most difficult for English learners to correctly use.

Present Perfect

The *present perfect* tense is formed with a present form of *have* (i.e., *has* or *have*) and a past participle of the main verb. It occurs with a time expression of duration, e.g., *for six years*, *since 1999*, *over the last six months*, and so on.

The present perfect has been treated, including in grammars written for English teachers, as expressing a number of meanings. These different meanings, which are shown on the next page, are due primarily to the lexical aspect of verbs.[12]

- **Expressing a situation that started in the past and continues to the present.** The duration of the situation is marked by phrases with either *for* or *since*, as shown in (45).

(**45**) a. They *have lived* in Chicago *since 1976*.
    b. My father *has been* a Cubs fan *for over 30 years*.
    c. I *have loved* her *since the day I first saw her*.
    d. She *has worked* for that company *for 15 years*.

Sentences (45a), (45b), and (45c) contain stative verbs, and (45d) contains an activity verb. Recall that both of these lexical aspects have potentially unlimited duration. We therefore interpret these sentences as describing past states or activities (situations) that have lasted up to the moment of speaking and may last into the future. The time phrases with *for* and *since* simply mark the past duration of the state or activity.

- **Expressing a recently completed action.** Typical examples of this meaning are shown in (46).

(**46**) a. The Japanese climbers *have reached* the peak of Mount Everest.
    b. Her plane *has arrived*.
    c. Alan *has* recently *written* an article on that very subject.
    d. She *has* just *drawn* a circle on the board.

Sentences (46a) and (46b) contain achievement verbs, which denote actions that occur instantaneously, hence the meaning of a recently completed action is imparted by the lexical aspect of these verbs. With accomplishment verbs, this meaning is somewhat less salient, but can be enhanced by adverbs such as *recently* and *just*, as (46c) and (46d) show.

- **Expressing an action that occurred at an unspecified time and has current relevance.** The notion of "current relevance" is also phrased as the action's being regarded by the speaker as noteworthy, as illustrated in (47).

(**47**) a. He *has read* all of Shakespeare's plays.
    b. John Le Carré *has written* a new novel.
    c. I *have* already *seen* that movie.

These sentences contain accomplishment verbs. The lexical aspect of the verbs thus accounts for the actions' having been completed. The fact that they have current relevance or are noteworthy is determined by the sentence content (e.g., reading all of Shakespeare's plays is surely a noteworthy accomplishment) and the discourse context (e.g., having seen a movie is relevant when someone suggests going to see it).

- **Describing an action that occurred over a period of time that is complete at the time of speaking.** Sentences exemplifying this meaning are shown in (48).

(**48**) a. The value of his house *has doubled* over the past two years.
    b. He *has grown* over two inches in the past six months.
    c. His condition *has improved* considerably in the last three days.

These sentences contain activity verbs that express actions involving inherent change over time. The sense of change is enhanced by the time expressions of duration. The perfect aspect imparts the meaning of completion, hence the interpretation that the evolving change is now complete.

Thus, we see that the lexical aspect of the verbs combines with the basic meaning of the present perfect to produce different semantic interpretations such as "started in the past and continues to the present," "occurred over a period of time that is completed at the time of speaking," and so on. The effect of the lexical aspect of verbs on the interpretation of sentences in the present perfect tense has implications for teaching. These will be discussed in the Suggestions for Teaching section.

Past Perfect

The *past perfect* tense is formed with the past tense form of the verb *have* (i.e., *had*) and a past participle.

Basic Meaning

The past perfect expresses a past action completed prior to another event or time in the past. Hence the past perfect often occurs in sentences with a main clause and a subordinate clause, where both clauses express the events in the past, as shown in (49).

> (**49**) a. She gave the book to his brother *after* she *had read* it.
> b. She *had* already mailed the letter *when* Hal called her.

The presence of the past perfect insures that the event it describes is interpreted as having occurred before the event in the other clause. Thus, the order in which the clauses appear does not affect the interpretation of which action occurred first. This can be seen by comparing (50a) with (50b) and (50c) with (50d).

> (**50**) a. When she arrived, he had already left.
> b. He had already left when she arrived.
> c. By the time she arrived, he had already left.
> d. He had already left by the time she arrived.

In subordinate clauses introduced by certain subordinators, such as *before*, *after*, and *as soon as*, it is often possible to use the simple past instead of the past perfect. The reason is that these subordinators themselves establish the sequence of the events. For example, most speakers would consider sentence (51b), in which the simple past tense occurs in the second clause, to have the same meaning as (51a), in which the past perfect tense occurs in the clause.

> (**51**) a. John left *as soon as* he *had spoken to* Edith.
> b. John left *as soon as* he *spoke to* Edith.

In some contexts, however, the past perfect is required. Notice that in (51b) *as soon as* establishes the temporal sequence between two events that have a comparatively short duration. However, if the second event has an inherently long duration, such as the accomplishment *write a dissertation*, then the past perfect is required, as the comparison in (52) shows.[13]

> (**52**) a. John left the country *as soon as* he had written his dissertation.
> b. *John left the country *as soon as* he wrote his dissertation.

Notice that when we make the duration of the second event short, by changing it to an achievement like *complete his dissertation*, in (53), the tense of the verb in the subordinate clause can be either the past perfect or the simple past. This supports the argument that both events should have about the same duration.

> (**53**) a. John left the country *as soon as* he had completed his dissertation.
> b. John left the country *as soon as* he completed his dissertation.

Additional Meaning

The past perfect also appears in *counterfactual conditional* sentences, which express speculations or regrets about unfulfilled events like the one in (54). Counterfactual conditionals are discussed in detail in Chapter 19.

(54) If I *had* only *worked* a little harder, I would have been promoted.

Future Perfect

The *future perfect* is formed with *will* followed by *have* and the past participle of the main verb. It is generally used to express an action that will be completed prior to or by some specified future time. Accomplishment verbs are especially common in sentences with the future perfect, as in (55). These verbs are often followed by gerundive complements, like *grading the papers* in the example.

(55) I *will have finished* grading the papers $\begin{Bmatrix} before \\ by \end{Bmatrix}$ 4:00 p.m.

However, the future perfect can also be used to express states that will have endured for a period of time as measured at some future date, as in (56), in which being married is the state.

(56) This coming January we *will have been* married for 30 years.[14]

As with the past perfect, sentences with a future perfect often have a main clause and a subordinate clause. In these sentences, the future action is completed prior to another action in a subordinate clause introduced by *before* or *by the time*. The verb in this subordinate clause may be in the present perfect, as in (57a), or the simple present, as in (57b).

(57) a. He *will have finished* grading all of his papers by the time you've *eaten* your lunch.
   b. He *will have completed* the negotiations by the time you *arrive*.

With some verbs (e.g., *finish*), the future perfect can be replaced by future forms such as *will + be +* an adjective formed from a past participle, as in (58b), or another, equivalent adjective, as in (58c). Sentences such as those in (58b) and (58c) occur frequently in spoken English.

(58) a. He will have finished by six o'clock.
   b. He will be finished by six o'clock.
   c. He will be through/ready by six o'clock.

SUMMARY

PERFECT ASPECT

Perfect aspect, formed with *have* + the past participle, expresses completed action and combines with present, past, and future time.

The **present perfect** is said to have several meanings. These meanings relate to the lexical aspect of verbs as follows:

• With stative and activity verbs, the present perfect expresses a **situation that started in the past and continues to the present**.
   I have lived in Geneva for over 35 years.
   John has worked for us since last December.

- With achievement and, to a lesser extent, accomplishment verbs, it expresses a **recently completed action**.
  Guess what? Joan's won the lottery.
  Al Gore has just written a book that contains a lot of information about that.

- With accomplishment verbs, it expresses an **action that occurred at an unspecified time and has current relevance** (the action is seen as noteworthy by the speaker).
  He has read every one of Shakespeare's plays.

- With activity verbs involving inherent change, it expresses an **action that occurred over a period of time completed at the time of speaking**.
  The value of that stock has tripled over the past year.

The **past perfect** expresses a **past event completed prior to another past event or past time**. Sentences with the past perfect often have a main clause and a subordinate clause introduced by *after*, *before*, *by the time* (*that*), *when*, and so on.
  Tom had already washed the dishes when Lucy asked if she could help him.

It also expresses speculations about unfulfilled conditions in **counterfactual conditionals**.
  I would have called him if I had had his number.

The **future perfect** expresses an **action that will be completed prior to or by some specified future time**.
  He will have read the entire book by five o'clock.

It can also express **states** that will have endured for a period of time as measured at some future date.
  They will have been married for 35 years this December.

EXERCISE 16.6

Identify the tense of the italicized verb in each sentence and state whether the sentence is grammatical or ungrammatical. If a sentence is ungrammatical, explain why and supply a correction.

Example: I *didn't see* her since Monday.

Answer: simple past; ungrammatical (Time expressions like *since Monday* do not occur with the simple past.)
Correction: I haven't seen her . . . .

1. I *have talked* to him about it last Tuesday.
2. She already *cooked* dinner when we came home.
3. I would have made a fortune in the stock market if I *bought* IBM back in 1972.
4. We *didn't get* any response on Monday.
5. My father and mother *will have been married* for over 40 years this coming August.
6. Tom *will be finished* by the time his wife comes home.

PERFECT AND PROGRESSIVE ASPECTS

The perfect and progressive aspects can be used together. They, too, intersect with the three times, forming the *present*, *past*, and *future perfect progressive tenses*. Reflecting the meaning of both aspects, these tenses express ongoing action to some point in time. They occur particularly with activity verbs, and they are often in sentences that include time expressions of duration (e.g., with *for* or *since*).

Present Perfect Progressive

The *present perfect progressive* tense is formed with *has* or *have* + *been* + the present participle. The present perfect progressive expresses *past activity that extends to the present*. Time expressions of duration, such as those mentioned in the previous paragraph, may be included, as in (59a), but need not be, as (59b) and (59c) show.

(**59**) a. He's *been going* to that health club $\begin{cases} since\ February. \\ for\ over\ six\ months. \end{cases}$
b. She's *been traveling* through Europe.
c. I've *been adjusting* the tension on this wire.

The present perfect progressive and present perfect are sometimes essentially interchangeable. The main difference may be that the present perfect progressive, which includes the progressive aspect, confers a sense of ongoingness. Thus, (60a), with the activity verb *work* in the present perfect progressive, and (60b), with *work* in the present perfect, have essentially the same meaning, although in (60a), the activity seems more continuous and ongoing.

(**60**) a. He *has been working* with our company for over 20 years.
b. He *has worked* with our company for over 20 years.

Often, however, the two tenses are not interchangeable. Consider the sentences in (61), in which the *for* prepositional phrase of duration in (60) has been omitted.

(**61**) a. He *has been working* with our company.
b. He *has worked* with our company.

Sentence (61a), with the present perfect progressive, still has the sense of the work continuing to the present; however, in (61b), with the present perfect, the work occurred at some time or times in the past.

Note that the sentences in (62) all contain an accomplishment verb, *write* (*a novel*).

(**62**) a. She *has been writing* a novel.
b. She *has written* a novel.
c. She *has been writing* a novel for more than 20 years.
d. *She *has written* a novel for more than 20 years.

In (62a) and (62b), we see the same type of meaning difference that was evident in (61a) and (61b): In (62a), she is still writing the novel; in (62b), writing the novel is a completed action. However, as (62d) shows, when a phrase indicating duration is used with an accomplishment verb, the present perfect is not possible.

Notice what happens when we make two changes to the sentences in (62). In (63), *write* is used as an activity verb and *novels* replaces *a novel*.

(**63**) a. She *has been writing* novels.
b. She *has written* novels.
c. She *has been writing* novels for more than 20 years.
d. She *has written* novels for more than 20 years.

In (63a) and (63b), we see the same meaning difference that (62a) and (62b) have – an action continuing in the present versus a past action. However, in contrast to (62d), (63d) allows the present perfect with a phrase indicating duration, and it essentially has the same meaning as the sentence in (63c) with the present perfect progressive.

The comparison of (62) with (63) demonstrates that, depending on the lexical aspect of the verb and differences in lexical items in sentences (e.g., singular vs. plural nouns), the present perfect may or may not have the meaning that is similar to that of the present perfect progressive.

Since the present perfect progressive suggests duration, it is preferred over the present perfect for questions beginning with *how long*. Thus, with the activity verb pairs in (64), (64b) is preferred over (64a) as is (64d) over (64c). Because stative verbs (e.g., *believe, know, possess, understand, want*) do not usually appear in the progressive aspect, questions with *how long* and these verbs appear in the present perfect, as illustrated in (65).

(**64**) a. ?How long have you studied?
b. How long have you been studying?
c. ?How long has it rained?
d. How long has it been raining?

(**65**) a. How long have you known him?
b. *How long have you been knowing him?

Past Perfect Progressive

The *past perfect progressive*, formed with *had* + *been* + the present participle, expresses an ongoing action in the past that is related to another past action, which is often expressed in the simple past tense. This other action frequently occurs in a subordinate clause, particularly with *when*, as in (66).

(**66**) Kennedy *had been trying* to interest a publisher in his novel for over two years, when, discouraged by the many rejections he had received, he finally asked Saul Bellow for help.

Time expressions of duration are common, as in (66) and (67), in which the past progressive occurs in sentences without subordinate clauses.

(**67**) a. At that point, Jack *had* already *been studying* for 20 hours straight.
b. When I came down the stairs, I saw that there was at least a foot of water in the basement. Jack was standing under a pipe, and a steady stream cascaded into his face. For the past 45 minutes, he *had been working* unsuccessfully to staunch the leak.

Future Perfect Progressive

The *future perfect progressive*, formed with *will* + *have* + *been* and a present participle, expresses an action that will continue into the future up to a specific time. The duration of the action is usually specified in a time expression with *for*. The point at which the action will be complete often is stated in the simple present tense in a subordinate clause introduced by *when* or *by the time* (*that*), as in (68a).

(**68**) a. He *will have been studying* and *practicing* medicine for over ten years when he finally completes his residency next month.
b. By March, we *will have been using* the new system for a full year.

The future perfect progressive tends not to be used much in either spoken or written English.

SUMMARY

PERFECT AND PROGRESSIVE ASPECTS

The **perfect progressive** tenses combine both progressive and perfect aspect with present, past, and future time.

Present perfect progressive expresses ongoing past action that continues up to the present. It often occurs with time expressions beginning with *for* and *since*.
   He's been taking lessons for about three weeks.

Past perfect progressive expresses a past ongoing action that happens prior to another past action or time. A subordinate clause, beginning with, for example, *when*, often marks a past action that is related in some way.
   She had been working on her paper for over an hour when Jack came home.

Future perfect progressive expresses an action that will continue in the future up to some specific time. That time is frequently indicated in a subordinate clause beginning with *when* or *by* (*the time*).
   When she finally lands in Australia, she will have been traveling for over 14 hours.

EXERCISE 16.7

Indicate whether each sentence is grammatical or ungrammatical. If a sentence is ungrammatical, explain why and supply a correction.

Example: They will be driving for over 16 hours when they complete the next stage of the Paris to Dakar race.

Answer: ungrammatical (The future perfect progressive, not the future progressive, should be used to express an action that will continue in the future up to a specific time.) correction: They will have been driving . . .

1. She has been studying for over four hours when she decided to take a short nap.
2. I have been reading your article. It's very good, but there are a couple of points that need to be clarified.
3. I've been studying since noon, so I think it's time to stop and do something else.
4. Cheryl has been working on that paper since January.
5. He will be traveling for about 18 hours when he lands in Sidney tomorrow.

EXERCISE 16.8

Explain the difference in meaning between each of the following pairs of sentences.

Example: a. How long has he been studying biology?
           b. How long did he study biology?

Answer: Question (a), with the present perfect progressive, indicates that he is still studying biology; (b), with the simple past, indicates his study is now complete.

1. a. How long have you been waiting for me?
   b. How long did you wait for me?

2. a. How long had he been living in London?
   b. How long has he been living in London?
3. a. She has been working for him for a little over two months.
   b. She has worked for him for a little over two months.
4. a. They have built a small house on the edge of town.
   b. They have been building a small house on the edge of town.

SEQUENCE OF TENSE RULES

The tense of one verb may be partly determined by the tense of another. This is what happens in *reported speech*, in which a speaker or writer reports what someone has said or thought. Reported speech is given in a complement clause following a *reporting verb* (*said, asked*, etc.). Through what are known as *sequence of tense* rules, the tense of the verb in the complement clause is affected by the tense of the reporting verb in the main clause. In particular, with a past tense reporting verb, tenses of verbs in the reported speech are *backshifted*, as mentioned earlier on page 359, that is, present tense forms become past tense forms and so on, as we shall see. Reported speech involves other changes as well, reflecting differences between the time of the original speech and its reporting as well as any other relevant differences, as in the speakers and place. Thus, for example, the sentence *I am applying for the job in your office today* might be reported as *She said she was applying for the job here last week*, with backshifting of *am applying* and changes in pronouns and time and place adverbials.

Shifts in Tenses

The main shifts in verb forms from the original utterance to reported speech are shown in (69) through (72):

(69) a. Al said, "I *like* her."   *simple present*
       BECOMES
     b. Al said (that) he *liked* her.   *simple past*

(70) a. Joan said, "I'*m working* on my book."   *present progressive*
       BECOMES
     b. Joan said she *was working* on her book.   *past progressive*

(71) a. Al said, "I *finished* my report on time."   *simple past*
       BECOMES
     b. Al said he *had finished* his report on time.   *past perfect*

(72) a. Susan said, "Al *has* finally *finished* his report.   *present perfect*
       BECOMES
     b. Susan said Al *had* finally *finished* his report.   *past perfect*

In addition, the present perfect progressive shifts to the past perfect progressive (e.g., *Susan said that Al had been working on his report*) and verbs in passive sentences undergo the same shifts (e.g., *Susan said, "Al's report has been published"* BECOMES *Susan said Al's report had been published*). However, shifts do not occur with past perfect or past perfect progressive verbs, as no shifts would be possible.

As mentioned, these rules apply in sentences that have past tense reporting verbs. When the reporting verb is in the present tense, no change occurs in the verb tense of the original utterance, as shown in (73).

(73) a. John said, "I *went* to the movies last night."
 b. John *says* (that) he *went* to the movies last night.

Shifts in Modals

Shifts also occur with certain modal auxiliaries. The main shifts with modals are as follows:

- *May* is changed to *might* when the meaning is possibility, as shown in (74a) and (74b). *May* is changed to *could* when the meaning is permission, as in (74c) and (74d).

  (74) a. Fred added, "I *may* go with her."   *possibility*
   b. Fred added that he *might* go with her.
   c. The secretary said, "You *may* go in."   *permission*
   d. The secretary said that we *could* go in.

- *Can* is changed to *could* when the meaning is ability, as in (75).

  (75) a. Alice said, "I *can* hold my breath for two minutes."
   b. Alice said that she *could* hold her breath for two minutes.

- *Shall* is changed to *would* when the meaning is future time, as in (76a) and (76b). When it represents a suggestion, it is changed to *should*, as in (76c) and (76d).

  (76) a. The headwaiter said, "I *shall* speak to the chef about it."   *future time*
   b. The headwaiter said that he *would* speak to the chef about it.
   c. "*Shall* we include Bill in our plans?" Alice asked.   *suggestion*
   d. Alice asked if we *should* include Bill in our plans.

- *Will* is changed to *would*, as in (77).

  (77) a. Judy said, " I *will* see Mike tomorrow."
   b. Judy said that she *would* see Mike tomorrow.

- *Must* is changed to *had to*, as in (78).

  (78) a. The conductor told the opera singer, "You *must* sing with gusto!"
   b. The conductor told the opera singer that she *had to* sing with gusto.

Exceptions to Backshifting

In certain situations, the sequence of tense rules are relaxed and backshifting is not required. Essentially, backshifting is not required if a statement about the present or future still holds. Thus, backshifting is merely optional if:

- The statement expresses something thought to be a *general truth*. Thus, in (79), because Torrecelli's conclusion is recognized as a general, scientific truth, both the present tense *is* and the past tense *was* are permissible.[15]

  (79) Torrecelli concluded that the atmosphere $\begin{Bmatrix} is \\ was \end{Bmatrix}$ a sea of air pressing down on the surface of the earth.

  However, if the belief expressed does not have this status, as is the case for *is* in (80), the backshifted version is preferred.

  (80) In Columbus's time, most people believed that the earth $\begin{Bmatrix} was \\ ?is \end{Bmatrix}$ flat.

- The speaker knows or believes what the sentence expresses is *still true* in the present, as in (81).

(**81**) Fred said he $\begin{Bmatrix} drives \\ drove \end{Bmatrix}$ a 1956 Belchfire Special.

The present tense verb in (81) could be used by someone who believes that Fred still drives that 1956 Belchfire Special. Someone who thinks Fred's statement no longer holds could only use the past tense verb.

- The speaker knows or believes that what the sentence expresses about the future is *still possible*. Again, as (82) shows, a shift is not required even though it is permissible.

(**82**) The forecast a couple of days ago said we $\begin{Bmatrix} will \\ would \end{Bmatrix}$ be having rain all weekend.

The version in (82) with *will* rather than *would* can be uttered, for example, on Thursday by someone who believes that Tuesday's weekend forecast still holds but not by someone who knows the forecast has been changed.

In (83), which reports a sentence in which the present progressive is used to express a future plan, note that shifting to the past progressive is similarly optional. In fact, the use of present or future time adverbs expressions, as in (83), may favor the use of the version without shifting.

(**83**) Fred said he $\begin{Bmatrix} \text{'s going} \\ was\ going \end{Bmatrix}$ on a diet *next week*.

- The speaker repeats something that was just said. Such speech, as in (84), rarely undergoes backshifting.

(**84**) John: I like opera.
   Bill: Sorry, I wasn't listening. What did you say?
   John: I said I *like* opera.

SUMMARY

SEQUENCE OF TENSE RULES

Reported speech changes the tense in spoken speech by sequence of tense rules. Tense shifts normally occur by what is known as **backshifting**.

- Simple present becomes simple past.
  Al said, "I like her."   BECOMES   *Al said (that) he liked her.*

- Present progressive becomes past progressive.
  Joan said, "I'm working on my book."   BECOMES   *Joan said she was working on her book.*

continued

Certain **modal auxiliaries** are also backshifted:

- *May* for possibility becomes *might*, and *may* for permission becomes *could*.
  Fred added, "I may go with her."   BECOMES   *Fred added that he might go with her.*
  The secretary said, "You may go in."   BECOMES   *The secretary said that we could go in.*

- *Can* becomes *could*.
  Alice said "I can do that too."   BECOMES   *Alice said she could do that too.*

- *Will* becomes *would*.
  Judy said, "I will see Mike tomorrow."   BECOMES   *Judy said she would see Mike tomorrow.*

- *Must* becomes *had to*.
  He told her, "You must finish it today!"   BECOMES   *He told her that she had to finish it today.*

A shift is not necessary if:

- the original statement is a general truth.
  Torrecelli concluded that the atmosphere is/was a sea of air pressing down on the earth.

- the speaker is reporting something that is still true.
  Fred said he drives/drove a 1956 Belchfire Special.

- the speaker is reporting something still possible for the future.
  The forecast said we will/would be having lots of rain.

- the speaker repeats something he or she just said.
  John: I like opera.
  Bill: What did you say?
  John: I said I like opera.

EXERCISE 16.9

Indicate whether the tense shift or lack of shift in each (b) sentence is appropriate and explain why.

Example: a. Waiter: You may smoke in this area but not in that room over there.
  b. The waiter told us that we could smoke in this area but not in that room over there.

Answer: shift is appropriate (*May* is shifted to *could* when the meaning is permission.)

1. a. John: I still have that dictionary you gave me when I was 16 years old.
   b. John said he still has that dictionary you gave him when he was 16 years old.
2. a. Perry: I could still run a mile in under five minutes if I had to.
   b. Perry added that he could still have run a mile in under five minutes if he had had to.
3. a. Alice: I have been around the world three times in the last four years.
   b. Alice replied that she had been around the world three times in the last four years.

4. a. Galileo believes all bodies, regardless of their mass, fall at the same rate toward the center of the earth.
   b. Galileo believed that all bodies, regardless of their mass, fall at the same rate toward the center of the earth.
5. a. Dreyfus: I am innocent! (Dreyfus is then stripped of his rank and led away.)
   b. Bystander: Dreyfus said that he is innocent.

PROBLEMS THAT ESL/EFL STUDENTS HAVE WITH TENSE AND ASPECT

Research over the past decade indicates that several factors converge to shape ESL/EFL students' attempts to master tense and aspect in English. More specifically, the lexical aspect of verbs plays a role along with the influence of the students' L1 and the input that students receive in class. This third factor, particularly in intensive courses, involves not only the instruction that the students receive from teachers and materials but, more specifically, the frequency with which, within this instruction, certain types of verbs are associated with particular tense forms.[16]

The way in which lexical aspect influences students' learning of tenses has been the focus of research by Kathleen Bardovi-Harlig and her colleagues (Bardovi-Harlig 1998, 1999, 2000; Bardovi-Harlig & Bergström 1996; Bardovi-Harlig & Reynolds 1995). Bardovi-Harlig and Reynolds' study involved 182 ESL students who represented 15 different L1s and six proficiency levels from beginning to advanced. In looking at students' learning of simple past tense forms, Bardovi-Harlig and Reynolds found that students were initially most successful at correctly producing these forms with telic verbs – that is, achievement and accomplishment verbs. With atelic verbs – stative and activity verbs – students were less likely to correctly use the simple past tense forms when needed.[17] They substituted progressive forms with the stative verbs and bare infinitive and simple present tense forms with the activity verbs. The progression of learning past tense forms was telic verbs, then stative verbs, and finally activity verbs. Interestingly, Bardovi-Harlig and Reynolds found that learners were not sensitive to frequency adverbs as clues indicating the need for a past tense form. Students' difficulties with stative verbs have been confirmed by other researchers. For example, Collins (2002, 2005) found that students frequently did not put tense endings on stative verbs.

Bardovi-Harlig and Reynolds suggest that their research has at least two important implications for teaching tense to ESL students:

- More attention should be devoted to teaching verbs that pose more difficulty for students – activity verbs and stative verbs in the case of the simple past tense.
- Frequency adverbs should be focused on as clues to tense, since students tend not to consistently use these cues until much later in their learning.

While Bardovi-Harlig's general view of stages in the acquisition of tense, and especially of past tense as spreading from telic to atelic verbs, has been supported by subsequent studies (e.g., Robinson 1995; Collins 2002), we continue to learn more about other factors that affect this acquisition. One important factor that interacts with lexical aspect was clearly evident in a large-scale study with 136 French-speaking university students in Canada (Collins, 2002). Employing the same methodology as

Bardovi-Harlig and Reynolds, Collins found that these students used present perfect forms for telic verbs in contexts in which the simple past is obligatory in English. An example from Collins' data is shown in (85).

(85) *When I was more young I *have gone* with my friend and his parents camping . . .
*At this place we *have met* some people who was very sympathetic.

The most likely explanation for the errors is that in French the tense that would be used in a context like the one shown in (85) is the *passé composé*, which in form resembles the English present perfect. Hence, Collins's results indicate that students' L1s also influence the acquisition of English tenses. In the following sections, we look at other examples of problems stemming from L1 influence.

L1 Does Not Mark Tense on Verbs (Chinese)

Some languages, including Chinese, do not indicate tense through overt markers, or inflections, on verbs. The Chinese sentence in (86) shows that past time is indicated by a time expression, *jien tien*, not by an inflection like the English -*ed*.

(86) *Ta   zao tian   chu   zhigiageo.*
she/he   yesterday   go   Chicago
"She/He went to Chicago yesterday."

An error that Chinese speakers frequently make is to use bare infinitive forms rather than verbs inflected for the simple present and past, as in (87).

(87) a. *She go (to) Chicago every day.
b. *She go (to) Chicago yesterday.

Although this kind of error is thought to be characteristic of beginners, one study by Lardiere (1998) found relatively infrequent use of tense markers on verbs (only 34 percent of the time they were required) in the speech of a Chinese woman who had come to the United States 10 years before at age 20.

L1 Has One Tense Corresponding to Two Tenses in English (German)

In German, the simple present is used not only in the contexts in which it is used in English but also in those in which English uses the present progressive. Thus, in (88), in German, the simple present is used in a sentence with a time expression corresponding to *right now*.

(88) *Er   arbeitet   jetzt   und   darf   nicht   gestört   werden.*
he   works   now   and   may   not   disturbed   become
He is working right now and can't/must not be disturbed.

Although German speakers have no trouble acquiring the -*ing* form, they have trouble using the two English tenses in the appropriate contexts. A common error is to overgeneralize the progressive to contexts in which time expressions require a simple form, as shown in (89), from Bland (1988).

(89) A: Do you know Sapsucker Woods?
B: *Yes, my wife *is often going there* with the children.

Alternatively, German speakers may err by using the simple present, the tense they would use in their L1. The error in (90) is taken from a letter by a native speaker of German who has a good command of English. The intent was to express *"I am enclosing/sending you a photo . . ."*

(**90**) *I send you a photo of Rita taken in Berlin.

L1 Requires Different Tense with Equivalent English Time Expressions (German)

Problems can occur when the L1 and English have corresponding tenses and corresponding time expressions, but the time expressions in the L1 and English require different tenses. For example, German has a present perfect tense formed, like the present perfect in English, with the present tense of the verb *haben* ("have") and the past participle of the main verb. English requires the present perfect tense with activity and stative verbs accompanied by expressions of duration beginning with *since* and *for*. Example (91a) shows the classic case of a state that began in the past and lasts up to the present. However, these expressions of duration in German require the simple present, as can be seen in (91b).

(**91**) a. *I have lived* in Vienna $\left\{\begin{array}{l}\textit{since 1970.}\\ \textit{for 25 years.}\end{array}\right\}$

    b. Ich *wohne seit* 1970 in Wien. OR   Ich *wohne seit 25 Jahren* in Wien.
      I *live* since 1970 in Vienna OR I *live*   for 25 years   in Vienna

As a result, German speakers may fail to use the present perfect in these English contexts and, overgeneralizing the use of the present progressive, may make errors like those shown in (92).

(**92**) a. *I am living in Vienna since 1970.
    b. *I am living in Vienna for 25 years.

English and German are practically an exact match on word order, and this provides opportunities for a pernicious kind of transfer that would not be found with other languages such as Japanese and Korean.

L1 Has Two Possibilities Where English Has One (German)

German uses the verb *werden* ("become") as the primary means of expressing future action. However, when describing an action that will occur in the near future in conversation, German speakers often use the present tense in English instead. If a German speaker applies this L1 possibility in an equivalent context in English, the result may be an error like the one made by speaker B in (93).

(**93**) A: Can you come to my place on Tuesday?
    B: *I have a look and let you know.

L1 Tense Transfers Throughout a Discourse (French, German)

In English, when we establish an event as in the past, we continue on with the simple past tense to report it. Thus, if someone asks "What did you do last night?" the answer is generally in the simple past tense, for example, "Well, I finished my composition, and then I watched television because there was a good program on." In French, there is also continuity of tense in this situation; however, as illustrated in (94), the tense generally used is the *passé composé*, which, as we have seen, in form is similar to the English present perfect.[18] This continuity of tense can continue through longer stretches of discourse.

> (94) A: *Qu'est-ce que vous   avez fait   hier soir?*
>   what is it   you   have done   last night
>
>   B: *J'ai fini   ma   composition,   puis j'ai   regardé   la télévision*
>   I *have finished*   my   theme   then *I have*   *watched*   television
>   *parce   qu'   il y   avait   un   bon   programme.*
>   because   there   was   a   good   program

Because French speakers frequently use the English present perfect where the past tense is required over a stretch of discourse, the errors accumulate. Hence, an English rendering by a French speaker of B's response in (94) could be entirely in the present perfect, which would be ungrammatical. Collins (2002) reports that for French speakers in her study, the present perfect was substituted as "the most common alternative to the simple past for telics," and that this "L1 influence . . . increased once learners began to develop some productive use of the simple past in English" (pp. 32–33).

Substitution of the present perfect for the simple past in stretches of discourse is also very common for German speakers learning English, for a similar reason. In German, the present perfect is often used in reporting past events, a fact that has led to its being referred to as the "informal," or "conversational," past tense.

L1 Choice Differs in Complex Sentences (Arabic)
Fakhri (1995) notes that Arabic has a perfective tense associated with complete or past action and an imperfective associated with action that is incomplete. As a result, speakers of Arabic may establish the following equivalencies: Arabic perfective = English simple past tense; Arabic imperfective = English simple present or present progressive tense. Fakhri examined Arabic complex sentences in discourse and found the perfective to be the dominant form for verbs in main clauses but the imperfective to be the dominant form for verbs in subordinate clauses. If Arabic speakers transfer this pattern, they should show fairly accurate tense usage in main clauses of complex sentences but far less accurate usage in subordinate clauses, where they may incorrectly substitute the English simple present or present progressive. An examination of 28 narratives written by Arabic-speaking ESL students revealed that 71 percent of the errors made reflected this L1 pattern. Thus, errors were typically of the sort *He left the house while it rains* or *He left the house while it is raining.*

Difficulties with Sequence of Tense Rules
Some languages do not have backshifting constraints as English does. Speakers of these languages sometimes do not follow the English backshifting rules described previously, producing tense sequences across clauses that sound ungrammatical or inappropriate. This type of error is sporadic but frequent enough to warrant some emphasis by ESL teachers.

Lack of Backshifting in Complements (Japanese, Russian)
In Japanese, the sequencing of tenses in sentences that have main verbs other than the reported speech verb *said* is not as restricted as English. Ogihara (1996) has

argued that past tense morpheme *-ta* is relative in terms of the time it expresses. In single-clause sentences, such as *John read the book yesterday*, it expresses perfect action just like English. However, as shown in (95), in Japanese sentences with complements, the *ta* can be interpreted as *has* or *had* in the *that* complement, which is bracketed.

(95)   *Taroo-wa*   [*zibun-ga   gan-dat   ta   to*]   *sitte   i-ta.*
       Taroo (topic)   self (num.) cancer-be (past) that   know   (past)
   a. Taroo knew [that he *has* cancer].
   b. Taroo knew [that he *had* cancer].

When Japanese speakers apply their L1 sequence-of-tense rule in forming English sentences with *that* complements, they may produce unacceptable tense sequences as shown in (96). We tend to view (96a) as ungrammatical because the verb in the *that* clause is not backshifted to *had*. Similarly, (96b) sounds much better if we change the tense of the main verb to the simple present (i.e., *knows*), or backshift the verb in the *that* complement to *had*.

(96) a. *He *remembered* that he *has* to turn out the light.
     b. *He *knew* that John *has* been working since five o'clock.

Similar errors have been noted with other languages such as Russian and Polish.

SUGGESTIONS FOR TEACHING TENSE AND ASPECT

The research cited earlier suggests a number of important points for improving the teaching of verb forms and tense and aspect.

Teaching could be improved by taking into account the role that lexical aspect plays in learning. In its simplest form, this would entail giving extensive examples of the four types of verbs – stative, activity, achievement, and accomplishment – and showing how the different types can produce different meanings when they appear in a particular tense, for example, in the present perfect.

Greater focus should be placed on the tenses that are commonly confused by English learners – for example, the simple past and the present perfect, and the simple present and the present progressive. Collins (2002) suggests that, if students have "attained a minimal threshold in their productive use of the simple past tense," there should be activities that are "designed to target the inappropriate use of the [present] perfect in past contexts."

While not denying the importance of Bardovi-Harlig and Reynold's discovery that students do not pay attention to adverbs as clues to appropriate tense use, it should be noted that quite a few English language teaching textbooks attempt to show which adverbs occur with particular tenses. Of course, some adverbs can occur with both tenses, as (97) shows.

	Simple Past	*Present Perfect*
(97)	I $\begin{Bmatrix} just \\ finally \end{Bmatrix}$ saw him.	I've $\begin{Bmatrix} just \\ finally \end{Bmatrix}$ seen him.
	I saw him *recently* at school.	I've seen him *recently* at school.
	Did you see him *yet*?	Have you seen him *yet*?

Biber et al. (1999, p. 436) state that the LSWE corpus shows a preference by speakers of British English for the present perfect tense with adverbs such as those in (98), whereas speakers of American English favor the simple past tense with them.[19] This preference is borne out in a study by Elsness (1999), who asked speakers of these two dialects to judge the acceptability of pairs of sentences differing only in tense, simple past or present perfect. The study also found that speakers of both groups strongly reject the simple past tense as possible in sentences with time expressions beginning with *since*, thereby validating its usefulness as a pedagogical clue for teaching the present perfect. The results for sentences with adverbs indicating a specific time in the past (e.g., *yesterday*, *last year*) are less conclusive for both dialects, since it appears that Elsness did not include many sentence pairs with these in his test.[20]

An important point that Elsness did not address is that some adverbs and temporal adverb phrases can occur with both the simple past and the present perfect, but each tense requires a different context. Presumably speakers of American and British English would have indicated the differences if the test that Elsness administered had provided them with this opportunity. For example, the sentences with *never* in (98) are identical except for tense. Sentence (98a) is not an appropriate answer to the question *Have you ever seen this man before?*, but (98b) is; and the sentence in (98b) is not an appropriate answer to the question *Are you absolutely sure that you didn't see him at the party?*, but (98a) is.

(**98**) a. No, I never saw him.
      b. No, I've never seen him.

Similarly, time expressions with *for* are permissible with the simple past as well as with the present perfect, but their use with one or the other tense requires a different context. Consider, for example, the sentences in (99) with *for a long time*. Sentence (99a), with the present perfect, might appear as an answer to the question *Have you seen him lately?* Sentence (99b), with the simple past, would make sense in reference to a previously mentioned past event or time (e.g., *I saw him at your wedding in 1994, and then I didn't see him for a long time*).

(**99**) a. I haven't seen him for a long time.
      b. I didn't see him for a long time.

The comparisons in (98) and (99) suggest that instruction on tenses that are frequently confused, such as the simple present and the present perfect, should include activities that ask students to identify contexts in which pairs of sentences can occur.

Another important finding that came out of Collins's (2005) study concerns the kind of instruction that might be most productive in teaching problem tenses. She correctly notes that most textbook exercises designed for tense instruction are "'fill-in-the-blank' sentence-level production [activities] which primarily involve the manipulation of form." However, her research showed that students who knew the appropriate forms did not always perform well on these exercises, "either [providing] different forms or, in some cases, no form at all."

Why did students not perform well on the fill-ins? Collins (2005) used controlled written production and judgment tasks with over 200 ESL students to investigate factors that influenced how they processed and interpreted tense forms. She asked the students to explain why they had sometimes changed their minds about a correct choice they had made or why they had not supplied a tense marking for a stative verb. The results revealed that students in intensive courses are influenced by the frequency of the input they have been receiving. For example, students who wrote present tense forms of stative verbs in contexts that required simple past tense forms reported that they were used to seeing these verbs in the present tense and were not really sure that they had past tense forms.

Collins's findings suggest that, instead of relying on fill-ins, it may be more productive to expose students to relevant contrasts in contexts, as previously recommended. Her findings also support the value of allowing students to voice their own hypotheses about tense usage and giving them "timely feedback that can help them revise their hypotheses when necessary."[21] Activities 3, 5, and 7 follow her recommendation for using production activities and eliciting student judgments about the appropriateness of tense forms.

Activity 1: Using the Simple Present in a Description (Beginning Through Low Intermediate)

A good activity that forces the use of the simple present is to have students prepare a description of themselves to present to the class. This description should include (1) the city or town where they used to live; (2) the school/university they attend at home; (3) their family; (4) their eating habits; (5) their usual activities with friends; and (6) their personal likes (movies, music, sports, etc.). Students can start by writing down information for each category and comparing information with a partner to stimulate ideas. Encourage partners to ask questions, such as "Do you have brothers and sisters?" and "What do you do with your friends?"[22] Afterward, have students present their descriptions to the class.

Activity 2: Using the Present Progressive in Postcards and Weather Reports (Intermediate)

A good activity for mixing the present progressive with activity verbs and simple present with stative verbs is a report of the current local or international weather (*It's raining in London*; *It's sunny in Rome*; *It's snowing in Moscow*; *The temperature is 29 degrees in Singapore*; etc.). This activity can also be used to practice future prediction with *will* and *be going to*. If you have access to international weather reports on SCOLA or the Weather Channel, you can develop an oral form of a *dicto-comp* (see Chapter 3). Record several weather reports to play for the class. After playing them, replay them with the sound off and at various points freeze a picture of the weather map. The students can then take turns describing the weather throughout the world. Alternatively, you can create a TBLT activity in which the students make a weather chart listing places, as well as symbols for rain, snow, sunshine, clouds, and so on, that can be placed on the chart. Each day bring a newspaper to class with international weather information and have the students take turns using the information and their chart to report the weather.

Activity 3: Focusing on Stative Verbs and Simple Present–Present Progressive Confusion (Intermediate)

Collins (2002) discovered that "a disproportionate percentage of errors" involving use of a progressive form instead of the simple present involved a small number of stative verbs that can also be activity verbs, for example, *look*, *smell*, and *think*. (The verb *look*, e.g., is a stative verb in *It looks good* but an activity verb in *I am looking at it*.)

Because students come across these verbs in the progressive aspect as activity verbs, they incorrectly use the progressive when these verbs are statives.

To address this problem, you might start by presenting students with a detailed listing of the stative verbs and emphasizing that, as stative verbs, they do not occur in the present progressive. Some textbooks are beginning to take this approach.[23] Next, you might try a combination of activities to call attention to the inappropriate use of statives in the present progressive.

One such activity involves short written first-person narratives that have stative verbs used correctly and incorrectly. If you write three different narratives, students can work in groups of three and take turns presenting them. Include statives from all categories (mental perception verbs such as *know*, *think*, and *understand*; measurement verbs such as *contain*, *measure*, *weigh*, etc.). An example of such a narrative is shown in (100).

> (**100**) I think I might be sick. Everything I eat is tasting bad or having no taste at all. I ache all over my body, and every medicine I take is not seeming to help me. Maybe I'm having the flu. I don't know. Do you think I should go see a doctor?

Give a narrative to one student in each group who will be the presenter. The objective is for the listeners to pick out the statives that incorrectly appear in the progressive aspect. The student who is presenting reads the narrative through silently, then says to one of the other students, "Ask me how I feel today." To answer the question, the presenter reads the narrative aloud as realistically as possible, only glancing at the paper. The other two students point out the mistakes that they heard. If the presenter notices anything they missed, the sentence containing the missed error can be reread.

Finally, try a processing instruction activity in which the students respond to sentences that you give them orally with, "Yes, that's OK," or "No, that's not OK." You can present sentences singly or in two- and three-way contrasts. For example, a three-way contrast might be "I am thinking of a number between 1 and 10"; "I think of you every day"; *"I'm thinking of her every day."

Activity 4: Using the Simple Past to Tell a Story (Beginning Through Low Intermediate)

A common and effective way of practicing the use of the simple past is to have the students role-play a situation in which one student, taking the part of a policeman or a reporter, asks another, playing an eyewitness, to describe an event, for example, a car accident, a robbery, or a fire. The teacher can prime the discussion by showing a videotape of an event or having the students read a short description of the event that is written on the board or projected on the wall with an overhead projector.

Another favorite approach uses a storyboard. Arrange a series of pictures depicting actions that could constitute a short story. The students relate what happened using the simple past tense.

A TBLT variation on this activity is a role play in which students have to report on events in their lives in response to questions. For example, pairs of students can take turns playing themselves and a university counselor soliciting data for a form. The questions asked might include the following: "Where were you born?" "What city/

town did you grow up in?" "Where did you go to high school?" "Did you attend any other school after high school?" "If so where?" "How long did you study there?" "When did you come to the United States?" "Where did you stay when you arrived?" "What was the first job you had in this country?" Remind students to answer the questions in full sentences.

Activity 5: Using the Past Progressive (High Intermediate)

Review with students key points about the past progressive use – for example, that this tense is often used in sentences in which there is a clause with a simple past tense verb indicating an interruption of the activity expressed by the progressive tense, and that it does not occur with durational time phrases like *since 2001*. Follow this review with processing instruction activities that contrast the past progressive with the present perfect. For example, show two sentences such as *He has worked there since 2001* and **He was working there since 2001* and ask about each one, "Is this a good sentence?"

Role plays can also be useful for practicing sentences with the past progressive and simple past in clauses and sentences that contain the past progressive in both clauses. In a variation of Activity 4, the student who plays an investigator asks another student a series of questions about what he or she was doing at the time of a crime (accident, etc.). For example, the investigator might ask, "What were you doing when you heard the alarm go off?" "What was your wife doing?" "Where were you standing exactly when he was talking to Mrs. Jones?" This role play provides both the students practice in using the past progressive.

Activity 6: Contrasting the Simple Past with the Present Perfect (High Intermediate Through Advanced)

We have already seen that ESL/EFL students persistently use present perfect forms in contexts in which a simple past form is required. To tackle this, you might begin by reviewing the fact that the present perfect tense occurs with time expressions introduced by *since*. Then present students with pairs of sentences about which they make grammaticality judgments, as shown in (101). For each pair, ask, "Which is a good sentence? Or are both of these OK?"

(**101**) a. I have lived here since 1999. vs. **I lived here since 1999.*
      b. **I didn't see her since last Friday.* vs. I haven't seen her since last Friday.
      c. The plane just arrived. vs. The plane has just arrived.

To demonstrate the effect of context on the choice between the simple past and present perfect, you could begin with pairs of sentences containing a stative verb and a temporal phrase of duration beginning with *for*, for example, *I have lived in Montreal for six years* vs. *I lived in Montreal for six years*. Point out that the sentence with the present perfect implies that you are still living in Montreal, but the sentence with the simple past tense states that you lived there sometime in the past. Then you could present a short dialog like the one in (102) and ask which choice is more appropriate.

(**102**) A: How's our friend Francesco?
      B: I don't know for sure.   a. I haven't seen him for a long time.
                                   b. I didn't see him for a long time.

Following Collins's suggestion on page 384, students could be asked to supply a reason for choosing one tense over the other. In this case, they should choose (a), as the context indicates that B has not seen the friend for a period of time that has lasted up to the present. If the student chooses (b), you might point out that this option would work only in a context like (103), in which speaker A's comment indicates that you are talking about a specific past event.

(**103**) A: So, how often did you see him after that?
        B: I didn't see him for a long time. Until, maybe, five or six years later.

Finally present pairs of sentences like those in (104), (105), and (106) and ask the students to supply contexts in which each sentence would be a proper continuation.

(**104**) a. I've worked in that office for 17 years.
        b. I worked in that office for 17 years.

(**105**) a. I never met him.
        b. I've never met him.

(**106**) a. He still hasn't finished it.
        b. He still didn't finish it.

Sentence (104a) is appropriate as an answer to the question *How long have you worked in that office?* It implies that you have worked there up to the present and may still be working there. Sentence (104b) is appropriate as a description of what you did in the past. There is no implication that you are still working there (e.g., *I worked in that office for 17 years, but then I got a better job with the company I am working for now*). The appropriate context for (105a) might be a situation in which you failed to meet the person in question in the past (e.g., *I met a lot of famous movie stars when I was in Hollywood, but I never met him*), whereas (105b) is an appropriate response to the question: *Have you ever met George Clooney?* Answer: *No, I've never met him.* The sentence in (106a) is an appropriate answer to the questions: *How is he coming along with that report? Is it finished yet?* Sentence (106b) is most appropriate as part of a past narrative (e.g., *You know, I remember back in 1992, we asked him over and over again to finish a report that we needed, but in spite of all our pleading and cajoling, he still didn't finish it*).

ENDNOTES

[1] Other aspects are *inceptive*, which signals the beginning of an action, and *inchoative*, which signals entrance into a state. Inchoative verbs are what we have been referring to as *ergative verbs*.

[2] See Cowan and Schuh (1976), p. 333.

[3] The concept of inherent, or lexical, aspect as applied to classifications of verbs is developed in Vendler (1967). The properties of inherent/lexical aspect are intended to apply to verbs in all languages, that is, they are presumed to be universal. Here we illustrate them only for English. The description of these properties and some of the examples presented here are modeled on Brinton (2000), pp. 143–147.

[4] Goodwell (1987), pp. 316–317 notes that the conversational historical present is the pragmatically correct tense for telling jokes because it creates the immediacy needed for comic effect.

[5] Wolfson (1979).

[6] Annen (1992).

[7] *Blood Simple: The Screenplay.* (1988). Joel Coen and Ethan Coen, p. 47.

[8] Biber et al. (1999), p. 362, list the following verbs as *communication verbs* that "involve communication activities" like speaking and writing: *ask, announce, call, discuss, explain, say, shout, speak, suggest, talk, tell,* and *write.* Not all of these can be used in the present tense to talk about events that happened in the past.

[9] The term *stative progressive* and the observations concerning stative progressives are largely due to Bland (1988).

[10] Bland (1988) claims that this use is more prevalent with speakers of American English than speakers of British English.

[11] The example comes from Bland (1988).

[12] All of these phrasings are taken directly from Celce-Murcia and Larsen-Freeman (1983), p. 64, and (1999), p. 116.

[13] See Huddleston and Pullum (2002), p. 147, for further discussion. The acceptability of contrasts like (51) seems to influence native speaker judgements in cases like (52), but the prevalent choice is for the past perfect.

[14] In some American dialects, a pattern consisting of *will + be +* the past participle, which expresses the state of being, is substituted for future perfect. Thus, instead of (56), one is often likely to hear *In January we will be married for 30 years.*

[15] See Riddle's (1986) explanations and generalizations on relaxing tense sequencing rules.

[16] A fourth factor that may constrain students' acquisition of tense is cognitive principles that constrain hypotheses that learners make about associating tense markers with certain activities and actions (Anderson and Shirai, 1994). The validity of these principles is debated. For a discussion, see Pienemann (2003).

[17] To some degree, this development reflects the "Aspect Hypothesis" (Anderson, 1991; Anderson and Sharai 1994, 1996), which predicts that past tense (*-ed*) and perfect forms (*have +* past participle) will be first associated with telic verbs and then proceed to activity verbs and eventually to statives. The acquisition of progressive forms like *–ing* will be applied first to stative and activity verbs and then spread to achievement verbs.

[18] In French, the equivalent of English *to be* (*être*) is used with certain verbs of motion and change of state (e.g., *aller, venir, arriver, mourir*) to form the *passé composé.* French ESL/EFL learners consistently use the English present perfect for the English equivalents of these verbs (see examples in [85]) where the simple past is required, but only with English *have.* This shows that they are following the French discourse constraint but not transferring French auxiliary form (*être*). The same situation exists in German for these verbs. German learners of English make the same transfer errors as the French learners.

[19] This is also mentioned in a footnote in Huddleston and Pullum, (2002), p. 146, as a "relatively small difference" that affects only a few cases such as talking about the immediate past, for example, with *just.*

[20] These conclusions are based on the sentence pairs in the experiment described at the end of Chapter 3 in Elsness (1999). It is not clear whether Elsness used enough pairs to feel confident in the validity of the test he designed, even though sample size seems adequate.

[21] Collins (2005), p. 12.

[22] This was suggested by De Oliveira (2004).

[23] A good example of how this is currently being done is Fuchs and Bonner's (2001) *Grammar Express* (pp. 10–13). Similar treatments with not quite as many activities can also be found in textbooks such as Riggenbach and Samuda (2000), *Grammar Dimensions.*

REFERENCES

Anderson, R. (1991). Developmental sequences: The emergence of aspect marking in second language acquisition. In T. Huebner & C. A. Furguson (Eds.), *Cross-currents in second language acquisition and linguistic theories* (pp. 305–324). Amsterdam: John Benjamins.

Anderson, R. & Shirai, Y. (1994). Discourse motivation for some cognitive acquisition principles. *Studies in Second Language Acquisition, 16.* 133–156.

Anderson, R. & Shirai, Y. (1996). The primacy of aspect in first and second language acquisition: The pidgin-creole connection. In W. C. Ritchie & T. K. Bhatia (Eds.), *Handbook of second language acquisition* (pp. 527–570). San Diego, CA: Academic Press.

Annen, G. (1992). Graveyard Utopia: Review of Günter Grass's *The Call of the Toad.* New York Review of Books, *39*(19), 19.

Bardovi-Harlig, K. (1998). Narrative structure and lexical aspect: Conspiring factors in second language acquisition of tense-aspect morphology. *Studies in Second Language Acquisition, 20,* 471–508.

Bardovi-Harlig, K. (1999). From morpheme studies to temporal semantics: Tense-aspect research in SLA. *Studies in Second Language Acquisition, 21,* 341–382.

Bardovi-Harlig, K. (2000). *Tense and aspect in second language acquisition: Form, meaning, and use.* Malden, MA: Blackwell.

Bardovi-Harlig, K., & Bergström, A. (1996). Acquisition of tense and aspect in second language and foreign language learning: Learner narratives in ESL and FFL. *Canadian Modern Language Review, 52,* 308–330.

Bardovi-Harlig, K., and Reynolds, D. (1995). The role of lexical aspect in the acquisition of tense and aspect. *TESOL Quarterly, 29,* 107–131.

Bland, S. K. (1988). The present progressive in discourse: Grammar versus usage revisited. *TESOL Quarterly, 22*(1), 53–68.

Brinton, L. J. (2000). *The structure of modern English: A linguistic introduction.* Amsterdam/ Philadelphia: John Benjamins.

Celce-Murcia, M., and Larsen-Freeman, D. (1983). *The grammar book: An ESL/EFL teacher's course.* Rowley, MA: Newbury House.

Celce-Murcia, & Hilles, S. (1988). *Techniques and resources in teaching grammar.* Oxford: Oxford University Press.

Chung, S., & Timberlake, A. (1985). Tense, aspect and mood. In T. Shopen (Ed.), *Language typology and syntactic description*, Vol. 3 (pp. 202–258). Cambridge: Cambridge University Press.

Collins, L. (2002). The roles of L1 influence and lexical aspect in the acquisition of temporal morphology. *Language Learning 52*(1), 43–94.

Collins, L. (2005). Assessing second language learners' understanding of temporal morphology. (To appear in *Language Awareness.*)

Comrie, B. (1976). *Aspect: An introduction to the study of verbal aspect and related problems.* Cambridge: Cambridge University Press.

Comrie, B. (1985). *Tense.* Cambridge: Cambridge University Press.

Cowan, J. R., & Schuh, R. (1976). *Spoken Hausa.* Ithaca, NY: Spoken Language Services, Inc.

Dahl, Ö. (1985). *Tense and aspect systems.* Oxford: Blackwell.

De Oliveira, C. P. (2004). Implementing task-based assessment in a TEFL environment. In B. L. Leaver and J. R. Willis (Eds.), *Task-based instruction in foreign language instruction* (pp. 253–279). Washington, D.C.: Georgetown University Press.

Elsness, J. (1999). *The use of the present perfect and the preterite in present-day English*. Berlin/ New York: Walter de Gruyter, Inc.

Fakhri, A. (1995). Tense and aspect in Arab ESL learners' discourse. *Eleventh Annual International Conference on Pragmatics and Language Learning*. University of Illinois at Urbana-Champaign.

Fuchs, M., & Bonner, M. (2001). *Grammar express*. White Plains, NY: Pearson.

Huddleston, R., & Pullum, G. K. (2002). *The Cambridge grammar of the English language*. Cambridge: Cambridge University Press.

Goodwell, E. W. (1987). Integrating theory with practice: An alternative approach to teaching reported speech in English. *TESOL Quarterly, 21.2*, 305–325.

Lardiere, D. (1998). Case and tense in the "fossilized" steady-state. *Second Language Research, 14*, 1–26.

McCawley J. D. (1971). Tense and time reference. In C. J. Fillmore & D. T. Langendoen (Eds.), *Studies in linguistic semantics*. New York: Holt, Rinehart & Winston.

Meisel, J. M. (1987). Reference to past events and actions in the development of natural language acquisition. In Carol W. Pfaff (Ed.), *First and second language acquisition processes* (pp. 206–224). Cambridge, MA: Newbury House.

Ogihara, T. (1996). Tense, attitude, and scope. Dordrecht: Kluwer.

Pienemann, M. (2003). Language processing capacity. In C. J. Doughty & M. H. Long (Eds.), *The handbook of second language acquisition* (pp. 679–714). Malden, MA: Blackwell.

Riddle, E. (1986). The meaning and discourse function of the past tense in English. *TESOL Quarterly, 20*(2), 267–286.

Riggenbach, H., & Samuda, V. (2000). *Grammar dimensions 2*. Boston: Heinle & Heinle.

Rinvolucri, M. (1992). *Grammar games: Cognitive, affective and drama activities for EFL students*. Cambridge: Cambridge University Press.

Robison, R. (1995). The aspect hypothesis revisited: A cross-sectional study of tense and aspect marking in interlanguage. *Applied Linguistics, 16*, 344–370.

Vendler, Z. (1967). *Linguistics in philosophy*. Ithaca, NY: Cornell University Press.

Wolfson, N. (1979). The conversational historical present alternation. *Language, 55*, 168–186.

CHAPTER 17

Passive Sentences

INTRODUCTION

Passive sentences, that is, sentences in the *passive voice*, are an important part of every English language teaching grammar syllabus. In this chapter, we consider the most important aspects of the English passive that a teacher must understand. These include when passive sentences are used, restrictions on their formation, and the most common errors that English language learners make in forming sentences in the passive voice. We will begin by discussing passives with *be*, the most common type of passive in English,[1] but then turn to passives with *get* and to other passive and passive-like structures.

FORMING PASSIVE SENTENCES

Let's begin by looking at how passive sentences with *be* are formed. The *active voice*, as shown in (1), has a subject NP followed by a verb and an object NP.

       Subject NP   *Verb*   *Object NP*
(**1**) [Anders Celsius] [invented] [the centigrade thermometer].

This sentence may be changed into the *passive voice*, as shown in (2).

       Subject NP   *Verb*   *Agent* By *Phrase*
(**2**) [The centigrade thermometer] [was invented] [by Anders Celsius].

Notice that this change – the passivization of the active sentence – involved these steps:

- The object NP in the active sentence moved into subject position in the passive sentence.
- The subject NP moved to the end of the sentence and *by* was inserted before it – the sentence now has an *agent* by phrase.
- The main verb was changed to its past participle form and the appropriate form of *be* (here, *was*) was inserted before it.

In keeping with subject-verb agreement, the passive sentence verb agrees in number with the NP that has been moved into subject position. Thus, whereas in (3a) the singular *fires* agrees with *the dean*, in passive (3b), the plural *are* agrees with *our professors*.

(3) a. The dean often *fires* our professors.   *active*
     b. Our professors *are* often *fired* by the dean.   *passive*

Passive sentences can occur in all of the tense-aspect combinations discussed in Chapter 16. The form of *be* is determined by the verb in the active sentence from which the passive sentence is formed, as follows:

- If the verb in the active sentence is in the simple present or simple past, so is the form of *be* that precedes the part participle of the main verb. For example, *are* in (3b) corresponds to the simple present *fires* in (3a); *was* in (4b) corresponds to the simple past *fired* in (4a).

    (4) a. The dean *fired* our professor.   *active*
         b. Our professor *was fired* by the dean.   *passive*

- If the verb in the active sentence is in the progressive aspect, then *being* is inserted between the progressive form of *be* and the past participle of the main verb. This is illustrated in (5b) for present progressive and in (5d) for past progressive.

    (5) a. The dean *is firing* our professor.   *active*
         b. Our professor *is being fired* by the dean.   *passive*
         c. The dean *was firing* our professor.   *active*
         d. Our professor *was being fired* by the dean.   *passive*

- If the verb in the active sentence is in the perfect aspect, then *been* is inserted between the form of *have* and the past participle of the main verb, as is shown in (6b) for the present perfect and in (6d) for the past perfect.

    (6) a. The dean *has fired* our professor.   *active*
         b. Our professor *has been fired* by the dean.   *passive*
         c. The dean *had fired* our professor.   *active*
         d. Our professor *had been fired* by the dean.   *passive*

- Perfect progressives, although rare in passive sentences, include *being* before the past participle (e.g., active *has/had been firing* becomes passive *has/had been being fired*).
- If the active sentence contains a modal followed by a bare infinitive verb, as in (7a), then in the passive sentence the modal is followed by the bare infinitive form of *be*, as in (7b) and (7d).

    (7) a. The dean *should fire* our professor.   *active*
         b. Our professor *should be fired* by the dean.   *passive*
         c. The dean *will fire* our professor.   *active*
         d. Our professor *will be fired* by the dean.   *passive*

Passive Subjects

Most English sentences have as their subject an NP that is an *agent* – the thing that causes the action in the sentence. As we will see in more detail, passive sentences enable NPs that have other roles – typically the *theme*, or the thing experiencing the action of the verb – to be the subject of the sentence and the agent to move out of subject position. Consider, for example, the pairs of sentences in (4) through (7). In these sentences, *the dean* is the agent, bringing about the action of firing, and *our professor* is the theme, experiencing that action. The passive versions of these sentences move *our professor* into subject position. (For more on thematic roles, see Chapter 8.)

In terms of grammatical function, the passive may promote to subject position one of several active sentence constituents.

A Direct Object

In the examples that we have looked at so far, the direct object in the active sentence becomes the subject of the passive sentence. Indeed, it is usually the direct object that is promoted to subject position.

An Indirect Object

Sentence (8a) exhibits what we referred to in Chapter 15 as the *dative movement pattern*, in which the indirect object precedes the direct object. When a sentence with this pattern is made passive, the IO is moved into subject position, as illustrated in (8b). In this case, the NP that becomes subject has the thematic role of goal.

	IO	DO	

(**8**) a. Warren gave [*Suzy*] [a beautiful present].   *active*
       b. *Suzy* was given a beautiful present by Warren.   *passive*

An Object of a Preposition

In (9b), the object in the prepositional phrase *in this bed* is moved into subject position.

	PP

(**9**) a. Herbert Hoover slept [in *this bed*].   *active*
       b. *This bed* was slept in by Herbert Hoover.   *passive*

A Complement

The entire *that* complement in (10a), which is the object of the verb *recognized*, is moved into subject position in the passive version in (10b). Different syntactic patterns that result from passivizing complements will be discussed in greater detail in Chapter 21.

That Complement

(**10**) a. Everyone recognized [*that John couldn't possibly win*].   *active*
        b. *That John couldn't possibly win* was recognized by everyone.   *passive*

Two Types of Passive Sentences

The passive sentences that we have looked at so far all have an agent *by* phrase. Many passive sentences, however, do not. Thus, along with the pattern in (11a), we have the more common pattern in (11b).

(**11**) a. These spare parts were manufactured in Thailand *by highly trained workers*.
        b. These spare parts were manufactured in Thailand.

Passives Without Agent *By* Phrases

Agentless, or *short*, passives, as illustrated in (11b), are more common in both written and spoken English than are passives with an agent phrase, called *long* passives.[2] Why might native speakers decide to use these agentless passives? The passive itself enables speakers to move the agent from subject position to a less prominent position in the sentence. If this information is not needed, the agentless passive gives speakers a way of omitting it. Reasons why a native speaker may decide to use short passives in speech and writing include the following:

- The most obvious reason for not including the agent is that the *speaker does not know who the agent is*. In (12), for example, it would be pointless to include "by someone" or "by a thief."

 (12) His car was stolen in Detroit.

- The *speaker does not want to reveal who the agent is*. For example, he or she may use the agentless passive to avoid assigning blame, as in (13).

 (13) Rather than dwelling unnecessarily on the causes of this fiasco, let's just say that *mistakes were made*.

- The *identity of the agent can be assumed or understood*, so it is not necessary to mention the agent. This is the case in (14).

 (14) a. Our grapes are usually harvested in late August.
  b. Diagnostic tests are used to identify students' strengths and weaknesses.[3]
  c. It is known that supercooled moisture forms ice.

 In (14a), the speaker assumes that listeners can infer that farmhands or workers do the harvesting. Similarly, in (14b), the writer assumes that the readers will understand that the missing agent must be a noun like *educator*s or *teacher*s. In (14c), the agent is universal – that is, the fact is known by everyone or by people generally – so, again, it is unnecessary to mention the agent.

- The *speaker is interested more in the action being reported than in the agent* that carries it out. A good example of this is shown in (15), which comes from a report of an experiment.

 (15) The animals were first given a cue for an orientation, and then a series of gratings was presented.[4]

 Notice that another reason for the agentless passives in (15) is likely that readers can assume the agents to be the researchers. Not surprisingly, short passives occur more frequently in academic prose than in any other genre of writing.[5] Writers of academic prose are often more concerned with generalizations, methods, and results than with individuals.[6]

Passives with Agent *By* Phrases

Why might native speakers use passives with agent *by* phrases, or long passives? Generally, the reason speakers and writers choose to keep the agent *by* phrase in a passive sentence is that it represents new information that is important in some way. For example, in (16), the fact that the person who beat a top-ranked tennis player like Andre Agassi didn't have a high ranking is important, so the writer leaves this information in by including the *by* phrase.

 (16) In the French Open, Agassi beat Sampras, but *he was later beaten by a young man from Singapore who was ranked 102 in the world*.

In the clause beginning with *but*, the writer has used the passive here because this puts information that is new and long (*a young man from Singapore* . . .) after the information that is old (Agassi), which is represented by the pronoun *he*.

The fact that an agent is famous can qualify him or her as important enough to be mentioned in a *by* phrase. This is illustrated in (17), a passive sentence which implies that the NP promoted to subject and the event described are interesting (at least to the speaker) because of their connection with the agent.[7]

(**17**) This bed was slept in by George Washington, our first president!

An agent can also be deemed important enough to mention if the speaker wishes to imply that the agent caused some harm or annoyance to the NP promoted to subject.[8] Sentence (18) implies that there is some unpleasant evidence in the cave, such as litter, that would have been left behind by woodchucks.

(**18**) This cave has clearly been lived in by woodchucks. (There's no way we can camp in here tonight. It's too dirty.)

USING PASSIVE SENTENCES

Passive sentences frequently occur in news reports and, as previously noted, in academic writing. As a result, they are often emphasized in ESL writing courses. Students often want to know what causes a native speaker to use a passive sentence instead of an active sentence. The answer lies mainly in two principles, both introduced in earlier chapters that have to do with how discourse is structured in English.

The Given–New Contract

The overriding principle that favors the choice of a long passive over a corresponding active sentence is the *given–new contract*.[9] That is, the passive voice is used to insure that the given (or old) information comes first in a sentence and new information comes after it. Recall that in (16), the passive was used in part to put *he*, referring to Agassi, into subject position because *Agassi* was old information, having been introduced in *Agassi beat Sampras*.

The given–new contract is often involved in the choice of passives in written discourse such as fiction, newspaper articles, and academic articles. A typical example is shown in (19a). *Fame* appears as new information at the end of the first sentence in the paragraph. It reappears in the second sentence, in the form of a pronoun *it*, at the beginning of the sentence, the position for old information. In the second clause of this sentence, the writer uses the passive voice, thereby putting this repeated instance of the pronoun in the position of old information, before the new information *the Rube Goldberg apparatus of the inner ear.*

(**19**) a. Light always travels at the same speed, but fame travels at dozens. It travels at the speed of sound, carrying the Apollo-prizewinner's voice through the air and, then, humming on the fine tympanies of eardrums, *it is converted by the Rube Goldberg apparatus of the inner ear* into the voice of Arthur Blaine, speaking, laughing, reading.[10]

   b. . . . It travels at the speed of sound, carrying the Apollo-prizewinner's voice through the air, and then, . . . *the Rube Goldberg apparatus of the inner ear converts it into the voice of Arthur Blaine* . . .

Compare the italicized sentence in (19a) with its active version in (19b), in which the agent remains in subject position in the clause. This active sentence is awkward – by presenting new information first, it seems to switch topics in midsentence.

In (19), the object that was moved into subject position as old information was the pronoun *it*, which refers to an earlier *it* and the noun *fame*. A passive subject that is old information does not have to refer to a specific noun or pronoun in a previous clause or sentence. Consider, for example, the sentences in (20a), taken from a review of a movie:

(**20**) a. In the time-warping thriller *Frequency*, a lonely son talks to his dead father across three decades with a ham radio. *This connection* has somehow been established by sunspots. . . .
b. . . . a lonely son talks to his dead father across three decades with a ham radio. *Sunspots have somehow established this connection.*

In (20a), a passive sentence is used to continue the topic described in the first sentence – the theme of a son and his dead father talking to each other. The passive voice enables the writer to place the old information (*this connection*) first. Again, notice the awkwardness of the italicized active alternative in (20b).

It is important to emphasize that the use of passive sentences to maintain the given–new contract is only a tendency, not a grammatical requirement. Nonetheless, it is a very strong tendency,[11] as, indeed, the comparisons of the passive and active versions of (19) and (20) suggest.

The Principle of End Weight

Particularly in written discourse, the end weight principle may also bias a choice in favor of a long passive sentence over its corresponding active version, although it appears to be less important than the given–new contract. According to the end weight principle, a long, complex (or "heavy") noun phrase is placed at the end of a sentence, to facilitate processing. In Chapter 15, we saw that applying the dative movement rule can move a long direct object NP from the middle of a sentence to the end, yielding a more comprehensible sentence. Writers may choose to use the passive voice for this same result, as a comparison of (21a) and (21b) illustrates.

(**21**) a. *A senator of Bologna, Petrus Crescentius, whose book was one of the most popular treatises on agriculture of any time*, condensed Roman writings on agriculture into one volume.
b. Roman writings on agriculture were condensed into one volume by *a senator of Bologna, Petrus Crescentius, whose book was one of the most popular treatises on agriculture of any time.*

For most native speakers, (21b) is preferable to (21a). Why? Sentence (21a) requires the reader to process and retain a lot of information that is part of the subject NP while reading on to reach the verb. Its passive version, (21b), in contrast, has just a short subject NP before the verb and, as a result, is easier to process.

SUMMARY

FORMING PASSIVE SENTENCES; USING PASSIVE SENTENCES

Passive sentences are formed from active sentences by:

- moving the subject to the end of the sentence and placing *by* in front of it.

- moving the object into subject position.

- changing the main verb to a past participle and inserting an appropriate form of *be* before it.
  The performance shocked the audience.   active
  The audience was shocked by the performance.   passive

Sentences with verbs in any tense can be made passive.
  Those children were reprimanded by their parents.
  Those children are being reprimanded by their parents.
  Those children have been reprimanded by their parents.

Subjects of passive sentences in the corresponding active sentences may be:

- direct objects
  The professor was dismissed by the dean.

- indirect objects
  Suzy was given many presents by her friends.

- objects of prepositions
  This bed has been slept in by presidents.

- object complements
  That he had special privileges was resented by everyone.

Short, or agentless, passives do not have an agent *by* phrase.
  The performance shocked the audience.   active
  The audience was shocked.   passive

Short passives are used when:

- the agent is unknown.
  His wallet was stolen in Philadelphia.

- the speaker does not want to reveal the agent.
  I was given some top-secret information.

- the agent is understood.
  The mail was delivered to my doorstep.

- the writer is interested more in the action being reported than in the agent.
  The subjects were each given a pencil and a sheet of paper.

Long passives have an agent *by* phrase.
  This picture was painted by van Gogh.
  This package was dropped off by a strange-looking woman.

The agent phrase is included when the agent is important new information, such as when the agent is a famous person or has caused harm or annoyance to the subject.

That search engine was developed by a young college student.
This old soccer ball is signed by the great Brazilian player Pelé.
I was kept up all night by my screaming neighbors.

Passive sentences may be used to comply with:

- the **given–new contract**, according to which old information comes before new information.
  For dessert I had a piece of a wonderfully delicious cake. It was made by the new pastry chef.

- the **end weight principle**, according to which long, complex NPs are moved to the end of the sentence.
  I was approached by a man wearing dark glasses, a wide-brimmed hat, and a black scarf.

EXERCISE 17.1

For each sentence, indicate the grammatical function (direct object, indirect object, complement beginning with *that*, object of the preposition) the subject played in its corresponding active sentence.

Example: This bridge has been flown under by that stunt pilot, Fearless Fred.

Answer: object of the preposition *under*

1. The exams were corrected for the professor by the teaching assistants.
2. That he had already left on Tuesday was discovered only later by the police.
3. For her birthday, Alice was given a beautiful blue necklace by her mother.
4. Centre Court at Wimbledon has been played on by some of the greatest players in the history of tennis.
5. That watch was bought for me by my grandfather on my 16th birthday.
6. That the two boys were in serious danger was recognized by everyone.

EXERCISE 17.2

For each sentence, indicate the probable reason why the speaker included or omitted an agent *by* phrase.

Example: I really don't like being leaned over by people who are buying popcorn at the movies.

Answer: The agent is important as it causes annoyance to the subject.

1. Guess what? This porch was walked on by "Old Rough and Ready," Teddy Roosevelt.
2. I hate to tell you this, but I'm afraid that I lost all that money you gave me to invest. I was given some bad advice.
3. This chair has definitely been sat on by someone who is very heavy. Look at that leg! It's cracked.
4. For several decades, the tachistoscope has been used to investigate how much visual information can be gained from a single fixation of the eyes.
5. The prime minister's house was broken into at some point during the night.

EXERCISE 17.3

Indicate, based on discourse principles, which alternative is the better continuation for the sentences shown.

Example: In the first round of the World Cup, the Danes beat the Germans by a score of 3 goals to 1. But in the second round . . .

      a. the French narrowly beat them.

      b. they were narrowly beaten by the French.

Answer: b

Discourse 1

PUNTA ARENAS, Chile

A small plane fitted with skis landed safely Tuesday night at the South Pole on a mission to rescue an ailing American doctor. After a 10-hour delay, the weather improved and . . .

    a. the doctor was flown to Rothera and from there to Punta Arenas.

    b. they flew the doctor to Rothera and from there to Punta Arenas.

Discourse 2

Ralph had been having a terrible day. He got up with a stiff neck and a headache. Then he burned his toast at breakfast. He was 20 minutes late to work, which earned him a chewing-out from his boss. A few minutes later, when he opened his mail, he found a letter from the IRS informing him that he was due for an audit. Then, to top it all off, as he was crossing the street at noon to have lunch at a nearby restaurant, . . .

    a. a passing bicyclist hit him.

    b. he was hit by a passing bicyclist.

Discourse 3

A recent report from the National Climatic Data Center predicts ever-harsher droughts, floods, heat waves, and tropical storms as the atmosphere continues to warm. "The trend is likely to become more intense as the climate continues to change and society becomes more vulnerable to weather and climate extremes," said the Center's David Easterling. . . .

    a. This vulnerability is underscored by a financial forecast from the world's sixth-largest insurance company.

    b. A report from the world's sixth-largest insurance company underscores this vulnerability.

CONSTRAINTS ON FORMING PASSIVE SENTENCES

The previous discussion makes clear that in English no active sentence can be made into a passive sentence unless its verb is followed by either an NP, a PP, or a complement. That is, there must be an object to move into the subject position in the passive version. Generally, the verb must be transitive, although there are certain exceptions as with *sleep* in (9) (*This bed was slept in by Herbert Hoover*). In addition to this basic constraint, there are a number of other constraints on the conversion of active sentences to passive sentences. This section looks at some of these.

Stative Verbs

Active sentences with certain stative verbs – for example, *contain, cost, equal, fit, lack, last,* and *resemble* – do not have corresponding passive versions.[12] This is illustrated in (22) with the verb *resemble*. The resistance of these verbs to passivization has been attributed to the fact that in order to be used in a passive sentence, a verb must affect the object in some way. These stative verbs do not really affect their objects and thus are not found in passive sentences.[13]

(22) a. In many ways, Agnes resembles my mother.   *active*
   b. *In many ways, my mother is resembled by Agnes.   *passive*

Multiword Verbs

In Chapter 9, we looked at various categories of multiword verbs. The categories that take objects differ in the extent to which they allow passive sentences. In some categories, most verbs can appear in passive sentences, but in others many or most verbs cannot.

- Active sentences that contain *separable transitive phrasal verbs* can usually be converted into passive sentences. Consider, for example, (23) with the verb *bring up*.

  (23) a. At the meeting, someone brought up the matter of the missing $20.
     b. At the meeting, the matter of the missing $20 was brought up.   *passive*

- Most members of the small class of *inseparable transitive phrasal verbs* can appear only in active sentences, as is illustrated in (24) and (25). Possible exceptions are *look after* ("care for"), *look into* ("investigate"), and *pick on* ("mistreat").

  (24) a. John fell for a tall blonde with icy blue eyes.
     b. *A tall blond with icy blues eyes was fallen for (by John).   *passive*

  (25) a. In the course of the investigation, he came across an
          incriminating letter.
     b. *In the course of the investigation, an incriminating letter
          was come across (by him).   *passive*

- Some *permanently separated transitive phrasal verbs* – for example, *ask* (someone) *out*, *let* (someone) *off* – can appear in passive sentences. However, others – for example, *get* (someone) *down*, *see* (something) *through* – do not passivize well, as shown in (26) and (27).

  (26) a. The criticism and complaints are getting him down.
     b. *He is being gotten down by the criticism and complaints.   *passive*

  (27) a. The sales team saw the project through to its conclusion.
     b. ?The project was seen through to its conclusion by the sales team.   *passive*

- Most *prepositional verbs* can appear in passive sentences; however, a few cannot or do not sound very good, as shown in (28b) and (29b). These verbs include *abide by*, *adjust to*, *agree with*, *bank on*, and *run for*.

  (28) a. Last fall, John ran for the office of mayor.
     b. *Last fall, the office of mayor was run for by John.

  (29) a. Even family members couldn't adjust to his weird habits.
     b. ?His weird habits couldn't be adjusted to even by family members.

- A few *phrasal prepositional verbs* such as *look forward to* can appear in passive sentences, but others, such as *break up with*, *close in on*, *come down with*, *cut down on*, *end up with*, *get along with*, *get down to*, *go in for*, and *put up with*, cannot, as seen in (30b) and (31b).

  (30) a. Everyone got along with him.
     b. *He was gotten along with by everyone.

(31) a. The crew put up with the noisy passenger.
   b. ?The noisy passenger was put up with by the crew.

For Dative Verbs

As we saw earlier, active sentences in the dative movement pattern can be passivized, with the indirect object becoming the passive subject. Active sentences in the prepositional pattern can, of course, also be passivized, with the direct object becoming the passive subject. Thus, the active *to* dative sentences in (32a) and (32b), which show both patterns, each have a passive equivalent, as illustrated in (33a) and (33b).

                                     DO   IO
(32) a. The old woman gave [a piece of candy] to [the little girl]. *prepositional pattern*
                                    IO   DO
    b. The old woman gave [the little girl] [a piece of candy]. *dative movement pattern*

(33) a. A piece of candy was given to the little girl by the old woman.
   b. The little girl was given a piece of candy by the old woman.

However, when the verb is a *for* dative verb (e.g., *bake*, *catch*, *find*), speakers of American English judge as grammatical only passives converted from active sentences in the prepositional pattern. Thus, in American English an attempt to convert the dative movement pattern sentence in (34b) to a passive results in an ungrammatical sentence, as shown in (35b).

                           DO   IO
(34) a. Susan found [a nice apartment] for [John]. *prepositional pattern*
                        IO   DO
    b. Susan found [John] [a nice apartment]. *dative movement pattern*

(35) a. A nice apartment was found for John by Susan.
   b. *John was found a nice apartment by Susan.

This constraint on sentences with *for* dative verbs causes difficulties for English learners. Students are often unable to recognize sentences like (35b) as ungrammatical.

PASSIVE LOOK-ALIKES

Some sentences with *be* followed by a past participle may look like passives when they are in fact active sentences. In sentences like this, the past participle form is actually a participial adjective. For example, (36) looks like a short passive sentence, but it isn't.

(36) The library *is located* on the other side of the campus.

One way we know this is not a passive is that it cannot be changed into a corresponding active sentence. If we attempt to change (36) into an active sentence, we end up with something like (37), which does not have the same meaning.

(37) Someone locates the library on the other side of campus.

Sentences like (36) express the idea that the subject of the sentence is in a certain state, condition, or, in this case, place. For this reason, such sentences have sometimes been referred to as *stative passives*.[14] This label is perhaps misleading since this is simply a case in which the past participle is a participial adjective in predicative position following *be*. In Chapter 12, we saw that these cases are common as there are many such participial adjectives (e.g., *he was frightened/amazed*). We also saw that another way of distinguishing them from passives is that adjectives often can be preceded by adverbs such as *very* or *too*. The presence of these or other degree adverbs (e.g., *a little*, *somewhat*, *quite*) is thus a good way of identifying passive look-alikes.

Sentence (36), with *located*, is unambiguously a sentence with a participial adjective; it has no sensible passive interpretation. However, as was also mentioned in Chapter 12, some sentences are ambiguous: *The shop is closed at five o'clock* could mean either that at five o'clock the shop is not open (the adjective interpretation) or that someone closes it at 5:00 (the passive interpretation). In such cases, context will usually enable you to disambiguate the sentence. For example, context clarifies *the vase was smashed* as part of an active sentence with a predicative adjective in (38a) and as part of a passive sentence in (38b).

(38) a. When Mrs. Dalyrimple walked into the room, she saw that *the vase was smashed*. It lay in a thousand pieces on the floor next to the table.

   b. In the struggle between the thief and Mrs. Dalyrimple, *the vase was smashed* into a thousand pieces.

SUMMARY

CONSTRAINTS ON FORMING PASSIVE SENTENCES; PASSIVE LOOK-ALIKES

Passive sentences cannot be formed if the active sentence verb is not followed by an NP, PP, or complement clause. In addition, passive sentences are not usually possible with:

- **stative verbs** that are not seen as affecting the object (e.g., *contain*, *cost*, *equal*, *resemble*, *weigh*).
  John resembles his father. active
  His father is resembled by John. passive

- many **multiword verbs**, especially phrasal verbs that are inseparable (e.g., *come across*, *fall for*) or permanently separated (e.g., *get . . . down*, *see . . . through*), and phrasal prepositional verbs (e.g., *get along with*, *put up with*).
  *In the course of the investigation, an incriminating letter was come across by him.
  *He was gotten down by the news.
  *He was gotten along with by everyone.

- **for** dative verbs (e.g., *bake*, *catch*, *find*) in the dative movement pattern.
  They found her a nice apartment. active (dative movement pattern)
  She was found a nice apartment by them. passive

The sequence *be* + past participle does not always signal the passive voice. Some past participles are adjectives.
  He saw that the pitcher was smashed to bits. verb + adjective
  The pitcher was smashed to bits by the angry woman. passive

EXERCISE 17.4

Indicate whether each sentence can be passivized. If it can, write the passive version. If it cannot, explain why.

Example: He found her a nice apartment.

Answer: no (Active sentences in the dative movement pattern with a *for* dative verb cannot be passivized.)

1. Susan baked Fred a big chocolate cake.
2. The company offered a huge salary bonus to the workers.
3. The producer sent her a telegram.
4. That new suit cost a lot of money.
5. A famous Swedish architect designed a radically different house for my boss.
6. She made me a sandwich.
7. He came down with a bad cold.

EXERCISE 17.5

For each pair, indicate whether each sentence is a passive, an active sentence with a predicate adjective, or ambiguous as to the two interpretations.

Example: a. The shop is opened at five o'clock.
          b. The shop is closed at five o'clock.

Answer: a. = passive; b. = ambiguous

1. a. Another 10 percent of the population is gathered around this new elite.
   b. Another 10 percent of the grape harvest is gathered in small baskets in late August.
2. a. The boxes are stacked on top of the bench in that corner.
   b. The boxes are assembled on top of the bench in that corner.
3. a. Those birds are found in warm climates.
   b. Those birds are found by a special electronic homing device.
4. a. The shutters on the window were closed before the storm began.
   b. The shutters were closed as soon as the storm began.

Get Passives

While *be* passives are the most common type of passive in English, passive sentences may also be formed with the verb *get. Get* passive sentences are formed with the appropriate form of *get* followed by a past participle. They occur in the same range of forms as *be* passives, as the examples in (39) suggest.

(**39**) a. John *got arrested.*
     b. John *is getting arrested.*
     c. John *has gotten arrested.*
     d. John *will get arrested.*
     e. By this time tomorrow, John *will have gotten arrested.*

Get passives are generally considered more informal than *be* passives and occur mostly in spoken English.[15] They are frequently used to talk about events that affect the subject in an adverse way, like the event in (39) and those in (40).[16]

(**40**) a. John got mauled by a vicious dog.
     b. My car got stolen.
     c. Susan got fired.

However, *get* passives can also express events that have no adverse implication, as in (41a), (41b), and (41c), as well as actions that benefit the subject, as in (41d).

(**41**) a. Fred got examined by a specialist.
     b. The mail gets delivered every day.
     c. My letter to the editor got published in the Sunday *Times*.
     d. Janice got promoted last week.

Get passives cannot occur with verbs that describe cognition (e.g. *comprehend, know, understand*, etc.). Compare (42a) with (42b).

(**42**) a. His solution to the problem was $\begin{Bmatrix} known \\ understood \end{Bmatrix}$ by everyone.

     b. *His solution to the problem got $\begin{Bmatrix} known \\ understood \end{Bmatrix}$ by everyone.

In most cases, *get* passives have the same meaning as passive sentences formed with *be*. For example, the two sentences in (43) have the same meaning.

(**43**) a. Our house got broken into last year.
     b. Our house was broken into last year.

However, *get* passives with human subjects can sometimes imply that the subject is responsible in some way for the action expressed in the sentence. Compare (44a) to (44b).

(**44**) a. I got invited to Sharon Stone's big New Year's Eve party.
     b. I was invited to Sharon Stone's big New Year's Eve party.

Sentence (44a) with *get*, but not (44b) with *be*, may be interpreted as implying that the subject undertook some action in order to secure an invitation. If a speaker intends to indicate willful self-involvement on the part of the subject, he or she may insert a particular adverbial expression such as *deliberately* or *on purpose*, as in (45).

(**45**) a. John deliberately got fired from his job.
     b. Sally got arrested on purpose.

Get Passive Look-Alikes

As with *be* passives, sentences that look like *get* passives may actually be active sentences. In the main type of look-alike, *get* means "become" and is followed by a participial adjective.

Get + Participial Adjective/Adjective

Sentence (46) looks like a short *get* passive, but it is in fact an active sentence in which the past participle form *complicated* is an adjective.

(**46**) His explanation is getting complicated.

Here the verb *get* expresses the idea of becoming or of coming into a state or condition.[17] Sentence (46) may, for instance, be paraphrased as in (47).

(**47**) His explanation is becoming complicated.

As with *be* passives, there are several tests that help distinguish passive look-alikes from passive sentences:

- Sentences in which *get* means "become" do not have active counterparts; that is, they cannot be changed into active sentences while maintaining the same meaning. Thus, (48a) does not mean the same thing as (48b).

(**48**) a. He got stuck in the elevator.
   b. Someone stuck him in the elevator.

- In sentences in which *get* means "become," the participle can be preceded by words and expressions that relate to becoming – for example, *gradually* (*more/less*), *increasingly* (*more/less*), *less* (*and less*), and *more* (*and more*).[18] These are adverbs modifying the participial adjective. Insertion of these words and expressions is not possible with a passive sentence.

If, for example, we insert *more and more* between *getting* and the participle in (49), the resulting sentence remains grammatical, so (49) is not a passive.

(**49**) a. Education is getting specialized.
   b. Education is getting *more and more* specialized.

In contrast, if we do this with (50a), the resulting sentence in (50b) is ungrammatical, so (50a) is in fact a *get* passive.

(**50**) a. We're getting paid.
   b. *We're getting *more and more* paid.

- Participial adjectives after *get* usually can be modified by adverbs indicating degree, such as *more* and *less*, mentioned earlier, and *very*, *a little*, *somewhat*, *moderately*, and so on. Notice that these adverbs can modify *specialized*, in (49). Moreover, some participial adjectives are especially common with *get* – including, for example, *alarmed*, *complicated*, *depressed*, *interested*, *lost*, *tired*, and *worried*. Thus, when we see *get* used with these past participles, as in (51a), we can suspect the sentence is not a passive, and we can confirm it by adding a relevant adverb, as in (51b).

(**51**) a. After waiting an hour she got *worried*.
   b. After waiting an hour she got *a little* worried.

Ambiguities are possible. Thus, *they got frightened*, which is likely to be *get* + an adjective, as in (52a), could be a passive sentence, as in (52b).

(**52**) a. They got very frightened.
   b. They got frightened out their wits by a bunch of skinheads.

Get is also followed by a number of regular adjectives like *angry*, *anxious*, *busy*, *chilly*, *cold*, *hungry*, *old*, and so on. In all of these cases, *get* has the meaning "become." So *It suddenly got cold* means "It suddenly became cold."

Idiomatic Expressions with *Get*

Get passives may also need to be distinguished from a range of idiomatic expressions with get, including prepositional verbs such as *get around* ("avoid"), *get over* ("forget/ recover from"), and intransitive phrasal verbs such as *get by* ("subsist"), *get down* ("descend"), *get going* ("start"), and *get up* ("arise").

Although it may seem obvious that *get* + participial adjective sentences are not passives, some English language textbooks present them along with *get* passives. This is inaccurate, and it confuses students who haven't been shown what real *get* passive sentences look like and mean. It is important to teach students the meanings and uses of *get* passives and to separate these passives from look-alike structures and idiomatic expressions. As we've seen, this separation involves focusing on both meaning and form.

SUMMARY

GET PASSIVES; *GET* PASSIVE LOOK-ALIKES

Get passives are formed with the appropriate form of *get* followed by a past participle. They are more informal than *be* passive sentences and are frequently, although not necessarily, used to talk about events that affect the subject in an adverse way.

> *The mail gets delivered every day before noon.*
> *He got fired by Mr. Sanders last week.*

Get passives usually do not occur with stative verbs of cognition.

> **The solution to the problem got known by everyone.*
> **The question got understood by no one.*

In **get passive look-alikes**, past participles that are adjectives follow *get*. *Get* in these sentences has the meaning "become." The sentences are not *get* passives.

> *He gets confused easily.* (= He becomes confused easily.)
> *Joe got stuck in the elevator.* (= Joe became stuck in the elevator.)
> *It's getting chilly.* (= It's becoming chilly.)

Idiomatic expressions with *get* such as the intransitive phrasals *get up*, *get down*, and *get going* are not *get* passives.

> *He got up at six o'clock.*
> *She got hungry, so she made herself a sandwich.*

EXERCISE 17.6

Identify each sentence below as a *get* passive or a *get* passive look-alike meaning "become."

Example: She got examined by a specialist.

Answer: get passive

1. Calm down! You're getting all worked up about a very trivial matter.
2. The situation is getting more and more complicated.
3. He got stuck in traffic on the freeway.
4. He got promoted last week.
5. He got increasingly frustrated by all the petty politics in his department, so he resigned.
6. She got hungry, so she stopped working and had something to eat.
7. He got reprimanded for not following company policy.

EXERCISE 17.7

You are in charge of choosing a grammar textbook for English language learners. In the course of examining a textbook that some of your colleagues like, you encounter the following description of the passive with *get*. What, if anything, is wrong with it?

The Passive with *Get*

Passive sentences can also occur with *get*. These passives are more common in spoken English, and in some cases, they may not be appropriate in written English. The passive with *get* has two forms:

Get is followed by a past participle.

When she didn't show up on time, John got worried.
After working for 16 hours, she got tired and took a break.

Get is followed by certain adjectives, for example, *angry, anxious, busy, full*, and *hungry*.

Jean has gotten fat. She eats too much.
She got so sleepy that she couldn't concentrate on the lecture.

OTHER TYPES OF PASSIVE SENTENCES

In this section, we will look at structures that differ from the *be* and *get* passives discussed earlier. These include complex sentences that contain passivized complements, a unique passive that occurs with *have* and *got*, and a sentence that has the meaning but not the structure of a passive.

Passives in Complements Following *Get* and *Have*

The verbs *get* and *have* can be followed by a complement. In such sentences, *get* and *have* have a causative meaning; that is, the sentence subject is understood as causing the action in the complement. As (53b) and (54b) show, the complements in brackets in (53a) and (54a) may be passivized without changing their meaning.

(53) a. Fred had [a mechanic at Jiffy Lube repair his car].   *active*
    b. Fred had [his car repaired by a mechanic at Jiffy Lube].   *passive*

(54) a. Alice got [someone to cut her hair].   *active*
    b. Alice got [her hair cut by someone].   *passive*

In many sentences, including (53b) and (54b), *get* and *have* are interchangeable. However, if both the sentence subject and the subject in the passivized complement are human, the choice of verb can affect the sentence meaning. Consider (55) with *got*.

(55) Shortly after she started working there, Ellen *got* Stan fired.

Here, Ellen did something that resulted in Stan's losing his job. She may have assigned someone the task of firing Stan or, for example, she may have simply behaved in some way that resulted in Stan's getting fired. Now consider (56) with *had*.

(56) Shortly after she started working there, Ellen *had* Stan fired.

This sentence can only be interpreted to mean that Ellen assigned someone the task of firing Stan. Hence, the active version of (56) is . . . *Ellen had someone fire Stan.*

Happenstance Passives

The sentences in (57) are examples of *happenstance passives*.[19]

> (**57**) a. My partner had his office broken into last week.
> b. I got my pocket picked in Penn Station.

In both of these sentences, the subject (*my partner*/*I*) experiences some event, expressed after *have* or *get* (*his office broken into*, *my pocket picked*). As in these sentences, happenstance passives usually describe unfortunate events that the subject did not intentionally cause. A happenstance passive can be paraphrased as a *be* passive; for example, (58a) and (58b) mean the same thing as (57a) and (57b).

> (**58**) a. My partner's office was broken into.
> b. My pocket was picked in Penn Station.

Happenstance passives always occur with *have* or *got* + NP + past participle. They may occur without agent phrases, as in (57), or with them, as in (59).

> (**59**) I got my pocket picked by someone who sounds a lot like the man you're describing.

Because they look so similar, it is sometimes difficult to distinguish between a happenstance passive and a sentence with a passive complement following causative *get* or *have*. Consider (60).

> (**60**) I $\begin{Bmatrix} had \\ got \end{Bmatrix}$ my car towed away by the police.

Most native speakers would probably interpret (60) as a happenstance passive, because the police frequently tow away cars that are illegally parked. However, there is a second, albeit more remote, possibility: the speaker might have asked the police to tow the car. In this case, the sentence would be interpreted as containing a passive complement after causative *had* or *got*. If the sentence context doesn't make clear the intended interpretation, the surrounding context will.

The Concealed Passive

There is one construction with the verbs *need*, *require*, and *want* that has the meaning of a passive sentence, although it is not a true passive. In this construction, the verb is followed by a present participle, as illustrated in (61).

> (**61**) This essay *needs* careful *checking* by the editor.

The sentence in (61) has the same meaning as the passive shown in (62).

> (**62**) This essay needs to be carefully checked by the editor.

Sentences like (61), which are sometimes called *concealed passives*, occur frequently in British English.[20]

> # SUMMARY
> ## OTHER TYPES OF PASSIVE SENTENCES
>
> **Passives in complements following *get* and *have*** have a causative meaning.
> *Susan got her nails done.*
> *James had the house painted.*
>
> **Happenstance passives** describe unfortunate events that the subject of the sentence did not intentionally cause.
> *I had my wallet stolen in Chicago.* (= My wallet was stolen in Chicago.)
> *Rob got his car towed away last night.* (= Rob's car was towed away last night.)
>
> **Concealed passives** occur with *need*, *require*, and *want*, especially in British English. They are not true passives but have the same meaning as passives.
> *This essay needs careful checking by the editor.*
> (= This essay needs to be carefully checked by the editor.)

EXERCISE 17.8

Indicate whether each sentence contains a causative verb with a passive complement, a happenstance passive, or a concealed passive.

Example: Mika got her laptop fixed, and it's as good as new.

Answer: causative *get* with a passive complement

1. Last year, Phil had his tax return audited by the Internal Revenue Service.
2. Al had his tax return prepared by a certified public accountant.
3. I got my car serviced at a gas station near the mall.
4. They had their house in Oakland completely destroyed by that huge fire that burned out of control for so many days.
5. This house really needs painting.

PROBLEMS THAT ESL/EFL STUDENTS HAVE WITH PASSIVE SENTENCES

We have seen that passivization in English moves an object into the subject position and that the active sentence subject may then appear in an agent *by* phrase. This change of position seems to be a characteristic of passive structures in many other languages as well. For example, in French, the verbs *être* ("be") and *avoir* ("have") combine with a past participle, so that a French passive sentence can look almost like a carbon copy of its English counterpart, as seen in (63).

> (63) *Cette lettre a été écrite par mon ami.*
>   that letter has been written by my friend
>   "That letter was written by my friend."

However, even with languages whose passives show a high degree of similarity to the English passive, there are differences in usage. In French and Spanish, the passive voice is not used as frequently as in English. This is, in part, because other grammatical structures are used in contexts in which English uses the passive voice. Thus, in French and Spanish active sentences with reflexive verbs express some English passives (e.g., *Ce garçon s'appelle Jean = This boy is called Jean*). German uses *man* ("one") in the active voice to express so-called impersonal passives – for example, *Man tut das nicht* (one doesn't do that) = "That isn't done." Farsi has a passive very similar to English, but speakers rarely use it.

All of these facts suggest that English language learners from many L1 backgrounds should have no real difficulty learning the basic subject-object switching aspect of English passives. These same students may still, however, have problems deciding when it is appropriate to use the English passive voice, and may not know whether a particular English verb can be used in the passive. Moreover, constraints on passivization vary from language to language, and these differences between the L1 and English can lead to difficulties.

Pseudo-Passive Constructions (Chinese)

Yip (1995) notes that Chinese speakers tend to create ungrammatical sentences like (64a) that look like "abortive attempts" at producing English passives as in (64b). These so-called *pseudo-passives*[21] do not include the verb *be* or the past participle form of the main verb.

> (**64**) a. *These ways can *classify* into two types.   *pseudo-passive*
>   b. These ways can *be classified* into two types.   *passive*

However, Yip presents evidence that ungrammatical sentences like (64a) are not instances of incorrect passive formation; rather they are active sentences involving L1 transfer. They are modeled on a common Chinese *topicalization*[22] structure shown in (65).

> (**65**) *Zhexie   fangfa   keyi   fen   liang   zhong.*
>   these   ways   can   separate   two   types

As was discussed in Chapter 13, in Chinese it is possible to omit subject and object pronouns whose antecedents have already been mentioned. Thus, the ungrammatical English sentence in (64a) results from following the pattern of the Chinese topicalization structure in (65), which has omitted pronouns *one/we* and *them*, as shown in (66).

> (**66**) These ways, (one/we) can classify (them) into two types.
>   "We can classify these ways into two types."

According to Yip, these pseudo-passives are produced by Chinese speakers with a low level of English proficiency. As the students' proficiency increases, these ungrammatical constructions usually disappear. However, see also Han (2000) and Ju (1999).

Ungrammatical Passives with Ergative Verbs (Korean)

Korean speakers frequently produce passive sentences containing ergative verbs, although these are ungrammatical in English. Typical examples, taken from compositions of advanced-level students, are shown in (67).

> (**67**) a. *It is ridiculous that most women in developing countries *are suffered* from extreme poverty.
>   b. *For the last decades, instructional environments *have been* enormously *evolved* with the development of various electronic communication media, especially in colleges, business training and continuing education institutes.

Many Korean verbs that are commonly passivized correspond in meaning to English ergative and change-of-state verbs. These Korean verbs take the passive morphemes *~toy-ta* (e.g., *change, compromise, consist, decrease, happen, increase, occur*), *-pat-ta* (*suffer*), and *-i-*, *-hi-*, *-li-*, and *-ki-* (*appear, disappear*). Thus, Korean speakers frequently follow the L1 pattern and produce an English sentence with *be* followed by the past participle when only the verb itself is required (e.g., **The expression on her face was suddenly changed from sadness to rage* instead of *The expression on her face suddenly changed from sadness to rage*). Data from Cowan, Choi, and Kim (2003) show that these errors are highly persistent, occurring in the writing of Korean graduate students.

SUGGESTIONS FOR TEACHING PASSIVE SENTENCES

The discussion in this chapter suggests that teachers should focus primarily on the following points:

- The appropriate use of *be* and *get* passives. With *be* passives in particular, this topic would include the most important biasing factor, the given–new contract. Constraints on forming passives would also be included.
- The differences between *get* passives and *get* + past participle constructions that have a "become" meaning to insure that students can produce both in the appropriate environments.
- The use and meaning of sentences containing *had* and *get* followed by passivized complements, including the differences between these sentences and happenstance passives.
- A review of sentences with indirect objects with reference to the passive.

In addition, focused practice that addresses problems caused by L1 transfer may also be desirable, particularly in the case of the Korean students.[23] Covering these issues will entail revisiting the passive voice several times with different activities.

Activity 1: Introducing the Form of Passive Sentences (Low Intermediate)

In introducing the passive rule, it is useful to choose a discourse context with plenty of transitive verbs, including in sentences in which passives with the agent *by* phrase will be appropriate. You might begin by showing the students a picture of Pierre-Auguste Renoir, such as in the following drawing. Explain that he was a famous French painter, and then show students a reproduction of one of his paintings.

Present students with the following sentences about Renoir on a handout or write them on the board.

**Pierre-Auguste Renoir
1841–1919**

1. Pierre-Auguste Renoir painted this picture.
2. The critics praised his pictures.
3. Many people bought his paintings.
4. His fellow painters admired him.
5. In 1886, the American public saw his pictures.
6. Toward the end of his life, the Louvre purchased one of his pictures.
7. When he was an old man, many famous artists visited him.

Explain that there is another way to say sentence 1 to emphasize the painting. Write the passive form on the board and explain how to form the passive. Pointing to the picture, say, "This picture was painted by Pierre-Auguste Renoir." Next, show students how to make sentence 2 passive. Then call on individual students to form passive versions of the other sentences. After they have finished, have a volunteer retell the entire sequence in the passive. Then have students in pairs retell the sequence to each other.

Use a similar procedure to introduce Camille Pissarro. Then call on individual students to change the sentences on Pissarro into passive sentences.

Camille Pissarro
1830–1903

1. Camille Pissarro painted this picture.
2. The critics did not appreciate his paintings.
3. Very few galleries exhibited his pictures.
4. Only a few people bought his paintings.
5. His artist friends did not understand his work.
6. However, his fellow Impressionist painters respected him.
7. Most of all, his colleagues admired him as a fine teacher.
8. Today, art critics recognize his importance.

Activity 2: Passive Voice and the Given–New Contract (Intermediate)

This activity conveys the substance of the given–new contract (and how it may favor a choice of passive sentences over active counterparts) without entailing a complicated explanation of this information-structuring principle. It should be conducted with students who have had some previous exposure to the passive voice. Prepare several short passages like (68) and hand them out to students.

(68) Miao Fen needed some fresh vegetables, so she decided to stop at the grocery store on the way home after work. She finished work at 4:30 and began to walk home. She went down Market Street and stopped at the corner to wait for the stoplight to change. When it was green, she stepped off the curb. Suddenly, as she was halfway across the street . . .
   a. a big gray car hit her.
   b. she was hit by a big gray car.

Read this short passage aloud, but stop before reading (a) and (b). Ask the students, "Does it make any difference if we use (a) or (b) to finish the story?" Explain that while both options would be grammatically correct, most people would complete the story with the passive sentence in (b) because the story is really about Miao Fen, not the car, which has not been mentioned before. Miao Fen, by contrast, is mentioned in all of the previous sentences. (Circle the subject pronouns in the preceding sentences as you make this observation.) Present the other examples you have prepared, asking the students which choice is preferable. Follow up with group or pair work in which the students have to write endings to paragraphs like (68).

Activity 3: Introducing and Practicing *Get* Passives (Intermediate)

Given its frequency in conversation, the *get* passive deserves more extensive coverage than it gets in textbooks and courses. Introduce the *get* passive after *be* passives have been practiced. Demonstrate the equivalence of these two structures by selecting examples as in (69).

(69) a. The mail is delivered every day except Sunday.
   b. The mail gets delivered every day except Sunday.

Hand out a list of transitive verbs + possible objects – for example, *accept* (*a person to a college*), *check* (*answers, results*), *deliver* (*a package*), *examine* (*a person*), *inspect* (*baggage*), *know* (*an answer*), *pick up* (*garbage*), *promote* (*a person*), *reward* (*a person for his/her honesty*), *understand* (*an answer*). Point out, with a few well-chosen examples, that *get* passives are not formed with verbs such as *know* and *understand*. Have the students form active and *be* passive sentences with the verbs. Working in pairs, they should then decide which *be* passive sentences can be converted into *get* passives and present their findings to the class.

Activity 4: Introducing and Practicing *Had/Get* + Passivized Complement (Intermediate)

These *have/get* structures are usually covered in ESL/EFL textbooks. One approach that seems fun and is easy to implement is to show a pair of before and after pictures – for example, pictures of a house or a room before and after it was renovated. Working in pairs, the students compare the pictures and use the passivized complement structures to describe all of the things that have been done (e.g., *He's had the roof repaired*, *He had the shutters on the windows fixed*, *He's had the house repainted*).

Activity 5: Practicing the Happenstance Passive (Advanced)

The happenstance passive receives little or no attention in most textbooks and syllabi, possibly because it is considered to be a marginal construction. If you want to expose your students to this construction, you could begin by modeling the structure with an example like (70).

(**70**) I had my car stolen in Chicago.

Point out that this means "My car was stolen in Chicago," and that kind of passive describes something unexpected and usually unpleasant that happens to the subject. The unfortunate, or bad, experience comes after *had*. Supply some more examples such as *She had her house broken into. He had his pocket picked. They had their house destroyed by a tornado.* Point out that this passive occurs with the verb *have* and that it looks like the construction they are familiar with in (71), but with one big difference – in (71) the subject has someone else do the action that comes after *had*, but in (70), the action after *had* happens to the subject.

(**71**) I had my car repaired in Chicago.

Now give the students a number of regular passive sentences that describe unfortunate events that could happen to someone without any advance notice, as in (72).

(**72**) My husband's arm was broken in three places in a car accident.
My taxes were audited by the IRS.
My brother's wallet was stolen in the library.
My parents' house was broken into and all of their credit cards were stolen.

Have students orally produce happenstance passives for these sentences. Finally, say, "Imagine that you have had a really terrible day – one of the worst days you've had in a long time. What bad things happened? Write three sentences like the ones we have been using that describe what happened to you." Have students read their sentences in groups or as a class.

Activity 6: Tackling the Ergative Verb Problem (Advanced)

For Korean speakers who are overpassivizing ergative verbs, a grammatical judgment task may be helpful. As the term *ergative* would likely be confusing, simply list examples of ergative verbs and point out that in each case, the subject of the verb experiences the action.

Prepare a passage like the one in (73), with paired and unpaired ergative verbs that have been passivized. Tell the students to read it, circle the verbs that are incorrect, and correct the errors.

> (73)   A Memorable Experience
>
> One of the most memorable experiences in my life was happened last year when I was visiting my friends in Los Angeles. They live in Santa Monica near the Pacific Ocean. One day we were sitting in their house eating dinner when everything started to shake. It was an earthquake. A glass on the edge of the table was fallen off and hit the floor. The shaking was continued for about 15 or 20 seconds before it stopped. My friends laughed when they saw how scared I was. They told me that this was just a small earthquake. They said that you have to get used to earthquakes if you live in Los Angeles because they are occurred there almost every day.

With the passage in (73), the errors discovered by the students can lead into a discussion of the three unpaired ergative verbs – *fall*, *happen*, and *occur* – which cannot appear in passive sentences. You might mention other such verbs – for example, *appear*, *arise*, *die*, *disappear*, *emerge*, *erupt*, and *suffer*.

Next, move to a discussion of paired ergative verbs. Explain that verbs such as *continue* can also be transitive, as shown in (74b):

> (74) a. The storm continued for three hours.   *no object, action happens to the subject*
>
> b. The school continued the course for three weeks   *object, the course,* because they found more money to pay the teacher.   *to which action happens*

Explain that the verb *continue* in (74a) is just like *die*, *fall*, *stumble*, and so on – the action happens to the subject. Thus, (74a) doesn't have a passive version; that is, you cannot say **The storm was continued for three hours.* Then explain that, in contrast, *continue* in (74b) is a transitive verb and has a direct object, *the course*. Thus, (b) has a passive version: *The course was continued for three weeks (by the school).* Present a few more example sentences with other paired ergative verbs (e.g., *boil*, *bounce*, *close*, *dry*, *fracture*, *hang*, *move*, *open*, *roll*, etc.).

Next, present sets of sentences that contain paired ergative verbs to check whether students have grasped the point. One sentence should show the verb in its ergative sense, as in (75a); the other should show it as an incorrectly passivized ergative, as in (75b). You can add other sentences that show the transitive counterpart used correctly in an active sentence, as in (75c), or in a passive sentence. The students' task is to identify which sentences are ungrammatical and explain why. This can be a pair or group activity.

> (75) a. He dropped the tennis ball, and it bounced a few times before coming to rest.
>
> b. He dropped the tennis ball, and it was bounced a few times before coming to rest.
>
> c. He bounced the ball several times before he served it.

Activity 7: Practicing Passive Patterns Used in Academic Writing (Advanced)

Advanced students, particularly those preparing to write at the university level, may benefit from practicing the two passive patterns favored in academic English (Biber et al. 1999: 732, 1019–1020). Here is a sample lesson designed to practice these in composition classes.

Stage 1

Point out that a common pattern in academic writing is a passive sentence such as in (76):

(**76**) In the 17th century, light was thought to be colorless.

Explain that such sentences come from active sentences with a main verb such as *assume*, *believe*, *consider*, *discover*, *find*, *suppose*, or *think* followed by a clause. Then show the active counterpart of the preceding passive sentence in (77).

(**77**) In the 17th century, scientists thought (that) light was colorless.

Explain that to create the passive sentence in (76), we make the following changes:

- Move the noun *light* from the *that* complement clause into the subject position in the main clause.
- Omit the active sentence subject, *scientists*.
- Change the verb *thought* to *was thought*.
- Change the verb *was* to the infinitive *to be*.

Next, hand out a paragraph like the one shown in (78) that contains only active sentences. At least one of the sentences should be passivizable in the pattern shown here. Have the students work in pairs to rewrite the paragraph so that it is composed of passive sentences. Tell them to omit active sentence subjects whenever possible. When students have finished, they can compare their rewrites with other pairs.

(**78**) In the 17th century, scientists had made a great deal of progress toward understanding optics, the science of seeing. However, scientists did not understand the origin of color very well. Most scientists attributed color to some sort of change that occurred when light interacted with other matter. Scientists thought pure light was colorless. But, for example, when the setting sun passed through the atmosphere, this contact supposedly changed it to an orange or red color. Scientists did not explain this change very well.

An example of a good rewrite is shown in (79).

(**79**) In the 17th century, a great deal of progress had been made toward understanding optics, the science of seeing. However, the origin of color was not understood very well. Color was attributed to some sort of change that occurred when light interacted with other matter. Pure light was thought to be colorless. But, for example, when the setting sun passed through the atmosphere, it was supposedly changed to an orange or red color. This change was not explained very well.

Stage 2

Write the sentence in (80) and explain to students that it is an example of another passive sentence pattern they will often see in academic writing.

(**80**) It was believed that light was a mixture of colors.

Point out that this passive sentence pattern resembles the previous pattern in that it comes from active sentences in which main verbs such as *assume, believe, discover, find, know, suppose,* and *think* are followed by a clause. Then show the active sentence in (81) that corresponds to (80).

(**81**) Most scientists believed that light was a mixture of colors.

Explain that to create the passive sentence in (80), we make the following changes to the active sentence:

* passivize the sentence by moving the *that* complement to the head of the sentence and omitting *by most scientists*
* change the verb *believed* to *was believed*
* insert *it* at the beginning of the sentence where the *that* complement was

Next, give students a paragraph like the one shown in (82) and ask them to rewrite it so that it contains passive sentences in the second pattern.

(**82**) For some time scientists have known that exercise is good for the body. Until recently, researchers believed that the main benefit of exercise to older people was maintaining body strength and endurance. However, recently, a number of studies have shown that exercise even benefits the mental health of the aging. In one study, researchers found that regular exercise can make the brain younger. In a recent study at the University of Illinois, investigators discovered that regular exercise by older people produced brain patterns typically found in 20-year-olds. Now the question seems to be, "What kinds of exercise produce the greatest cognitive benefits for older people?"

An example of a good rewrite is shown in (83).

(**83**) For some time it has been known that exercise is good for the body. Until recently, it was believed that the main benefit of exercise to older people was maintaining body strength and endurance. But recently it has been shown that exercise even benefits the mental health of the aging. In one study, it was found that regular exercise can make the brain younger. In a recent study at the University of Illinois, it was discovered that regular exercise by older people produced brain patterns typically found in 20-year-olds. Now the question seems to be, "What kinds of exercise produce the greatest cognitive benefits for older people?"

Activity 8: Revisiting Dative Movement Verbs (Intermediate)

You will need to revisit dative movement verbs in the course of teaching the passive voice to make clear that *for* dative verbs, which have two active patterns, have only one passive. After explaining this, you could have your students read a text that contains a mixture of *to* dative and *for* dative verbs in active sentences and ask them to change the active sentences into passives wherever possible. Point out that some of the sentences will sound better as short passives. This activity serves as a review of both types of verbs that take indirect objects. If you include a second step in which students discuss whether it is in fact a good idea to change each of the passivizable active sentences, you can also use the activity to review how the given–new contract affects the choice between active and passive sentences.

ENDNOTES

[1] See Biber et al. (1999), p. 475.

[2] See Table 11.9 in Biber et al. (1999), p. 938, for an overview of the frequency of occurrence of different types of passive sentences.

[3] This example is from Hughes (1991), p. 13.

[4] This example is from Kosslyn (1994).

[5] See Biber et al. (1999), p. 938.

[6] Biber et al. (1999), p. 938, advance this argument.

[7] This example is adapted from Davison (1980). The observation is hers.

[8] The observation and example are due to Davison (1980).

[9] Biber, et al. (1999), pp. 942–43.

[10] Lourie (1987).

[11] This is borne out by the passive data in Cowan (1995), p. 35.

[12] Of course, some stative verbs such as *weigh* have transitive counterparts, and these can undergo passivization (e.g., *Each sack is weighed twice before it is loaded on the truck*).

[13] There are, however, stative verbs that can, and often do, occur in the passive voice (e.g., *believed, desired, hated, known, loved, perceived, preferred, regarded, seen, thought,* and *understood*). Interestingly, these all have to do with states of knowing, feeling, and perceiving.

[14] For example, Celce-Murcia and Larsen-Freeman (1983), p. 229.

[15] Biber et. al. (1999), p. 476.

[16] In certain languages – for example, Chinese – some passives are often used only in adverse situations. See Reed and Cowan (1989) and Cowan and Reed (1990). Pei and Chi (1987) argue that this is changing under the influence of English.

[17] This structure is sometimes referred to as the *resulting copula* (Quirk et al., 1972, p. 803).

[18] See Quirk et al. (1972), pg. 803.

[19] The term *happenstance passive* was perhaps first introduced by Gee (1974).

[20] See Huddleston and Pullum (2002), p. 1429.

[21] The term *pseudo-passive* was introduced by Schachter and Rutherford (1979) who provided one of the first discussions of the phenomenon.

[22] English has topicalization structures that move objects to the beginning of the sentence (e.g., *Bill, I like*; *Susan, I don't*). However, Chinese uses topicalization structures much more frequently than passives sentences, and it hence is often referred to as a "topic prominent language." See Li & Thompson (1976) and Yip (1995).

[23] Cowan, Choi, & Kim (2003) have shown that CALL programs can effectively improve Korean students' ability to identify and correct these errors.

REFERENCES

Biber D., Johannson, S., Leech, G., Conrad, S., and Finegan, E. (1999). *Longman grammar of spoken and written English*. Essex, UK: Pearson.

Celce-Murcia M., and Larsen-Freeman, D. (1983). *The grammar book: An ESL/EFL teacher's course*. Rowley, MA: Newbury House.

Cowan, R. (1995). What are discourse principles made of? In P. Downing and M. Noonan (Eds.), *In word order and discourse* (pp. 29–50). Amsterdam/Philadelphia: John Benjamins.

Cowan, R., Choi, H. E., & Kim, D. H. (2003). Four questions for error diagnosis and correction in CALL. *CALICO Journal, 20*(3), 451–463.

Cowan, R., & Reed, B. (1990). Experimental evidence of the transfer of L1 implicature in L2 acquisition. In K. Hall, J. P. Koenig, M. Maecham, S. Reinman, & L. A. Sutton (Eds.), *Proceedings of the sixteenth annual meeting of the Berkeley Linguistics Society* (pp. 94–102). Berkeley, CA: Berkeley Linguistics Society.

Davison, A. (1980). Peculiar passives. *Language*, *57*, 42–65.

Gee, J. P. (1974). Get passive: On some constructions with 'get.' University of Indiana Linguistics Club, MS 1–14.

Han, Z-H. (2000). Persistence of the implicit influence of L1: The case of the psuedo-passive. *Applied Linguistics*, *21*(1), 47–77.

Huddleston, R. and Pullum, J. (2002). *The Cambridge grammar of the English language*. Cambridge: Cambridge University Press.

Hughes, A, (1991). *Testing for language teachers*. Cambridge: Cambridge University Press.

Ju, M-K. (1999). Overpassivization errors by second language learners: The effect of conceptualizable agents in discourse. *Studies in Second Language Acquistion*, *22*, 85–111.

Kosslyn, S. A. (1994). *Image and brain: The resolution of the imagery debate*. Cambridge, MA: MIT Press.

Li, C. N., & Thompson, S. A. (1976). Subject and topic: a new typology of language. In C. N. Li (Ed.), *Subject and topic* (pp. 457–489). New York: Academic Press.

Lourie, R. (1987). *Zero gravity*. San Diego/New York/London: Harcourt Brace Jovanovich.

Pei, Z . Z., & Chi, F. W. (1987). The two faces of English in China: Englishization of Chinese and the nativization of English. *World Englishes*, *6*, 111–126.

Quirk, R., Greenbaum, S., Leech, G., & Svartvik, J. (1985). *A comprehensive grammar of the English language*. New York: Longman, Inc.

Reed, B., & Cowan, R. (1989). Applying an experimental approach to the investigation of syntactic change. In T. J. Walsh (Ed.), *Georgetown University round table on languages and linguistics*, *1988* (pp. 260–267). Washington, D.C.: Georgetown University Press.

Schachter, J., & Rutherford, W. (1979). Discourse function and language transfer. *Working Papers in Bilingualism*, *19*, 1–12.

Yip, V. (1995). *Interlanguage and learnability: From Chinese to English*. Amsterdam/Philadelphia: John Benjamins.

CHAPTER 18

Relative Clauses

INTRODUCTION

Relative clauses are clauses that modify noun phrases. In this chapter, we will look at different kinds of relative clauses and at how they can be shortened and moved around to create different complex sentences. Relative clauses are used widely in written and spoken English, thus, it is important for teachers to have a good knowledge of their various forms and functions.

FORM AND FUNCTION

In Chapter 2, we saw that complex sentences consist of a main, or independent, clause and one or more subordinate, or dependent, clauses. Relative clauses are one kind of dependent clause. They are introduced by a special set of pronouns, the *relative pronouns – that*, *which*, *who*, *whom*, and *whose*. Relative clauses have the same function as adjectives, and for this reason are sometimes called "adjective clauses." They add information to the head nouns of noun phrases. However, relative clauses differ from adjectives in where they occur – adjectives come before head nouns (i.e., are prenominal modifiers), and relative clauses come after them (i.e., are postnominal modifiers). This difference is illustrated in (1), in which two adjectives precede the head noun *problem*, and in (2), in which these adjectives appear in a relative clause following *problem*.

    Art   *Adj*   *Adj*   *Head Noun*
(**1**) a   *difficult* and *perplexing*   problem

    Art Head Noun   *Relative Clause*
(**2**) a   problem   [*that is difficult and perplexing*]

The noun phrase modified can have any grammatical function in the sentence; it can be a subject, object, indirect object, or object of a preposition. Thus, for example, we can have both *A problem that is difficult and perplexing can take time to solve* and *We gave him a problem that is difficult and perplexing*. In the first of these sentences, the relative clause modifies a noun phrase that is the subject of the main clause; in the second, it modifies an object. The former also exemplifies a "center-embedded" relative, or relative clause that occurs in the middle or center of the main clause, as opposed to at the end, as in the latter.

Restrictive Versus Nonrestrictive Relative Clauses

English relative clauses are classified as *restrictive* or *nonrestrictive* depending upon their function. A *restrictive relative clause* is one that serves to restrict the reference of the noun phrase modified. In (3), the restrictive relative clause *who lives in Canada* restricts *my sister* by specifying the sister in Canada. The sentence implies that the speaker has more than one sister, but only one sister in Canada is a biologist. It could be an answer to the question *Which of your sisters is a biologist?* The information added by the relative clause identifies the sister.

(3) My sister *who lives in Canada* is a biologist.

Sentence (4) contains a nonrestrictive relative clause, indicated as such by the commas around it. A *nonrestrictive relative clause* adds information about the noun modified. The noun's reference is already clear; the clause does not restrict it. Thus, in (4) the relative clause is just an added comment to the main clause content *my sister is a biologist*. The relative clause in essence says "Oh, by the way, she lives in Canada." There is no implication that the speaker has other sisters.

(4) My sister, *who lives in Canada*, is a biologist.

The commas around nonrestrictive relatives reflect the pauses in speech and a falling intonation pattern at the end of the clause, as shown in (5). There is no pause at the beginning or end of a restrictive relative clause, and falling intonation occurs only at the end of the sentence, as shown in (6).

nonrestrictive relative clause intonation

(5) The students, *who had to take final exams today*, are tired.

restrictive relative clause intonation

(6) The students who had to take final exams today are tired.

These two criteria – punctuation in written sentences and intonation in spoken sentences – are traditionally applied to distinguish restrictive from nonrestrictive relative clauses. Later, we will see additional criteria distinguishing the two. However, the criteria do not constitute a foolproof method of determining whether a clause was intended as essential or merely supplementary information.

Forming Relative Clauses

The formation of relative clauses can be described by means of a rule of *wh- movement*, which we saw earlier in the formation of questions in Chapter 4. This rule moves the NP in the relative clause that corresponds to the NP in the main clause to the front of the relative clause, leaving a "gap" at the place from which it was moved. The NP fronted by *wh-* movement is replaced by a relative pronoun.[1] Examples of the application of *wh-* movement are shown in (7), (8), and (9).

(7) The movie [*that* we saw *the movie*] was really scary.

(8) I'm looking for the box [*that* he puts all his stuff in *the box*].

(9) That bed [*that* I slept on *that bed*] was really soft.

In (7), (8), and (9), the NP that corresponds to the main clause noun functions within the relative clause as an object NP of some sort. When the NP is instead the subject of the relative clause, as in (10), *wh-* movement does not apply, but the subject NP is replaced by a relative pronoun.

> (**10**) The car [~~the car~~ crashed into the streetlight] was destroyed.
>   *that*

If the NP being replaced is human (or, for example, a pet), *that* or *who* (and *whom*, if the NP is an object) can be used. This is despite the prescriptivist rule that only *who* be used for human NPs; in actuality, *who* occurs more frequently in writing, but *that* is used almost as frequently as *who* in spoken English.[2] With other NPs, *that* or *which* can be used. As will be discussed later, *whose*, which expresses possession, is used for all NPs but is preferred for those that are human. With the exception of *that*, all the relative pronouns can be used in restrictive or nonrestrictive relative clauses; *that* can only be used in restrictive relative clauses. With many relative clauses there is also, as discussed later, the option of omitting the relative pronoun.

We will now turn to a discussion of the types of relative clauses in English – looking first at restrictive relative clauses and some variations, and then at nonrestrictive clauses.

RESTRICTIVE RELATIVE CLAUSES

Restrictive relative clauses are far more common than nonrestrictive clauses. The restrictive relative clauses that we look at in this section all modify a head noun in the main clause, include one of the relative pronouns mentioned previously, and have a main verb that is not an infinitive.

Types of Restrictive Relative Clauses

Restrictive relative clauses can be classified in terms of the grammatical function of their relative pronouns. Based on this classification, English has six types of restrictive relative clauses, also found in many other languages of the world.[3] These relative clause types are the following: subject (S), direct object (O), indirect object (IO), object of the preposition (OP), possessive (POS), and object of comparison (OC). We will look at each in turn. Keep in mind that these types are based on the grammatical function of the relative pronoun in its clause and that the NP the relative clause modifies may have any of a range of functions in the main clause. Thus, for example, a subject relative clause may modify an NP that is a subject or object in the main clause.

Subject (S) Relative Clauses

As we have seen, *subject (S) relative clauses*, in which the relative pronoun replaces the subject of the clause, do not require *wh-* movement. In S relative clauses, the relative pronouns *who* and *that* replace human NPs, as in (11a) and (11b).

> (**11**) a. The guy [*who* hired Robert] was the manager of the supermarket.
>   b. The guy [*that* hired Robert] was the manager of the supermarket.

The relative pronouns *which* and *that* replace inanimate NPs, as in (12). *That* seems to be preferred, at least for American English.

> (**12**) The tornado [$\begin{Bmatrix} that \\ which \end{Bmatrix}$ struck the town] destroyed several homes.[4]

Object (O) Relative Clauses

In *object (O) relative clauses*, the relative pronoun replaces the object of the verb. The relative pronouns *who*, *whom*, and *that* introduce O relative clauses that modify human nouns. In spoken English, the relative pronoun used is generally *who* or *that*, as in (13a) and (13b).

> (**13**) a. At the party there were many people [*who* he did not know].
> b. At the party there were many people [*that* he did not know].

As early as 1928, the *Oxford English Dictionary* observed that *whom* was "no longer in natural colloquial speech" as a relative pronoun introducing O relatives. Today, *whom*, as in (14), tends to be used mostly in written English.[5]

> (**14**) At the party there were many people [*whom* he did not know].

For inanimate nouns, again, *which* and *that* are both used, as in (15), with *that* occurring more frequently in American English.

> (**15**) The dress [$\left\{{which \atop that}\right\}$ Sonya was wearing] was very colorful.

Indirect Object (IO) Relative Clauses

In *indirect object (IO) relative clauses*, the relative pronoun comes from the indirect object position following the preposition *to* or *for*. As with O relative clauses, *which*, *that*, *who*, and *whom* are all used. However, two patterns are possible, and which is chosen affects the use of relative pronouns.

In one pattern, shown in (16), when *wh-* movement occurs, the preposition – *to* or *for* – remains behind, or is "stranded," as in shown in (16b). *Whom* is seldom used in this pattern.

> (**16**) a. The girl [*who/that* we gave the candy *to*] is Fred's sister.
> b. The girl [_____ we gave the candy *to the girl*] is Fred's sister.
> c. The institution [*that/which* she left the most money *to*] is the Blanchard Foundation.

In the other pattern, shown in (17), the preposition, too, is moved to the front of the clause. Only *whom* and *which* can occur in this pattern; *who* and *that* are not possible.

> (**17**) a. The student [*for whom* Alice baked a cake] is my roommate.
> b. The student [_____ Alice baked a cake *for the student*] is my roommate.
> c. The store [*for which* she bakes her cakes] is located nearby.

Relative clauses with *to whom/for whom* sound formal to many native speakers; hence they tend to be confined to written English. In spoken English, speakers avoid such clauses by using the relative clause pattern with clause-final prepositions, as in (16c).

Object of the Preposition (OP) Relative Clauses

Object of the preposition (OP) relative clauses have the same two patterns as IO relatives, so we might easily collapse IO and OP relatives into one category. The difference is, of course, that IO relatives are limited to two prepositions, *to* and *for*, inasmuch as the indirect object is always a goal or beneficiary, whereas with OP relatives many prepositions can occur.

As with IO relative clauses, the first OP pattern, with the preposition stranded at the end of the clause, shown in (18a) and (18b), is more typical of spoken English. The second pattern, shown in (18c) and (18d), is found more often in written English.

(**18**) a. The mattress [*which/that* he slept *on*] had several broken springs.
b. The people [*who/that* he aimed his weapon *at*] were very frightened.
c. The mattress [*on which* he slept] had several broken springs.
d. The people [*at whom* he aimed his weapon] were very frightened.

When *way* or *manner* is the object of the preposition *in*, the preposition must be moved and cannot be stranded, as shown by the contrast between (19a) and (19b).

(**19**) a. The manner *in which* he spoke was shocking.
b. *The manner *which* he spoke *in* was shocking.

Most phrasal prepositional verbs do not permit the elements following the verb to be moved, as (20) illustrates.

(**20**) a. A preposition is an abomination which we will not *put up with*.
b. ?A preposition is an abomination *with which* we will not put *up*.
c. *A preposition is an abomination *up with which* we will not put.[6]

Possessive (POS) Relative Clauses

In *possessive* (*POS*), or *genitive*, relative clauses,[7] the relative pronoun replaces an element that expresses possession. The relative pronoun may be *whose* or may be *which* preceded by *of*.

POS RELATIVE CLAUSES INTRODUCED BY *WHOSE*

The relative pronoun *whose* is typically used when the head noun is human or animate, as in (21a), or is a collective noun such as a club, agency, corporation, or society, as in (21b). However, we can also find it used with inanimate head nouns, as in (21c) and (21d).

(**21**) a. Last week I met a girl [*whose* brother works in your law firm].
b. He bought stock in a company [*whose* profits had increased dramatically for the last three quarters].
c. A crystal is a piece of matter [*whose* boundaries are naturally formed plane surfaces].[8]
d. Let ABC be a triangle [*whose* sides are of equal length].[9]

Possessive relative pronouns are part of a noun phrase. *Whose* functions as a possessive determiner, such as *my*, *your*, *our*, and so on.

If the relevant noun phrase is in subject position, *whose* simply replaces its determiner. Thus, in (22a), *that girl's*, the possessive determiner in the NP *that girl's brother*, is replaced by *whose*, as in (22b).

(**22**) a. I just met *that girl* [[*that girl's* brother] is a chef].
b. I just met that girl [[*whose* brother] is a chef].

If the NP is elsewhere in the clause, *wh-* movement is needed to produce a sentence such as in (23).

(**23**) The author [*whose* last three books Peter reviewed] won a Pulitzer Prize.

As (24) and (25) show, the NP that contains the determiner that will become *whose* is the object of the verb in the relative clause, and *wh-* movement applies to the entire NP.[10] When *whose* replaces *the author's*, we get the sentence in (23).

(**24**) The author [Peter reviewed [*the author's last three books*]] won an award.

(**25**) The author [[*the author's last three books*] Peter reviewed _____] won an award.

As (26) and (27) show, the constituents before the noun may include not only the words that are replaced by *whose* but also, for example, a quantifier, such as *several*, plus the preposition *of*, and these, too, are moved to the front of the clause. Thus, the sentence in (26) is a result of the process shown in (27) followed by the replacement of *the author's* with *whose*.

(**26**) The author *several of whose books Peter reviewed* won a Pulitzer.

(**27**) a. The author [Peter reviewed [several of *the author's* books]] won a Pulitzer.
　　　 b. The author [*several of the author's books* Peter reviewed _____] won a Pulitzer.

In sentences like (23) and (26), there is a strong tendency to add pauses around the center-embedded relative clause and to give it the falling intonation typical of a nonrestrictive relative clause. The pauses may reflect native speakers' expectation that center-embedded restrictive relatives should have no more than one word (preferably a preposition) separating a relative pronoun from the NP that it modifies.[11] Thus, in sentences like these, it may be difficult to determine whether the speaker had a restrictive or nonrestrictive relative clause in mind.[12]

POS RELATIVE CLAUSES INTRODUCED BY *OF WHICH*

As we saw in Chapter 10, there are two ways to indicate possession with nouns: a noun may be inflected with *'s* or an apostrophe, as in (28a), or it may be preceded by *of*, as in (28b).

(**28**) a. the reports' size
　　　 b. the size of the reports

We have already seen that (28a) is the source of the relative pronoun *whose*. The option in (28b) is the source of an alternative possibility for POS relative clauses – *of which*. These two ways of introducing POS relative clauses are shown in (29).

(**29**) a. The reports [*whose size* the government prescribes] are boring.
　　　 b. The reports [*the size of which* the government prescribes] are boring.

The relative clauses in (29) arise as a result of applying *wh-* movement to the object NP in (30).

(**30**) The reports [the government prescribes [$\begin{Bmatrix} \textit{the reports' size} \\ \text{the size } \textit{of the reports} \end{Bmatrix}$]] are boring.

Thus, following *wh-* movement, *the reports'* is replaced by *whose*, as in (29a), or *the reports* is replaced by *which*. In the latter case, three patterns are possible. The relative pronoun may be moved alone, leaving the *of* stranded, as in (31a). Alternatively, *of* may also be moved, as in (31b).[13]

(**31**) a. The reports [*which* the government prescribes *the size of* _____] are boring.

　　　 b. The reports [*of which* the government prescribes *the size* _____] are boring.

Finally, the material moved may be the entire NP, as occurs with *whose* clauses, resulting in the sentence shown in (32).[14]

(32) The reports [*the size of which* the government prescribes _____] are boring.

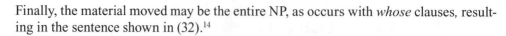

At some point, you may want to discuss with your advanced students that relative clauses such as (31b) or (32) should be written without surrounding commas if intended to be restrictive rather than nonrestrictive.

Object of Comparison (OC) Relative Clauses

Object of comparison (*OC*) *relative clauses* include comparative structures, discussed in Chapter 24. The NP that is replaced by the relative pronoun originates after the conjunction *than*. The relative pronouns used are *who*, *whom*, and *that* for NPs referring to humans, as in (33a), and *which* and *that* for those referring to inanimate things, as in (33b).

(33) a. The girl [*who/that* Susan was faster *than*] won the 100 meter dash.
 b. The sports car [*which/that* the Alfa Romeo was faster *than*] was a Porsche.

Unlike prepositions in IO and OP relative clauses, the conjunction *than* cannot move to the front of the clause with the relative pronoun; it must remain at the end. Thus, *wh*- movement shown in (34) results in (33b); the inclusion of the conjunction results in **The sports car than which the Alfa Romeo was faster*, which is ungrammatical.

(34) The sports car [_____ the Alfa Romeo was faster *than the sports car*]

was a Porsche.

Additional Facts About Restrictive Relative Clauses

Two kinds of relative clauses that you will encounter differ from the standard form that we have seen. They are typical of spoken rather than written English.

What as a Relative Pronoun in Nonstandard English

In spoken English, *what* is also used as an alternative to *which* and *that* in nonstandard dialects. *What* is more common in British English than in American English, and it is used in both S and O relative clauses, as shown in (35a) and (35b).[15]

(35) a. And you see that truck *what just went by*.[16]
 b. That geezer *what we met down at the bar* is me old Dad.

Resumptive Pronouns

In spoken English, native speakers sometimes produce relative clauses that contain a resumptive pronoun, such as the *it* in (36).

(36) *Usually they give you a thing . . . , you know, a thing *that you don't want it*.[17]

A *resumptive pronoun* is a pronoun that occupies the position that the NP replaced by the relative pronoun had before it underwent *wh*- movement. In (36), the pronoun *it* at the end of the relative clause is unnecessary and inappropriate, since the clause begins with a relative pronoun *that*, which corresponds to the NP *a thing*.

The sentences in (37) are typical of those in which resumptive pronouns occur.

(37) a. *What about the guy *who they don't know whether he wants to come?*[18]
  b. *You mean the lawyer *who he and his wife had dinner here last night.*

Notice that, in these two examples, unlike in (36), omitting the resumptive pronouns would not be enough; there is no way to repair the relative clauses without rephrasing the sentences. Researchers have hypothesized that native speakers use resumptive pronouns to complete sentences begun in a way that makes completion with a grammatical English relative clause impossible.[19] The use of resumptive pronouns, in other words, may be a performance strategy that speakers resort to under the pressure of planning and producing complex sentences.[20] This idea gains some support from the fact that relative clauses with resumptive pronouns are found primarily in spoken English.[21] Relative clauses with resumptive pronouns can be heard quite frequently, thus, it is probably worth having a discussion about them with advanced students. A key point to emphasize is that this spoken version is nonstandard English and should never be used in writing.

SUMMARY

FORM AND FUNCTION; RESTRICTIVE RELATIVE CLAUSES

Like adjectives, **relative clauses** modify nouns; they differ from adjectives in that they are clauses and that they follow the noun they modify. They can modify any noun in the main clause.
  A problem that is difficult to solve is a challenge.
  He gave us a problem that was difficult to solve.

A **restrictive relative clause** functions to identify the noun it modifies; a **nonrestrictive relative clause**, separated by commas or pauses, functions to add information about the noun it modifies.
  The students who had to take exams are tired.
  The students, who had to take exams, are tired.

Relative clauses can be described as formed through **wh- movement**, which moves an NP corresponding to the noun modified to the front of the clause and replaces this NP with an appropriate relative pronoun.
  The movie [that/which we saw the movie] was really scary.

The **relative pronouns** are *that* (for humans and inanimate things), *who* and *whom* (for humans), *which* (for inanimate things), and *whose* (possessive form for humans and inanimate things).

Restrictive relative clauses can be classified by the grammatical function of their relative pronouns into six types:

• **Subject (S) relative clauses**, in which *who*, *that*, or *which* replaces the subject of the clause.
  The guy who/that hired Robert was the manager of the supermarket.
  The tornado that/which struck the town destroyed several homes.

continued

- **Object (O) relative clauses**, in which *who*, *whom*, *that*, or *which* replaces the object of the clause.
  At the party, there were many people whom/who/that he did not know.
  The car which/that Ted bought has a very powerful engine.

- **Indirect object (IO) relative clauses**, in which *who*, *whom*, *that*, or *which* replaces an indirect object following the preposition *to* or *for*. Two patterns are possible:
  The girl to whom we sent the e-mail lives in Seattle.
  The girl who/that we sent the e-mail to lives in Seattle.

- **Object of the preposition (OP) relative clauses**, which have the same two patterns as IO clauses but may have a range of prepositions.
  The girl with whom he went to the dance is my sister.
  The bed that/which I slept on once belonged to Abraham Lincoln.

- **Possessive (POS) relative clauses**, in which the relative pronoun replaces an element that indicates possession. These clauses take two forms:

  - **POS relative clauses introduced by *whose***, used especially but not exclusively for possessors that are human or otherwise animate.
    Last week I met a girl whose brother works in your law firm.
    The author one of whose last three books Peter has reviewed is very famous.
    Let ABC be a triangle whose sides are of equal length.

  - **POS clauses introduced by *of which***, used with inanimate possessors. Three patterns are possible when *of* + *which* is part of an object NP:
    The reports which the government prescribes the size of are boring.
    The reports of which the government prescribes the size are boring.
    The reports the size of which the government prescribes are boring.

- **Object of comparison (OC) relative clauses**, in which *who*, *whom*, *that*, or *which* replaces an NP following the comparative conjunction *than*.
  The girl who/whom/that Susan was faster than won the 100 meter dash.
  The sports car which/that the Alfa Romeo was faster than was a Porsche.

Relative clauses in speech occasionally include:

- ***What* as an alternative to *which* and *that*** in nonstandard dialects.
  And you see that truck what just went by.

- **Resumptive pronouns**, pronouns inappropriately used in a clause along with a relative pronoun and occurring in the position the relative pronoun came from.
  *Usually they give you a thing . . . , you know, a thing that you don't want it.
  *What about the guy who they don't know whether he wants to come?

EXERCISE 18.1

Label each restrictive relative clause in the sentences as an S, O, IO, OP, POS, or OC relative clause.

Example: The girl who Jack bought a watch for never thanked him.

Answer: IO relative clause

1. Fred knew the woman who Alan eventually married.
2. The girl who is smarter than Fred won the poetry contest.
3. The man who invented pizza is no longer living.
4. That professor who Ed is taking a course from is really weird.
5. The girl who Fred is smarter than won the poetry contest.
6. Bill went out with the girl who I gave his phone number to.
7. The professor whose son is studying at Princeton teaches my class.
8. The T-shirts the colors and sizes of which are determined by the athletic department are on sale at a store on campus.

EXERCISE 18.2

Diagram each sentence to show the constituents that undergo *wh-* movement or replacement by a relative pronoun.

Example: John met the guy who Norma is engaged to.

John met the guy [who Norma is engaged to <u>the guy</u>].

1. The scientist to whom they gave the award was from Sweden.
2. Iris bought the car that Fred had previously sold to Susan.
3. The guy whose brother is engaged to Joan owns a big house.
4. I know that girl whose sister Alan eventually married.
5. John admired the dresser in which Alice kept her sheets.
6. Alan found an ancient manuscript the last few pages of which had several beautiful illustrations.
7. The actor whose last three movies I had seen and enjoyed gave a surprisingly bad performance in this play.

POSITION AND REDUCTION OF RESTRICTIVE RELATIVE CLAUSES

In this section, we look at some variations in the positions of restrictive relative clauses within the sentence and then at several ways in which restrictive relative clauses can be reduced.

Extraposed Relative Clauses

Restrictive relative clauses sometimes do not always appear directly after the head noun they modify. Occasionally a writer or, more often, a speaker may place them farther away, for example, as in (38b), rather than (38a).

(**38**) a. A man *who has red hair* just came in.
   b. A man _____ just came in *who has red hair*.

Relative clauses that have been moved away from the head nouns they modify are called *extraposed relatives*.[22] Often, the relative clause is separated from its NP by a single word, for example, by an adverb, such as *yesterday* in (39b), or a main verb, such as *happened* in (40b).

(**39**) a. I saw someone *who I hadn't seen for years* yesterday.
   b. I saw someone yesterday *who I hadn't seen for years*.

(**40**) a. Something *that I can't really talk about* happened.
    b. Something happened *that I can't really talk about.*

However, the separation can be longer, as in example (41b), in which the relative clause has been moved away from the subject noun around a verb phrase containing not only the verb *is studying* but also a prepositional phrase, *with me*.

(**41**) a. A girl *who has an IQ of 200* is studying with me.
    b. A girl is studying with me *who has an IQ of 200.*

Various explanations of why native speakers create extraposed relative clauses have been proposed. Perhaps native speakers move the clause into the position of "new information," where it receives more attention.[23] Another explanation involves the principle of end weight, which we saw earlier in Chapters 15 and 17. In keeping with this principle, a lengthy center-embedded relative clause moves to the end of the sentence.

Although we cannot say precisely how far a relative clause can be moved, there is one restriction that cannot be violated: a relative clause cannot be moved into a position in which it could have originated, that is, following another noun. This restriction exists because such a move could change the meaning of the original sentence. For example, if the relative clause in (42a) is moved away from the noun *a pole* to the end of the sentence, as in (42b), a change in meaning occurs. This is because the relative clause is now directly after another noun, *a workman,* and now the workman, not the pole, is nine feet tall.

(**42**) a. A pole *that must have been nine feet tall* fell on a workman.
    b. A pole fell on a workman *that must have been nine feet tall.*

Extraposed relatives can be a source of amusing errors in freshman English rhetoric courses. Freshman English students not infrequently write sentences like (42b). Thus, college rhetoric teachers admonish their students never to write relative clauses that are "removed from the nouns they modify." In reality, there is nothing wrong with writing sentences like the (b) sentences in (38) through (41), even though English instructors might insist that they are stylistically bad. Of course, sentences like (42b) should be avoided because they don't express the writer's intent.

Stacking

Relative clauses are frequently strung together, one clause after the other, as shown in (43) and (44). This phenomenon, which appears to occur more frequently in conversation than in writing, is called *stacking*.

(**43**) The people [who take the course] [who Dana likes] usually come from local high schools.

(**44**) The book [that I like] [which everyone else in the class hates] was written by Joan Didion.

Notice that stacked relative clauses modify the same noun, *people* in (43) and *book* in (44). Notice, as well, that the sentences each involve only two relative clauses. Although there is probably no limit to the number of relative clauses that could be linked in this way, in general native speakers do not stack more than two relatives.

Omission of Nonsubject Relative Pronouns

In all types of clauses except S relative clauses, it is possible to delete the relative pronoun, with the relative clause thus beginning with the subject NP. Such clauses are sometimes said to have a "zero relative pronoun."

Deletion of the relative pronoun is possible in any O relative, for example, in (45a) to produce (45b).[24] Compare this example to (46), in which the relative pronoun is the clause subject.

(**45**) a. We just met that woman [*who/whom/that* Alan likes so much].
    b. We just met that woman [Alan likes so much].

(**46**) a. We just met that woman [*who/that* likes Alan so much].
    b. *We just met that woman [likes Alan so much].

Deletion is also possible with any OC relative, as in (47):

(**47**) a. The sports car *which/that* the Alfa Romeo was faster than won the Le Mans 24-hour race.
    b. The sports car the Alfa Romeo was faster than won the Le Mans 24-hour race.

In IO and OP relatives, reduction can occur only in the patterns that have the preposition stranded at the end of the clause, as (48) and (49) show with IO relatives.

(**48**) a. The student *who* the dean sent a message *to* is out of town.
    b. The student the dean sent a message *to* is out of town.

(**49**) a. The student *to whom* the dean sent a message is out of town.
    b. *The student to the dean sent a message is out of town.

Similarly, *of which* POS relatives with stranded prepositions can be reduced, as is illustrated by (50). However, POS relatives introduced by *whose* cannot be reduced, as (51) shows.

(**50**) a. The reports *which* the government prescribes the size *of* are boring.
    b. The reports the government prescribes the size *of* are boring.

(**51**) a. Last week I met a girl *whose* brother works in your law firm.
    b. *Last week I met a girl brother works in your law firm.

Reduction in Subject Relative Clauses

Although we have previously seen that the relative pronoun cannot be omitted in S relatives, in certain S relatives, it appears that the relative pronoun can be omitted if an additional change is made. We look first at some clear cases of such reduction and then at some possible cases.

Reduction in Clauses with *Be*

In S relative clauses, the relative pronoun and a form of *be* may be deleted when they are followed by:[25]

- a present participle, as in (52a).
- a past participle in a passive sentence, as in (53a).
- an adjective followed by a prepositional phrase, as in (54a), including past participial adjectives, as in (55a).[26]

These deletions produce postnominal modifiers like those shown in the (b) versions of (52) through (55).

(**52**) a. That man *who is standing over there* knows the Prime Minister.
   b. That man *standing over there* knows the Prime Minister.

(**53**) a. The bills *that were passed by the House yesterday* died in the Senate.
   b. The bills *passed by the House yesterday* died in the Senate.

(**54**) a. Senators *who are familiar with details of the proposal* believe that it has a good chance of passing.
   b. Senators *familiar with details of the proposal* believe that it has a good chance of passing.

(**55**) a. He is considered to be a prophet *who is descended from heaven*.
   b. He is considered to be a prophet *descended from heaven*.

Postnominal Modifiers with a Stative Verb in *-ing* Form

As we saw in Chapter 16, present participles of stative verbs (*cost, equal, measure, resemble, weigh*, etc.) do not normally appear in the progressive aspect. However, sequences beginning with the present participle form of stative verbs often appear after nouns, as in (56). These sequences appear to be reduced relative clauses like those previously discussed: their missing subject always corresponds to the head noun they modify, and they always have the same meaning as a relative clause with the same verb in a tensed form (e.g., [56] has the same meaning as *A woman who resembles your wife is sitting in front of me*).

(**56**) A woman *resembling your wife* is sitting in front of me.

Clearly, we would not want to say that *resembling your wife* in (56) arises from the application of the same reduction rule that produces the (b) versions in (52) through (55). If we did, we would be claiming that (56) is a reduced version of the ungrammatical sentence **A woman who is resembling your wife is sitting in front of me*. Nonetheless, as we've just seen, syntactic and semantic evidence seems to argue for such an analysis. There appear to be historical explanations for the development of these postnominal constructions with stative verbs, but we will not go into them here.[27]

SUMMARY

POSITION AND REDUCTION OF RESTRICTIVE RELATIVE CLAUSES

Extraposed relatives are relative clauses that have been moved away from the nouns they modify.
   A man just came in who has red hair.

Stacking of relative clauses regularly occurs in spoken English.
   The only person who I like whose kids Dana is willing to put up with is my neighbor Pat.

Omission of nonsubject relative pronouns is possible in all O and OC relatives and in IO, OP and *of which* POS relatives that have a stranded preposition.
   We just met the woman Alan likes so much.
   We know the student the dean sent the message to.

Reduction of S relatives occurs by deleting the relative pronoun and a following form of the verb *be*, leaving a present participle, a past participle, or an adjective followed by a prepositional phrase.

> *The guy standing next to Fred is a famous poet.*
> *The bill passed by Congress was vetoed.*
> *He's someone familiar with the details.*

Postnominal modifiers with stative verbs in present participle form might be a special type of reduced relative clause.

> *A shark weighing over 400 pounds washed up on the beach.*

EXERCISE 18.3

For each sentence, if omission of the relative pronoun or reduction of the clause is possible, show the resulting sentence. If neither is possible, state why.

Example: The woman who was very mysterious got up and left.

Answer: neither is possible (The relative pronoun is the subject of the relative clause.)

1. The rules that the committee must follow are set down in the constitution.
2. The guy who John was stronger than challenged him to an arm-wrestling contest.
3. The other day we ran into that girl who you lent your textbook to.
4. Alan finally came up with a good answer to that problem that was so tough to solve.
5. The person for whom he bought the ring is none other than your sister.
6. The paramedic treated several of the passengers who were injured in the accident.
7. The man who was the manager of the hotel gave us a nice room.

EXERCISE 18.4

Indicate whether each sentence can undergo relative clause extraposition. If it cannot, say why.

Example: The girl who loved me slapped the secretary.

Answer: no (Extraposition would move the relative clause after *the secretary*, and this would change the meaning of the sentence.)

1. A guy who was wearing the cap you reported stolen just walked in.
2. A dwarf who must have been about three feet tall kicked a giant.
3. Anyone who wants to come is welcome.
4. A woman who was pregnant left with her sister.
5. Mary met a soldier who she really likes at the party.
6. I met a man who says he knows you the other day.

OTHER TYPES OF RESTRICTIVE RELATIVE CLAUSES

There are grounds for recognizing other structures as restrictive relative clauses even though some of them, like the reduced clauses we looked at in the previous section, do not begin with relative pronouns. We will discuss these structures in this section.

Infinitival (Infin) Relative Clauses

The types of restrictive relative clauses considered earlier in the chapter all have verbs with tense. The sentences in (57) have what appear to be infinitive clauses (with verbs in infinitive forms) following and modifying a head noun. These are examples of *infinitival (INFIN) relative clauses*. Notice that the particular examples in (57) are similar to OP relatives; the head noun modified corresponds to a prepositional object in the infinitival relative clause.

(**57**) a. Here is a chair *to sit on*.
b. We need a sack *to carry the money in*.
c. John is not the right person *to confide in*.

Although the clauses in (57) do not have relative pronouns, they have versions that do have relative pronouns, shown in (58). In each case, the preposition and its object have been moved to the front of the infinitive clause by *wh-* movement, as illustrated in (58a). Thus, the versions in (57) can be considered INFIN relative clauses that have undergone relative pronoun deletion.

(**58**) a. Here is a chair [on which to sit _____].

b. We need a sack *in which to carry the money*.
c. John is not the right person *in whom to confide*.

Notice that a relative pronoun is possible only if the preposition moves to the front; we cannot add relative pronouns to the stranded versions in (57) (e.g., **Here is a chair which to sit on*).

The infinitival relative clauses in (59) are similar to O relatives; in each sentence in (59) the head noun corresponds to the object of the relative clause verb. The sentences in (59) also show that infinitival relative clauses can optionally have subjects, shown in parentheses, that follow *for*. Notice that the relative clauses in (57) can all have subjects, however, the versions with the fronted preposition and relative pronoun, as in (58), cannot. If there is no overt subject, the subject is interpreted as "people in general" or as corresponding to the appropriate noun in the main clause.

(**59**) a. I found something interesting (*for us/you*) *to read*.
b. That is not a very good way (*for you/him*) *to begin*.
c. A computer programmer wouldn't be such a bad thing (*for one/her*) *to be*.

There are also infinitive relative clauses similar to S relatives, as illustrated by (60), in which the clause subject corresponds to the noun the clause modifies, the first *person*. The sentence therefore has no alternative version with *for*, but the infinitive clause has an S relative clause paraphrase: *John is not the first person who (has) noticed that*.

(**60**) He is not the first person *to notice that*.

Adverbial (Adv) Relative Clauses

Nouns that denote a place, a time, or a purpose may be followed by OP relative clauses, as shown in (61).

(**61**) a. That's the gas station *at which* I'm working now.
b. How well I remember the day *on which* he was born.
c. I have forgotten the reason *for which* the trust fund was established.

The preposition + *which* combinations in (61a), (61b), and (61c) can be replaced by *where*, *when*, and *why*, as shown in (62a), (62b), and (62c). Since these three words have an adverbial function, grammarians often refer to the clauses they introduce as *adverbial (ADV) relative clauses.*

> (**62**) a. That's the gas station *where* I'm working now.
> b. How well I remember the day *when* he was born.
> c. I've forgotten the reason *why* the trust fund was established.

Some English language teaching textbooks explain the correspondence between sentences such as those in (61) and (62) by positing a *relative adverb substitution* rule, through which, in the appropriate contexts, preposition + *which* becomes *where*, *when*, or *why*.[28] However, along with adverbial relative clauses with *where*, *when*, and *why*, there are also clauses beginning with *how*, which can be seen as corresponding to OP relatives modifying the noun *way*. An attempt to derive these *how* adverbial clauses by applying the relative adverb substitution rule to an OP relative clause, such as the one in (63a), is problematic, because it would produce the ungrammatical sentence in (63b). In (62b) and (62c), *the day* and *the reason* may optionally be deleted. In contrast, with *how*, deletion of *the way* is obligatory. That is, we would have to apply an additional head noun deletion rule to (63b) to produce the grammatical sentence in (63c). (Alternatively, with *how* as with the other adverbials, we can omit the adverbial, yielding, e.g., *I remember the day he was born* or *I liked the way she expressed herself.*)

> (**63**) a. I liked the way *in which* she expressed herself.
> b. *I liked *the way how* she expressed herself.
> c. I liked *how* she expressed herself.

A further problem for this analysis of clauses with *how* is that changing *in which* to *how* is possible only with a very limited number of head nouns, all of which have the same general meaning, such as *way* and *manner*. In contrast, an entire range of nouns can precede *when* or *where* clauses. For this and other reasons, clauses like the one in (63c) are generally not considered to be adverbial relative clauses.[29]

Free Relative Clauses

Free relative clauses (also called *nominal relative clauses*) stand alone, rather than following and modifying a head noun. There are two types of free relative clauses.

Definite Free Relative Clauses

The first type of free relative clause, the *definite free relative clause*,[30] is introduced by a *wh-* word such as *what*, *where*, or *when*, as shown in (64).

> (**64**) Mark eats *what he orders.*

Several tests enable us to distinguish definite free relatives from other structures beginning with *wh-* words. One such test is that verbs that are followed by definite free relatives beginning with *what* must be capable of being followed by nonhuman NPs. *What Jim chose* in (65a), a free relative, passes this test, as shown by (65b).

> (**65**) a. Sally ordered *what Jim chose.*
> b. Sally ordered *a hamburger/coffee/a piece of pie.*

Another test for definite free relatives is substituting *that* (*thing*) *which* for *what*, as shown in (66).

(**66**) Sally ordered *that* (*thing*) *which Jim chose.*

Definite free relatives beginning with *where* must be replaceable with a locative phrase like that in (67b). Definite free relatives beginning with *when* must be replaceable with a time phrase like that in (67d).

(**67**) a. Mick Jagger stayed *where Carly Simon had wanted to stay.*
b. Mick Jagger stayed *at the Ritz Hotel/in Paris.*
c. The president applauded *when Emanuel Axe stopped playing the piano.*
d. The president applauded *then/at that time.*

Indefinite Free Relative Clauses

The second type of free relative clause is an *indefinite free relative clause*, also called a *conditional free relative clause* because the words that introduce the clause (*who*(*m*) *ever, whatever, whichever, whenever, wherever,* and *however*) can be paraphrased with *if,* as shown by (68a) and (68b), or *regardless of,* as shown by (68c) and (68d).[31]

(**68**) a. Joan dances with *whoever asks her to dance.*
b. *If someone asks Joan to dance with him,* she dances with him.
c. Fred eats *whatever Alice offers him.*
d. *Regardless of what Alice offers Fred,* he eats it.

SUMMARY

OTHER TYPES OF RESTRICTIVE RELATIVE CLAUSES

Infinitival (INFIN) relative clauses have a verb in its infinitive form and are not always introduced by relative pronouns.
Here is a chair to sit on.   OR   *Here is a chair on which to sit.*
Susan is the ideal person (for you) to talk to about that.

Adverbial (ADV) relative clauses are introduced by *where, when,* and *why,* rather than by relative pronouns.
That's the motel where we stayed.
How well I remember the day when he was born.
I've forgotten the reason why the trust fund was established.

Free relative clauses stand alone rather than following and modifying a head noun. There are two types:

• **Definite free relatives** are introduced by *what, where,* and *when.*
He eats what he orders.
Alice goes where she wants to go.
They applauded when he stopped playing.

• **Indefinite free relatives** introduced by *who*(*m*)*ever, whichever, whatever, wherever,* and *whenever.*
He eats whatever she offers him.
Joan dances with whoever asks her to dance.

EXERCISE 18.5

In each sentence, change the infinitival relative clause into an alternative form.

Example: I am looking for an essay question with which to challenge the students.

Answer: I am looking for an essay question to challenge the students with.

1. That's not the best area to build a house in.
2. We need a freezer in which to put the ice cream.
3. That is a good place for you to begin your trip from.
4. I found a great video for us to watch on Saturday.
5. They cleared some space in which to spread out their papers.

EXERCISE 18.6

In each sentence identify each relative clause as an adverbial relative clause, a definite free relative clause, or an indefinite free relative clause.

Example: The reason why the law was originally proposed is not entirely clear.

Answer: adverbial relative clause

1. That's the restaurant where I met her.
2. The king can sit wherever he wants to sit.
3. Fred is buying what Jane bought.
4. They always stay where we stay.
5. Alan buys whatever he wants to buy.

NONRESTRICTIVE RELATIVE CLAUSES

Thus far we have focused on restrictive clauses, which, indeed, account for a majority of relative clauses and for much of the variety in relative clause form. Now we turn to the other major type of relative clause, nonrestrictive relative clauses. As discussed at the beginning of the chapter, *nonrestrictive relative clauses* add information about the noun modified rather than identifying the noun as restrictive relative clauses do.

Form Criteria Distinguishing Nonrestrictive and Restrictive Relative Clauses

Several form criteria distinguish nonrestrictive relative clauses from their restrictive counterparts. Beginning with the two best-known criteria, these may be listed as follows:

- **Punctuation.** Nonrestrictive relative clauses have commas around them, as in (69a). Restrictive relative clauses must not be separated by commas, as shown in (69b).

    (69) a. My sister, who lives in Canada, is a biologist.
         b. My sister who lives in Canada is a biologist.

- **Intonation.** As mentioned earlier, nonrestrictive relative clauses are marked by pauses and by a falling intonation pattern at the end of the clause, as shown in (70a). Restrictive relative clauses, as in (70b), do not have this special intonation pattern.

    nonrestrictive clause intonation pattern

    (70) a. The students, *who had to take final exams today*, are tired.

    restrictive clause intonation pattern

    b. The students who had to take final exams today are tired.

- **Modification of proper nouns.** Nonrestrictive relative clauses can modify proper nouns, as in (71a); restrictive relatives, as in (71b), cannot.

    (71) a. John, who is a linguist, was not impressed by Professor Fish's arguments.
    b. *John who is a linguist was not impressed by Professor Fish's arguments.

- **Modification of *any, every, no,* etc.** Nonrestrictive relative clauses may not modify *any, every,* or *no* + noun or indefinite pronouns such as *anyone, everyone,* or *no one,* as shown by (72a); restrictive relatives may, as shown in (72b).

    (72) a. *Any man, who goes back on his word, is no friend of mine.
    b. Any man who goes back on his word is no friend of mine.

- ***That* as relative pronoun.** Nonrestrictive relative clauses may not be introduced by *that,* as shown by (73a); restrictive relatives may, as in (73b).

    (73) a. *The plan, that we discussed yesterday, will be adopted.
    b. The plan that we discussed yesterday will be adopted.

- **Stacking.** Nonrestrictive relative clauses cannot be stacked. Stacking results in ungrammatical sentences like (74a). Restrictive relatives can be stacked, as in (74b).

    (74) a. *They gave the job to Rob, who is very qualified, who starts next month.
    b. I really like that car that you have that your wife is always zipping around town in.

- **Sentence modification.** Nonrestrictive relative clauses may modify an entire sentence, that is, a preceding independent clause, as in (75a). Restrictive relatives like (75b) may only modify noun phrases.

    (75) a. Professor Fish gave everyone an A, which was just fine with Alice.
    b. *Professor Fish gave everyone an A which was just fine with Alice.

Relative Pronouns in Nonrestrictive Relative Clauses

With the exception of the restriction on the use of *that,* nonrestrictive relative clauses have the same relative pronouns that occur in restrictive relatives. It is quite common for several words, such as a quantifier + *of,* to precede the relative pronoun of center-embedded nonrestrictive relatives, as shown in (76). This fact supports our earlier observation that relative clauses with many words preceding the relative pronoun will usually be viewed as nonrestrictive.

    (76) a. The boys, *some of whom* were not more than 10 years old, stood silently in a long line.
    b. The planes, *a few of which* seemed to be too old and rickety to fly, were parked on the side of the runway.

In nonrestrictive relative clauses, reductions by deleting a relative pronoun, possible in restrictive clauses, are generally not possible. Deletion of the relative pronoun results in the ungrammatical sentence shown in (77b). Reducing the nonrestrictive relative clause in (78a) by deleting *who* + *was* results in the participial clause in (78b). However, for most native speakers, this is no longer a relative clause, rather it is an adverbial clause that has the meaning: *John's lawyer, while he was packing his suitcase, heard the telephone ring.* These reduced participial clauses are discussed in Chapter 23.

(77) a. The thief, *who(m)* they finally managed to apprehend, was so frightened that he could hardly speak.
   b. *The thief, they finally managed to apprehend, was so frightened that he could hardly speak.

(78) a. John's lawyer, *who was packing his suitcase*, heard the telephone ring.
   b. John's lawyer, *packing his suitcase*, heard the telephone ring.

SUMMARY

NONRESTRICTIVE RELATIVE CLAUSES

Nonrestrictive relative clauses are relative clauses that merely add information about the nouns they modify.

The following characteristics distinguish nonrestrictive relative clauses:

- In writing, they are set off by commas.
  My sister, who lives in Canada, is a biologist.

- In speech, they are set off by pauses and falling intonation at the end of the clause.
  My sister, who lives in Canada, is a biologist.

- They can modify proper nouns.
  John, who is a lawyer, was not impressed by Professor Fish's arguments.

- They cannot modify *any, every, no* + noun or indefinite pronouns such as *anyone, everyone, no one*, etc.
  *Any man, who goes back on his word, is no friend of mine.

- They cannot be introduced by *that*.
  *The plan, that we discussed yesterday, will be adopted.

- They cannot be stacked.
  *They gave the job to Rob, who is very qualified, who starts next month.

- They can modify an entire sentence.
  Susan is afraid of dogs, which doesn't surprise me at all.

The relative pronouns used in nonrestrictive relatives are the same as those used in restrictive relatives, except for *that*.
  *The plan, that we discussed yesterday, will be adopted.

Reduction is not possible in nonrestrictive relative clauses.
  *The thief, they finally managed to apprehend, was terrified.

EXERCISE 18.7

Indicate whether each of the sentences below is grammatical or ungrammatical. If a sentence is ungrammatical, explain why.

Example: The car, that was parked in my parking space, belongs to Joy.

Answer: ungrammatical (Nonrestrictive relative clauses can't be introduced by *that*.)

1. The men at the shop, two of whom John knew, were very helpful.
2. Any man, who loves children and dogs, would make a good husband.
3. Susan who knows a lot about modern art thought the painting was a fake.
4. He finally agreed to come on the trip with us which made everyone very happy.
5. The authors, whose books have sold well, who I like, are few and far between.

PROBLEMS THAT ESL/EFL STUDENTS HAVE WITH RELATIVE CLAUSES

Relative clauses in the L1s of many students differ from English relative clauses in a number of ways. These differences may influence students' attempts at producing English relative clauses. The following are well-attested examples of relative clause errors made by ESL students with different L1s.

Resumptive Pronouns (Farsi, Arabic, Turkish)

Languages such as Farsi, Arabic, and Turkish have a single subordinator that marks the beginning of the relative clause. The grammatical function of the relative clause is indicated by a resumptive pronoun within the clause, not by a relative pronoun as in English. This is illustrated in an example from Farsi in (79), in which the relative clause is introduced by a subordinate clause marker, *ke*. The object pronoun *eš*, which means "him/her/it," marks the direct object in this O relative.

(**79**) *maerdi   ke   diruz   did   im   eš   pedar   aem   e.*
    man   yesterday   saw   we   him   father   my   is
    "The man who we saw yesterday is my father."

A persistent transfer error made by native speakers of these languages (Gass, 1979, 1984; Hyltenstam, 1984; Khalil, 1985) is the production of corresponding resumptive pronouns in English relative clauses. The examples in (80) were produced by Arabic-speaking university students recorded by Khalil (1985). In (80a), we have a subject resumptive pronoun, and in (80b), we have an object resumptive pronoun.

(**80**) a. *I've learned that I shouldn't do things that *they* hurt them.
    b. I learned many things at the university. *The first was scientific knowledge which I got *it* from the courses.

Although these errors have been claimed for students with other L1s, they seem to be particularly persistent in the speech and writing of speakers of these typologically similar languages. This persistence suggests that some pedagogical intervention to raise these students' consciousness about them is warranted.

Forms Introducing Adverbial Relative Clauses (Japanese)

An error corpus assembled by Miura (1989) reveals that Japanese high school students use *which* in English adverbial relative clauses instead of preposition + *which* combinations (e.g., *in which*, *on which*) or their corresponding relative adverbs *when* and *where*, as shown in (81).

(81) a. *The day which we arrived was a holiday.
     b. *This is the house which Shakespeare was born.
     c. *June is the month which it often rains in Japan.

Two factors appear to conspire to create these errors.[32] The first is that Japanese does not have any relative pronouns. As a result, Japanese speakers may have trouble distinguishing relative adverbs *when* and *where* from relative pronouns. The second factor is that *particle ellipsis* (deletion) occurs in Japanese relative clauses. Japanese has particles that indicate the grammatical functions of nouns. For example, the locative particle *ni* follows the noun *kooen* in the sentence in (82). Here it marks the goal and would be represented in English by the preposition *to*.

(82) *Mary-ga   kooen-ni   itta.*
     Mary (nom)   park (loc) went
     "Mary went to the park."

This particle is omitted in sentences with relative clauses, as shown by (83), in which the relative clause is in brackets. (In Japanese, relative clauses precede the noun they modify.)

(83) [*Mary-ga   itta*]   *kooen.*
     Mary (nom)   went   park
     "the park to which Mary went"

Japanese speakers who carry over their L1 tendency for ellipsis when producing English adverbial relative clauses may produce the errors shown in (81). Since this error was found in the work of high school students, it is possible that the error will eventually disappear as students receive more input.

Omission of Relative Pronouns in S Clauses (Chinese)

Schachter and Rutherford (1979) found a surprisingly high number of errors like those shown in (84) in the compositions of Chinese speakers enrolled in English classes at the University of Southern California. Moreover, Bunton (1989) states that such errors are common in Hong Kong English.

(84) a. *There are many people in Hong Kong want to emigrate.
     b. *There are episodes in fiction tell the readers about the discussion.
     c. *There are many people like syntax.

Note that in each case the sentence begins with nonreferential *there is/are* and the error is an omitted relative pronoun in an S relative clause modifying the noun following *be*. Thus, for example, for (84a) we would need to add *who* after *many people in Hong Kong* to produce the grammatical *There are many people in Hong Kong who want to emigrate.*

Yip (1995) points out that Chinese uses the verb *you* ("exist") and a following indefinite NP to express the equivalent of English *there is/are* + indefinite NP sentences, as shown in (85).

	V		*NP*		*V*	*NP*
(85)	*you*	[*hen*	*duo*	*ren*]	*xihuan*	*yufa*
	exist	very	many	people	like	syntax

An equivalent of (85) in English could be a sentence with *there are* + the indefinite *many people* and a following relative clause – that is, *There are many people who like syntax*. Chinese speakers apparently follow the L1 pattern when forming sentences with *there is/are*, and the result is ungrammatical sentences like those in (84). This appears to be a persistent error that deserves pedagogical attention.

Gisborne (2000) notes that a common error in the Hong Kong database of the International Corpus of English is the omission of relative pronouns in subject relative clauses, as shown in (86).

(**86**) a. *This is the student did it.
b. *Hong Kong is a small island has a large population.

The source of this error is not absolutely clear, but Newbrook (1998) confirms that it occurs with high frequency in the written English of Hong Kong ESL students.

SUGGESTIONS FOR TEACHING RELATIVE CLAUSES

Relative clauses, sometimes called "adjective clauses" in English language teaching text-books,[33] are usually introduced after students have attained a beginning level of proficiency. Although they are practiced orally, relative clauses take on a greater significance for writing with upper-intermediate and advanced students. Hence, they are usually part of the grammar included in intermediate- and advanced-level composition textbooks. Textbook discussions of relative clauses often fail to treat infinitival and free relatives or to cover the formation of complex POS relative clauses like those in (23) through (33). Some grammar textbook series contain editing exercises in which students read a passage and find and correct errors in relative clauses. Unfortunately, often, many of the errors in these passages are not the types of errors students actually make. Teachers of students whose native languages are implicated in the errors discussed previously should consider developing focus-on-form activities to help students eliminate the errors. Here are some activities that may be useful for practicing spoken and written relative clauses.

Activity 1: Practicing Restrictive Relative Clauses (Intermediate)
In this favorite activity, students will use relative clauses to describe pictures taken from magazines or other sources. Collect pictures of famous people (film or sports stars, politicians, etc.) and/or famous places (buildings, structures, etc.) that are familiar to students. You will need at least eight pictures per group of six students. Review how relative clauses are formed. Then divide each group of six in half. Give each subgroup half of the pictures. The students in one subgroup describe one of their pictures with a sentence that includes a relative clause (e.g., "This is a picture of a building that is in Paris"), and the students in the other subgroup try to guess who or what is depicted in the picture.

To practice adverbial relative clauses, give pairs of students a list of offices and organizations that they are familiar with. One student asks what an office or organization is (e.g., "What is the motor vehicle bureau?"), and the other student answers using an adverbial relative clause (e.g., "The motor vehicle bureau is a place where you go to get a driver's license").

Activity 2: Sentence Combining Plus (High Intermediate)
Enginarlar (1994) recommends an activity called "sentence combining plus" for practicing writing paragraphs that have sentences with relative clauses. Select a text that is at

least a paragraph long and that is developed around a central idea. Expository or narrative texts are best, since they have clear organization and coherence. Write all the simple sentences in the text on one piece of paper. Then take all of the complex sentences and break each of them down into simple sentences. Write these simple sentences on another piece of paper. You will have two sets of sentences, on two separate pieces of paper. Divide the students up into groups of three or four. Conduct the activity in the following stages.

Stage 1

Give each group the two sets of sentences. Indicate the paper with sentences that were originally simple, and tell the students to put it aside for later use. Tell students to combine the sentences on the second paper (those that were formerly complex) into one or more complex sentences. Tell them that they may delete words and replace nouns with relative pronouns. Remind them of specific relative clause structures that could help them combine the sentences.

Stage 2

Ask the students to make a meaningful text by integrating the complex sentences that they have formed with the simple sentences that they had set aside.

Stage 3

Ask one or two groups to read their completed texts, or go through the text, sentence by sentence, as a class. When the order of the text has been agreed upon, you can go over the possible alternatives for the complex sentences. Conclude the activity by distributing a copy of the original text to the class.

Activity 3: Addressing the Resumptive Pronoun Problem (Intermediate)

To tackle the resumptive pronoun problem that speakers of languages such as Farsi, Arabic, and Turkish have when forming English relative clauses, you might try a processing instruction approach. First, highlight the problem in forming English relatives and caution the students against inserting a resumptive pronoun as they would in their native languages. Next present them with a picture description task. You will need to prepare a number of appropriate erroneous sentences to alternate with grammatical sentences. To begin, show students, for example, a picture of a boy talking to a girl in a red sweater. Then say, "I am going to describe this picture: the girl who the boy is talking to her is wearing a red sweater." Ask, "Is that okay?" Don't supply the correct answer when a student does not recognize a sentence as ungrammatical. Let students debate any disagreements. Help them only by referring back to your original explanation of the problem. (This technique can also be used to tackle the problems that Japanese students have forming adverbial relative clauses.)

Activity 4: Addressing Relative Pronoun Omission (High Intermediate)

This writing activity focuses on the problem discussed earlier that Chinese speakers often have. To prepare for the activity, collect examples of relative pronoun omission errors from your students' compositions. Write a paragraph containing several errors like those you have collected. On the board or with an overhead projector, show an example or two of the errors and explain why students are making the errors. Then hand out the paragraph you have created and tell your students that it was written by a fellow Chinese student who has asked a friend to help proofread the paragraph before the student hands it in. Say, "Let's see if we can help this student. Can you spot any errors like the ones we just looked at?" These errors can also be effectively addressed by CALL programs such as the ESL Tutor described in Cowan, Choi, and Kim (2003).

Activity 5: Reduction of Restrictive Relatives (Intermediate)

This simple but enjoyable activity uses "Droodles," a type of drawing conceived in the 1950's by Roger Price, a humorist and publisher.[34] The activity was devised by Bill Rutherford, a consistent contributor to the teaching of English and second language learning, to practice the production of reduced relative clauses. Students look at the pictures shown below either on a handout or on a transparency projected with an overhead projector. Explain to students that the object of the activity is to describe what they think each droodle illustrates, using the relative clause structure that they have covered. Pointing to the first picture, for example, say, "I'll show you what I mean. This first picture looks like a mother pyramid feeding its baby, but if you look closely you can see that it could also be a ship arriving too late to save a drowning witch."[35] Then encourage your students to offer their guesses about what the other droodles might represent. If they give an answer that works but doesn't contain a reduced clause, say, "That's good. Now how can we say that using the structure we have been practicing?" You could follow this activity up with the homework assignment of drawing some droodles to bring in and share with the class. Emphasize that every droodle must depict something that can be expressed in a reduced relative clause structure.

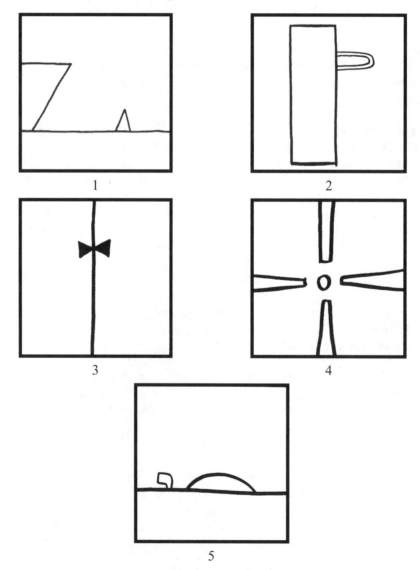

Possible descriptions for the pictures
2. A man playing a trombone in a telephone booth.
3. A butterfly sitting on a high tension wire, or a man wearing a bow tie who stood too close to the elevator doors.
4. Four elephants inspecting a grapefruit or four hunters with large guns waiting for a rabbit to come out of his hole.
5. A submarine cruising the ocean at sundown or a fat man lying on a soft bed smoking a pipe.

Activity 6: Introducing and Practicing Nonrestrictive Relative Clauses (Intermediate)

A popular activity for introducing nonrestrictive relative clauses is a geography game. Ask one of the students in your class where he comes from. If the student says, for example, "the Philippines," ask him to state, in simple sentences, some facts about the Philippines. Write down the short sentences that the student supplies on the board – for example, "It is an English-speaking country," "It has many islands," "It produces a lot of coffee," "It is always hot." (You can help the student by asking questions like "What is the chief agricultural product?") Now ask, "How can we combine these first two sentences into a sentence beginning with 'The Philippines'?" Give an example: "The Philippines, which is an English-speaking country, has many islands." Point out that the information within the commas is "extra" information and can be changed. Show this by creating another sentence with a different nonrestrictive relative selected from the sentences on the board – for example, "The Philippines, which produces a lot of coffee, has many islands." Repeat the process with another student. Then have the students work in groups of four to six to ask similar questions of each other and to use the responses to form sentences with nonrestrictive relative clauses.[36]

Activity 7: Forming Complex Nonrestrictive Relative Clauses (Advanced)

This activity is designed to practice forming sentences with complex nonrestrictive relatives in which the relative pronoun is preceded by a number or a quantifier such as *a few*, *both*, *many*, *none*, or *some*. Prepare beforehand three or four suitable pictures to show to the class. Show, for example, a picture of four people sitting on a beach, three of them smiling and one who looks sad. Show students how to construct a sentence that uses an appropriate nonrestrictive relative in describing the picture, for example, *These people, three of whom are happy, are all sitting on the beach*. Show the other pictures and ask students to form similar sentences. Then move to the following TBLT activity.

Tell the students to download some advertisements for cars from the Internet. Working as a class, they should find ads for three or four roughly comparable models of different makes of cars, for example, a four-door model of a Toyota, Honda, Chrysler, and BMW. They should then make a list of various features that some or all of these cars have (e.g., an engine with more than 200 hp, antilock brakes, dual front and side door airbags, power windows, sunroof, a certain gas mileage). Then, working in small groups, students use the lists to write about the cars in sentences with complex nonrestrictive relatives such as those in (87).

(87) a. These four cars, *three of which have engines with at least 200 horse power*, get from 18 to 22 miles to the gallon.
   b. The Toyota and the Honda, *both of which have sun roofs*, cost under $28,000.

Using the facts in the list, each group tries to write more sentences than the other groups and to come up with a judgment as to which car gives you more for your money. Some other commodity conducive to the activity could be used instead of cars.

ENDNOTES

[1] See Radford (1998) pp. 484–492, for an alternate treatment of *wh- movement*.

[2] Biber et al. (1999), p. 610.

[3] See Keenan and Comrie (1977) for the different types of relative clauses found in many languages.

[4] The relative clauses in (11) and (12) are examples of center-embedded relatives. Like any relative clause, S relative clauses can occur at the end of a main clause (e.g., *Yesterday we met the girl* [*who John married*]).

[5] Biber et al. (1999) show *whom* as virtually absent in conversation and barely used in most forms of written English. See charts on pp. 610 and 611 and examples and discussion on pp. 614 and 615.

[6] This sentence is attributed to Winston Churchill who was making a joke about a prescriptive grammar rule that prohibited the use of preposition stranding because it was "bad style."

[7] This is often referred to by the abbreviation GEN, for *genitive*.

[8] Biber et al. (1999), p. 617.

[9] Quirk et al. (1972), p. 863.

[10] The movement of other constituents along with the relative pronoun in an NP or a PP is called "Pied Piping." It is discussed in detail by Ross (1967).

[11] Cowan, Edwards, and McCune (2001).

[12] This fact has also been noted by Biber et al. (1999), p. 602.

[13] The Longman corpus indicates that *of which* appears far less frequently than *whose*, but it occurs almost as frequently in academic prose (Biber et al., 1999, p. 618).

[14] These examples are due to Ross (1967). Cowan, Edwards, and McCune (2001) hypothesize that, as more words intervene between the relative pronoun and the NP that it refers to, the likelihood increases that the clause will be viewed as nonrestrictive.

[15] Biber et al. (1999).

[16] This example is from Biber et al. (1999), p. 609. The other is modeled on Radford (1988), p. 522.

[17] This example is from Biber et al. (1999), p. 622.

[18] These examples are from McCawley (1988), p. 444.

[19] This hypothesis was first proposed by Kroch (1981).

[20] This position is taken by Biber et al. (1999), section 14.2, who view these clauses as "disfluencies" that are due to the complexity of complex sentence production. This position is implicit in Kroch's explanation.

[21] Sentences such as (36) are not easily explained by Kroch's and Biber's hypothesis, since, as McCawley (1988), p. 444, points out, they would be grammatical without the resumptive pronoun. Perhaps resumptive pronouns are increasing in the speech of native speakers.

[22] The rule of extraposition will be explained in greater detail in Chapter 21.

[23] Kiss (2003). Relative clause extraposition occurs in other languages, for example, German. See also Kathol & Pollard (2000).

[24] This rule has been called *wh- deletion*.

[25] This reduction rule has been called *wh-is deletion*.

[26] Sag (1997) also proposes that prepositional phrases like the one shown in (1b) should be derived from *wh-is deletion* on sentences like (1a).

(1) a. The voters *who were in Rome* were opposed to the plan.

   b. The voters *in Rome* were opposed to the plan.

[27] A historical description of the development of the *-ing* ending attached to verbs is found in Scheffer (1975).

[28] For example, Celce-Murcia and Larsen-Freeman (1999), p. 598.

[29] Quirk et al. (1972), McCawley (1988), and others have pointed to this argument for rejecting *how* as a relative clause introducer.

[30] The term, argument, and examples (64) and (65) are from Baker (1995).

[31] For further discussion of conditional free relatives, see McCawley (1988), pp. 354–356; Baker (1995), pp. 210–212; and Grosu (2002), pp. 6–9.

[32] I am indebted to Teruake Muto for this observation.

[33] ESL/EFL textbook authors who adopt this practice justify this as being more "descriptive," i.e., more indicative of the function of relative clauses. They usually label restrictive and nonrestrictive clauses as "defining" and "nondefining" adjective clauses. See, for example, Master (1996).

[34] Visit www.Tallfellow.com for more information.

[35] Some students may not comprehend the second description of this particular picture because they are not familiar with the stereotypical image in American culture of witches wearing pointed hats.

[36] This activity was designed by Ben Wiley.

REFERENCES

Baker, C. L. (1995). *English syntax*. 2nd ed. Cambridge, MA: MIT Press.

Biber, D., Johansson, S., Leech, G., Conrad, S., & Finegan, E. 1999. *Longman grammar of spoken and written English*. Essex: Pearson Education Limited.

Bunton, D. (1979). *Common English errors in Hong Kong*. London: Longman.

Celce-Murcia, M., & Larsen-Freeman, D. (1999). *The grammar book: An ESL/EFL teacher's course*. 2nd ed. Heinle & Heinle.

Cowan, R., Edwards, C., & McCune E. (2001). The disappearance of "of which" relatives: Positing a psycholinguistic basis for synchronic change. Paper presented at the *Annual Conference of the American Association of Applied Linguistics*, St. Louis, MO. March, 2000.

Cowan, R., Choi, H-Y., & Kim, D-Y. (2003). Four questions for error diagnosis and correction in CALL, *CALICO Journal*, *20*(3), 451–463.

Enginarlar, H. (1994). Sentence combining plus: A new use for an old technique. *ELT Journal*, *48*(3), 214–224.

Gass, S. (1979). Language transfer and universal grammatical relations. *Language Learning*, *29*, 327–347.

Gass, S. (1984). A review of interlanguage syntax: Language transfer and language universals. *Language Learning*, *34*, 115–132.

Gisborne, N. (2000). Relative clauses in Hong Kong English. *World Englishes*, *19*(3), 357–370.

Grosu, A. (2002). Strange relatives at the interface of two millennnia. State-of-the-Article, *GLOT International* 6, (6), 145–167.

Hyltenstam, K. (1984). The use of typological markedness conditions as predictors in second language acquisition: The case of pronominal copies in relative clauses. In R. Anderson (Ed.), *Second language: A cross-linguistic perspective* (pp. 39–45). Rowley, MA: Newbury House.

Kathol, A., & Pollard, C. (2000). Extraposition via complex domain formation. Ohio State University.

Keenan, E., & Comrie, E. (1977). Noun phrase accessibility and universal grammar. *Linguistic Inquiry 8*, 63–77.

Khalil A. (1985) Communicative error evaluation: Native speaker evaluation and interpretation of written errors of Arab EFL learners. *TESOL Quarterly*, *19*(2), 335–351.

Kiss, T. (2003). Phrasal typology and the interaction of topicalization, *wh*-movement, and extraposition. In J. B. Kim & S. Wechsler (Eds.), *Proceedings of the 9th international conference on head-driven phrase structure grammar. CSLI Online Proceedings, pp. 235-246, Stanford CSLI Publications.*

Kroch, A. (1981). On the role of resumptive pronouns in amnestying island constraint violations. *CLS 17*, 125–135.

Master, P. (1996). *Systems in English grammar: An introduction for language teachers.* Englewood Cliffs, NJ: Prentice Hall.

McCawley, J. D. (1988). *The syntactic phenomena of English.* Chicago and London: The University of Chicago Press.

Miura, S. (1989). Hiroshima English Learners Corpus. Department of English Education, Hiroshima University.

Newbrook, M. (1998). Which way? That way? Variation and on-going change in English relative clauses. *World Englishes*, *17*, 43–59.

Quirk, R., Greenbaum, S., Leech, G., & Svartvik, J. (1972). *A grammar of contemporary English.* New York/London: Seminary Press.

Radford, A. (1988). *Transformational grammar: A first course.* Cambridge: Cambridge University Press.

Ross, J. R. (1967). Constraints on variables in syntax. Ph.D. Thesis, MIT. Published in *Infinite syntax!* Hillsdale, NJ: Earlbaum.

Rutherford, W. (1974). Pragmatic syntax in the classroom. *TESOL Quarterly*, *8*(2), 177– 184.

Sag, I. A. (1997) English relative clause constructions. *Journal of Linguistics*, *33*, 431–483.

Schachter, J., & Rutherford, W. (1979). Discourse function and language transfer. *Working Papers in Bilingualism*, *19*, 1–12.

Scheffer, M. (1975). *The progressive in English.* Amsterdam/New York: Elsevier.

Yip, V. (1995). *Interlanguage and learnability: From Chinese to English.* Amsterdam/Philadelphia: John Benjamins.

CHAPTER 19

Conditional Sentences

INTRODUCTION

In this chapter, we will look at *conditional sentences*, sentences that express a condition and the result of the condition. We will utilize a system that has proved useful for classifying conditional sentences in English.[1] All languages have something like conditional sentences, but these do not correspond exactly to English conditionals. We will examine why many English language learners have difficulty producing some kinds of conditional sentences.

THE FORM OF CONDITIONALS

The most common type of *conditional sentence* has two clauses, a main clause and a subordinate clause that begins with *if* or a similar word. The *if clause* contains a proposition known as the condition, and the *result clause* contains a proposition stating what happens if the condition is fulfilled.[2] The conditional sentence has the meaning "If *x* occurs, then *y* occurs." A typical example is shown in (1).

                 Condition   *Result*
(**1**) a. [If John leaves now], [he will arrive at the airport in time to make his flight.]

In spoken English, there is no preference for one clause or the other in initial position, but in written English there is a slight tendency for *if* clauses to occur first. Alternatives to *if* include *provided* (*that*), *as long as*, and *assuming* (*that*), as illustrated in (2). (For convenience, we use "*if* clause" even when the clause has an alternative to *if.*)

(**2**) a. *As long as* John leaves now, he will arrive at the airport in time to make his flight.
    b. John will arrive at the airport in time to make his flight *provided that* he leaves now.

Conditional sentences refer to present, past, and future time. The contingencies they express divide them into two major categories – *real*[3] and *unreal* conditionals. We look at each in turn.

REAL CONDITIONALS

Real conditionals are conditionals in which the condition, and hence the result, can be fulfilled. Real conditionals describe condition–result relationships that always or frequently obtain (*generic* and *habitual conditionals*); conclusions or implications that can be drawn if a condition in the *if* clause is fulfilled (*inference conditionals*); and the probability of something happening in the future (*future conditionals*). The boundaries between these subtypes of conditionals can be blurry; in certain cases, context may determine whether a sentence belongs to one or another subtype. Nonetheless, the subtypes give us a way of understanding the meanings and functions of conditional sentences and the uses of modals and tense-aspect combinations within them.

Generic Conditionals

Generic conditionals express a fact that appears to be a scientific truth. They are used primarily in academic prose, as illustrated in (3) through (6). The *if* clause of generic conditionals specifies general conditions under which the phenomena described in the result clause will occur or hold.

(**3**) The monitor *does not function* if the contact strip *is* not moist.

(**4**) If a gas *is* heated, it *expands*.

(**5**) If the temperature *falls* below 32 degrees Fahrenheit, water *freezes*.

(**6**) If light *is moving* in the direction labeled *z* in the figure, it *has* two distinct possibilities of polarization.[4]

Although the verbs in both clauses are usually in the simple present tense, as shown in (3) and (4), this is not a hard-and-fast rule. For example, in (6) the verb in the *if* clause is in the present progressive tense, while the verb in the result clause is in the simple present. The modal *will* can also occur in the result clause; hence, (3) could be recast as *The monitor will not function if the contact strip is not moist.*

Habitual Conditionals

Habitual conditionals express situations or events, in the present or past, as being the usual but not inevitable result of a condition being met, as illustrated in (7) and (8), respectively.

(**7**) If she *is* his bridge partner, they (usually) *lose* big.

(**8**) If he *had* business in Baltimore, he (usually) *stayed* at the Hyatt.

The simple present tense occurs in both clauses in habitual conditionals that describe present situations, as in (7). However, a habitual conditional that describes a past situation may have the simple past tense in both clauses, as in (8), or, alternatively, the past tense in the *if* clause and the modal *would* followed by the bare infinitive in the result clause, as shown in (9).

(**9**) If he *had* business in Baltimore, he *would* (usually) stay at the Hyatt.

Habitual conditionals have a paraphrase with *whenever*, as shown in (10). This is because habitual conditionals express conditions and results that occur repeatedly.

(**10**) a. *Whenever* she is his bridge partner, they (usually) lose big.
　　　b. *Whenever* he had business in Baltimore, he would (always) stay at the Hyatt.

Habitual conditionals can also be used to describe a policy that has been established. In (11), a teacher is explaining a school policy about plagiarism. In this use, the result clause can appear in the present tense, as in both sentences in (11), or with the modal *will*.

> (**11**) If a new student is caught plagiarizing, he or she gets a warning and some instruction about why this is not acceptable. If one of our current students plagiarizes, he or she comes up before a disciplinary board.

Inference Conditionals

In *inference conditionals*, the proposition in the result clause is inferred from the proposition in the *if* clause. That is, inference conditionals say "If *x*, then *y* follows." Of course, *x* may or may not be true (i.e., as with other conditionals, it may or may not be fulfilled), but if *x* is true, the speaker is saying, then so is *y*, since it can be reasonably inferred from *x*. Inference conditionals can be about the present or the past. Moreover, the result clause can be stated as being, in the event the condition is true, a certainty or merely a possibility, with different degrees of likelihood. Thus, inference conditionals have more possibilities for modals and tense-aspect combinations than do generic or habitual conditionals. As an example of an inference conditional, consider (12).

> (**12**) If we *can save* the bald eagle from extinction, we *can* certainly *ensure* the survival of other endangered species.

The speaker in (12) infers our ability to save other species from our ability to save the bald eagle. We may or may not have the ability to save the bald eagle, but if we do have the ability to save the bald eagle, then we have the ability to save other species. Notice that in this inference conditional both clauses contain the ability modal *can*.

In (13), the inference conditional is about a past situation. The speaker is inferring Jane and Bill's quick trip home from the condition of their having left before rush hour. The speaker is saying that if the condition was fulfilled, the result followed – if they did leave before rush hour, they probably had a quick trip home. Both clauses have past tense verbs.

> (**13**) If Jane and Bill *left* before rush hour, they probably had a quick trip home.

In (14), the inference conditional is about the present, in which both clauses in both sentences have verbs in the simple present. As indicated by the inclusion of *probably* in the second sentence, the speaker in (14) feels more comfortable inferring a liking for Italian wine from a liking for Italian food than a liking for Italian opera from a liking for Italian food and wine. Other adverbs (e.g., *possibly*) and modals (e.g., *might*) would convey other degrees of likelihood.

> (**14**) If he *likes* Italian food, then he *likes* Italian wine. If he *likes* Italian food and wine, he probably *likes* Italian opera.

A speaker does not need to know the condition is true in order to make an inference. Consider, for example, (15), (16), and (17).

> (**15**) If that call*'s* for me, it*'s* my wife.

> (**16**) If John*'s* in Baltimore, he *should/must be* at the Hyatt.

> (**17**) If Ann *is wearing* a wedding ring, she and Bill $\begin{Bmatrix} got \\ have\ gotten \\ must\ have\ gotten \end{Bmatrix}$ *married*.

Sentence (15) could be said by someone who has just heard the phone ring and doesn't know who the call is for. Similarly, (16) could be uttered on hearing that John is in Baltimore, and (17) on being told that Ann was seen wearing a wedding ring. The proposition in the result clause is inferred as likely – whether the inference is from a known proposition or a possible one – perhaps because in (15), the speaker is expecting a call from his wife, and in (16) and (17), respectively, the speaker knows that John habitually stays at the Hyatt when in Baltimore, and that Ann and Bill have been thinking about getting married.

The grounds for making the inference may be fairly strong, as in (18a), in which they lie in the definitions of *brother*, *son*, and *nephew*, but for the most part, inferences are made on special knowledge that the speaker has, as in (13) through (17) or has just been given, as in (18b).

> (**18**) a. If John *is* your brother and Bill *is* his son, then Bill *is* your nephew.
> b. You said there are only two points of entry to the room. Well, if the door *was* locked, then the thief *must have/had to have come* through the window.

As shown by the examples in this section, the *if* and result clauses in inference conditionals can contain modals and present or past tense forms, depending on whether present or past time is involved. The inference in the result clause is often expressed with modals of inferred probability such as *should*, *must*, *must have*, *has got to have*, and *had to have* (see Chapter 14).

Sarcastic statements often take the form of inference conditionals in the present tense. In (19), the speaker wants to imply that she or he does not believe the claim that Alan has an IQ of 182. The intended meaning is "He does not have an IQ of 182, because I am certainly not another Einstein."[5] In other words, with these conditionals, the falseness of the proposition in the result clause means that the proposition in the *if* clause, from which it is inferred, must also be false.

> (**19**) If Alan has an IQ of 182, then I'm another Einstein!

Future Conditionals
Future conditionals express predicted future results of conditions, which are often, but not necessarily, in the future. They also have several special uses.

Expressing Future Results
Future conditionals expressing future results may be about plans, as in (20a), or other contingencies, as in (20b). Typically, the *if* clause expresses an event with a verb in the simple present, and the result clause, which contains the modal *will* or, less often, *be going to*, expresses a future event that depends on the condition being fulfilled.

> (**20**) a. If you *don't leave* now, you *will miss* your plane.
> b. If we *get* more rain, the river *is going to flood*.

Different probabilities for the predicted outcome can be expressed depending upon the modal used in the result clause. The modals in (21) express different degrees of likelihood that the event in the result clause will occur.

> (**21**) a. If you start now, you *should* get there on time.   *good probability*
> b. If you start now, you *may* get there on time.   *possibility*
> c. If you start now, you *might* get there on time.   *weak possibility*

In the typical future conditional, the *if* clause expresses an event in the present, thus the verb is in the simple present. However, it is possible to talk about a future result that depends upon something that happened in the past. In such cases, the verb in the *if* clause could be in the simple past, as in (22a), or the present perfect, as in (22b).

(22) Fred: Do you think I will get a raise this year?
    (a) Bill: It depends. If you *did* a good job on that project last summer, you'll get a raise.
    (b) Bill: It depends. If *you have done* everything your boss asked you to do and *done* it well, then you'll get a raise.

Special Uses: Expressing Instructions, Questions, and Suggestions

In some future conditionals, an *if* clause, typically in the simple present and denoting a possible future event, is followed by an instruction, question, or suggestion. For example, the *if* clause in (23) is followed by an instruction.

(23) If I'm late, don't wait up.

Particularly in British English, the modal *should* is sometimes used in the *if* clause instead of the simple present, so that (24a) would be said instead of (24b).

(24) a. If you *should see* him, tell him I want to talk to him.   *British English*
    b. If you *see* him, tell him I want to talk to him.   *American English*

In (25a), the *if* clause is followed by a question. In (25b) and (25c), it is followed by a suggestion and a strong recommendation, respectively.

(25) a. If he calls, what do I tell him?
    b. If you intend to do it, you ought to do it soon.[6]
    c. If she agrees to our proposal, we should close the deal. If she doesn't, we should refuse to continue negotiating.

SUMMARY

THE FORM OF CONDITIONALS; REAL CONDITIONALS

Conditional sentences express a condition, in an *if* **clause**, and its result, in a **result clause** (i.e., *if* x *occurs*, *then* y *occurs*). Both major categories – real and unreal conditionals – can refer to the past, present, or future.
If John leaves now, he'll get to the airport on time.

Real conditionals – conditionals in which the condition and result can be fulfilled – can be categorized into four types:

- **Generic conditionals** express facts considered scientific truths.
  If water is cooled to 32 degrees Fahrenheit, it becomes a solid.
  If light is moving in the direction labeled z, *it has two possibilities of polarization.*

- **Habitual conditionals** express situations or events as being usual results of conditions being met. They have paraphrases with *whenever.*
  If / Whenever they go out to eat, they always go to a Chinese restaurant.
  If he had business in Baltimore, he often stayed at the Hyatt.

continued

- **Inference conditionals** express situations or events as logically following from conditions being fulfilled.
  If we can clean up the pollution in this river, we can clean up the waterways all over the world.
  If that call is for Susan, it must be her new boyfriend. He's been calling every five minutes.
  If the door was locked, then the thief must have come through the window. There's no other way to get in.

- **Future conditionals** express predicted future results of conditions which are also often in the future.
  If you don't leave now, you'll miss your plane.

The *if* clauses in future conditionals can also be followed by instructions, questions, and suggestions.
  If you see him, tell him I want to talk to him.
  If he calls, what do I tell him?
  If you intend to do it, you ought to do it soon.

EXERCISE 19.1

Identify each sentence as a generic, habitual, inference, or future conditional.

Example: If she's in the lobby, the plane must have arrived early.

Answer: inference conditional

1. If Alice calls while I'm out, tell her I'll be back in about an hour.
2. If he was in the room with her, he must have seen how she got out.
3. If they go on a trip, they usually get into a fight over where to stay.
4. If the air temperature is cooled to a point where it has 100 percent humidity, fog or clouds form.
5. If we can eliminate air pollution in cities like Los Angeles and Mexico City, then we can eliminate it everywhere.
6. If he's an expert on impressionist art, then pigs can fly.
7. If it's Tuesday, then this must be Belgium. It says in the brochure that we will cross the border into Belgium on Tuesday.
8. If he finishes the exam before the allotted time, take his paper and tell him that he can leave.
9. If you touch me again, I'll slap you silly.
10. If you've done a really good job on that paper, I'm sure you'll get an A.

UNREAL CONDITIONALS

Unreal conditionals are conditionals in which the proposition in the *if* clause is an imagined condition and the proposition in the result clause is its imagined outcome. Like real conditionals, unreal conditionals can express present, past, and future time. There are two types of unreal condtionals, *hypothetical conditionals* and *counterfactual conditionals*.

Hypothetical Conditionals

Hypothetical conditionals express speculations about imagined possible events or states in the present and future. They contrast with future conditionals, which express future results of real plans or contingencies. Typical examples of this kind of unreal conditional are shown in (26).

> (**26**) a. If I *found* a wallet on the subway, I *would return* it to the owner.
>   b. If you *drove* to the city on Monday, you *would miss* all the weekend traffic.

In (26a), the speaker imagines a hypothetical situation that could happen in the future – finding a wallet – and declares what he or she would do in this case. The speaker in (26b) knows that the person he or she is addressing is traveling to the city sometime in the future. The utterance expresses a hypothetical plan for doing so that has the advantage of avoiding weekend traffic.

Although the verb in the *if* clause of a hypothetical conditional about the future is usually in the simple past tense, it can take other forms – for example, be accompanied, by a modal like *should*, or consist of *happened*, *managed*, or *were* and a following infinitive, as shown in (27). *If I should* + verb is more typical of British English than American English. The result clause typically has the modal *would*, but can also have *could* or *might*.

> (**27**) If I $\left\{\begin{array}{l} \textit{happened to get} \\ \textit{were to get} \\ \textit{got} \\ \textit{should get} \\ \textit{should happen to get} \\ \textit{managed to get} \end{array}\right\}$ enough money, I'*d spend* a year in Paris and *study* art.

Hypothetical conditionals that comment or speculate on present states are illustrated in (28). Hypothetical conditionals about present states differ from real conditionals, in which the condition and result obtain.

> (**28**) a. If you *had* the photographs with you, I *could see* my grandson.
>   b. If I *knew* Joan's telephone number, we *could call* her.
>   c. If I *understood* that chapter, I *would explain* it to you.

Each of these sentences talks about a present state by presenting a condition and result that evidently don't obtain. Thus, in (28a), the speaker regrets that the listener does not have the photographs; in (28b), the speaker states that he or she does not have Joan's telephone number, and she can't be called; in (28c), the speaker states that he or she lacks the understanding required to explain the chapter to the listener. Hypothetical conditionals that express comments and speculations about current states have stative verbs in the *if* clause, as in (28).[7] They cannot have the variety of verb forms in the *if* clause shown in (27), rather the stative verb is always in the past tense.

Hypothetical conditionals can also comment on present events, as shown in (29).

> (**29**) If the Mets were winning, I would be enjoying this game a lot more.

This sentence is spoken by someone who is watching an ongoing baseball game in which the Mets are not winning. The *if* clause expresses a condition that is presently not real, but, if fulfilled, could result in the imaginary result in the following clause. Notice that the verb in the *if* clause has the past tense form *were* followed by a present participle and the result clause contains *would be* followed by a present participle. Other modals like *could* or *might* could also appear in the result clause.

Counterfactual Conditionals

Many *counterfactual conditionals* about the past talk about past events that did not obtain. Typical examples are shown in (30).

> (**30**) a. If I *had seen* you at the mall, I *would have said* hello.
>   b. If you *had locked* the side door before we left for the movie, the burglar *would* not *have gotten in*.

Notice that these sentences involve actual events: the speaker in (30a) was at the mall, and the speaker and the listener in (30b) left the house for a movie. However, the conditions in the *if* clauses did not obtain: the speaker did not see the listener at the mall; the side door did not get locked. The two sentences can thus be understood as having the respective implications of: "I did not see you, so I did not say hello" and "You didn't lock the door when we left, so the burglar got in." Affirmative statements in the clauses, in other words, imply the corresponding negative statements, and negative statements imply the corresponding affirmative statements.

The tense sequence in counterfactual conditionals about the past is as follows: past perfect in the *if* clause and *would* + *have* + past participle in the result clause. Other modals such as *could* and *might* also occur in the result clause, as shown in (31).

> (**31**) a. If you *had left* the party early, we *might* never *have met*.
>   b. If the voting machines *hadn't been rigged*, we *might have had* a very different outcome.
>   c. If he *hadn't run* in and *pulled* her out of the burning house, she *could have been killed*.

Counterfactual conditionals can also express speculations about impossible states or situations in the present, as shown in (32).

> (**32**) a. If Mozart *were* living/alive today, he *would be writing*/*would write* music for the movies.
>   b. If I *were* president, I *would sell* the White House's Limoges china to fund education.[8]

The *if* clause in (32a) describes an impossible present state, inasmuch as we know that Mozart is dead, and speculates about his activities were he still living. In (32b), the chances of my becoming president are virtually impossible, and here I imagine an action that I would carry out if this impossible state were somehow to become possible.

The *if* clause has a past tense form *were* with third- and first-person singular subjects, as shown in (32b). *Was* is often heard in spoken American English (e.g., *if Mozart was living today*), but most editors and writers still consider this use of *was* to be unacceptable. Progressives (i.e. *were* + *present participle*), as in (32b), are quite common. The result clause containing the impossible speculation generally includes the modal *would* (or *could* or *might*) + *be* + present participle, as in (32a), or *would* + verb, as in (32b).

Counterfactual conditionals can also contain speculations about present states that would or could have resulted had past events been different, as shown in (33).

> (**33**) If the French *had won* the battle of Quebec, we *would* probably *be speaking* French today instead of English.

The Canadian speaker in (33) is speculating about the reversal of a historical event, something that is not possible. The French lost the battle of Quebec, and this led to British dominance over the territories that later became Canada. But what if the French had won? A reasonable speculation is that they would have gained control over all of what became present-day Canada, and today Canadians would be speaking French as their primary language rather than English.

In conditionals about impossible present states resulting from the reversal of a past event, the verb in the *if* clause has the same tense as in counterfactuals about the past – the past perfect. However, the verb form in the result clause is a modal + verb combination that describes an impossible outcome in the present. Compare (33) with (34), a speculation about the same imaginary condition but an imaginary past result.

> (34) If the French *had won* the battle of Quebec, they *would have attacked* the remaining British forces below Lake Champlain.

Variations in Form in Unreal Conditionals

Potentially contributing to the difficulties of unreal conditionals are two variations in form – one associated with spoken English, the other primarily with written English.

Substitution of *Would Have* + Past Participle for the Past Perfect

A change that is becoming extremely common in spoken American English is the substitution of *would have* + past participle for the past perfect in the *if* clause of counterfactual conditionals about the past. That is, the form that is generally used in the result clause of these conditionals is used in the *if* clause as well. A typical example is shown in (35), where *would have had* replaces *had had*.

> (35) *If I *would've had* a little more time, I would've told him about it.

So pervasive has this substitution become that many native speakers will refuse to acknowledge that sentences like those in (35) and in (36), following, are ungrammatical.

> (36) a. *If it *would've been* a real fight, the referee would've stopped it.
> b. *If I *would've had* the right tools, I could've finished the job properly.

Whether this development in spoken English will lead to a permanent change in the grammar of these counterfactual *if* clauses is not yet clear, but sentences like those in (35) and (36) are still considered ungrammatical in written English. Teachers should tell their students that, even though they may hear native speakers utter sentences like these, they should not follow this practice in writing, since such sentences will not be viewed as "educated" English.

Ellipsis of *If* and Subject–Aux Inversion

Ellipsis of *if* is possible in hypothetical and counterfactual conditional sentences, provided that subject–aux inversion also occurs, as shown in (37).

> (37) a. If I had known you were coming, I'd have baked a cake.
>   *Had I* known you were coming, I'd have baked a cake.
> b. If I were in your position, I wouldn't say anything.
>   *Were I* in your position, I wouldn't say anything.
> c. If things should turn out badly, you could always try again.
>   *Should things* turn out badly, you could always try again.

The sentences without *if* in (37) sound somewhat antiquated and poetic, rather like the first line in Andrew Marvell's (1621–1678) famous poem "To His Coy Mistress," shown in (38).

(**38**) *Had we but world enough, and time,*
　　　　This coyness, Lady, were no crime.[9]

Unreal conditionals with ellipsis of *if* and subject–aux inversion may occur more frequently in British English, since, as we saw in Chapter 4, this dialect forms *yes/no* questions with *have* by subject–aux inversion. Although unreal conditionals with ellipsis and subject–aux inversion are occasionally heard in spoken English, as in (39a) and (39b), this stylistic variation is more frequently found in writing, especially with counterfactual conditionals such as (39c), which comes from a book review.

(**39**) a. *Were I* to live another 10 years, I would be 95.
　　　　b. *Should I* leave for only a minute to attend to something, I would be fired.[10]
　　　　c. *Had Galbraith* devoted more effort to gathering empirical evidence to support his views and to finding ways to test them statistically, his influence on economics would have been greater.[11]

ADDITIONAL FACTS ABOUT CONDITIONAL SENTENCES

In this section, we look at two possible sources of confusion related to conditionals – a structure called *speech act conditionals* and the use of *unless* instead of *if* (*not*) in conditional sentences.

Speech Act Conditionals

Speech act conditionals[12] resemble future conditionals, but their clauses do not have a condition–result relationship. The *if* clause in a speech act conditional functions as a preface to different speech acts[13] that occur in the following clause. It gives the listener the option of reacting to these speech acts while making the entire sentence more polite or appropriate.[14] Typical speech acts in the following clauses include instructions, as in (40); requests, as in (41); corrections, as in (42); and hedged opinions, as in (43). Notice that the modal *will* appears in the *if* conditional preceding the instruction in (40), whereas the simple present would be found in a regular future conditional.

(**40**) *If you'll step over here*, I'll give you an application.
　　　　(= Please step over here, and I'll give you the application.)

(**41**) *If you are going my way*, I could use a lift. My car is in the shop.
　　　　(= I don't want to inconvenience you, and I would appreciate a lift.)

(**42**) *If you recall your Greek mythology*, it was Zeus who was Athena's father, not Poseidon.
　　　　(= Actually, according to Greek mythology, it was Zeus who was Athena's father.)

(**43**) John is a little too abrupt with people, *if I may say so*.
　　　　(= In my opinion, John is a little too abrupt with people.)

The *if* clause in these sentences can lead to the mistaken impression that they are conditionals, with a condition and a result, when in fact they are structures used to perform the speech acts mentioned previously. Speech act conditionals are probably not worth including in a syllabus, but teachers should be able to recognize them and to explain why they are not real conditionals.

Unless Does Not Equal *If Not*

English language teaching textbooks often treat clauses with *unless* and *if* clauses with *not* as having the same meaning and being interchangeable.[15] Typically, pairs of sentences like those in (44) are presented to illustrate the formula *if . . . not = unless*.

(44) a. We will go on a picnic *if* it *doesn't* rain.
     b. We will go on a picnic *unless* it rains.

Unfortunately, the equation, which works with future conditionals, does not always hold with other types of conditionals.[16] For example, in many counterfactual conditionals *unless* cannot be substituted for *if . . . not* without an ungrammatical result, as shown in (45).

(45) a. If it hadn't been for the quick action of Jack Armstrong, we would have been involved in a terrible accident.
     b. *Unless it had been for the quick action of Jack Armstrong, we would have been involved in a terrible accident.

To make matters worse, some counterfactual conditionals do not have the same meaning when *if . . . not* is substituted for *unless*. Consider (46),[17] spoken by a well-known bank robber who had been apprehended by the police shortly after a robbery took place in downtown Chicago. He is protesting his innocence to an officer who pulled him over in Kankakee, a town 45 miles south of Chicago. In the first sentence he is claiming that it is impossible that he could have traveled from the site of the robbery in downtown Chicago in such a short time without the aid of high-speed transportation like a helicopter. Since he is presently in a car, it follows that he must be innocent.

(46) Look, I couldn't possibly have pulled off the job and gotten all the way down here in ten minutes *unless, maybe, I'd had a helicopter*. And you don't see a helicopter around here, do you?

However, in (47) the same thief, who was freed because of lack of evidence, is explaining to a group of colleagues in Kankakee (where he is holding a master class on the technology of modern bank robbery) that he needed a helicopter to escape after pulling off this particular job. Here, the meaning of the conditional sentence is that he did commit the crime.

(47) Look, I couldn't possibly have pulled off the job and gotten all the way down here in ten minutes *if I hadn't had a helicopter*. You have to use the best in modern getaway equipment if you want to outsmart the cops.

Examples (45) and (47) demonstrate that clauses with *unless* are not equivalent to counterfactual conditional *if* clauses containing *not*. *Unless* is best understood as meaning "except in the case that." It is perhaps the equivalence of *unless* and *if . . . not* clauses in future conditionals such as (44) that has led to the presentation of *unless = if . . .*

not as an invariable equation. Students must be warned against substituting *unless* for *if . . . not* in counterfactual conditionals so that they do not produce sentences that are ungrammatical or do not express the meaning they had intended. One way to do this is to teach them that *unless = except if* or *except in the case that.*

SUMMARY

UNREAL CONDITIONALS

Unreal conditionals express an imagined condition and its imagined outcome. They have verb forms in the *if* and result clauses that differentiate them from real conditionals. Unreal conditionals can be seen as falling into two basic types:

- **Hypothetical conditionals**, which express speculations about the present or the future.
  If I found someone's wallet I would return it.
  If we knew her telephone number, we could call her right now.
  I would be enjoying this game a lot more if the Mets were winning.

- **Counterfactual conditionals**, which express speculations about past events that did not obtain or impossible states or situations in the present.
  If he had been paying attention, he wouldn't have crashed.
  If Mozart were alive, he would be writing music for films.
  If Gore had won the 2000 election, we would all be driving cars that get 50 miles per gallon of gas.

Ellipsis of *if* and subject–aux inversion can occur in unreal conditionals with *have*, *be*, or *should*.
  Had she checked her facts, she would have discovered the error.
  Were I to die here in your arms, I would be content.

EXERCISE 19.2

Identify each sentence as either a hypothetical or a counterfactual conditional.

Example: If I had enough time, I could probably get into shape. But I don't, so I can't.

Answer: hypothetical conditional

1. If I were you, I would help her.
2. If I saw a crime being committed, I would call the police.
3. If we went and talked to the dean about the project, he would probably help us.
4. If the British had won the Revolutionary War, the United States would probably have a parliamentary system of government instead of the one we have.
5. If he had broken the vase, I would have definitely have asked him to pay for it.
6. If he broke something valuable like that vase, he would definitely pay for it.
7. I would be feeling a lot better about the way this game is going if Brazil were leading by two points.
8. If I knew how to fix it, I would fix it right now.

EXERCISE 19.3

Indicate whether each sentence is grammatical or ungrammatical. If a sentence is ungrammatical, indicate the change that is needed and supply it.

Example: If antibiotic drugs like penicillin were available during World War I, many more lives could be saved.

Answer: ungrammatical (Change the verb in the *if* clause to make it a counterfactual conditional in the past.)
correction: If antibiotic drugs like penicillin had been available during World War I, many more lives could have been saved.

1. If I happen to run into her, I would tell her where you live.
2. "He came at me with an ax over his head," Webster said. "He would have chopped my head off if I wouldn't have been armed with a 12-gauge shotgun. This guy was totally berserk."[18]
3. If I was in your position, I would probably agree to do it.
4. If Napoleon had won the Battle of Waterloo, a lot more people would be speaking French in Europe today.
5. I wouldn't have gotten so wet if I remembered to bring my umbrella.
6. Had she spoken to him earlier, he could have done something about the problem. But it is too late now.
7. If I see him, I wouldn't speak to him.
8. I certainly wouldn't have invited him to watch the Super Bowl on TV at my house had I known that he disapproves of contact sports.

PROBLEMS THAT ESL/EFL STUDENTS HAVE WITH CONDITIONAL SENTENCES

ESL/EFL students have considerable difficulty producing correct tense sequences across *if* and result clauses in English conditional sentences, despite the fact that a great deal of emphasis is placed on the form of real and unreal conditionals in English language teaching textbooks and courses. One cause of this problem may be that some learners have difficulty going from a small number of tenses used in conditionals in their L1 to the larger number of tense sequences required for expressing specific conditional meanings in English. Although all languages have ways of expressing the idea of an outcome being contingent upon some condition, not all do this through such a variety of tense sequences. A logical consequence of this would be that speakers of L1s whose conditionals are grammatically similar to those of English will be more successful in learning conditionals than speakers of L1s whose conditionals use a more limited number of tenses. The latter, because they might rely on the surrounding context to interpret differences indicated by tense sequences in English conditionals, may have difficulty mastering appropriate tense sequences across clauses. This seems to be the case. Speakers of languages such as French, which forms conditional sentences much like English, apparently acquire English conditionals with greater accuracy than speakers of Chinese, who depend primarily on context to distinguish between real and unreal conditionals. Other learners may make false equations between L1 tenses and English tenses and apply these in their production of English conditionals. In what follows, we look at just a few of the types of attested errors that ESL/EFL students make in attempting to form English conditionals that may be attributed to the grammar of conditionals in the L1.

Equating English Past Tense with Perfect Tense in L1 Conditionals (Arabic)

In Arabic, the perfect (complete action) tense occurs in conditional clauses after the subordinators *ʔidhaa* and *law*, as illustrated in (48a) and (48b). Note that *perf* = perfect aspect, *prt* = particle, and *imperf* = imperfect aspect.

(**48**) a. *ʔidhaa ʔaDaa'a lkitaaba sa-ʔu 'aaqibuhu.*[19]
   if lose (perf) the book (prt) punish (imperf) him
   "If he loses the book, I (will) punish him."
  b. *law ʔaDaa'a lkitaaba la- 'aaqabtuhu.*
   if lose (perf) the book (prt) punish (perf) him
   "If he had lost the book, I would have punished him."

Fakhri (1995) suggests that transfer errors may arise when Arabic speakers establish a correspondence between the English simple past tense and their L1 perfect tense when producing English clauses introduced by *if*. This equation leads to confusing sentences like the one shown in (49), where, given the tense in the following clause, we would anticipate the simple present tense in the *if* clause (i.e., *if we take transportation*).[20]

(**49**) *If we took transportation, for example, women are not allowed to drive any type of motor vehicles in my country . . .

Mixing L1 Tenses Occurring in More Than One L1 Conditional (Korean)

In Korean, future conditionals and hypothetical conditionals have the same morphemes affixed to the result clause verb: *(u)l + ke + ya* or *(u)l + teyn + tey*. This leads to the production of English conditionals that begin with an *if* clause in the simple present tense but have a following result clause that is suitable for a hypothetical conditional (i.e., the inclusion of *would*), instead of a future conditional, which appears to be what the learner in (50) wants to say.

(**50**) *If international students improve their vocabulary, deal wisely with outside pressures, and understand the American meaning of friendship, *they would easily adjust* to life in the United States.

In Korean, counterfactual conditionals have past tense morphemes in both clauses. Korean speakers often create what appear to be hypothetical conditionals in which the context of the discourse clearly indicates the need for a counterfactual conditional. In (51), the first sentence establishes a context that requires a following counterfactual conditional, but the student appears to have supplied a hypothetical conditional instead. This suggests that he or she is following the L1 tense pattern.

(**51**) Although it was a painful experience for me during my elementary and middle school life, it [studying English] gave me chance to see how I have talent in learning English. *If I was not forced to learn, I would never have chance to learn English, and I would not be studying at University of Illinois.*

Lack of Grammatical Distinction Between Future, Hypothetical, and Counterfactual Conditionals (Chinese)

Chinese does not distinguish between future, hypothetical, and counterfactual conditionals about the past by the use of auxiliary verbs and tense markers. Native speakers infer the meaning of conditional sentences from the proposition of the second clause and the speaker's "knowledge of the world and of the context in which the sentence is being used" (Li & Thompson, 1981, p. 641). As result, the sentence shown in (52a) could be interpreted as any one of the three conditionals in (52b) depending upon the surrounding context.[21] Note the following abbreviations in brackets: *3sg* = third person singular; *perf* = perfect aspect.

(**52**) a. *Ruguo ni   kan dao wo meimei ni   yiding   zhidao ta   huiyun le.*
     if   you see   I   younger you certainly know   (3sg) pregnant (perf)
                         sister

    b. "If you *see* my younger sister, *you'll* certainly know that she is pregnant."
      "If you *saw* my younger sister, *you'd* certainly know she was pregnant."
      "If you *had seen* my younger sister, *you would have* certainly known that she was pregnant."

Research (Tseng & Cowan, 1999; Tseng 2001; Tseng & Cowan, to appear) has shown that Chinese learners of English who have a very advanced competence continue to produce ungrammatical English conditionals. On oral and written discourse completion tasks that required students to create conditional sentences appropriate to various contexts, 20 native speakers of Chinese, who were graduate students and had been in the United States for over three years and whose original admission TOEFL scores had ranged from 583 to 663 (only two students had TOEFL scores below 603), produced numerous errors. Almost all of these were like the sentences in (53), in which the tenses in the two clauses do not constitute a sequence that could be grammatical in English conditionals.

(**53**) a. *If I had studied harder, I would pass.
    b. *If I had worn my glasses, I will greet you.
    c. *If I had studied industrially, I can get a high score.
    d. *If I studied harder, I could have passed the test.
    e. *If I wore more clothes, I would not have caught another cold.

The performance of these students was then compared with that of another group of 20 Chinese graduate students who had just arrived in the United States, a group of 20 newly arrived French graduate students, and a group of native speakers of English. Both of the newly arrived groups had TOEFL scores that were not significantly different from those of the original group. The French students performed as well as the native speakers, but neither of the Chinese groups performed as well as the French students. Furthermore, there was no significant difference between the performance of the newly arrived Chinese students and that of the group that had been in the United States. Since conditional sentences are extremely important for academic writing, the results of this test strongly suggest that Chinese learners require focused English instruction on the forms of conditionals and the contexts in which they are appropriate.

SUGGESTIONS FOR TEACHING CONDITIONAL SENTENCES

ESL/EFL textbooks usually address all real conditionals. Hypothetical conditionals and counterfactual conditionals are often lumped under the rubric "hypothetical conditionals." There is nothing wrong with this provided that the basic meaning of the two types are differentiated. Counterfactual conditionals that speculate about impossible present situations related to past conditions that did not occur are not often taught, perhaps because of the difficulty of the tense structure. Of the various types of real conditionals, inference conditionals can be especially difficult to teach, because of the range of forms involved, but they can certainly be taught to high-intermediate and advanced-level students, for example, through Activity 4 in this section. In teaching future conditionals, it is probably a good idea to point to the difference between regular future conditionals and future conditionals expressing commands, instructions, and questions. As we have seen, *unless* should not be taught as equivalent to *if . . . not*, or it should be taught as equivalent only for future conditionals. Students whose L1 is Chinese will require some extra work in fitting forms to context and more focus on appropriate tense sequences across clauses. It is not necessary or even desirable in teaching conditionals to use the terms for them that we have used here (i.e., *inference*, *counterfactual*). What is important is to explain the meaning of the type of conditional being focused on, the possible tense sequences it can have, and the contexts in which it occurs.

Activity 1: Generic Conditionals (Intermediate)

To introduce generic conditionals through this common and effective activity, begin by writing on the board a conditional sentence that contains a familiar scientific condition and result – for example, *If you cool water to 0 degrees centigrade, it freezes*. Next, write two columns of conditions and results as in (54). The items in the "Result" column can be completed or left incomplete, as shown, so that the students can provide the missing content.

	Condition	*Result*
(54)	you go toward the Equator	the weather gets . . .
	you get closer to the North/South Pole	the weather becomes . . .
	you climb higher up a mountain	the air gets . . .
	you dive deep under the water in a submarine	the water pressure . . .

You can also ask questions about general facts that involve personal experience – for example, "If you run very fast, what happens?" Have students answer in full sentences. After the students have answered these questions, have them form groups and write down as many examples of generic conditionals as they can. Encourage them to come up with everyday examples.

Activity 2: Habitual Conditionals (Intermediate)

A TBLT activity for practicing habitual conditionals is to have students list things that they do at school and on vacation. For this purpose, hand out sheets with about 10 items like those in (55) to each student:

(55) If I have some free time in the middle of the week, I . . .
    If I go out with friends, we usually . . .
    If I need to study for a test, I usually go . . .
    If I feel the need for some exercise, I . . .
    If I go home on vacation, I . . .
    If I don't go home on vacation, I . . .

Have everyone write completions for all items and hand them to you with their names on the top. Select two of these completed sheets. Make enough typed copies of each sheet for half the class. Keep the originals. After you have done this, which can be the next day, divide the class into two teams, making sure that the students who supplied the completions are not on the same team. Hand out copies of each student's paper to the team that the student is not a member of. The task for each team is to identify the "mystery student" on the other team who wrote the responses on their paper.

The contest begins with one student asking a student from the other team a question that will elicit one of the list items – for example, "If you need to study for a test, where do you usually go?" Remind students that the questions must always be phrased to include an *if* clause. Since all the team members have a copy of the list with the mystery student's completions, they can note the names of people who give answers that match what is on the list. Then a student from the other team asks a question. The game proceeds until one team thinks that they have enough answers that match the list of their mystery student. They then declare who the mystery student is.

Activity 3: Future Conditionals Expressing Suggestions (Intermediate)

The use of future conditionals for expressing suggestions is often taught by getting students to provide a list of suggestions about what to do in a city they are familiar with (e.g., *If you like jazz, try the following clubs . . .* ; *If you are interested in outdoor activities, take a walk through Grant Park*). Students can also be asked to write suggestions for traveling in a country (e.g., *If you have want to travel cheaply but comfortably, buy a Eurail Pass*; *If you are going to be in Berlin for over a week, buy a weekly pass for the U-Bahn*).

Activity 4: Inference Conditionals (High Intermediate)

Solving mysteries is one way to set up the use of inference conditionals. Demonstrate to the class how they can create short stories that contain clues that lead to the formation of inference conditional sentences. Start by reading a short passage that describes an unsolved mystery, such as in (56a).

(56) Lady Milford Smythe's precious jewels were stolen from her room at the Hotel Danford while she was eating in the hotel's dining room. When she returned to her room, she discovered that the jewels were missing. The police report stated that the door to her room was locked, and there was no evidence of forced entry. One window was unlocked, but it was shut. How did the thief get into her room? (*Possible Solution*: If the door was locked but the window was unlocked, then the thief must have come through the window and gone out the same way. We might find his fingerprints on the window.)

Ask the students to state the evidence that points to a solution. Restate what they come up with as an extended inference conditional like the solution shown.

Then have the students break into groups and work together to create a short report of an unsolved incident. The story should have enough clues to suggest at least one reasonable answer that can be stated in the form of an inference conditional. When two groups have written down their stories and their solutions, they exchange them. One member of each group is chosen as the reader and is given the story and the solution. The reader reads the story and the other members listen and offer solutions. The reader checks these against the correct solution. Groups continue to exchange stories until all of the stories have circulated to all of the groups. Monitor the groups to ensure that the students summarize their solutions in the form of inference conditionals. Since coming up with and writing down the story can take some time, it may be best to allot two periods to this activity – one for creating the mysteries and one for exchanging and solving them.

Although mysteries based on crimes have high interest value, you can use other events that appear regularly in the news – forest fires (evidence of careless campers), fires started in buildings (evidence of arson), airplane crashes (evidence of sabotage or pilot error), and so on. Random acts of kindness or honesty can also be included (e.g., a person loses his wallet, but it is mysteriously returned to his hotel; he last remembers taking it out to pay the cab driver when he arrived).

Activity 5: Future Conditionals (Low Intermediate)

A simple way of practicing future conditionals is to ask students questions about an event in their future that could have two possible outcomes, each of which could in turn lead to other outcomes. For example, after asking someone what university he or she is applying to, you can ask, "What will you do if you are accepted to that university?" When the student provides an answer, ask about what would happen in the event of the other outcome: "What will you do if you are not accepted to that university?" The student will probably say something like, "Then I'll go to another university." Next, build on this by making up a table of potential outcomes for an imaginary student, as shown in (57). Give the student a name, and begin to develop a narrative of what the student plans to do. As shown in (57a), write the first condition and result. Under that line write an alternative condition – the condition that obtains if the condition on the line above is not fulfilled – and its result. Ask students to state these conditions and results as conditional sentences. Afterward, as shown in (57b), write a second pair of alternative conditions and results, with the conditions based on the results of the first pair.

	Condition	Result
(57) a.	passes this exam	applies to enter the university
	doesn't pass	takes one more English course, gets a higher score; applies again
b.	is accepted	studies biology
	is not accepted	applies to another university, is accepted, studies biology
c.	aces all exams	graduates as a biologist
	has difficulty on exams	changes major to business

Give the students enough examples so that they can see how the narrative is developing. Then have them work together in groups to construct variations on this story by adding alternative conditions and results. When all the groups have finished, as a class compare the different ways the story can develop.

A sports playoffs scenario can also be used for this activity, since the seeding diagrams of tournaments are available in newspapers or on the Internet (i.e., *If Oregon beats UCLA, they will play Kansas in the semifinals*, and so on).

Activity 6: Hypothetical Conditionals (Intermediate)

One of the most widely used approaches for practicing hypothetical conditionals involves having students work in pairs and supply results for hypothetical conditionals written on slips of paper. Each slip has a phrase such as *win five million dollars in the lottery, get a pilot's license and be able to fly a plane, become friends with a movie star like Jackie Chan*, and so on. Students work in pairs producing hypothetical conditional sentences describing what they would do if these things came about (e.g., *If I got a pilot's license and could fly a plane, I would* . . . ; *If I became friends with a movie star like Jackie Chan, I would* . . .). As students work, monitor the activity closely to ensure that they use the past tense in the *if* clause.

Activity 7: Unreal Conditionals of Advice (Intermediate)

Create unreal conditionals with the expression *if I were you* through a highly focused problem-solving activity. Make up – or ask students to brainstorm – typical problems students have like the one in (58). Have students work in pairs. One student presents the problem and asks, " If you were me, what would you do?" The other student offers advice by answering, "If I were you . . . " Provide them with an example first.

> (58) Problem: My roommates are very noisy. I can never study in my room.
> Advice: If I were you, I would get some new roommates.
> If I were you, I would ask them to be quiet so you can study.
> If I were you, I would move out of the dorm.

Activity 8: Counterfactual Conditionals About the Past (High Intermediate)

To introduce counterfactuals, create a series of linked statements describing what happened to someone, and have the students work in pairs to create conditional sentences that describe what the outcome would have been if the circumstances in each condition had not occurred, as shown in (59b).

> (59) a. Sheila didn't set her alarm clock for seven a.m. So she got up late.
>
> b. If she had set her alarm for seven a.m., $\begin{cases} \text{she wouldn't have gotten up late.} \\ \text{she would have gotten up on time.} \end{cases}$
>
> c. She was in a hurry to get the airport. So she forgot some important papers.
>
> d. She had to go back to get the papers. So she lost some more time.
>
> e. She got to the airport 10 minutes late. So she missed her flight.

As a follow-up activity, create a text to use as a departure point for a discussion that forces the use of unreal conditionals about the past.[22] An example is shown in (60).

> (60) **Pleasantville Then and Now**
> Pleasantville is a city that has made many improvements, so that life there has changed a great deal. Formerly, Pleasantville did not have very good schools, so it increased taxes. The extra money raised was used to improve schools. There were no parks in Pleasantville, but the mayor convinced a real estate developer and the owner of a construction company to donate their services to create one. Now the citizens have a large and beautiful park where they can take their children to play. The lake at the edge of the town was not used except by the citizens for fishing. However, the mayor decided to give a large tourist company a tax break. As a result, many tourists were attracted to the lake during the summer, and this has created a lot of new businesses that serve the tourists in the summer. As a result of the improved schools and the new park, a company that makes plastic bottles has moved to Pleasantville. Now many citizens of Pleasantville work in that factory. However, a lot more people from out of state have come into the city to work, so the population is growing. The schools are becoming crowded. The park is too. Life is not quite as pleasant in Pleasantville.

Have students read this text and then make sentences that describe what would not have happened in Pleasantville if some of the changes described had not happened. Provide them with an example such as (61).

> (**61**) If the people of Pleasantville had not raised taxes, they wouldn't have been able to improve their schools.

If the text concludes in the present, as this one does, you can expand the activity to incorporate future conditionals. With this text, for example, you would simply also tell students to list things that describe what will happen or might happen if the people of Pleasantville don't make more changes.

Activity 9: Unreal Conditionals (High Intermediate)

This activity forces students to recognize what verb forms in unreal conditionals are appropriate in the context of a particular discourse and to produce an accurate version of the unreal conditional required. Construct contexts that force hypothetical and counterfactual conditionals such as shown in (62) and ask students to supply a sentence beginning with *if* that fits the context. It is important that the context does not contain a verb form clue that gives away which kind of conditional is appropriate. Thus, the first example shown here does *not* contain the obvious clue "tell your friends how you would feel *if you had an air conditioner.*" This activity can be done in small groups or in pairs. It can be quite helpful for students who are having trouble making correct tense sequences across clauses in unreal conditionals.

> (**62**) a. Outside, the temperature is 100° Fahrenheit. Because your air conditioner is broken, you are really suffering from the heat. You envy your friends who don't have this problem and are enjoying nice cool air inside their homes right now. How would you express this?
>   Possible answer: If I had an air conditioner, I wouldn't be suffering from the heat.
>
> b. While driving through a school zone, you exceeded the limit of 20 miles per hour because you did not look at your speedometer. A police officer pulled you over and wrote you a ticket for speeding. How would you express your frustration about getting this ticket?
>   Possible answer: If I had been paying attention to how fast I was going, I wouldn't have gotten a ticket.

Activity 10: Counterfactuals with Past Conditions and Present Results (Advanced)

First, show how the verb forms in the result clauses of counterfactuals with past conditions and present results differ from those with past conditions and past results. After presenting several example sentence pairs, have the students research various historical events (battles, elections, etc.) and the political issues surrounding them. Ask the students to describe these issues and propose speculations that reflect what might have happened if the historical event had turned out differently. For example, research into the 2000 presidential election would discover that the loser, Al Gore, is an advocate for cleaner energy. After describing this, the students might produce the conditional structures shown in (63).

> (**63**) If Al Gore had won the 2000 election,
>   • we would all be driving cars that get 50 miles per gallon of gas.
>   • we would be using greener sources of electric power like wind power.

ENDNOTES

[1] The system used here draws on the analyses proposed in Dancygier (1999), perhaps the most comprehensive treatment of English conditionals to date, and others. The terms used in this chapter – *real* and *unreal, generic, habitual, inference, hypothetical,* and *counterfactual conditionals* – may be found in English language teaching textbooks and pedagogical grammars, and in treatments of conditionals by linguists and philosophers.

[2] Traditionally, the content of the *if* clause is usually called the *protasis,* and that of the following clause the *apodosis.* These terms are derived from Greek. The relationship between the two clauses is often discussed in terms of truth conditions: *if P, then Q.* See Comrie (1986).

[3] Quirk et al. (1972) and Quirk and Greenbaum (1975) and Huddleston and Pullum (1999) refer to these as "open" conditionals.

[4] Example (6) comes from the LSWE corpus as reported in Biber et al. (1999), p. 825.

[5] Quirk and Greenbaum (1975), p. 319, call this a "rhetorical conditional" since it makes a strong assertion of an absurd statement that is not intended to be believed.

[6] Intended future action can also be expressed by *going to* (e.g., *If you're going to do it, you should do it now*).

[7] See Dancygier (1999) and Filmore (1990).

[8] This example is from Dancygier (1999), p. 83.

[9] Notice that *were* means "would be" here.

[10] This example is modeled on Green (1982), p. 135.

[11] Madrick (2005), p. 15.

[12] The term is used in Dancygier (1999); see her discussion, pp. 89–93.

[13] "Speech acts" are utterances that have illocutionary force, such as requests, orders, and questions. They were first proposed by Austin (1962). For a summary of the issues in the study of speech acts, see Cole and Morgan (1975).

[14] This is Dancygier's (1999, p. 90) characterization of the function of *if* clauses in speech act conditionals.

[15] See, for example, Azar (1989), p. 333.

[16] Some unreal conditionals with *were* (*If he weren't so stubborn, . . .*) and inference conditionals (*If he doesn't write you much, it must be because he has broken his arm*) also do not allow the substitution of *unless* for *if . . . not.* See Geis (1973) for a more detailed discussion. We will not discuss these cases because they are rather marginal in terms of teaching English.

[17] Examples (46) and (47) are modeled after Whitaker (1970).

[18] *News-Gazette,* p. A3, October 1, 2000.

[19] In this transcription the author uses [?] for a glottal stop and ['] for a voiced pharyngeal fricative.

[20] Kaharma and Hajjaj (1989) also note that speakers of Arabic make a large number of errors producing English unreal conditionals that would be expressed in Arabic with *Iðaa* and *law.*

[21] Chinese does have the equivalent of a future time marker that appears in conditionals like (1). Not surprisingly, the Chinese subjects in this experiment produced more correct English future conditionals than hypothetical or counterfactual conditionals.

    (1) ruguo wo kao guo   ceyan, wo *hui* gu Chicago.

          if   I   pass (comp) exam I   (fut) go Chicago

      "If I pass my exam, I will go to Chicago."

[22] This activity was suggested by Megan Hardy.

REFERENCES

Austin J. (1962). *How to do things with words*. New York and London: Oxford University Press.

Azar, B. S. (1989). *Understanding and using English grammar*. 2nd ed. Englewood Cliffs, NJ: Prentice Hall Regents.

Biber, D., Johansson, S., Leech, G., Conrad, S., & Finegan, E. (1999). *Longman grammar of spoken and written English*. Essex: Pearson Education Limited.

Cole, P., & Morgan, J. (1975). Speech acts. *Syntax and Semantics*, *3*, New York: Academic Press.

Comrie, B. (1986). Conditionals: A typology. In E. C. Traugott, A. T. Meulen, J. S. Reilly, & C. A. Ferguson (Eds.), *On conditionals* (pp. 77–102). Cambridge: Cambridge University Press.

Dancygier, B. (1999). *Conditionals and prediction: Time, knowledge and causation in conditional constructions*. Cambridge: Cambridge University Press.

Fakhri, A. (1995). Tense and aspect in Arab ESL learners' discourse. Paper presented at the *Eleventh Annual International Conference on Pragmatics and Language Learning*, University of Illinois at Urbana-Champaign. March 1995.

Fillmore, C. 1990. Epistemic stance and grammatical form in English conditional sentences. *Papers from the Twenty-sixth Regional Meeting of the Chicago Linguistic Society*, 137–162.

Geis, M. (1973). Unless and if not. In B. Kachru, R. Lees, Y. Malkiel, A. Pietraangeli, and S. Soporta (Eds.), *Issues in lingusitics: Papers in honor of Henry and Renée Kahane*. Urbana: University of Illinois Press.

Green, G. (1982). Colloquial and literary uses of inversions. In D. Tannen (Ed.), *Spoken and written language* (pp. 119–153). Norwood, NJ: Ablex.

Huddleston, R., & Pullum, G. K. (2002). *The Cambridge grammar of the English language*. Cambridge: Cambridge University Press.

Kaharma, N., & Hajjaj, A. (1989). *Errors in English among Arabic speakers: Analysis and remedy*. Essex: Longman.

Li, C. N., & Thompson, S. A. (1981). *Mandarin Chinese: A functional reference grammar*. Berkeley: University of California Press.

Madrick, J. A. (2005). Mind of his own, *New York Review of Books*.

Quirk, R., & Greenbaum, S. (1975). *A concise grammar of contemporary English*. New York: Harcourt Brace Jovanovich, Inc.

Quirk, R., Greenbaum, S., Leech, G., & Svartvik, J. (1972). *A grammar of contemporary English*. New York/London: Seminary Press.

Tseng, M. F. (2001). Investigating L2 learners' acquisition of tense constraints in English conditionals. Paper presented at the *Annual Convention of the American Association of Applied Linguistics*.

Tseng, M. F., & Cowan, R. (1999). Using the DTC to investigate Chinese ESL students' errors with English conditionals. *Annual Conference of the American Association of Applied Linguistics*. Stamford, CT.

Whitaker, S. F. (1970). Unless. *English Language Teaching Journal*, *24*(2), 154–160.

CHAPTER 20

Subject Clauses and Related Structures

INTRODUCTION

In this chapter, we will look at subordinate clauses that can be *subject clauses* – that can appear in subject position in sentences. (In Chapter 21, we will see that these same types of clauses can also function as complements of verbs and adjectives.) The four types of clauses together are sometimes called *noun clauses*, because they typically occur in the places that noun phrases occur. We will also examine certain structures that can be used instead of sentences with subject clauses and look at discourse factors that favor the use of subject clauses and of these related structures. Subject clauses and most of the other structures are taught in English language teaching textbooks; however, some of the related structures, in particular, cause problems for ESL/EFL students in their writing and speaking.

TYPES OF SUBJECT CLAUSES

All verbs allow noun phrases to occur as subjects, as shown in (1).

NP as Subject	*Verb*	*Object*
(1) {*John/He* / *Alan's sister*}	bought	a plane ticket.

Some verbs also permit subordinate clauses to appear in this position. In (2), the clause in subject position is introduced by *that*.

Clause as Subject	*Verb*	*Object*
(2) [That she did not reply immediately]	doesn't surprise	him.

Unlike NP subjects, clauses in subject position generally cannot undergo subject–aux inversion, as (3) demonstrates.

(3) *Doesn't [that she did not reply immediately] surprise him?

However, they have quite a few other properties of subjecthood in common with NPs. In addition to appearing before the verb, they display agreement with it (taking a singular verb), have a pronoun reflex (*it*) in tag questions, and can be part of a coordinate structure. As with other subjects, if they are removed from a sentence, the sentence becomes ungrammatical.

There are four types of subordinate clauses that appear in subject position. We will look at each in turn. For each, we will see some of the verbs that are among those commonly found in main clauses when the clause type is in subject position. In addition to occurring with particular main clause verbs, subject noun clauses also occur with combinations of *be* and particular adjectives or nouns, and we will look at some common examples of these as well.

Infinitive Clauses

Infinitive clauses, as the name indicates, are clauses that contain a verb in its infinitive form. They are a type of *nonfinite clause* in that their verb, being in the infinitive form, does not carry tense. Infinitive clauses may have a subject, which is preceded by *for*, as shown in (4a). The *for* is a *complementizer* – a type of subordinator whose only function is to introduce dependent clauses. Far more frequently, infinitive clauses have no overt subject, as in (4b), in which case the subject is typically understood as "people in general."

> (4) a. *For John to ignore her advice* would be foolish.
> b. *To write good poetry* requires as much practice as talent.

Infinitive clauses can appear in subject position before verbs including *amuse*, *cause*, *delight*, and *occur*, as in (5a). They can also appear before *be* + adjectives including *easy*, *difficult*, *foolish*, *good*, and *impossible*, as in (5b), as well as before *be* + nouns including *error*, *mistake*, *offense*, and *task*, as in (5c).

> (5) a. *To ask someone for help* simply wouldn't occur to my father.
> b. *To fool him* is not particularly difficult.
> c. *To get a simple yes or no answer out of her* is a real task.

Gerund Clauses

Gerund clauses contain a verb in the present participle form. Like infinitive clauses, they are nonfinite clauses, not marked for tense. Gerund clauses may contain as their subject a noun in the possessive form – for example, *Alan's* in (6a) – or a possessive pronoun – for example, *his* in (6b). If a gerund clause has no overt subject, it begins with a present participle, as shown in (6c).

> (6) a. *Alan's refusing our invitation* took us completely by surprise.[1]
> b. *His refusing our invitation* took us completely by surprise.
> c. *Writing good poetry* requires as much practice as talent.

Gerund clauses can occur with many of the same verbs and *be* + adjective or noun combinations as infinitive clauses, as in (6a) and (6b) respectively. Consequently, many subject infinitive clauses have gerund clause counterparts, as illustrated in (7).

> (7) a. *To get an interview with him* is practically impossible.
> b. *Getting an interview with him* is practically impossible.

That Clauses

That clauses are introduced by the complementizer *that* and include a subject and a past or present tense verb, as in (8a) and (8b), or a modal, as in (8c). Because they have a tensed verb, *that* clauses are a type of *finite clause*. Verbs before which *that* clauses appear include *amaze*, as in (8a), and also *bother*, *deter*, *illustrate*, *indicate*, and *surprise*.

That clauses also occur before *be* + adjectives including *apparent, clear, disconcerting, evident, important,* and *remarkable,* as in (8b); and before *be* + nouns, including *accident, asset, factor, miracle, result (of),* as in (8c), and *source (of)*.

(8) a. *That he continues to visit her regularly after all these years* amazes me.
   b. *That he managed to get his degree at all* is truly remarkable.
   c. *That he would say such a thing* is the result of his utter lack of understanding.[2]

Interrogative Clauses

Interrogative clauses, or *embedded question clauses,* begin with a *wh-* element and, like *that* clauses, are finite clauses, having a present or past tense verb or a modal. Verbs including *bother, concern, depend on, determine, interest,* and *matter* can take interrogative clause subjects, as exemplified in (9a). Interrogative clauses can also precede *be* and adjectives, such as *arguable, certain, clear, debatable, important, obvious, relevant, significant,* as exemplified in (9b); and *be* + nouns, such as *concern, issue, matter,* and *problem,* as exemplified in (9c). The main clause is often negative, as is the case with (9b) and (9c).

(9) a. *Whether he can get a scholarship* will depend on his grade.
   b. *How he plans to do that* is not clear.
   c. *Whether he completes it today or tomorrow* is not the issue.

SUMMARY

TYPES OF SUBJECT CLAUSES

Subject clauses are subordinate clauses that occur as subjects of sentences. They are possible with some verbs and some combinations of *be* + adjective and *be* + noun.

Four types of clauses appear as subject clauses:

• **Infinitive clauses** are clauses that have a *to* + verb. They may occur with or without a subject preceded by the complementizer *for.*
   For John to believe such a lie is unthinkable.
   To write good poetry requires considerable talent.

• **Gerund clauses** have a verb in the present participle form. They may include a possessive noun or possessive pronoun as their subject.
   Alan's refusing our invitation took us completely by surprise.
   Writing good poetry isn't easy.

• ***That* clauses** are introduced by the complementizer *that* and include a modal or tensed verb.
   That he would even consider doing it surprises me.
   That he managed to get his degree is truly remarkable.

• **Interrogative (embedded question) clauses** begin with a *wh-* element and include a modal or tensed verb.
   How he plans to do that is not clear.
   Whether he completes it today or tomorrow is not the issue.

EXERCISE 20.1

Underline the subject clause in each sentence and identify its type (infinitive, gerund, *that*, or interrogative).

Example: Iraq's invading Kuwait set off a war.

Answer: <u>Iraq's invading Kuwait</u> set off a war.   gerund clause

1. That Bush got so many votes surprised everyone.
2. For Alan to spread such an outright lie would be unthinkable.
3. Whether they will take disciplinary action against him has not been decided yet.
4. To take offense at such a harmless joke is really silly.
5. Ted Turner's refusing Rupert Murdoch's offer took him completely by surprise.
6. Taking an extra week of vacation wasn't such a good idea after all.

USE OF SUBJECT CLAUSES IN DISCOURSE

Subject clauses are infrequent, especially in spoken English.[3] Their infrequency likely relates to the end weight principle discussed in earlier chapters with regard to NP subjects: when possible, long complex elements are placed at the end of sentences to facilitate processing. As we will see shortly, a rule in fact enables subject clauses to be shifted to the end of the sentence.

Subject clauses occur in the prototypical position for old information – sentence initially. Thus, when used in written discourse, they typically contain an NP that has already been mentioned and make an assertion about it that is clear from the preceding discourse or is information readers can be assumed to know. We see an example of this in the use of the *that* subject clause in (10).

(**10**) There are many players who might win the Masters, many who could. But the feeling about Faldo is that if he is at the top of his game, he should win it.

That he is ranked only No. 4 in the world at the moment is due to the eccentricity of the system. His first Masters win has now slipped from his ranking points.

The subject clause has as its subject the pronoun *he*, which refers to the golfer Nick Faldo, discussed in the previous paragraph and hence old information. The rest of the clause gives information the writer assumes golf-savvy readers will know. The subject clause in this way makes a connection to the previous paragraph and simultaneously shifts the topic – from Faldo's chance to win the Masters to his professional ranking and the reason for it, which is given by the rest of the sentence. The following sentence continues the new topic of ranking.

Not surprisingly, subject clauses are typically used to begin a new paragraph that follows previous information but not in the lead-in sentence that begins a text. Because these subject clauses contain some reference to preceding information or shared knowledge, writers often use them to shift from a previous topic, to which they are connected, to something new, introduced in the main clause that follows.

In (11), which is from an academic text, the subject clause recapitulates the information just presented (that meteorites are all of the same age), and the rest of the sentence, after the main clause verb *suggests*, shifts to an explanation of this information.[4]

(11) One of the triumphs of radioactive dating emerged only gradually as more and more workers dated meteorites. It became surprisingly apparent that all meteorites are of the same age, somewhere in the vicinity of 4.5 billion years old. *That there are no meteorites of any other age, regardless of when they fell to earth*, suggests that all meteorites originated in other bodies of the solar system that formed at the same time that the Earth did.

The example in (12) involves an infinitive clause. Notice that the object NP *this goal* is old information, referring to *finding a cure for this dreaded disease* and thus linking to the preceding sentence, and that the rest of the sentence completes the shift to a related topic – the difficulty of achieving the goal.

(12) The scientific community is now focusing intently on finding a cure for this dreaded disease. *To accomplish this goal* will not be easy. It will require very expensive research.

As a last example, consider the gerund clause in (13), which is taken from a book review. The reviewer has described a political crisis in India that was precipitated by the publication of textbooks containing descriptions that members of some religious groups found offensive. Having provided a detailed account of the political crisis, the author of the review then shifts the topic to an additional complication associated with this problem – the lack of unbiased published histories of India. This shift is accomplished by a gerund clause at the start of a new paragraph: *the problem* links to the previous content, and *exacerbating* introduces the shift to the lack of histories, which is completed in the main clause of the sentence.

(13) *Exacerbating the problem in the long term* is a lack of accessible, well-written and balanced histories of India. The most widely available introductions to the subject – the two Penguin histories . . . are both fine works but somewhat dull and hard going.

In short, the choice of subject clauses by writers may often be due to the information structuring principle by which sentences in a discourse have old information preceding new information. Subject clauses are a vehicle for linking new information to old information.

MOVEMENT OF SUBJECT CLAUSES

As already noted, the subject clause of a sentence can sometimes be moved, creating an alternative version of the sentence. In this section, we look at the rule involved and at factors that influence which version is used.

Extraposition

Clauses in subject position can be moved to the end of a sentence. When this happens, the subject position is filled by the word *it*. The rule that makes this change is known as *extraposition*. It is illustrated in (14) for an infinitive clause and in (15) for a *that* clause. For descriptive purposes, we will refer to sentences like (14b) and (15b) as having the *extraposition pattern*. Notice that the *it* in extraposition pattern sentences is not anaphoric (it has no referent) – for this reason, it is often called a *dummy it*.[5]

(**14**) a. *For John to ignore her advice* would be stupid.
b. *It* _____ would be stupid *for John to ignore her advice*.

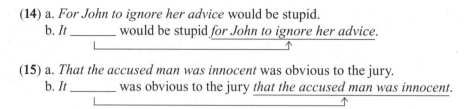

(**15**) a. *That the accused man was innocent* was obvious to the jury.
b. *It* _____ was obvious to the jury *that the accused man was innocent.*

With infinitive clauses, this rule applies to sentences with main clause verbs including *amuse, bother, delight, disturb, embarrass,* and *please,* as exemplified in (16), and *be* followed by adjectives including *difficult, easy, foolish, good,* and *impossible,* as exemplified in (17).

(**16**) a. *For the committee to even consider doing something like this* would bother me.
b. It would bother me *for the committee to even consider doing something like this.*

(**17**) a. *To understand this lesson* is easy.
b. It is easy *to understand this lesson.*

Gerund clauses generally resist extraposition, as can be seen in (18), with the ungrammaticality of (18b) and (18d). Nevertheless, exceptions can be found; (19b) is fully grammatical.

(**18**) a. *Understanding this lesson* was easy.
b. *It was easy understanding this lesson.
c. *Herb's winning the gold medal* came as a complete surprise to his coach.
d. *It came as a complete surprise to his coach Herb's winning the gold medal.

(**19**) a. *Protesting the new policies* would be no use.
b. It would be no use *protesting the new policies.*

With *that* clauses, extraposition is possible with main clause verbs such as *amaze, bother,* and *surprise,* as exemplified in (20), and with *be* followed by a range of adjectives including *apparent, clear, evident,* and *important,* as exemplified in (21).

(**20**) a. *That anyone can still believe her* amazes me.
b. It amazes me *that anyone can still believe her.*

(**21**) a. *That his efforts are doomed to fail* is now readily apparent.
b. It is now readily apparent *that his efforts are doomed to fail.*

Interrogative clauses can be extraposed when they are followed by *be* with adjectives such as *clear, important, obvious,* and so on, as illustrated in (22).[6] However, extraposition of interrogative clauses in sentences with transitive verbs often produces ungrammatical, or at best marginally acceptable, sentences such as (23b).

(**22**) a. *How they will manage to do that* is not clear.
b. It is not clear *how they will manage to do that.*
c. *Whether he completes it today or tomorrow* is not important.
d. It is not important *whether he completes it today or tomorrow.*

(**23**) a. Whether he gets a scholarship will depend on his grades.
b. ?It will depend on his grades whether he gets a scholarship.

A small number of intransitive verbs – *appear, come about, develop, happen, seem, transpire, turn out* – occur in sentences with extraposed *that* clauses but cannot appear in sentences in which the *that* clauses are in subject position, as illustrated in (24) and (25).

(**24**) a. It turns out *that he can't come.*
   b. **That he can't come* turns out.

(**25**) a. It appears *that she won't be joining us.*
   b **That she won't be joining us* appears.

Use: Extraposition Pattern Sentences Versus Sentences with Subject Clauses

Some verbs or adjectives are possible only with extraposed clauses or only with subject clauses. Others can occur with either, so that the writer or speaker has a choice between two possible versions. Extraposition pattern sentences occur far more frequently in speech and writing than sentences with clauses in subject position. We have already touched on the main reason for their greater frequency in our discussion of the use of subject clauses in discourse: extraposition moves a clause to the end of the sentence, and the result is in keeping with the principle of end weight, which, as we have seen, facilitates the processing of sentences that have long, heavy constituents. Furthermore, extraposition makes it possible to create sentences with multiple embedded clauses that would be virtually incomprehensible in subject position. For example, a sentence like (26) is ungrammatical.[7]

(**26**) **[That [that he was angry] was so obvious]* embarrassed her.

However, if we first extrapose the entire subject *that* clause with the embedded clause *that he was angry*, and then extrapose this embedded clause, we get (27), which is quite comprehensible.

(**27**) It embarrassed her [*that it was so obvious* [*that he was angry*]].

Although subject clauses are the less frequent choice, we have already seen one factor that can favor their use: the desire to link to previous discourse and to shift to a new topic. The example given earlier in (10) is repeated in (28) with the subject clause extraposed. Notice that the extraposition version in (28) is much less effective than the original in (10).

(**28**) There are many players who might win the Masters, many who could. But the feeling about Falco is that if he is at the top of his game, he should win it.

   It is due to the eccentricity of the system *that he is ranked only No. 4 in the world at the moment.* His first Masters win has now slipped from his ranking points.

Another factor favoring the use of subject clauses is a complex constituent in the main clause following the verb. Notice, for example, that (29a), with a subject clause, is far easier to understand than an extraposed version, as shown in (29b), would be.

(**29**) a. *To include that issue in the forthcoming Student Loans Bill* would make the measure hybrid and deny it any prospect of a swift passage through Parliament.[8]
   b. It would make the measure hybrid and deny it any prospect of a swift passage through Parliament *to include that issue in the forthcoming Student Loans Bill.*

In short, speakers and writers generally will opt for the extraposition structure, since this allows them to place a heavy element at the end of a sentence; however, at any given point in a discourse, other factors, including some favoring subject clauses, may also be involved.

SUMMARY

USE OF SUBJECT CLAUSES IN DISCOURSE; MOVEMENT OF SUBJECT CLAUSES

Subject clauses are used to make a connection to previous discourse and to introduce a new topic.

> *The scientific community is now focusing intently on finding a cure for this dreaded disease. To accomplish this goal will not be easy. It will require expensive research.*

The rule of **extraposition** moves a clause in subject position to the end of a sentence, substituting a dummy *it*.

> *That they were not interested in our offer was quite clear.* →
> *It was quite clear that they were not interested in our offer.*

Extraposition applies to *that*, infinitive, and interrogative clauses, but only infrequently to gerund clauses.

> *That he likes her is quite obvious.* →
> *It is quite obvious that he likes her.*
>
> *To write good poetry requires considerable talent.* →
> *It requires considerable talent to write good poetry.*
>
> *How he does it is not important.* →
> *It is not important how he does it.*
>
> *Getting him to agree will be no problem.* →
> *It will be no problem getting him to agree.*
>
> BUT
>
> *Herb's winning first prize was a complete surprise.* →
> **It was a complete surprise Herb's winning first prize.*

A few verbs such as *appear*, *develop*, *happen*, *seem*, and *turn out* can appear only in the extraposition pattern with *that* clauses.

> *It turns out that he won't be coming to the party after all.*
> **That he won't becoming to the party after all turns out.*

Extraposition pattern sentences are much more frequent than subject clause sentences. They are used to:

- move heavy clauses to the end, in keeping with the end weight principle.
  > *It's not important whether he completes it today or tomorrow.*

- create sentences with multiple embeddings.
  > *It embarrassed her that it was so obvious that he was angry.*

Subject clauses are favored over extraposition when there is a complex constituent in the main clause following the verb.

> *To include that issue in the forthcoming Student Loans Bill would make the measure hybrid and deny it any prospect of a swift passage through Parliament.*

EXERCISE 20.2

Indicate whether each of the following sentences has an extraposed counterpart. If so, give the extraposed counterpart; if not, explain why.

Example: Insulting the boss in front of everyone was really a dumb idea.

Answer: no (Gerund subject clauses do not extrapose well.)

1. To be awarded first prize in this contest is a great honor.
2. For Alan to be denied the right to a fair trial would be outrageous.
3. Paying off our mortgage has markedly improved our financial position.
4. How they managed to finish on time is not clear to us.
5. That the senator enjoys such popularity among the general public surprises many conservatives.

EXERCISE 20.3

Indicate whether each of the following sentences has a counterpart with a subject clause. If so, give the counterpart; if not, explain why.

Example: It turns out that she won't be coming after all.

Answer: no (*Turn out* is a verb that occurs only in the extraposition pattern.)

1. It just so happens that he is a friend of the president.
2. It's really quite easy to solve that problem.
3. It appears that she knew all along where the money was.
4. It's obvious that he is upset with her.
5. It seems that he will win after all.

RELATED STRUCTURES WITH NOUN PHRASE SUBJECTS

We have seen that extraposition pattern sentences are an alternative to sentences with subject clauses. In this section, we look at two other structures that are alternatives. Both involve the movement of an NP from an extraposed subject clause into subject position in the main clause. These structures are possible only in sentences with certain main clause verbs or certain adjectives or nouns following *be*.

Tough Movement Sentences

The object of an infinitive clause in an extraposition pattern sentence like that shown in (30a) may be moved out of its clause into the position occupied by *it*, to produce a sentence that has an identical meaning as shown in (30b). The rule that does this is called *tough movement*.[9]

infinitive clause
(**30**) a. It is easy [to understand *this lesson*].

    b. *This lesson* is easy [to understand _____].

Although the infinitive clause in (30) has no overt subject, *tough* movement also operates on infinitive clauses with subjects, as illustrated in (31).

(**31**) a. It's easy for John to understand this lesson.
    b. This lesson is easy for John to understand.

Moreover, the object that is moved into main clause subject position can be the object of a preposition in the infinitive clause, as in (32).

(32) a. It's a real pleasure to work with John.
b. John is a real pleasure to work with.

Tough movement cannot be applied to all extraposition pattern sentences with infinitive clauses. For *tough* movement to apply, the main clause must have *be*, or a similar verb, followed by either

- an *ease/difficulty adjective* such as *dangerous, difficult, easy, fun, hard, impossible, pleasant, simple, tough,* or *wonderful,* or
- an NP that has a similar "ease/difficulty" meaning, for example, *a chore, a cinch, a joy, a pain, a piece of cake, a pleasure, a snap.*

Applying *tough* movement to sentences in which *be* is followed by an adjective or NP that is not a member of the ease/difficulty set results in ungrammatical sentences, as illustrated in (33) and (34).

(33) a. It is *possible* to see the director.
b. *The director is possible to see.

(34) a. It is *a real honor* to work with Professor Hobson.
b *Professor Hobson is a real honor to work with.

Tough movement sentences are common in both conversation and academic prose.[10] The subject of a *tough* movement sentence is frequently a pronoun that refers back to something that has been mentioned previously, as shown in (35), in which *it* refers to *John's birthday.* (The lack of an object after *remember* confirms that this *it* is not a dummy *it.*) This suggests that *tough* movement gives speakers and writers a way to put old information that would otherwise come later in a sentence in its typical position, at the start of a sentence.

(35) A: Do you know when John's birthday is?
B: It's easy to remember. December 25th, Christmas Day.

Subject Raising Sentences

In (24) and (25), earlier in the chapter, we saw that when the verbs *appear, happen,* and *seem* occur with *that* clauses, they are restricted to the extraposition pattern, as in (36).

$$(36) \text{ It} \begin{Bmatrix} seems \\ happens \\ appears \end{Bmatrix} [that\ Edith\ enjoys\ my\ company].$$

There is another possibility for these verbs: they can also occur in sentences with a following infinitive clause, the subject of which has been moved to subject position in the main clause. Thus, in addition to (36), we can have (37). Notice that (37) has the same meaning as (36).

$$(37) \text{ Edith} \begin{Bmatrix} seems \\ happens \\ appears \end{Bmatrix} to\ enjoy\ my\ company.$$

To derive (37), we can start with a structure such as the one shown in (38) and apply a rule called *subject raising*, which moves the subject of the infinitive clause into subject position in the main clause.[11]

(**38**) a. It seems [*Edith* to enjoy my company].
b. *Edith* seems [_____ to enjoy my company].

The subject raising rule also applies to sentences with *be* followed by an adjective that expresses a degree of probability, such as *certain*, *likely*, or *unlikely*, as shown in (39).

(**39**) The value of the dollar is $\begin{Bmatrix} likely \\ unlikely \\ certain \end{Bmatrix}$ [*to go up in January*].

This sentence can be seen as the result of applying subject raising, as shown in (40).

(**40**) a. It is likely [*the value of the dollar* to go up in January].
b. *The value of the dollar* is likely [_____ to go up in January].

As with the verbs, with many of these adjectives, equivalent sentences with extraposed *that* clauses are possible. For example, along with (39), we can have *It is likely that the value of the dollar will go up in January.* However, with some probability adjectives, such as *sure* and *apt*, only the subject raising pattern with an infinitive is possible, as (41) illustrates.

(**41**) a. He is $\begin{Bmatrix} sure \\ apt \end{Bmatrix}$ to complain about something.

b. *It is $\begin{Bmatrix} sure \\ apt \end{Bmatrix}$ that he will complain about something.

Use: Subject Raising Sentences Versus Sentences with Extraposed *That* Clauses

Subject raising sentences are much more frequent than sentences with extraposed *that* clauses, both with verbs like *seem* and *appear* and with adjectives such as (*un*)*likely* and *certain*, in both spoken and written English.[12] The given–new contract appears to be a factor favoring a subject raising construction – that is, the NP that subject raising positions at the start of the sentence, in the position of old information, is often one that has an anaphoric link to the preceding discourse. Consider, for example, (42). The pronoun *she* in the subject raising sentence is more directly linked to the antecedent *Marge* in the previous sentence than it would be in the alternative with extraposition – *It wasn't likely that she would take a taxi to Naples.*

(**42**) The first thing he thought of when he woke up was Marge. *She wasn't likely to take a taxi to Naples.*[13]

Although less common, the extraposition pattern may be favored due to several specific factors. For example, to attribute a perception to someone or something, a writer or speaker can use *seem* or *appear* followed by a *to* prepositional phrase and then the extraposed *that* clause, as shown by (43).

(**43**) It seemed *to her* that she was losing control of her temper all the time.

Moreover, the principle of end weight favors the extraposition pattern when the *that* clause subject is a long, complex noun phrase, as subject raising would move this NP to an initial position. For the most part, such sentences, including that in (44), originate in academic prose.

(**44**) The report states that it is likely that *more than half of all conventional gas reserves that will be ultimately produced in the United States* have already been produced.[14]

Sentences That Look like *Tough* Movement or Subject Raising Structures

Both *tough* movement and subject raising structures have the grammatical pattern NP *is* + Adj [infinitive clause]. Not all sentences that have this pattern are one of these two sentence types.

Sentence (45) has the same pattern as (46a), a subject raising sentence, and (46b), a *tough* movement sentence.

(**45**) John is *eager* to please.

(**46**) a. John is *certain* to please.
b. John is *easy* to please.

However, unlike (46a) and other subject raising sentences, (45) does not have a grammatical extraposed counterpart with a *that* clause, as (47) demonstrates. Thus, it cannot be a subject raising structure.

(**47**) *It is eager that John will please.
(Cf. It is certain that John will please.)

Unlike (46b) and other *tough* movement sentences, (45) does not have a grammatical extraposed version with an infinitive complement, as (48) shows. Moreover, whereas in *tough* movement sentences, the subject was originally the infinitive clause object, as in (45), *John* clearly is not understood as the object of *please*. Thus, (45) also cannot be a *tough* movement structure.

(**48**) *It is eager to please John.
(Cf. It is easy to please John.)

Sentence (45), in short, has a different structure, as illustrated in (49b). Unlike the other structures shown, this one does not relate to a structure with a subject noun clause; the NP *John* originates in subject position.

(**49**) a. John is eager to please.
b. John is eager [(John) to please (someone)] .

The structure in (49b) reflects our intuitions that the subject of the infinitive complement in square brackets is identical to the main clause subject. Sentences like (45) always have adjectives of willingness or ability (e.g., *able, eager, eligible, free, ready, welcome, willing*) between the main clause verb *be* and a following infinitive clause.

SUMMARY

RELATED STRUCTURES WITH NOUN PHRASE SUBJECTS

In addition to extraposition pattern sentences, speakers and writers can use the following alternatives to sentences with subject clauses:

- *Tough* **movement sentences**, in which an object of an infinitive clause in an extraposition pattern sentence moves into subject position in the main clause. *Tough* movement sentences occur with *be* + either an ease/difficulty adjective or an NP with an ease/difficulty meaning.

extraposition	tough *movement*
It is fun to work with him.	*He is fun to work with.*
It is a pleasure to work with him.	*He is a pleasure to work with.*

- **Subject raising sentences**, in which an NP that is the subject of an infinitive clause following a verb or *be* + adjective moves into subject position in the main clause. They correspond to sentences with extraposed *that* clauses. Subject raising occurs with verbs, such as *appear*, *happen*, and *seem*, and with *be* + probability adjectives including *(un)likely* and *certain*.

extraposition	*subject raising*
It seems that Edith likes me.	*Edith seems to like me.*
It is likely that John will succeed.	*John is likely to succeed.*

Subject raising sentences are much more common than sentences with extraposed *that* clauses, perhaps because an initial subject linking to previous discourse fits the given–new contract.

I'd love to see my brother. But he isn't likely to be here.

In sentences with *be* + an adjective of willingness or ability and a following infinitive clause, the main clause subject is also the subject of the infinitive clause.

Alan is eager to participate. (= *Alan is eager* [*(Alan) to participate*].)

EXERCISE 20.4

Identify each of the following sentences as a *tough* movement sentence, a subject raising sentence, or a sentence with *be* + a willingness/ability adjective.

Example: The stock market is not likely to peak when the Dow reaches 10,000.

Answer: subject raising

1. She happens to be his sister.
2. He is sure to notice all those mistakes in the report.
3. This lesson is really hard to understand.
4. Suddenly he remembered Susan. She was likely to show up at any moment.
5. She's certain to lose the election.
6. A good, "politically correct" man is really hard to find today.
7. John is really easy to work with.
8. Andy Roddick is able to do anything on the tennis court – serve, volley, or lob.

> **EXERCISE 20.5**
>
> 1. Write two original sentences that involve *tough* movement and two that involve subject raising.
> 2. Compare the *tough* movement rule with the subject raising rule. How are they similar and how are they different?

> **EXERCISE 20.6**
>
> Indicate whether the sentences in each pair are the same or different in structure. Support your answer by indicating what structure(s) they have.
>
> *Example:* a. Bill is likely to spoil the surprise party by saying something to Susan.
>   b. Bill is apt to spoil the surprise party by saying something to Susan.
>
> *Answer:* same (subject raising)
>
> 1. a. Well, he's certainly welcome to try!
>   b. Well, he's certainly willing to try!
> 2. a. Fred is sure to win.
>   b. Fred is determined to win.
> 3. a. He's easy to forget.
>   b. He's eager to forget.
> 4. a. Alice isn't ready to enter the contest.
>   b. Alice isn't likely to enter the contest.
> 5. a. Bill is eligible to enter the contest.
>   b. Bill is ready to enter the contest.

PROBLEMS THAT ESL/EFL STUDENTS HAVE WITH SUBJECT CLAUSES AND RELATED STRUCTURES

Subject clauses do not seem to be a problem for ESL/EFL students, perhaps because they are not used that frequently and they occur mostly in written English. However, extraposition and *tough* movement structures, which occur frequently in spoken as well as in written English, do pose problems for ESL/EFL students. When attempting to express the equivalent of an English extraposition or *tough* movement structure, students often fall back on the structures of their L1, and this can result in strange-sounding English sentences. We will look at some well-documented errors and their probable causes.

"Pseudo-*Tough*-Movement" Structures (Chinese)

Yip (1995) reports that Chinese ESL students have been heard to use sentences like (50a) when they want to express the meaning conveyed by the English extraposition structure in (50b) or the *tough* movement structure in (50c).

> (**50**) a. *I am difficult to learn English.
>   b. It is difficult for me to learn English.
>   c. English is difficult for me to learn.

Similar errors made by Chinese intermediate level students are shown in (51).

> (**51**) a. *If there is a job, they are very easy to take it.
>   b. *You may be hard to catch what they are talking about.

The ungrammatical sentences in (50a) and (51) have been called *pseudo*-tough-*movement structures* because they contain *tough* movement adjectives. The Chinese speakers who produced them appear to have moved the subjects of the infinitive clauses into subject position rather than the objects, as (52) illustrates.

(52) a. It is difficult [for *me* to learn English]. → **I am difficult to learn English.*
    b. If there is a job, it is very easy [*for them* to take it]. → ** . . . they are very easy to take it.*

Chinese does not have extraposition or *tough* movement structures. It uses *topicalization* instead. In English, topicalization is the movement of an NP to the beginning of the sentence to give it prominence. For example, if we want to emphasize the direct objects in the sentence *I don't like **him**; I like **her***, we could use sentence stress, or we could use topicalization to move the direct object pronouns to the start of their respective clauses, yielding *Him I don't like, her I do.* This kind of movement is less common in English than in Chinese. The topicalization structure shown in (53) would be used to express the English sentence *It is very difficult for her to find a room.* The topic, *ta*, is moved to the beginning of the sentence, as is the infinitive clause subject in English subject raising.

(53) *Ta   hen   nan   zhaodao   fangzi*
     she/he very difficult find   room
     "It is very difficult for her/him to find a room."

The linear arrangement of the Chinese topicalization structure in (53) – NP (*is*) adjective (*to*) verb – is almost identical to that of English *tough* movement structures. The Chinese speakers may follow the pattern in (53) when producing English sentences that contain *tough* movement adjectives, thus putting the subject of the infinitive clause at the beginning of the sentence. This would explain the pseudo-*tough*-movement structures, and it would predict that the Chinese speakers would frequently assign an incorrect meaning to English *tough* movement structures. This is exactly what Yip found. When asked what the *tough* movement sentence *He is difficult to see* meant, one Chinese ESL student insisted that the correct meaning was "it is difficult for him to see" rather than "it is difficult to see him." Yip's study suggests that Chinese speakers follow the L1 topicalization pattern when they create sentences with *be* and following *tough* movement adjectives. They also extend the pseudo-*tough*-movement structure to non-*tough*-movement adjectives in English, creating sentences such as **I am not convenient to come to school this week.*

The pseudo-*tough*-movement problem has been found with English learners with other L1s. For example, Korean speakers in a required writing course at an American university wrote the sentences in (54).

(54) a. *Many Koreans are difficult to learn English because of pronunciation.
    b. *Other children are easy to seek things faster and faster.
    c. *Poor families are hard to afford to buy a computer and cooperate.

Like Chinese, Korean has no extraposition pattern. Korean uses a single structure with either a nominal postposition marker (*-i/ka*) or a topic marker (*–eykey-nun*). The pseudo-*tough*-movement structures are a persistent error for Korean speakers, occurring in the compositions of undergraduate and graduate students at American universities.[15]

Pseudo-*Tough*-Movement with Passivization (Chinese)

The ungrammatical sentences in (55) were also produced by Chinese speakers. They differ from the pseudo-*tough*-movement structures we have looked at in that they are passives.

> (55) a. *The instrument is easy to be performed.
> b. *The second sentence is not that easy to be expressed in gesture language.
> c. *Communication tools are difficult to be commercialized.

In Chinese, some topicalization structures are ambiguous. In order to give them a single, unambiguous meaning, Chinese speakers passivize them.[16] The Chinese speakers who produced the sentences in (55) apparently transferred this preference for passivizing to English.

Omission of *It* in Extraposition Structures (Spanish)

Spanish does not have extraposition structures with a dummy *it*. Instead it uses *es*, as illustrated in (56).

> (56) *Es tan difícil   para mí porque   las gramáticas   no son   iguales.*
> is so difficult   for me because   the grammars   not are   the same
> "It's so difficult for me because the grammars are not the same."

Spanish speakers will often omit the *it* required in extraposition structures, thereby making errors like the one in (57), from the composition of an intermediate-level ESL student.

> (57) *Is very hard to live without privacy.

This particular type of error is fairly common with low-intermediate and intermediate-level students. We would expect it to disappear as students gain greater proficiency. In fact, this expectation is supported by an examination of an error corpus[17] consisting of errors made by Spanish-speaking university students. These students no longer dropped dummy *it* in simple sentences like those in (57). Nonetheless, when they wrote longer and more complex sentences in their compositions, they still dropped the *it* in embedded clauses, as shown in (58). Retention of dummy *it* in complex clauses may therefore be something that writing teachers should address.

> (58) *To answer that, is important to make a clear distinction between . . .

SUGGESTIONS FOR TEACHING SUBJECT CLAUSES AND RELATED STRUCTURES

Certain structures we have looked at are of greater importance than others for the teaching of writing to advanced-level students. Swales and Feak (2005, p. 86) point out that, in the reports that many students will need to write, extraposition structures with *that* clauses are typically used to comment on the strength of data (e.g., *It is certain/likely/quite probable/possible that* . . .). Subject raising structures, too, are common in academic writing. In short, students who are going to be writing about research will need, as the authors put it, "the linguistic resources" to do so, and these include extraposition and subject raising structures. Furthermore, as we have seen, *that* and infinitive clauses in subject position are not infrequently used in academic writing. This suggests that subject clauses and extraposition and subject raising should be introduced at the high-intermediate/advanced level as well as incorporated into the writing instruction provided for many ESL students in undergraduate and graduate programs. The activities that follow, all intended for high-intermediate and advanced-level students, are divided into two sets – one to practice the structures in this chapter (extraposition, subject raising, and *tough* movement) and the other to work on common errors.

Introducing and Practicing Structures

Activity 1: Using a Poem to Focus on Subject Infinitive Clauses and *Tough* Movement and Extraposition Structures (High Intermediate Through Advanced)

The primary objective of this activity is to use the short poem shown in (59) to draw attention to subject infinitive clauses and *tough* movement structures, each of which occurs once in the poem, and to show how subject infinitive clauses can be paraphrased with extraposition and *tough* movement structures. However, this activity is also intended to be fun; the overall effect intended by the poet should not be neglected. There is certainly no need to turn the class into a session on literary criticism, but you can ask questions and point out things that the poet has done to create humor. For example, you could ask, "What two words does the poet repeat several times to create a humorous effect? What does the poet do in the last line of the poem to make us laugh?"

(59) The Pecan, The Toucan
    Very few can
    Tell the Toucan
    From the Pecan –
    Here's a new plan:
    To take the Toucan from the tree,
    Requires im-mense a-gil-i-tee,
    While anyone can pick with ease
    The pecans from the pecan trees.
    It's such an easy thing to do,
    That even the Toucan he can too.

        Robert Williams Wood

Stage 1

Have the poem written on the board or on a handout or projected on a wall. The picture of the toucan can also be displayed this way. Read the poem aloud with the proper pauses, at the line breaks, while the students read it silently. This allows them a chance to experience the oral effect of the poet's choice of words.

Stage 2

Read the poem through in semantic units; that is, combining lines that make complete statements. The goal of this second reading is to ensure complete comprehension of all lines and to draw attention to the subject infinitive clause and the *tough* movement structure. This is done through questions that force the students to explain the complete meaning of truncated lines. The questions also get the students to restate the two structures by using a possible alternative (extraposition in one case, a subject infinitive clause in the other). A reading and questioning session might proceed as follows:

- Read "*Very few can / Tell the Toucan / From the Pecan*," and ask, "What does that mean – 'very few'? Very few what? [Answer: people.] That's right, very few people can tell the Toucan from the Pecan." Ask a student, "Can you tell a toucan from a pecan? Yes, I bet you can. It's pretty easy, isn't it?"

- Read "*Here's a new plan*," and say, "A new plan for what? What is this new plan for? . . . Right! It's a new plan to tell the difference between a toucan and a pecan."

- Read "*To take the Toucan from the tree, / Requires im-mense a-gil-i-tee.*" Say, "Look how the poet has written 'immense.' What does 'immense' mean? Right, 'a lot of.' The reason he put a hyphen in there was so we would stretch the word out when we read it. And notice how 'agility' is spelled and that it has hyphens in it. That tells us that we are supposed to read it like this: 'ah-GIL-ah-tee.' That way it has the same number of beats as the other lines. It fits into the poem better that way." Reread the two lines and ask, "What's another way of saying that?" If no answer is forthcoming, prompt: "It requires immense agility . . ." This will usually elicit the extraposition structure. Say, "Good. So we can say either 'To take the Toucan from the tree requires immense agility' or 'It requires immense agility to take the Toucan from the tree.' Why does it take immense agility to take the Toucan from the tree?" The students answer.

- Read "*While anyone can pick with ease / The pecans from the pecan trees*," and then ask, "Is that right? Why can anyone pick pecans from the trees they grow on?"

- Read "*It's such an easy thing to do / That even the Toucan he can too*," and ask, "What's such an easy thing to do?" This will probably elicit the answer "pick the pecans." You can respond with something like "Right! It's so easy to pick the pecans from the tree that even the Toucan can do it."

Stage 3

Read the poem aloud one more time, emphasizing the rhythm and the pauses which enhance the intended humorous effect. Ask a student to read it aloud. Finally, if you did not use handouts, give a copy of the poem to each student.

Activity 2: Practicing *Tough* Movement Sentences (High Intermediate Through Advanced)

This activity can begin in small groups and evolve into a whole-class activity. Before beginning, demonstrate the extraposition and *tough* movement patterns on the board, and show students that sentences in the two patterns mean the same thing. Divide students into groups of three, and give each group a paper with an activities list, such as the one shown below.

study English	talk to my teacher	watch television
solve a crossword puzzle	learn a foreign language	listen to music
do my homework assignment	read a good book	meet new friends
fly an airplane	learn about history	ride a motor scooter
lift a ton (2,000 pounds)	read a newspaper	play video games
beat an army single-handedly	make a sandwich	book a hotel on the Internet
write a 500-page novel in 2 hours	open a bottle	
eat 10 large pizzas in an hour	change a lightbulb	

On the board, write *tough* movement adjectives that could be used to characterize the activities: *boring, dangerous, easy, fun, hard/difficult, impossible, interesting.*

Tell the students to look at the lists and think about which activities would fit with which adjectives. The members of each group then ask each other questions about how they would characterize the activities. The student asking a question uses one pattern – extraposition or *tough* movement – and the student responding uses the other pattern. For example, student A asks, "Is it easy to learn a foreign language?" and student B answers, "No. Foreign languages are hard to learn."

As students ask and answer questions, move from group to group, and check to see that they are using both patterns. If the group is only using the extraposition pattern, you can say, "What's another way of saying that?" Don't take sides in any disputes about whether an activity fits a particular adjective; instead, allow students to disagree about even impossible activities and to argue about answers.

Activity 3: Finding Real Examples of Extraposition Structures (High Intermediate Through Advanced)

After introducing extraposition structures, you may find it useful to show students how often these structures appear in the written English they come across every day in newspapers and magazines. Collect examples from simple advertisements like those shown in (60). Have the students bring in other examples and discuss them in class.

(60) a. **Introducing L'eggs wear**
   Tights, trouser socks, opaques, and socks.
   Now it's more fun to put yourself together.
   [from an advertisement for L'eggs hosiery]

   b. **Best bet in stretching**
   It's crucial to stretch these five muscles before running: hamstrings, hip flexors, quadriceps, groin, and achilles tendons. Get off to a running start with the New Balance 665, a highly shock absorbing running shoe with excellent cushion and energy return.
   [from an advertisement for New Balance shoes]

Activity 4: Practicing Subject Raising Structures (High Intermediate Through Advanced)

To practice subject raising sentences with the verbs *seem* and *appear*, collect from magazines pictures that you can use to ask students questions that use these verbs, for example, "What does she seem to be doing? Does the night appear to be foggy?" Almost any picture will be satisfactory provided that you can come up with questions about it that can be answered with an affirmative response, for example, "She seems to be looking at something/bending down to pick up something" or a negative response with a clarification, for example, "No, the night doesn't appear to be foggy, but it appears to be rainy."

To practice subject raising with probability adjectives such as *likely* and *certain*, find pictures that allow predictions about the likelihood of some event occurring. For example, you might use a picture that shows someone getting ready to dive into a swimming pool. Ask, "Is she likely to jump?" Tell the students to reply with a full sentence ("Yes, she's likely to jump"). You can then ask, "Why is it likely that she will jump?" Students can reply with another extraposed *that* clause ("It's likely that she'll jump because . . . ") or with a subject raising sentence ("She's likely to jump because . . . ").

Activity 5: Hedging, Estimating, and Predicting Using Extraposition and Subject Raising Structures (High Intermediate Through Advanced)

Academic discourse often involves making hedges, giving estimates, and making predictions, including in sentences that have (1) *seem* or *appear*, sometimes preceded by a modal like *would*, and an extraposed *that* clause (e.g., *It would appear that . . .*); (2) probability adjectives such as *certain*, *likely*, *possible*, or *probable*, preceded by *be*, or *seem* or *appear*, and followed by a *that* clause (e.g., *It is highly/quite likely that . . .*); (3) subject raising structures with *certain* or *likely* and an infinitive clause (e.g., *The situation is likely to . . .*).

To practice these structures using TBLT, find a short passage about a topic (this can be taken from a written text or a video) along with a chart or graph that relates to it. You can present the passage orally, show the video, or give students the passage in writing to read. The students then pair off or work in groups to answer a series of questions that relate to the passage and visuals. For example, if you present a passage on greenhouse gases and global warming, the students might be asked, "What trend, if any, is apparent in the output of carbon dioxide in the atmosphere over the last 40 years? What is an implication of this trend? If the trend continues, what can we predict will happen by the year 2030? How likely do you think it is that this will happen?" Have the students frame their answers in sentences that use extraposition and subject raising and that accurately reflect the relative strength of claims based on the data in the passage and visuals (e.g., *It appears that carbon dioxide has increased by 20 percent from . . .* ; *Global warming seems to have . . .* ; *According to the graph, it is possible/quite likely that by 2030 . . .* ; *The level of carbon dioxide appears to have increased by 20 percent . . .*). Then have students compare their answers in a class discussion. Finally, ask each student to write a short report based on the findings.

Use this activity as the basis of a complete TBLT lesson in which the students study some other aspect of the topic. Ask students to select the aspect of the topic they want to study, find appropriate source material, evaluate the scientific data, and make an oral report, including charts, in which they present and comment on the data.

Activity 6: Choosing Extraposition Versus Subject Raising in Discourse (Advanced Writing)

To begin this advanced-level consciousness-raising activity for writing classes, present the discourse-based reasons why writers would choose either a subject raising structure with an infinitive clause or a corresponding extraposition structure. Give students examples such as those in (42), (43), and (44) earlier in this chapter. Then give them a passage in which they have to choose between the structures at various points. This exercise could have either of two formats: students can change all the extraposition structures that would be more appropriate as subject raising structures or they can cross out the structure that is not appropriate, as shown in (61).

> **(61)** ~~Apple seems to have~~ / It seems that Apple has contradicted the prediction of Wall Street analysts, who felt that the tiny company would not be able to compete with the bigger PC manufacturers like Dell and IBM. But unlike the PC companies, Apple's profits have continued to grow over the last three quarters. ~~It appears that this is due~~ / This appears to be due in part to Apple's ability to produce new products that are a hit with the both the younger and older generations. The Ipod is an excellent example of this. It has been a big success with young and old. ~~It seems that everyone likes~~ / Everyone seems to like the idea of tuning out the world around them and listening to their own tunes.

Working on Common Errors

Activity 7: Targeting Pseudo-*Tough*-Movement and Related Errors (High Intermediate Through Advanced)

Particularly if you are teaching Chinese or Korean students, it might be a good idea to target errors such as **I am interesting to know more about biology* and **I am boring to study*, since they involve participles that are frequently used incorrectly. Explain that these present participles cannot be used in this way. Explain what *I am interesting* and *I am boring* mean (e.g., *I am interesting* means "I am an interesting person"). Provide students with examples of the correct usage of participles: *I am interested in* + gerund (*knowing, studying*, etc.), *It is boring (for me) to study*, and *Studying is boring (for me)*. This presentation can be extended to pseudo-*tough*-movement errors with, for example, *easy* and *hard* (e.g., **I am easy to forget things*). After you have discussed these errors, provide students with a short passage that contains instances of these errors and ask them to correct any errors they see. The passage can be similar to (62) in Activity 8. Follow up this error detection activity with a processing instruction activity in which the students judge the grammaticality of sentences that include errors such as **I am easy to play piano*, **I am hard to remember*, and **She is difficult to remember things*.

Activity 8: Addressing the Pseudo-*Tough*-Movement and *It* Omission Problems (High Intermediate Through Advanced)

To focus on the problems of pseudo-*tough* movement and *it* omission, prepare a short passage that includes some pseudo-*tough*-movement structures and/or incomplete extraposition structures. If you are working with Chinese students, you can also include some errors that involve incorrect passivization. An example of this is shown in (62). Tell the students that they are supposed to read through this composition written by a friend and help her by spotting any errors and correcting them. Create your passages using errors that you have collected from student compositions (the passage below was written by a Chinese student).

(62) The other day I so embarrassed! I was supposed to go to a music recital given by my friend, but I forgot all about it. When I am very busy, I am easy to forget things. And I have been very busy recently. Every day after I finish my classes I have to go to work and then I have to go to my music lesson. I am learning to play the violin, and this instrument is so difficult to be performed.

ENDNOTES

[1] Some native speakers may prefer to use an alternative construction to a gerund clause in subject position. This alternative, often referred to as an "action" nominalization, involves changing the verb to a verbal noun. The action nominalizations for (6a) would be: *Alan's **refusal** of our invitation . . .*

[2] *That* clauses can often be expressed as gerund and infinitive clauses. For example, sentence (8c) can be expressed as *His saying such a thing/for him to say such a thing is the result of his utter lack of understanding*. However, these alternatives are not always possible. For example, an infinitive clause version of (8a), *For him to continue to visit her amazes me*, sounds nearly ungrammatical and at best much worse than *That he continues to visit her amazes me*. This shows that because they contain tensed verbs and modals, *that* clauses are capable of providing information that infinitive and gerund clauses can't.

[3] Biber et al. (1999), p. 660.

[4] This example is from Biber et al. (1999), p. 677.

[5] The *it* in extraposition structures is also referred to as *filler it* or a *pleonastic pronoun*.

[6] For many speakers, extraposition with *important* requires the bare infinitive, often called the *subjunctive* form (e.g., *It is important that he complete the entire course*).

[7] The observation and example in (26) is due to Huddleston and Pullum (2002) p. 1406.

[8] This example is from Biber et al. (1999), p. 727.

[9] The name "*tough* movement" comes from the fact that *tough* is one of the adjectives that permits this movement.

[10] Biber et al. (1999), p. 728.

[11] Subject raising is also referred to as *raise-subject-to-subject* in the syntactic literature.

[12] Biber et al. (1999), pp. 731–734.

[13] Biber et al. (1999), p. 731.

[14] Biber et al. (1999), p. 734.

[15] Schachter and Celce-Murcia (1977) mention a similar error (**Americans are easy to get guns*) made by a Japanese speaker. Cooper, Olshtain, Tucker, and Waterbury (1975) examined adult Egyptian and Israeli ESL students' comprehension of *tough* movement structures and found it to be very low in relation to comprehension of other structures. It is interesting that English *tough* movement sentences like *The pyramids are easy to see* are expressed by a passive in Arabic (i.e., *The pyramids are easy to be seen*). Additional examination of pseudo-*tough*-movement sentences by speakers of other languages will eventually reveal whether the L1 and language typology are the source of these errors.

[16] The sentence may be passivized provided that the predicate allows this (i.e., the verb is of a particular type) and the subject is "affected" by the action. For a more detailed explanation of this error with additional examples, see Yip (1995), pp. 155–160.

[17] This corpus, as mentioned in Chapter 1, consists of slightly over 36,000 words. It consists of compositions written by Spanish ESL students at three distinct proficiency levels: pre-university, undergraduate, and graduate. See Cowan & Leeser (2007) for a more extensive description.

REFERENCES

Biber, D., Johansson, S., Leech, G., Conrad, S., & Finegan, E. (1999). *Longman grammar of spoken and written English*. Essex: Pearson Education, Ltd.

Cooper, R. L., Olshtain, E., Tucker G. R., & Waterbury, M. (1975). The acquisition of complex English structures by adult speakers of Arabic and Hebrew. *Language Learning 29*, 255–275.

Cowan, R., & Leeser, M. (2007). The structure of corpora in SLA research. In R. Facchinetti (Ed.), *Corpus linguistics 25 years on* (pp. 289–303). Amsterdam: Rodopi.

Huddleston, R., & Pullum, G. K. (2002). *The Cambridge grammar of the English language*. Cambridge: Cambridge University Press.

Schachter, J., & Celce-Mercia, M. (1977). Some reservations concerning error analysis. *TESOL Quarterly 11*, 441–451.

Swales, J. M., & Feak, C. B. (2005). *Academic writing for graduate students: A course for non-native speakers of English*. Ann Arbor: The University of Michigan Press.

Yip, V. (1995). *Interlanguage and learnability: From Chinese to English*. Amsterdam/Philadelphia: John Benjamins.

CHAPTER 21

Complements

INTRODUCTION

This chapter deals with a key building block in English language teaching courses and textbooks – *object complements*, subordinate clauses that follow verbs. The types of clauses we saw as subject clauses in Chapter 20 can all be object complements as well; thus, there are *that*, infinitive, gerund, and interrogative complements. In this chapter, we look at the first three of these, as choosing among them is the main source of student difficulties with complements. (A main use of interrogative clauses as complements is for questions in reported speech; see Chapter 16 for examples.)

Verbs are limited as to the kinds of complements they can take. Consider, for example, the verbs *want*, *enjoy*, and *think*, shown in (1), (2), and (3). As (1) shows, the main clause verb *want* can take an infinitive complement but not a gerund or a *that* complement. As (2) shows, *enjoy* takes only a gerund complement, not an infinitive or a *that* complement. Finally, as (3) shows, *think* takes only a complement introduced by *that*, not an infinitive nor a gerund complement.

> **(1)** a. He wants *to watch television.*   infinitive complement
> b. *He wants *watching television.*
> c. *He wants *that he will watch television.*

> **(2)** a. He enjoys *watching television.*   gerund complement
> b. *He enjoys *to watch television.*
> c. *He enjoys *that he watches television.*

> **(3)** a. He thinks *that he will watch television.*   that complement
> b. *He thinks *to watch television.*
> c. *He thinks *watching television.*

Adding to the potential difficulties for English language learners, some verbs can take more than one type of complement. (Thus, in this chapter, the examples of verbs that take the different complement types are necessarily limited, and verbs mentioned for one complement type may occur in other types as well.) To construct grammatical sentences with complements, a student must know which kind of complements can appear after a verb. We will now turn to a discussion of the types of complements in English, focusing on the verbs that take each type and, at points, including adjectives as well.

THAT COMPLEMENTS

Many verbs take complements introduced by *that*. As discussed in Chapter 20, *that* is a complementizer (it can be distinguished from the relative pronoun *that* in that it follows verbs rather than nouns and cannot be replaced by *which*). *That* complements contain overt subjects, which need not be identical to the subject of the sentence, as illustrated in (4a). Except when following verbs from a particular subset that we will discuss, *that* complements are *finite clauses* – the verb in the clause is inflected for tense, as in both (4a) and (4b).

> **(4)** a. He thinks *that she is beautiful.*
>   b. I regret *that I had to punish him.*

In that they contain a subject and a verb inflected for tense, *that* complements are like the *that* subject clauses we saw in Chapter 20. There is, however, a difference: the complementizer *that* can often be omitted from the complement, especially in informal speech, so that, for example, (4) can be rendered as *He thinks she's beautiful.*

In the sentences in (4) and many other sentences with *that* complements, the complement immediately follows the main clause verb. With certain verbs, however, an NP or *to* + NP may intervene, as illustrated in (5).

> **(5)** a. He told her *that she is beautiful.*
>   b. He mentioned to me *that he would be leaving early.*

Main clause verbs that report speech – for example, *reply*, *say*, and *tell*, as in (6a) – occur with *that* complements (see Chapter 16). Also common with *that* complements are verbs that express mental acts – for example, *believe*, *comprehend*, *feel*, *find*, *guess*, *know*, *see*, *think*, and *understand*, as shown in (6b). Certain of these verbs that take *that* clauses have been called "factive predicates" because their complement is assumed to be a fact.[1] Examples include *bear in mind*, *comprehend*, *know*, *regret*, and *understand*, as illustrated in (6c). For some native speakers, sentences with factive predicates are unacceptable when the complementizer is omitted, as in (6d) and (6e).

> **(6)** a. She replied *that he must have been mistaken.*
>   b. She comprehended *that this would mean a big change in her lifestyle.*
>   c. I regret *that I had to punish him.*
>   d. ?She comprehended this would mean a big change in her lifestyle.
>   e. ?I regret I had to punish him.

Yet other verbs that take *that* complements are distinguished by the form of the verb in the complement clause. It is to these verbs that we now turn.

Complements After Verbs of Request or Demand

A subset of verbs that we can call *verbs of request or demand* – for example, *ask*, *demand*, *insist*, *recommend*, and *stipulate* – must be followed by a *that* complement containing a bare infinitive, as shown in (7).[2]

> **(7)** We *recommend* that she *accept* his offer.

That is, the verb in the *that* complement is not inflected for tense, and the complement clause is therefore a *nonfinite* clause. The bare infinitive form in such clauses is often referred to as the *subjunctive* form.

Raising *Not* from *That* Complements

As we saw earlier in Chapter 5, with some main clause verbs, the negative element *not* may be moved from a *that* complement into the main clause without changing the meaning of the sentence, as exemplified by (8a) and (8b). The diagram in (9) shows how *not* is moved from the complement in (8a) into the main clause to create (8b).[3] The rule that does this is called *negative raising* or *not transportation* (see also Chapter 5).

(8) a. I imagine *that he won't want to come.*
    b. *I don't imagine* that he will want to come.

(9) I do *not* imagine *that he will* ___ want to come.　　*negative raising*

Negative raising can occur only with a few main clause verbs, such as *anticipate*, *believe*, *expect*, *imagine*, *suppose*, and *think* and with several verbs such as *appear* and *seem* with extraposed *that* complements. With verbs other than these, moving the *not* out of the complement would result in a change of meaning, as a comparison of (10a) and (10b) demonstrates.

(10) a. We forgot that she doesn't like him.
     b. We didn't forget that she likes him.

SUMMARY

THAT COMPLEMENTS

Complements are subordinate clauses that follow verbs or adjectives and complete their meaning. *That*, infinitive, gerund, and interrogative clauses may all be complements. Verbs are limited as to the kinds of complements they can take.

***That* complements** occur after many verbs, including reporting verbs and verbs expressing mental acts. They have an overt subject and most are finite clauses. The complementizer *that* often can be deleted.
　He knew that they would come.　OR　*He knew they would come.*

After main verbs of request and demand, the complement verb has the bare infinitive, or **subjunctive**, form (the clause is nonfinite).
　We recommended that he buy a less expensive car.

Negative raising, or ***not* transportation**, moves the negative element *not* out of a *that* complement and into the main clause without changing the meaning of the sentence. It is possible only with certain verbs.
　I think that he won't come.　OR　*I don't think that he will come.*

EXERCISE 21.1

Indicate for each sentence whether negative raising can or cannot apply, and if not, explain why.

Example: We believe that she isn't coming.

Answer: can apply

1. It appears that she doesn't want to compromise.
2. She knew that she didn't have a chance.
3. She thought that she didn't have a chance.
4. She seemed not to care what he thought about her paper.
5. John realized that he could not answer all of the questions on the exam.

INFINITIVE COMPLEMENTS

Many verbs take *to* clauses beginning with infinitives as complements. As discussed in Chapter 20, these nonfinite clauses may or may not have an overt subject. Infinitive complements can be subclassified in terms of the verbs that take them. We can identify four types, each of which follows a particular group of verbs. Complements of the four types differ in whether they have an overt subject and, if not, what the subject is understood as being. More specifically, as we shall see, they differ with regard to three questions:

- Is there an NP following the main clause verb?
- If so, is this NP the object of the main clause verb?
- What is the subject of the infinitive complement?

Type 1 Complements: *Persuade* Verbs

A large number of verbs, such as *advise, authorize, cause, compel, convince, order, persuade,* and *tell* are transitive, and, therefore, must have an NP object, as shown in (11).

   (**11**) Alice persuaded John to come to the party.

We can confirm that *John* is the object of *persuade* through passivization, which moves *John* into subject position in the main clause. The result is shown in (12).

   (**12**) John was persuaded (by Alice) [to come to the party].

Since *John* is the object of *persuade*, the infinitive complement in (11) has no overt subject. However, *John* is understood as being its subject. The diagram in (13) reflects our intuition that the missing subject of the complement is identical to the object of the main clause (parentheses indicate an understood subject).[4]

   (**13**) Alice persuaded *John* [(*John*) to come to the party].

In short, we can characterize sentences with *persuade* verbs as having the following pattern: NP_1 V NP_2 [*to* V], with NP_2 understood as the complement subject.

In terms of their meaning, *persuade* and the other verbs that take this complement type have been called *influence,* or *manipulative, verbs* because their object is usually influenced by the main clause subject to carry out the action expressed in the complement. Usually an animate subject does the influencing or manipulating, as shown in (11), but this is not always the case. In (14), inanimate subjects influence the object.[5]

   (**14**) a. Ignorance of thermodynamics compelled Susan to enroll in a physics class.
           b. A desire to learn more about poetry induced Bruce to seek the advice of his old English teacher.

The proposition expressed in the complement does not have to be an action. It can be a state resulting from the influence of the subject on the object, as shown in (15).

   (**15**) His pituitary condition caused him to be nine feet tall.

Type 2 Complements: *Want* Verbs

Another group of verbs that include *hope*, *like*, *promise*, and *want*, either can or must occur without a following NP, as shown in (16). Other verbs in this group include *arrange*, *desire*, *expect*, *love*, *need*, *plan*, *prefer*, *refuse*, *vow*, *want*, *wish*, and *yearn*.

(16) Joan $\begin{Bmatrix} wanted \\ hoped \end{Bmatrix}$ to write a letter to the mayor.

The bracketing in (17) reflects our intuition that the missing subject of the complement is identical to the main clause subject. What Joan wanted was that she herself write a letter to the mayor.[6]

(17) *Joan* wanted [(*Joan*) to write a letter to the mayor].

Some verbs in this group, including *expect*, *need*, *promise*, and *want*, can also have a following NP, as shown in (18).

(18) Joan $\begin{Bmatrix} wanted \\ expected \\ needed \end{Bmatrix}$ Bill to write a letter to the mayor.

What is the NP following the verb? Notice that if we ask the question *What did Joan want?*, we get the answer *for Bill to write a letter to the mayor*. Thus, the NP *Bill* is not itself the object of *want* but is instead the subject of the infinitive complement, as shown in the bracketing in (19).

(19) Joan wanted [Bill to write a letter to the mayor].

Passivization supports this conclusion. The only way to apply the passive rule to (18) is within the infinitive complement, so that the complement object, *a letter*, is moved into subject position, as is shown in (20a). If *Bill* were the object of *want*, the passive in [20b] would be grammatical, but it clearly is not.

(20) a. Joan wanted [a letter to be written to the mayor (by Bill)].
     b. *Bill was wanted (by Joan) [to write a letter to the major].

The passive test thus allows us to confirm whether a verb takes a type 1 or a type 2 infinitive complement. With *persuade* verbs, the passive applies to the main clause, as in (12); with *want* verbs it applies to the complement, as shown in (20).

In the case of some *want* verbs (including *arrange*, *like*, *love*, *plan*, and *prefer*), the complementizer *for*, discussed in Chapter 20, can appear at the beginning of the complement, as illustrated in (21).

(21) a. We will arrange *for* your group to have access to the conference room.
     b. I won't plan (*for*) you to be back in time to go with us.
     c. I will arrange (*for*) us to be away while they do the cleaning.

One *want* verb is somewhat of an exception to the pattern discussed – namely, *promise*. When *promise* occurs without a following NP, it clearly is like the other *want* verbs, since, for example, the meaning of (22a) is (22b), in which the bracketed complement means that he (Bill) would write a letter to the mayor.

(22) a. Bill promised to write a letter to the mayor.
     b. Bill promised [(Bill) to write a letter to the mayor].

Like many other *want* verbs, *promise* can also be followed by an NP. A comparison of the sentence with *promise* in (23) with the sentences with other *want* verbs in (18) reveals the difference.

(**23**) Bill promised Joan to write a letter to the mayor.

The NP after *promise* (i.e., *Joan*) is clearly the object of *promise*, and the subject of the complement is missing but is understood as identical to the main clause subject (*Bill*). Thus, (23), with *promise*, has the structure that is illustrated in (24).

(**24**) Bill promised Joan [(Bill) to write a letter to the mayor].

With *want* verbs, then, we have three patterns:

- *hope*: NP_1 V [*to* V], with NP_1 understood as the complement subject, as in (16);
- *want*: which has the same pattern as *hope* verbs and also the pattern NP_1 V [NP_2 *to* V], as in (18);
- *promise*: which has the same pattern as *hope* and *want* verbs, and also the pattern NP_1 V NP_2 [*to* V], with NP_1 understood as the complement subject, as in (23).

In terms of meaning, verbs that take type 2 complements can be said to include *commitment verbs* (e.g., *agree, decline, promise, refuse*) and *expectation verbs* (e.g., *desire, expect, hope, want*). These groupings are discussed with others in the activities in the Suggestions for Teaching Complement Clauses section at the end of this chapter.

Type 3 Complements: *Believe* Verbs

A number of verbs, including *acknowledge, believe, consider*, and *judge*, have an infinitival complement that contains *be* plus an NP or an adjective, as shown in (25). With these verbs, as in (25), there is always an NP.

(**25**) Everyone believed Einstein to be $\begin{Bmatrix} a\ genius \\ brilliant \end{Bmatrix}$.

The NP that follows the verb is the subject of the complement, not the object of the verb. This is expressed in the bracketing in (26).

(**26**) Everyone believed [Einstein to be a genius].

In other words, what everyone believed was not Einstein but the proposition that Einstein was a genius. With these verbs, the pattern is thus NP_1 V [NP_2 *to be* NP/adj].

Notice, however, sentence (27), a passive version of (26). Although *Einstein* is the subject of the infinitive complement in (26) rather than the object of *believe*, passivization can move it to subject position.

(**27**) Einstein was believed to be a genius (by everyone).

To account for sentences such as (27), grammarians have proposed a rule called *raise-subject-to-object*, or *subject-to-object raising*. The operation of this rule is shown in (28); once *Einstein* has become the object, passivization can operate on it, producing (27).

(**28**) Everyone believed Einstein [_____ to be a genius].   *raise-subject-to-object*

The raise-subject-to-object rule also accounts for the fact that when the subject of the main clause is identical to the subject of the complement clause, the latter is a reflexive pronoun, as shown in (29). As discussed in Chapter 13, a reflexive pronoun occurs in the same clause as its antecedent. After the subject of the infinitive clause, *Tom*, is raised into object position in the main clause, as shown in (30a), it can be converted into the reflexive pronoun *himself* shown in (30b). Notice that in sentences such as this, the pattern is NP$_1$ V [NP$_1$ *to be* NP/adj] – that is, the NP originating in the complement is the same as the main clause subject.

(**29**) Tom considers himself to be a genius.

(**30**) a. Tom considers Tom [____ to be a genius].

b. Tom considers himself to be a genius.

With some *believe* verbs (e.g., *consider, judge*), *to be* can be omitted, as shown in (31). Judgments about which *believe* verbs permit the omission of *to be* vary among native speakers.

(**31**) a. We consider him to be an expert in these matters.
b. We consider him an expert in these matters.

Verbs in the *believe* group typically have animate subjects who take a certain stance (of belief, acknowledgment, acceptance, etc.) toward the proposition expressed in the complement.

Type 4 Complements: *Make* Verbs

A few verbs, such as *have*, *let*, and *make*, take a complement with a bare infinitive, as shown in (32). The NP that occurs after the verb is the subject of the complement. Thus, sentences with these verbs generally have the pattern NP$_1$ V [NP$_2$ V NP$_3$].

(**32**) Bill $\begin{Bmatrix} had \\ let \\ made \end{Bmatrix}$ Susan *revise* the article she had submitted.

Along with *get*, these verbs are often referred to in ESL/EFL textbooks as "causative verbs."[7] Semantically, they belong to the same influence/manipulative verb group as the *persuade* verbs we discussed earlier: their subjects manipulate someone or something to carry out the action in the complement. Except for *get*, however, syntactically these "causatives" behave differently from *persuade* verbs, by taking the bare infinitive. Furthermore, as we saw in Chapter 17, page 404, these verbs only permit passivization of the complement, e.g., *Bill had* [*Susan revise the letter*] → *Bill had* [*the letter revised by Susan*]. The verb *make* is an exception since its only possible passive is closer to that of *persuade* verbs. For those native speakers who find the sentence ?*Susan was made to revise the letter by Fred* acceptable, the causative verb *make* is a type 1 *persuade* verb. The syntactic and semantic similarity of *make* to type 1 *persuade* verbs may explain one of the most common grammatical errors made by English language learners. Sentences like **He made me to revise the article* result from learners' following the pattern of *persuade* verbs by inserting *to* in complements following *make*.

A group of perception verbs (e.g., *hear*, *observe*, *see*, *watch*) also take bare infinitive complements. Because they in addition take gerund complements, they are discussed in a section later in the chapter.

Verbs with Complements Similar to *Believe* Verbs

Although these verbs are not followed by an infinitive complement, they are included in this section because English language learners may overgeneralize and apply an infinitive complement structure to them.

Description/Classification Verbs

A number of verbs, such as *accept*, *characterize*, *classify*, *describe*, *intend*, *recognize*, *regard*, *treat*, and *use*, take objects that are followed by an adjective or an NP. Sentences with these verbs look very similar to sentences with *believe* verbs from which *to be* has been omitted, the only obvious difference being the inclusion of *as*, as a comparison between (33a) and (33b) shows.

(33) a. I would *describe/characterize* him *as* intelligent/a diligent student.
    b. I would *consider* him (to be) intelligent/a diligent student.

Because the adjective or NP after *as* describes or classifies the preceding NP object, these verbs are referred to as *description*, or *classification*, *verbs*.

Naming Verbs

A group of so-called *naming verbs*,[8] such as *appoint*, *baptize*, *christen*, *crown*, *elect*, and *name*, take complements consisting of two successive NPs, the second of which names or designates a title or office that the preceding NP holds. Examples are shown in (34).

(34) a. They elected him president.
    b. The board appointed him secretary pro tem.

SUMMARY

INFINITIVE COMPLEMENTS

Infinitive complements are nonfinite clauses with *to*; they may or may not have an overt subject. Different groups of verbs take different types of infinitive complements:

- **Type 1 complements** follow *persuade* verbs. These verbs are called *influence* (*manipulative*) verbs.

  Pattern: NP_1 V NP_2 [*to* V]; complement subject $= NP_2$
  Alice persuaded John to come to the party.

- **Type 2 complements** follow *want* verbs.

  Pattern: NP_1 V [*to* V]; complement subject $= NP_1$
  Joan hopes to leave the party early.

  Plus, for some verbs including *want*:
  NP_1 V [NP_2 *to* V]
  Joan wanted Bill to leave the party early.

  Or, for *promise*:
  NP_1 V NP_2 [*to* V], complement subject $= NP_1$
  Bill promised Joan to write a letter.

- **Type 3 complements** follow *believe* verbs. The complement verb is *be*; *to be* may be omitted. The rule of subject raising moves the complement subject.

  Pattern: NP_1 V $\begin{Bmatrix} [NP_2 \ (to\ be)\ NP/adj] \\ [NP_1 \ (to\ be)\ NP/adj] \end{Bmatrix}$

  We consider Allen (to be) an expert in these matters.
  He considered himself (to be) an expert in these matters.

continued

> • **Type 4 complements** follow *make* verbs. They involve a bare infinitive.
>
>   Pattern: NP$_1$ V [NP$_2$ V NP$_3$]
>
>   Two groups of verbs that do not take infinitive complements but that may be confused with those that do are
>
>   ▪ description/classification verbs.
>   *I would describe him as intelligent.*
>
>   ▪ naming verbs.
>   *We appointed her secretary treasurer.*

EXERCISE 21.2

Indicate for each pair whether the sentences have the same patterns. If they do not, say why by identifying the pattern types.

Example: a. John wanted Susan to fix dinner.
          b. John persuaded Susan to fix dinner.

Answer: no; (a) = type 2 (or *want* verb) complement, (b) = type 1 (or *persuade* verb) complement

1. a. Alice refused to undertake the job.
   b. Alice vowed to undertake the job.
2. a. John promised Susan to finish the project by Tuesday.
   b. John ordered Susan to finish the project by Tuesday.
3. a. Fred told Alan to conduct an investigation.
   b. Fred expected Alan to conduct an investigation.
4. a. He ordered John to take the job.
   b. He wanted John to take the job.
5. a. She considered him to be brilliant.
   b. She needed him to be brilliant.

EXERCISE 21.3

Indicate whether each of the following sentences is grammatical. If a sentence is not grammatical, explain why.

Example: We elected him to be president of our club.

Answer: ungrammatical (The naming verb *elect* must be followed by two successive NPs.)

1. I believe her very knowledgeable about wine.
2. She described him to be highly intelligent.
3. He expected her to call him when she was finished.
4. She promised him to wait until he returned.
5. They appointed her to be secretary treasurer of the club.

GERUND COMPLEMENTS

Certain verbs take *gerund complements*, clauses with verbs in the present participle form. As discussed in Chapter 20, gerund clauses are nonfinite clauses and may or may not include an overt subject. When a gerund complement is lacking an overt subject, the subject is generally understood to be the main clause subject.

Certain verbs can only take gerund clauses. Examples include *avoid, delay, dislike, enjoy, favor, finish, practice,* and *resist*. In addition to such single-word verbs, prepositional verbs and prepositional phrasal verbs that can take clauses must take gerund complements (see Chapter 9 for more on prepositional verbs and prepositional phrasal verbs). Prepositional verbs that take gerund complements include *agree on, count on, decide on, depend on,* and *insist on*; relevant phrasal prepositional verbs include *look forward to* and *get away with*. Thus, along with sentences with single-word verbs, as shown in (35), we have sentences with prepositional verbs, as shown in (36a) and (36b), and phrasal prepositional verbs, as shown in (36c) and (36d).

(35) a. He dislikes *our telling him what to do.*
     b. They enjoy *playing baseball.*

(36) a. They insisted on *paying their share of the check.*
     b. We counted on *receiving some help from him.*
     c. We look forward to *seeing you next week.*
     d. He got away with *telling a terrible lie.*

Similarly, gerund complements can occur after verb and preposition combinations that have an NP between the verb and preposition (e.g., *accuse* NP *of, thank* NP *for, warn* NP *against/about*), as shown in (37).

(37) a. He accused them of *stealing the jewels.*
     b. She thanked him for *telling her about the deal.*

With certain verbs, for example, *finish* and *practice,* the gerund complement does not have an overt subject, and the subject is understood as identical to the main clause subject. Thus, the gerund complement in (38a) has *the movers* as its subject, and that in (38b) has *the kids.*

(38) a. The movers still haven't finished *bringing in the boxes.*
     b. The kids need to practice *catching fly balls.*

With many verbs that take gerund complements, the complement can occur with or without an overt subject. Among these verbs are *anticipate, discuss, enjoy, imagine, mind, remember,* and *risk*. In each of the (a) sentences in (39), (40), and (41), the subject of the complement is understood as identical to the main clause subject, whereas in each of the (b) sentences, the complement has an overt subject, different from the main clause subject. Notice in the (b) sentences, the complement subjects appear in their possessive form.

(39) a. You don't mind calling me Tony, do you?
     b. You don't mind *my* calling you Tony, do you?

(40) a. We discussed leaving all of our money to charity.
     b. We discussed *Alan's* leaving all of his money to charity.

(41) a. You risk being arrested.
     b. I won't risk *their* being arrested.

However, many speakers of American English regularly use nonpossessive forms of nouns and object pronouns instead of possessive forms. Thus, you will also hear the (b) sentences produced as shown in (42).

(**42**) a. You don't mind *me* calling you Tony, do you?
  b. We discussed *Alan* leaving all of his money to charity.
  c. I won't risk *them* being arrested.

Moreover, with some verbs, such as *catch*, *find*, *hear*, *keep*, and *leave*, the complement subject cannot occur in possessive form, as is illustrated by (43).

(**43**) a. She caught *him* breaking into her car.
  b. *She caught his breaking into her car.

Finally, with a few verbs, such as *advise*, *advocate*, *encourage*, *recommend*, and *suggest*, complements occur with or without a subject. When there is no subject, the understood subject is not the subject of the main clause. In (44), for example, there is no overt complement subject, and the subject is understood as "you," "they," "anyone who wants to eat lunch there." The precise interpretation of these subjects depends on the context in which the sentence appears.

(**44**) I would recommend calling the restaurant the day before. They are usually very busy at lunch time.

Verbs that take gerund complements can be grouped by meaning. Prominent among these groups are *interception verbs*, such as *behold*, *discover*, *catch*, *come upon*, and *find*; and *mental imagery verbs*,[9] such as *conceive of*, *imagine*, *picture*, *recall*, *remember*, and *see* (= *visualize*). As shown in (45), verbs whose gerund complements have nonpossessive subjects are often from these two groups.

(**45**) a. They found the children sleeping on the back porch.
  b. We can easily imagine Fred doing something like that.
  c. I can still see her standing on the platform waving good-bye as the train pulled out of the station.

SUMMARY

GERUND COMPLEMENTS

Gerund complements are nonfinite clauses that have verbs in the present participle form. They may or may not include a subject. Verbs that take gerund complements include:

- **single-word verbs** (e.g., *avoid*, *delay*, *dislike*, *enjoy*, *favor*, *finish*, *practice*)
  Alan enjoys watching football on television.

- **prepositional verbs** (e.g., *agree on*, *count on*, *decide on*)
  He counted on receiving his check today.

- **phrasal prepositional verbs** (e.g., *look forward to*, *get away with*)
  They are looking forward to seeing you next week.

The **subject of gerund complements** depends on the verb:

- With some verbs (e.g., *finish, practice*), there is no overt subject, and the subject is understood as the main clause subject.
  We finished unpacking the boxes.

- With some verbs, there may or may not be an overt subject. If there is no overt subject, the subject may be understood as the main clause subject (e.g., with *anticipate, discuss, enjoy*) or as the listener or people in general (e.g., with *advise, recommend*).
  We discussed paying the bill.   OR   *We discussed your paying the bill.*
  I recommend calling for an appointment.   OR   *I recommend their calling for an appointment.*

Overt subjects are:

- **possessives** for most verbs, although often nonpossessive forms are used in speech.
  We discussed John's/his leaving early.   OR
  We discussed John/him leaving early. (speech)

- **nonpossessive forms** for certain verbs (e.g., *catch, keep, find*).
  She heard them telling a lie.

Verb groups that take gerund complements include **interception** and **mental imagery verbs**.
  She caught him breaking into her car.
  I can easily imagine Fred doing something like that.

EXERCISE 21.4

Indicate whether each of the following sentences is grammatical. If a sentence is not grammatical, explain why and supply a correction.

Example: She avoided to commit a crime.

Answer: ungrammatical (*Avoid* takes a gerund complement.)
          correction: She avoided committing a crime.

1. The police caught him break into her apartment.
2. She risks to lose all of her money.
3. She didn't approve of their staying out until two o'clock in the morning.
4. Alan warned us about talking to strangers.
5. He delayed to leave for school.

VERBS THAT TAKE BOTH GERUND AND INFINITIVE COMPLEMENTS

To this point, we have focused on the various complement types, discussing each in conjunction with verbs that commonly take them. As was mentioned earlier, many verbs, including some listed in the previous sections, take more than one complement type. In this section and the next, we focus on verbs that take both gerund and infinitive complements and on differences in meaning that can be created by choosing one complement type or the other. This section focuses on the difference between gerund complements and infinitive complements with *to*, the next on the difference between gerund complements and bare infinitive complements.

A number of verbs – e.g., *begin, continue, hate, like, love, prefer, remember, start, try* – take both gerund and infinitive complements. Depending on the verb, the choice of complement may or may not make a difference to the meaning of the sentence.

Different Complements with Similar Meanings

With stative verbs of emotion (e.g., *bear, detest, dislike, hate, like, love, stand*), gerund and infinitive complements can be used with no difference in meaning. The sentence pairs in (46) and (47) are each identical in meaning.

(**46**) a. He hates to mow the lawn.
  b. He hates mowing the lawn.

(**47**) a. She can't stand to be alone at night.
  b. She can't stand being alone at night.

Certain verbs that describe the beginning or progression of an action – for example, *begin, start,* and *continue* – often occur with both types of complements with little or no difference in meaning. In (48), with *continue,* the meaning of both sentences is the same. In (49), with *start,* the (a) and (b) pair seem to have the same meaning, but the (c) and (d) pair may be slightly different. In (49c), he definitely spoke. Example (49d) may also have this meaning, but it can also be interpreted as "he changed his mind before actually speaking."

(**48**) a. She continued arguing her client's case.
  b. She continued to argue her client's case.

(**49**) a. He took a few steps and started jogging.
  b. He took a few steps and started to jog.
  c. He started speaking.
  d. He started to speak.

Complements with Different Meanings

Sentences with some verbs that take both infinitive and gerund complements have different meanings, depending upon which complement is chosen. The difference in each case relates to the general difference of gerunds as imparting a sense of actuality to the event expressed while infinitives impart a more hypothetical or future sense.

Remember

When *remember* is followed by an infinitive complement, the meaning is that the need to carry out some action was remembered before it was carried out, as illustrated in (50).

(**50**) John remembered to mail the letter.
  (= He remembered he had the task and then did it.)

With a gerund complement following *remember,* the action occurred before the remembering, as in (51).

(**51**) John remembered mailing the letter.
  (= He did the task and then remembered doing it.)

Forget

Forget usually has an infinitive complement. In this case, the sentence subject did not carry out the action in the complement because he or she did not remember to.

(52) I forgot to lock the door.
  (= I did not lock the door because it slipped my mind.)

When *forget* takes a gerund complement, the action did occur. *Forget* can be followed by a gerund complement only when the main clause includes a negative word like *never* or *not* with a modal. The content of the complement must describe something that was a special experience for the speaker, as in (53).

(53) I'll never forget seeing Olivier on the stage at the Old Vic Theater in London.
  (= I can't forget that experience.)

When these conditions do not occur, the gerund complement sounds ungrammatical, as illustrated by (54).

(54) *He forgot mailing the letter.

Try

When an infinitive complement follows *try*, the implication is that the action in the complement was attempted but may not have been carried out. With a gerund complement, the implication is that the action was carried out.[10] Thus, in (55), the blank can be filled with (a), with the infinitive complement, because the following clause confirms that Julia did not slap Fred's face. It cannot be filled with (b), the gerund complement, whose implication that the action was carried out conflicts with the following clause. (The # before [b] indicates that it is inappropriate for this reason.)

(55) Julia was furious at Fred's treatment of her. When he came back into the room, her rage boiled over into action. _____, but he dodged the blow and laughed at her.
  a. She tried to slap his face.
  b. #She tried slapping his face.

In (56), the discourse following the complement indicates that its action was carried out. Notice that here, (b), with the gerund complement, can be inserted in the blank, whereas (a), with the infinitive complement, cannot be.

(56) Harry suddenly began to choke. Alarmed, Fred asked what the matter was. Harry continued to make choking noises as he pointed to the fish on his plate. Fred realized that Harry must have a bone lodged in his throat. Some kind of first aid was needed! _____, but to no avail. Harry's eyes were beginning to bug out of his face. This was getting serious.
  a. #Fred tried to pound him on the back.
  b. Fred tried pounding him on the back.

For the infinitive complement to be appropriate, the discourse following it would need to be something like (57), in which the meaning is that the complement action was not carried out.

(57) . . . but he really couldn't reach him very well over the gigantic torso of Francis, who was sitting between them.

In both American and British English, "try and" can be heard instead of an infinitive complement, as illustrated in (58).

(58) a. I'm going to *try and* talk him out of it.
  b. I'm going to try to talk him out of it.

Stop

The verb *stop* takes a gerund complement, as shown in (59a). It also takes what appears to be an infinitive complement, as shown in (59b).

(59) a. He stopped eating at that restaurant.
b. He stopped to eat at that restaurant.

The two sentences in (59) are very different in meaning. Sentence (59a) means "he did not eat at that restaurant again," whereas (59b) means "he stopped in order to eat at that restaurant." The infinitive in (59b) answers the question *Why did he stop?* Infinitive clauses that can answer a *why* question posed about the main clause are called *adjuncts of purpose*, or *purpose clauses*. They are a shortened version of clauses introduced by *in order*, formed by omitting *in order*. Since they are not complements of verbs, they can appear after verbs that do not take complements, as in (60a), and after object NPs, as in (60b), as well as in other positions that will be discussed in greater detail in Chapter 23.

(60) a. He studied (in order) to pass the test.
b. Alice played the Rachmaninov Sonata in G Minor to please her mother.

Infinitive complements cannot be answers to this kind of *why* question posed about the main verb. Thus, the verb *stop* really takes only one complement – a gerund. Like many other verbs, it can also be followed by an adjunct of purpose.

SUMMARY

VERBS THAT TAKE BOTH GERUND AND INFINITIVE COMPLEMENTS

Some verbs can be followed by infinitive or gerundive complements, with **little or no difference in meaning**.

He hates to go to the dentist. OR *He hates going to the dentist.*
She continued to work out every day. OR *She continued working out every day.*

Other verbs take both complements but with a **difference in meaning**:

- *Remember* + infinitive complement means the remembering occurred before the action; *remember* + gerund complement means the remembering occurred after the action.
  He remembered to mail it. (= He remembered he had the task and then did it.)
  He remembered mailing it. (= He did the task and then remembered doing it.)

- *Forget* + infinitive complement means the subject did not carry out the action. *Forget* + gerund complement means the action did occur (the main clause must have a negative element, and the action must be special to the subject).
  He forgot to call his girlfriend. (= He didn't call her because it slipped his mind.)
  I'll never forget saying good-bye to my family on the day I left to go to America. (= I said good-bye that day, and I will always remember.)

> • **Try** + infinitive complement means the subject attempted but did not necessarily carry out the complement action; *try* + gerund complement means the subject did carry out the action.
> *She tried to slap his face.* (= Her attempt wasn't necessarily successful.)
> *She tried slapping his face.* (= She did slap his face.)
>
> **Stop** takes only gerund complements. Although *stop* and other verbs take what look like infinitive complements, these are in fact **adjuncts of purpose**, with the meaning "in order to."
> *He stopped visiting his mother.*
> *He stopped to visit his mother.*   *adjunct of purpose* (= *He stopped in order to visit his mother.*)
> cf. *He continued to eat at that restaurant.*   *infinitive complement*

EXERCISE 21.5

Indicate whether the sentences in each pair have the same meaning or a different meaning. Explain any differences.

Example: a. We stopped to have lunch at that restaurant.
b. We stopped having lunch at that restaurant.

Answer: different; Sentence (a) means we stopped in order to have lunch. Sentence (b) means we did not eat there again.

1. a. I hate exercising early in the morning.
   b. I hate to exercise early in the morning.
2. a. I remembered to put the keys in my coat pocket.
   b. I remembered putting the keys in my coat pocket.
3. a. I'll never forget going to the theater on Sunday morning.
   b. I'll never forget to go to the theater on Sunday morning.
4. a. Bruce continued to talk to his wife.
   b. Bruce continued talking to his wife.
5. a. Tom started to work out at the gym.
   b. Tom started working out at the gym.

EXERCISE 21.6

State which of the two sentences fits the discourse, and explain why.

When Alice walked into the room, she found Fred lying on the bed, dead to the world. At the foot of the bed lay a small plastic bottle with the top off. She picked it up and read the label: "sleeping pills." Alice gasped as she realized that Fred had probably swallowed the contents of the bottle in an attempt at ending his life. Time was of the essence; she had to take immediate action to revive him! _____ But neither action had any effect. Fred slumbered on.

a. First she tried to slap him, and then she tried to throw water in his face.
b. First she tried slapping him, and then she tried throwing water in his face.

VERBS THAT TAKE BOTH GERUND AND BARE INFINITIVE COMPLEMENTS

A small set of *perception verbs*, including *feel, hear, listen to, notice, observe, overhear, see,* and *watch,* can be followed by bare infinitive or gerund complements.[11] Compare (61a) with (61b).

> (**61**) a. We saw him resisting the policeman.
> b. We saw him resist the policeman.

For most native speakers, the sentence with the gerund complement expresses an "in progress" action (i.e., we saw him in the act of resisting the policeman). That is, the gerund takes on the aspectual sense of the progressive *-ing*. In contrast, the sentence with the bare infinitive complement is interpreted as simply a report of an action that took place (i.e., we saw him do something – he resisted a policeman). In addition to this general difference, sentences with perception verbs can have other fairly distinct meanings depending on the type of verb that appears in the complement.

Single Instance Versus Repeated Action

If the verb in the complement is a punctual achievement verb (i.e., a verb whose action ends as soon as it begins – *bat, blink, hit, kick, shoot, slap, snap, strike,* etc.), in a gerund complement its action will be interpreted as happening repeatedly, whereas in a bare infinitive complement, its action its understood as a single occurrence. To see the difference, compare (62a) and (62b).

> (**62**) a. I saw Mr. Hanks snapping his fingers agitatedly just before he turned and walked into the dining room.   *repetition of the action*
> b. I saw Mr. Hanks snap his fingers agitatedly just before he turned and walked into the dining room.   *single instance of the action*

Completed Action Versus In-Progress Action

If the complement contains an accomplishment verb, in a gerund complement the verb's action is in progress, whereas in a bare infinitive complement its action is complete. *Drown* is one such verb; compare (63a), in which it occurs in a bare infinitive complement, with (63b), in which it occurs in a gerund complement. The bare infinitive complement is not an appropriate beginning for the sentence because it conveys the meaning that the action is complete: the boy has drowned; pulling him out of the pool will not save his life. In contrast, the gerund complement makes sense in relation to the rest of the sentence, since it implies that the action of drowning is still in progress – hence the rescue attempt is justified and can be successful.

> (**63**) a. #I saw the boy drown in the pool, so I reached out, pulled him in, and saved his life.
> b. I saw the boy drowning in the pool, so I reached out, pulled him in, and saved his life.

With some verbs in some contexts, both complements will work with little difference in meaning. This is the case in (64), presumably because the action of diving, unlike that of drowning, inevitably involves a completion. However, some native speakers will see a difference in meaning; (64b) will be interpreted as in-progress action, whereas (64a) will be seen simply as a report of the event.

> (**64**) a. I looked up and saw this young kid dive off a cliff that was 175 feet above the sea.
> b. I looked up and saw this young kid diving off a cliff that was 175 feet above the sea.

Assuming a Position Versus Being in a State

Verbs that express an activity involving physical position (e.g., *lean*, *lie*, *sit*, *stand*) describe a state when they appear in a gerund complement but the action of assuming the position when they appear in a bare infinitive complement. In (65a), the basketball player is in the position of leaning against the locker. In (65b), the basketball player takes up the position of leaning against the locker.

> (**65**) a. I saw the tired basketball player leaning against the locker.
> b. I saw the tired basketball player lean against the locker.

SUMMARY

VERBS THAT TAKE BOTH GERUND AND BARE INFINITIVE COMPLEMENTS

When the main clause has a **perception verb** such as *feel*, *hear*, *notice*, and *see*, there are differences in interpretation between gerund and bare infinitive complements:

- A gerund complement expresses **in-progress action**. A bare infinitive complement simply gives a **report of the action**.
  He saw him breaking the window.
  He saw him break the window.

- A punctual verb (e.g., *hit*, *kick*, *snap*) is interpreted as expressing **repeated action** if in a gerund complement but a **single instance** if in a bare infinitive complement.
  I saw him kicking the tires.
  I saw him kick the tires.

- An accomplishment verb (e.g., *dive*, *drown*) is interpreted as expressing **action in progress** in gerund complements, **completed action** in bare infinitive complements.
  I saw him drowning, so I dived in and saved him.
  I saw him drown. I couldn't do anything to save him.

- With verbs expressing physical positioning (e.g., *lean*, *lie*, *sit*), a gerund complement denotes a **state**, whereas a bare infinitive denotes the act of **assuming a position**.
  I saw him leaning against the wall.
  I saw him lean against the wall.

EXERCISE 21.7

Indicate whether the sentences in each pair have the same meaning or different meanings. Explain any differences.

Example: a. She saw him hit the tennis ball against the backboard.
          b. She saw him hitting the tennis ball against the backboard.

Answer: different; Sentence (a) means she saw him hit the ball once. Sentence (b) means she saw him hit the ball repeatedly.

1. a. We saw him kicking the flat tire furiously. Then he went around to the back of the car, opened the trunk, and took out a jack.
  b. We saw him kick the flat tire furiously. Then he went around to the back of the car, opened the trunk, and took out a jack.
2. a. I saw the janitor lean the ladder against the wall.
  b. I saw the janitor leaning the ladder against the wall.
3. a. They heard someone pound on the door.
  b. They heard someone pounding on the door.

EXERCISE 21.8

Indicate which choice better fits each discourse, and explain why.

Example: _____, so he rushed over and picked her up. She seemed a little bruised but was otherwise all right.
        a. He saw her falling down the stairs
        b. He saw her fall down the stairs

Answer: Sentence (b) is better because the bare infinitive complement indicates completed action. The gerund complement in (a) indicates the action is still in progress, which doesn't fit the content that follows.

Discourse 1
    Nancy had not fastened her seatbelt, so she was thrown forward when the car crashed into the tree, and she hit her head on the dashboard. She got out of the car, staggered forward a few steps, and then seemed to lose consciousness. Jim saw her _____, so he reached out and caught her before she hit the ground.
      a. fall over
      b. falling over

Discourse 2
    _____, so she fastened a tourniquet around his arm. Later, one of the paramedics who took over told her that her knowledge of first aid had saved the man's life.
      a. Alice saw the policeman bleed to death
      b. Alice saw the policeman bleeding to death

Discourse 3
    As she stepped out onto the balcony, Helen noticed dark clouds rolling in. A storm was brewing. She went back into the apartment, closed the door to the balcony, and went to bed. Before she turned off the light, _____.
      a. she heard the rain fall on the roof.
      b. she heard the rain falling on the roof.

PROBLEMS THAT ESL/EFL STUDENTS HAVE WITH COMPLEMENTS

We have a limited amount of data on the kinds of errors ESL/EFL students make producing English complements. Two possible sources of documented errors are overgeneralization to semantically similar verbs and transfer from L1.

Overgeneralization Based on Semantic Categories

Celce-Murcia and Larsen-Freeman (1999) cite attested examples of errors like that shown in (66).

(66) *My father demanded me to do it.

Such errors suggest that students sometimes overgeneralize on the basis of semantic grouping. An ESL/EFL student might reasonably assume that *demand* is one of a group of influence/manipulative verbs that we saw earlier – verbs such as *command*, *compel*, and *order*. Like these other verbs, *demand* describes a state of affairs in which the main clause subject influences someone to carry out the action expressed in the complement. Thus, (66) might occur when the learner acts on this assumption by applying the complement pattern for influence/manipulative verbs to *demand*. What he or she must do is learn that *demand* takes a *that* complement.

L1 Transfer Resulting in Bare Infinitive Complements Instead of *To* Infinitive or Gerund Complements (Spanish, Portuguese)

Errors with verb complements might also be caused by L1 transfer. This seems quite plausible with students who speak Spanish and Portuguese. For example, in Portuguese, many verbs that only take infinitive complements are equivalent in meaning to English verbs that only take gerund complements (e.g., *avoid*, *discuss*, *finish*, *risk*). Examples are shown in (67).

(67) a. *terminar:*   *Ela terminou*   *de estudar por volta das dez.*
       finish   she finished   to study   about   ten
    b. *evitar:*   *Ele evitou*   *responder*   *minha*   *pergunta.*
       avoid   he avoided   to answer   my   question
    c. *discutir:*   *Eles discutiram a possibilildade*   *de abrir*   *um novo negócio.*
       discuss   they discussed the possibility   to open   a new business
    d. *arriscar:*   *Ela arriscou perder todo o seu dinheiro.*
       risk   she risked to lose all   her money

If Portuguese and Spanish speakers apply the L1 complement verb form when producing equivalent English sentences, we would expect to find infinitive complements after these verbs. This actually occurs in our corpus of errors made by Spanish speakers. The example in (68) was made by a graduate student in an advanced composition class for graduate students.

(68) . . . but he rejects *to include* Erasamus's murders in his discussion.

The vast majority of complement errors made by Spanish-speaking students at all proficiency levels consist of the use of bare infinitive complements in place of infinitive or gerund complements. Typical examples are shown in (69). Examples (69a) and (69b) were made by students in high-intermediate and advanced writing classes in an intensive English institute, and (69c) comes from a composition written by a student in a freshman composition course at an American university.

(69) a. *I prefer *do* exercise, watch TV or go out.
    b. *Sometimes when the people study several hours they *prefer read* a book or walk with other people.
    c. *It is a controversial technique that *consists in advise* the kid first and face him next.

The errors in (68) and (69) suggest that the acquisition of verb complements may proceed in stages (rather like we saw with tense acquisition), at least for students with these L1s. Thus, students at lower proficiency levels, like those in (69), may form complements with bare infinitives. As their proficiency increases, they will begin to produce more complements correctly. However, when using verbs whose complement structure they are unsure of, they may follow the L1 pattern, which has an infinitive. There may be some vacillation between the bare infinitive and the infinitive before they begin to use the correct complements for these verbs.

SUGGESTIONS FOR TEACHING COMPLEMENTS

Complements are part of every grammar textbook series and course, with some coverage of *that* complements but more emphasis on verbs that take infinitive and gerund complements. Coverage of the latter usually begins with verbs that take infinitive complements and then moves on to verbs that take gerund complements and, finally, to verbs that take both. Most of the activities in textbooks consist of fill-in-the-blank or sentence completion exercises. Realistic tasks that require the use of complements are sometimes lacking, presumably because they can be difficult to create, as there is often little semantic relationship among verbs taking a particular complement. In order to construct task-based activities, a teacher must find a common theme that encompasses a number of verbs within each complement type. This requires a great deal of creativity, and, even so, many common verbs will not be covered – hence, the reliance in textbooks on fill-in-the-blank and sentence completion exercises to pick up verbs that could not be worked into the tasks.

The following activities, which are designed for students at intermediate to advanced levels, are divided into two sets. The first set simply builds on the traditional approach described in the preceding paragraph. The second seeks to overcome some of the limitations of the traditional approach by focusing on meaning-based groups of verbs.

Activities Based on a Traditional Approach

The following three activities – the first dealing with a range of verbs, the others with single verbs – exemplify the possibility of using more communicative, task-based activities with the traditional, syntactic grouping approach.

Activity 1: Complements That Take Gerunds and/or Infinitives (Intermediate Through Advanced)

Questioning can be used to focus on the form of the complements that different verbs take. Select three sets of verbs: a set including *hate*, *like*, *love*, and *prefer*, which takes both infinitive and gerund complements; a set including *avoid*, *dislike*, *enjoy*, and (*not*) *mind*, which is restricted to gerund complements; and a set including *hope*, *intend*, and *plan*, which takes only infinitive complements. Use these sets together in a single activity. First, have students make a list of things they like, dislike, and plan to do. Then, working in pairs or small groups, have students ask each other questions such as "What do you really like to do?" "What do you dislike/avoid doing?" "What do you intend to do this weekend?" Next, the class as a whole can discuss their likes, dislikes, and plans. Point out restrictions regarding which complement(s) these verbs can take.

Activity 2: *Forget* + Infinitive Versus Gerund Complements (Intermediate Through Advanced)

You could apply the approach in Activity 1 to teach and practice the meaning difference between *forget* with an infinitive versus a gerund complement. After explaining this meaning difference, ask some students to give examples of things that they would not forget to do every day – for example, eat breakfast, answer e-mails, and so on. If they do not come up with any examples, prompt them by asking "Would you forget to . . . ?" about various appropriate activities. Then ask students to make a list of things that they did at some time that were very important, fun, or unusual (e.g., visiting the Grand Canyon, skydiving, dancing in the streets during Mardi Gras, etc.). Give a few examples of your own to start them off. After students have completed their lists, ask them to share their experiences with the class or in small groups using the structure *I'll never forget* + gerund complement. Provide a few examples (e.g., "I'll never forget dancing in the streets during Mardi Gras").

Activity 3: *Try* + Infinitive Versus Gerund Complements (Intermediate Through Advanced)

The meaning differences between *try* with infinitive and gerund complements can be illustrated and practiced by creating very short contexts that signal one of two possible choices as being appropriate like those in Exercise 21.8 or the example in (70).

> (**70**) Alice knew that Fred would be late for work if he didn't get up right away. But he was sleeping so soundly. She tried _____ but he kept on sleeping. He was really tired.
> a. to shout at him and shake him
> b. shouting at him and shaking him

Have students read the paragraph aloud, choosing the correct complement form. Then ask them to explain why the alternative is not appropriate in this context and to make up a context that illustrates the appropriate use of the other complement.

Activities Based on Semantic Grouping of Verbs

An alternative to the organization of complements typically found in English language teaching textbooks is to present them in a way that reveals how a group of verbs is similarly related to the main clause subject and the complement clause content. For example, *influence* or *manipulative verbs* (e.g., *advise, compel, persuade*) usually express the idea that the subject of the main clause influences the object to carry out the action expressed in the complement, and they all take type 1 infinitive complements. We could use the semantic relationship as the basis for teaching the complement structure of these verbs. Similarly, verbs which we could call *want* or *expect verbs* (e.g., *desire, expect, hope, long, need, want, wish,* and *yearn*) express some expectation or desire on the part of the main clause subject toward the content in the complement; they all take type 2 infinitive complements. The group we called *believe* verbs – including *acknowledge, believe, consider, find, hold, judge*, and *know* – typically have subjects that believe or otherwise accept the proposition in the complement to be true. These verbs can all take infinitive or *that* complements. A group of verbs which we could call *commitment verbs*[12] – including *agree, attempt, contract, decline, pledge, promise, refuse, swear*, and *vow* – typically have subjects that commit or refuse to commit to performing an action described in the complement. Like the expectation verbs, these take type 2 infinitive complements.

There are, of course, verbs that take the same complements as other members of a group but are not similar in meaning to those members, such as those we mentioned earlier. Within the groups that we have just looked at, there are some verbs that can take other complements as well (e.g., *expect* but not *need* can take *that* as well as infinitive complements). Nonetheless, presenting the verbs in this way could allow the teacher to come up with activities that connect the verb meaning to the complement form – and connecting grammatical form and meaning is generally thought to be what second language learners seek to do. Also, from a practical standpoint, larger groups of semantically related verbs make it easier for the teacher to devise meaningful task-based activities. If you are interested in trying this approach, here are some activities for using these groupings.

Activity 4: Influence/Manipulative Verbs and Their Complements (Intermediate Through Advanced)

This activity allows the teacher to teach meanings of influence/manipulative verbs that students may not be familiar with, while demonstrating that they have the same complement structure. Prepare a series of open-ended questions that could be appropriately answered with the verbs and that are followed by a more specific question using one of the verbs, as in the example that follows. Write the verbs (*advise, authorize, force, get, have, make, order, persuade, tell, urge*, etc.) on the board. Underneath the verbs, write both the open-ended and specific questions, for example, "What would you do if you wanted to go to a party with a good friend who didn't want to go with you? Would you order him or her to come with you?" Ask a student these questions. The student will probably answer "no" to the second question. Reply by saying, "No, you wouldn't *order* him or her, would you? You don't usually order a friend to do something you want to do, do you? What's a better verb?" When someone says "urge" or "persuade," say, "Yes, you would persuade your friend to come with you." Proceed in this manner with questions whose answers could contain other verbs you listed, including some that the students may not know – for example, "Can a boss authorize an employee to destroy valuable information that might conceal a crime?" or "What would you do if your daughter refused to clean up her room?" Help students if they form answers with incorrect complements. For instance, if a student says, "*I would make her to clean it up," point out that *make* is an exception to the general pattern of influence verbs.

Activity 5: Expectation Verbs and Their Complements (Intermediate Through Advanced)

Self-improvement sorts of activities could serve as a basis for practicing expectation verbs such as *want, expect, hate*, and *hope*. Ask the students to suggest things that people might do to improve themselves, for example, lose weight and exercise more. Then demonstrate the activity by describing an imaginary course of improvement that you and a friend undertook, as shown in (71). The object of the activity will be to practice both patterns that can occur with these verbs.

(71) I *wanted* to learn how to defend myself and get in shape, and my friend wanted to do this, too. So we both decided to take a karate class. When we started, I *expected* to earn my black belt in a few weeks. My friend *expected* to earn her black belt in a few weeks, too. But I just couldn't keep up with her. She was in better shape than I was, and she really learned all the moves faster than I did. I really *hoped* to keep up with her, but I couldn't. She already has her black belt, but I still don't have one.

Have the students pair off and describe an imaginary self-improvement project that they undertook with a friend. They can add as many details as they wish as long as they use some expectation verbs.

Activity 6: Verbs That Take *That* Complements and Gerund Complements (Intermediate Through Advanced)

Verbs of advice, such as *advise*, *recommend*, and *suggest*, can be followed by a *that* complement with a bare infinitive verb or by a gerund complement. An advice activity enables students to practice the verbs with both of these complement types. The activity requires that you prepare two lists of requests for advice as well as a list of responses to the requests in one of these lists.

Tell the class that you need some help. For example, say "I'm going to Chicago next week, and I need to get a room at a good hotel downtown – one that is not too expensive. What would you suggest that I do?" A student may supply an answer such as "Go to the Internet," naming some dot-coms that specialize in hotels and travel. You could then respond with a sentence using *suggest* followed by a *that* complement – for example, "OK, so you suggest that I look for a good, reasonably priced hotel on the Internet." Ask for other advice, and again paraphrase a student's response, this time using *recommend* followed by a gerund complement. Write the two sentences with *suggest* and *recommend* on the board. Point out that they have a *that* + NP + bare infinitive form of the verb. Then show students that with these verbs there is a second possibility, one with a gerund complement – for example, *I suggest/recommend looking for a good, reasonably priced hotel on the Internet*. If you include *advise*, point out that with this verb there is actually a third possibility – an infinitive complement (e.g., *I would advise you to look for a good, reasonably priced hotel on the Internet*).

Have the students pair off, and give one student in each pair a list of sentences that are requests for assistance and the other student a list of possible responses to the requests, one response for each request. For example, the first list might include the request *I have a friend who wants to sell his car. What should he do?* The second would have among its responses *I would suggest/recommend that he place an ad in the newspaper.* When the first student makes a request, the second finds and gives the appropriate response.

Next, give the pairs a new list of requests, and tell them that this time they will need to create their own responses. Have students take turns asking for and giving advice using the two kinds of complements. Walk around the classroom and coax students to use both complements if they look as if they are favoring one.

Activity 7: Perception Verbs with Bare Infinitive Versus Gerund Complements (Intermediate Through Advanced)

This role-play activity focuses on the meaning differences that occur when perception verbs are followed by bare infinitive versus gerund complements. (In presenting this verb group to students, you may want to use a simpler name such as "four senses verbs," i.e., *hear, see, touch, smell*.) To address the meaning differences with punctual verbs in the complement following the perception verb, prepare cards that have a sentence with a perception verb followed by either a bare infinitive or a gerund complement on each one. Examples of such sentences are shown in (72). Give each pair of students one set of cards.

(72) She saw him kicking the wall.   She saw him hit the policeman.
     He saw her bounce the ball.   He heard her scratch the blackboard.
     She felt something biting her arm.   He saw her pounding on the table.
     She saw him blow off the chalk dust She saw him snapping his fingers.
     from the eraser.

Working in pairs, students choose a card from the pile and decide how they will role-play the sentence. They write the subject and verb of the sentence – but nothing else – on the board and then act out their sentence for the class. The rest of the class guesses what the sentence is using the correct complement verb form. If the class guesses incorrectly or the card is incorrectly acted out, help students by asking questions that can lead to the correct answer.[13]

ENDNOTES

[1] The term *factive predicate* originates with Kiparsky and Kiparsky (1970). A test for whether a verb is a factive predicate is that the truth of the complement remains unchallenged regardless of whether the higher clause that precedes it is affirmative, negative, or interrogative. In addition to verbs, factive predicates include adjectives such as (*be*) *clear*, *odd*, and *significant* in sentences with extraposed subject clauses (e.g., *It is significant that the value of exports is increasing*).

[2] This verb form is also required for complements that occur after necessity adjectives such as *essential*, *imperative*, *important*, *necessary*, and *vital* in sentences with extraposed subject clauses (e.g., *It is essential that he receive your report no later than 3 p.m.*).

[3] To the best of my knowledge, *not* transportation was first discussed by Lakoff (1970). Lakoff points out that it is a "minor" rule operating only on a "handful" of verbs. Some linguists have claimed that *not* transportation applies to certain extraposed *that* clauses with *be* + adjective combinations (e.g., *be likely*). For them, sentences such as *It is likely that John won't come* and *It isn't likely that John will come* have the same meaning. *Not* transportation also appears to apply with some verbs that take infinitival complements, as illustrated by sentence pairs such as *They want us not to talk to the reporters* and *They don't want us to talk to the reporters*. For some native speakers, myself included, the former sentence sounds awkward.

[4] These complements are also referred to as being under "object control" because the subject of the complement is filled by an NP that is an object in the main clause, in this case, *John*.

[5] The observation and examples in (14) are from Sag and Polard (1991).

[6] These complements are said to be under "subject control" since the subject of the complement is the main clause subject (cf. note 4).

[7] Huddleston and Pullum (2002), pp. 1235–1236, refer to them as "verbs of causation." See their discussion.

[8] The term *naming verbs* comes from Quirk et al. (1972).

[9] See Quirk et al. (1972: 842) and Celce-Murcia and Larsen-Freeman (1983: 476).

[10] The difference in implication between *try* followed by an infinitival complement and *try* followed by a gerundive complement was apparently first noted and tested by Bolinger (1968).

[11] The observation comes from Kirsner and Thompson (1976). They use the term *sensory verbs*.

[12] The descriptions of the semantic relationships, as well as the terms *commitment, expectation*, and *influence*, are based on Sag and Polard's (1991) analysis of complements.

[13] This activity was suggested by Bhiyyihi Phillips and Sheila Lebadenko.

REFERENCES

Bolinger, D. (1968). Entailment and the meaning of structures. *Glossa, 2*(2), 119–127.

Celce-Murcia, M., & Larsen-Freeman, D. (1983). *The grammar book: An EFL/ESL teacher's course*. Rowley, MA: Newbury House Publishers.

Celce-Murcia, M., & Larsen-Freeman, D. (1999). *The grammar book: An ESL/EFL teacher's course*. 2nd ed. Boston: Heinle & Heinle.

Huddleston, R., & Pullum, G. K. (2002). *The Cambridge grammar of the English language*. Cambridge: Cambridge University Press.

Kirsner, R. S., & Thompson, S. A. (1976). The role of pragmatic interference in semantics: A study of sensory-verb complements in English. *Glossa, 10*(2), 200–240.

Kiparsky, P., & Kiparsky, C. (1970). Fact. In M. Bierwisch and K. Heidolf (Eds.), *Progress in linguistics* (pp. 143–173). The Hague: Mouton.

Lakoff, G. (1970). *Irregularity in syntax*. New York: Holt, Rinehart and Winston, Inc.

Quirk, R., Greenbaum, S., Leech, G., and Svartvik, J. (1972). *A grammar of contemporary English*. NewYork/London: Seminar Press.

Sag, I., & Polard, C. (1991). An integrated theory of complement control. *Language, 67*(1), 63–113.

CHAPTER 22

Focus Structures

INTRODUCTION

In previous chapters, we have seen structures such as passive sentences (in Chapter 17) and extraposition pattern sentences (in Chapter 20) that are the result of constituents being moved around, often for specific reasons related to the presentation of information. As we saw, two important reasons are making sure that what comes first in a sentence has a link with previous information (the given–new contract) and that long, heavy elements come toward or at the end of a sentence so the sentence is easier to process (end weight). In this chapter, too, we will look at grammatical structures created through movement of consituents and/or other changes for reasons relating to presenting information, including some structures that depart substantially from the basic S-V-O word order of English. The sentence types discussed in this chapter have been referred to as *focus structures* because they place certain elements of the basic version of the sentence in different positions in order to make them more prominent.[1] Focus structures are widely used in both conversation and writing; thus ESL/EFL teachers should understand the grammar of these structures and how they are usually used. We will look first at *cleft sentences*, formed through movement of constituents and other changes, and then at sentences with *fronting* and *inversions*, both involving only movement.

FORM OF CLEFT SENTENCES

Cleft sentences, or *clefts*, are a variation of basic declarative sentences, differing from them in that constituents have been made prominent through changes that include splitting, or "clefting," the sentence. This can be seen by comparing the declarative sentence in (1a) to its cleft versions in (1b) and (1c). Also illustrated in (1) are the two types of clefts in English: *it clefts*, which have the structure shown in (1b), and *wh- clefts*, with the structure in (1c).

(1) a. He bought *a small red convertible.*
    b. It was *a small red convertible* that he bought.   it *cleft*
    c. What he bought was *a small red convertible.*   wh- *cleft*

The formation of clefts can be described by looking at a declarative sentence as divided into two parts. For example, to describe the formation of the clefts in (1b) and (1c), we would describe (1a) as divided into the two parts shown in (2).[2]

Part 1   Part 2
(2) [He bought] [a small red convertible].

The cleft sentences in (1b) and (1c) have *a small red convertible* as their *focused element*. Thus, here, the subject and verb, *he bought*, make up one part, and the object, *a small red convertible*, as the element to be focused on, makes up the other. Both types of cleft have a more complex structure than the basic sentence, but the details of the added complexity and the placement of the focused element differ.

It Clefts

In an *it cleft*, *it* plus some form of *be* is inserted at the beginning of the sentence and is followed by the part of the sentence that is to be the focused element, which is itself followed by *that* and the rest of the original sentence, as shown in (3b). This generally means that what we have called the two parts of the sentence are switched around.

Part 1   Part 2
(3) a. [He bought] [a small red convertible].

Part 2   Part 1
b. *It was* [a small red convertible] *that* [he bought].

In the resulting sentence in (3b), part 2 is brought into focus – made the focused element – by being placed after initial *it + be*, and part 1 is moved into the background by being made part of a structure resembling a relative clause. Although *it* clefts generally have *that*, they occasionally occur with *who* and *when*, as shown, respectively, in (4b), in which the focused element is a person, and (4c), in which it is a time adverb.

(4) a. John saw Bill yesterday.

b. It was Bill $\begin{Bmatrix} that \\ who \end{Bmatrix}$ John saw yesterday.

c. It was yesterday $\begin{Bmatrix} that \\ when \end{Bmatrix}$ John saw Bill.

As is also clear from (4), different constituents can become the focused elements in *it* clefts. Examples (5) through (11) illustrate some of these. Notice in (5) and (10) that the focused element can be the subject, in which case the parts of the sentence are not switched around. Certain kinds of constituents are less conducive than others to being the focused element in an *it* cleft. For example, although an adjective phrase is shown in (9), *it* clefts with adjective phrases are relatively rare.

(5) a. *John* saw Bill yesterday.   *(subject) noun phrase*
    b. It's *John* who saw Bill yesterday.

(6) a. He got his promotion *six months ago.*   *time adverb*
    b. It was *six months ago* that he got his promotion.

(7) a. They aren't changing the rules *to make life easier for us.*   *adjunct of purpose*
    b. It is not *to make life easier for us* that they are changing the rules.

(8) a. He put up with the extra work load *for the bonus.*   *prepositional phrase*
    b. It was *for the bonus* that he put up with the extra work load.

(9) a. Her favorite color is *flaming red.*   *adjective phrase*
    b. It's *flaming red* that is her favorite color.

(10) a. *How you play the game* matters.   *subject interrogative clause*
   b. It is *how you play the game* that matters.

(11) a. They decided to intervene *because they were deeply concerned about his welfare.*   *adverbial subordinate clause*
   b. It is *because they were deeply concerned about his welfare* that they decided to intervene.

Wh- Clefts

Wh- clefts, also referred to as *pseudo-clefts*, are formed by placing *what* (or, less often, another *wh-* word) in front of part 1 and inserting some form of *be* before part 2, which becomes the focused element. This process is illustrated in (12).

           Part 1   *Part 2*
(12) a. [He bought] [a small red convertible].
   b. *What* he bought *was* a small red convertible.

As with *it* clefts, different kinds of constituents can become the focused elements of *wh-* clefts, as shown in (13) through (20). Notice in (18) and (19) that if the subject becomes the focused element, the parts of the sentence are switched around, with the subject moving to follow *be*. Sentence (19), with a person as the focused element, has *who* rather than *what*. Notice in (20) that a VP can be the focused element and that this requires the insertion of the appropriate form of *do*.

(13) a. She wanted *a glass of milk.*   *(object) noun phrase*
   b. What she wanted was *a glass of milk.*

(14) a. He promised *to have it ready today.*   *infinitive complement*
   b. What he promised was *to have it ready today.*

(15) a. I said *that I was hungry.*   *that complement*
   b. What I said was *that I was hungry.*

(16) a. I don't know *why they decided to do it today.*   *interrogative complement*
   b. What I don't know is *why they decided to do it today.*

(17) a. I really dislike *having to listen to nonsense like that.*   *gerund complement*
   b. What I really dislike is *having to listen to nonsense like that.*

(18) a. *Having to fill out all these forms* really annoys me.   *subject gerund clause*
   b. What really annoys me is *having to fill out all these forms.*

(19) a. *Bob* won't be at the party.   *(subject) noun phrase*
   b. *Who* won't be at the party is *Bob.*

(20) a. He *sells cars.*   *verb phrase*
   b. What he *does* is *sell cars.*

Adjective phrases, as in (21), are not easily focused by *wh-* clefts, nor are prepositional phrases in general unless they are locative or temporal, as shown in (22).

(21) a. Her boss, in my opinion, is *extremely arrogant.*   *adjective phrase*
   b. What her boss is, in my opinion, is *extremely arrogant.*

(22) a. I do most of my writing *in the morning.*   *prepositional phrase*
   b. When I do most of my writing is *in the morning.*

Some *wh-* cleft structures do not have corresponding noncleft sentences, as shown in (23) and (24).

(**23**) a. What I like about it is its smooth lines.
     b. *I like about it is its smooth lines.

(**24**) a. What I object to is that the judge won't consider a mistrial.
     b. *I object to that the judge won't consider a mistrial.

Wh- clefts often have a second version, called a *reversed wh- cleft*, or *reversed pseudo-cleft*, in which the focused element occurs at the beginning followed by *be + what*. We can see in (25) how a reversed *wh-* cleft, as shown in (25c), differs in form from the corresponding declarative sentence, in (25a), and regular *wh-* cleft, in (25b).

(**25**) a. I really need a vacation.
     b. What I really need is *a vacation*.   wh- *cleft*
     c. *A vacation* is what I really need.   *reversed* wh- *cleft*

Reversed *wh-* clefts are used primarily in conversation, as in (26), and fiction. They are not as common as *it* or *wh-* clefts.[3]

(**26**) A: You can't fly to Birmingham on Wednesday.
     B: Yeah? Why not?
     A: They don't have any flights to there on Wednesday. But they've got plenty on Friday and Sunday. *A weekend flight is what you want.*

SUMMARY

FORM OF CLEFTS

Cleft sentences give prominence to a **focused element** through changes that include splitting the sentence. Cleft sentences are of two basic types: *it* clefts and *wh-* clefts.
    It was a small red convertible that he bought.
    What he bought was a small red convertible.

***It* clefts** are formed from regular sentences by adding *it + be* at the start, moving the focused element to follow, and following the focused element with an added *that +* the rest of the sentence.
    He bought a small red convertible.
    It was a small red convertible that he bought.

Elements that can be focused include noun phrases, time adverbials, adjuncts of purpose, prepositional phrases, and adverbial subordinate clauses.
    It was John who spoke to Bill.
    It was last year that he got promoted.
    It is not to make life easier that they're changing the rules.
    It wasn't for the bonus that he did it.
    It is because he was worried that he called you.

continued

Wh- clefts are formed from regular sentences by adding *what* at the start and *be* before the focused element.

He bought a small red convertible.
What he bought was a small red convertible.

Elements that can be focused include noun phrases, infinitive complements, interrogative complements, gerund complements, and verb phrases.

What she wanted was a glass of milk.
What he promised was to have it today.
What I don't know is why they decided to do it today.
What I really dislike is listening to nonsense.
What he does is sell cars.

Reversed wh- clefts exist for many *wh-* clefts. The focused element occurs at the beginning followed by *be + what.*

A vacation is what I really need.
(Cf. *wh-* cleft: *What I really need is a vacation.*)

EXERCISE 22.1

From each regular sentence, form as many cleft sentences as possible with the italicized constituent as the focused element. Sentences may take one, two, or all three types of clefts (*it*, *wh-*, and reverse *wh-*).

Example: She likes *mushrooms*.

Answer: It's mushrooms that she likes. What she likes is mushrooms. Mushrooms are what she likes.

1. You find some of the longest rivers in the world *in South America*.
2. He accepted the position *with considerable misgivings*.
3. I really love *making people happy*.
4. The columnist in the *Times* predicted *that Alan would lose the election*.
5. I can't understand *how you were able to refinance your house with such a lousy credit rating*.

USES OF CLEFT SENTENCES

The basic function of cleft sentences is to make certain elements more prominent. However, in filling this basic function, cleft sentences have more specific uses in discourse, and *it* clefts and *wh-* clefts differ somewhat in these uses.

Uses of *It* Clefts

The focused element in an *it* cleft may contain old information or new information. Depending on whether the focused element contains old or new information, the *it* cleft will be used by speakers and writers for different purposes.

Contradict

It clefts are often used to contradict something that has been said or written. In (27), speaker B's response contradicts the information presented by speaker A – that a particular person is going to be fired as a result of a scandal. Notice that here the focused element is new information, whereas the information in the clause beginning with *who* is old information, given in the previous sentence.

(**27**) A: This has blown up into an enormous scandal. I hear that they are going to fire the secretary of state.

B: No, *it's the secretary of defense who they want to fire*, not the secretary of state.[4]

Argue a Point

In persuasive writing, *it* clefts are frequently used to argue a point. In (28), the writer wants to make the point that there is a cause-and-effect relationship between wing shape and the maximum speed that a jet airplane can attain. The writer does this by first asking a question about shape and then answering it in a new sentence containing an *it* cleft. Here the focused element (*the shape*) is the old information, and new information – the reason why the shape of the wing is important – follows in the clause beginning with *that*.

(**28**) But why is the shape of the wing so important? *It is the shape that determines the maximum speed that can be attained by a jet airplane.*

Establish a Topic

An *it* cleft sentence may serve to establish the writer's topic, for example, as a lead-in sentence to an article. In such cases, all of the information in the sentence is new. Thus, in (29), the material following *that* and the focused time adverbial establish the topic – that the concept "the weekend" began with Henry Ford about 90 years ago. The writer goes on to elaborate this topic in the following sentence and the rest of the paragraph.

(**29**) *It was just about 90 years ago that Henry Ford gave us the weekend.* On September 25, 1926, in a somewhat shocking move for that time, he decided to establish a 40-hour work week, giving his employees two days off instead of one.[5]

Uses of *Wh-* Clefts

Generally, in *wh-* clefts, the clause beginning with *what* is old information, and the focused element is new information. *Wh-* clefts are used primarily in conversation for a range of specific uses, including those described here.

Resume a Topic

Wh- clefts are used to resume a topic that was being discussed.[6] In (30), speaker B asks a question that causes speaker A to shift from the topic of the beverage to the bowls that it was served in. The new topic is continued for a while until speaker A uses a *wh-* cleft to resume the original topic – the beverage. The new information – its alcoholic nature – is in the focused element.

(**30**) A: Well, they served us some kind of white beverage in these interesting-looking bowls.

B: What kind of bowls?

A: Well, they were all covered with beautiful colors and designs.

B: They were painted on?

A: No. They were more like carved on. . . . I can't think of the word.

B: "Inlaid"?

A: Yeah. "Inlaid." Well, *what I didn't realize at the time was that the beverage was alcoholic.*

Present the Gist

Wh- clefts are also used to present the gist of preceding conversation. In (31), speaker A launches into a description of why he doesn't want to go over to his parents' house. Speaker B then utters a *wh-* cleft sentence that expresses what he believes is the gist of what speaker A is trying to say.

> (31) A: Well, you know, if I go there, my mom will be asking me what I'm doing with myself. And then both my mom and my dad will start to ask me why I don't have a steady job yet. And then when I tell them that I'm trying, but I just haven't had any luck yet, they will give me that kind of look, you know. Kinda skeptical and all.
>
> B: So, *what you're saying is that they will never get off your case.*
>
> A: Right. I can't stand a whole day of that.

Contradict Something Said and Present an Alternative Interpretation

Speakers may use a *wh-* cleft to contradict something that has been said in the conversation and then, possibly, present what they believe is an alternative interpretation. For example, in (32), speaker B doesn't believe that speaker A's previous statement is accurate. She responds with a *wh-* cleft that indicates disagreement and, at the same time, states her view of what happens. *Wh-* clefts used for this purpose will often contain verbs such as *happen, occur,* and *develop.*

> (32) A: When people reach retirement age, they usually slow down and become less interested in things like physical appearance and a lifestyle that includes things like dating and fast cars.
>
> B: Actually, *what often happens is that older people become more interested in regaining some of their youthful appearance and lifestyle.* They have more money, so they often spend it on changing their appearance, buying sports cars, and, not infrequently, getting back into the dating game.

Clarify a Possible Misunderstanding

Speakers may also use *wh-* clefts to clarify, rather than contradict, when it appears that something they have said has been misunderstood or not fully comprehended by their listeners. In the dialog in (33), speaker B uses an *it* cleft to repair a misunderstanding that arose from his question in response to speaker A's request to borrow a DVD.[7]

> (33) A: So I was wondering if you could lend me a DVD.
>
> B: A DVD?
>
> A: Yeah.
>
> B: WHAT DVD?
>
> A: You have a lotta DVDs, doncha?
>
> B: Yeah.
>
> A: Well . . .
>
> B: *What I meant was WHICH DVD.*
>
> A: Oh. Well, I was thinking I could watch that one you like so much.

Express the Speaker's Stance

Wh- clefts are frequently used to express a speaker's attitude, or "stance," regarding something mentioned in the conversation. As shown in (34), this use is reflected in the inclusion of verbs and nouns that express attitude, such as *surprise, love, dislike, fear,* and *hesitation.*

(34) A: So I guess you'll be happy to start drawing your Social Security check next
month.

B: Yeah.

A: You've looked into it, I suppose?

B: Yeah. You have to register to get it. *What surprises me is that the amount you
get actually goes up every year.*

SUMMARY

USES OF CLEFT SENTENCES

It **clefts** have the following uses, depending on the distribution of old and new information in the sentence to:

- **contradict** (with the focused element containing new information; the *that/who*
  clause, old information).
  A: Bob must have recommended him as department chairman.
  B: Actually, it was Betty who recommended him.

- **argue a point** in persuasive discourse (with the focused element containing old information; the *that* clause, new information).
  *But why is shape of the wing so important? It is the shape that determines the
  maximum speed.*

- **establish a topic** that is going to be elaborated (with the entire sentence containing
  new information).
  It was just about 90 years ago that Henry Ford gave us the weekend. On September 25, 1926, in a somewhat shocking move . . .

Wh- **clefts**, in which new information is generally in the focused element, are used
especially in conversation to:

- **resume a topic** temporarily relegated to the background.
  *A: Well, they served us some kind of white beverage in these interesting-looking
  bowls.*
  B: What kind of bowls?
  *A: They were all covered with beautiful colors and designs. Well, what I didn't
  realize at the time was that the beverage was alcoholic.*

- **present the gist** of preceding conversation.
  *A: If I go there my mom will be asking me what I am doing with myself. And then
  both my mom and my dad will start to ask me why I don't have a steady job yet.*
  B: So what you're saying is that they will never get off your case.

- **contradict** something that has been said and possibly **present an alternative**
  explanation.
  *A: When people reach retirement age, they usually slow down and become less
  interested in things like physical appearance and lifestyle.*
  *B: Actually, what often happens is that older people become more interested in
  regaining some of their youthful appearance and lifestyle.*

continued

> • To **clarify a possible misunderstanding** or an imperfect understanding.
> *A: So I was wondering if you could lend me a DVD.*
> *B: A DVD?*
> *A: You have a lotta DVDs, doncha?*
> *B: Yes I do. What I meant was WHICH DVD do you want?*
>
> • To **express the speaker's stance**, or attitude, regarding something in the conversation.
> *A: So I guess you'll be happy to start drawing your Social Security check. You've looked into it, I suppose?*
> *B: Yeah. What surprises me is that the amount you get actually goes up every year.*

EXERCISE 22.2

In each of the following texts and dialogs, identify the use (contradict, argue a point, establish a context) of the *it* cleft sentence.

Example: It was just over 100 years ago that Orville and Wilbur Wright made the first flight in a powered aircraft. This historic event inaugurated a new era in transportation.

Answer: establish a topic

1. The new XJ that will be introduced this year resembles other cars on the market. It has a low silhouette with sleek aerodynamic lines, twin headlights, and dual exhausts. Even the grill doesn't differ much from other models. But you can still tell that this is a Jaguar. It's the distinctive hood ornament that immediately establishes its identity.
2. A: I was just as surprised as you are that he took the job. I couldn't imagine why someone with his talent could even consider working for that company.
   B: What are you talking about? It was you who told him that he would be lucky to get a job with as many benefits as they offer! That's what convinced him to take the position.
3. A: I read in the newspaper that Boeing is going to make a new jumbo jet that can carry 800 people.
   B: No, it's that French company that makes Airbus that's going to do that. Boeing is going to make a smaller plane that goes almost as fast as the old Concorde.
4. It was just a little more than 50 years ago that the Battle of Britain was in full swing. Bombing raids were being carried out on large cities on a daily basis, and the only defense against this was the Royal Air Force (RAF). Though equipped with fighter planes that were equivalent to their adversary's, the RAF was woefully outnumbered.

EXERCISE 22.3

In each of the following dialogs, identify the use of the *wh-* cleft sentence.

Example: A: You must be pretty happy about your promotion.
   B. Well, naturally, I am very pleased. More than pleased. What really puzzles me is that they didn't promote Bill over me. He's done a lot more for the firm than I have.

Answer: express a stance

1. A: Everyone believes that the plane crash was due to mechanical failure.
   B: But that isn't true. What actually happened was that the pilot flew into bad weather and lost control of his aircraft. That's the main cause of most small airplane accidents.

2. Policeman: Did you see the accident?

   Bystander: Yeah. I was standing right over there. I saw the whole thing.

   Policeman: OK. Could you describe what you saw?

   Bystander: Well, that little green car was halfway through the intersection when a big blue car ran a red light and smacked into it. He never stopped for the light and never stopped after he hit that little car. Just drove off. I got part of his number, though.

   Policeman: Good. You say it was red?

   Bystander: Red? No, it was blue. I think it was a BMW.

   Policeman: What I meant was are you sure that the light was red when the other car hit that green one over there?

3. A: So how do you feel about the promotion system at your university?

   B: Well, to be perfectly honest, I have mixed feelings about it. I think it's a good idea that we use scholarship and teaching as our two major criteria for promotion. We always stress these two things as being most important in the decision to promote someone. But, you know, I've seen too many situations where someone seems pretty weak in the scholarship area and he gets promoted anyway. Maybe because he works hard at being friendly with an important professor in the department or he knows the dean real well or he has a wife who already has tenure, and she makes noise about leaving if her husband isn't promoted. Things like that, you know?

   A: So what you're saying is that the criteria of scholarship and teaching can be swayed or even neutralized by politics. Right?

4. A: So, after I had passed through airport security successfully, this guy comes over and shows me his badge and identifies himself as an FBI agent. He asked me if I would step into this room because he wanted to ask me a few questions.

   B: Did the badge have a photo of the guy on it?

   A: Um . . . I think so.

   B: Did you take a good look at it?

   A: Not really, but, as I remember, it looked pretty official.

   B: You should have taken a good look at it.

   A: Probably. Well, anyway, what I didn't realize at the time was that I fit the description of someone the FBI was looking for. So that was why the guy wanted to talk to me. He told me so later.

FRONTING

Fronting gives an element greater prominence by moving it to the beginning of a sentence. As it involves only the movement of a constituent and not the addition of elements to a sentence, it is a simpler device than clefting. Fronting applies to a range of constituents and has several specific uses. It is relatively rare in speech but quite common in writing.

Commonly Fronted Constituents

Examples showing constituents that are frequently fronted in speech and writing are shown in (35) through (42).

(35) a. I don't understand *this/him*.   *pronoun object*
   b. *This/Him* I don't understand.

(36) a. You forget *some things*.   *object noun phrase*
   b. *Some things* you forget.

(37) a. They galloped *across the plains.*　*prepositional phrase*
　　　b. *Across the plains* they galloped.

(38) a. He wasn't *skillful.*　*adjective phrase*
　　　b. *Skillful* he wasn't.

(39) a. We interviewed his mother *to get more information.*　*purpose adjunct*
　　　b. *To get more information*, we interviewed his mother.

(40) a. I don't recall *why he changed his mind.*　*interrogative complement*
　　　b. *Why he changed his mind* I don't recall.

(41) a. I don't doubt *that he knows the answer.*　*that complement*
　　　b. *That he knows the answer* I don't doubt.

(42) a. The new substance, *which was discovered quite by accident*, has revolutionized
　　　　the computer industry.　*reduced relative clause*
　　　b. *Discovered quite by accident*, the new substance has revolutionized the com-
　　　　puter industry.

Uses of Fronting

Fronting is usually done for one of three reasons. The speaker or writer may want to emphasize the fronted element, to emphasize a contrast between two elements, and/or to introduce a new topic or a topic shift while maintaining a bridge to previously mentioned information.

Emphasize an Element

Fronting emphasizes elements both because it moves them to sentence-initial position – a position of prominence – and because it violates the usual word order. In (43) and (44), the emphasizing effect of fronting for two different kinds of constituents that are often fronted is shown.

In (43), a fronted demonstrative pronoun serves to emphasize something that has already been mentioned in the previous sentence. In this way, it simultaneously puts old information before new information, and links the sentences more tightly.

(43) I work outside in the fresh air, which I really enjoy, and I don't have anyone telling
　　　me what to do every minute. *That* I also like.

In (44a), fronting an interrogative complement clearly has the effect of emphasizing its content more than if it had appeared in normal word order, as shown in (44b).[8]

(44) a. *Why he chose to do it that way* we will probably never know.
　　　b. We will probably never know *why he chose to do it that way.*

Emphasize a Contrast

Fronting can apply in successive clauses or sentences. Speakers and writers make use of this to emphasize a contrast between two elements, as well as to stress the elements themselves. The contrast is further emphasized when, as in (45) and (46), the fronted elements are the same kinds of constituents.

In (45), the speaker uses fronting to highlight two NPs that are contrasted. Notice here that the fronted elements not only are both NPs but are also directly related – *some things* and *other things*. In (46), the two elements that are contrasted are adjective phrases. Notice that the contrast between them is reinforced by the parallel wording in the remainder of the two short clauses.

> **(45)** *Some things* you miss because you're in a hurry; *other things* you miss because you're tired or careless.

> **(46)** *Pretty* they aren't, but *affordable* they are.

In (47), the first sentence of speaker B's response contains a fronted *that* complement, which contains old information linked to what speaker A just said. Speaker B then uses a parallel fronted *that* complement in the next sentence.

> **(47)** A: One thing that I admire about him is that he really argues very forcefully for what he believes in.
>
> B: *That he is able to present arguments for his positions forcefully*, I do not doubt. *That they will hold up under closer examination* is not clear.

Notice, in (48), that without the fronting, to establish contrast would have required a contrastive conjunction such as *still* – and the effect would have been far less powerful.

> **(48)** B: I do not doubt *that he is able to present arguments for his positions forcefully*. Still, it is not clear *that they will hold up under closer examination*.

Introduce a Topic or Topic Shift

Fronted reduced relative clauses like (42b) frequently introduce topics of newspaper articles in the first sentence of initial paragraphs. A typical example is shown in (49). Here the author uses the fronted reduced relative clause to highlight a serious problem, which is elaborated on throughout the article.

> **(49)** *Racked by drug scandals, rider departures, team withdrawals, and fighting among the leaders of the sport,* the 94th Tour de France ended Sunday as one of the most tumultuous races in the event's history.[9]

These fronted reduced relative clauses are connected to the main clause by a comma, like free adjuncts that will be discussed in Chapter 23. This punctuation convention is not always observed with purpose adjuncts, which are sometimes followed by no comma.

Other types of clauses, particularly purpose adjuncts, also frequently appear in the first sentence of a new paragraph within an article to provide a bridge to old information while simultaneously introducing a topic shift. A typical example is shown in (50).

> **(50)** Researchers in the U.K. and the Netherlands who have conducted reviews of the science, including one published last month, conclude there are no rigorous, long-term studies proving that pulling symptom-free impacted teeth is beneficial. But there are known drawbacks. . . . [The rest of the paragraph describes the drawbacks.]
>
> *To get more definitive answers*, the American Association of Oral and Maxillofacial Surgeons is sponsoring continuing research.[10]

The first paragraph in (50) begins with a topic sentence that indicates there are no solid data to support dentists' contention that pulling wisdom teeth is beneficial. The lead-in sentence of the second paragraph begins with a fronted purpose adjunct, which provides a bridge back to the old topic introduced in the previous topic sentence while introducing a shift to a new topic – that research is being undertaken to get better data. The rest of the second paragraph describes what this new research has discovered to date. Although the purpose adjunct is connected to the main clause by a comma in (50), many writers might omit the comma.

SUMMARY
FRONTING

Fronting moves a constituent to the start of a sentence to give it prominence.

Object noun phrases, prepositional phrases, adjectives phrases, and various complements and reduced relative clauses are among the constituents that are commonly fronted.
This/Some things/Him I don't understand.
Across the plains they galloped.
Skillful he wasn't.
That he knows the answer I don't doubt.

Speakers and writers often use fronting to:

- **emphasize an element**
  Why he chose to do it that way we will probably never know.

- **emphasize a contrast**
  Pretty they aren't, but affordable they are.

- **introduce the topic of an article**
  Racked by drug scandals, rider departures, team withdrawals, and fighting among the leaders of the sport, the 94th Tour de France ended Sunday as one of the most tumultuous races in the event's history.

- **introduce a topic shift** while providing a bridge to old information (as at the start of a new paragraph)
  Theories of global warming have been challenged by a small group of scientists. They claim that the warming occurs at various times and then slacks off for even longer periods of time.
  *   To test this theory, two scientists have mapped average climate temperature over several centuries. . . .*

EXERCISE 22.4

Identify what has been fronted in the following sentences.

Example: A: I always see you in a turtleneck sweater. Do you ever wear anything else?
        B: Sure. I have a lot of other clothes. Most of my stuff my wife gets at Bergner's.[11]

Answer: Most of my stuff

1. Today's cars are comfortable and stylish, but cheap they are not.
2. I moved to Los Angeles three months ago. I am still trying to get used to the smog and the constant sunny weather. The smog I can do without. I don't have any problems with the sunny weather.

3. That she displays tremendous enthusiasm for the project I don't dispute. It's her qualifications for leading it that I am not so sure of.
4. Exactly what she intended with that remark we will probably never be sure of. Nevertheless, it made a profound impact on the audience.
5. A: What can I get you?
   B: Can I have a cappuccino?
   A: Sorry, we can't heat the milk. The machine is broken.
   B: How about an espresso?
   A: An espresso I can give you.
6. To emphasize the point, he pounded his fist on the table.

INVERSIONS

Inversion moves elements into a position of prominence at the beginning of a sentence, as does fronting, and, in addition, it simultaneously moves the subject to follow the verb. Depending on the inversion, the verb may be a main verb or may be an auxiliary; examples of both follow. (With an auxiliary, the inversion in effect involves the subject–aux inversion rule, which is used to form *yes/no* questions; see Chapter 4.) This process of creating an inversion structure from a sentence with normal declarative S-V-O word order is shown in (51): With the movement of the element *sprawled in the foreground* to the beginning of the sentence, the subject, *George Price*, moves to follow the verb, *is*, as shown in (51b).

> (51) a. George Price is sprawled in the foreground.[12]
>   b. *Sprawled in the foreground* is *George Price*.

Notice that the inverted subject, at the end of the sentence, seems emphasized along with the constituent moved to the beginning. In (51b), the subject is evidently also new information, which inversion has moved to the end. As (51) thus suggests, inversions, like the other structures we have looked at, give writers and speakers another option that can serve a range of purposes related to conveying information.

We can identify three types of inversions, which we will refer to as *lexical*, *stylistic*, and *information packaging* inversions. Although there is some overlap among these types, they can help us understand the uses of inversions.

Lexical Inversions

Lexical inversions are inversions triggered by the presence of a particular word. These words fall into several groups.

A very few locative adverbs – *here*, *there*, and possibly *yonder* – trigger inversions, as illustrated in (52).

> (52) a. *Here* come the cops!
>   b. *There* goes another SUV.

The sentences in (52) are clearly formulas for expressing the ideas *the cops are coming*, and *another SUV is passing by*. Their formulaic nature is reflected in the fact that we don't have corresponding sentences such as *The cops come here!* or *Another SUV goes there*. Moreover, they are limited formulas, requiring not only one of these three adverbs but also one of just a few verbs, such as *go, come, be,* or *lie.* If other adverbs or verbs are substituted, we get ungrammatical sentences, as (53) demonstrates.[13]

(53) a. **Around* come the cops!
b. ***There *speeds* another SUV.

A second group consists of negative adverbs such as *never, seldom, rarely,* and *not often,* as well as *only.* As we saw in Chapter 5, sentences beginning with one of these adverbs trigger subject–aux inversion; (54) offers further examples. We can now see that these sentences are lexical inversions, resulting from the movement of the adverb to the front.

(54) a. *Never* have I witnessed such a stunning upset.
b. *Seldom* will you see a performance as good as that.
c. *Only* with a bank loan will we be able to buy the car.

A third group can be characterized as words that link content across clauses – *not only, neither, nor, so,* and *as,* all of which are shown in (55). The clauses in (55b), (55c), and (55d) of course involve ellipsis as well as inversion, so that, for example, (55c) corresponds to *and we can do it (, too).* For many native speakers, inversion after *as* is no longer obligatory, at least with the auxiliary *do,* as illustrated in (55d).

(55) a. *Not only* am I unhappy with his behavior, but I frankly just don't understand it.
b. A: I don't understand why she reacted that way.

B: $\begin{Bmatrix} \textit{Neither} \text{ do I.} \\ \textit{Nor} \text{ do we.} \end{Bmatrix}$

c. She can do it, and *so* can we.

d. He believes firmly in the goals of the project, $\begin{Bmatrix} \textit{as} \text{ do I.} \\ \textit{as} \text{ I do.} \end{Bmatrix}$ *inverted*
uninverted

Stylistic Inversions

In the lexical inversions, positioning a particular word at the start of a sentence makes the inversion of the subject and verb obligatory. What we are calling *stylistic inversions* involve the utilization of an optional grammatical pattern, which enables a writer to achieve a stylistic effect. The resulting structures may represent greater or lesser departures from the expected, with the stylistic effect varying accordingly.

A fairly common type of stylistic inversion is one that we have already seen in Chapter 19 – namely, that triggered by the deletion of *if* in hypothetical and counterfactual conditional sentences. As we saw in Chapter 19, this inversion is used in poetry (as in, e.g., Andrew Marvell's "Had we but world enough and time . . ."), but it also is common in discursive writing, as in (56a), and turns up in spoken English, as in (56b) and (56c). Notice that this type of inversion differs from the others we have seen in that the auxiliary that has switched with the subject is itself the sentence-initial element.

(56) a. Had Galbraith devoted more effort to gathering empirical evidence to support his views and to finding ways to test them statistically, his influence on economics would have been greater.[14]
b. Were I to live another 50 years, I would be 95.
c. Should I leave for only a minute to attend to something, I would be fired.[15]

Inversions with initial prepositional phrases are not infrequently used in poetry to achieve dramatic effects. Perhaps the most famous example is the line from Alfred Lord Tennyson's poem "The Charge of the Light Brigade": "Into the valley of death rode the six hundred. . . ." Compare the effect of this line with that of the mundane uninverted version: *The six hundred rode into the valley of death.*

Information Packaging Inversions

Information packing inversions are simply the many different inversions whose primary purpose is to "package," or distribute, the information in the sentence in a way that is somehow more appropriate to effectively conveying it. Thus, as we shall see, the speaker or writer may use an inversion for such purposes as facilitating accuracy in spoken communication, facilitating a connection between old and new information, or providing a particular perspective to the reader. We will look at a use in spoken English and then at several uses that are particularly characteristic of written English.

Spoken English

The sentences in (57) represent a special use of inversions in spoken English – their use by sportscasters in describing an ongoing game. The inversion puts the action first and gives sportscasters more time to accurately identify the players.[16]

> (57) a. Down with the ball comes Roan.
> b. Into the game for New Trier West is Brenner.
> c. Trying to save it was Shelly Tunsen.

Written English

Like the other focus structures we have considered in this chapter, inversions may serve more than one purpose. This is all the more likely in carefully crafted prose – whether journalism, academic prose, or fiction. Each of the examples in (58) through (63) highlight a particular use.

AVOIDING LONG SUBJECT NPs

Inversions are a favorite device of journalists because they provide a concise and seamless means of connecting new information to old information. Inversions allow the writer to avoid a discontinuity with the preceding sentence that would occur if a long, complex subject appeared in its normal position. Typical examples are shown in (58).

> (58) a. Investigators were at the scene of the crash by ten o'clock. *Dead were the pilot, Ralph Halsott, 29, Kankakee, Ill.; and two passengers, Susan Galston, 43, Milwaukee, Wis.; and William Johnson, 52, Chicago, Ill.*
> b. The committee members argued about the bill late into the evening hours. *At issue was section 405, which appeared to be an attempt to weaken the Controlled Substances Act.*

In each case, the sentence with the inversion keeps the connection to the previous sentence and allows the writer to place the new – and heavy – information at the end. Recasting the sentences so that they have the normal word order would lead to considerable clumsiness and to processing difficulties. For example, compare (58a) to (59).

> (59) Investigators were at the scene of the crash by ten o'clock. *The pilot, Ralph Halsott, 29, Kankakee, Ill.; and two passengers, Susan Galston, 43, Milwaukee, Wis.; and William Johnson, 52, Chicago, Ill., were dead.*

EMPHASIZING A RELATED POINT

In journalism and academic expository prose, inversions commonly serve the function of emphasizing a point related to what preceded. The example in (60) involves an adjective phrase.

(**60**) Reports show that many passengers sustain trauma to the body and broken limbs in this type of roll-over accident. *Far more serious* are the severe head injuries that cause bruising of the brain.[17]

Here, the use of the inversion emphasizes the importance of the new information that follows the expression *far more serious*. The sentence with the inversion also signals a topic shift within a paragraph, where the seriousness of head trauma may then be expanded on in the following sentences.

TOPIC SHIFT

Writers of descriptive and expository prose commonly employ inversions, often with present and past participles, for the purpose of introducing a new topic. Sentence (61) begins a new paragraph, and shifts the topic from the problem the White House is having exerting pressure on China to alter its economic policies to a related problem – the growing hostility in Congress, which is making it difficult for the president to gain support for his policy.

(**61**) *Complicating the White House calculus is soaring hostility on Capitol Hill, which some officials call "off the charts."* Congress has largely deferred to the president's foreign policy priorities, but China is one area where legislators are demanding a change of course, particularly on trade.[18]

Notice that the present participle and object NP of the verb phrase have been moved to the start of the sentence in (61). The uninverted sentence is shown in (62).

(**62**) Soaring hostility on Capitol Hill, which some officials call "off the charts," is complicating the White House calculus.

As is underscored by a comparison between the versions, in (61) an initial link to the previous paragraph is made through the NP *the White House calculus* and, at the same time, the subject of the sentence, *soaring hostility on Capitol Hill*, is placed in the position of new information. It is the new topic, which is expanded in the following sentence. The inversion has yet another benefit; the NP *the soaring hostility . . .* , made heavy by its nonrestrictive relative clause, is easier to process because it is now at the end of the sentence.

IMMEDIATE OBSERVER EFFECT

Inversions can also be used to create the illusion for readers that they are witnessing an event or an action unfold before their eyes. The writer's description can mirror the perception of objects or events as they might appear in a movie where a camera pans across a room. This "immediate observer effect" is created by placing the description in successive inversions, as shown in (63).[19] Notice that the successive inversions each have an initial prepositional phrase of location, which seem to take the reader first behind the plate and then inside the bag to the bags inside.

(**63**) Ludo is conscientious. He bends closely to his work. He unscrews the plate and removes it from the door. *Behind the plate is a chiseled cavity. Inside the cavity is a polythene bag. Inside the bag are several smaller bags. Inside each of them is a. . . .*

This stylistic effect, formerly the province of fiction, is becoming more common in newspaper writing.

SUMMARY

INVERSIONS

Inversion moves elements to the front of the sentence and simultaneously moves the subject after the verb.

There are several types of inversions:

- **Lexical inversions** are inversions triggered by the presence of a particular word, including:

  - locative adverbs *here/there* (with *come*, *go*, etc.), in formulaic sentences.
    Here come the cops!
    There goes another SUV.

  - negative adverbs (e.g., *never, not only, seldom*).
    Never have I witnessed such a stunning upset.
    Seldom will you see a performance as good as that.

  - *not only, neither, nor, so,* and *as* used to link content across clauses.
    He doesn't understand, and neither do we.
    She can do it. So can we.

- **Stylistic inversions** are alternatives to specific grammatical structures, chosen for a specific effect. These include:

  - conditional sentences in which *if* is deleted.
    Were I to live another 50 years, I would be 95.

  - inversions with initial prepositional phrases, used in poetry.
    "Into the valley of death rode the six hundred."

- **Information packaging inversions** distribute information in a sentence in a way more appropriate to the discourse context. These include inversions used:

  - by sports commentators.
    Down with the ball comes Roan.

  - to avoid the creation of a long subject NP.
    The committee members argued about the bill for days. At issue was section 405, which appeared to be an attempt to weaken the Controlled Substances Act.

  - to emphasize a point related to preceding information.
    Reports show that many passengers sustain trauma to the body and broken limbs in this type of rollover accident. Far more serious are the severe head injuries that cause bruising of the brain.

continued

- to shift the topic at the start of a paragraph.

  Complicating the White House calculus is soaring hostility on Capitol Hill, which some officials call "off the charts." Congress has largely deferred to the president's foreign policy priorities, but China is one area where legislators are demanding a change of course, particularly on trade.

- to achieve the immediate observer effect – where readers have the illusion that they are witnessing an event unfold.

  Ludo is conscientious. He bends closely to his work. He unscrews the plate and removes it from the door. Behind the plate is a chiseled cavity. Inside the cavity is a polythene bag. Inside the bag are several smaller bags. Inside each of them is a. . . .

EXERCISE 22.5

Identify the constituents that were moved to the start of the sentence by inversion, and explain the speaker or writer's purpose in doing this.

Example: Into the game comes number 51, and that will be Mike Matakitis.

Answer: into the game (to buy time to identify the player)

1. A group of councilors, along with the council officials from North Down, recently met with the Board to discuss the move. Present at the meeting were outgoing Mayor Ellie McKay, deputy mayor Jane Copeland, and council members Rob Noth, Steven Jenks, Harold Hyde, and Minnie McPartland.
2. Instruction at every business school emphasizes theory. Presumably, no businessman can be successful if he does not understand the theories of how to make money. So different, however, are the theories from the practice of ordinary business that much of what he learned will have to be unlearned later.
3. On the far side of the room stood a battered, upright piano. In front of it was a yellow wooden piano bench.
4. Trying to get inner-city teenagers to avoid violence is a difficult problem. There are several factors that may influence a teenager to go down the wrong path. For one thing, many teenagers who may be open to committing violent acts do not have parents to provide guidance to them. Often, one or both parents may be in jail, so the children are raised by their grandparents, whose ages and lifestyles may be hard for the children to relate to.

   Adding to the challenges are music, movies, and video games that glamorize violence and the gangster lifestyle. These are powerful influences on children who live in areas where the sound of a gunshot is as common as the sound of a car.
5. Representing the American team was Arnold Crumholz, the captain who had scored five goals in the previous matches leading up to this semifinal game.
6. Here comes the judge.

EXERCISE 22.6

Write a sentence with an inversion for each situation.

Example: Alan was hungry. A small diner was across the street next to a pool hall. That would have to do.

Answer: Alan was hungry. Across the street next to the pool hall was a small diner. That would have to do.

1. Can you do me a favor? A letter that has to be mailed today is up in my room on the nightstand.
2. He shoots. The ball bounces off the rim and . . . Collins comes down with the rebound.
3. The car struck a van after running a red light. Emory L. Ensley, 46, and Hazel Ensley, 41, both of Mohamet, are reported in satisfactory condition today at Mercy Hospital.
4. Steven P. Hurley, court-appointed public defender, will be representing Mayberry in the trial next week.
5. You will seldom see a performance as good as that by a man of 75.

PROBLEMS THAT ESL/EFL STUDENTS HAVE WITH FOCUS STRUCTURES

Although the problems that ESL/EFL students have producing and using English focus structures have not been widely investigated, new research is emerging that may reveal a clearer picture of what these might be. One research project that holds potential for shedding light on the acquisition of English focus structures in an EFL environment is described by Callies (2002). Using a battery of judgement, error identification, production and introspection tasks, Callies and his colleagues are examining the competency of advanced-level German learners of English in forming *wh-* cleft, *it* cleft, fronting, and inversion structures. German and English are closely related, consequently these focus structures are virtually syntactically identical in the two languages. Klein (1988), Plag and Zimmermann (1998), and Zimmermann (2000) have suggested that advanced learners are not fully competent with regard to the restrictions on focus structures, nor are they sufficiently aware of their discourse functions. Plag and Zimmermann have stated that learners avoid marked (infrequent) structures such as focus constructions, do not use them productively, and overuse specific structures such as fronting. Callies and his group are investigating these hypotheses. Although there are some reports of SLA research on the use of specific focus structures by speakers of other L1s, these are not always sufficiently detailed to warrant our consideration. This leaves a tantalizing gap in our knowledge about how English focus constructions are learned by speakers of non-Indo European languages. One exception to this was discussed in Chapter 20. There we saw that when Chinese speakers follow the linear arrangement of one of their L1 focus structures, a topicalization structure, ungrammatical English sentences that look like imperfect *tough* movement structures are produced.

One grammatical problem that ESL/EFL teachers have noted has to do with inversions triggered by the use of negative adverbs in subject position.

Inversion with Negative Adverbs (Portuguese, Spanish)

In Portuguese sentences that begin with negative adverbs, subject–verb inversion does not occur, as the examples in (64) illustrate.

> (**64**) a. *Raramente o Jorge   esquece   de fazer o seu   dever de casa.*
>   rarely   George forgets   to do   his   homework
>   b. *Somente com   um empréstimo bancário nó poderemos   comprar   o carro.*
>   only   with a   loan   bank   we can   buy   the car

Portuguese speakers follow the uninverted word order in their native language when they produce English sentences that begin with negative adverbs. The results are sentences like **Rarely George forgets to do his homework* and **Only with a bank loan we can buy the car*. This is apparently a persistent problem for Portuguese speakers up to advanced-level proficiency in English. It was also found in our corpus of compositions produced by Spanish speakers.

SUGGESTIONS FOR TEACHING FOCUS STRUCTURES

Although focus structures may seem unimportant as a grammar topic, in fact, many of these structures occur frequently enough in spoken and written English to justify their inclusion in a grammar curriculum. As we have seen, clefting occurs widely in conversation. *It* clefts can be incorporated in regular oral grammar practice and in composition instruction. *Wh*-clefts used to contradict something that has been said are good candidates for oral grammar activities. Fronting of prepositional phrases, adverbs, and reduced relative clauses is used often in academic and popular writing, as are inversions; thus, a knowledge of how to use these two focus structures could help your advanced students tó improve their writing skills. Some ways of working on focus structures are given in the following activities.

Activity 1: Contradicting with *It* Clefts (Advanced)

The use of *it* clefts for contradicting is worth teaching because it is the easiest use for the students to understand, as well as the one they will probably encounter most frequently. Create a list of sentences that make correct or incorrect statements about political, sports, or entertainment events. The list, which should be quite long, should have an equal number of correct and incorrect statements. For example, you could make an incorrect statement about a movie by writing *Robert Redford was the star of* Saving Private Ryan – that is, substituting *Robert Redford* for the correct *Tom Hanks*. It is important to choose events that you believe are well known to the students.

Begin by writing on the board an incorrect statement like the previous one about Robert Redford. Ask the students if the statement is correct. When someone says no, ask what is wrong with it. If the student says that Robert Redford wasn't in the movie or that Tom Hanks was the star, you agree and show them that they can supply a correction by saying *It was Tom Hanks who was the star of* Saving Private Ryan, *not Robert Redford*. Write that sentence on the board.

Explain that we use this kind of *it* sentence to disagree with or to correct something that someone else has said. Show how the sentence is formed. "We begin with *it* and a form of *be*. Next, place the alternative answer after the form of *be* and add a relative clause that begins with *that* or *who* and includes the rest of the sentence." To make sure that students see this, compare the two sentences on the board. Then demonstrate the last part of this procedure with a couple of other sentences that you have selected.

Now divide the class into two teams and hand out the list you have prepared. Give the teams a few minutes to go over the list and decide which sentences are incorrect and what the corrections should be. When this time is up, read a sentence to one of the teams. A student on the team must answer by agreeing with the statement or disagreeing by saying "No, that's not right" and following with a cleft structure: "It was/is X that/who . . ." Make up your own point system for correct and incorrect answers. The teams take turns answering, as do the students on a team. The team that gets the highest score wins the game. Be sure that you have enough sentences and that you ask each team an equal number of incorrect sentences.

You can follow this up by presenting a short narrative that has several individuals who have different roles in the narrative and perform different actions. Ask questions such as "Did Dick Ackley drop out of prep school?" This elicits a response with an *it* cleft: "No, it was Holden Caulfield that dropped out of prep school." [20]

Activity 2: Contradicting with *Wh-* Clefts (Advanced)

This activity is an alternative to Activity 1. It practices the use of *wh-* clefts for contradicting and correcting a previous account. Think of a situation that everyone in the class can relate to that could be seen from two viewpoints. On separate sheets of paper, compile two parallel lists that describe the opposing viewpoints about a past event. Each list should contain about six or seven statements in each column. For example, a plane trip scenario might have the two lists under the headings shown in (65).

(65) *How A Saw It*	*How B Saw It*
We drove to the airport and got there in plenty of time for our flight.	The freeway was jammed with traffic, so we didn't really have all that much time.
We parked in the parking garage.	The parking garage is almost full, so we spent a lot of time looking for a parking space.
We checked our luggage in at the ticket counter.	There was a long line to check in, so we lost more time.
We went through security.	The security line was enormous, and it took forever to get through.
We got to the gate and boarded the plane.	We barely made it to the gate on time. After the plane pushed back, we had to wait 45 minutes on the runway before we could take off because of heavy air traffic.
The plane arrived a little late.	The plane arrived almost an hour late.

Divide students into pairs. Give each partner a different list and let them look it over. Establish the rules of the dialog that will recount the event from the different perspectives. The student who takes part A must pause after each statement he or she makes to allow the other student to interject his or her perception of what happened in the form of a *wh-* cleft (where possible). The dialog could then proceed as in (66):

(66) A: We didn't have too much trouble getting to the airport.
    B: Well, actually we did, because there was a lot of traffic on the freeway.
    A: When we arrived, we parked in the parking garage and walked to the terminal.
    B: Well that's not quite accurate. What actually happened was that we had to drive around for a long time looking for a parking space because the parking garage was almost full.

As you can see, this activity allows for some variation in that speaker B doesn't always have to use a *wh-* cleft as a contradiction to speaker A's account of the events; however, you should stress that student B should use it several times. The students should have a feeling that they are engaged in a longer conversation in which they can use *wh-* clefts in this discourse function.

Activity 3: Introductory Sentences in Compositions (Advanced)

Tell students that *it* clefts are sometimes used to begin paragraphs that present a historical perspective. Choose an *it* cleft that begins such a paragraph, and show students (on the board, an overhead projector, or other screen) how the sentence would look in its regular word order. For example, show the sentence in (67).

> (**67**) *Henry Ford gave us the weekend just about 90 years ago.* On September 25, 1926, in a somewhat shocking move for that time, he decided to establish a 40-hour work week, giving his employees two days off instead of one.

Then show students the *it* cleft version of the sentence: *It was just about 90 years ago that Henry Ford gave us the weekend.* Point out that this version emphasizes the time phrase *just about 90 years ago* and also finishes up with the information the paragraph is going to be about – Henry Ford's introducing the 40-hour work week and hence, the weekend. Compared to the first version, it provides a more dramatic opening and leads more effectively into the rest of the paragraph.

Next, provide the students with similar paragraphs, as in (68), with a first sentence that could be effectively rewritten with an *it* cleft, and have them change that sentence into an *it* cleft (*It was over a hundred years ago that Orville and Wilbur Wright made the world's first successful flight.*)

> (**68**) *Orville and Wilbur Wright made the world's first successful flight over a hundred years ago.* On December 17, 1903, they flew a little over 120 feet and remained in the air for 12 seconds at Kitty Hawk, North Carolina. Only five people were interested enough to watch the flight, and few newspapers wrote anything about it.

Give students a short writing assignment on a historical theme in which they have to use an *it* cleft in the opening paragraph.

Activity 4: Using Fronted Purpose Adjuncts and Reduced Relative Clauses for Topic Shifts (Advanced)

Fronted purpose adjuncts are commonly used in academic and other writing to introduce an attempted solution to a problem that was described, often in the previous paragraph. Mastering this use of fronted purpose adjuncts will enable your students to improve their writing; moreover, it is fairly easy to teach.

Explain to students that fronted purpose adjuncts can be used when a writer presents a problem in one sentence and wants to shift to the related topic of an attempt to solve this problem. Show a typical example of a purpose adjunct (you can call it a "purpose clause") in the form *in order to* . . . . For example, on the board write the sentences in (69).

> (**69**) Scientists don't really understand how tornadoes work. They are undertaking research *in order to learn more about how tornadoes work.*

Then show the reduced version in sentence (70a) and then the fronted version in (70b).

(**70**) a. Scientists don't really understand how tornadoes work. They are undertaking research *to learn more about them.*

b. Scientists don't really understand how tornadoes work. *To learn more about them*, they are undertaking research.

Explain that the sentence in (70b) with the fronted purpose clause makes a smoother connection to the previous sentence than does (70a). It begins with information related to the previous sentence – learning more about tornadoes, which scientists don't really understand, and it ends with something new – the solution of undertaking research. For this reason, sentences with fronted purpose clauses frequently serve as transition sentences showing a shift in the topic.

Next, present via handout or projector two paragraphs that illustrate how such sentences are effective in shifting the topic from one paragraph to another. Keep the paragraphs short, and use simple current events topics that you can find in newspapers or on the Internet. An example is shown in (71).

(**71**) Who talks more, men or women? Men claim women talk so much that they can never get a word in edgewise. Women claim that they have to talk a lot more because men never listen to them. For many years, it was thought that women used about 20,000 words a day, while men only used about 7,000. So who really talks more?

To find the answer to this question, researchers at the University of Texas at Austin strapped an unobtrusive digital recorder to 400 students and recorded their conversations from 1994 to 2004. When they analyzed the transcripts of the conversations, they found that both women and men use on average about 16,000 words a day.

Point out how the sentence with the fronted purpose clause makes a much smoother transition than would the alternative. Next, present the students with an account of some research and ask them to write two paragraphs based on the research similar to those shown in (71).

Fronted reduced relative clauses also frequently appear at the beginning of a paragraph, where they shift to a new topic. You can modify the procedure described above to teach students how to effectively use these clauses in their writing.

Begin by showing students the main characteristics of reduced relative clauses – that is, they have participles and are related to fuller versions of relative clauses. Find a fronted reduced relative clause in the lead-in sentence of a paragraph that shifts to a new topic. Show it first as a full nonrestrictive relative clause, as shown in (72), and then demonstrate how this clause can be reduced and fronted, as shown in (73).

(**72**) The researchers, *who were encouraged by these results*, decided to investigate how elevated sea surface temperature (SST) of water might increase the amount of rain that hurricanes drop.

(**73**) *Encouraged by these results*, the researchers decided to investigate how elevated sea surface temperature (SST) of water might increase the amount of rain that hurricanes drop.[21]

In order to demonstrate the topic shift function of a fronted reduced relative clause, give the students a handout that shows the sentence in its context – with both the paragraph preceding the topic sentence and the text that follows it. The text for (73) is shown in (74).

(74) The researchers first attempted to see if there was any connection between elevated sea surface temperature (SST) and the strength of big hurricanes like Katrina. They took the real data of hurricanes occurring in 2004 and 2005 and fed them into a computer. Then they added the SST data and the time Katrina had spent over the Gulf of Mexico. This resulted in a computer model that closely resembled the track the real hurricane Katrina took.

Encouraged by these results, the researchers decided to investigate how an elevated sea surface temperature (SST) of water might increase the amount of rain that hurricanes drop. They calculated that a 1° C increase in SST raised the vapor in the atmosphere by 7° C. The maximum winds also rose. Together these two increases showed that a one degree rise in SST would raise the amount of rain by about 19 percent.

Follow this up with more examples of fronted reduced relative clauses that are used in sentences that shift the topic. Then present students with a short passage that you have prepared in which several paragraphs that shift the topic begin with sentences that contain a full nonrestrictive relative clause like that in (74). Have the students read the passage and change these sentences to sentences with fronted reduced relative clauses. Finally, assign a short composition of the students' choice in which the students must include at least one paragraph-initial topic shifting sentence with a fronted reduced relative clause.

Variations of this approach can be extended to show other fronted structures (e.g., fronted adjectives and prepositional phrases) used for purposes of topic shift. It can also be extended to inversions, for example, inversions with prepositional phrases, as in the sentence *Among the most successful biotechnology drugs are monoclonal antibodies*. Each teacher must decide how many of these structures should be covered based on his or her students' needs and the time available.

ENDNOTES

[1] These structures have also been termed *information-packaging structures* by Huddleston and Pullum (2002). They use the term to refer to sentences that have a corresponding S-V-O, or "basic canonical form," counterpart and are used for several functions: (1) maintaining given–new flow of discourse; (2) focusing; (3) shifting heavy NPs; and (4) topicalizing.

[2] The origin of the term *cleft* sentence comes from Jesperson (1968) who observes that the proposition expressed by the sentence is "cleft" (split) into two parts. No precise rule for the formation of both types of clefts has been proposed as far as I know. My description is modeled on the description in Huddleston and Pullum (2002). However neither Huddleston and Pullum nor I claim that this is a general rule. See also Geluykens (1988) and Gundel (1977).

[3] See Biber et al. (1999), pp. 960–961, from which this example is adapted.

[4] Huddleston and Pullum (2002), p. 1424. Note that the prominence given to the element that is foregrounded in an *it* cleft like (27) has the same function as contrastive stress. We could rephrase speaker B's contradiction as *No, THE SECRETARY OF DEFENSE is going to be fired, not the secretary of state*. Contrastive stress and *it* clefts converge in cases where the intent is to contradict.

[5] This example is from Prince (1978), p. 898. I have altered only the number of years in the original example, which comes from a daily newspaper, the *Philadelphia Bulletin*.

[6] This observation is from Kim (1995). The uses in this section are proposed by Kim; the examples are either Kim's or based on those in his article.

[7] This example is adapted from Kim (1995), pp. 262–263.

[8] See Biber et al. (1999), p. 901.

[9] The *New York Times*, page D1, July 30, 2007.

[10] This example is from "The Wisdom of Pulling Teeth," *The Wall Street Journal*, May, 17, 2005, D6.

[11] This example is adapted from Huddleston and Pullum (2002), p. 1373.

[12] This example is from Green (1980).

[13] The observation and the term *formulaic* is due to Green (1982), p. 129.

[14] This example is from J. Madrick, "A Mind of His Own," *New York Review of Books*, p. 15, May 26, 2005.

[15] This example is modeled on Green (1982), p. 135.

[16] Green (1982), pp. 132–133.

[17] This example is adapted from Biber et al. (1999), p. 902.

[18] This example is taken from "Engaging China is a Delicate Dance," The *Wall Street Journal*, May, 18, 2005.

[19] The term *immediate observer effect inversion* comes from Kreyer (2007), who has used a corpus comprised of two genres of the British National Corpus to analyze various inversions. His article on types of inversions is instructive. This kind of inversion has also been discussed by Dorgeloh (1995, 1997) as the *eyewitness perspective* and the *camera effect*.

[20] This activity was suggested by Howard Williams.

[21] These examples are adapted from K. Trenberth, "Warmer Oceans, Stronger Hurricanes," *Scientific American*, July 2007, Vol. 297(1), pp. 50–51.

REFERENCES

Biber, D., Johansson, S., Leech, G., Conrad, S., & Finegan, E. (1999). *Longman grammar of spoken and written English.* Essex: Pearson Education, Ltd.

Callies, M. (2002). Information structure and discourse-pragmatics in German-English interlanguage. Paper presented at the *Conference on the Pragmatics of Interlanguage English (ConPILE)*, Münster, September 22–25.

Dorgeloh, H. (1995). Viewpoint and the organization of informative discourse. On the discourse function of full inversion in English. In B. Warvik, S. K. Tanskanen, & R. Hiltunen (Eds.), *Organization in discourse: Proceedings from the Turku conference* (pp. 223–230). Turku: University of Turku.

Dorgeloh, H. (1997). *Inversions in English: Form and function.* Amsterdam: John Benjamins.

Geluykens, R. (1988). Five types of clefting in English discourse. *Linguistics, 26*, 823–841.

Green, G. (1980). Some wherefores of English inversions. *Language, 56*, 582–601.

Green, G. (1982). Colloquial and literary uses of inversions. In D. Tannen (Ed.), *Spoken and written language: Exploring orality and literacy*. Norwood, NJ: Ablex.

Gundel, J. K. (1977). Where do cleft sentences come from? *Language, 53*, 543–559.

Huddleston, R. & Pullum, G. K. (2002). *The Cambridge grammar of the English language.* Cambridge: Cambridge University Press.

Jespersen, O. (1968). *Analytic Syntax.* New York: Holt, Rinehart and Winston.

Kim, K-H. (1995). *Wh-* clefts and left-dislocation in English conversation. In P. Downing & M. Noonan (Eds.), *Word order in discourse*, pp. 247–296. Amsterdam/Philadelphia: John Benjamins.

Klein, E. (1988). A contrastive analysis of focus phenomena in English and German on a functional basis and some implications for didactic grammar. *Die Neueren Sprachen, 87*(4), 371–386.

Kreyer, R. (2007). Inversion in modern written English. In R. Faccinetti (Ed.), *Corpus linguistics 25 years on* (pp. 189–203). Amsterdam/New York: Rodopi.

Plag, I., & Zimmermann R. (1998). Wortstellungsprobleme in der lernersprache Englisch-frontierung und inversion. In W. Börner & K. Vogel (Eds.), *Kontrast und äquivalenz: Beiträge zu sprachvergleich und übersetzung* (pp. 208–232). Tübingen: Narr.

Prince, E. F. (1978). A comparison of *wh-* cleft and *it* cleft in discourse. *Language, 54*, 883–906.

Zimmermann, R. (2000). Pseudo-spaltsätze: Norm und lernersprache. In H. Ditwell, C. Gnutzmann & F. G. Königs (Eds.), *Dimensionen der didaktishen grammatik. Festschrift für Günther Zimmermann zum 65 Geburtstag* (pp. 391–414). Bochum: AKS Verlag.

CHAPTER 23

Adverbial Subordinate Clauses

INTRODUCTION

In this chapter, we will look at *adverbial subordinate clauses* – subordinate clauses that have an adverbial function (i.e., like adverbs, they answer questions such as *How? When?* and *Why?*). Just as relative clauses are introduced by a specific set of words, *relative pronouns*, adverbial subordinate clauses are introduced by specific *subordinators*. After looking at clauses with subordinators, we will turn to *free adjuncts*, related structures that lack a subordinator. The former type of clause, common in spoken and written English, is part of every English language teaching syllabus; the latter type, frequently used in written English, is sometimes touched on in ESL grammar textbooks and treated in composition courses.[1]

ADVERBIAL SUBORDINATE CLAUSES WITH SUBORDINATORS

The set of subordinators that introduce adverbial subordinate clauses includes single words such as *when*, *since*, *while*, and *because*, as well as multiword members such as *as soon as*.[2] These subordinators establish the relation between the events or conditions in the subordinate clause and those in the main clause. We will look first at the form of adverbial subordinate clauses and then look at their meanings.

Form

Adverbial subordinate clauses usually have an overt subject and a verb with tense or a modal, as illustrated in (1). Most adverbial subordinate clauses may follow or precede a main clause, so that both (1a) and (1b) are possible.

> *Main Clause*　　*Adverbial Subordinate Clause*
> (**1**) a. She called him *after she had finished her dinner.*

> *Adverbial Subordinate Clause*　　*Main Clause*
> b. *After she had finished her dinner,* she called him.

However, in addition to these finite clauses, we find adverbial subordinate clauses that have an infinitive or a past or present participle instead of a tensed verb, and that lack overt subjects, as shown in (2). Notice that in each case there is an implied subject – the subject of the main clause (*we, he, you*).

(2) a. We'll go on Tuesday *in order to avoid the Thanksgiving traffic.*
 b. *Although angered by their refusal*, he managed not to lose his temper.
 c. *When visiting Washington*, be sure to make a stop at the Library of Congress.

Meaning

Adverbial subordinate clauses are usually classified into different groups according to the relationship expressed by their subordinator. The main types of adverbial subordinate clauses are clauses of *time, manner, cause (purpose, reason), result, concession,* and *condition.* We will look at each of these, with the exception of clauses of condition, which have already been discussed in Chapter 19. Some adverbial subordinate clauses have parallels in prepositional phrases; in fact, many of the subordinators (e.g., *after, before, until*) are also prepositions that are heads of prepositional phrases with the same meaning. Thus, for example, (1b) can also be stated as *After dinner, she called him*, with the clause replaced by a prepositional phrase. Some prepositional phrase equivalents are included in what follows.

Clauses of Time

Clauses of time (also called *temporal clauses*) are introduced by the following subordinators: *after, as, as soon as, before, once, since, until, when, whenever,* and *while.* These subordinators establish a time sequence relationship between the events or conditions in the main and the subordinate clauses. For example, the action in an adverbial clause introduced by *after*, as in (3), will occur prior to the action in the main clause.

    Main Clause   Adverbial Subordinate Clause
(3) I will go see him *after I have registered.*

Different subordinators establish different time sequence relationships.

AS

Adverbial clauses introduced by *as* describe actions that are in progress at the time that the event in the main clause occurs or occur simultaneously with it, as in (4).

    (4) a. She called *as I was leaving.*
 b. *As they entered the salon*, the two officers ran past a group of children on their way home after school.[3]

AS SOON AS/ONCE

Adverbial clauses introduced by *as soon as* specify an action that occurs right before the main clause action is carried out, as in (5).

    (5) a. I'll finish the paper *as soon as I have cleaned up this mess.*
 b. I called *as soon as I got your message.*

The subordinator *once* marks an action that occurs prior to the main clause action. It is basically interchangeable with *as soon as*, as (6) illustrates.

    (6) We'll invite you over $\begin{Bmatrix} once \\ as\ soon\ as \end{Bmatrix}$ *we are settled in.*[4]

If *once* is followed by *be* and a prepositional phrase, the clause subject and *be* can be deleted to produce a shortened clause, as illustrated in (7). Such verbless adverbial clauses are also possible with certain other subordinators.

(**7**) a. *Once ~~they were~~ in bed*, they promptly fell asleep.
  b. *Once in bed*, they promptly fell asleep.

BEFORE

The action in an adverbial clause introduced by *before* occurs after the action in the main clause, as shown in (8). *Before* is also a preposition (e.g., *before five p.m./noon*).

(**8**) a. He voted *before he came to work*.
  b. *Before he left the room*, he checked to see if his tie was straight.

SINCE

Clauses introduced by *since* mark the beginning of a time during which the main clause action occurred – the action occurs during a span of time that starts with the point in the adverbial clause, as shown in (9). Thus, for example, in (9a), Joan's 500 hours of flying have occurred during the period subsequent to the point in time that she got her pilot's license. *Since* is also a preposition (e.g., in *I've been here since 2007*).

(**9**) a. Joan has flown over 500 hours *since she got her pilot's license*.
  b. *Since reading Dostoyevsky*, I've been looking for an author I like as much.

UNTIL

Clauses introduced by *until* designate the end point of an action described in the main clause. In (10a), the point at which George could no longer stand is when the work stopped, and, in (10b), the sitting and chatting stops when the brother shows up. *Until* is also a preposition (e.g., in *They danced until midnight*).

(**10**) a. George worked *until he couldn't stand on his feet anymore*.
  b. They sat and chatted *until his brother showed up*.

WHEN/WHILE

The subordinators *when* and *while* can both introduce a clause that specifies a period during which the action in the main clause occurred. Thus, in (11a), the action of running across the ad occurs within the larger period of reading the newspaper. However, if the action of the verb in the adverbial clause has a very short duration, as, for example, *regain consciousness* in (11b), *when* means "simultaneously, right after." *While*, which only introduces clauses that have duration, cannot be used, as shown by the unacceptability of (11c).

(**11**) a. He ran across the ad *when/while he was reading the newspaper*.
  b. *When he regained consciousness*, he found himself in a hospital bed.
  c. **While he regained consciousness*, he found himself in a hospital bed.

As we saw in Chapter 18, *when* can also be a relative adverb modifying an NP, like *the day* in (12a), and introducing definite free relatives, such as the one in (12b).

(**12**) a. I can still remember the day when I first laid eyes on her.
  b. She hates when he snores.

WHENEVER

The subordinator *whenever* means "regardless of/irrespective of the time, no matter what time," as can be seen from (13a) and its paraphrase in (13b).

(**13**) a. He was determined to go to her wedding, *whenever it was*.
  b. He was determined to go to her wedding, *no matter/regardless of what time it was scheduled to occur*.

Whenever can also be a relative adverb in indefinite free relative clauses (see Chapter 18). In this case, *whenever* means "on any occasion, every time." This use of *whenever* is shown in (14a), as paraphrased in (14b).

(**14**) a. He blushes whenever he sees her.
b. He blushes on any occasion/every time that he sees her.

The distinction between the meaning of *whenever* in adverbial subordinate clauses and its meaning in indefinite free relatives is subtle but significant and may not be recognized by ESL teachers and their students.

Participles After Subordinators

Adverbial clauses of time that are introduced by *while* or *when* and have *be* plus a present or past participle have short forms in which the subject and *be* are omitted.[5] Thus, corresponding to (15a) and (16a), we have (15b) and (16b), with shortened clauses.

(**15**) a. *While he was waiting for the bus*, he read the newspaper.   *present participle*
b. *While waiting for the bus*, he read the newspaper.

(**16**) a. *When he was asked to take on a larger teaching load*,
he refused.   *past participle*
b. *When asked to take on a larger teaching load*, he refused.

Now consider the clauses in (17), introduced by *after*, *before*, and *since*. Like those in (15), they have a present participle and no overt subject.

(**17**) a. *After studying for 13 hours*, he collapsed.
b. *Before leaving for lunch*, she signed the papers.
c. *Since leaving the firm*, she has set up her own business and is doing very well.

Notice, however, that these do not seem to correspond to longer versions with subject and *be* omitted, the way (15b) did. For example, (17c) clearly corresponds not to *since she was leaving the firm* but, rather, to *since she left the firm*. Notice, too, in (18), that we can substitute an NP for the words following *after*, *before*, and *since*, as the sentence pairs demonstrate.

(**18**) a. After *studying for 13 hours*, he collapsed.
b. After *the exam*, he collapsed.

c. Before *leaving for lunch*, she signed the papers.
d. Before *lunch*, she signed the papers.

e. Since *leaving the firm*, she has set up her own business and is doing very well.
f. Since *last year*, she has set up her own business and is doing very well.

Thus, although the clauses in (17) look like the shortened adverbial clause in (15b), they have a structure that is much closer to that of a prepositional phrase.

In contrast, in adverbial clauses introduced by subordinators such as *as soon as*, *when*, and *while*, words following the subordinator cannot be replaced by an NP, as (19b) shows.

(**19**) a. While *waiting for the bus*, he read the newspaper.
b. *While *the wait* he read the newspaper.

This substitution test indicates that *after*, *before*, and *since* in (17) are prepositions; the clauses in (17) are different from the reduced adverbial clauses in (15) and (16) in that they are more like prepositional phrases.

ON/UPON

The prepositions *on/upon* can introduce time clauses that have essentially the same meaning as clauses introduced by *when*. Thus, for example, (20a) means the same thing as (20b). However, unlike the other introducing words we have seen, *on* can introduce only clauses that have a present participle and do not have an overt subject. Corresponding finite clauses with a subject and a tensed verb are ungrammatical, as (20c) demonstrates.

> (**20**) a. *On hearing of his death*, she suffered a nervous breakdown.
> b. *When she heard of his death*, she suffered a nervous breakdown.
> c. **On she heard of his death*, she suffered a nervous breakdown.

Clauses of Manner

Adverbial subordinate clauses of manner are introduced by the compound subordinators *as if* and *as though*, as in (21). They answer questions posed with *how*. For example, (21b) answers the question *How were they treated?*

> (**21**) a. The guests ran out of the burning building $\begin{Bmatrix} as\ if \\ as\ though \end{Bmatrix}$ *they were abandoning ship.*
>
> b. They were treated $\begin{Bmatrix} as\ if \\ as\ though \end{Bmatrix}$ *they were citizens of the United States.*

Inserting a pronoun that matches the main clause subject and *would* between *as* and *if*, as in (22), brings out the "in the manner" meaning that these subordinators have.

> (**22**) a. The guests ran out of the burning building *as they would if* they were abandoning ship.
> b. They were treated *as they would be if* they were citizens of the United States.

The preposition *like*, which means "similar to" (e.g., *John is like his brother*), is often substituted for the subordinator *as if*, especially in spoken American English. Thus, for (21b), one may hear (23).

> (**23**) *They were treated like they were citizens of the United States.*

SUMMARY

ADVERBIAL SUBORDINATE CLAUSES: TIME AND MANNER CLAUSES

Adverbial subordinate clauses are subordinate clauses that have an adverbial function. They are introduced by **subordinators**, and on that basis are grouped into types: **time**, **cause** (**purpose**, **reason**), **result**, **concession**, and **condition**. These clauses often may either follow or precede a main clause.

She called him after she had finished her dinner.
After she had finished her dinner, she called him.

continued

Clauses of time, or **temporal clauses**, are introduced by subordinators including:

- *as*   *She called as I was leaving.*

- *as soon as*   *I'll finish the paper as soon as soon as I have cleaned up this mess.*

- *before*   *He voted before he came to work.*

- *once*   *We'll invite you over once we have moved in.*

- *since*   *Joan has flown over 500 hours since she got her pilot's license.*

- *until*   *George worked until he couldn't stand up anymore.*

- *when*   *When he was asked to take on a larger teaching load, he refused.*

- *whenever*   *He was determined to go to her wedding, whenever it was.*

- *while*   *He ran across the ad while he was reading the newspaper.*

Clauses of time introduced by *while* and *when* have shortened versions in which the subject and *be* are omitted.

While waiting for the bus, he read the newspaper.
When asked to take on a larger teaching load, he refused.

Clauses that have a present participle and no overt subject and are introduced by *after*, *before*, *since*, or *on/upon* have a structure closer to PPs.

After studying for 13 hours, he collapsed.
Since leaving the firm, she's been doing well.

Clauses of manner, which answer the question *how*, are introduced by the compound subordinators *as if* and *as though*.

The guests ran out as if they were abandoning ship.
They were treated as though they were citizens of the United States.

EXERCISE 23.1

Rewrite each sentence so that it has an adverbial subordinate clause that is connected to the main clause by an appropriate subordinator. (There may be more than one correct answer.)

Example: I was leaving, and at that moment she walked into the room.

Answer: As I was leaving, she walked into the room.

1. We will get together, but first we have to unpack our furniture and set up our house.
2. She watched television up to the time that her taxi arrived.
3. I will give you a ride to the airport regardless of what time you have to leave.
4. We visited her prior to coming here.
5. She heard that he had been severely injured, and she fainted.
6. Her application was reviewed as it would be if it had been submitted by a foreign student.
7. She arrived at the same time that I was leaving.

Clauses of Cause

Clauses of cause answer a *why* question. In (24), both sentences contain an adverbial subordinate clause that answers the question *Why did you get up early?* Most grammarians recognize two kinds of causes – purpose and reason. *Clauses of purpose*, such as (24a), usually imply some intention or plan by the subject of the main clause. *Clauses of reason*, such as (24b), do not.

(**24**) a. I got up early *so I would get to the airport on time.*   **purpose**
     b. I got up early *because the birds were making so much noise outside.*   **reason**

CLAUSES OF PURPOSE

The main subordinators that introduce purpose clauses are *so* and *in order*, as illustrated in (25).

(**25**) a. I got up early *in order to get to work on time.*
     b. I got up early *so I wouldn't be late.*

In (25a), the subordinator *in order* is followed by an infinitive. As discussed in Chapter 21, *in order* can be omitted from such a clause, yielding what we called an *adjunct of purpose* – in the case of (25a), *I got up early to get to work on time.* *In order* can also introduce purpose clauses followed by *that* and, generally, a modal + a bare infinitive, as in (26).

(**26**) He decided to postpone his trip a few days *in order that he might have enough time to finish writing his report.*

The subordinator *so* is often optionally followed by *that*. Thus, (25b) could also be phrased as *I got up early so that I wouldn't be late.* Similarly, (27a) can be phrased with or without the *that*. These finite clauses with *so* (*that*) often have a modal such as *can* or *could*, as is the case with both (25b) and (27a). Alternatively, *so* can be followed by *as* and introduce an infinitive purpose clause, as shown in (27b).

(**27**) a. I sent everyone an e-mail *so* (*that*) *we could be sure of a quorum.*
     b. I sent everyone an e-mail *so as to be sure of a quorum.*

PURPOSE CLAUSES OF AVOIDANCE

Purpose clauses of avoidance are a special class of purpose clauses which express the idea that an action in the main clause has the purpose of avoiding a possible undesirable outcome in the adverbial clause. The subordinator *before* occurs primarily in time clauses, as shown in (8) earlier in the chapter, but it is also used in directives that imply the need for avoidance. In (28), for example, the speaker warns the listener of something bad that may occur if he or she doesn't follow the directive in the main clause. The meaning here is similar to that of a purpose clause with *so that*: "Step away from the machine so that you won't get hurt."

(**28**) Step away from the machine *before you get hurt.*

Clauses introduced by *lest* also convey the idea of avoidance. They generally contain a bare infinitive verb, as in (29). This particular subordinator is viewed as rather antiquated by most native speakers, so it is seldom heard.

(**29**) When he heard the guard coming, he quickly ejected the CD and turned the computer off, *lest they discover that he had been trying to break into their data bank.*

The idiomatic expression *for fear* also introduces clauses that imply avoidance. *For fear* is optionally followed by *that*, which often include a modal, as in (30a), or is followed by *of* and a present participle, as in (30b).

(**30**) a. He never joined in their games *for fear* (*that*) *he would be ridiculed as an unath-letic nerd who couldn't catch a football.*
   b. He never joined in their games *for fear of being ridiculed as an unathletic nerd who couldn't catch a football.*

In contrast to other purpose clauses, purpose clauses of avoidance are usually not included in ESL/EFL grammar textbooks.

CLAUSES OF REASON

The main subordinators that introduce reason clauses are *because, for, inasmuch as, seeing as/that,* and *since.* Typical examples are shown in (31).

(**31**) a. . . . *as they were not an extension of the central government,* their hold was weakened with the introduction of national policies and the strengthening of the formal organization of the district administration.[6]
   b. They had to cancel the lecture *because she missed her plane.*
   c. She kept quiet, *for she was afraid of annoying him.*
   d. *Inasmuch as you have apologized,* I will consider the matter closed.
   e. *Seeing as/that you have already done a lot of work on this project,* you might as well finish it.
   f. *Since Mars has an elliptical orbit,* its distance from the sun varies considerably.[7]

Clauses introduced by *for* must appear after the main clause, as shown in (31c), but clauses with all of the other reason subordinators can appear before or after the main clause. *As* is most frequently used as a time clause subordinator (see [4], earlier in the chapter), but it also introduces reason clauses such as (31a), appearing in this function more frequently in British English than in American English.[8] *Seeing* may occur alone or with either *that* or *as,* as shown in (31e), with dialect possibly affecting the choice.

Clauses of Result

Clauses of result are introduced by either the conjunction *so* or the idiomatic expression *with the result.* The former may or may not be followed by *that,* the latter must be, as shown in (32).

(**32**) a. It had rained heavily the night before, *so* (*that*) *the track was covered with water.*
   b. He's lived a very frugal life, *with the result that he now has a lot of money.*

Although, as we saw earlier, *so* (*that*) can also introduce purpose clauses, the result and purpose uses can be distinguished on the basis of syntactic tests and intonation. A result clause with *so that* cannot precede the main clause, as shown in (33), because this places the result before the cause.

| *Cause* | *Result* |
(**33**) a. It rained last night, *so* (*that*) *the track was covered with water.*
   b. **So* (*that*) *the track was covered with water,* it rained last night.

In contrast, purpose clauses with *so that* can precede the main clause, as (34) illustrates.

(**34**) a. He got up earlier *so that he wouldn't be late for work on his first day.*
   b. *So that he wouldn't be late for work on his first day,* he got up early.

In order to can be substituted for *so that* in a purpose clause with no change of meaning, as (35) shows. It cannot be substituted in the result clause, as this would create an ungrammatical sentence, as (36) illustrates, or change the intended meaning of the sentence.

(35) He left early *in order not to be late for work on his first day.*

(36) *It rained last night *in order to the track was covered with water.*

Result clauses with *so* (*that*) also have falling intonation and a small pause before the *so*, but this does not occur with *so that* purpose clauses, as is shown in (37a) and (37b).

(37) a. He had just cashed his paycheck [pause], so he had more than enough money to pay the bill.   *result*
   b. He had cashed his paycheck so that he could pay the bill.   *purpose*

Clauses of Concession

Clauses of concession, or *concessive clauses*, express a contrast with the main clause. They are usually referred to as *contrast clauses* in ESL/EFL textbooks. The main subordinators introducing clauses of concession are *although*, *even* (*though*), *whereas*, and *while*.

A typical example of the kind of contrast that a concessive clause creates is shown in (38).

(38) Mehri doesn't speak Farsi although she grew up in Tehran.

In light of the content of the clause introduced by *although*, the statement in the main clause is unexpected. We would expect Mehri to be able to speak Farsi if she grew up in Tehran. A key feature of concessive meaning is that the truth of the concessive clause would lead a person to expect that the main clause would be false. Concessive clauses can appear sentence initially as well as finally, so (38) could be stated as (39).

(39) *Although she grew up in Tehran*, Mehri doesn't speak Farsi.

The subordinator *though* alternates with *although*, with some native speakers considering *though* more formal. When *though* is preceded by *even*, as in (40), the statement in the main clause is made to seem yet more surprising or unexpected.

(40) *Even though he had excellent athletic ability, access to the best coaches and equipment, and trained for years*, he never really developed into a competitive athlete.

While, primarily a temporal subordinator, and *whereas* also introduce contrasting clauses, as in (41a) and (41b).

(41) a. $\left.\begin{array}{l}\textit{While} \\ \textit{Whereas}\end{array}\right\}$ *the salad was tasty*, the main course was rather bland.

   b. $\left.\begin{array}{l}\textit{While} \\ \textit{Whereas}\end{array}\right\}$ *many Afghanis speak Farsi*, hardly any can speak Chinese.

While and *whereas* differ from *although* and (*even*) *though* clauses in one way: they do not suggest that the main clause might be expected to be false; they simply express a contrast. For this reason, *whereas*, in particular, cannot always be used in place of *although*, as (42) illustrates.

(42) **Whereas she grew up in Tehran*, she doesn't speak Farsi.

Clauses with *although*, *though*, or *while* that have *be* can sometimes be shortened by omitting the subject and *be*. Thus, (43a) can be reduced to (43b).

(43) a. *Although/Though/While it was expensive*, it was not particularly well made.
   b. *Although/Though/While expensive*, it was not particularly well made.

The meaning conveyed by adverbial clauses of concession can also be conveyed by the preposition *despite* or prepositional collocation *in spite of* followed by *the fact* and a *that* clause, as shown in (44a) and (44b).[9] *Despite* and *in spite of* also introduce clauses beginning with a present participle, as (44c) illustrates.

(**44**) a. *In spite of the fact that she grew up in Paris*, she doesn't speak French.
     b. *Despite the fact that she really didn't like him*, she decided to marry him.
     c. *In spite of/despite having grown up in Paris*, she doesn't speak French.

SUMMARY

ADVERBIAL SUBORDINATE CLAUSES: CAUSE, RESULT, AND CONCESSION CLAUSES

Clauses of cause answer questions posed with *why*. There are two types:

- **Purpose clauses** imply intent. They are introduced by the subordinators *so* (*that/as*) and *in order* (*to/that*).
  She went to bed early so that/in order that she might get plenty of sleep.
  She went to bed early so as/in order to get plenty of sleep.

- **Purpose clauses of avoidance** convey the idea that the purpose for doing something is to avoid an undesirable outcome. They are introduced by *before*, *for fear* (*of/that*), and *lest*.
  Step away before you get hurt.
  He never joined in for fear of being ridiculed/that he would be ridiculed.
  He quickly ejected the CD lest they discover he had been copying the data onto it.

- **Reason clauses** do not imply intent by the speaker. They are introduced by the subordinators *as, because, for, inasmuch as, seeing as/that*, and *since*.
  She couldn't sleep because/as/for there was too much noise coming from the street.
  Inasmuch as/Seeing that/Since you have apologized, I'll consider the matter closed.

Clauses of result describe results without implying intent. They are introduced by *so* (*that*) and *with the result that*.
  It had rained heavily the night before, so that the track was covered with water.
  He's lived a very frugal life, with the result that he now has a lot of money.

Clauses of concession convey a contrast with the content of the main clause. Clauses introduced by *although, though*, and *even though* present information that makes the main clause content unexpected. Clauses introduced by *while* and *whereas* simply express a contrast.
  Although/(Even) though she grew up in Tehran, she doesn't speak Farsi.
  While/Whereas the salad was tasty, the main course was rather bland.

Concession can also be conveyed through the prepositions *despite* and *in spite of* followed either by *the fact* and a *that* clause or by a participial clause.
  In spite of the fact that she grew up in Paris, she doesn't speak French.
  Despite having grown up in Paris, she doesn't speak French.

EXERCISE 23.2

Rewrite each sentence using a subordinator that won't change the meaning of the sentence. Other changes may be needed. (There may be more than one correct answer.)

Example: Despite the fact that she was very rich, she had an unhappy life.

Answer: Although she was very rich, she had an unhappy life.

1. He couldn't visit her very often because she lived over on the other side of town.
2. Since she wanted to be sure that there were no errors in the report, she proofread it twice.
3. While many older people like classical music, very few young people do.
4. The elections were held on time, though many polling places did not have ballot boxes.
5. He refused to sign the petition for fear of being branded a troublemaker.
6. In spite of trying like mad to please her superiors, Lucy never received a promotion.

EXERCISE 23.3

In the following pairs, identity the kind of clause that the subordinator introduces in each sentence.

Example: a. He left the office early *so that he could have some time to spend with his son.*
      b. He left the office late, *so he didn't have any time to spend with his son.*

Answer: (a) = purpose clause; (b) = result clause

1. a. You had better give me that carving knife. You might cut yourself.
    b. You had better give me that carving knife *before I leave this afternoon.* Otherwise, I might forget to return it to the caterer.
2. a. *Since you have already started work on this project,* I guess you should be allowed to finish it.
    b. *Since you have started work on this project,* I have heard nothing but good things about it.
3. a. A storm was brewing, so a stiff breeze was blowing.
    b. He went back inside so he could warm up.
4. a. *While he was handsome,* he really wasn't very intelligent. So he was never very popular with women, except those who liked good-looking men.
    b. *While he was handsome,* he was popular. However, with the passage of time, his popularity waned.

FREE ADJUNCTS

Free adjuncts, sometimes called *supplementive clauses,* are adverbial subordinate clauses that are loosely tied to the main clause in that they are not introduced by a subordinator.[10] The main clause in (45) is preceded by a free adjunct. The looseness of the tie is semantic since, as we have seen, subordinators clarify the relationship between the main and subordinate clauses.

(45) *Waiting for the bus,* he read a newspaper.

Free adjuncts are used almost exclusively in written English. They appear in fiction, newspaper reports and, to a lesser extent, in academic writing.[11]

Form

In terms of form, free adjuncts have the following characteristics:

- They are not introduced by a subordinator as are regular subordinate clauses.
- They contain a present participle.

- They have no overt subject, but in most cases the missing subject is felt to be identical to the main clause subject. (This identity was found in 90 percent of cases in a study of native speaker judgments of over 1,400 adjuncts.[12] The remaining 10 percent may be due in part to one kind of adjunct, discussed in what follows, whose missing subject is different from the main clause subject.)
- They can precede or follow the main clause and are set off from it by a falling intonation and a pause, represented by a comma in writing.

These characteristics of free adjuncts are apparent in the examples in (46).

(46) a. *Backing out of the parking space*, he bumped into a passing car.
    b. The train stopped suddenly, *throwing some of the passengers out of their seats*.

Meaning

As with the other clauses in this chapter, the relationships that free adjuncts have to main clauses are largely adverbial. Like regular adverbial subordinate clauses, the adjuncts answer *how*, *when*, or *why* questions about the main clause.

Because free adjuncts do not have subordinators to specify a meaning connection to the main clause, it is sometimes possible to paraphrase a sentence with a free adjunct with more than one subordinator. However, as we will see, often the possible meanings of a specific adjunct in its context are fairly restricted.

The types of adverbial relationships that free adjuncts have to main clauses can be usefully divided into time relationships and several other types.[13] We will consider each in turn. As we will see, native speakers' interpretations of the relationship of a free adjunct to its main clause are often significantly influenced by the lexical aspect of the verbs in both clauses. The position of the free adjunct in relation to the main clause also plays a role in how free adjuncts are used and understood. The free adjuncts discussed here typically occur before the main clause; in the next section, on use, we will also look at adjuncts that occur after the main clause, and we will see the special uses of adjuncts in each of the two positions.

Time Relationships

Many free adjuncts constitute a possible answer to a *when* question posed about the main clause. That is, the action in the main clause occurs at a time relative to the event that is in the free adjunct. Two kinds of temporal relationships can be recognized: *concurrent action* and *sequential action*.

CONCURRENT ACTION

The *concurrent action* relationship between clauses occurs when the main clause action goes on while the action in the adjunct is happening, as shown in (47a). Notice that both verbs, *drive* and *gaze*, are activity verbs: They have inherent duration that potentially can go on indefinitely. The main clause action, gazing, is going on concurrently to the action of driving. The free adjunct answers the question *When did Alvin gaze upon the countless fruit trees?* As we saw earlier in the chapter, *while* and *as* are subordinators of ongoing action, so the relationship of the free adjunct to the main clause in (47a) can be paraphrased, as in (47b), in a sentence with either of these two subordinators.

(47) a. *Driving through the countryside*, Alvin gazed upon countless fruit trees that were in full bloom.
    b. *While/As* (he was) *driving through the countryside*, Alvin gazed upon countless fruit trees that were in full bloom.

Concurrent action may also be expressed if the adjunct contains a stative verb, since states, too, have inherent duration. Thus, in (48a), the free adjunct has the stative verb *lie* and the main clause, as in (47), has an activity verb, namely, *reflect*. The action of reflecting occurs during the state denoted in the free adjunct, and a paraphrase with *while* or *as* is again possible, as (48b) illustrates.

(**48**) a. *Lying between the satin sheets of her bed*, Veronica reflected on the joys of being fabulously wealthy.
   b. *While/As she lay between the satin sheets of her bed*, Veronica reflected on the joys of being fabulously wealthy.

Thus, when a free adjunct has a stative or activity verb and the main clause has an activity verb, the free adjunct tells what the main clause activity was concurrent with.

SEQUENTIAL ACTION

The *sequential action* time relationship occurs when the main clause action closely follows the action in the free adjunct. In sentences with a sequential action relationship, typically the free adjunct and the main clause contain achievement or accomplishment verbs. Since both types imply an action with an end point, the action in the main clause is seen as the second of two actions that occur in succession. This relationship can be seen clearly in (49a) and (50a), which have achievement verbs in both clauses. It is also evident in the paraphrases with the coordinate conjunction *and* optionally followed by *then*, illustrated in (49b) and (50b). Various paraphrases express the idea of successive actions; *and* (*then*) is the most basic of these.

(**49**) a. *Taking the bartender hostage*, the gunman fled into the street.
   b. The gunman took the bartender hostage *and* (*then*) fled into the street.

(**50**) a. *Opening the drawer*, he took out the manuscript.
   b. He opened the drawer *and* (*then*) took out the manuscript.

In (49) and (50), the paraphrases with *and* (*then*) work particularly well because the actions in both clauses have a relatively short duration. Consider now the sentence in (51a), in which the verb in the free adjunct (*reaching*) is a change-of-state, rather than punctual, achievement verb; thus, a period of time is involved. Notice that, while a coordinate paraphrase is also possible for (51a), as (51c) shows, paraphrases with *as soon as*, *when*, and (*up*)*on*, shown in (51b), are equally valid, since these subordinators are appropriate with an achievement verb that involves longer duration prior to the end point. In any case, regardless of which subordinator a native speaker favors in a paraphrase, the interpretation of the relationship between the two clauses in (51a) is sequential action, as it is for (49a) and (50a), with the main clause action following the adjunct action.

(**51**) a. *Reaching the river*, they pitched camp for the night.

   b. *As soon as they reached* / *When they reached* / *Upon reaching* the river, they pitched camp for the night.

   c. They reached the river, *and* (*then*) pitched camp for the night.

A sequential action interpretation also occurs with a common type of free adjunct beginning with *having* + past participle, as shown in (52a). Because the verb is in the perfect form, the free adjunct denotes an action that occurred before the main clause action.

Moreover, because sequence is thus established, these clauses may have not only telic (accomplishment or achievement) verbs but also atelic (stative or activity) verbs. A paraphrase that expresses the relationship between the free adjunct and the main clause in (52a) would be (52b), with the subordinator *after* or *as soon as.*

(52) a. *Having considered the entrances and escape routes*, Kurtz decided he must rent the lower flat too. . . .[14]

b. $\left.\begin{array}{l}\textit{After} \\ \textit{As soon as}\end{array}\right\}$ *he had considered the entrances and escape routes*, Kurtz decided he must. . .

Other Relationships

In addition to the time relationships we have looked at, free adjuncts can be interpreted as having *reason*, *instrumental*, or *conditional* relationships to the main clause.

REASON

Free adjuncts can also be interpreted as expressing a reason for the main clause action. Thus, in (53a), Pierre's desire not to draw attention to himself was the reason for his action of moving back into the crowd, and in (54a), Tom's belief about Susan was the reason he took his time. Such interpretations are common when free adjuncts have stative verbs of cognition such as *believe, desire, dislike, doubt, feel, guess, know, prefer, see, suppose, think*, and *understand* or stative verbs of desire such as *desire, want*, and *wish*. In these cases, the adjunct answers a *why* question posed about the main clause, and can be paraphrased with adverbial subordinators of reason such as *because* and *since*, as shown in (53b) and (54b).

(53) a. *Not wanting to draw attention to himself,* Pierre began to move back into the crowd that was gathering at the scene of the accident.
b. *Because/Since he didn't want to draw attention to himself,* Pierre began to move back into the crowd that was gathering at the scene of the accident.

(54) a. *Believing that Susan would be late as usual,* Tom took his time getting ready for their date.
b. *Because/Since he believed that Susan would be late as usual,* Tom took his time getting ready for their date.

INSTRUMENTAL

An *instrumental relationship* between the clauses occurs when the free adjunct expresses the means for the action in the main clause. For example, in (55a), *twisting her body* is Susan's means for freeing herself, and in (56a), *using a crowbar* is Hal's means for opening the crate. The verb in the free adjunct denotes an action to bring about a result described in the main clause. The free adjunct is thus the answer to a *how* question posed about the main clause, for example, for (55a), the question *How did she free herself from his grip?* This instrumental relationship is facilitated by main clause verbs that denote accomplishments – *free herself* in (55a) and *pry open* in (56a). The subordinator that brings out this interpretation is *by*, as shown in the paraphrases (55b) and (56b).

(55) a. *Twisting her body sideways,* Susan freed herself from his grip.
b. *By twisting her body sideways,* she freed herself from his grip.

(56) a. *Using a crowbar,* Hal pried open the top of the crate.
b. *By using a crowbar,* Hal pried open the top of the crate.

CONDITIONAL

With free adjuncts introduced by a few verbs (e.g., *assume, consider, grant,* and, possibly, *suppose*), we can have a *conditional relationship* between the clauses; that is, the truth of the content of the main clause is expressed as having the condition given in the free adjunct. Thus, in (57), the inference that Chicagoans are experiencing alarm is dependent on newspaper accounts being an accurate reflection of public opinion. This relationship is promoted by the presence in the main clause of the modal *must* in its inferred probability meaning (see Chapter 14). When clauses have a conditional relationship, the sentence can be paraphrased with the subordinator *if,* as shown in (57b). As the paraphrase reveals, with these conditional relationship sentences, the missing subject of the free adjunct is *one* or *we,* rather than the main clause subject, as in other free adjuncts.

> (**57**) a. *Assuming that newspaper accounts are an accurate reflection of public opinion,* Chicagoans must have been alarmed at the rise of property-related crimes over the past year.
>
> b. *If one/we assume(s) that newspaper accounts are an accurate reflection of public opinion,* Chicagoans must have been alarmed at the rise of property-related crimes over the past year.

Use

Free adjuncts, as already mentioned, are used almost exclusively in writing. The effects to which writers use them are dependent in large part upon the position of the adjunct in relation to the main clause.

In Sentence-Initial Position

Particularly in journalistic writing, adjuncts that are in sentence-initial position frequently occur in sentences at the beginning of paragraphs, in which they serve two important purposes related to information structuring considerations we looked at in Chapter 22.

In sentences that begin the first paragraph of an article, an initial free adjunct can draw the reader in by vividly setting the scene in a sentence that is introducing the topic. Thus, in (58), the free adjunct evokes a vivid image that further gains effectiveness by contrasting with the shocking fact revealed following the main clause. That is, the adjunct vividly and concretely conveys the unremarkableness of the city, and this unremarkableness contrasts with the dangerous radioactive material stored beneath it, the topic of the article, which is thereby introduced

> (**58**) *Rising out of the central plateau in a jumble of dusty apartment blocks and crowded roads,* this is an unremarkable city in every respect but one – the caverns beneath it house hundreds of barrels of highly radioactive fuel rods.

The free adjunct in (59), which also opens an article, in addition to helping to paint a vivid image, lends a sense of immediacy, much like a TV camera trained on the person who was interviewed in the article. This is the immediate observer effect that we saw in Chapter 22 with inversions.

> (**59**) *Looking up from his daily routine of selling coffee, chocolates, and vegetables in his tiny, unheated kiosk,* Petre Simion nods at his idol, who is towering nearby, and swells with inspiration.

In sentences that start later paragraphs in a text, initial free adjuncts are often used to link to information in the previous paragraph while introducing a topic shift, as exemplified in (60).

(**60**) *Hoping to get a better handle on the hunt,* agencies and hunting groups in 1999 embarked on a cooperative program called community-based management.[15]

The paragraph preceding sentence (60) had described the problems that Canada's Department of Fisheries and Oceans (DFO) has had monitoring the annual hunt that the Inuit conduct to harvest narwhals, a species of whale. The DFO suspected that the narwhal population was becoming reduced by the annual hunt to a point where the species was becoming endangered. However, it was difficult to confirm this because the DFO staff was very small and the agency is regarded with suspicion by the Inuit. The sentence with the free adjunct in (60) begins a new paragraph and, while linking to these past problems, it shifts the topic to a new initiative that the DFO has started, which will hopefully provide more accurate information about how many narwhals are killed and build trust with the Inuit.

After the Main Clause

Free adjuncts that follow main clauses have the same types of adverbial relationships as adjuncts that precede main clauses. In terms of use, free adjuncts following the main clause serve purposes that have been labeled *addition* and *elaboration*.[16] That is, the free adjunct is used to add to the meaning of the main clause or to expand it in some way.[17]

In (61), the free adjunct provides further information about the action in the main clause. The information in the adjunct in (61) is about manner; it answers the question *How did he answer their questions?*

(**61**) He answered their questions, *smiling, frowning, and occasionally laughing heartily.*

In (62), the free adjunct provides an elaboration of the event described in the main clause. Again, the relationship the two clauses expressed could be considered to be one of manner; the adjunct presents a more detailed description of how Microsoft was hit hard.

(**62**) Microsoft was hit hard today, *falling from yesterday's price of 30 at one point to a new low of 25, but eventually recovering to 28.*

Finally, in (63) and (64a), the action in each sentence-final free adjunct is a further action that results from the action in the main clause. Thus, there is a cause-and-effect relationship between the actions in the two clauses. Notice that (64a) can be paraphrased with a clause beginning *with the result*, as in (64b).

(**63**) High waves whipped up by hurricane-force winds swamped the pleasure boats, *sinking several and carrying others out into the Bay of Biscayne.*[18]

(**64**) a. The retro-rockets fired prematurely, *throwing the craft into a spin.*
     b. The retro-rockets fired prematurely, *with the result that the craft was thrown into a spin.*

SUMMARY

FREE ADJUNCTS

Free adjuncts are adverbial subordinate clauses that are loosely tied to the main clause because they are not introduced by a subordinator. Free adjuncts begin with a present participle, have no overt subject, and are attached to main clauses by a comma. They may come before or after the main clause.

Many free adjuncts can be interpreted as having two **time relationships** and several other relationships to the main clause. These interpretations are:

- **Concurrent action**, with the main clause action going on when the free adjunct event is. In these sentences, the free adjunct has an activity verb or stative verb, and the main clause has an activity verb.
  Driving through the countryside, Alvin gazed upon the fruit trees. (= *While/As he was driving through the countryside, Alvin gazed upon the fruit trees.*)

- **Sequential action**, with the main clause closely following the action of the free adjunct. Generally, the free adjunct and main clause have achievement or accomplishment verbs. A wider range is possible when the free adjunct has a perfect form.
  Opening the drawer, he took out the manuscript. (= *He opened the drawer and took out the manuscript.*)
  Reaching the river, they pitched camp for the night. (= *As soon as they reached the river, they pitched camp for the night.*)
  Having considered the escape routes, Kurtz decided he must rent the lower flat. (= *After he had considered the escape routes, Kurtz decided he must rent the lower flat.*)

- **Reason**, with the free adjunct expressing a reason for the main clause action. The free adjunct usually has a stative verb of cognition or desire.
  Believing that Susan would be late as usual, Tom took his time getting ready for their date. (= *Because he believed that Susan would be late as usual, Tom took his time getting ready for their date.*)

- **Instrument**, with the free adjunct expressing the means for the main clause action. The main clause usually has an accomplishment verb.
  Twisting her body sideways, she freed herself from his grip. (= *By twisting her body sideways, she freed herself from his grip.*)

- **Condition**, with the truth of the main clause depending on the condition in the free adjunct. The free adjunct verb is *assume*, *grant*, *consider*, or *suppose*.
  Assuming that newspaper accounts reflect public opinion, Chicagoans must have been alarmed at the increase in property-related crime. (= *If we/one assume(s) that newspaper accounts reflect public opinion . . .*)

In **sentence-initial position**, free adjuncts are used at the start of:

- the first paragraph of a text, to vividly paint the scene and give a sense of immediacy.
  Rising out of the central plateau in a jumble of dusty apartment blocks and crowded roads, this is an unremarkable city in every respect but one.

- subsequent paragraphs, to link to previous content while introducing a new topic.
  Hoping to get a better handle on the hunt, agencies and hunting groups in 1999 embarked on a cooperative program called community-based management.

After the main clause, free adjuncts are used for **addition** and **elaboration** – that is, to provide information in addition to, and elaborate on, the content in the main clause.
  He answered their questions, smiling, frowning, and occasionally laughing heartily.
  Microsoft was hit hard today, falling from yesterday's price of 30 at one point to a new low of 25, but eventually recovering to 28.

Rewrite each sentence to replace the free adjunct with a clause with an appropriate subordinator. Make any necessary changes. (There may be more than one correct answer.)

Example: Realizing that the plane was dangerously close to stalling, the pilot pushed the nose down to gain speed.

Answer: Because he realized that the plane was dangerously close to stalling, the pilot pushed the nose down to gain speed.

1. Backing out of the driveway, Alice ran over her daughter's bike.
2. Having disembarked from the ship, the German tourists set off to find a comfortable hotel.
3. Driving through the streets of London in her Rolls Royce and watching the heads turn as she passed by, Deborah was struck by how easily people are impressed by an expensive car.
4. Arriving at the cabin, they immediately started a fire in the fireplace.
5. Inserting the credit card between the door and the lock and pushing it upward, the thief was able to unlock the door and gain access to the room.
6. Knowing that they might have to repel a counterattack, the lieutenant arranged his men in a defensive position and told them to dig in.
7. Assuming that they left on time, they should now be somewhere between Dayton and Columbus.

Rewrite each sentence so that it has a sentence-final free adjunct.

Example: The room clerk stiffened, and she straightened her shoulders as she did this.

Answer: The room clerk stiffened, straightening her shoulders.

1. He wrote about the problem in his book, and he argued for a different solution that incorporated diplomacy rather than conflict.
2. "There's a lot more division than I expected on the court," said Georgetown University law professor David Law, and this echoed the sentiments of several legal experts.
3. Since the Enlightenment, there has been a steady spread of rationality and humanitarianism that has, in turn, affected religious belief, and this has led to a wider spread of religious tolerance.
4. West Germany resisted broadening the treaty, and this unleashed efforts from the American delegation to influence the other delegates.
5. Yugoslav troops reopened Montenegro's main airport, and this eased a confrontation with Serbia's independence-minded partner in the Balkan federation.

PROBLEMS THAT ESL/EFL STUDENTS HAVE WITH ADVERBIAL SUBORDINATE CLAUSES

We do not have extensive corpus data on the problems that ESL students have with adverbial subordinate clauses, thus no strong statements about general trends can be made. It appears that many of the more frequently used adverbial subordinate clauses may be learned quite quickly. An examination of compositions written by ESL students at the university level revealed three kinds of problems. The following discussion focuses on these problems, using as illustrations errors from our corpus made by learners whose L1s were Spanish, Portuguese, and Korean. Although some examples of free-standing subordinate clauses were found in the corpus, there were too few of these to enable any conclusions as to whether this is a recurrent problem. Our corpora included only one example of a free adjunct, which may indicate that even students with advanced proficiency seldom use free adjuncts in writing.

Connection to the Main Clause

Students sometimes produce sentences with a grammatically correct subordinate clause but a faulty connection between subordinate and main clauses. This is the case in (65), from the composition of a Spanish-speaking undergraduate student. Notice that omitting "it is why" would greatly improve the connection of the subordinate clause to the main clause.

> (65) *Because I was not prepared when I arrived to UIUC it is why the low temperatures in October began to make effect on me.

There are not many errors like this in our corpus, so it is not clear that there is strong need for teachers to address the connection between subordinate and main clauses.

Subordinator Choice

Students sometimes choose the wrong subordinator or even confuse subordinators with other words. In (66a), the writer uses the subordinator *even though* rather than *even*, creating a subordinate clause where none was intended. In (66b) and (66c), in contrast, the writers intend *even though* but use *even* and *even that* instead, thus failing to produce a subordinate clause. (The context of [66c] indicates that the writer's use of *my joint process* is intended to mean "my integration into American society.") In (66d), the writer uses *while* instead of *when*.

> (66) a. *Even though* for the unskilled immigrants, there are lots of jobs and opportunity, which can be accomplished.
> b. *Even* I will not work at group teams as much as I would in companies as the described above, I will receive a continuous education which will satisfy my knowledge in structures.
> c. *Even that* my joint process has not been the worst; I had a huge impression when I deal with the absolute reality at UIUC.
> d. *While* you select one track in the engineering market, you are also missing the rest of the other possibilities you may have.

Verb Forms in Subordinator + Participle Structures

Students sometimes use verb forms other than present participles in structures in which these are required, as exemplified in (15), (16), and (17) earlier in the chapter. For instance, in (67), the student follows *while* with *should make* instead of the present participle *making* (i.e., *while making a strong system to prevent . . .*)

> (67) *The government should do their best to solve the social problems caused by the illegal immigrants, while they should make a strong system to prevent an increase of illegal immigrants.

In (68), following *after*, the student has selected the infinitive form *to see* rather than the present participle *seeing*. This appears to be an L1 transfer error, since in the corresponding sentence in Spanish the infinitive follows *después de*.

(68) Después de ver   una película,   él fue   a   ver   a   su madre.[19]
After   to see   a film,   he went   to see   his mother.

Such errors may suggest that more attention should be given to the teaching of subordinators that have more than one meaning (e.g., *while*) and to subordinators followed by participles.

SUGGESTIONS FOR TEACHING ADVERBIAL SUBORDINATE CLAUSES AND FREE ADJUNCTS

Adverbial clauses are treated as advanced-level structures in grammar books and in textbooks designed to teach writing. The categories used in this chapter (i.e., clauses of time, reason, purpose, etc.) are found in ESL grammar books and courses. However, concessive clauses are often labeled "contrastive," and the distinction between true concession and simple contrast is not always shown. The main types of activities used for practicing adverbial subordinate clauses are exercises requiring students to fill in the blanks with appropriate subordinators, sentence combination exercises, and sentence completion drills.

Probably the most effective way of teaching adverbial clauses is through classroom activities that emphasize the different subordinators that express a particular relationship – time, reason, purpose, and so on. Tasks that induce students to make sentences with as many subordinators as possible for each category should foster comprehensive learning of different subordinators. Rather than relying solely on the types of exercises in textbooks, you should devise relevant and realistic tasks that involve speaking and writing. Examples of how this might be done are shown in the activities that follow.

Activity 1: Using Concessive Clauses to Express Apparent Contradictions (High Intermediate Through Advanced)

To work on concessive clauses, begin by modeling clauses with the subordinator *although.* Use an example that is truly concessive, such as shown in (69):

(69) *Although he is an American citizen*, he has never lived in the United States.

Explain that the meaning of an *although* clause is almost the same as that of a *but* clause except for one difference: with *although*, the contrast between the *although* clause and the main clause is unexpected or surprising; *but* simply expresses a contrast. In (69), *although* is very appropriate because we would not expect an American citizen never to have lived in the United States. Ask students how this is could be possible. If they don't come up with a good answer, you can tell them that children of American citizens are citizens even if they are born outside of the country.

Next, model concessive clauses with *despite* and *in spite of.* Show students that *despite* and *in spite of* can be followed by *the fact that*, as shown in (70). Point out that these clauses, like those with *although*, can come before or after the main clause.

(70) a. He has been unable to obtain a government job *despite the fact that he is a close friend of the secretary of state.*
   b. He has been unable to obtain a government job *in spite of the fact that he is a close friend of the secretary of state.*

Use the sentences in (70) to show that *despite* and *in spite of* can also be followed by a present participle, as shown in (71). Have students compare the clause containing the gerund form with the clause containing *the fact that*.

(71) He has been unable to obtain a government job, *in spite of being a close friend of the secretary of state.*

(= He has been unable to obtain a government job, *in spite of the fact that he is a close friend of the secretary of state*.)

Provide pairs of contrastive sentences and have the students form concessive clauses with all three subordinators (*although, despite, in spite of*). Make sure that the contrasts are striking, as in the examples in (72).

(72) We are in an economic depression. The travel industry is booming.

He has very little money. He lives in a huge house.

He is quite plain looking. He is married to a beautiful woman.

She is not very athletic. She managed to win an athletic scholarship.

Move to examples based on current events. For instance, you might draw on statements that politicians have made about their positions and actions they have taken or programs they have supported that contradict these statements. These examples can be taken from newspaper or Internet articles, short summaries, and even video clips. Have the students use this material to make statements containing a concessive clause with a subordinator. This activity can be done in small groups or in pairs in which both students have a list of things that politicians or governments have said they support as well as another list of actions that clearly contradict these. One student says "Senator X says he wants a cleaner environment. He is quoted as saying . . ." (the student reads the quote). The second student says, "Yes, but look at this. Although he says he supports a cleaner environment, he voted against the Clean Air Act." The students take turns using the contradictory facts to create sentences that contain a concessive clause. Stress that they should use all three subordinators and the clauses with *despite/in spite* followed by a present participle.

As a follow-up, you can have the students research some current event in which contradictions abound and present their findings in short oral or written reports.

Activity 2: Using Alternative Subordinators in Discourse (High Intermediate Through Advanced)

An activity in which students replace subordinators in a discourse with acceptable alternatives may help them review what they have been taught. The discourse for this activity can take the form of a short paragraph that includes subordinators of different types. The students read the paragraph and replace each underlined subordinator with an alternative, rewording the sentences as needed. For example, in the paragraph in (73), *although* in the first sentence can be replaced by *in spite of the fact/despite the fact* (*that*). In that same sentence, *in order* can be restated as *so* (*that*), which would necessitate the omission of *to* and the insertion of *he could*. In the second sentence, *because* can be replaced by *since*; in the third sentence, *since* can be replaced by *because*; and in the last sentence, *after* can be replaced by *as* *as soon as*.

(73) Although he was still recovering from the flu, John came in early in order to catch up on the work that had piled up during the last three days he had been out of the office. He didn't really have to do this because he was, after all, the boss and either

his assistant or one of his division managers could have attended to these matters for him. But, <u>since</u> he was the boss, he felt that he should keep on top of everything that was going on in the business. <u>After</u> he got to his office, he began reading the new contracts that had been put on his desk.

Hand out several such paragraphs of varying lengths which contain a variety of subordinators. Call on students to read their revised sentences and ask the class whether their revisions were similar or different.

Activity 3: Determining Meaning with Subordinators with More Than One Meaning (High Intermediate Through Advanced)

A variation of the preceding activity can serve to review the meanings of adverbial subordinators that have more than one meaning, such as *since*, which introduces time and reason clauses, or *while*, which introduces time and concession clauses. First, review the types of relationships established by each group of subordinators to which the subordinator belongs. Next, present the subordinator and illustrate that it belongs to each group. Here is an example with *while*.

First point out that *while* introduces time clauses. In (74), the action in the *while* clause is happening when the action in the main clause occurs. Tell students that *when* or *as* can have the same meaning as *while* here.

While *Clause*	Main *Clause*

(74) *While he was listening to her*, he jotted down some notes.
(= *When/As he was listening to her*, he jotted down some notes.)
(Meaning: *He was listening to her, and at the same time* he was jotting down some notes.)

Next, point out that adverbial clauses beginning with *while* also express action that contrasts in some way with the action in the main clause, as shown in (75). It can therefore be paraphrased with *although* or *even though*.

(75) *While the first act of the play was exciting*, the last act was dull and disappointing.
(= *Although/Even though the first act was exciting*, the last act was dull and disappointing.)
(Meaning: *The first act was exciting, but* the last act was dull and disappointing.)

For the activity itself, you will need to have constructed sentences with *while* clauses that establish a concessive relationship and sentences with *while* clauses that establish a temporal connection. You will need at least 12 sentences for each meaning. With each sentence, you will probably need to supply an additional sentence to bring out the interpretation, as illustrated in (76).

Concessive
(76) a. *While he was handsome*, he really wasn't very intelligent. So he was never very popular with women, except those who liked good looking men.

Temporal
b. *While he was handsome*, he was popular. But with the passage of time, his popularity waned.

Read one of the sentences, and ask, "What is another way of saying that sentence?" Prompt the students to restate the sentence with another subordinator that has the same meaning (e.g., *although* for [76a], *when* for [76b]). If you get a wrong answer, ask, "Is that OK?" As soon as the students have grasped the purpose of the activity, have them pair off and take turns deciding which meaning is correct in each sentence and providing a paraphrase using a temporal or concessive subordinator other than *while*.

If desired, repeat the activity using another subordinator that has two meanings. For example, you could review and practice *before* used to introduce temporal clauses (e.g., *He locked the door before his left the house*) and *before* as a subordinator in purpose clauses of avoidance (e.g., *You'd better stop before you get hurt*).

Activity 4: Teaching Free Adjuncts (Advanced Composition)

There are pros and cons to teaching free adjuncts in advanced composition classes. Two arguments against teaching them are the following: (1) they are used most frequently in genres in which many ESL/EFL students will not be writing, and (2) they may seem an intimidating topic to teach since more than one paraphrase is possible with many sentence-initial free adjuncts. Arguments in favor of teaching them are that they improve and enliven students' prose and that they are used frequently for various functions (some of which we also saw with fronting, in Chapter 22); that is, in topic sentences, including to provide topic shift, and as a means of adding descriptive content to a sentence in a way that is easy to process.

If you decide to do some instruction on free adjuncts, you should probably confine yourself to those that are less conducive to several interpretations – the best candidates are generally adjuncts that express temporal relationships and adjuncts that express reason relationships. Provide your students with examples of verbs that commonly appear in adjunct clauses that express the particular relationship (e.g., *believe, feel, think, understand, want* for adjuncts expressing a reason for the main clause action), and show them the subordinators that can be used in adverbial subordinate clauses expressing the relationship (e.g., *since* and *because* for adjuncts expressing reason). (In discussing the verbs used in the adjunct clauses, rather than using terms related to lexical aspect, use descriptions that students will readily understand, for example, "verbs that describe an activity that can continue for some time" for activity verbs, or "verbs that occur quickly at a single moment" for achievement verbs.) Write on the board sentences with free adjuncts that include a variety of relevant verbs. Elicit paraphrases that are introduced by the appropriate subordinators and write these on the board. Thus, for example, show students a sentence such as (77a), ask them what they think the adjunct and sentence mean, and then encourage them to produce paraphrases such as (77b). Be sure to go over enough sentences with adjuncts so that students can identify the clues to the meaning of the adjuncts.

(**77**) a. *Believing that Susan would be late as usual,* Tom took his time getting ready.
   b. *Because/Since he believed that Susan would be late as usual,* Tom took his time getting ready.

To give students practice, look in newspapers or other publications for sentences with free adjuncts expressing relationships you have covered and have students paraphrase the sentences using appropriate subordinators (as a model, see Exercise 23.4). Then reverse the process, giving the students sentences with sentence-initial subordinate clauses and asking for paraphrases that have free adjuncts. For example, the sentence *As they swarm onto the ice, the narwhals wield their tusks carefully* would be paraphrased as *Swarming onto the ice, the narwhals wield their tusks carefully.*

After you have completed these sentence activities, present the students with paragraphs that you have found that include several free adjuncts that you have converted to subordinate clauses. Thus, if you were to use the paragraph in (78), you could convert the free adjunct in the first sentence to *As we crouched on the boat deck during the first night of our experiment*, and the sentence-final adjunct in the second sentence to *and it snapped the T in its jaws*. Provide enough prior context for these paragraphs to enable your students to understand their content. In the case of (78), this would mean supplying at least the preceding paragraph or a couple of sentences that describe the purpose of the experiment and the apparatus.

(78) Crouching on the boat deck during the first night of our experiment, we peered into the hole as a great blue shark circled and then zeroed in on the scent of ground fish flowing from the apparatus. It swam straight toward the odor and at the last instant veered sharply to the right, snapping the T in its jaws. The shark shuddered and thrashed and abruptly released the apparatus. In the final moment of the attack, the predator had ignored the odor source and instead turned to bite the electrode.[20]

Ask the students to work in pairs to decide which sentences have clauses that can be converted to free adjuncts and to rewrite them using appropriate free adjuncts. After they have completed this assignment, go over it in class. Through questioning, establish the functions of the free adjuncts in the paragraph in (78): to introduce a topic (sentence 1) and to add information to the main clause (sentence 2). This assignment and discussion can be a departure point for assigning a composition that must include at least two free adjuncts that are used correctly.

Since sentence-final adjuncts occur more frequently than sentence-initial adjuncts in popular and academic writing, it might be useful to concentrate solely on them. You can use the same procedure described previously to show students how they are formed and what they do. On the board, write a sentence like the one in (79), in which main clauses are joined by *and*.

(79) When you read something, your eyes move rapidly from left to right in small hops, and this brings each word into focus. These small hops are called "seccades."

Point out that the clause beginning with *and* in the first sentence simply adds information to the preceding clause. Explain that you can keep the meaning of the sentence by omitting *and this* and changing the verb of the second clause to the *-ing* form, as shown in (80).

(80) When you read something, your eyes move rapidly from left to right in small hops, bringing each word into focus.

Explain that this is a common stylistic alternative to a coordinate sentence when the second clause adds information to the previous clause. Provide several more examples in which clauses joined by *and* are rephrased with a sentence-final free adjunct. Then hand out a prepared paragraph that includes sentences with clauses that can be converted to sentence-final free adjuncts that add to or elaborate on the content of the previous clause. Have the students identify the clauses that can be changed into free adjuncts and make these changes. Finally, have your students write a paragraph that contains at least one sentence-final free adjunct. Expand on this lesson in subsequent practice sessions in which you show examples of sentence-final free adjuncts in real texts. First, review the functions of free adjuncts. Then present students with coordinate sentences that would be good candidates for conversion to sentence-final adjuncts and some that would not be good because the clauses do not add or elaborate. Ask the students, "Can we change this one?" Ask students to make an immediate oral conversion to a free adjunct where appropriate.

ENDNOTES

[1] See, for example, Pollock and Eckstut (1997), p. 124.

[2] This traditional view of adverbial clauses being introduced by subordinators should be contrasted with Huddleston and Pullum's (2002, pp. 1014–1017) view of adverbial clauses. They adopt a point that was first developed by Emonds (1976) that subordinators are prepositions. Although some of Huddleston and Pullum's arguments are interesting and, in certain cases, compelling, I feel that the more traditional term, *subordinator*, is still quite useful for pedagogy. Still, I have incorporated some of Huddleston and Pullum's observations at various points throughout this chapter.

[3] Adapted from Biber et al. (1999), p. 847.

[4] Huddleston and Pullum (2002), p. 697.

[5] Clauses with present participles whose missing subjects are seen to be the same as the main clause subject can also occur when the verb in the adverbial clause is in the simple present or past tense (e.g., *While he waits/waited for the bus, he reads/read his newspaper* can be rephrased as *While waiting for the bus, he reads/read his newspaper*). This shows that participial clauses are not always the result of eliding the subject and object of a more fully specified adverbial clause.

[6] This example is from Biber et al. (1999), p. 847.

[7] The example is adapted from Huddleston and Pullum (2002), p. 731.

[8] Biber et al. (1999), p. 846.

[9] *Despite* and *in spite of* also head prepositional phrases (e.g., *Despite/In spite of his surly attitude, he was really a kind man*).

[10] *Supplementive clauses* is, for example, the term that Quirk et al. (1972) and Biber et al. (1999) use.

[11] Biber et al. (1999), p. 826.

[12] Kortmann (1991), p. 48.

[13] The different classifications presented here are based on Kortmann (1991), Thompson (1983) and my own research, part of which is in Cowan (2001). One type of sentence-initial free adjunct that seems to be ambiguous between an adverbial or adjectival interpretaton is shown in (1).

(1) *Consisting of over 50 paintings and drawings by Cézanne, Monet, Pissarro, Renoir, van Gogh, and Gauguin,* Mr. Waxman's private collection of Impressionist art is reputed to be the largest in the world.

This type of adjunct contains stative verbs with a strong "static" meaning like *amount* (*to*), *belong, cluster, consist of, cost, include, contain, dominate, equal, measure, possess, range, resemble, weigh,* etc. It might be considered to be a free adjunct, since the subjectless clause answers the question posed of the main clause: *Why is Mr. Waxman's private collection reputed to be the largest collection of Impressionist art in the world?* However, it could also be argued that it modifies the subject of the main clause, in which case it should be a fronted reduced relative clause. There may be additional classifications that have other interpretations not covered here. Obviously, some writers produce sentence-initial free adjuncts that do not have any discernable semantic connection to the main clause.

[14] J. le Carré, (1983), *The Little Drummer Girl*, p. 47, from Kortmann's corpus.

[15] Paul Nicklen, "Arctic Ivory: Hunting the Narwhal," in *National Geographic*, August 2007, p. 126.

[16] Halliday (1985), p. 203; Mann and Thompson (1987), p. 52.

[17] A number of different kinds of addition or elaboration have been recognized. Among these are *attendant circumstance*, *manner*, and *specification*. Some of them are not easily distinguishable from others, and the context of the sentence plays an appreciable role. For a more comprehensive discussion, see Kortmann (1991), chapters 9–11.

[18] This example is from Kortmann's corpus.

[19] This error is cited in Swan and Smith (2002), p. 108. It is not clear whether it has been drawn from a corpus that the author of this chapter, Norman Coe, has assembled, or whether it is actually made up on the basis of his knowledge of errors that Spanish learners of English might make.

[20] R. D. Fields, "The shark's electric sense," in *Scientific American*, August 2007, p. 80.

REFERENCES

Biber, D., Johansson, S., Leech, G., Conrad, S., & Finegan, E. (1999). *Longman grammar of spoken and written English*. Essex: Pearson Education, Limited.

Cowan, R. (2001). The interaction of syntax and discourse: How I learned to write Wall Street journalese. Paper presented at the *Georgetown University Roundtable on Languages and Linguistics*, Georgetown University, March 8–10.

Emonds, J. (1976). *A transformational approach to English syntax*. New York: Academic Press.

Halliday, M. (1985). *An introduction to functional grammar*. London: Edward Arnold.

Huddleston, R., & Pullum, G. K. (2002). *The cambridge grammar of the English language*. Cambridge: Cambridge University Press.

Kortmann, B. (1991). *Absolute adjuncts and absolutes in English: Problems of control and interpretation*. London/New York: Routledge.

Mann, W., & Thompson, S. A. (1987). *Rhetorical structure theory: A theory of text organization*. University of Southern California Marina del Rey: Information Sciences Institute.

Pollock, C. W., & Ekstut, S. (1997). *Communicate what you mean: A concise advanced grammar*. 2nd ed. White Plains, NY: Prentice Hall Regents.

Quirk, R., Greenbaum, S., Leech, J., & Svartvik, J. (1972). *A grammar of contemporary English*. London: Longman.

Swan, M., & Smith, B. (2002). *Learner English: A teacher's guide to interference and other problems*. 2nd ed. Cambridge: Cambridge University Press.

Thompson, S. A. (1983). Grammar and discourse: The English detached participial clause. In F. Klein-Andreu (Ed.), *Discourse perspectives on syntax* (pp. 43–65). New York: Academic Press.

CHAPTER 24

Comparatives and Superlatives

INTRODUCTION

In this chapter, we will look at the grammatical structures used to compare things in English. There are a number of ways that comparisons can be made, and it is important for ESL teachers to be familiar with them. We will look first at several kinds of *comparatives* and then at *superlatives*, focusing on the details of form that can make these structures difficult for students.

TYPES OF COMPARISONS

Comparisons are of different types, depending on whether the things being compared are seen as different or similar on the dimension on which they are being compared. The two main types of comparisons are thus *inequality comparisons* and *equality comparisons*.

Inequality Comparisons

An *inequality comparison* presents one of two things being compared as being greater than or less than the other in some respect.[1] For example, in (1), Bill and John are compared in the respect of height, which has different degrees on a scale represented by the adjective *tall*. The comparison in (1) states that, on the scale of tallness, John exceeds Bill.

       Clause 1   Clause 2
(**1**) John is taller than Bill is.
     (= John is tall to degree *x*, and Bill is tall to degree *y*; degree of tallness *x* exceeds degree of tallness *y*.)

As exemplified in (1), the second clause of an inequality comparison, a subordinate clause, is a reduced version of the preceding clause, with omission of content that is like the content in the first clause. Thus, (1) can be seen as the reduction of (2a) to (2b), and further reduction is also possible: *be* can be deleted along with the adjective, so we hear (2c) as well as (2b). Notice in (3) that with another main verb, such as *exercise*, when the reduction does not omit the verb, it replaces it with *do*, so we have (3b) along with (3c). (Reductions in sentences with equality comparisons work in the same way, and the details are discussed later in the chapter.)

(2) a. John *is taller* than *Bill is tall.*
    b. John is taller than *Bill is.*
    c. John is taller than *Bill.*

(3) a. John *exercises* more than *Bill exercises.*
    b. John exercises more than *Bill does.*
    c. John exercises more than *Bill.*

Inequality comparisons that have the meaning "*x* is greater than *y*" show a *superiority* relationship, as demonstrated in (4a). Comparisons that express the meaning "*x* is less than *y*," as in (4b), show an *inferiority* relationship. The terms *superiority* and *inferiority* have nothing to do with the meanings "better" and "worse," referring only to *x* being greater than *y* or less than *y.*

(4) a. John is *more intelligent* than Bill is.   superiority
    b. Bill is *less intelligent* than John is.   inferiority

Superiority Relationships

Superiority relationships are expressed by *more,* or *-er* on certain adjectives and adverbs, and with *than* introducing a second clause, as shown in (5). (The use of *more* versus *-er* with adjectives and adverbs is discussed in detail in the next major section of the chapter, Comparative Forms of Adjectives and Adverbs.) In comparisons expressing superiority relationships, as in all the other comparisons we will look at, the element on which things are compared can be one that is expressed by an adjective, as in (5a) and (5b); an adverb, as in (5c) and (5d); a noun, as in (5e); or a verb, as in (5f). Adjectives used in these and other comparisons need to be gradable adjectives; the small number of absolute adjectives that cannot be graded on a scale (e.g., *ultimate*) cannot be used in the comparative structures (see Chapter 12).

(5) a. Fred is *smarter than* Alice.   adjective (with -er)
    b. George is *more considerate than* Alan is.   adjective
    c. She tries *harder than* Susan does.   adverb (with -er)
    d. She speaks *more fluently than* he does.   adverb
    e. John has *more problems than* I do.   noun
    f. He *talks* a lot *more than* she does.   verb

Although generally expressed with comparative sentences, superiority relationships can also be expressed by certain verbs, such as *surpass, prefer* (*x* to *y*), and *favor* (*x* over *y*), and certain combinations of *be* + adjective + *to,* such as *be preferable/superior to,* as illustrated in (6).

(6) a. I *prefer* opera *to* the ballet.
    b. His entry *was superior to* hers.
    c. The solution he suggested *is preferable to* the one you just made.

Inferiority Relationships

Inferiority relationships are expressed by *less* – or with count nouns, *fewer* – followed by *than* introducing the second clause. Examples are shown in (7); (7c) and (7d) illustrate the use of *less* and *fewer* with noncount and count nouns, respectively.

(7) a. The first estimate was *less expensive than* the second.   adjective
    b. He drives *less cautiously than* I do.   adverb
    c. She has much *less money than* you do.   noncount noun (with less)
    d. Alice has *fewer friends than* Susan does.   count noun (with fewer)
    e. She *contributes* much *less* to the discussion *than* her
       husband does.   verb

Although the rule for *less* and *fewer* with nouns is that, as shown in (7c) and (7d), *less* is used with noncount nouns and *fewer* with count nouns; in spoken English, *less* is sometimes used instead of *fewer*. For example, (8b) might be used in place of (8a).

(8) a. On the midterm exam, he made *fewer mistakes* than the other students.
    b. ?On the midterm exam, he made *less* mistakes than the other students.

It is possible that the use of *less* in place of *fewer* may relate to the fact that *less*, rather than *fewer*, is used in contexts such as those in (9), where *numeral + noun* is treated as a unit rather than as a plural count noun preceded by a numeral.[2]

(9) a. We can be there in *less than 20 minutes.*
    b. *We can be there in *fewer than 20 minutes.*
    c. She's *less than 14 years old.*
    d. *She's *fewer than 14 years old.*
    e. We were traveling *less than 30 miles an hour* when we hit the other car.
    f. *We were traveling *fewer than 30 miles an hour* when we hit the other car.

Expressions such as *ten years*, *five dollars*, *two pounds of flour*, etc., are treated as single units, so we say *Ten years is a long time*, not **Ten years are a long time*; *Five dollars is too much*, not **Five dollars are too much*; *Thirty miles an hour is too fast*, not **Thirty miles an hour are too fast*, and so on. It therefore makes sense that with such expressions we would use *less* rather than *fewer*. We would say *It is less than ten years ago that I saw him*, not **It is fewer than ten years ago that I saw him*; or *I need a little less than five pounds of flour to make a pizza that big*, not **I need a little fewer than five pounds of flour to make a pizza that big*. This, along with the fact that percentages can be preceded by *fewer* or *less* (*Less/fewer than 30 percent of the students who took the test passed it*) may be contributing to what appears to be a rise in the use of *less* in American English inferiority comparisons.

Equality Comparisons

When we present two things as being equal in some respect, we make *equality comparisons* – that is, equality comparisons say that in some respect *x* is equal to *y*. Equality comparisons are expressed through *as . . . as*, which links the two clauses. Adjectives and adverbs simply come between the two instances of *as*, as in (10a) and (10b), respectively; nouns are preceded by *much* (or *little*) if noncount, as in (10c), or by *many* (or *few*) if count, as in (10d); and verbs are followed by *much* (or *little*), as in (10e).

(10) a. The hat was *as expensive as* the sweater.   *adjective*
     b. This course covers the material *as thoroughly as*
       that other course.   *adverb*
     c. He has *as much/little money as* she does.   *noncount noun* (with *much/little*)
     d. They have *as many/few friends as* we do.   *count noun* (with *many/few*)
     e. He contributed *as much/little* to the discussion
       as Susan did.   *verb*

Equality comparisons sometimes have a metaphorical meaning, including in such idioms as *He is as honest as the day is long*, which can create difficulties even for advanced ESL students.[3]

In addition to being expressed with these comparative sentences, equality comparisons can be made in a number of other ways, for example, with *be* or a similar verb followed by *the same* + noun + *as*, as in (9a); *similar to* or *equal/identical to*, as in (11b) and (11c); or (*just*) *like*, as in (11d).

(**11**) a. Susan's car *is the same color as* the car we saw in front of Steve's house.
    b. His views on that matter *are similar to* those of the other speaker.
    c. His raincoat *is identical to* mine.
    d. He *is just like* his sister.

However, whereas sentences with *as . . . as*, such as those in (10), state that the two things compared are at a similar point on a scale (of cost, of thoroughness, of amount of money, number of friends, etc.), these alternative equality comparisons, as in (11), state only the equality.

Because equality comparisons with *as . . . as* are comparisons on a scale, they can be changed to sentences that express inequality comparisons by inserting *not* in the first clause. Thus, when *not* is added to the sentences in (10), these sentences express inequality comparisons, as illustrated in (12). As shown in (12a), in sentences with *not*, *so* adjective + *as* is a variant of *as* + adjective + *as*.

(**12**) a. The hat was *not as/so expensive as* the sweater.
    b. This course *doesn't* cover the material *as thoroughly as* that other course.
    c. He *doesn't* have *as much money as* she does.
    d. They *don't* have *as many friends as* we do.
    e. He *didn't contribute as much* to the discussion *as* Susan did.

Notice that each sentence in (12) not only says that *x is not equal to y* but also implies superiority and inferiority relationships. For example, (12a) implies the inferiority comparison *The hat was less expensive than the sweater* as well as the superiority comparison *The sweater was more expensive than the hat.*

In contrast, with the alternative equality comparisons with *the same as, similar to,* and so on, if *not* is added, the comparisons simply state that one thing is not the same or like the other, and, by implication, that they are different. This difference is clear from the sentences in (13), formed by adding *not* to those in (11).

(**13**) a. Susan's car *isn't the same color as* the car we saw in front of Steve's house.
    b. His views on that matter *aren't similar to* those of the other speaker.
    c. His raincoat *isn't identical to* mine.
    d. He *isn't just like* his sister.

SUMMARY

TYPES OF COMPARISONS

Inequality comparisons present two things being compared as at different points on a scale related to the dimension on which they are being compared. Inequality comparisons may express:

- **a superiority relationship** (i.e., *x* is greater than *y*)
  John is taller than Bill.

- **an inferiority relationship** (i.e., *x* is less than *y*)
  Alice has fewer friends than Susan does.

Superiority relationships are expressed with *more* or, for certain adjectives and adverbs, *-er* followed by *than* introducing a second clause.

> *Bill is calmer/more patient than John is.*
> *She worked faster/more quickly than the others.*
> *Bill has more friends than I do.*
> *John exercises more than Bill does.*

Inferiority relationships are expressed with *less* or, for count nouns, *fewer*, followed by *than* introducing a second clause.

> *John is less tolerant than Bill.*
> *He speaks less fluently than she does.*
> *Susan has less money/fewer friends than Bill.*
> *John exercises less than Bill does.*

Equality comparisons present two things as being equal in some respect (i.e., *x* is equal to *y*). They are expressed with *as . . . as* linking clauses. Nouns in this structure are preceded by *much* or *little* if noncount nouns or by *many* or *few* if count nouns.

> *The hat is as expensive as the sweater.*
> *He prepared as thoroughly as I did.*
> *He has as much money as/as many friends as she does.*
> *He contributed as much as she did.*

Not in the first clause of an equality comparison implies an inequality comparison.

> *John is not as intelligent as Bill.*
> (Implies *John is less intelligent than Bill* and *Bill is more intelligent than John.*)

EXERCISE 24.1

Indicate whether each sentence conveys an inequality relationship, an equality relationship, or just a difference.

Example: Her opinion on that matter is definitely different from that of the editorial board.

Answer: just a difference

1. He is not as diplomatic as his boss is.
2. Bill is less judgmental than Alan is.
3. Sally is definitely more ambitious than Marcia is.
4. NASA's successful landing of a robot explorer on Mars does not really surpass some of its previous accomplishments, such as landing a lunar module.
5. He isn't really like his brother at all.
6. A snowshoe hare is just as fast as a lynx. They escape them about 50 percent of the time.

COMPARATIVE FORMS OF ADJECTIVES AND ADVERBS

Mention has already been made of the difficulties in forming inequality comparisons with adjectives and adverbs. As we shall now see, the choices between *more* and *-er* involve rules, but the rules are not always clear-cut.

More Versus *-er* with Adjectives; *Less* with Adjectives

Inequality comparisons of superiority with adjectives are a frequent type of comparison in both spoken and written English. Thus, the choice between the inflectional *-er* and *more* with adjectives is an important one. English language learners are taught these comparisons fairly early, and their attempts to produce comparisons often result in errors such as *I am more old than my brother and *For me is more easy to see what I am learning. To see more precisely what these errors involve, let's review the rules that determine the comparative forms for use with particular adjectives. Inequality comparisons of inferiority with *less* tend to occur with some adjectives and not with others, so we will look at this as well.

Single-Syllable Adjectives

Several single-syllables adjectives – notably, *good*, *bad*, and *far* – have special comparative forms: *better*, *worse*, and *farther/further*. For these adjectives, forms with *more* are ruled out (*more good, *more bad, *more far), as are forms with *-er*.

For the remaining single-syllable adjectives, *-er* tends to be preferred over *more*:

- With many adjectives, for the most part only *-er* is heard. These include *big*, *clean*, *cold*, *cool*, *fast*, *fat*, *great*, *high*, *large*, *long*, *old*, *short*, *slow*, *small*, *tall*, *thick*, *thin*, *wide*, and *young*.
- Some adjectives do commonly occur with either *-er* or *more*. These include *quick* (*quicker/more quick*) and *fierce* (*fiercer/more fierce*).

Inferiority relationships, which are expressed with *less*, tend not to be expressed with single-syllable adjectives; for example, native speakers usually would not say *less tall*. Instead, they would more likely do either of the following:

- Use an antonym with the *-er* ending, for example, *shorter* for *tall*, *warmer* for *cold*, thereby expressing the same meaning but as a superiority relationship.
- Use *not* with *as . . . as*, for example, *not as tall as*, *not as cold as*.

Thus, instead of *Bill is less tall than John*, we usually hear *Bill is shorter than John* or *Bill isn't as tall as John*.[4]

Two-Syllable Adjectives

With two-syllable adjectives, some must form the comparative with *more* whereas others tend to form it with *-er*:

- An *-er* is preferred with adjectives that are stressed on the first syllable and end in *-y*, *-ly*, *-le*, or *-ow*. Examples include the following:[5]

-y	angry–angrier; dirty–dirtier; easy–easier; funny–funnier; happy–happier
-ly	costly–costlier; deadly–deadlier; friendly–friendlier; likely–likelier; lovely–lovelier
-le	able–abler; ample–ampler; gentle–gentler; noble–nobler; simple–simpler
-ow	mellow–mellower; narrow–narrower; shallow–shallower; yellow–yellower

This preference is stronger for some of the groups than others. Significant variation between comparative forms in *-er* and *more* has been noted in adjectives ending in *-ly*, such as *costly*, *deadly*, *friendly*, *lonely*, *lovely*, *lowly*, and *ugly*. Thus, one native speaker may say *He wanted something livelier*, while another may use *more lively* in the same context.[6]

Inferiority relationships with adjectives having two or more syllables are usually formed with *less*, e.g., *less foolish, less faithful, less articulate.*

- *More* is required for most other two-syllable adjectives, including those that are stressed on the first syllable and end in *-ful, -ish, -al, -ic,* or *-ous.* The following are some examples.

-ful	bashful–more bashful (*bashfuller); careful–more careful (*carefuller); faithful–more faithful (*faithfuller); harmful–more harmful (*harmfuller)
-ish	brutish–more brutish (*brutisher); fiendish–more fiendish (*fiendisher); foolish–more foolish (*foolisher); sheepish–more sheepish (*sheepisher)
-al	central–more central (*centraler); global–more global (*globaler); lethal–more lethal (*lethaler); normal–more normal (*normaler); rural–more rural (*ruraler); vital–more vital (*vitaler)
-ic	caustic–more caustic (*causticer); chronic–more chronic (*chronicer); epic–more epic (*epicer); magic–more magic (*magicer); tragic–more tragic (*tragicer)
-ous	anxious–more anxious (*anxiouser); cautious–more cautious (*cautiouser); conscious–more conscious (*consciouser); famous–more famous (*famouser); nervous–more nervous (*nervouser)

Still, stress placement and the ending of the base form are not always solid predictors of what the comparative form will be. As the following example pairs show, adjectives with the same stress pattern (stressed first syllable) and the same endings (*-id, -on, -er, -ed,* or *-ant*) in some cases take either *-er* or *more* and in others must take *more.*

-id	placid–more placid (*placider); stupid–stupider/more stupid
-on	common–commoner/more common; wanton–more wanton (*wantoner)
-er	clever–cleverer/more clever; eager–more eager (*eagerer)
-ed	rugged–more rugged (*ruggeder); wicked–wickeder/more wicked
-ant	mordant–more mordant (*mordanter); pleasant–pleasanter/more pleasant

Adjectives with More Than Two Syllables

If an adjective has more than two syllables, the comparative form will be made with *more,* for example, *suspicious–more suspicious* (*suspiciouser); *important–more important* (*importanter*). There are very few exceptions to this, the most notable being three-syllable adjectives that were formed by adding the prefix *un-* to a two-syllable adjective that forms its comparative in *-er.* For example, *un* + *happy* yields *unhappy,* which has the comparative form *unhappier.*[7]

Participial Adjectives

Many adjectives are formed from present or past participles; *amazing* and *interesting* exemplify the former, *amazed* and *interested* the latter. Participial adjectives have only comparative forms with *more,* as illustrated in (14).

(14) a. When she heard that the plane was overdue, she became even *more worried.*
 b. *When she heard that the plane was overdue, she became even *worrieder.*

 c. The game turned out to be *more exciting* than we had anticipated.
 d. *The game turned out to be *excitinger* than we had anticipated.

There are a few exceptions to this. For example, the comparative form of *tired* is either *more tired* or *tireder.*

Double Comparatives

More and a following *-er* comparative form of the adjective are sometimes heard in conversation, even though this is not considered acceptable in educated English. Attested examples such as those in (15) suggest that such *double comparatives* may be more frequent with single-syllable than with bisyllabic base forms.[8] If they generally occur, as in these examples, with the addition of *more* to a form that takes *-er*, this may indicate a movement toward the use of *more* as the default or preferred means of making comparative forms. Notice the difference between these forms and the erroneous comparative forms produced by ESL students as cited earlier.

(**15**) a. This way it is *more easier* to see.
     b. It's much *more warmer* in there.
     c. She's a bit *more nicer* than Mrs. Jones.

More Versus *-er* with Adverbs

Adverbs used in comparisons fall into two types and form comparatives accordingly:

- The adverbs *well*, *badly*, and *far* have the same comparative forms as the adjectives *good*, *bad*, and *far* – namely, *better*, *worse*, and *farther/further*.
- A small number of single-syllable adverbs have identical adjective counterparts; these include *fast*, *hard*, *late*, and *long*. As with the adjectives, the comparative forms of these adverbs are made by adding *-er*, yielding *faster*, *harder*, and so on.
- The vast majority of adverbs are derived by adding *-ly* to adjectives (i.e., *quickly* from *quick*, *quietly* from *quiet*, *regularly* from *regular*, etc.). These adverbs form their comparatives with *more* (e.g., *more quickly*, *more fluently*) and *less*, (e.g., *less lively*, *less likely*, *less easily*). In colloquial speech, certain of these adverbs (e.g., *easily*, *quietly*, and *quickly*) sometimes lose their *-ly* and hence their *-ly* comparative form. Thus, in conversation, a person is as likely to hear the (b) versions of (16) and (17) as the (a) versions.

(**16**) a. Snowmobiles are running more quietly than they used to.
     b. Snowmobiles are running quieter than they used to.

(**17**) a. Snow melts more quickly than ice does.
     b. Snow melts quicker than ice does.

SUMMARY

COMPARATIVE FORMS OF ADJECTIVES AND ADVERBS

The **comparative forms of adjectives** follow these rules:

- *Good*, *bad*, and *far* have the comparative forms *better*, *worse*, and *farther/further*.

- **Single-syllable adjectives** (e.g., *big*, *fast*, *large*, *clean*) usually take *-er* rather than *more*: *bigger*, *faster*, *larger*, *cleaner*.

- Inferiority relationships are usually expressed with antonyms with the *-er* ending or with *not + as . . . as*.
  That movie is shorter than this one.   OR   *That movie isn't as long as this one.*
  NOT USUALLY   *That movie is less long than this one.*

- **Two-syllable adjectives** can occur with one or both forms:

  - Adjectives that have a stressed first syllable and end in *-y*, *-ly*, *-le*, or *-ow* usually take *-er*.
    funny–funnier; *friendly–friendlier*; *narrow–narrower*; *simple–simpler*

  - Most adjectives that have a stressed first syllable and end in *-ful*, *-ish*, *-al*, *-ic*, or *-ous* must take *more*.
    more careful (*carefuller); more famous (*famouser); more foolish (*foolisher); more lethal (*lethaler); more tragic (*tragicer)

- **Adjectives with more than two syllables** form their comparatives with *more*. An exception is adjectives formed from *un-* added to an adjective that takes *-er*.
  more suspicious (*suspiciouser), more important (*importanter)
      BUT   *unhappier*

- **Participial adjectives** form their comparatives with *more*.
  more amazing (*amazinger); more worried (*worrieder)

The **comparative forms of adverbs** follow these rules:

- *Well*, *badly*, and *far* have the comparative forms *better*, *worse*, and *farther/further*.

- **Single-syllable adverbs** with identical adjective counterparts (e.g., *fast*, *hard*, *long*) add *-er*.
  faster, harder, longer

- **Adverbs ending in -ly** (e.g., *enthusiastically*, *quickly*, *regularly*, *softly*) form comparatives with *more*.
  more enthusiastically, more quickly, more regularly, more softly

---

EXERCISE 24.2

Indicate whether the comparative form in each sentence is acceptable. If not, explain why.

Example: The problem was more easier than I thought.

Answer: unacceptable (*more* is unnecessary; this is a double comparative)

1. The Art Institute of Chicago has a more complete collection of Impressionist paintings than the museum in Minneapolis has.
2. He was supposed to arrive at two o'clock, but he didn't. At 2:30 he still hadn't come, and we were getting anxiouser and anxiouser.
3. It is simpler and more efficient to learn the rules and abide by them than to ignore them.
4. Today it is actually more warmer outside the house than inside.
5. That lecture turned out to be boringer than I had expected.
6. She was even more strong than I thought. She could lift her own weight.
7. Mr. Cruise's performance in his latest film is less risky than his performance in *Risky Business*.
8. That use of *dude* as an address is a lot commoner in American English than in British English.
9. Many movie stars are less impressive in person than they are when you see them on the big screen.

THE FORM OF COMPARATIVE SENTENCES

As we saw earlier, the second clause of a sentence containing a comparison is a reduced clause, with the deletion of content corresponding to content in the first clause. Both inequality and equality comparisons take this form. We can explain the different patterns of comparative sentences by picturing longer versions that are shortened.

Inequality Comparisons

Let us look at different possibilities for repetition across clauses and hence reduction. For simplicity, we will use only superiority comparison sentences; however, sentences that make inferiority comparisons work the same way.

In (18), the subjects of the two clauses in each sentence differ, but the verb phrase that follows them (*enjoyed the concert*) are identical. As (18b) shows, the second clause is reduced by replacing the repeated verb phrase with a form of *do* or simply omitting it.

> (**18**) a. I *enjoyed the concert* more than Susan *enjoyed the concert*.
> b. I enjoyed the concert more than Susan (*did*).

The sentences in (19) each also have different subjects and identical verb phrases in their clauses. They differ from (18) only in the verbs they include. Notice that modals, auxiliary verbs, and *be* are not replaced by *do*.

> (**19**) a. John *is taller* than Bill *is tall*.
> b. John is taller than Bill (*is*).
> c. John *has* more *problems* than Bill *has problems*.
> d. John has more problems than Bill (*does/has*).
> e. John *has been going there* longer than Bill *has been going there*.
> f. John has been going there longer than Bill (*has*).
> g. John *can finish it* more quickly than Bill *can finish it*.
> h. John can finish it more quickly than Bill (*can*).

In the sentences in (20), the verb phrases in the two clauses include some contrasting constituents – both (20a) and (20c) have different prepositional phrases following the two verbs. These prepositional phrases are retained in the shortened versions in (20b) and (20d).

> (**20**) a. They *spend* more *time* in Europe than we *spend time* in New York.
> b. They spend more time in Europe than we *do* in New York.
> c. He *can get through* more *work* in an hour than I *can get through work* in a day.
> d. He can get through more work in an hour than I *can* in a day.

In each sentence in (21), the two clauses have the same subjects. The subject can therefore be elided (deleted) from the second clause, and the verb, which in these sentences is also the same in the two clauses, can be deleted. Thus, what remains following the *than* is just the contrasting constituent: a prepositional phrase in (21b), an adjective in (21d), and a noun in (21f).[9] (Of course, fuller versions are also possible; thus, (21b) could be phrased *They spend more time in Europe than they do in New York*.)

> (**21**) a. They spend more time *in Europe* than they spend *in New York*.   prep phrase
> b. They spend more time in Europe than in New York.
> c. He seems to play better *drunk* than he seems to play *sober*.   adjective
> d. He seems to play better drunk than sober.

    e. He has more *friends* than he has *enemies.*   *noun*
    f. He has more friends than enemies.

In (22), two sets of contrasting constituents enter into the comparison – the direct objects (*postcards–letters*) and the indirect objects (*friends–his mother*).

    (22) a. He sent more *postcards* to *his friends* than he sent *letters* to *his mother.*
        b. He sent more postcards to his friends than letters to his mother.

An entire clause that is embedded in the second clause may be omitted, as occurs in (23b) with the *that* complement clause.

                                               Complement Clause
    (23) a. *The matter is* more *serious* than we had expected *that it would be* (*serious*).
        b. The matter is more serious than we had expected.

When the second clause has a pronominal subject and the verb of the clause is omitted, there is also the matter of the form of the pronoun. As an example, consider (24). If *am*, included in the comparative sentence in (24a) is deleted, the subject pronoun *I* often changes to the object pronoun *me*, as in (24b). According to the prescriptivist rule, the pronoun should remain *I* as in (24c), but in speech the object pronoun form is far more common.

    (24) a. He is older than *I am.*
        b. He is older than *me.*
        c. He is older than *I.*

Equality Comparisons

The same reduction rules that were illustrated for inequality comparisons are applied to form reduced equality comparisons with *as . . . as.* The sentences in (25) give some examples.

    (25) a. He enjoyed the concert as much as Susan *enjoyed it.*
        b. He enjoyed the concert as much as Susan (*did*).
        c. He has said as many nice things about her as you *have said about her.*
        d. He has said as many nice things about her as you (*have*).
        e. They spend as much time here as *they spend in Europe.*
        f. They spend as much time here as (*they do*) *in Europe.*
        g. The board's decision affected John as much as *it affected me.*
        h. The board's decision affected John as much as (*it did*) *me.*
        i. They finished the job as quickly as *it had been expected that they would finish it.*
        j. They finished the job as quickly *as* (*had been*) *expected.*

Equality comparisons such as (26) cannot be reduced; (26b) is not a good sentence.

    (26) a. The pool is as wide as it is deep.
        b. *The pool is as wide as deep.

SUMMARY

THE FORM OF COMPARATIVE SENTENCES

In comparative sentences, the second clause is generally reduced, with the omission of elements that are the same as those in the first clause.

With inequality comparisons:

- When the subjects of the two clauses differ but the verb phrases are the same, the second verb phrase is omitted or, alternatively, it is replaced by *do* or an auxiliary is left behind. If there are contrasting constituents within the verb phrase, they are retained.
  I enjoyed the concert more than Susan enjoyed the concert. →
  I enjoyed the concert more than Susan (did).
  I enjoyed the concert more than Susan had enjoyed the concert. →
  I enjoyed the concert more than Susan (had).
  I enjoyed the concert last week more than Susan enjoyed the play this week. →
  I enjoyed the concert last week more than Susan did the play this week.

- When the subjects and verbs of the two clauses are identical, they can both be omitted, with the unlike constituent retained.
  They spend more time in Europe than they spend in New York. →
  They spend more time in Europe than in New York.
  He has more friends than he has enemies. →
  He has more friends than enemies.

- An entire clause that is embedded in the second clause of a comparative sentence may be elided.
  The matter is more serious than we had anticipated that it would be. →
  The matter is more serious than we had anticipated.

Equality comparisons with *as . . . as* follow the reduction rules for inequality comparisons.
  He enjoyed the concert as much as Susan enjoyed it. →
  He enjoyed the concert as much as Susan (did).
  They spend as much time here as they spend in Europe. →
  They spend as much time here as (they do) in Europe.
  Their decision affected him as much as it affected me. →
  Their decision affected him as much as (it did) me.

EXERCISE 24.3

Form a shorter comparison of each of the following sentences. (There may be more than one correct answer.)

Example: She talked to him a lot longer than you talked to him.

Answer: She talked to him a lot longer than you did.   OR   She talked to him a lot longer than you.

1. She liked what we told her a lot more than she liked what she eventually saw.
2. He is late more often than the other boys are late.
3. The project is turning out to be much more expensive than they had predicted that it would be.
4. It would be more profitable to accept their proposal than it would be to refuse it.

5. I am just as fit as he is fit.
6. Alan fears his father more than he respects his father.
7. He loaned more money to his sister than his father loaned her.
8. The president's speech contributed as much to the outcome of the election as it contributed to the decision to go to war.
9. She corrected more papers in an hour than he was able to correct in three days.
10. More time was spent on planning for the conference than it was necessary to spend on it.

SUPERLATIVE FORMS

Sentences with *superlative* forms single out a particular thing in relation to all other members of a group of things rather than comparing one thing to another. Thus, for example, (27a) is a superlative and differs from the related comparative in (27b).

(**27**) a. This test was *the most difficult* of all this semester.
b. This test was *more difficult* than the last one.

Superlative forms can be thought of as indicating the top or the bottom of a scale, for *superlatives of superiority* and *superlatives of inferiority*, respectively. With superlatives, we have *most* and *-est*, corresponding to *more* and *-er* for comparatives, and *least*, corresponding to *less*. Hence, *most* and *-est* occur in superlatives of superiority and *least* in superlatives of inferiority. Sentences (28a) and (28b) are about things at the top of scales of ease and difficulty, respectively, while (28c) is about something at the bottom of the scale of difficulty.

(**28**) a. That is the *easiest* solution of all.   *superlative of superiority*
b. That is the *most difficult* problem of all.   *superlative of superiority*
c. That is the *least difficult* problem of all.   *superlative of inferiority*

As in (27a) and (28), superlative forms are usually preceded by *the*, and sentences with these forms often include the prepositional phrase *of all*. This prepositional phrase signals the entire group (e.g., of tests, solutions, problems) and signals the item as being at an end (high or low) of the scale as it applies to the items in the group. That is why we find the boy's answer in the last panel of the cartoon funny.

The rules governing the superlative forms of adjectives – the use of *-est* versus *most* – follow those we saw for creating comparative forms with *-er* and *more*:

• The adjectives *good*, *bad*, and *far* have their unique superlative forms – *best*, *worst*, and *farthest/furthest*. Other single-syllable adjectives generally form superlatives with *-est* (e.g., *biggest*, *cleanest*, *coldest*, *fastest*).

- Two-syllable adjectives that have a stressed first syllable and end in *-y*, *-ly*, *-le*, and *-ow* tend to take *-est* (e.g., *angriest, deadliest, simplest, narrowest*), although with *-ly* there is considerable variation between superlatives with *-est* and *most* (e.g., between *friendliest* and *most friendly*). Two-syllable adjectives that have a stressed first syllable and end in *-ful*, *-ish*, *-al*, *-ic*, and *-ous*, take *most* (e.g., *most careful, most foolish, most central, most tragic, most cautious*). Many two-syllable adjectives ending in *-id*, *-ome*, *-on*, *-er*, *-ed*, and *-ant* can form superlatives with *-est* as well as with *most* (e.g., *most stupid/stupidest*).
- Adjectives with more than two syllables and participial adjectives form superlatives with *most* (e.g., *most important, most used, most exciting*).

The superlative forms of adverbs, too, follow the same rules as comparative forms:

- *Well*, *badly*, and *far* have the forms *best, worst*, and *farthest/furthest*.
- Single-syllable adverbs form superlatives by adding *-est* (e.g., *fastest, hardest, latest*).

Adverbs ending in *-ly* form superlatives with *most* (e.g., *most quickly, most fluently*).[10] (These superlative forms of adverbs often appear as modifiers of participial adjectives, e.g., *most frequently cited*, in *The most frequently cited example of this problem is discussed in his book*.)

So far we have looked at *most* and *least* as used in forming superlative adjectives and adverbs. *Most*, *least*, and *fewest*, preceded by *the* can also be used before nouns, as in (29a), (29b), and (29c). In this use, they indicate a superlative amount or quantity of the noun, generally as possessed by one member of a group relative to the rest of the group.

(**29**) a. He has *the most money* of all my friends.
   b. He displayed *the least patience* of anyone present.
   c. This plan poses *the fewest* potential *glitches*.

The variation between *least* and *fewest* is similar to what was described earlier for *fewer* and *less* – the prescriptive rule specifies the use of *fewest* before plural count nouns, but sentences such as (30b) are not infrequently heard in place of sentences such as (29c).

(**30**) a. She made *the fewest errors* on the entrance exam.
   b. ?She made *the least errors* on the entrance exam.

Many occurrences of *most* are not in fact instances of the superlative *most*. As discussed in Chapter 10, *most* is also a quantifier, meaning "the vast majority of." This use is exemplified in (31a), in which *most* occurs before the noun *Germans*, and in (31b), in which it signifies most of the thousands of young men referred to in the previous sentence.

(**31**) a. *Most* Germans like bratwurst.
   b. Thousands of young men went off to the war. *Most* were killed.

Most is also a degree adverb like *very* and *extremely*; in this use it precedes adjectives, as in (32). Notice, in (33), that in this intensifier use *most* occurs after an indefinite article *a/an*, as in (33a), while in its superlative use it follows a definite article, as in (33b).

(**32**) You are *most kind*. (= *You are very kind*.)   *degree adverb*

(**33**) a. That's *a most beautiful sunset*.   *degree adverb*
   b. That's *the most beautiful sunset* I've ever seen.   *superlative of adjective*

SUMMARY

SUPERLATIVE FORMS

Sentences with **superlative** forms single out a particular thing in relation to all other members of a group as at the top or bottom of a scale.

> *He's the kindest person I know.*

Superlatives of superiority indicate the top of a scale and use *-est* or *most*; **superlatives of inferiority** indicate the bottom of a scale and use *least* (*fewest* with count nouns).

> *That's the easiest test I've ever taken.*
> *That's the most difficult test I've ever taken.*
> *That is the least complicated explanation I can give you.*

Sentences with superlative forms usually have *the* preceding the form and often have *of all*, indicating the group.

> *That was the nicest compliment of all!*

The prescriptivist rule specifies *least* before noncount nouns and *fewest* before count nouns.

> *He displayed the least patience.*
> *She made the fewest errors.*

Superlative forms of adjectives follow the same rules as those for comparatives:

- *Best, worst,* and *farthest/furthest* are the superlatives for *good, bad,* and *far.*

- Single-syllable adjectives usually form superlatives with *-est* (e.g., *biggest*).

- Two-syllable adjectives with *-y, -ly, -le,* and *-ow* tend to take *-est* (e.g., *angriest*); those with *-ful, -ish, -al, -ic,* and *-ous* take *most* (e.g., *most careful*).

- Adjectives with more than two syllables and participial adjectives take *most* (e.g., *most beautiful, most bored, most exciting*).

Superlative forms of adverbs also follow the rules for comparatives:

- *Best, worst,* and *farthest/furthest* are the superlatives for *well, badly,* and *far.*

- Single-syllable adverbs add *-est* (e.g., *hardest, fastest, latest*).

- Adverbs ending in *-ly* add *most* (e.g., *most frequently*).

EXERCISE 24.4

Indicate whether the superlative form in each sentence is correct. If it is not correct, say why.

Example: That's the most easiest test I've ever had.

Answer: not correct (*Easiest* is the superlative form, so *most* is unnecessary.)

1. Albert Einstein is the most commonly cited example of a scientific genius.
2. This is the beautifulest orchid in the entire greenhouse.
3. This is the least people I have ever seen turn out for a rock concert.
4. The essay part of the example was the most difficult.
5. The frequentliest asked question is "Who is buried in Grant's tomb?"

PROBLEMS THAT ESL/EFL STUDENTS HAVE WITH COMPARATIVES AND SUPERLATIVES

The most frequently cited errors that ESL/EFL students make are incorrect renditions of comparative and superlative forms of adjectives and adverbs. Among the students who have problems with these forms are speakers of Romance languages. Here we look at how the patterns used in Romance languages – patterns that are in keeping with one set of English forms but not the other – may contribute to students' problems with the English forms. The Spanish and Portuguese data drawn on tend to confirm that these errors occur largely with beginning and intermediate students, becoming very infrequent when students reach advanced-level proficiency.[11] If these data are indicative, it may be unnecessary for teachers to make a special pedagogical intervention to eradicate the errors.

Comparatives (Spanish, Portuguese, Italian)

In Spanish, comparative forms of adjectives and adverbs are made by placing *más* ("more") or *menos* ("less") before the adjective or adverb. Thus, the comparative of *fast* (*rápido*) would be *más rápido*, as shown in (34).

(34) *Es   más   rápido   ir   en   taxi.*
    is   more   fast   to go   in   taxi
    "It's faster to go by taxi."

Spanish speakers equate *más* with English *more* when producing comparative forms of English adjectives. For many adjectives, this works, but as we saw, one-syllable adjectives and certain two-syllable adjectives in English, such as those ending in *-y*, form their comparatives by adding *-er*. In our corpus of essays written by Spanish speakers at the intermediate level, we commonly find errors of the sort shown in (35), in which *more* is placed before high frequency two-syllable adjectives such as *easy* or *happy*. We also occasionally find *more* used with single-syllable adjectives.

(35) a. *For me is *more easy* to see what I am learning.
     b. *The children who go with their fathers to a football game are *more happy*.

The same situation obtains with Portuguese. The error shown in (36), with the single-syllable adjective *rare*, was made by a Portuguese-speaking EFL student in an intermediate-level composition class.

(36) *We have more options but they are getting *more rare* . . .

Similarly, in Italian, comparatives are formed with *più* ("more") and *meno* ("less") preceding an adjective or an adverb, as in (37).

(37) *Sei   più   ricco   di   me.*
    you're   more   rich   than   me
    "You're richer than I am."

As with Spanish and Portuguese speakers, Italian speakers have no problem when they insert the English equivalent of *più* before many adjectives but encounter difficulties with others, such as the single-syllable *old*, as shown in (38).

(38) *He is much *more old* than me.

Superlatives (French, Portuguese)

Superlatives of French adjectives are formed by adding *la/le/les plus* ("the most") and *la/le/les moins* ("the least") in front of adjectives. With certain English adjectives, this process works; with others, however, such as single-syllable adjectives, it may lead to the sort of error shown in (39).

(39) *I am *the most short* person of the class.[12]

There are similar errors in our Portuguese corpus, as can be seen in (40). This error was made by a student who was in an advanced-level course in Brazil.

(40) *Friendship is a spontaneous growth, so I am convinced that *the most strong* friends are people that grow with us in our childhood.

SUGGESTIONS FOR TEACHING COMPARATIVES AND SUPERLATIVES

Comparative and superlative forms of adjectives and adverbs are introduced in beginning and low-intermediate level English language teaching textbooks. Some textbooks spread out the teaching of different types of comparatives over several levels; others try to present them in fairly close succession.[13] Coverage focuses largely on comparative and superlative forms of adjectives and adverbs. The concepts of superiority, equality, and inferiority comparison are almost always introduced through simple (presumably easy-to-comprehend) formulas such as *x* is greater than *y*, *x* is equal to *y*, and *x* is less than *y*. Many authors make a point of treating superlatives separately after comparative forms have been covered.[14]

Since the basics of teaching comparatives and superlatives are presented in English language teaching textbooks, it is probably best to focus on developing activities that expand on the basic information and show how these structures are used in writing. Some suggestions follow.

Activity 1: Practicing Comparative and Superlative Forms (Beginning Through Low Intermediate)

Many of the exercises included in textbooks are of the fill-in-the-blanks type, and, as was pointed out earlier, it may not be such a good idea to rely too much on these as a measure of whether your students command a structure. Learning may be facilitated more by activities that force accurate production of comparative and superlative forms in realistic contexts.

You could begin with a common adjective such as *tall*. Have three students stand up and point to the tallest one. Ask, "Is he tall?" When you get an affirmative answer, point to one of the other students, and ask, "How about Marco? Is he as tall as Antonio?" When you get a negative answer, say, "Yes, that's right. Antonio is taller." On the board, write *Marco is tall. Antonio is taller.* Then ask, "Of these three, who is tallest?" When the students answer "Antonio," say, "That's right, Antonio is the tallest. He is the tallest student." Write *Antonio is the tallest* on the board. Explain that with adjectives like *big, clean, cold, cool, fast, fat, great, high, large, long, old, short, slow, small, tall, thick, thin, young,* and *wide,* we use the adjective with *-er* to compare two things. Explain that when you compare three or more things with these adjectives, *-est* is added to them to talk about the thing that has the most of a quality – that is, the biggest, tallest, or so on. You can draw stick figures on the board to demonstrate this. Next, ask students to practice these two forms using pictures from various sources that you have prepared (photocopies, slides, or transparencies).

In a later lesson, repeat this activity, this time using it to introduce and practice two-syllable adjectives that take *-er* and *-est*. Point out that adjectives that have two syllables with the stress on the first syllable and that end in *-y* or *-ly* usually have these comparative and superlative forms. List common adjectives, including *angry, easy, friendly, funny,* and *pretty*. Continue on with examples of two-syllable adjectives ending in *-le* and *-ow* (*able, simple, yellow,* etc.). To practice the forms, you could expand from classroom and other familiar objects to include comparisons of, for example, countries, climates, and flowers (for color).

Many of the adjectives ending in *-ful, -ish, -al,* and *-ous* are not used in beginning classes, thus, low-intermediate classes might be the appropriate place to teach that these only have comparative and superlative forms with *more/most* and *less/least*. For an initial lesson, you could find pictures of people that could be described using adjectives with these endings – for example, as *anxious, cheerful, famous, graceful, harmful,* and *nervous* – and elicit or introduce the relevant adjectives. For example, show a picture of Albert Einstein and ask, "Who is this man? Is he famous?" Then take a picture of a rock star or an actor and ask, "Is this person more famous than Einstein?" Finally, add another picture and ask, "Who is the most famous of these three people?" Help students answer and write the sentence on the board. Tell students that they are going to learn some new adjectives that end in *-ous, -ful, -ish,* and *-al* and list examples on the board. Explain that adjectives with these ending always form their comparatives with *more* and their superlatives with *most*, and that they never take *-er* or *-est*.

Proceed with more pictures that can be used to make comparisons. For adjectives that are not readily depicted, use short stories, fables, or jokes; for example, *foolish* can be introduced through a story about the way three people handle a dangerous situation. At the end of the story or joke, always ask one question that forces a comparative form and another that forces a superlative form.

Activity 2: Practicing *More/Less Than*, *the Most/Least*, and *As Much As* with Verbs (Intermediate)

Think of several general categories that have obvious subcategories – for example, *entertainment* (with subcategories such as movies, plays, opera, ballet, rock concerts), *music* (e.g., pop, rock, jazz, classical, hip-hop), *sports, TV programs, movie stars, movies I have seen this year* – and write them on the board. Have the students supply entries under each category. When you have at least six entries in each of the categories you have chosen, have a student pick out three entries that are within a category and that he or she is familiar with – for example, three sports that the student has played or likes to watch. Demonstrate the task by ranking the three entries – for example, write *1* in front of *basketball*, *2* in front of *wrestling*, and *3* in front of *boxing*. Say "Basketball is my top choice and boxing is my bottom choice." Then write sentences using comparatives and superlatives on the board, showing students how these sentences can have more than one version. For example, write sentences with unreduced and reduced comparative structures (*I like wrestling more than I like boxing, but I like basketball the most* versus *I like wrestling more than boxing, but I like basketball the most*) and sentences with inferiority comparatives and superlatives (*I like wrestling less than I like boxing. I like boxing the least*). Next ask the students to choose three items in a category, rate them, and compare them using the structures. When you feel that students have begun to produce the structures accurately, have them continue the activity in pairs or small groups.

Repeat this procedure to incorporate equality comparisons. For example, after writing *1* next to both *wrestling* and *boxing* and *3* next to *basketball*, write *I like boxing as much as wrestling. I like basketball the least.* Now, ask a few students to rate their choices under a category and compare them using the structures. When you feel that the students have begun to produce the structures accurately, have them carry on the activity in pairs or in small groups. To facilitate the activity, you may want to give them handouts with the categories and some of the options for structures.

As a follow-up, you could next move to ranking entries under a category with *more/less* and *most/least* before adjectives such as *popular*, *famous*, and so on.

Activity 3: Practicing the Form of Comparative Sentences (Intermediate)

Hand out a chart, as shown in (41), that shows the amount of time three students each spent on a number of activities.

(41)

John's Activities	*Bill's Activities*	*Susan's Activities*
studied for exam 1 hour	studied for exam 50 min.	studied for exam 2 hours
watched television 3 hours	watched television 2 hours	watched television 30 min.
answered e-mail 45 min.	answered e-mail 1 hour	answered e-mail 30 min.
talked on phone 20 min.	talked on phone 40 min.	talked on phone 3 hours
worked on paper 2 hours	worked on paper 35 min.	worked on paper 1½ hours
stayed in library 35 min.	stayed in library 1 hour	stayed in library 2 hours
worked on project 10 min.	worked on project 1 hour	worked on project 1 hour

Ask students to form comparisons such as the following in (42).

(42) Susan studied for her exam more/longer than John or Bill did.
Susan talked on the phone longer than John studied for his exam.
Bill spent less time in the library than Susan (did).
John spent as much time studying for his exam as Bill did in the library.
Bill worked longer on his project than on his paper.

The activity can be expanded to include practice with superlatives of time, for example, *Susan spent the most time in the library*; *John spent the least time in the library*.

A slightly different chart, as shown in (43), could be used to practice forming reduced comparatives (e.g., *John spent more time watching television than he had planned/ expected to*).

(43)

Activity	*Planned/Expected to Spend*	*Actually Spent*
watch television	30 minutes	2 hours
work on paper	2 hours	1 hour
study for exam	1 hour	3 hours

Activity 4: Comparative Structures with Passivized Verbs (Advanced)

The content of the chart in Activity 3 can be modified slightly, as shown in (44), to provide advanced-level students practice in forming reduced passive structures such as *The bridge was completed/finished (six months) sooner than expected.* You can use the prepared chart in (44) or, preferably, modify the chart to include actual projects with which students are familiar. Hand it out to students and explain that the government has undertaken a number of projects and the chart shows the original time frame for completing them and how long it actually took to complete them. On the board, demonstrate how the table can be used to produce sentences like *The bridge was completed sooner than it was anticipated that it would be completed* and how these can then be shortened to produce sentences like *The bridge was completed sooner than anticipated*. Write examples on the board. Explain that verbs such as *assume, expect, indicate, intend, plan, predict, require,* or *schedule*, can also be used in sentences and provide some example sentences.

(44) Project	Expected Completion Date/Time	Actual Completion Date/Time
Bridge	November 1987	October 1988
Highway	2 years	1 year
Dam	December 2000	June 1999
Office building	3 years	4 years

This activity can be the beginning of a TBLT activity where students are told to go to the Internet and look up any historical construction project (e.g., the Empire State Building in New York, the Aswan Dam in Egypt, the Three Gorges Dam in China, etc.) for which they can find a planned completion date. Students bring in a short account of the project and write the conclusion with a passivized sentence that reports whether it was concluded sooner or later than originally projected.

Activity 5: Comparison/Contrast Essays (Advanced Composition)

The so-called comparison/contrast essay, which is part of any ESL writing curriculum, provides a perfect vehicle for practicing comparisons in complex sentences like those in activities 3 and 4. Writing textbooks often focus on the discourse connectors of comparison and contrast (to be discussed in Chapter 26) when dealing with this type of essay, but we might start with a simpler version in which the students use the basic comparison grammar discussed in this chapter. One way to do this might be through a simplified TBLT activity involving a comparison of items that most students are familiar with. To demonstrate the activity, we will use Macs and PCs.

After explaining the basic organization of the comparison/contrast essay, assign the task of writing a short composition that might be informative to someone interested in buying a new computer. Explain that students must first brainstorm the advantages and limitations of Macs and PCs, and list them under columns labeled "Similarities" and "Differences." The students can work together in small groups to make lists like those shown in (45). Should you choose, you could give them a few criteria to help them with the lists by pointing out things that a prospective buyer would want to know about, such as cost, availability, compatibility with programs, and access to service.

(45) Similarities	Differences
1. Both provide access to the Internet.	1. Macs are very user friendly; PCs are less so.
2. Both run Microsoft programs.	2. PCs are widely available; Macs are less so.
3. Both run good e-mail programs.	3. Macs are virtually virus proof; PCs aren't.
4. Both have ports for printers.	4. Lots of computer video games are written for PCs; not so many are written for Macs.
5. Both have flat screens.	5. PCs are relatively cheap; Macs cost more.
6. Both come with audio (speakers).	6. Macs have cool graphics programs; not so many are available for PCs.

After the students are finished, go over the organization of the comparison/contrast essay again – the first paragraph states the topic of the essay, subsequent paragraphs separately state the similarities and differences, and the final paragraph should state a conclusion. Quickly review inequality and equality comparisons that will be used. Then have students write the essay. When they have finished, have them exchange compositions and do peer editing and then hand them in to you. Have a quick look at the essays to check for grammatical accuracy and then hand them back. Pick out a good one for demonstration purposes and go over it in class while they compare it with theirs. Repeat this procedure with other topics that are appropriate for your class, for example, changes that have gone on in their lives. Keep the topics fairly simple at first.

ENDNOTES

[1] The terms *comparisons of equality* and *comparisons of inequality* are suggested by Huddleston and Pullum (2002).

[2] Huddleston and Pullum (2002), p. 1127.

[3] Howard Williams, personal communication.

[4] Still, with some single-syllable adjectives you may hear *less + adjective* (e.g., *In a fight, a badger is less fierce than a wolverine*), although many native speakers would probably prefer the negated *as . . . as* alternative: *In a fight, a badger is not as fierce as a wolverine*.

[5] For a more complete listing, see, for example, Huddleston and Pullum (2002), p. 1583.

[6] Biber et al. (1999), p. 523, provide examples such as the following:
  (1) She thought that Blackpool would be somewhat *livelier* and possibly safer and cheaper from other reports.
  (2) The photographer wanted something *more lively*, though, a picture of an actual capture.
  In (1), it seems clear that the following *-er* comparatives with *safe* and *cheap* help force the choice in favor of *livelier* over *more lively*.

[7] Huddleston and Pullum (2002), p. 1584.

[8] These examples are from Biber et al. (1999), p. 525.

[9] Examples are from Huddleston and Pullum (2002), p. 1112. See also McCawley (1988), p. 683.

[10] It is also possible to form superlatives by placing *more* in front of adverbs ending in *-ly* in comparisons. To do this, some form of the indefinite *any* (e.g., *any other + NP, anyone else*) must appear after *than*. An example of this would be: *He comes more frequently than any other member/anyone else*.

[11] The Portuguese data come from a corpus of errors made by students at a binational center in Brazil. The Spanish data come from a corpus referred to in Chapter 1. The errors here are from compositions by students in an intensive English institute who were preparing for entry into American universities. Their proficiency level was placed at intermediate.

[12] Cited by Walter (2001), p. 67.

[13] The *Grammar Dimensions* series is a good example of the more spread-out approach. The first book presents the comparative forms of adjectives, and then other aspects of inequality and equality comparisons are presented in books 2 and 3. *Grammar Sense*, Pavlik, (2005) extends the introduction in Book 1 and expands it in Book 2.

[14] Celce-Murcia and Larsen-Freeman (1999), p. 750, claim that delaying the presentation of superlatives until after comparatives have been taught should improve acquisition of both, and in the *Grammar Dimensions* series, which Larsen-Freeman supervises, this practice is followed. Other grammar textbook series present comparative and superlative formation in contiguous chapters.

REFERENCES

Biber, D., Johansson, S., Leech, G., Conrad, S., & Finegan, E. (1999). *Longman grammar of spoken and written English.* Essex: Pearson Education, Ltd.

Celce-Murcia, M., & Larsen-Freeman, D. (1999). *The grammar book: An ESL/EFL teacher's course.* 2nd ed. Boston: Heinle & Heinle.

Huddleston, R., & Pullum, G. K. (2002). *The Cambridge grammar of the English language.* Cambridge: Cambridge University Press.

McCawley, J. (1988). *The syntactic phenomena of English.* Vol. II. Chicago University Press: Chicago.

Pavlik, C. (2005). *Grammar sense 1.* New York: Oxford University Press.

Pavlik, C. (2005). *Grammar sense 2.* New York: Oxford University Press.

Walter, C. (2001). French Speakers. In M. Swan & B. Smith (Eds.), *Learner English: A teacher's guide to interference and other problems* (pp. 52–72). Cambridge: Cambridge University Press.

CHAPTER 25

Coordination

INTRODUCTION

Coordination is the joining of constituents of the same type – for example, clauses, noun phrases, verb phrases, or prepositional phrases – by *coordinating conjunctions*, or *coordinators*.[1] The coordinators are of two types: *single-word coordinators*, such as *and*, *but*, *or*, and *yet*; and *multiword coordinators*, such as *either . . . or*, *neither . . . nor*, and *both . . . and*. In this chapter, we will look at the various coordinators, and we will focus especially on the coordination of clauses – on how clauses are commonly joined and shortened in English. The clauses joined by coordination are main clauses; this is in contrast to subordination, which, as discussed in Chapter 23, joins a main clause and a subordinate clause. In traditional grammar, sentences that have coordinated clauses are called *compound sentences*.[2]

SINGLE-WORD COORDINATORS

In this section, we will discuss the form and meaning of sentences joined by the single-word coordinators *and*, *or*, *but*, *nor*, and *yet*.

Form

Almost any constituent can be joined with its syntactic equivalent; (1) through (4) give just a few of the possibilities. Sentences (1), (2), and (3) are examples of *phrasal coordination*, or coordination at the phrase, rather than the clause, level. As already mentioned, our focus will be mainly on *clausal coordination*, exemplified in (4).

(1) [His brother] *and* [my sister] design computer software. *noun phrases*

(2) Your car keys are [in your purse] *or* [on the dresser]. *prepositional phrases*

(3) They performed [very energetically] *yet* [unconvincingly]. *adverb phrases*

(4) [John went to the party], *but* [Felicia stayed home]. *clauses*

With *and* or *or*, coordination can link more than two clauses or other constituents.[3] In (5), five independent clauses are joined into a single sentence. Notice that commas separate the clauses and that the coordinator, as is usually although not always the case, occurs only between the last two clauses.

(5) Fred worked hard, Alan studied, Joan watched television, Herman ate lunch, *and* I finished my term paper.

The normal position for a coordinator is between two clauses, as in (4) and (5) and in (6a). A coordinator and its following clause may not be moved over a preceding clause, as in (6b).

(6) a. She joined a nearby gym, *but* she didn't work out very often.
b. *But she didn't work out very often, she joined a nearby gym.

Although sentences often begin with coordinators, such sentences are coordinate with a previous sentence, as (7) shows.

(7) Of course the U.S. long ago replaced the rattler [rattlesnake] with the stars and stripes. *But* this old symbol and the motto ["Don't tread on me"] still lurk behind the newer flag, like a rattler under a slab.[4]

Sentences with an initial coordinator, like the one in (7), traditionally have been considered bad form for written English but are gaining acceptance. One reason for this may be that spontaneous conversations, which are constructed on the basis of thoughts popping into a speaker's mind, usually consist of single sentences, some of which are prefaced by a coordinator that relates that sentence to previous utterances, as shown in (8).

(8) I had always wanted to visit New Zealand. *And* then I finally got the chance. *But* I was so committed to other projects that I couldn't go.

Sentence-initial coordinators, such as that in (9), avoid overly long and complex sentences or the use of discourse connectors (e.g., in this example, *in addition* or *moreover*), which could result in too formal a tone.

(9) Future unmanned aircraft may be used as so-called surrogate satellites, dispatched during crises to fly in the upper reaches of the earth's atmosphere for days at a time. *And* UAVs [unmanned aerial vehicles] could be "weaponized," allowing them to launch missiles and drop bombs for less money and less risk than manned aircraft.[5]

In journalistic writing, sentences beginning with single-word coordinators are now not uncommonly used to introduce new paragraphs. Thus, for example, in (10), *but* introduces a sentence that announces a topic shift from the preceding paragraph, from Chrysler's becoming profitable in the 1980s through smart production decisions to its contrasting stumbles by 1998.

(10) In the 1980s, Chrysler clawed its way back from bankruptcy by parlaying the guts of a single vehicle known as the K-car into what it sold as half a dozen models. A decade later, cost-conscious creativity saved the company again, producing sport-utility vehicles and pickups that were bolder than the competition's just as SUVs and trucks were catching on with suburban consumers.

But by 1998, as it was negotiating to sell itself to Daimler-Benz, Chrysler was stumbling.

Thus, in discussing coordinators, ESL/EFL teachers should explain the prescriptivist rule (never start a sentence with a coordinator) but also show students that, depending on the written register, coordinators such as *and* and *but* may appear at the beginning of sentences for reasons like those mentioned here.

Meaning

Coordinators establish a relationship between the clauses or other elements they connect. In this way, coordinators contribute to the meaning of sentences whose elements they join. Some of the relationships established when clauses are joined by the coordinators *and, or, nor, but,* and *yet* are described in what follows.

And

And is the most frequently used coordinator in spoken and written English.[6] Its inclusion can establish any of a range of meaning relationships between two clauses. Some of the most basic of these are *addition, temporal succession, cause and effect, condition,* and *concession.*

By *addition* we mean that the content of the clause after *and* adds information to or elaborates on the content of the clause that precedes it, as in (11).

> **(11)** She has written a lot of books, *and* one of them has been turned into a successful screenplay.

When two clauses contain events that could occur in close *temporal succession,* the one preceding *and* is likely to be interpreted as occurring before the following one, as in (12).

> **(12)** He jumped on the horse, *and* then he rode off into the sunset.[7]

Similarly, when the event that occurs before *and* can be seen as causing the action or outcome expressed in the following clause, a *cause and result* interpretation is possible. In (13), the reader will interpret the first action – the premature firing of the retro-rockets, as cause of the action in the second clause, the spacecraft being thrown into a spin.

> **(13)** The retro-rockets fired prematurely, *and* the spacecraft was suddenly thrown into an uncontrollable spin.

A *conditional* interpretation can occur when the first clause can be seen as a condition which, when fulfilled, could result in the action or outcome expressed in the second clause. Notice that (14) can be rephrased as a future conditional sentence.

> **(14)** You tell me what you have heard, *and* I'll tell you everything that I know about the deal.
> (= If you tell me what you have heard, then I will tell you everything that I know about the deal.)

Another possible meaning is *concession.* As we saw in Chapter 23, the clauses contrast in such a way that the content of one makes the content of the other surprising. In (15), the clause after *and* is surprising given the preceding clause; one normally expects that eating a lot of anything will result in weight gain.

> **(15)** You can eat as much of this as you want, *and* you won't put on weight.

The discourse context in which a sentence with two clauses joined by *and* occurs may allow yet other implied meanings, in addition to those listed here.[8]

Or

Or introduces a clause that expresses an option that is an alternative to the option or options expressed in one or more preceding clauses. *Or* frequently expresses the exclusivity of the options. In (16a), if a person takes one means of transportation, then obviously, he or she will not take the other. *Or* can also have a conditional interpretation, with nonfulfillment of the event in the first clause being a condition that could result in the outcome expressed in the second clause. Thus, (16b) can be rephrased as a conditional. At times, this conditionally interpreted *or* is used to express a warning, as illustrated in (16c).

(**16**) a. I'll go by train, *or* I'll go by bus.
    b. She should leave now, *or* she'll miss her plane.
      (= If she doesn't leave now, she will miss her plane.)
    c. Start coming on time, *or* you're going to find yourself out of a job.
      (= If you don't start coming on time, you're going to find yourself out of a job.)

Nor

Nor introduces a clause that adds information to a preceding negative clause. The clause it introduces is also negative, but it lacks *not* because *nor* carries the negative meaning. Subject–aux inversion occurs after *nor*, as shown in (17). This use of *nor* is quite rare and is considered by most speakers to be very formal.[9]

(**17**) The public wasn't happy with the court's decision, *nor* was the governor very pleased about it.

But

But introduces a clause whose content contrasts with that of the previous clause, as shown in (18).[10]

(**18**) Alan enjoyed the opera, *but* his parents didn't like it at all.

Yet

Yet can also introduce a contrast. It sometimes combines with *and*, as shown in (19).[11]

(**19**) a. He worked for peace all his life, (and) *yet*, sadly, he died by a gun.[12]
    b. I look healthy, (and) *yet* I feel terrible.

SUMMARY

SINGLE-WORD COORDINATORS

Coordination uses **single-word coordinators** (e.g., *and*, *but*, *or*) and **multiword coordinators** (e.g., *either . . . or*, *both . . . and*) to join constituents of the same type. Thus, coordination may be:

- **phrasal coordination**.
  Your car keys are in your purse or on the dresser.

- **clausal coordination** (linking main clauses)
  John went to the party, but Felicia stayed home.

More than two clauses can be joined by a single coordinator.
    Fred worked hard, Alan studied, Joan watched television, Herman ate one pizza after another, and I finished my term paper.

Coordinators including *and* and *but* sometimes appear sentence initially in written texts despite the prescriptivist rule.
    I had always wanted to visit New Zealand. And then I finally got the chance. But I was so committed to other projects that I couldn't go.

Different meaning relationships between clauses or other constituents linked by coordinators are established by the different coordinators:

- **And** establishes relationships of addition, successive action, cause and effect, condition, and concession.

  She has written a lot of books, and one of them has been turned into a successful screenplay.

  He jumped on the horse, and he rode into the sunset.

  The retro-rockets fired prematurely, and the spacecraft was thrown into an uncontrollable spin.

  You tell me what you've heard, and I'll tell you everything I've heard.

  You can eat as much of this you want, and you'll never put on weight.

- **Or** introduces an option that is an alternative to the content in the preceding clause and can also have a conditional interpretation.

  I'll go by train, or I'll go by bus.

  She should leave now, or she'll miss her plane.

- **Nor** adds information to a preceding negative clause and expresses negative meaning for the clause it introduces.

  The public wasn't happy with the decision, nor was the government very pleased about it.

- **But** and **yet** introduce clauses whose content contrasts with that of the preceding clause.

  Alan enjoyed the opera, but his parents didn't like it at all.

  He worked for peace all his life, yet, sadly, he died by a gun.

EXERCISE 25.1

Indicate whether the relationship between the joined clauses in each of the following sentences is best described as one of addition, condition, contrast, temporal succession, or cause and effect.

Example: The principal came in, and everyone immediately stopped talking.

Answer: cause and effect

1. The book was finished three years ago, yet it still hasn't been published.
2. You do that, and you're fired.
3. To steady himself, he grabbed onto the cord above the light, and suddenly a shower of plaster rained down on his head.
4. She didn't attend the committee's special meeting, nor was she informed of its decision.
5. She left at three o'clock, but he stayed until six.
6. John climbed over the bridge railing, and he jumped into the water.
7. He corrected the typos in the manuscript, and he penciled in a few comments in the margin.

MULTIWORD COORDINATORS

The types of meaning relationships established between constituents by the single-word coordinators are sometimes established by several words. *Correlative coordinators* (*both . . . and, neither . . . nor, either . . . or, not only . . . but*) have two parts: a single-word coordinator preceding the first of the constituents joined and another part preceding the second. This use of a part before each constituent adds emphasis to the conjoined constituents. As we will see, there are yet other ways of joining constituents and expressing relationships of addition, alternatives, contrast, and concession.[13]

Addition

Along with the coordinator *and*, the correlative coordinator *both . . . and* expresses addition, and other words may be involved in joining constituents. The correlative coordinator used in negative sentences is *neither . . . nor*.

Both . . . and

Both . . . and can join constituents with the exception of main clauses, as is illustrated by the grammaticality of (20a), which joins NPs, and (20b), which joins infinitive complements, and the ungrammaticality of (20c). Notice that, if (20a) and (20b) had *and* rather than *both . . . and*, there would be less emphasis on the constituents joined and their additive relationship; (20c) is, of course, possible only in the alternative version with *and*.

(**20**) a. *Both* Bob's family *and* his friends attended his graduation.
    b. You need *both* to complete the assignments *and* to pass a final exam.
    c. **Both he'd been feeling sick, *and* he was up all night.

Neither . . . nor

Neither . . . nor is used to express an additive relationship between two negative elements that are joined. As with *both . . . and*, the constituents joined cannot be main clauses, so that (21a) and (21b) are grammatical, but (21c) is not. Notice that, as *neither* and *nor* have a negative as well as additive force, the sentences in (21a) and (21b) could be paraphrased with *not* and *and*, as shown in (22).

(**21**) a. *Neither* the public *nor* the governor liked the court's decision.
    b. He *neither* knew *nor* cared about it.
    c. **Neither* the buses were running *nor* were any taxis available.

(**22**) a. The public *didn't* like the court's decision, *and* the governor *didn't* like it.
    b. He *didn't* know about it, and he *didn't* care about it.

Other Ways of Expressing Addition

The second of two affirmative clauses linked by *and* often includes *too* or *so*, particularly in shortened versions, as discussed in the next section of the chapter. As shown in (23), *too* follows the second clause whereas *so* occurs after *and*. Notice that *so* requires subject–aux inversion in the clause.

(**23**) a. The public was happy with the court's decision, *and* the governor liked it, *too*.
    b. The public was happy with the court's decision, *and so* was the governor.

Among the other means of joining constituents in an additive relationship are the three-word expressions *as well as* and *just as . . . so*. *As well as* is used to join constituents other than clauses – for example, VPs, as in (24a), and NPs, as in (24b). *Just as . . . so*, is used to join clauses, and, as shown in (24c), it is generally used when two clauses are making a similar point. Notice that all of the following sentences could be paraphrased with *and*.

(**24**) a. She means what she says *as well as* says what she means.[14]

    b. Abstraction *as well as* Impressionism were Russian inventions.

    c. *Just* as they must lower their voices, *so* we must try to be a little more understanding.

We saw that sentences with *neither . . . nor* can be paraphrased with *not* and *and*, so that the sentences in (21) could be paraphrased as in (22). These paraphrases with *not* and *and* can be made more emphatic with *either* following the second constituent that is conjoined. Thus, (22) also has the version shown in (25).

(**25**) The public *wasn't* happy with the court's decision, *and* the governor *didn't* like it *either.*

Alternatives

The correlative coordinator corresponding to *or* is *either . . . or*. Thus, sentences with constituents joined by *either . . . or* state alternatives. For example, (26a) implies that either of the two alternatives expressed is acceptable. Like *or*, *either . . . or* can link several constituents, as (26b) shows, although according to the prescriptivist rule, *either . . . or* should link only two constituents. *Either . . . or* can link main clauses, as (26c) shows.

(**26**) a. You can *either* pay cash right now *or* use your credit card.

    b. You can *either* go to the movies, read a good book, listen to some music, *or* take a walk. There are lots of ways to relieve stress.

    c. *Either* you tell him, *or* I will.

Either . . . or, to a greater extent than *or* alone, implies an exclusive meaning – that is, only one of the alternatives stated is possible. For example, in (27), the implication is that I won't both stay at home and go to Venice.[15]

(**27**) I will either go to Venice or stay home this summer.

Either . . . or, like *or* alone, can be used to express a warning. In (28), the second clause warns of a possible outcome that will occur if the action in the first clause is not fulfilled. The meaning is similar to that of a conditional sentence with a negative condition clause.

(**28**) *Either* he leaves now *or* he will suffer the consequences.

    (= If he doesn't leave now, he will suffer the consequences.)

Contrast

Not . . . but can be used to contrast two constituents that are joined, as in (29) and (30). Example (30), in which two subordinate clauses are joined, shows the use of this structure to dispute information by preceding it with *not* and contrasting it with the content following *but*.

(**29**) I finally found it *not* in my wallet *but* in my jacket pocket.

(**30**) A: I always thought Rachael married John because she loved him.

    B: No. She married him *not* [because she loved him] *but* [because she was lonely].

Concession

The correlative coordinator *not only . . . but (also)* expresses concession as well as addition. It is used particularly when the speaker or writer wishes to convey the content of the first of the coordinated constituents as being unexpected and that of the second as being even more unexpected, as in (31) and (32).[16] Notice, in (32), that when *not only* is used with a clause, subject–aux inversion is triggered.

(31) That child must be sick! He turned down *not only* the cake *but* (*also*) the ice cream.

(32) No one expected that either of the girls would make it to the state finals. Much to everyone's surprise, *not only* did Alice win the 400-meter high hurdles, *but* Edith won the high jump and the broad jump.

SUMMARY

MULTIWORD COORDINATORS

Constituents can be joined by **correlative coordinators** and other multiword entities. Like the single-word coordinators, these express the meaning relationships of:

- **addition** (***both . . . and***, ***neither . . . nor*** with negatives, ***and . . . too***, ***and so***, ***as well as***, [***just***] ***as . . . so***).
  Both his family and his friends were there.
  He neither knew nor cared about it.
  The public was happy with the decision, and the governor liked it, too.
  The public was happy with the decision, and so was the governor.
  Just as they must lower their voices, so we must try to be more understanding.
  His friends as well as his enemies were surprised by the news.

- **alternatives** (**either . . . or**).
  You can either pay cash right now or use your credit card.

- **contrast** (***not . . . but***).
  She married him not because she loved him but because she was lonely.

- **concession** (**not only . . . but** [**also**]).
  Much to everyone's surprise, not only did Alice win the 400-meter high hurdles, but Edith won the high jump and the broad jump.

EXERCISE 25.2

Rewrite each of the following sentences or sentence pairs as a single sentence joined by *both . . . and, neither . . . nor, either . . . or, just as . . . so,* or *not . . . but.*

Example: The public wasn't happy with the court's decision, and the governor didn't seem very pleased about it.

Answer: Neither the public nor the governor seemed very pleased about the court's decision.

1. Sandra has two options. She can pay the speeding ticket now. Alternatively, she can protest it in court.
2. Rick won a Booker Prize, and he won a National Book Award, too.
3. Miron wouldn't read those kinds of books, and his wife wouldn't read those kinds of books either.
4. It wasn't because he didn't like the job that he quit. It was because he wasn't earning enough money.
5. We will have to lower our expectations somewhat. On the other hand, they will have to raise their productivity.
6. Alan didn't understand her explanation, and he didn't really listen to her explanation.

SHORTENING SENTENCES THAT INVOLVE COORDINATION

Sentences that involve coordination tend to be efficient, in that material that could be repeated generally is not. Thus, instead of (33a), which repeats *Alice* and *the silverware*, we would generally use (33b), which does not.

(33) a. *Alice* washed *the silverware*, and *Alice* dried *the silverware*.
    b. Alice washed and dried the silverware.

One way of describing changes that create different, shortened patterns like those shown in (33b) is to assume that they result from a rule that elides identical elements from longer sentences like (33a). However, it is difficult to formulate a rule that will account for the many different configurations that can occur. In many cases, the best rule seems to be: to form reduced versions of longer conjoined sentences, omit identical constituents on both sides of the conjunction.[17] We will examine some of the ways that English coordinate sentences can be shortened.

Conjunction Reduction

The shortening shown in (34), (35), and (36) seems to be similar to what we find in (33).

(34) a. John kissed Martha or John hugged Martha.
    b. John kissed or hugged Martha.

(35) a. We like turnips, but we don't like rutabagas.
    b. We like turnips but not rutabagas.

(36) a. Phil didn't buy that Jag, and Phil didn't lease that Jag.
    b. Phil neither bought nor leased that Jag.

The most general rule we could formulate to explain all of the shortened versions in (33) through (36) is that English sentences with clauses conjoined by *and, or, neither . . . nor*, or *but not*, and which are identical except for one constituent, can be combined so that the unlike constituents are connected by the coordinators. This rule has been called *conjunction reduction*. As we shall see later, it turns out that conjunction reduction works only if the unlike elements are verbs; it cannot be extended to sentences in which the unlike elements are NPs.[18] (See Joint Coordination, page 608.)

Verb Phrase Ellipsis

Some shortened sentence patterns arise from *verb phrase ellipsis*, in which a repeated verb phrase is omitted. Thus, it is possible to reduce sentences (37a), (38a), and (39a), which have conjoined clauses and repeated verb phrases. Notice in the reduced versions, (37b), (38b), and (39b), that when there is a modal or other auxiliary, that auxiliary remains.[19]

(37) a. Alice can come to the party, and John *can come to the party*, too.   *modal*
    b. Alice can come to the party, and John *can*, too.

(38) a. Alice is coming to the party, and John *is coming to the party*, too.   *auxiliary*
    b. Alice is coming to the party, and John *is*, too.

(39) a. Alice had left the party, but John *hadn't left the party*.   *auxiliary*
    b. Alice had left the party, but John *hadn't*.

When a modal and more than one auxiliary are present, they can be elided only up to a point where the intended meaning of the second clause can be recovered. Thus, for example, verb phrase ellipsis applied to (40a) can produce (40b), but (40c) is prohibited. This is because the deletion of *have* would result in a sentence that could seem to have come from, and to mean, *John may have gone home for the summer, and Alicia may go home for the summer, too.*[20]

(**40**) a. John may have gone home for the summer, and Alicia *may have gone home for the summer*, too.
b. John may have gone home for the summer, and Alicia *may have*, too.
c. *John may have gone home for the summer, and Alicia *may*, too.

When the verb phrase does not have a modal or other auxiliary or main verb *be*, the appropriate form of *do* must be included in the second clause to represent the elided material, as illustrated in (41), (42), and (43). (Notice that, as discussed earlier, subject–aux inversion occurs following *so*.)

(**41**) a. John went home, and Peter *went home*.
b. John went home, and so *did* Peter.

(**42**) a. First John quit the job, and Peter *quit the job*, too.
b. First John quit the job, and Peter *did*, too.

(**43**) a. John likes the food in the cafeteria, but Fred *doesn't like the food in the cafeteria*.
b. John likes the food in the cafeteria, but Fred *doesn't*.

Verb phrase ellipsis is still being investigated.[21] It is considered a kind of anaphora (see Chapter 13) whereby the elided material has an antecedent. It is not limited to clauses that are joined by particular coordinators, and it occurs across sentences, as in (44) and in other constructions.

(**44**) A: I can't understand why Susan won't eat rhubarb pie.
B: I can't either.

Delayed Right Constituent Coordination

Sentences with conjoined clauses that have different verbs but identical elements following – for example, object NPs or *that* complements – can be shortened by a stylistic rule called *delayed right constituent coordination* or *right node raising*. In delayed right constituent coordination, the identical constituent that is in the first clause is omitted, as is illustrated in (45), (46), and (47). Pauses in speech and commas in writing come after what remains of the first clause and before the identical constituent in the second clause.[22] Notice that in (45), the identical material in the second clause is actually the object in an infinitive complement that is itself part of a relative clause.

(**45**) a. Alex owned *a vintage 1939 Bentley*, and Sue knew a guy who wanted to buy *a vintage 1939 Bentley*.   object NP
b. Alex owned, and Sue knew a guy who wanted to buy, *a vintage 1939 Bentley*.

(**46**) a. Professor Schmidt has conjectured *that Susan's theory is correct*, and the director of the institute has stated unequivocally *that Susan's theory is correct*.   that complement
b. Professor Schmidt has conjectured, and the director of the institute has stated unequivocally, *that Susan's theory is correct*.

(47) a. Sandra denied *that the faculty knew about Bill's research*, but Fred affirmed *that the faculty knew about Bill's research*.   that complement
    b. Sandra denied, but Fred affirmed, *that the faculty knew about Bill's research*.

Gapping

If conjoined clauses have identical verbs, the verb and any other identical constituent immediately preceding or following the verb can be elided from the second clause. This leaves a gap in the middle of that clause, as shown in (48b), so this process is referred to as *gapping* or as *gapped coordination*.[23]

(48) a. John *ordered* carrots, and Fred *ordered* peas.
    b. John ordered carrots, and Fred _____ peas.

Often the elided element is just the verb, as in (48) through (51).

(49) a. Bill *gave* a nickel to Alice, and Fred *gave* a dime to Sue.
    b. Bill gave a nickel to Alice, and Fred a dime to Sue.

(50) a. John *asked* if Bill would leave, and Sam *asked* if Sue would apologize.
    b. John asked if Bill would leave, and Sam if Sue would apologize.

(51) a. I *went* by car and Alan *went* by train.
    b. I went by car and Alan by train.

A gap can comprise more than just a verb – a verb and a prepositional phrase, for example, as in (52). As (53) and (54) show, a gap can also include the subject.

(52) a. She *came to Canada* in 1999, and her parents *came to Canada* in 2001.
    b. She came to Canada in 1999, and her parents in 2001.

(53) a. On many occasions *they've served us* snapper, and a couple of times *they've served us* abalone.
    b. On many occasions they've served us snapper, and a couple of times abalone.

(54) a. In February *he went* to Beijing, and in March *he went* to Tokyo.
    b. In February he went to Beijing, and in March, to Tokyo.

Gapping is possible with more than two coordinate clauses. The gaps occur in the clauses after the first, as (55) illustrates.

(55) a. Bill *is* a doctor, his brother *is* a dentist, and his sister *is* a professor.
    b. Bill is a doctor, his brother a dentist, and his sister a professor.

Gapping cannot be applied to sentences with infinitive or gerund complements, as illustrated by (56) and (57), respectively.[24]

(56) a. John *asked* Bill to leave, and Sam *asked* Sue to apologize.
    b. *John asked Bill to leave, and Sam Sue to apologize.

(57) a. Ed *kept on* eating, and Marcia *kept on* arguing.
    b. *Ed kept on eating, and Marcia arguing.

SUMMARY

SHORTENING SENTENCES THAT INVOLVE COORDINATION

Sentences with clausal coordination can be shortened in various ways:

- **Conjunction reduction** shortens sentences with clauses conjoined by *and, or, neither . . . nor,* and *but not,* which are identical except for one constituent. Clauses are combined so that the unlike constituents are connected by these coordinators.
  John kissed Martha or John hugged Martha. → *John kissed or hugged Martha.*
  We like turnips, but we don't like rutabagas. → *We like turnips but not rutabagas.*

- **Verb phrase ellipsis** deletes a verb phrase identical to a previous one, with an auxiliary or modal (or more if required for recoverability) remaining or an appropriate form of *do* inserted.
  John is coming to the party, but Sue isn't coming to the party. → *John is coming to the party, but Sue isn't.*
  John went home, and Peter went home, too. → *John went home, and Peter did, too.*

- **Delayed right constituent coordination** is a stylistic rule applying where clauses have different verbs but some identical elements following, for example, in object NPs or *that* complements. This material is deleted from the first clause.
  Al owned a VW, and Sue knew someone who wanted to buy a VW. → *Al owned, and Sue knew someone who wanted to buy, a VW.*

- **Gapping** can apply when clauses have the same verbs. It deletes from the second clause the verb and any other identical constituents immediately before or after it.
  John ordered carrots, and Fred ordered peas. → *John ordered carrots, and Fred peas.*
  Often they've served us snapper, and a couple of times they've served us abalone. → *Often they've served us snapper, and a couple of times abalone.*

EXERCISE 25.3

Shorten each of the following sentences using conjunction reduction, verb phrase ellipsis, delayed right constituent coordination, or gapping.

Example: The director didn't write that letter, and he didn't approve that letter either.

Answer: The director didn't write or approve that letter.
    The director neither wrote nor approved that letter.

1. He's suggesting that you are wrong, and I am stating that you are wrong.
2. Mark likes opera, but Al doesn't like opera.
3. Alan bought that motor bike, or he rented that motor bike.
4. John is coming with us, and Sandra is coming with us, too.
5. Stephen mowed the lawn, and he watered the lawn.
6. John expects to get an A, and Bill expects to get a B.

EXERCISE 25.4

State which rules were used to form these shortened coordinate sentences (conjunction reduction, verb phrase ellipsis, delayed right constituent coordination, gapping).

Example: On Tuesday, John had sushi, and on Friday oysters.

Answer: gapping

1. Melany is interested in, and Fred has done some minor research on, the politics of Germany after reunification.
2. The first group was given picks, and the second shovels.
3. Alice stamped and mailed the letter.
4. She could have said that, and he could have, too.
5. Alan went to Hong Kong, and Paul to Jakarta.
6. He often rents Iranian movies and sometimes German movies.
7. Sandra is going to the party, and her roommate is, too.

ADDITIONAL FACTS ABOUT CLAUSAL COORDINATION

As the preceding sections have suggested, coordination raises a number of issues and questions. Here we deal with three of these.

Respectively

There is one lexical item that can occur only in coordinate sentences in which two elements are conjoined by *and*. The adverb *respectively* pairs elements in conjoined structures. In (58a), *Alan* is paired with *first prize* and *Cynthia* with *second prize*, so (58a) means (58b).

> **(58)** a. Alan and Cynthia won first and second prize, *respectively*.
> b. Alan won first prize, and Cynthia won second prize.

Respectively can also pair constituents other than noun phrases. For example, nouns and verbs may be linked, as in (59), as may nouns and prepositional phrases, as in (60).

> **(59)** Alan and Cynthia paint and sculpt, respectively.
> (= Alan paints, and Cynthia sculpts.)

> **(60)** Alan and Cynthia are going to Tucson and to Santa Fe, respectively.
> (= Alan is going to Tucson, and Cynthia is going to Santa Fe.)

Respectively can pair two following NPs with a single preceding NP, as in (61).[25]

> **(61)** For the two subsequent years, the government has set the planning levels at 110,000 and 125,000, respectively.

Here, although the two years are not specified, it is clear that the level of 110,000 is set for the first year, and 125,000 for the second.

Subject–Verb Agreement

According to prescriptive grammars, in sentences in which subject noun phrases are joined by (*either* . . .) *or* or by (*neither* . . .) *nor*, subject–verb agreement is determined by the proximity principle – that is, the main verb should agree in number with the noun phrase that immediately precedes it. Thus, along with (62a), which has a singular verb, and (62b), which has a plural verb, we have (62c), with a plural verb agreeing with *the members*, and (62d), with a singular verb agreeing with *the president*.[26]

(**62**) a. Neither *geologic evidence* nor *physical theory supports* this conclusion.
b. Neither *the pilots* nor *the machinists appear* interested.
c. Neither *the president* nor *the members of the cabinet were* informed.
d. Neither *the members of the cabinet* nor *the president was* informed.

Native speakers may not always follow the proximity principle when joining NPs with these coordinators. One small study found that while native speakers always provided plural agreement in sentences with two plural noun phrases, for sentence (62c), 28 percent of 50 subjects supplied a verb that agreed with the first NP, *the president*, producing the sentence in (63).[27]

(**63**) *Neither the president nor the members of the cabinet was informed.

Joint Coordination

The sentence in (64) is an example of what has been referred to as *joint coordination*, that is, coordination in which the two elements, in this case the NP *Alex and Chris*, function as a unit. Thus, the sentence would not be paraphrasable with each of the coordinated elements in its own clause.[28]

(**64**) Alex and Chris are a happy couple.

Unlike sentences in previous sections, (64) cannot be rephrased with coordinate clauses – we cannot have **Alex is a happy couple, and Chris is a happy couple*. For this reason, sentences with joint coordination are, as mentioned earlier, evidence against the idea that the conjunction reduction rule could be extended to NPs. *Alex and Chris* is a unit that must be the result of phrasal, not clausal, coordination.

Joint coordination occurs only with *and*, and it does not permit certain modifiers that could otherwise appear with coordinated elements, such as *too, as well, especially*, or *probably* (e.g., **Alex and probably Chris as well are a happy couple*).[29] More than two NPs can be joined – for example, *John, Steven, and Alice met in New York* involves joint coordination.

Sentences with two NPs joined by *and* in subject position can be ambiguous. Consider, for example, (65a). Without a context, it can be interpreted as the equivalent of (65b) or as an instance of joint coordination having the meaning of (65c).

(**65**) a. *Steven Spielberg and George Lucas* have made a lot of successful movies.
b. Steven Spielberg has made a lot of successful movies, and George Lucas has made a lot of successful movies.
c. Steven Spielberg and George Lucas (together) have made a lot of successful movies.

PROBLEMS THAT ESL/EFL STUDENTS HAVE WITH COORDINATION

Little research has been done on the kinds of problems that ESL/EFL students encounter when they attempt to produce English coordinate sentences. It is tempting to speculate, for example, on the types of errors that might occur when coordinate structures are shortened by the rules described here. Thus, German and Dutch both have a rule that corresponds to the English verb phrase ellipsis rule but does not insert a form like *do*, instead simply deleting the verb and leaving behind the equivalent of *too* (*also = ook* in Dutch, *auch* in German). These rules yield sentences like the Dutch *John eet kaas, en Harry ook* or the German *John ißt kase, und Harry auch* ("John eats cheese and Harry also").[30] However, whether EFL learners who speak German or Dutch produce English sentences like **John eats cheese and Harry, too* has not been verified. Until more data on errors in coordinate structures exist, we can only report on some documented errors and speculate on whether they warrant pedagogical intervention.

Overuse of Coordinators in Sentence-Initial Position (Korean)

An analysis of our corpus of Korean ESL students' written compositions reveals that *but* appears more frequently than in large corpora of English native speakers' writings.[31] Moreover, in the Korean students' compositions, *but* appears more frequently in sentence-initial position than sentence internally as a joiner of clauses. A typical illustration is the two paragraphs in (66), written by a Korean undergraduate student in a composition course.

(66) From my perspective, young students in U.S. were very lucky, because they didn't have to do too much work, and had enough time to do extra-curricular activities. *But*, after reading this essay "The Big Score," I felt that the pressure from tests became worldwide issue. *But* in any circumstances, test is necessary to learn something, for we can look over the whole content and check what part should be made up.

Ideally speaking, it's not desirable to study only in the test period, *but* it's true that we spend much time to study when we prepare exam. There are various range of students from very advanced the test, they have to standardize those questions for all level of students. *But*, no matter what the level of questions, taking test help students actually learn.

It is not clear what causes the overuse of *but* in sentence-initial position; perhaps the fact that English *but* has several corresponding forms in Korean, or instructional practices in Korea may favor *but* over other English contrastive alternatives. The students may also be influenced to some degree by examples of sentences beginning with *but* that they see in written English. Although examples such as those in (66) are not, strictly speaking, grammatical errors, they reveal that the students do not know how to appropriately use this coordinator. The corpus analysis reveals that this "overbutting" persists at the undergraduate and graduate level, so it might be worth addressing.

Correlative Coordinators (Spanish, German)

Correlative coordinators still appear to cause problems for ESL students who are undergraduates in American universities. For example, when using *not only . . . but (also)* in sentence-initial position, students may fail to apply subject–aux inversion after *not only*. The result is the sentence in (67), written by a Spanish-speaking student. (Notice, too, that in this sentence, *it* needs to come between *but* and *also*.)

(67) **Not only* it will make the U.S. lost its advantage, *but also* it will cause another problem.

A German speaker made the error shown in (68) when attempting to produce a sentence with *neither . . . nor*.

(68) **Neither* I gave him coffee *or* his wife cake.

The student uses *or* rather than the *nor* that *neither* requires and does not follow any of the patterns possible in English (e.g., *I neither gave him coffee nor gave his wife cake* or *Neither did I give him coffee nor did I give his wife cake*).

Errors such as these two suggest that multiword coordination, especially forms that can trigger subject–aux inversion, should receive extra emphasis in teaching.

SUGGESTIONS FOR TEACHING COORDINATION

Most English language teaching textbooks provide some coverage of English coordination. Typically, treatment of coordination first focuses on teaching the meaning of the more frequently used coordinators – *and* (including with *so* and *too*), *but*, *or*, *either . . . or*, and *neither . . . nor*. The meaning relationships established by coordinators in sentences are taught by examples supplemented with definitions such as *but = contrast, or = choice, and = addition*. Some grammar textbook series cover more conjunctions by teaching them at different levels. This is a good idea, and one you might want to keep in mind when preparing syllabi.[32]

Even if books have adequate coverage, it is probably a good idea to provide students with additional practice, especially with correlative coordinators, and to extend this to writing practice through editing/rewriting activities. You can take your cue as to which areas need more expanding by examining the textbooks you are using to see how their coverage matches the inventory of coordinate structures discussed in this chapter. Fill in any gaps with new activities. Since the essence of coordination is the joining of equal units, most activities involve finding ways of providing elements that can be joined by one or more coordinators. Realistic tasks for this can involve students' listening to TV programs or reading articles in newspapers and magazines or on the Internet.

Activity 1: Introducing Simple Coordination (Beginning)

To introduce making sentences with coordinating conjunctions, show the class a picture and make a comment about it – for example, "There's a man in the picture." Call on a student to repeat the comment and to add a comment following *and*, forming a sentence conjoined with *and* – for example, "There's a man in the picture, and there's a woman in the picture." Ask another student to make a comment about some other aspect of the picture, and then call on yet another student to add a comment using *but*. This new sentence might be something like "The man looks happy, but the woman doesn't look happy." You can facilitate this activity by pointing out aspects of the picture that could be the source of comments (e.g., asking "What about the man? Is he tall?"). The activity not only introduces the students to forming longer sentences with coordinators but also stimulates the use of new vocabulary and keeps the class discourse going.[33]

Activity 2: Practicing the Rules for Shortened Versions (Intermediate)

A number of strategies have been suggested for teaching shortened coordinate sentences. All of them use either comments elicited from students or material clipped from newspapers. The strategy described here is particularly suitable for practicing patterns with *and, both . . . and, but*, and *neither . . . nor* and verb phrase ellipsis patterns with *and so, and . . . too, and neither, and not either*, and *nor*.

Begin by asking the students to name different sports that they enjoy playing or watching. (You may have to supplement this list somewhat so that it will be large and diverse enough.) After a list has been compiled, ask two or three students which sports they like and which they do not. Write the name of each of these students on the board, and under each name, write two column heads, *likes* and *doesn't like*. Under each head list the likes and dislikes of the student. The result might look something like (69).

(69)

Ali		Fernando		Alicia	
likes	doesn't like	likes	doesn't like	likes	doesn't like
boxing	horseback	soccer	wrestling	tennis	boxing
soccer	riding	skiing	cycling	swimming	soccer
swimming	tennis	baseball	swimming	skiing	baseball
motocross	baseball	boxing	horseback	biking	American
football	cycling		riding	American	football
tennis			motocross	football	motocross
			snowboarding		
			American		
			football		

Have the students whose names are on the board form a few sentences that compare their likes and dislikes (e.g., *I like soccer, and Fernando likes soccer*; *I like soccer, but Alicia doesn't like soccer*). Then call on other students to compare their likes and dislikes to those of the students listed on the board. The patterns in (70) can be practiced:

(70) ***and (both); both . . . and; and . . . too; and so***
Alicia and Ali (both) like tennis.
Both Alicia and Ali like tennis.
I like soccer, and Fernando does, too.
Ali likes soccer, and so does Fernando.

but . . . not; not . . . but
Alicia likes American football, but Fernando doesn't.
Fernando doesn't like American football, but Alicia does.

not . . . and neither; not . . . either; not . . . nor; neither . . . nor
Ali doesn't like cycling, and neither does Fernando.
Ali doesn't like cycling, and Fernando doesn't either.
Ali doesn't like cycling, nor does Fernando.
Neither Ali nor Fernando likes cycling.

Next, have students pair off and make lists of topics that can be used for creating conjoined sentences. Any topic that the students are familiar with can be used to practice different patterns (e.g., appearances of famous people, preferences for studying or spending free time, responsibilities in jobs or in a living unit, personalities of friends or of parents). Articles about health care may present options that lend themselves to conjunction with *or* and *either . . . or* (e.g., *You can either see the doctor or a nurse practitioner*; *You can get that drug in a generic or in the more expensive original form*).

Activity 3: Rewriting Activities (High Intermediate Through Advanced)
Upper-intermediate and advanced-level students may benefit from some controlled writing activities that use coordination patterns found in written English. In particular, such activities can help them use coordination patterns that present the information more succinctly, for example, conjoined NPs instead of conjoined clauses, as well as VP ellipsis and other ways of shortening coordinate sentences. What is important here is to provide

some contextualization for the structures you intend to focus on. You could use a short paragraph, such as in (71), that tells a story and that includes sentences that could be rewritten using particular patterns. Before students start working on the passage, give them some examples of the particular reduced patterns that they can use in rewriting the passage. Have enough example sentences to give students a good feel for what they should be looking to reduce. Many students who don't enjoy studying grammar nonetheless really enjoy this kind of rewriting exercise. A rewritten paragraph for (71) is shown in (72).

(71) Student Life

John was a student at the University of Michigan. In his freshman year, he lived in a dormitory. His roommate, Al, was a few years older than John, but the two young men had many common interests. They did a lot of things together. They went to movies, and they went to basketball games, and they sometimes went to concerts. At the end of the spring semester, John and Al decided to room together in an apartment. The following fall, John became friendly with a girl named Alicia from Australia. John started to spend more and more time with her. He went out sometimes with Al and Alicia, but he went out usually just with Alicia. John and Alicia liked to sit in the coffeehouse near the music building and talk about "important things." Of course, a few topics were "off limits." John talked to her about politics, but he didn't talk to her about religion. That was something that did not interest him. After about a year, John decided to ask Alicia to marry him. He was convinced that she would say yes, and Al was sure that she would say yes. Unfortunately, Alicia said no. John was crushed. For a while he continued to go out with Alicia, but they eventually broke up.

(72) Student Life (Rewrite)

John was a student at the University of Michigan. In his freshman year, he lived in a dormitory. His roommate, Al, was a few years older than John, but the two young men had many common interests. They did a lot of things together. *They went to movies, to basketball games, and sometimes to concerts.* At the end of the spring semester, John and Al decided to room together in an apartment. The following fall, John became friendly with a girl named Alicia from Australia. John started to spend more and more time with her. *He went out sometimes with Al and Alicia but usually just with Alicia.* John and Alicia liked to sit in a coffeehouse next to the music building and talk about "important things." Of course, a few topics were "off limits." *John talked to her about politics but not about religion.* That was something that did not interest him. After about a year, John decided to ask Alicia to marry him. *He was convinced, and Al was sure, that she would say yes.* Unfortunately, Alicia said no. John was crushed. For a while he continued to go out with Alicia, but they eventually broke up.

ENDNOTES

[1] The term *coordinator* is used in Huddleston and Pullum (2002).

[2] In traditional, prescriptive grammars, sentences with subordination are called *complex sentences*, and sentences that have both coordinated and subordinated clauses are called *compound-complex sentences*.

[3] This is also referred to as *multiple coordination*.

[4] *Scientific American*, September 1999, Vol. 281, No. 3, p. 24.

[5] *Scientific American*, September 1999, Vol. 281, No. 3, p. 34.

[6] Biber et al. (1999), p. 81.

[7] The example is from Blakemore and Carston (2005).

[8] For more of these meanings, see Blakemore and Carston (2005).

[9] Biber et al. (1999), p. 81.

[10] Huddleston and Pullum (2002), p. 1310, refer to this as *adversive coordination*.

[11] Based on Huddleston and Pullum (2002), p. 1310, who argue that *yet* is an adverb.

[12] Huddleston and Pullum (2002), p. 1320.

[13] Biber et al. (1999), p. 80; Huddleston and Pullum (2002), p. 1276.

[14] Examples (a) and (b) from Huddleston and Pullum (2002), p. 1316.

[15] Still, this is just an implication, so the notion of exclusiveness is not absolute. As Huddleston and Pullum point out (2002, p. 1307), a sentence such as *You can get two-gallon watering cans at either Menards or Lowes*, certainly does not rule out the possibility that watering cans are obtainable at both stores.

[16] Quirk et al. (1972).

[17] Van Oirsouw (1987) makes a case for a single rule formulated as "delete identical material in coordination." This rule would apply to left-peripheral, right-peripheral, and medial sites and is constrained by a *Partial Deletion Constraint*.

[18] Sentences conjoined by *but not* are an exception to this, as in (35).

[19] Verb phrase ellipsis occurs in noncoordinate sentences (e.g., *If you study, I will study, too* → *If you study, I will, too*). Its use in such sentences is more restricted, however.

[20] Example (47d) demonstrates a universal constraint – deletions must be recoverable under identity with other constituents. Sag (1976) points out that the progressive form of the auxiliary sounds ungrammatical. Compare **Alan's application is being discussed and Susan's is being, too* with *Alan's application is being discussed and Susan's is, too*.

[21] The list of articles is far too long to cite here. For an overview, see Johnson (2007).

[22] *Right node raising* is not viewed as a deletion rule in the theoretical literature. See McCawley (1988), pp. 526–532, for a more complete discussion of how it works. Huddleston and Pullum (2002), pp. 1343–1345, have renamed it *delayed right constituent coordination*.

[23] Ross (1967) and Jackendoff (1971) coined the term *gapping*, and Huddleston and Pullum (2002), p. 1337, refer to *gapped coordination*.

[24] *Gapping* in English does not seem to work very well with pronoun subjects.

    (1) John ordered carrots and I ordered peas.

    (2) *John ordered carrots and I peas.

However it is permissible in other languages (e.g., Arabic), as Ross (1967) notes:

    (3) *ana   kalt   bamya   wi   huwwa   ruzz*
        I   ate   ladyfingers   and   he   rice
        "I ate ladyfingers and he rice."

This small difference between essentially the same rule in these two languages might possibly lead Arabic learners of English to produce sentences like the English version of (3) which, to me, sounds questionable if not ungrammatical.

For other difficulties in formulating this rule, see McCawley (1988), pp. 526–528.

[25] The example is from Huddleston and Pullum (2002), p. 1557.

[26] Examples (a) and (b) are from Biber et al. (1999), p. 183.

[27] Tsai (1980).

[28] The term *joint coordination* is from Huddleston and Pullum (2002), p. 1282.

[29] Huddleston and Pullum, (2002), p. 1282.

[30] These examples are from Van Oirsouw (1987).

[31] The comparison, carried out by Kent Lee, is between the Illinois corpus for Korean ESL students and the Loch Ness corpus.

[32] The *Focus on Grammar* series (1995) Pearson Longman, spreads conjunctions over intermediate- and high intermediate-level books and presents a summary in their advanced-level book. It presents the most comprehensive treatment of coordination that I am aware of.

[33] This activity was suggested by Howard Williams.

REFERENCES

Biber, D., Johansson, S., Leech, J., Conrad, S., & Finegan, E. (1999). *Longman grammar of spoken and written English*. Essex: Pearson Education, Ltd.

Blakemore D., & Carston, R. (2005). The pragmatics of sentential coordination with *and*. (to appear in *Lingua*)

Celce-Murcia, M., & Larsen-Freeman, D. (1983). *The grammar book*: *An ESL/EFL teacher's course*. Rowley, MA: Newbury House.

Huddleston, R., and Pullum, G. K. (2002). *The Cambridge grammar of the English language*. Cambridge: Cambridge University Press.

Jackendoff, R. S. (1971). Gapping and related rules. *Linguistic Inquiry*, *2*, 21–31.

Johnson, K. (2007). What VP elipsis can do, and what it can't, but not why. http://people.umass.edu/kbj/homepage/Content/what_vp_can_do.pdf

McCawley, J. D. (1988). *The Syntactic phenomena of English*: *Volume 1*. Chicago: University of Chicago Press.

Ross, J. R. (1967). *Constraints on variables in syntax*. Ph.D. dissertation. Massachusetts Institute of Technology. Published in 1987 as *Infinite syntax!* Hillsdale, NJ: Erlbaum.

Sag, I. (1976). *Deletion and logical form*. Ph.D. Dissertation. Massachusetts Institute of Technology.

Tsai, P. (1980). Neither Jane nor I are happy? *English Teaching Forum 18*(1), 19–21.

Quirk, R., Greenbaum, S., Leech, G., & Svartvik, J. (1972). *A grammar of contemporary English*. London: Longman.

Van Oirsouw, R. R. (1987). *The syntax of coordination*. New York: Croom Helm.

CHAPTER 26

Discourse Connectors and Discourse Markers

INTRODUCTION

Discourse connectors are words and phrases that, typically, connect information in one sentence to information in previous sentences. They have also been referred to as *cohesive elements*,[1] *connectives*,[2] *logical connectors*,[3] *linking adverbials*,[4] and *conjunctive adverbials*.[5] Accurate use of English discourse connectors is essential for ESL/EFL students writing academic and technical English, in addition to being important in spoken discourse. After looking at these connectors, we will look at *discourse markers*, words that are used to perform certain functions in a conversation, for example, repairing an utterance, shifting to a different topic, or pausing to consider what to say next.[6]

DISCOURSE CONNECTORS

Discourse connectors are connectives like subordinators and coordinators (discussed in Chapters 23 and 25, respectively). They differ from these other connectives not only in their ability to link a sentence to a larger piece of discourse, but also because they are less restricted in terms of where they may occur in a sentence. As we will see, discourse connectors may be classified in terms of the semantic relationships they establish.

Form

Whereas coordinators occur between the clauses they connect and subordinators occur at the beginning of the clause they introduce, discourse connectors can occur at the beginning of a sentence, within it, and sentence finally, as illustrated by (1a), (1b), and (1c). In all of these positions, discourse connectors are set off from the rest of the sentence by a comma or a set of commas.

(**1**) Sonja was discouraged when the committee vetoed her plan.
    a. *However*, this time she was not going to let herself be beaten.
    b. This time, *however*, she was not going to let herself be beaten.
    c. She was not going to let herself be beaten this time, *however*.[7]

Example (1) also reflects the ability of discourse connectors to link ideas across sentences. Sentence (1a), (1b), or (1c) could not be fully understood without the idea in the preceding sentence, *Sonja was discouraged*, nor would the relationship between the sentences be clear without the *however*. Moreover, just as *however* links across sentences here, an occurrence of *however* in the first sentence of a paragraph can link ideas across paragraphs and even larger segments of discourse.

Discourse connectors may also serve as a link between clauses within a sentence. For example, the first sentence in (1) can be combined with any of (a), (b), and (c) as two main clauses separated by a semicolon if the writer perceives the ideas as closely connected (e.g., *Sonja was discouraged when the committee vetoed her plan; however, she was not going to let herself be beaten*). Thus, such sentences are essentially just alternatives to representing the main clauses as separate sentences. In addition, some discourse connectors can serve as links within a main clause as, for example, does *hence* in *She felt tired and hence discouraged*.

Meaning: Cohesive Relationships

Discourse connectors establish semantic relationships between the sentence they appear in and preceding sentences. By establishing these relationships, discourse connectors contribute to *cohesion* – they help the ideas in the discourse hang together and clarify how they hang together. For example, the discourse connector *however* in (1a), (1b), and (1c) establishes a cohesive relationship of contrast with the preceding sentence. Some of the more common relationships and the discourse connectors that establish them are shown in what follows.

Ordering

Ordering discourse connectors indicate and order the main points that speakers or writers want to make. These connectors include the following: *first, firstly, second, secondly, third, thirdly, in the first place, in the second place, first of all, for a start, for one thing, for another thing, to begin with, then, next, finally, last, lastly, last of all*.[8] The example in (2) comes from a letter to the editor of a newspaper. The writer lists a series of objections to an article that appeared in the newspaper. In the original letter, each sentence shown in (2) begins a separate paragraph which describes an objection.

> (2) *First*, your article fails to fully describe the manner in which independent fund directors are selected for fund boards. . . .
>
> *Second*, the article pejoratively characterizes the fact that many directors sit on boards that oversee multiple funds. . . .
>
> *Third*, the article implies that fund management fees and expenses are increasing. . . .
>
> *Finally*, you state that directors rarely spend more than 100 to 200 hours per year on their fund duties. . . . [9]

These connectors can also indicate a sequence of steps in a process, in this case establishing a temporal relationship between sentences, as shown in (3).

> (3) *First*, you have to take these two boards and place them side by side. *Second/Next*, you have to insert these flat head screws in these holes. And, *finally*, you have to take this special key wrench and screw them in.

The steps indicated by ordering connectors do not have to each be completed before the next, as illustrated by the guidelines for losing weight in (4).

> (4) If you really want to lose weight you have be prepared to do three things. *First*, you have to commit to making a commitment. *Second*, you have to be able to undergo the discomfort of cutting back on your food intake. And, *third*, you have to be prepared to assume a new life style that incorporates the other two commitments.

Summary

Summary discourse connectors establish content that follows as summarizing or providing a conclusion to preceding information. These connectors include *all in all*, *in conclusion*, *overall*, *to conclude*, *finally*, *in sum*, *in summary*, *to summarize*, and *to sum up*. They may, but do not necessarily, follow a list of points. A typical example from an academic article is shown in (5).

> (5) *To summarize*, verbs such as *roar*, *bark*, *laugh*, and *cry* in the vocal expression (unergative) class take periphrastic causatives in both Vietnamese and English.[10]

Additive

Additive discourse connectors show information as parallel to and building on preceding information. The most common additive discourse connectors are *also*, *in addition*, *further*, *furthermore*, *moreover*, and *too*. Informal expressions used in spoken English include *what is more*, *on top of that*, *to top it off*, and *to cap it all*.

The contexts in which the various additive connectors can be used differ. The connector *in addition* is appropriate for the purpose of simply adding some parallel material. For example, in (6), *in addition* introduces another benefit of the new technologies, parallel to those that preceded.

> (6) These new technologies show great promise for expanding our overall knowledge of how L1 transfer develops. They will enable us to determine whether the predictions made by current SLA theory are accurate. *In addition*, they can provide us with authentic examples that may be incorporated in second language instruction.

In contrast, the connector *moreover* works well when the sentence is adding information that, rather than being merely parallel to what preceded, is potentially contributing to some thesis or conclusion, which need not be explicitly expressed. Notice that *moreover* works well in the third sentence in (7). Here, following the second sentence, on the climbers' dissatisfaction with their leader, *moreover* introduces the information that bad weather obscured the view – so the two sentences together can be seen as contributing to a conclusion that the climbers were dissatisfied with their ascent of Mount Hood.

> (7) Last week the Mountaineers Club tackled the ascent of Mount Hood. The climbers were not happy with their leader, who displayed uncertainty at several points during the climb. *Moreover*, the weather was bad, which meant that the beautiful view they had been anticipating was obscured on the way up and during the descent.

In contrast, in (8) *moreover* is no longer appropriate. Since the third sentence simply supplies information parallel to that in the second sentence, *in addition* is more appropriate (# indicates material that is grammatical but inappropriate).

> (8) Last week the Mountaineers Club tackled the ascent of Mount Hood. A few climbers from the Idaho chapter of the club joined the group. $\begin{Bmatrix} \textit{In addition,} \\ \textit{\#Moreover,} \end{Bmatrix}$ a few Californians showed up for the climb.

Notice that the use of *moreover* in (8) becomes more acceptable if we add a final clause like *So the group tackling the ascent was a more heterogeneous one than usual*. It is more acceptable because this final clause makes the sentence about Californians not just another parallel piece of information, but evidence toward a conclusion.

Furthermore functions like *moreover*, but generally it links the last two points when more than two exist, as in (9).

(9) The annual ascent of Mount Hood by the Mountaineers Club was not as enjoyable as in past years. The climbers were not happy with their leader, who displayed uncertainty at several points during the climb. Certain of the trails used seemed too steep and dangerous for some of the club members' level of experience and expertise. *Furthermore*, the weather was bad, which meant that the beautiful view they had been anticipating was obscured on the way up and during the descent.

Exemplification and Restatement

Discourse connectors of *exemplification* and *restatement* signal that information following in some way clarifies the information that preceded. The clarification may take the form of examples or of some expansion or other explanation of what preceded. These discourse connectors are sometimes also referred to as *appositive connectors* or *adverbials of apposition*.[11]

The most common connectors of exemplification are *for example* and *for instance*. *Namely* and *that is* can introduce examples if these are followed by an expression such as *and so on*. A typical example of use of a discourse connector of exemplification is shown in (10).

(10) There are ways in which you might improve your chances of gaining financing for your project. *For example*, you could try to bring the focus of your research more in line with the goals of the request for proposals that our agency announced on the Internet.

The connectors of restatement include *that is, in other words, more precisely, which is to say, that is to say*, and *namely*. They expand on previously presented information, often providing a more comprehensive explanation, as in (11).

(11) If you had accepted their offer, they would have given you a $14,000 moving allowance. *In other words*, the total amount of compensation that you would have received would have been greater than what you finally accepted.

That is often appears sentence internally, as must *which is to say*. Like certain other connectors, *that is* is used mainly in writing; in spoken discourse, *I mean* often serves the same function. As in (12) and (13), *that is* often clarifies a prior statement by elaborating on it, whereas *in other words* often clarifies by rephrasing the prior statement in shorter form.

(12) All of the Hispanic students who took the foreign language section of the ACT would receive an extra 15 points; *that is*, they would boost their overall chances for admission by 30 percent and also meet the undergraduate foreign language requirement if admitted.   *elaborating*

(13) All of the SUVs had a tendency to roll up on two wheels at lower speeds. *In other words*, they flunked the rollover test.   *rephrasing*

Namely generally adds information in the form of an NP and thus usually appears sentence internally, as in (14).

(14) But there was something else that they had to consider – *namely*, the lack of a legal justification for starting a war.

Result

Result discourse connectors – for example, *accordingly, consequently, hence, therefore, thus, as a consequence, as a result,* and *so* – introduce information that is a consequence of preceding information. In (15), the fact that some English passives cannot be recast as passives in Chinese is the result of semantic restrictions on the Chinese passive.

> (15) The Chinese passive is semantically restricted to cases where the subject is adversely affected by the action. *Consequently,* some English passives are anomalous in Chinese.[12]

When the result is an event that follows from a situation or action that was described, *consequently* and *as a result* tend to be used, as in (16a), in which the decision made follows from the decreasing visibility. When the result is, instead, an inferential consequence, *therefore* and *thus* tend to be used, as in (16b). *So* can readily be used in either context.

> (16) a. It was getting dark, and visibility was rapidly decreasing. *Consequently/As a result,* they decided to call off the search until the following morning.
> b. You have three, and I have two; *therefore/thus,* we have five altogether.

Thus and *hence* are often used for asides meaning "so, for this reason" in a formal register and in this use occur sentence internally, as in (17), or may even be represented as a sentence fragment.

> (17) He has a lot of money tied up in that company – *thus/hence* his intense interest in how the stock is doing.

Concession

The *concessive* discourse connectors *nevertheless, nonetheless, in spite of that, despite that,* and *still* introduce information that is surprising or unexpected in light of previous information. Example (18) is typical. *Nevertheless* (or any of the other concessive connectors) introduces content (i.e., Laura did not get admitted to Harvard) that is surprising in light of the content in the previous sentence (i.e., Laura had the third highest ACT score in the country).

> (18) Laura had the third highest score on the ACT test in the country. *Nevertheless/In spite of that/Still,* she did not get admitted to Harvard.

Contrast

Discourse connectors of *contrast* include *in contrast, by way of contrast, conversely, by comparison, however, instead, on the contrary,* and *on the other hand.* As with other sets of connectors, contrast connectors differ considerably in formality and use. For example, *instead* and *on the contrary* are frequently used in speaking, whereas *conversely, in contrast,* and *by way of contrast* are viewed as more formal and therefore appear largely in written English. They link information viewed as contrastive, whether the contrast is between different aspects of a subject or one or more aspects of different subjects, as in (19a), which contrasts the temperature of Rio with that of Alaska. The difference between contrast connectors and concessive connectors is clear from comparing (19a) and (19b): concessive connectors, such as *nevertheless, despite that,* and *still,* make no sense in the context of this straight contrast that does not involve surprise, as in (19b).

> (19) a. In terms of annual mean temperature, Alaska is cold. *However/By contrast,* Rio is clearly hot.
> b. In terms of annual mean temperature, Alaska is cold. *#Nevertheless/Despite that/Still,* Rio is clearly hot.

Instead often introduces an action that contrasts with a previously mentioned action. Typical examples are shown in (20).

> (**20**) a. He doesn't do any work at all. *Instead*, he sits all day in front of his computer and plays games or reads the news on the Internet.
> b. She told us she was going to join us tonight. *Instead*, she went out with her boyfriend.

On the contrary can preface a remark that reflects the speaker's stance of contradiction to something that has been said, as in the dialog in (21). It usually carries falling intonation and a pause before the rest of the sentence, which contains the speaker's conflicting opinion.

> (**21**) A: She is really very witty and intelligent.
> B: *On the contrary*, I found her to be quite boring and a bit slow on the uptake.

In contrast is often used when two subjects or aspects of a subject differ in one or more respects.[13] In (22), the contrast is between American cars, which are large and have powerful engines, and European cars, which are small and have engines that are less powerful.

> (**22**) The American automobile companies have been focusing on developing cars that are big and comfortable and have powerful engines. *In contrast*, European automakers have been emphasizing economy so their cars are small and underpowered by American standards.

Notice that with the looser sort of contrast in (23) we can use only *however*; we cannot use *in contrast* or any of the other connectors of contrast mentioned here.

> (**23**) a. He wanted to take a trip to Europe. *However*, he didn't have enough money.
> b. He wanted to take a trip to Europe. #*In contrast*, he didn't have enough money.

The discourse connector *on the other hand* is used in spoken as well as written English and should, according to the prescriptivist rule, appear after *on the one hand*. This discourse connector is used in contrasting qualities or aspects of a single subject, as in (24a) and (24b), respectively. Often, as in these examples, the contrast involves pros and cons.

> (**24**) a. *On the one hand*, Utah has a dry and arid climate. *On the other hand*, it has some of the most beautiful scenery in the United States in parks such as Bryce and Zion.
> b. Coaching athletes is a tricky business. *On the one hand*, you want to give all of your athletes the opportunity to develop their talents. *On the other hand*, you have to win games, so you may be forced to favor those athletes that seem to have the greatest natural talent.

Cognitive Stance

Cognitive stance, or *attitudinal*, discourse connectors express the writer's cognitive stance (attitude) regarding the truth of the preceding content and introduce content in support of the stance.[14] These connectors include *as it happens, indeed, in fact, actually, in actual fact*, and *in reality*.

As it happens, indeed, and *in fact* can all be used to signal the stance that the preceding content is true and to introduce information that emphasizes and presents support for its truth. *Indeed* is perhaps the most common; it is considered equivalent to the paraphrase *I might even go so far as to say* . . . . Typical uses of these connectors are shown in (25) and (26).

(25) The dean did not object to the proposal. *Indeed*, what he said in the ensuing discussion seemed to support it.

(26) The previously accepted hypothesis that hemispheric lateralization is not complete before the onset of puberty is now being questioned. *In fact*, there are a number of studies that challenge this hypothesis.

Along with *as it happens* and *in fact*, the connectors *actually*, *in actual fact*, *really*, and *in reality* can indicate that the material that preceded is not accurate or true and introduce information that presents the real truth.[15] Often, the preceding material is in a sentence that includes an adverb such as *officially*, *ostensibly*, *formally*, *nominally*, *outwardly*, or *theoretically*, which suggests that it may not be accurate or true and contrasts with the connector that follows, as shown in (27).

(27) *Ostensibly,* he is in charge of the entire unit. *In reality*, his secretary makes all of the decisions and runs everything.

Abrupt Topic Shift

A few discourse connectors such as *incidentally*, *by the way*, *by the by*, and *apropos of* + NP are used to preface an abrupt shift to another topic, which is often peripherally related to the topic described in the preceding sentences, as in (28). These connectors are typical of spoken English.

(28) I will be going to College Park next week to give a short talk on our research. *By the way*, have you finished the analysis of the native speaker data yet? I could use that in my talk.

SUMMARY

DISCOURSE CONNECTORS

Discourse connectors link information in the sentence in which they occur to information in preceding sentences. They can occur at various points in the sentence, separated from the rest by a comma or a set of commas:

Sonja was discouraged. However, she wouldn't let herself be beaten./She, however, wouldn't let herself be beaten./She wouldn't let herself be beaten, however.

Discourse connectors contribute to the **cohesion** of a discourse and express various types of relationships:

- **Ordering** connectors (e.g., *first, firstly, second, secondly, third, thirdly, next, then, finally*) signal the order of main points the speaker or writer wants to make or of steps in a process.
  - *First, you get some vegetables. Next, you chop them up. Then, you throw them in a pot of boiling water.*

- **Summary** connectors (e.g., *all in all, in conclusion, finally, overall, to conclude, in sum, in summary, to summarize, to sum up*) indicate that a summary or conclusion follows.
  - *In conclusion, your analysis of the situation is badly flawed.*

continued

- **Addition** connectors (e.g., *also, in addition, further, furthermore, moreover*) add information to what comes before. *Moreover* and *furthermore* are often not interchangeable with *in addition*, as *in addition* simply introduces added parallel information whereas they introduce information that builds toward a conclusion.
  - *Last week the Mountaineers Club tackled the ascent of Mount Hood. The climbers were not happy with their leader, who displayed uncertainty at several points. Moreover, the weather was bad, which meant that the view was obscured.*
  - *Last week some climbers from the Idaho chapter of the club joined the group. In addition, a few Californians showed up for the climb.*

- **Exemplification and restatement** connectors (e.g., *for example, for instance, namely, that is*) provide examples or an expansion or other clarification of something previously stated.
  - *There are ways you might improve your chances of gaining financing for your project. For example, you could try to bring its focus more in line with the goals of the request for proposals.*
  - *All of the SUVs had a tendency to roll up on two wheels at lower speeds. In other words, they flunked the rollover test.*

- **Result** connectors (e.g., *accordingly, consequently, hence, therefore, thus, as a consequence, as a result, so*) introduce information that is the consequence of preceding information. For inferential consequences, *thus* and *therefore* tend especially to be used.
  - *The Chinese passive is semantically restricted to cases where the subject is adversely affected by the action. Consequently, some English passives are anomalous in Chinese.*
  - *You have three, and I have two; therefore, we have five altogether.*

- **Concession** connectors (e.g., *nevertheless, nonetheless, in spite of that, despite that, still*) introduce surprising or unexpected information.
  - *She had the third highest score on the ACT test in the country. Nevertheless, she did not get admitted to Harvard.*

- **Contrast** connectors (e.g., *by way of contrast, in contrast, conversely, instead, however*) introduce information that is in some way contrastive with previously stated information. The contrast may be between subjects (e.g., with *in contrast*) or between aspects of a subject (e.g., with *on the other hand*). *Instead* is used especially with actions. With loose contrasts, only *however* is used.
  - *The highest temperature in Alaska in January is minus 7 degrees. In contrast, the highest temperature in Arizona for that month is 68 degrees.*
  - *On the one hand, Arizona's climate is very hot. On the other hand, the humidity is low.*
  - *He doesn't do any work. Instead, he plays games on his computer.*
  - *He wanted to take a trip to Europe. However, he didn't have enough money.*

- **Cognitive stance (attitudinal)** connectors (e.g., *actually, certainly, indeed, in fact, in actual fact, as it happens*) express the writer's attitude regarding the truth of the previous information and introduce information supporting the stance.
  - *The dean did not object to the proposal. Indeed, what he said seemed to support it.*
  - *The hypothesis that age limits the acquisition of a second language is now being questioned. In fact, one new study seriously challenges this hypothesis.*

- **Abrupt topic shift** connectors (e.g., *incidentally, by the way, by the by, apropos of*) mark a sudden transition from one topic to another, possibly loosely connected, topic.
  - *Next week I will give a short talk on our research. By the way, have you finished the analysis of the native speaker data? I could use that in my talk.*

EXERCISE 26.1

Identify the discourse connectors in the following sentences and indicate their function (abrupt topic shift, cognitive stance, concession, contrast, restatement, result, addition, or summary).

Example: All in all, it appears that the project is proceeding on schedule, and there is every reason to believe that the building will be finished on or possibly even before the projected completion date.

Answer: all in all = summary

1. The nation is more polarized than ever, or so conventional wisdom has it. Washington is said to seethe with snarling, snapping partisans.

   As it happens, this claim is roughly true.[16]
2. Most thought the movie a powerful work. "I was struck by the sophistication of the photography," notes Charles Kimball.

   Substantively, however, they were troubled by the film. The violence . . . bothered them.[17]
3. In terms of his natural skills, he had an excellent chance of winning the grand prize. Unfortunately, he did not have enough money to enter the tournament. Consequently, he never had the chance to prove to himself and others that he was a serious competitor.
4. It seems clear that we have no alternative except to go back and run this experiment again. Incidentally, one way to avoid the kind of problem that is forcing us to do this is to make sure that we follow basic procedures for assigning subjects to groups and that we follow the experimental design.
5. It had snowed heavily all day long for the past week, and they had been forced to stay in the cabin. Still, they refused to give up hope that the sun would come out sometime in the next three days and that they would at least get in some skiing before their vacation was over.
6. I had expected that she would at least speak up and offer some support in my defense. Instead, she remained silent during the attack that was coming from the other members of the committee.
7. Originally, many computer-based systems were viewed as having the role predominantly of providing the "design paperwork." That is to say, they operated in such a way to either confirm the proposed design or to generate the engineering information for production.[18]
8. To summarize, most theories of second language acquisition recognize that the native language can exercise a strong influence on production of second language learners' interlanguage. Moreover, a number of experiments indicate that the native language is the most likely source of ungrammatical utterances that second language learners produce. Thus, there are both theoretical and empirical grounds for recognizing the concept of "native language transfer" as a concept that shapes second language learning.

EXERCISE 26.2

Replace any italicized discourse marker in each of the following sentences that seems inappropriate in the context in which it appears with a connector that is more appropriate. Explain your reason for the substitution.

Example: A: I thought that movie was really excellent. Lots of action and great acting.

B: *Nevertheless*, I thought it was quite boring, and the acting wasn't particularly good either.

Answer: on the contrary (Since speaker B's opinion contrasts with speaker A's, the concessive connector *nevertheless* is inappropriate and a contrastive connector is needed.)

1. This summer, things are looking bleak for the owners of movie theaters. No large summer blockbuster film that would fill up multiplexes has appeared yet. *In addition*, the availability of recently released movies on DVD makes renting more appealing to a large part of the movie-going public. This has resulted in a 50 percent drop in the sale of theater tickets so far.
2. In terms of land mass, America is a large country; *nevertheless*, China is huge.
3. Some women have full-time jobs in addition to feeding, clothing, and looking after their children. *Consequently*, it is fair to say that they have a larger daily workload than women who have full-time jobs but no children.
4. She had wanted to invite John, too. *In contrast*, she couldn't find his telephone number, so she didn't know how to get in touch with him.
5. Fifty percent of the applicants scored under 200 on the screening – *that is*, they failed to qualify for admission.
6. A: I think he would make an excellent governor.
   B: *Instead*, I believe that he doesn't have the experience or the good judgment necessary for the office.
7. The opposition party is having a debate tomorrow night to let the public get a feel for the views of their candidates on different issues. *Furthermore*, did you see the interview that their leading candidate gave on TV last night? He made some terrible gaffes.

DISCOURSE MARKERS

Discourse markers, often called *discourse particles*, are words that are not an integral part of a sentence or its grammar but are inserted by a speaker for various reasons, including to indicate a pause before continuing, to signal a new phase in the conversation, to repair or wrap up what has been said, or to express disagreement with what the other speaker has said.[19] As this definition indicates, by and large, discourse markers are restricted to spoken English. They occur most frequently in sentence initial position but can also appear sentence internally.[20]

Functions of Discourse Markers

The same discourse marker can have more than one function.[21] Some of the more frequently used discourse markers and their functions in conversation are presented in what follows.

Well

Well fulfills several different functions. It can signal that a speaker is deciding how he or she should continue. Each instance of *well* in (29) marks a brief deliberation in which the speaker decides how to frame what comes next.

(**29**) The concept "fossilization"? *Well*, it's been widely used for some time, but the validity has been challenged by some people in the field, like, *well*, Long, for example . . . and, *well*, there's a seminal article by him in the new *Handbook of Second Language Acquisition* and, *well*, you could read that if you want to know the details of how it has been used. . . .

In a related function, *well* may also preface a response the speaker makes, particularly to something that requires some thought. In (30), speaker A confronts speaker B with an unexpected challenge. Speaker B wants to respond in a way that saves face, and *well* provides him or her with a short delay in which to formulate a response.

(**30**) A: Look, I don't know why you're asking me to solve this problem. YOU'RE the one who got us into this mess. So what are YOU going to do about that?
    B: *Well*, lemme think . . .

Well can also signal the speaker's desire to end a topic of discussion and move on to another activity, as in (31).

(**31**) *Well*, let's get started, shall we?

A speaker can also indicate disagreement by prefacing *well* to his or her response, as in (32) or in (33), in which it begins a sentence that is an evasion or perhaps an outright lie.

(**32**) A: You're always hungry.
    B: *Well*, I'm not now.[22]

(**33**) A: Can I borrow your textbook tonight?
    B: *Well*, I need it to study tonight.

Well also prefaces commands and remarks that indicate impatience, as illustrated in (34), and remarks that indicate that the other speaker's objections are irrelevant or insignificant, as shown in (35).

(**34**) *Well*, hurry up!

(**35**) A: But I think John may not be very happy with that.
    B: *Well*, that's no big deal.

I Mean

I mean is a repair marker that allows the speaker to rephrase his or her words, as exemplified in (36a). In addition, it can be inserted before an attempt to clarify meaning or provide additional explanation of a point. In this use, it is similar to *that is* or *in other words*. Example (36b) shows *I mean* used as a clarification that does not entail repair.

(**36**) a. It's to my advantage, *I mean*, it's to our mutual advantage, to work together.
    b. Let's think of another solution. *I mean*, fixing it this way just isn't going to work.

You Know (Ya Know, Y'know)

You know can preface information that the speaker assumes the listener may be aware of, as if to say "you probably know this," but it can also indicate that the speaker wants to make some fact very clear to the listener. This emphasizing function is probably involved in (37).

(**37**) *You know*, that really bugs me.

When *you know* appears sentence finally with falling intonation, it functions as a *conducive tag question* that invites confirmation or assumes that the person being addressed will assess the situation the same way that the speaker would (see Chapter 4). In (38), sentence-final *you know* may be functioning as a tag question.

(**38**) Our president is a dope, *you know.*

Like *well, you know* is often inserted, at different points in sentences, as a deliberation signal[23] to indicate that the speaker is in the process of formulating a continuation of the utterance. The frequent use of *you know* for this purpose, as shown in (39), is extremely irritating to many listeners, who may feel that the speaker is indecisive or incapable of forming a complete sentence. It may be worthwhile for ESL/EFL teachers to demonstrate this and warn students against overuse of *you know.*

(**39**) So I said, *ya know*, you oughta, *you know*, take care of that . . . 'cause, *ya know*, it could be dangerous, *ya know.* I mean, *ya know*, you could have an explosion from a gas leak like that.

Oh

Oh, which is generally used sentence initially, is a mental state marker[24] – that is, it can indicate that the speaker has realized or understood something from what has been said, as in (40a). A statement of the realization may then follow, as in (40b).

(**40**) a. *Oh*, I see.
  b. A: How can I get a grant for that?
    B: *Oh*, I didn't realize that you were looking for information about grants.

Oh may also be used to preface a repair, as in (41), or a clarification, as in (42).

(**41**) I think the law was passed in 1976. *Oh*, maybe it was 1978. I don't remember for sure.

(**42**) A: I saw this guy working as a waiter, with a Ph.D.! He couldn't get a good job!
  B: Really? What was his Ph.D. in?
  A: *Oh*, I didn't talk to him. The guy I was eating lunch with told me about him.

Okay

Okay is a used to wrap up a topic, as illustrated in (43). It also is used very frequently to indicate that the speaker has heard and understood what the previous speaker has said, as in (44).

(**43**) A: So that is a brief summary of everything that was said at the meeting.
  B: *Okay*, so let's move on to the next item on the agenda.

(**44**) A: Your mother wants you to come home.
  B: *Okay.*

Right

Right signals that the speaker is about to initiate a new phase in the conversation, often, as illustrated in (45), one that requires some kind of action.[25]

(**45**) A: I added that section you wanted – about the dangers involved in pursuing an aggressive foreign policy.
  B: *Right* . . . now you can sum up the pros and cons in the conclusion, and the report will be complete.

Right also has a function similar to *okay* as an indicator that the speaker has understood what has been said, as in (46). In American English, it can, in addition, signal agreement with what the previous speaker has said, as in (47).

(**46**) A: We still need to make our reservations for Siena.
B: *Right*, I'll get on it as soon as I finish this.

(**47**) A: So she must've known about the report . . .
B: *Right!*
A: . . . and she didn't tell him about it after all.
B: *Right!* She obviously didn't want him to know about it.

In addition, *right* is also a tag in a same polarity tag question (with rising intonation) where the speaker is seeking feedback from the person addressed (see Chapter 4).

(**48**) A: You know how to do this, *right*?
B: Yeah, you showed me yesterday.

Like

Similar to cleft sentences, discussed in Chapter 22, *like* marks information that is salient. A word or a phrase may be marked as salient because it is new information, emphasizes something, or stands in contrast to something previously mentioned. *Like* appears to have this salience use in (49a) and in (49b), in which it appears with *it's*.

(**49**) a. Okay, but that's not *like*, a law or anything?
b. I wake up, and it's *like*, no one's home, and I have no idea where anyone is.

Like can soften requests, as in (50), or mark an approximation, similar to stance adverbs *about*, *approximately*, and *roughly*, as in (51). In British English, *like* can appear at the end of a sentence to indicate the meaning "so to speak," as shown in (52).

(**50**) Could I *like* borrow your sweater?[26]

(**51**) a. This guy would follow me *like* every day until I had to call the police.
b. Some parts of Los Angeles really have a lot of palm trees. On this street I've seen *like* twenty-five already.

(**52**) My wee girl can swim, you know – she has her wings, *like*.[27]

Particularly in the speech of younger people, *like* currently appears to be a favored means of introducing reported speech, occurring in place of *says* and *said*. A present or past form of *be* precedes *like* when it is used for this purpose. In the first two sentences in (53), *he's like* and *I'm like* are equivalent to *he says* and *I say*. In the next two sentences, *he was like* and *they were like* are replaceable by *he said* and *they said*.

(**53**) a. So, then *he's like*, "No way!" And then *I'm like*, "Why not?" And *he was like*, "Cuz I don't wanna. I never do stuff like that." And then his mom and dad, *they were like*, "Oh, no? You've done things like that before."

SUMMARY

DISCOURSE MARKERS

Discourse markers are words that are not an integral part of a sentence and that are used in spoken English for a range of functions. One discourse marker can have several functions. Common discourse markers include the following:

- **Well** can signal the speaker's deliberation about how to continue, preface a response, indicate a desire to end a topic and shift activities, and preface a disagreement or evasion. It can also preface remarks that indicate impatience.
  The concept "fossilization"? Well, it's been widely used for some time.
  A: So what are you going to do about this mess? B: Well, lemme think. . . .
  Well, let's get started, shall we?
  A: You're always hungry. B: Well, I'm not now.
  A: Can I borrow your textbook tonight? B: Well, I need it to study tonight.
  Well, hurry up!

- **I mean** allows the speaker to rephrase in order to repair and/or clarify.
  It's to my advantage, I mean, it's to our mutual advantage, to work together.
  Let's think of another solution. I mean, fixing it this way just isn't going to work.

- **You know (ya know, y'know)** prefaces information that the speaker assumes is known or wants to emphasize, functions as a tag question, and signals deliberation.
  You know, that really bugs me.
  Our president is a dope, you know.
  So I said, ya know, you oughta, you know, take care of that . . . cause, ya know . . .

- **Oh** indicates the speaker has understood and is a repair or clarification marker.
  A: How can I get a grant for that? B: Oh, I didn't know you wanted a grant.
  I think the law was passed in 1976. Oh, maybe it was 1978.
  A: What was his Ph.D. in? B: Oh, I didn't ask him. Some other guy told me.

- **Okay** is used to wrap up a topic and to indicate the speaker has heard and understood.
  Okay, so let's move on the next item on the agenda.
  A: Your mother wants you to come home. B: Okay.

- **Right** signals that the speaker is about to initiate a new phase in the conversation, indicates comprehension and agreement, and is also a tag.
  A: I added that section you wanted. B: Right, now you can sum up the pros and cons.
  A: We still need to make our reservations. B: Right, I'll get on it now.
  You know how to do this, right?

- **Like** marks a word or a phrase that is salient, softens requests, marks an approximation, and introduces reported speech.
  I wake up, and it's like no one's home, and I have no idea where anyone is.
  Some parts of Los Angeles have a lot of palm trees. On this street, I've seen like twenty-five already.
  So, then he's like, "No way!" And then I'm like, "Why not?' And he was like, "Cuz I don't wanna."

EXERCISE 26.3

Identify the function of each italicized discourse marker in the following sentences.

Example: A: So I guess that's about everything I wanted to say.

B: *Right*, let's move on to the next item on the agenda.

Answer: Right indicates that the speaker is about to initiate a new phase in the conversation, one that may require some kind of action.

1. A: Who owns that black SUV that's blocking my driveway?
   B: So who wants to know?
   A: *Well*, I want to know.
2. A: That's a very nice Persian rug. It's a Nain, *right*?
   B: That's right. How much do you think I could get for it?
3. Susan, could you try to ease up a little on your criticism of Bill? Cuz *like*, it's really beginning to bug him. He says you're always on his case.
4. She's a real dope, *you know*.
5. He's very difficult to get along with – *I mean*, he's not the easiest person to get along with.
6. A: Can I help you?
   B: No, I just wanted to look at these items you have on sale.
   A: *Okay*. If there is anything you want to know about them, just ask.
7. Well, *you know*, these things aren't quite as simple as they seem, *you know*. There are a lot of variables that, *you know*, have to be taken into consideration.
8. So I was *like*, "Well do you or don't you?" And he was *like*, "I dunno, whadda ya want to do?" And I'm *like*, "You decide."

PROBLEMS THAT ESL/EFL STUDENTS HAVE WITH DISCOURSE CONNECTORS AND DISCOURSE MARKERS

A number of studies – for example, Altenberg (1986), Connor (1984), Crewe (1990), Field and Yip (1992), Kahlil (1989), Martel (1991), and Milton and Tsang (1993) – are beginning to provide us with insights into problems that students may have with discourse connectors. One interesting study by Granger and Tyson (1996) compared a corpus of essays written in English by native speakers of French (89,918 words) with a corpus of essays written by native-speaker college students (77,723 words). They discovered several trends in the French students' use of English discourse connectors that seem to be reflected to some degree in other studies and in our corpora.

Certain kinds of connectors were overused or underused, and these use patterns seemed to relate to the genre of the compositions that the students had written.

They also found evidence of L1 transfer. The French EFL students equated the English connectors *in fact* and *as a matter of fact* with French *en fait*, and overused them in their compositions, often creating connections that sounded odd or illogical. Their overuse of *on the contrary* was probably the result of equating it with *au contraire*, which is used in French to specify concessive and antithetical links. They often began an English sentence with an antithetical *on the contrary*, as shown in (54), where *however* is clearly more appropriate.

(54) This kind of union will be economic. Therefore I think nobody will have to fear for his cultural identity. #*On the contrary*, if Europe achieves a political union one day, the European citizen will have to destroy what made him belong to his previous nation. (Cf. *However*, if Europe achieves a political union one day . . .)

Another type of apparent L1 transfer error, which we found in our corpus of compositions written by Portuguese and Spanish speaking EFL students, was word-for-word translation of connectors consisting of several words in the L1. For example, one Brazilian graduate student created a connector *by another side*, in the sentence shown in (55). This connector is a word-for-word translation of the Portuguese *por outro lado*, the equivalent of the English connector *on the other hand*.

(55) *By another side*, Americans also has wrong idea about another people.

The EFL students in Granger and Tyson's corpus also did not seem to understand the contextual conditions that bias a choice of one connector within a group over another. For example, they did not grasp the fact that *moreover* works best when the sentences it links are supporting some conclusion, rather than just adding parallel information. They thus used *moreover* in contexts where a simple addition connector like *and* or *in addition* would be more appropriate.

The same EFL students exhibited a lack of sensitivity to style, often mixing more informal connectors like *anyway* with more formal connectors like *moreover*.

An examination of our corpus of compositions written by undergraduate Spanish and Korean students found quite a few examples of overuse of certain connectors and of mixing of informal connectors like *so* with formal connectors like *moreover*. The overuse of *so* can impart a disconcerting jerky quality to the writing, where a statement is immediately followed by a conclusion beginning with *so*. One gets the impression that students seize on certain connectors and use them preponderantly in certain types of writing assignments. It is not clear how this problem might be addressed except by showing students how paragraphs laced with too many discourse connectors, or too many instances of certain discourse connectors, could be rewritten.

SUGGESTIONS FOR TEACHING DISCOURSE CONNECTORS AND DISCOURSE MARKERS

Because discourse connectors and discourse markers are such different areas from the standpoints of use and pedagogy, in this discussion of suggestions for teaching, we take up first one and then the other.

Discourse Connectors

Discourse connectors are clearly important for writing instruction. Under various labels (e.g., "transition signals"[28]) they are always taught in advanced-level grammar textbooks and as part of the grammar that is covered in textbooks designed to teach writing skills. Textbook presentations usually group them, as in the first part of this chapter, according to the semantic relationships they establish, and sometimes show how certain coordinating conjunctions and subordinators establish these same relationships (e.g., that concession can be established with *yet* and *although* as well as with connectors such as *nonetheless*). Some textbooks devote several chapters to the topic, covering a large number of connectors in each semantic category as well as the proper punctuation of connectors. Despite the extensive coverage that discourse connectors receive in textbooks, students have difficulty using them correctly and make a range of errors, as we have just seen.

Part of the problem may stem from the way discourse connectors are taught in textbooks. As a rule, connectors having the same function are presented as a group, often in a table, without discussion of the differences in their use. Thus, for example, a textbook may present a group of "sentence connectors that signal addition and alternatives," including *also*, *in addition*, *furthermore*, and *moreover*. The textbook might have one example of each of these connectors used in a model sentence along with a general description of all of them as "simple additive connectors that have the general meaning of *too* and *also*." The textbook might then practice this group along with others, with students selecting any of them from a box of connectors to link sentences that logically have an additive relationship. However, as we have already seen, *moreover* is not interchangeable with *in addition*. Since the differences between them, and the contextual conditions that favor the choice of one or the other, have not been described, there is nothing to prevent students from using *in addition* in contexts where *moreover* is the appropriate choice, and vice versa. If the teacher does not demonstrate that *moreover* is the best fit for contexts where there is some logical conclusion to be drawn from the sentences linked, but not for contexts involving simple addition of parallel information, the students will not be any wiser and will insert *moreover* in the wrong contexts.

If this hypothesis is an accurate account of why students continue to have problems using discourse connectors, then there are two things that teachers can do to improve the teaching of this important syntactic topic. The first would be to explain contextual subtleties that influence choices from among the individual connectors within the specific groups. The second would be to provide more practice that forces students to speak and write sentences using discourse connectors. Two activities designed to do both are described in what follows.

Activity 1: Focusing on the Environment (Advanced)

From one of the groups of discourse connectors, select a connector that is used in particular kinds of contexts, different from those for the group as a whole, and describe these contexts. Then contrast this discourse connector with other members of the group. For example, to explain the use of *moreover*, begin by writing on the board the sentences in (56).

(56) 1. The climbers were unhappy with their guide because he took them up the most dangerous trail.
2. The weather was misty and rainy, so they couldn't see anything.
3. <u>Conclusion</u>: All in all, they didn't have a good time.

Explain that in this case *moreover* can link sentence 2 to sentence 1, because both sentences lead to the conclusion expressed in sentence 3. Insert *moreover* in front of sentence 2 and *so* in front of sentence 3, as shown in (57).

(57) 1. The climbers were unhappy with their guide because he took them up the most dangerous trail.
2. <u>Moreover</u>, the weather was misty and rainy, so they couldn't see anything.
3. <u>So</u>, all in all, they didn't have a good time.

Point out that other additive connectors like *in addition* are far less appropriate in this case. Explain that they are appropriate in sentences that are simple additions, and write the sentences in (58) on the board:

(58) 1. Last week the Mountaineers Club tackled the ascent of Mount Hood.
2. A few climbers from the Idaho chapter of the club joined the group.
3. Some Californians showed up for the climb.

Explain that since sentence 2 and sentence 3 only add information to sentence 1 and don't lead to any conclusion or support a particular idea, you can link sentence 3 by the discourse connector *in addition*. Insert *in addition* at the beginning of sentence 3.

Now present the students with sheets of paper that have triplets of sentences that you have prepared, and tell them to work in pairs to decide for each triplet which of the two discourse connectors is more appropriate to include.

Next, perhaps in another lesson, present them with further triplets, some connected with an inappropriate discourse connector and others appropriately connected. Have students decide whether each discourse connector used is appropriate or inappropriate. A class discussion should follow in which they justify their decisions. Other candidates for this activity include *instead* versus *in contrast*, *in contrast* versus *on the contrary*, and, going across groups, *however* versus *nevertheless*.

When teaching in an EFL context, there is no harm in pointing out that certain English connectors should not be equated with and used in the same way as a particular L1 connector. You can also address the L1 transfer problems shown in (54) and (55) by collecting a bank of examples drawn from compositions and then presenting them to your students and asking what the writer intended in each case. This can lead to a refocusing on the particular use of the English discourse connector that would have been appropriate in that context.

Activity 2: Open-Ended Practice (Advanced)

After you have taught the meanings of and contexts for different discourse connectors, a simple but effective practice involves getting students to produce sentences that are appropriate for the relationships established by different connectors by providing them with a sentence followed by several connectors, as shown in (59). The students use each connector to form a sentence that could be linked to the first sentence.

> (59) a. My brother has always been a good student.
>   1. On the other hand, _____
>   2. However, _____
>   3. Consequently, _____
>   4. In contrast, _____
>   b. Americans prefer big, gas-guzzling cars.
>   1. However, _____
>   2. What is more, _____
>   3. Conversely, _____
>   4. On the contrary, _____

Prepare the sentences in (59) as a handout. As a class, you might ask different students to supply an appropriate sentence for each connector, or you may have students work in pairs or small groups to create sentences. When students are ready, have them present their sentences and ask the class whether each sentence fits the context provided by the first sentence. Discuss any inappropriate choices.[29]

Although this kind of exercise may not appear to afford much opportunity for learning, it is actually an excellent way of finding out how much progress your students are making. It also has the benefit of letting students draw on their own experiences while allowing them to be creative with the linguistic resources at their disposal. You can vary the activity by including connectors from different groups, as in the second of the two examples. Since this is essentially a production activity, it is the next best thing to free writing and yet allows focus on form. Repeat this activity from time to time as you cover new groups of connectors.

A follow-up step would be to see what students can do with authentic samples of texts from which you have removed discourse connectors. You will need to collect texts with a number of examples of connectors from the groups that you want to practice. If possible, find texts that include connectors that link sentences within a paragraph, that occur within sentences, and that occur in the first sentence of a new paragraph and thus provide a transition to a new topic. Prepare a version of the passage without the discourse connectors, and pass it out to the class. Ask the students to insert appropriate connectors in the blank spaces. You can do this as a group task that culminates in a class discussion of why certain choices are appropriate, or this can be a teacher-fronted activity where everyone makes his or her choice and then you lead a summarizing discussion. Avoid producing a passage that has too many blanks, as the result may be unnatural or otherwise too difficult.

Discourse Markers

There are various reasons why ESL teachers might want to expose their students to at least a limited number of discourse markers: (1) discourse markers appear so regularly in spoken English that an ability to recognize high-frequency markers and their functions in conversation will enable students to improve their oral comprehension; (2) discourse markers may enable students to express themselves more naturally and colloquially; (3) students can use discourse markers, as native speakers can, to hold the floor more effectively in a conversation, make smoother transitions, and eliminate awkward pauses while searching for a word.[30] In an EFL context, students might be helped with their oral comprehension. Some English language teaching textbooks actually include quite a few examples of discourse markers[31] and even limited discussion of them.[32]

These arguments in favor of teaching discourse markers should be weighed against two counterarguments. First, it is quite possible that ESL students will pick up the use of many discourse markers just by listening to native speaker speech. Second, there is a strong stigma attached to frequent use of certain discourse markers. Although frequent use of *like* and *ya know* seems to be tolerated in preteens and teens, adults who pepper their speech with *like* and *ya know* may be viewed as inarticulate.

If you feel that your students could benefit from some instruction in discourse markers, the following lesson, designed for an ESL class, offers an example of how this could be done.[33]

Activity 3: Understanding and Using *Like* in Conversation (High Intermediate)

This activity is based on *like*, chosen because it has a range of functions that vary in acceptability. The process used here can be extended to other discourse markers.

Step 1: Review some of the different functions of *like* other than as a discourse marker: (1) a verb meaning "enjoy, appreciate, be fond of " (*I like classical music and jazz*); (2) a preposition meaning "in the manner of " (*That description fits him like a glove; Habit grips a person like an octopus*) and "with the characteristics of " (*I don't eat things like that*); (3) a conjunction of comparison meaning "the same way" (*She looks just like she looked the last time we saw her*) and "as if, as though" (*You look like you've seen a ghost*). Provide examples of these meanings and ask the students to describe them.

Step 2: Present a simple dialog that exemplifies the use of *like* as a discourse marker of salience, as shown in (60). You can perform the dialog yourself, or you can play a dialog that you have recorded. Television programs that feature teenagers can be a source of material or ideas. Here is part of a dialog from a TV program. A female high school student is discussing friendships.

> **(60)** I think a lot has to do with humor, 'cuz like, my best friend, we laugh at the dumb-est things that no one else would laugh at. And, I mean, that just like, creates a bond because you can laugh at the dumbest things.

Ask the students to guess the meaning of *like* and how it is being used. Repeat the dialog. You might show the dialog on an overhead projector and underline the words that come after *like*. If they have trouble explaining what they feel *like* means, point out that each instance of *like* comes before something that the speaker thinks is important.

Next model the "approximately" meaning of *like* in a sentence such as in (61):

> **(61)** Wow. Some parts of Los Angeles really have a lot of palm trees. On this street I've seen like twenty-five already.

Point out that this is a very common use of *like*.

Step 3: Now present another dialog, as shown in (62), this time with *like* used as a substi-tute for *said*.

> **(62)** He's like, "I dunno." And I'm like, "Well, you're supposed to be the big expert."

Ask the students if *like* in the sentences is being used in any of the ways that you have been talk-ing about. Then ask students what they think this *like* means. As you discuss its function here, you can stress the sociolinguistic aspects by asking students whether they think this is formal or informal English and who they think might be most likely to use *like* this way. These kinds of questions should lead the discussion in a direction that results in the students recognizing that this use of *like* is slangy and appears primarily in the speech of younger people. They should also realize that, while this use is not acceptable in formal contexts and although older people often don't like it, it is not necessarily "bad" English. You might want to talk about the situations in which this use of *like* or the overuse of *like* generally could prove irritating to listeners.

Although this familiarization activity is probably adequate, if the students want to try us-ing *like*, you should model the distinct intonation (quick, falling) that accompanies it. Some repetition practice of sentences with *like* in its salience use and sentences with *like* in its use with reported speech might be in order. Then split the students into groups of two to three and have them discuss informal topics such as friendships, dating, parents, and daily activities.

ENDNOTES

[1] Halliday and Hasan (1976).

[2] Huddleston and Pullum (2002).

[3] Quirk et al. (1985).

[4] Biber et al. (1999).

[5] Celce-Murcia and Larsen-Freeman (1999), p. 530.

[6] As Fraser (1999), p. 932, points out, over the past decade, dozens of articles on "discourse markers" have been produced. Many attempts to distinguish between what I am defining as discourse connectors and discourse markers blur the distinction between these two categories and include constituents like coordination conjunctions in sentence initial position as members of the former. The terms used to designate these two categories also vary considerably.

7 This example is from Halliday and Hasan (1976), p. 251.

8 These are often referred to as *enumerative conjuncts*.

9 "Independent, Diligent, Committed." in Letters to the Editor, the *Wall Street Journal*, March 26, 2004.

10 "Transfer in SLA and Creoles," Rena Helms-Park, *Studies in Second Language Learning*, 25, 2003, p. 220.

11 Quirk et al.'s term *appositive* (to indicate that the information they introduce is equivalent to previous information) is generally recognized. Biber et al. (1999), p. 876, refer to them as *adverbials of apposition*.

12 Yip (1995), p. 80.

13 Williams (1996).

14 The term *attitudinal* and the definition are from Quirk et al. (1974), p. 666.

15 This observation is due to Quirk et al. (1974), p. 676.

16 The *Wall Street Journal*, de Gustibus John H. Fund. March 26, 2004, W11.

17 The *Wall Street Journal*, March 25, 2004. Politics and People, Albert R. Hunt, A17.

18 Biber et al. (1999), p. 885.

19 I am indebted to Kent Lee for granting me permission to adapt much of his unpublished paper *Teaching, like, discourse markers*, which was presented at TESOL 2001. Some of the examples in this section are also his.

20 Green (2002).

21 A partial list of some of the research in this area would include Andersen (2000), Brinton (1996), Romaine and Lange (1991), König (1991), James (1983), Miller and Weinert (1995), Schiffrin (1987), Schourup (1983), and Wilson and Sperber (1993).

22 Biber et al. (1999), p. 1087.

23 This characterization comes from Biber et al. (1999), p. 1086.

24 Heritage (1977).

25 Biber et al. (1999), p. 1087.

26 Schourup (1983).

27 Miller and Weinert (1995).

28 For example, in Oshima and Hogue (1999).

29 This activity was suggested by Howard Williams.

30 These arguments are advanced by Lee (2001).

31 These are sometimes books that bill themselves as "conversation management" texts, for example, McClure (1996).

32 Carter, Hughes, and McCarthy (2000), pp. 178–179, for example.

33 Adapted from "Teaching the colloquial particle *like*." MS. Kent Lee.

REFERENCES

Altenberg. B. (1986). Contrastive linking in spoken and written English. In G. Tottie & I. Bäcklund (Eds.), *English Speech in Writing* (pp. 13–40). Uppsala: Semqvist & Wiksell International.

Andersen, G. (2000). The role of the pragmatic marker *like* in utterance interpretation. In G. Anderson & T. Fretheim (Eds.), *Pragmatic markers and prepositional attitude* (pp.1–22). Amsterdam: John Benjamins.

Biber, D., Johansson, S., Leech, G., Conrad, S., & Finegan, E. (1999). *Longman grammar of spoken and written English*. Essex: Pearson Education, Limited.

Blakemore, D. (2002). *Relevance and linguistic meaning: The semantics and pragmatics of discourse markers*. Cambridge: Cambridge University Press.

Brinton, L. J. (1996). *Pragmatic markers in English*. New York: Mouton de Gruyter.

Carter, R., Hughes, R., & McCarthy, M. (2000). *Exploring grammar in context: Grammar reference and practice upper-intermediate and advanced*. Cambridge: Cambridge University Press.

Celce-Murcia, M., & Larsen-Freeman, D. (1999). *The grammar book: An ESL/EFL teacher's course,* 2nd ed. Boston: Heinle & Heinle.

Connor, U. (1984). A study of cohesion and coherence in English as a second language students' writing. *Papers in Linguistics, International Journal of Communication, 17*(3), 301–316.

Crewe, W. (1990). The illogic of logical connectives. *ELT Journal, 44*(4), 316–325.

Field, Y., & Yip, L. M. O. (1992). A comparison of internal cohesive conjunction in the English essay writing of Cantonese speakers and native speakers of English. *RELC Journal, 23*(1), 15–28.

Fraser, B. (1999). What are discourse markers? *Journal of Pragmatics, 31*, 931–952.

Granger, S., & Tyson, S. (1996). Connector usage in the English essay writing of native and non-native EFL speakers of English. *World Englishes, 15*(1), 17–21.

Green, G. (2002). Discourse particles in natural language processing. www.linguistics.uiuc.edu/g-green/discours.pdf

Halliday, M. A. K., & Hasan, R. (1976). *Cohesion in English*. London: Longman.

Heritage, J. (1977). A change-of-state token and aspects of sequential placement. In J. M. Atkinson & J. Heritage (Eds.), *Structures of social action*. Cambridge: Cambridge University Press.

Huddleston, R., & Pullum, G. K. (2002). *The Cambridge grammar of the English language*. Cambridge: Cambridge University Press.

James, A. R. (1983). Compromises in English: A cross-disciplinary to their interpersonal experience. *Journal of Pragmatics, 7*, 191–206.

Kahlil, A. (1989). A study of cohesion in Arab EFL college students' writing. *System, 17*(3), 359–371.

König, E. (1991). *The meaning of focus particles*. New York: Routledge.

Lee, K. (2001). Teaching the colloquial particle *like*. MS.

Martel, G. (1991). Les connecteurs: Problèmes particuliers à l'analyse différentielle du discours. *Langues et Linguistique, 17*, 159–167.

McClure, K. (1996). *Putting it together: A conversational management text*. Upper Saddle River, New Jersey: Prentice Hall Regents.

Miller, J., & Weinert, R. (1995). The function of LIKE in dialogue. *Journal of Pragmatics, 23*, 365–393.

Milton, J., & Tsang, E. S. C. (1993). A corpus-based study of logical connectors in EFL students' writing: Directions for future research. In R. Pemberton & E. S. C. Tsang (Eds.), *Studies in lexis* (pp. 215–246). Hong Kong: The Hong Kong University of Science and Technology.

Oshima, A., & Hogue, A. (1999). *Writing academic English*. White Plains, NY: Addison Wesley Longman.

Quirk, R., Greenbaum, S., Leech, G., & Svartvik, J. (1972). *A grammar of contemporary English*. New York/London: Seminary Press.

Quirk, R., Greenbaum, S., Leech, G., & Svartvik, J. (1985). *A comprehensive grammar of the English language*. London: Longman.

Romaine S., & Lange, D. (1991). The use of *like* as a marker of reported speech and thought: A case of grammaticalization in process. *American Speech, 66*, 227–279.

Schiffrin, D. 1987. *Discourse Markers*. Cambridge: Cambridge University Press.

Schourup, L. (1983). Common discourse particles in English conversation. Working Papers in Linguistics, Vol. 28. Ohio State University.

Underhill, R. (1988). Like is, like, focus. *American Speech, 63.3*, 234–246.

Williams, H. (1996). *An analysis of English conjunctive adverbial expressions in English*. Ph.D. Dissertation, UCLA.

Wilson, D., & Sperber, D. (1993). Linguistic form and relevance. *Lingua, 90*, 1–25.

Yip, V. (1995). *Interlanguage and learnability: From Chinese to English*. Amsterdam/Philadelphia: John Benjamins.

Common Multiword Verbs

Phrasal Verbs

Separable Transitive Phrasal Verbs

They called off the meeting.   *They called it off.*

back up (= support)
bear out (= support)
beef up (= fortify)
blow up (= inflate)
break in (= make usable)
break out (= unveil,
  make available)
bring up (= broach)
bring off (= execute a task
  successfully)
brush off (= reject)
call off (= abandon, cancel)
call up (= telephone)
carry out (= execute)
clean up (= make clean
  and tidy)
clean out (= remove
  all objects)
clear up (= resolve)
carry out (= execute)
check out (= investigate)
empty out (= remove
  something from a container)
figure out (= solve, find
  a solution)
fill in (= supply information)
fill out (= complete a form)

get back (= reacquire)
give back (= return)
give up (= abandon)
hand in (= submit)
hand out (= distribute)
hand over (= give something
  to someone)
hold up (= delay)
jot down (= write)
keep out (= deny access)
leave out (= omit)
line up (= form in a line)
lock in (= secure)
look over (= examine)
look up (= find information)
make out (= discern,
  recognize)
make up (= fabricate)
open up (= unlock a door,
  show something hidden)
pay back (= settle debts,
  get revenge)
pick out (= select)
pick up (= acquire,
  obtain, fetch)
point out (= indicate)
put off (= postpone)

put on (= dress)
put out (= place outside,
  extinguish)
rule out (= eliminate)
set up (= arrange, erect)
sort out (= separate, solve)
spread out (= move apart,
  unfold)
take on (= undertake)
try on (= test for size)
try out (= test)
take off (= undress)
take on (= assume)
talk over (= discuss)
track down (= find, locate)
turn down (= refuse)
turn off (= deactivate)
turn on (= activate)
turn over (= place with
  other side up)
use up (= exhaust supply)
work out (= develop, solve)
work over (= beat badly)
wrap up (= cover, finish)
zip up (= close)

Inseparable Transitive Phrasal Verbs

I will look into it. **I will look it into.*

bump into (= encounter)
come across (= discover)
come by (= acquire)
come upon (= encounter)
get over (= recover from)
fall for (= become attracted to)
hit on (= make romantic overtures to)

level with (= tell the truth to)
look after (= care for someone)
look into (= investigate)
pick on (= mistreat)
run across (= discover)
run into (= encounter)
stand by (= support)

Permanently Separated Transitive Phrasal Verbs

All this arguing is getting Fred/him down. **All this arguing is getting down Fred/him.*

ask [someone] out (= invite)
do [something] over (= redo)
get [someone] down (= depress)
let [someone] off (= excuse or reduce punishment)
narrow[something] down (= reduce)
put [someone] on (= kid, fool)
see [something] through (= complete)
string [someone] along (= delude)

Intransitive Phrasal Verbs

PURE INTRANSITIVE PHRASAL VERBS

I don't know anyone who does that sort of thing, but I'll ask around.

ask around (= inquire)
back down (= retreat)
back up (= reverse direction)
bend over (= incline body forward)
branch out (= extend)
butt in (= interrupt)
butt out (= stop involving oneself)
check in (= register)
check out (= leave)
come forward (= present oneself)
come over (= visit)
drop around/by/over (= visit)
fight back (= resist)
forge ahead (= progress)
get away (= escape)
get by (= survive)
get together (= meet)
get up (= arise)

give in (= surrender)
hang around (= stay in one place)
hang out (= socialize, be with)
leave off (= stop)
line up (= form a line)
move on (= keep moving)
pay up (= make payment)
set off (= begin a journey)
settle down (= become calm)
shut up (= stop talking)
sit down (= seat oneself)
sit up (= elevate oneself from a prone position)
slip up (= make a mistake)
start off/out (= begin)
stay on (= continue)
strike out (= lose, begin a journey)
take off (= leave the ground)
throw up (= vomit)

Ergative Phrasal Verbs

UNPAIRED ERGATIVE PHRASAL VERBS

Finally, the storm began to die down.

break down (= stop functioning)
break up (= disintegrate)
catch on (= become popular)
come apart (= disintegrate)
come up (= arise)
crop up (= appear)
die down (= abate)
die out (= disappear)
doze off (= fall asleep)
drag on (= continue too long)
dry up (= end [supply of money,
   food, water, etc.])

end up (= finish)
fall behind (= lose ground)
fall out (= become loose and come out)
grow up (= mature, increase)
pass away (= die)
pass out (= become unconscious)
show up (= appear)
sink in (= become comprehensible)
taper off (= decrease)
wind down (= decrease)

PAIRED ERGATIVE PHRASAL VERBS

The ship blew up.   ergative   *The enemy blew up the bridge.*   *transitive counterpart*

blow up	cheer up	thaw out
break off	clear up (= weather)	wake up
break up	close down	warm up
build up	heat up	wear down
burn down	open up	wear out
burn up	slow down	

Prepositional Verbs

He laughed at her jokes.

abide by
account for
agree on
allow for
apply for
approve of
ask for
bank on
call for (= require)
call on (= visit)
comment on
conform to
consent to
consist of
contribute to
decide on
depend on
differ from
enlarge on (= expand in greater detail)
go through (= search, pass through)
hint at
hope for
insist on

laugh at
lead to
lie about
listen to
look at
look for
object to
part with
reason with
refer to
resort to
result in
see about (= attend to something)
serve as
smile at
stand for (= represent)
stare at
tamper with
wait for
wait on
watch for
worry about

Phrasal Prepositional Verbs

He got away with murder.

break in on (= interrupt)
cash in on (= take advantage of)
come in for (= be due or receive criticism/praise, etc.)
come up with (= produce, devise)
come down to (= amount to)
come down with (= contract)
cry out for (= seriously require)
cut in on (= interrupt)
do away with (= exterminate)
face up to (= acknowledge)
fall back on (= rely on if necessary)
get along with (= coexist peacefully)
get away with (= escape without punishment)
get in on (= become involved or a part of)
get out of (= avoid doing something, escape)
go along with (= accept, cooperate)
go out for (= become engaged in an activity)
go through with (= carry out, execute, e.g., a plan)
hold on to (= retain)
look down on (= hold in lesser esteem)
look forward to (= anticipate)
look in on (= visit, call on)
look up to (= admire)
measure up to (= meet a standard)
own up to (= admit)
pick up on (= comprehend)
play along with (= cooperate)
put up with (= tolerate)
run up against (= encounter)
stand up to (= withstand pressure or scrutiny)

They let him in on the secret.

bring (someone/something) in on (= enlist the help of someone/something)
put (someone) up to (= induce someone to do something)
put (something) down to (= ascribe something to)
play (someone) off against (= create strife between two people)
take (something) out on (= direct anger, frustration at someone)

Adjective Phrases

The following are some common adjective + preposition combinations. Adjectives preceded by an asterisk (*) are more limited to the combinations in which they are shown.[1] Many of these adjective + preposition combinations can be followed by a gerund, e.g., *He is afraid [of heights]* and *He is afraid [of frightening her]*.

Adjective [*about* NP]

He was happy about the result.

angry about	furious about	mad about
annoyed about	glad about	pleased about
concerned about	happy about	relieved about
cross about	irritated about	upset about
delighted about	knowledgeable about	

Adjective [*at* NP]

John is brilliant at chess.

*adept at	angry at	delighted at	*hopeless at	puzzled at
*aghast at	astonished at	disgusted at	*indignant at	skilled at
alarmed at	bad at	gifted at	mad at	superb at
amazed at	brilliant at	good at	marvelous at	talented at
amused at	clever at	great at	pleased at	terrible at

Adjective [*by* NP]

The other members of his department were unaffected by the changes.

amused by
*burdened by
distressed by
*unaffected by
*unperturbed by

Adjective [*for* NP]

Alan is responsible for the team's success this year.

answerable for	greedy for
*bad for	necessary for
difficult for	prepared for
eager for	*responsible for
easy for	sorry for
good for	

Adjective [*from* NP]

This one is completely different from the other one.

descended from	immune from
*different from	*remote from
*distant from	removed from
*divorced from	safe from
distinct from	separated from
free from	

Adjective [*in* NP]

She was quite confident in her abilities.

bathed in	*fortunate in
clothed in	*inherent in
confident in	interested in
covered in	*lacking in
*dressed in	lucky in
embroiled in	secure in
*engaged in	steeped in

Adjective [*of* NP]

She is afraid of large dogs.

afraid of	*cognizant of	*fond of	proud of	suggestive of
ashamed of	conscious of	full of	reminiscent of	supportive of
aware of	convinced of	ignorant of	representative of	sure of
capable of	desirous of	illustrative of	respectful of	tired of
certain of	*devoid of	indicative of	scared of	wary of
characteristic of	distrustful of	*mindful of	short of	worthy of

Adjective [*on/upon* NP]²

You were too easy on him.

based on/upon	big on
bent on/upon	easy on
contingent on/upon	hard on
dependent on/upon	keen on
incumbent on/upon	severe on
intent on/upon	sweet on

Adjective [*to* NP]

I'm allergic to shellfish.

*accustomed to	conducive to	hostile to	mean to	resistant to
adjacent to	connected to	*immune to	nice to	responsible to
allergic to	devoted to	impervious to	opposed to	*similar to
answerable to	*due to	inclined to	*prone to	*subject to
*attributable to	equal to	inferior to	proportional to	subordinate to
attuned to	equivalent to	injurious to	receptive to	subservient to
averse to	generous to	insensible to	reconciled to	superior to
close to	good to	integral to	related to	susceptible to
comparable to	hospitable to	kind to	resigned to	tantamount to

Adjective [*with* NP]

He was furious with his wife.

angry with	*consonant with	enchanted with	happy with	satisfied with
annoyed with	content with	familiar with	harsh with	sick with
bored with	*conversant with	fed up with	impatient with	skillful with
busy with	covered with	firm with	obsessed with	stricken with
careful with	cross with	*fraught with	occupied with	strict with
cautious with	delighted with	friendly with	parallel with	*taken with
comfortable with	disappointed with	furious with	pleased with	*tinged with
compatible with	disgusted with	gentle with	reckless with	
concerned with	effective with	good with	*riddled with	

---

¹ This list was compiled mainly from Huddleston and Pullum (2002) and the *Collins Cobuild English Grammar* (1994).

² The adjectives in the first column take *on* or *upon*. The adjectives in the second column are more informal and take only *on*.

Verbs That Take Indirect Objects

1. *To* **dative verbs** that optionally take the *dative movement* rule:

Send the money to my sister. *prepositional pattern*
Send my sister the money. *dative movement pattern*

allot	hand	play	slip
assign	hand back	preach	supply
award	issue	quote	take
bring	leave[1]	read	teach
cable	lend	rent	tell
cede	loan	sell	throw
feed	mail	send	toss
forward	offer	serve	type
give	owe	ship	wire
give back	pass	show	write
grant	pay	sing	

2. *To* **dative verbs** that are restricted to the prepositional pattern:

She explained the problem to us. *prepositional pattern*
*She explained us the problem.

administer	display	propose	roll
admit	donate	push	say
announce	explain	recite	slide
confess	extend	recommend	state
contribute	float	recount	submit
convey	haul	relay	suggest
communicate	illustrate	repeat	transfer
declare	indicate	report	transport
describe	introduce	restore	
deliver	mention	return	
demonstrate	narrate	reveal	

3. *For* **dative verbs** that optionally take the *dative movement* rule:

She baked a cake for him.   *prepositional pattern*
She baked him a cake.   *dative movement pattern*

bake	choose	draw	get	order	plow	save
boil	cook	draw up	guarantee	pack	prepare	sing
build	cut	fetch	hire	paint	print	spare
buy	design	find	leave	peel	quote	
call	dig	fix[2]	make	pick out	reserve	
catch	do	fry	mix	play	roast	

4. *For* **dative verbs** that are restricted to the prepositional word order:

She corrected the papers for him.   *prepositional pattern*
*She corrected him the papers.

acquire	collate	dance	kill	repeat	take over
answer	complete	eat	look over	retrieve	unload
capture	compose	examine	obtain	sacrifice	whistle
carry	copy	finish	plan	select	
cash	correct	fix[3]	recite	sew	
clean up	create	guard	remove	take down	

5. Idioms that are restricted to the *dative movement* word order:

She really gives me a pain.
*She really gives a pain to me.

drop someone a line (= write)   lend someone a hand (= help)
give someone flack (= admonish)   give someone a kick (= kick)
give someone a pain (= annoy)   give someone a shove (= shove)
give someone the ax (= fire, dismiss)   give someone a ring (= call)
give someone a wide berth (= avoid)

6. Idioms that are restricted to the prepositional word order:

He went to bat for me.
*He went me to bat.

give substance to something (= make believable)
give way to (= lead to something)
give credence to (= make believable)
give assistance to (= help)
give birth to (= have a baby)
give rise to (= lead to something happening)
go the extra mile for someone (= make an extra effort)
go to bat for someone (= help, assist, defend)
lend an ear to (= listen to)
lend support to (= support)
pay attention to (= attend to)
pay homage to (= honor)
stand up for someone (= defend)

---

[1] meaning = *bequeath*

[2] meaning = *prepare*

[3] meaning = *repair*

Answer Key to Exercises

CHAPTER 2 GRAMMATICAL TERMS

2.1, page 15

1. *governor* = noun
2. *put* = verb; *in* = preposition
3. *tall* = adjective; *spoke* = verb; *very* = degree adverb; *rapidly* = adverb
4. *ran* = verb; *across* = preposition; *bridge* = noun; *jumped* = verb; *into* = preposition; *red* = adjective
5. *Jan* = noun; *turned* = verb; *slowly* = adverb; *her* = possessive determiner; *sister* = noun

2.2, page 15

1. Ann bought a [new car].
   NP
2. [The young senator] sat [beside the president].
   NP   PP
3. His wife spoke [very softly].
   AdvP
4. [[The police]] [arrested [the two thieves]].
   NP   VP   NP
5. My brother is [in the library].
   PP
6. Mary is [extremely intelligent].
   AdjP

2.3, page 18

1. *those* = demonstrative determiner; *they* = personal pronoun; *these* = demonstrative pronoun; *fresh* = adjective
2. *That* = demonstrative determiner; *mine* = possessive pronoun
3. *All* = quantifier; *his* = possessive determiner
4. *this* = demonstrative pronoun; *the* = definite article; *those* = demonstrative determiner
5. *Reading a long paper* = gerund
6. *Our* = possessive determiner; *Yours* = possessive pronoun; *an* = indefinite article; *annual* = adjective
7. *she* = personal pronoun; *your* = possessive determiner

2.4, page 20

1. *the head of the department* = appositive; *the appointment* = direct object
2. *your glasses* = direct object; *the glove compartment* = object of the preposition *in*
3. *her sister* = indirect object; *an e-mail* = direct object
4. *my brother* = subject; *an anesthesiologist* = predicate nominal
5. *a large painting* = direct object; *the fireplace* = object of the preposition *over*

2.5, page 24

1. *take* = bare infinitive
2. *tries* = tensed verb; *to write* = infinitive
3. *helped* = past participle; *has* = auxiliary verb
4. *took* = tensed form of the irregular verb *take*
5. *to do* = infinitive
6. *haven't* = auxiliary verb; *talked* = past participle
7. *working* = present participle; *may* = modal verb; *be* = auxiliary verb

2.6, page 24

1. *knocked* = transitive; *broke* = paired ergative verb (transitive counterpart = *He broke
   the vase.*)
2. *hit* = transitive verb
3. *own* = stative verb
4. *weighs* = stative verb
5. *died* = unpaired ergative verb
6. *rolled* = paired ergative verb; (transitive counterpart = *She rolled the ball.*);
   bounced = paired ergative verb; (transitive
   counterpart = *She bounced the ball.*)
7. *signed* = transitive verb
8. *ran* = intransitive verb

2.7, page 26

1. *She sold the house* = independent clause
   because she needed the money = adverbial
   subordinate clause
2. *The professors will travel to Stockholm* =
   independent clause
   who were chosen by the Nobel committee =
   relative clause
3. *Susan stayed home* = independent clause
   Alice went to the basketball game =
   independent (coordinate clause)
4. *He grasped her firmly around the waist* =
   independent clause
   in order to lift her off the ground =
   adverbial subordinate clause
5. *I had never met the guy* = independent clause
   who sold her the car = relative clause

2.8, page 26

1. *to take a break* = infinitive complement
2. *that they will come to the reunion* = *that*
   complement
3. *watching sports on television* = gerund
   complement
4. *when he will finish it* = embedded question
   complement
5. *arguing about politics* = gerund complement

CHAPTER 4 QUESTIONS

4.1, page 66

1. expectation (He must have told you.)
2. no expectation
3. expectation (I thought she was coming.)
4. no expectation
5. expectation (I think someone might have
   called.)

4.2, page 66

1. to show surprise
2. to confirm information
3. to check information

4.3, page 70

1. falling (speaker expects interlocutor to
   agree)
2. rising (speaker is seeking information)
3. falling (speaker expects the interlocutor to
   agree)
4. starts low, jumps up (speaker has reached
   the conclusion stated in the question)
5. falling (speaker expects interlocutor to
   agree)

4.4, page 70

1. asking for information
2. polite request
3. making an observation that is obvious
   (British English)
4. suggestion
5. sarcastic statement
6. exclamation

4.5, page 75

1. information question — How do you get to New Orleans from here?

2. *elaborate please* question — Where in California?

3. information question — How much does this cost?

4. *elaborate please* question — When?

5. *repeat please* question — Who told you about it?

4.6, page 78

1. echo question   B: She always has lunch where?

2. alternative question   A: Do you like the blue one or the red one?

3. echo question   B: Have I seen your glasses?

4. display question   A: So this essay discusses what?

5. exclamatory question   A: Isn't she a beauty?

6. rhetorical question   B: Who hasn't?

CHAPTER 5 NEGATION

5.1, page 93

1. ungrammatical (*Much* is a negative polarity item.)
   correction: *She doesn't visit her grandmother much.*
2. grammatical
3. ungrammatical (*Yet* is a negative polarity item.)
   correction: *I haven't read the newspaper yet.*
4. grammatical
5. ungrammatical (*Some* is a positive polarity item.)
   correction: *There aren't any cherries in the bowl.*

5.2, page 96

1. debatable (*Not* should appear before the infinitive complement *to call*, but many native speakers prefer this word order)
2. grammatical (*Not* should appear before the infinitive complement, *to show up*; however, many native speakers prefer the order with *not* in the complement.)
3. grammatical
4. ungrammatical (*Not* should appear before *thinking.*)
   correction: *I sat on the bus not thinking about my destination.*
5. grammatical (The sentence means "*You must take the test.*")

5.3, page 97

1. Sentence (a) means she did delete all of her e-mail messages, but she didn't do it on purpose. Sentence (b) means that she purposely did not delete all of her e-mail messages.
2. Sentence (a) means exactly what it says: she doesn't dislike classical music. Sentence (b) implies that she dislikes other kinds of music but not classical music.
3. Sentence (a) means that the winner did not take credit for the changes and that she did this intentionally. Sentence (b) means that she did take credit for the changes, but she did not do this on purpose.
4. Sentence (a) means that my brother doesn't enjoy watching news programs on TV. Sentence (b) implies that I have other family members who do enjoy watching news programs, but my brother does not.

5.4, page 97

1. The sentences mean essentially the same thing even though many native speakers tend to prefer (b), which has undergone negative raising.
2. They have the same meaning.
3. The two sentences have different meanings because the verb *understand* in the main clause does not permit *negative raising*. Sentence (a) means she understood something, and that was that he did not want to come. Sentence (b) means that what she didn't understand was that he actually wanted to come.
4. The sentences mean essentially the same thing even though many native speakers tend to prefer (a), which has undergone negative raising.

5.5, page 102

1. There was no one that we knew at the party.
2. There are no more muffins left.
3. I saw nothing suspicious.
4. She was nowhere near the accident when it happened.
5. He saw neither John nor Susan.
6. None of the people who usually attend these concerts came this time.

5.6, pages 102–103

1. ungrammatical (Although often heard in spoken English, double negatives like this example may be considered to be examples of "uneducated" English.)
   correction: *I've never seen anything like that.*
2. ungrammatical (subject–aux inversion is needed when negative *not often* or *seldom* occur initially in a sentence.)
   correction: *Not often will you have a streak of luck like that.*
3. grammatical
4. ungrammatical (*indefensible*, not *undefensible*)
5. ungrammatical (As in item 1, double negatives may be considered examples of "uneducated" English.)
   correction: *I didn't do anything wrong.*
6. grammatical
7. grammatical

CHAPTER 6 IMPERATIVE SENTENCES
6.1, page 115

1. *let's* imperative
2. imperative with visible subject
3. emphatic imperative
4. basic imperative
5. open imperative (not a true *let* imperative)
6. imperative with visible subject
7. vocative imperative
8. *I need you* imperative

6.2, page 118

1. acceptance (accepting someone's decision although you disagree with it)
2. advice (advising someone who wants to play the stock market)
3. invitation (inviting someone to a social event)
4. command (giving a command in the military)

5. instructions (operating a machine such as a VCR)
6. wish (ending a conversation)
7. expository directive (making a point in a discussion)

6.3, page 120

1. noncontrastive (reassurance)
2. contrastive
3. noncontrastive (threatening)
4. noncontrastive (emphasizing importance)
5. noncontrastive (speaker A = irritation; speaker B = angry admonition)

CHAPTER 7 NONREFERENTIAL *IT* AND *THERE*
7.1, page 132

1. nonreferential
2. referential
3. nonreferential
4. nonreferential
5. referential
6. nonreferential
7. nonreferential

7.2, page 136

1. nonreferential
2. referential; *there* = hotel
3. nonreferential
4. nonreferential
5. referential; *there* = Caspian Sea

7.3, page 136

1. grammatical
2. ungrammatical (The verb *is* doesn't agree in number with *characters*.)
3. ungrammatical (The verb *is* doesn't agree in number with *ways*.)
4. grammatical
5. grammatical

7.4, page 138

1. shift the focus
2. call something to mind
3. respond to question regarding existence of something
4. introduce new information

CHAPTER 8 PREPOSITIONS

8.1, page 152

1. prepositional verb (A *who/whom* question can be formed and answered with a noun phrase: *On whom did she depend? Who did she depend on? Her neighbors.*)
2. prepositional phrase (A *where* question can be formed and answered with a prepositional phrase: *Where did they drive? Across the river.* The phrase *across the river* can be moved to the beginning of the sentence: *Across the river they drove.* [prepositional movement test])
3. prepositional verb (A *what* question can be formed and answered with a noun phrase: *What did you look at? His application.*)
4. prepositional verb (A *what* question can be formed and answered with a noun phrase: *What does UAE stand for? United Arab Emirates.*)
5. prepositional phrase (A *where* question can be formed and answered with a prepositional phrase: *Where are my keys? On the table.*)
6. prepositional phrases (*Where* questions can be formed and answered with prepositional phrases: *Where did you walk? Around the plaza. Where did you stop? Beside the monument.*)

8.2, pages 152–153

1. *in full* = Prep + Adj
2. *furious with* = Adj + Prep
3. *in return for* = Prep + NP + Prep (idiom)
4. *in compliance with* = Prep + NP + Prep (idiom)
5. *on the condition* = Prep followed by a *that* clause
6. *From inside* = Prep + Prep
7. *In brief* = Prep + adjective combination

8.3, page 161

1. *with* = instrumental
2. *at* = goal
3. *off* = source; *onto* = goal
4. *in* = fixed static location
5. *by* = static location
6. *to* = goal; *through* = intermediate location
7. *with* = comitative
8. *with* = instrumental

8.4, page 162

1. *by* = passing of time
2. *over* = spanning a period
3. *by* = no later than
4. *with* = location
5. *by* = a margin of
6. *under* = in (a little) less than
7. *by* = unit of measurement

CHAPTER 9 MULTIWORD VERBS

9.1, page 175

1. *dry up* = ergative
2. *came upon* = inseparable transitive
3. *made up* = separable transitive
4. *hand out* = separable transitive
5. *got away* = pure intransitive
6. *break up* = paired ergative
7. *stringing along* = permanently separated transitive
8. *getting together* = pure intransitive

9.2, pages 178–179

1. *figured out* = phrasal verb (transitive) (It takes particle movement: *He figured the answer out.* It doesn't take adverb insertion: **He figured the answer quickly out.* The particle can't occur at the beginning of a relative clause, **The answer out which he figured*, or a *wh-* question, **Out what did he figure?*)
2. *comment on* = prepositional verb (It doesn't take particle movement: **He commented the proposal on.* It takes adverb insertion: *He commented extensively on the proposal.* The preposition can occur at the beginning of a relative clause, *The proposal on which he commented*, or a *wh-* question, *On what did he comment?*)
3. *getting over* = phrasal verb (inseparable transitive) (It doesn't take particle movement: **The strain of flu over which he got.* It doesn't take adverb insertion: **He got quickly over the flu.* The particle can't occur at the beginning of a relative clause or a *wh-* question: **Over what did he get?*)
4. *catching on* = phrasal verb (intransitive) (Since *catch on* can't take a direct object and there are no intransitive prepositional verbs, this must be a phrasal verb.)
5. *getting John down* = phrasal verb (permanently separated) (As the NP *John* comes between the verb, *get*, and other element, *out*, this cannot be a prepositional verb.)

9.3, page 179

1. phrasal verbs
2. There are three subclasses of transitive phrasal verbs: separable (*fill out*), inseparable (*bump into*), and permanently separated (*brush [someone] off*). There are two subclasses of intransitive phrasal verbs: pure intransitives (*get away*) and ergatives (*break down*). Within the ergative subclass, there are unpaired and paired ergatives (*break down* and *wear out*, respectively).

9.4, page 180

1. *be aware of* = a construction that looks like a prepositional verb (*be* + Adj + *of* NP)
2. *listened to* = a prepositional verb
3. *scrub the pot clean* = a construction that looks like a prepositional verb (verb + NP + Adj)
4. *do away with* = a phrasal prepositional verb
5. *broke out* = intransitive phrasal verb followed by a prepositional phrase (You can say both *They broke out* and *They broke out of prison.*)
6. *looks down on* = a phrasal prepositional verb

CHAPTER 10 DETERMINERS

10.1, pages 188–189

1. *the* = article, *first* = ordinal number, *two* = cardinal number
2. *his* = possessive determiner, *both* = quantifier (The order of these two elements is incorrect. Quantifiers precede possessive determiners.) Correction: *Both (of) his sisters.*
3. *one-third* = fraction, *her* = possessive determiner, *last* = ordinal number
4. *that* = demonstrative determiner, *my* = possessive determiner, *brother's* = noun as possessive determiner; *twentieth* = ordinal number
5. *bags of* = partitive, *twice* = multiplier, *your* = possessive determiner
6. *a bunch* = partitive, *a loaf* = partitive

10.2, page 193

1. *tenth* = ungrammatical (Ordinal numbers are preceded by an article, usually a definite one.)
   correction: *the tenth* student
2. *this* = grammatical

3. *one* = ungrammatical (Cardinal numbers can't precede a noncount noun such as *luggage* unless there is another expression that specifies the unit.)
   correction: *one more piece of*
4. *half* = ungrammatical (Fractions cannot precede a noun. They are followed by an article such as *the*.)
   correction: *half the size*
5. *two* = ungrammatical (Cardinal numbers can't precede a noncount noun such as *furniture* unless there is another expression that specifies quantity.)
   correction: *two pieces of furniture*

10.3, page 193

1. *This guy* is new information.
2. *That summer* marks time farther back in the past. *This summer* indicates now.
3. *This* with the adjective *wonderful* conveys the idea that the book is of high relevance to the speaker.
4. *That* before the NP *theoretical point* is used to define a concept.
5. *Those* refers to mistakes that the listener knows about.

10.4, page 200

1. *Each* cannot appear after the infinitive *to go*.
   correction: *They each wanted to go.*
2. Quantifier pronoun–flip has not been applied. It should be applied.
   correction: *so she bought them all.*
3. *Each* can't appear after *cost*, but it could appear after *dollars*.
   correction: *Those T-shirts cost fifteen dollars each.*
4. *Both* cannot occur after the infinitive *to write*.
   correction: *I want you both to write . . .*
5. Quantifier floating cannot apply with *some*.
   correction: *Some of the students . . .*

10.5, page 200

1. He said that we should all come to his party.
2. My colleagues both received raises, but I didn't.
3. Their mother hoped that the girls would each marry rich men.
4. He had only one day to visit his relatives in Montreal, but he managed to visit them all.
5. The candidates must each study very hard if they want to get a scholarship.

10.6, page 203

1. not preferable (The inflected pattern, [*the dog's shiny red fur*], is usually used with humans and animals.)
2. The inflected pattern is preferred here, but the *of* + (*the*) noun pattern could also be heard. It is a toss-up with geographical places.
3. not preferable (The inflected pattern [*the player's eye*] is usually used with humans.)
4. preferable (The *of* + *the* noun pattern is the correct choice for NP's that refer to inanimate objects.)
5. not preferable (The *of* + *the* noun pattern is preferable here because the noun phrase is quite long.)

CHAPTER 11 ARTICLES

11.1, pages 219–220

1. error: *the Professor Granger* (Names preceded by professional titles do not take an article.)
2. This is grammatical in British English. (In American English, *university*, which is used here in its institutional sense, should be preceded by *the*.)
3. error: *an information* (Noncount nouns are not preceded by indefinite articles.)
4. no error
5. no error (However, the noncount noun *coffee* is normally preceded by *some* or the partitive *a cup of*. The use of the indefinite article alone is common in spoken English.)
6. This is grammatical in British English. (In American English, *hospital*, which is used here in its institutional sense, should be preceded by *the*.)
7. error: *in a class* (*Class* is evidently being used here in its institutional sense and therefore should be preceded by zero article.)
8. no error
9. error: *by the express mail* (Following the preposition *by*, nouns that denote modes of communication are preceded by zero article.)
10. error: *a homework* (Noncount nouns like *homework* are not preceded by indefinite articles.)

11.2, pages 225–226

1. immediate presence (The vase is visible to the speaker and listener.)
2. associative anaphoric use (The speaker assumes the hearer knows that diesel buses emit exhaust fumes.)
3. associative anaphoric use (The speaker assumes the hearer knows that laptops have screens.)
4. associative anaphoric use (The speaker assumes the hearer knows that a trip to Paris involves a journey.)
5. relative clause that specifies a noun (*Woman* is defined by the relative clause *who she works for.*)
6. part of larger context (The speaker assumes that the listener is familiar with the meeting place.)
7. ordinal (*Person* is preceded by the ordinal *first.*)
8. *that* clause (The noun *fact* is followed by a *that* clause.)

CHAPTER 12 ADJECTIVES AND ADVERBS

12.1, page 241

1. grammatical
2. ungrammatical (*Unique* is an *absolute adjective*, so it doesn't require *most* to form a superlative.)
3. grammatical
4. ungrammatical (The past participle adjective *worried*, takes *more* to form its comparative form: *more and more worried.*)
5. grammatical

12.2, page 246

1. grammatical
2. ungrammatical (*Afraid* is an *a*-prefix adjective that only occurs predicatively.)
3. grammatical
4. ungrammatical (*Ill* belongs to the small group of *health* adjectives that can only appear in predicate position.)
5. grammatical

12.3, page 248

1. ungrammatical (correction: worried about)
2. ungrammatical (correction: afraid of)
3. grammatical
4. ungrammatical (correction: responsible for)
5. ungrammatical (correction: glad about)

12.4, pages 252–253

1. *sharply* = manner adverb
2. *kind of* = hedge
3. *rarely* = frequency adverb
4. *wisely* = stance adverb
5. *typically* = stance adverb
6. *slowly* = manner adverb
7. *deliberately* = act-related adverb
8. *now* = time adverb
9. *only* = restrictive adverb

12.5, page 257

1. ungrammatical (Degree adverbs like *almost* appear before but not after verbs.)
2. grammatical
3. ungrammatical (*Seldom* in sentence-initial position requires subject–aux inversion.)
4. ungrammatical (Adverbs modifying verbs cannot appear between a verb and an object NP.)
5. ungrammatical (*Always* is a frequency adverb that does not occur in sentence-initial position. It comes before the verb.)

CHAPTER 13 PRONOUNS

13.1, page 270

1. *Joan*; intrasentential anaphora, forward
2. *Crows*; intersentential anaphora, forward
3. *girls*; intrasentential anaphora, backward
4. *bicycle*; intersentential anaphora, forward
5. *boys*; intrasentential anaphora, backward

13.2, page 271

1. not appropriate (should be *me*, as the conjoined noun and pronoun are the object of the preposition *with*)
2. not appropriate (should be *I*, as it is part of a conjoined subject and the preferred order would be: *this bloke and I*)
3. not appropriate (should be *me*, as it is part of a conjoined object of the preposition)
4. not appropriate (should be *I*, as part of a conjoined subject and the preferred order would be: *Susan and I*)
5. appropriate

13.3, page 275

1. Bruce
2. Cathy or Emily
3. Paul
4. Susan or Barbara
5. Alice

13.4, page 275

1. same meaning
2. not the same meaning (Sentence [a] means Francine told Alice all about someone else; sentence [b] means Francine told Alice about Alice or about Francine.)
3. not the same meaning (Sentence [a] means the Fred and Bill both felt that they both – together – were to blame; sentence [b] means that Fred blamed Bill and Bill blamed Fred.)
4. not the same meaning (Sentence [a] means that Alice showed Francine a picture of either Alice or Francine; sentence [b] means Alice showed Francine a picture of someone else.)
5. same meaning

13.5, pages 278–279

1. a difference (Sentence [a] seems to refer to one specific neighbor; in sentence [b], the neighbor is indefinite, rather than a specific neighbor.)
2. a difference (Sentence [a] implies an expectation that someone removed something; sentence [b] doesn't imply this expectation.)
3. no difference
4. no difference

13.6, pages 281–282

(Answers may vary)
1. no problem
2. problem (*Tweezers* is a noun that is plural in number.)
   correction: *I left the tweezers on this counter, and now they're gone.*
3. no problem
4. problem (*Committee* is followed first by the singular *it* but then by the plural *their*.)
   correction: *The committee has been putting in all the time it can and has been working diligently to get its report out by July.*
5. problem (The *his* referring to *anyone* is not gender-neutral writing.)
   correction: *Anyone who graduates in the top 10 percent of his or her class expects to get a good job.*

13.7, page 283

1. *near the village of Crécy*
2. entire preceding sentence

3. *the campus atmosphere at this university* OR the entire preceding sentence
4. *those gloves*
5. preceding quotation

CHAPTER 14 MODAL VERBS
14.1, page 302

1. *can't* = admonition
2. *couldn't have* = possibility
3. *may not* = permission
4. *can't* = disbelief
5. *might* = suggestion
6. *could* = ability
7. *can* = possibility
8. *might have* = criticism
9. *could* = possibility

14.2, pages 306–307

1. *must* = minimal requirement or condition
2. *should* = inferred probability
3. *should* = inferred probability
4. *should* = advice
5. *mustn't* = necessity/obligation
6. *should* = inferred probability
7. *should have* = reproach/reprimand
8. *must* = necessity/obligation

14.3, page 313

1. *gotta* = inferred probability
2. *oughta* = advice
3. *has to* = inferred probability
4. *(had)* *'d better* = advice
5. *(have)* *'ve gotta* = necessity/obligation
6. *need* = necessity
7. *have to* = necessity/obligation
8. *dare* = advice
9. *ought to* = inferred probability
10. *supposed to* = obligation
11. *(had)* *'d best* = advice

14.4, page 318

1. *would* = regular action in the past
2. *shall* = volition
3. *would* = regular action in the past
4. *would* = hypothetical result
5. *(would)* *'d* = inferred probability
6. *shall* = suggestion
7. *'m going to* = planned action; *'ll* = prediction
8. *would* = future from the perspective of the past

Activity 7, pages 326–327

The thief is Lady L.

CHAPTER 15 INDIRECT OBJECTS
15.1, page 336

1. yes
2. no
3. yes
4. no
5. no
6. no
7. yes

15.2, pages 336–337

1. *one*; yes
2. *them*; no
3. *some*; yes
4. *it*; no
5. *those*; yes

15.3, page 340

1. a (It puts the old information [*her*] before the new information [*some flowers*].)
2. b (It puts the old information [*him*] before the new information [*a gift certificate*].)
3. b (It puts the old information [*a package, a letter*] before the new information [*a Mr. Green, a Mrs. Harrison*].)
4. a (It puts the old information [*her*] before the new information [*a seat*].)

15.4, page 340

1. no (Move the heavy direct object NP to the end of the sentence. Dative movement isn't possible with *report*.)
   Rewrite: *John reported to the police the theft of his new sky-blue BMW convertible with the heated leather seats and the yellow fog lights.*
2. no (Move the heavy direct object NP to the end of the sentence. Dative movement isn't possible with *recommend*.)
   Rewrite: *The mediator recommended to the strikers an alternative solution for eliminating the barriers to a negotiated settlement of the dispute.*
3. no (Apply dative movement to move the heavy direct object NP to the end of the sentence.)
   Rewrite: *Alan found his grandmother a very comfortable apartment near a supermarket that was within walking distance of a lovely little park.*

CHAPTER 16 TENSE AND ASPECT

16.1, page 355

1. future; progressive
2. present; perfect
3. future; perfect
4. past; progressive
5. past; perfect

16.2, page 356

1. activity
2. state
3. accomplishment
4. achievement
5. accomplishment
6. achievement
7. activity
8. accomplishment

16.3, page 361

1. to describe a past event (conversational historical present)
2. to express a hypothetical condition (past tense)
3. to express politeness in the question (past tense of the auxiliary *do*)
4. to express habitual action (present tense)
5. to describe a story plot (historical/narrative present tense)
6. to express a state with the verb *seem* (present tense)

16.4, page 367

1. grammatical
2. ungrammatical (The past progressive tense does not appear with adverb phrases that mark the point in time when the action began, like *since noon*.)
3. ungrammatical (The present progressive tense [*it is expanding*] should be replaced by the simple present [*it expands*] which is appropriate for describing a scientific fact, which is the intent of the writer.)
4. grammatical
5. ungrammatical (The present tense does not describe a future event that is fixed or planned. The present progressive tense or the future expressed by *will* does.)

16.5, page 367

1. Sentence (a) expresses an action that will occur very shortly; (b) expresses an action that is planned for the future.

2. Sentence (a) expresses in-progress action or action that is planned for the future; (b) expresses an action that will occur in the future.
3. Sentence (a) expresses action that happened in the past; (b) emphasizes the repetitive aspect of the action that occurred in the past.
4. Sentence (a) expresses a usual state of behavior; (b) expresses a behavior that is a change from the norm.
5. Sentence (a) expresses future action and its duration; (b) emphasizes the repetitive aspect of the action that will continue for at least three years.

16.6, page 371

1. present perfect; ungrammatical (This tense does not occur with adverb phrases of time like *last Tuesday*.)
   correction: *I talked to him about it* . . .
2. simple past; ungrammatical (The past perfect should be used because the action in the main clause occurs before the action in the following clause.)
   correction: *She had already cooked dinner* . . .
3. simple past; ungrammatical (The past perfect should be used because this sequence is the only one correct for counterfactual conditionals.)
   correction: . . . *if I had bought IBM* . . .
4. simple past; grammatical
5. future perfect; grammatical
6. future (*will* + *be* + adjective); grammatical

16.7, page 374

1. ungrammatical (The tense of the verb in the first clause must be changed to the past perfect progressive to fit the termination of the past ongoing action in the second clause, which is in the simple past.)
   correction: *She had been studying for over four hours* . . .
2. grammatical
3. grammatical
4. grammatical
5. ungrammatical (The tense of the verb in the first clause must be changed to the future perfect progressive to match the prepositional phrase *for about 18 hours*, which expresses duration.)
   correction: *He will have been traveling for about 18 hours* . . .

16.8, pages 374–375

1. Sentence (a) is uttered when the person who is late arrives and apologizes; (b) is uttered at some later time when the person who was late wants to find out how long someone waited before finally leaving.
2. Sentence (a) describes ongoing activity in the past in relation to some other past action that is not expressed in the question (e.g., *How long had he been living in London when you met him?*); (b) conveys the meaning that the person in the question (*he*) is still living in London.
3. Sentence (a) emphasizes a sense of ongoing activity that is not present in (b).
4. Sentence (a) describes a recently completed activity; (b) emphasizes the ongoing nature of an activity that is not yet completed.

16.9, pages 378–379

1. Lack of shift is appropriate. (The speaker is reporting something that is still true.)
2. Tense shift is not appropriate. (The speaker is reporting something that is still possible in the future.)
3. Shift is appropriate.
4. Shift or no shift is appropriate. (Galileo's belief is a scientific fact.)
5. If the bystander reports Dreyfus's statement right after he makes it, no shifting is necessary. If the bystander reports this a little later he or she would probably choose the past tense: *Dreyfus said he was innocent.*

CHAPTER 17 PASSIVE SENTENCES
17.1, page 399

1. direct object
2. complement beginning with *that*
3. indirect object
4. object of the preposition *on*
5. direct object
6. complement beginning with *that*

17.2, page 399

1. The agent is a famous person.
2. The speaker wishes to conceal the identity of the person who gave the advice.
3. The agent is unknown but has caused some harm.
4. The writer is more interested in the activity than the agent.
5. The agent is unknown or assumed to be a thief.

17.3, page 400

1. a
2. b
3. a

17.4, page 404

1. no (It has the *for* dative verb *bake* in the dative movement pattern.)
2. yes (*A huge salary bonus was offered to the workers by the company.*)
3. yes (*She was sent a telegram by the producer.*)
4. no (It contains stative verb *cost*.)
5. yes (*A radically different house was designed for my boss by a famous Swedish architect.*)
6. no (It has the *for* dative verb *make* in the dative movement pattern.)
7. no (It contains a phrasal prepositional verb, *come down with*.)

17.5, page 404

1. (a) = active with a predicate adjective structure; (b) = passive
2. (a) = ambiguous; (b) = possibly ambiguous but most likely a passive
3. (a) = predicate adjective structure; (b) = passive
4. (a) = ambiguous; (b) = passive

17.6, page 407

1. *get* passive look-alike
2. *get* passive look-alike
3. *get* passive look-alike
4. *get* passive
5. *get* passive look-alike
6. *get* passive look-alike
7. *get* passive

17.7, page 408

The only thing accurate about the description is that the *get* passive is more common in spoken English. Everything else is wrong. There is not a single example of the true *get* passive. None of the examples has an active sentence counterpart. The *get* + past participle examples both have participial adjectives. Contrary to the explanation, *get* + adjective is never a passive.

17.8, page 410

1. happenstance passive
2. causative *had* passive with passive complement
3. causative *get* passive with passive complement
4. happenstance passive
5. concealed passive

CHAPTER 18 RELATIVE CLAUSES

18.1, pages 428–429

1. O relative clause
2. S relative clause
3. S relative clause
4. OP relative clause
5. OC relative clause
6. IO relative clause
7. POS relative clause
8. POS relative clause

18.2, page 429

1. The scientist [to whom they gave the award to the scientist] was from Sweden.

2. Iris bought the car [that Fred had previously sold the car to Susan].

3. The guy [~~the guy's~~ brother is engaged to Joan] owns a big house.
   whose

4. I know that girl [whose sister Alan eventually married that girl's sister].

5. John admired the dresser [in which Alice kept her sheets in the dresser].

6. Alan found an ancient manuscript [the last few pages of ~~the ancient manuscript~~ had
   which

   several beautiful illustrations].

7. The actor [whose last three movies I had seen and enjoyed the actor's last three movies]

   gave a surprisingly bad performance in this play.

18.3, page 433

1. The rules the committee must follow are set down in the constitution.
2. The guy John was stronger than challenged him to an arm-wrestling contest.
3. The other day we ran into that girl you lent your notebook to.
4. neither is possible (The relative pronoun is the subject of the relative clause, and this sentence does not contain one of the features which permit omission of the subject.)
5. neither is possible (The relative pronoun is preceded by the preposition *for*.)
6. The paramedic treated several passengers injured in the accident.
7. neither is possible (The relative pronoun is the subject of the relative clause, and this sentence does not contain one of the features which permit omission of the subject.)

18.4, page 433

1. yes
2. no (Extraposition would move the relative clause *who must have been three feet tall* after *a giant*, and this would change the meaning of the sentence.)
3. yes
4. no (Extraposition would move the relative clause *who was pregnant* after *her sister*, and this would change the meaning of the sentence.)
5. yes
6. yes

18.5, page 437

1. That's not the best area in which to build a house.
2. We need a freezer to put the ice cream in.
3. That is a good place to begin your trip from/from which to begin your trip.
4. I found a great video to watch on Saturday.
5. They cleared some space to spread out their papers in.

18.6, page 437

1. adverbial relative clause
2. indefinite free relative clause
3. definite free relative clause
4. definite free relative clause
5. indefinite free relative clause

18.7, page 440

1. grammatical
2. ungrammatical (Nonrestrictive relative clauses can't modify *any* + noun)
3. ungrammatical (Restrictive relative clauses can't modify proper nouns; nonrestrictive relative clauses must be set off by commas.)
4. ungrammatical (The nonrestrictive relative clause, which modifies the entire main clause, must be set off from it by a comma.)
5. ungrammatical (Nonrestrictive relative clauses can't be stacked.)

CHAPTER 19 CONDITIONAL SENTENCES

19.1, page 454

1. future conditional (instruction)
2. inference conditional
3. habitual conditional
4. generic conditional
5. inference conditional
6. inference conditional
7. inference conditional
8. future conditional (instruction)
9. future conditional
10. inference conditional

19.2, page 460

1. hypothetical conditional
2. hypothetical conditional
3. hypothetical conditional
4. counterfactual conditional
5. counterfactual conditional
6. hypothetical conditional
7. hypothetical conditional
8. hypothetical conditional

19.3, page 461

1. ungrammatical (Change the tense in the *if* clause to simple past to make it a hypothetical conditional.) correction: *If I happened to run into her, I would tell her where you live.* or (Change the modal in the result clause to make it a true future conditional.) correction: *If I happen to run into her, I will tell her where you live.*
2. ungrammatical (Change *would have been armed* in the result clause to *hadn't been armed* to make it a grammatical counterfactual.) correction: *He would have chopped my head off if I hadn't been armed with a 12-gauge shotgun.*
3. ungrammatical but heard in spoken English (*Was* should be changed to *were.*) correction: *If I were in your position, I would agree to do it.*
4. grammatical
5. ungrammatical (Change the tense in the *if* clause to the past perfect to make it a grammatical counterfactual.) correction: *I wouldn't have gotten so wet if I had remembered to bring my umbrella.*
6. grammatical
7. ungrammatical (Change the tense in the *if* clause to simple past to make it a grammatical hypothetical conditional.) correction: *If I saw him, I wouldn't speak to him* or (Change the modal in the result clause to *will* to make it a grammatical future conditional.) correction: *If I see him, I won't speak to him*).
8. grammatical

CHAPTER 20 SUBJECT CLAUSES AND RELATED STRUCTURES

20.1, page 474

1. That he got so many votes surprised everyone.   *that* clause
2. For Alan to spread such an outright lie would be unthinkable.   infinitive clause
3. Whether they will take disciplinary action against him has not been decided yet.   interrogative (embedded question) clause
4. To take offense at such a harmless joke is really silly.   infinitive clause
5. Ted Turner's refusing Rupert Murdoch's offer took him completely by surprise.   gerund clause
6. Taking an extra week of vacation wasn't such a good idea after all.   gerund clause

20.2, page 479

1. yes (*It is a great honor to be awarded first prize in this contest.*)
2. yes (*It would be outrageous for Alan to be denied the right to a fair trial.*)
3. no (Gerund subject clauses do not extrapose well.)
4. yes (*It is not clear to us how they managed to finish on time.*)
5. yes (*It surprises many conservatives that the senator enjoys such popularity among the general public.*)

20.3, page 479

1. no (*Happen* is a verb that occurs only in the extraposition pattern.)
2. yes (*To solve that problem is really quite easy.*)
3. no (*Appear* is a verb that occurs only in the extraposition pattern.)
4. yes (*That he is upset with her is obvious.*)
5. no (*Seem* is a verb that occurs only in the extraposition pattern.)

20.4, page 483

1. subject raising
2. subject raising
3. tough movement
4. subject raising
5. subject raising
6. tough movement
7. tough movement
8. *be* + willingness/ability adjective

20.5, page 484

1. Answers will vary.
2. The tough movement rule and the subject raising rule are similar in that they both move something out of an infinitive clause into subject (of the main clause) position. They are different in that tough movement moves the object of the infinitive clause whereas subject raising moves the subject of the infinitive clause.

20.6, page 484

1. same; (a) and (b) = *be* + willingness/ability adjective + infinitive clause
2. different; (a) = subject raising; (b) = *be* + willingness/ability adjective + infinitive clause
3. different; (a) = tough movement; (b) = *be* + willingness/ability adjective + infinitive clause

4. different; (a) = *be* + willingness/ability adjective + infinitive clause; (b) = subject raising
5. same; (a) and (b) = *be* + willingness/ability adjective + infinitive clause

CHAPTER 21 COMPLEMENTS

21.1, pages 496–497

1. can apply
2. cannot apply because the meaning of the sentence would change
3. can apply
4. can apply
5. cannot apply because the meaning of the sentence would change

21.2, page 502

1. yes
2. no; (a) = type 2 (*want* verb) complement; (b) = type 1 (*persuade* verb) complement
3. no; (a) = type 1 (*persuade* verb) complement; (b) = type 2 (*want* verb) complement
4. no; (a) = type 1 (*persuade* verb) complement; (b) = type 2 (*want* verb) complement
5. no; (a) = type 3 (*believe* verb) complement; (b) = type 2 (*want* verb) complement

21.3, page 502

1. ungrammatical (The NP after *believe* must be followed by *to be*.)
2. ungrammatical (The NP after *describe* must be followed by *as*.)
3. grammatical
4. grammatical
5. ungrammatical (The naming verb *appoint* is followed by an NP that names the office.)

21.4, page 505

1. ungrammatical (The interception verb *caught* takes an object NP followed by a gerund complement.)
   correction: The police caught him breaking into her apartment.
2. ungrammatical (*Risk* takes only a gerund complement.)
   correction: She risks losing all of her money.
3. grammatical
4. grammatical
5. ungrammatical (*Delay* takes only a gerund complement.)
   correction: He delayed leaving for school.

21.5, page 509

1. same
2. different. (a) means "I was supposed to put the keys in my pocket and I did"; (b) means "I remembered the act of putting the keys in my pocket."
3. different. (a) means "I will never forget the special occasion of going to the theater on Sunday morning"; (b) means "I will never forget that I am supposed to go to the theater on Sunday."
4. same
5. same

21.6, page 509

Sentence (b) should be inserted in this context because the gerund after *try* means she took these actions; an infinitive after *try* suggests that she wasn't able to slap him or throw water in his face.

21.7, page 512

1. different; (a) means we saw him repeatedly kick the tire; (b) means we saw him kick it once.
2. different; (a) means I saw the janitor perform the complete action; (b) means I saw him in the act of leaning it against the wall.
3. different; (a) means they heard someone pound once; (b) means they heard someone pound repeatedly.

21.8, page 512

1. Sentence (b) is better, because with the gerund complement the act of falling is in progress, so he could catch her (with the bare infinitive, it would be complete).
2. Sentence (b) is better, because with the gerund complement, the officer is in the act of bleeding to death and can still be saved (with the bare infinitive, the officer is dead).
3. Sentence (b) is better, because with the gerund complement the action of the rainfall is ongoing (the bare infinitive implies a single act that terminates immediately).

CHAPTER 22 FOCUS STRUCTURES
22.1, page 524

1. It's in South America that/where you find some of the longest rivers in the world.
   Where you find some of the longest rivers in the world is in South America.
   South America is where you find some of the longest rivers in the world.
2. It was with considerable misgivings that he accepted the position.
   What he accepted with considerable misgivings was the position.
   The position was what he accepted with considerable misgivings.
3. It's making people happy that I really love.
   What I really love is making people happy.
   Making people happy is what I really love.
4. What the columnist in the *Times* predicted was that Alan would lose the election.
   That Alan would lose the election was what the columnist in the *Times* predicted.
   It's that Alan would lose the election that the *Times* predicted.
5. It is how you were able to refinance your house with such a lousy credit rating that I can't understand.
   What I can't understand is how you were able to refinance your house with such a lousy credit rating.
   How you were able to refinance your house with such a lousy credit rating is what I can't understand.

22.2, page 528

1. argue a point
2. contradict
3. contradict
4. establish a topic

22.3, pages 528–529

1. contradict
2. clarify a possible misunderstanding
3. present the gist
4. resume a topic

22.4, pages 532–533

1. cheap
2. the smog
3. that she displays tremendous enthusiasm for the project
4. exactly what she intended with that remark
5. an espresso
6. to emphasize the point

22.5, page 538

1. *present at the meeting* (to avoid a long subject NP)
2. *so different* (to emphasize a related point)
3. *on the far side of the room, in front of it* (to create an immediate observer effect)
4. *adding to the challenges* (topic shift)
5. *representing the American team* (to avoid a long subject NP)
6. *here* (obligatory lexical inversion)

22.6, page 539

1. Up in my room on the nightstand is a letter that has to be mailed today.
2. Down with the rebound comes Collins.
3. Reported in satisfactory condition today at Mercy Hospital are Emory L. Ensley, 46, and Hazel Ensley, 41, both of Mohamet.
4. Representing Mayberry in the trial next week will be Steven P. Hurley, court-appointed public defender.
5. Seldom will you see a performance as good as that by a man of 75.

CHAPTER 23 ADVERBIAL SUBORDINATE CLAUSES

23.1, page 552

(Answers may vary.)
1. We will get together *as soon as* we unpack our furniture and set up our house.
2. She watched television *until* her taxi arrived.
3. I will give you a ride to the airport *whenever* you have to leave.
4. We visited her *before* we came here.
5. *On* hearing that he had been severely injured, she fainted.
6. Her application was reviewed *as if* it had been submitted by a foreign student.
7. She arrived *as I was leaving.*

23.2, page 557

(Other answers are possible.)
1. He couldn't visit her very often *since/as* she lived over on the other side of town.
2. *Because/As* she wanted to be sure that there were no errors in the report, she proofread it twice.
3. *Whereas* many older people like classical music, very few young people do.
4. The elections were held on time, *even though/although* many polling places didn't have ballot boxes.

5. He refused to sign the petition *lest* he be branded a troublemaker.
6. *Even though/Although* she tried like mad to please her superiors, Lucy never received a promotion.

23.3, page 557

1. (a) = purpose clause of avoidance; (b) = time clause
2. (a) = reason clause; (b) = time clause
3. (a) = result clause; (b) = purpose clause.
4. (a) = a concessive clause; (b) = time clause

23.4, page 564

(Other answers are possible.)
1. *As she was backing out of the driveway,* Alice ran over her daughter's bike.
2. *As soon as/After they had disembarked from the ship,* the German tourists set out to find a comfortable hotel.
3. *As she drove through the streets of London in her Rolls Royce and watched the heads turn as she passed by,* Deborah was struck by how easily people are impressed by an expensive car.
4. *Upon arriving at the cabin/When they had arrived at the cabin,* they immediately started a fire in the fireplace.
5. *By inserting the credit card between the door and the lock and pushing it upward,* the thief was able to unlock the door and gain access to the room.
6. *Because he knew that they might have to repel a counterattack,* the lieutenant arranged his men in a defensive position and told them to dig in.
7. *If we assume that they left on time,* they should now be somewhere between Dayton and Columbus.

23.5, page 564

1. He wrote about the problem in his book, *arguing for a different solution that incorporated diplomacy rather than conflict.*
2. "There's a lot more division than I expected on the court," said Georgetown University law professor David Law, *echoing the sentiments of several legal experts.*
3. Since the Enlightenment there has been a steady spread of rationality and humanitarianism that has in turn affected religious belief, *leading to a wider spread of religious tolerance.*

4. West Germany resisted broadening the treaty, *unleashing efforts from the American delegation to influence the other delegates.*

5. Yugoslav troops reopened Montenegro's main airport, *easing a confrontation* with *Serbia's independence-minded partner in the Balkan federation.*

CHAPTER 24 COMPARATIVES AND SUPERLATIVES

24.1, page 577

1. inequality
2. inequality
3. inequality
4. inequality
5. just a difference
6. equality

24.2, page 581

1. acceptable
2. unacceptable (two-syllable adjectives that have a stressed first syllable and end in -*ous* form the comparative with *more*.)
3. acceptable
4. unacceptable (*more* is unnecessary; this is a double comparative)
5. unacceptable (participial adjectives form the comparative with *more*)
6. unacceptable (two-syllable adjectives ending in -*y* form the comparative with -*er*)
7. acceptable (adjective of two or more syllables are usually formed with *less*)
8. unacceptable (adjectives with a first stressed syllable ending in -*on* form the comparative with -*er*)
9. acceptable

24.3, pages 584–585

(Answers may vary.)

1. She liked what we told her a lot more than what she eventually saw.
2. He is late more often than the other boys.
3. The project is turning out to be much more expensive than (they had) predicted.
4. It would be more profitable to accept their proposal than to refuse it.
5. I am just as fit as he is.

6. Alan fears his father more than (he) respects him, or Alan fears more than he respects his father.
7. He loaned more money to his sister than his father did.
8. The president's speech contributed as much to the outcome of the election as (it did) to the decision to go to war.
9. She corrected more papers in an hour than he was able to in three days.
10. More time was spent on planning for the conference than (was) necessary.

24.4, page 587

1. correct
2. not correct (Three-syllable adjectives form the superlative with *most*.)
3. not correct (*Fewest* is more appropriate with a count noun like *people*.)
4. correct
5. not correct; (Adverbs with -*ly* form the superlative with *most*: *most frequently* *asked question*.)

CHAPTER 25 COORDINATION

25.1, page 599

1. contrast
2. condition
3. cause and effect
4. addition
5. contrast
6. temporal succession
7. addition

25.2, page 602

(Answers will vary.)

1. She can either pay the speeding ticket now or protest it in court.
2. Rick won both a Booker Prize and a National Book Award.
3. Neither Miron nor his wife would read those kinds of books.
4. He quit not because he didn't like the job but because he wasn't earning enough money.
5. Just as we will have to lower our expectations somewhat, so they will have to raise their productivity.
6. Alan neither understood nor really listened to her explanation.

25.3, page 606

1. He is suggesting, and I am stating, that you are wrong.
2. Mark likes opera, but Al doesn't.
3. Alan bought or rented that motor bike.
4. John is coming with us, and Sandra is, too.
5. Stephen mowed and watered the lawn.
6. John expects to get an A and Bill a B.

25.4, page 607

1. delayed right constituent coordination
2. gapping
3. conjunction reduction
4. VP ellipsis
5. gapping
6. gapping
7. VP ellipsis

CHAPTER 26 DISCOURSE CONNECTORS AND DISCOURSE MARKERS

26.1, page 623

1. *as it happens* = cognitive stance
2. *however* = contrast
3. *consequently* = result
4. *incidentally* = abrupt topic shift
5. *still* = concession
6. *instead* = contrast
7. *that is to say* = restatement
8. *to summarize* = summary; *moreover* = addition; *thus* = result

26.2, page 624

1. *Moreover* (The sentence is supporting a thesis, rather than just adding information, so *moreover* is a better choice than *in addition*.)
2. *However* (In a straightforward comparison such as this, *however* is preferable to *nevertheless*.)
3. *Consequently* is appropriate.

4. *However* (*In contrast* is inappropriate here because it is used when two subjects are different in at least one respect – not finding his telephone number is related to not having invited him, so *however* is the appropriate choice.)
5. *That is* is appropriate.
6. *On the contrary* (*On the contrary* is more appropriate here than *instead* because it is the connector of contrast that signals a speaker's contradictory stance.)
7. *By the way* or *Incidentally* (*Furthermore* adds information whereas here the speaker is making an abrupt topic shift.)

26.3, page 629s

1. *Well* signifies impatience and prefaces a response following a challenge.
2. *Right* is a tag in a same polarity tag question.
3. *Like* marks something that is salient.
4. *You know* serves as a tag question that invites confirmation or assumes assent.
5. *I mean* is used to repair the first part of the utterance, which the speaker evidently thinks was perhaps too harshly worded.
6. Speaker A's *okay* is used to wrap up the topic.
7. All of these *you knows* are deliberation signals that indicate that the speaker is formulating the next part of the discourse.
8. *Like* is used here as substitution for *said/ say* to introduce reported speech.

Glossary of Grammatical Terms

Accomplishment verb A type of **dynamic verb**, expressing action that has a logical endpoint (*build, paint*). (*She wrote a novel.*)

Achievement verb A type of **dynamic verb**, expressing action that occurs instantaneously (*bounce, kick*) or involves a preliminary activity culminating in the act denoted by the verb (*find, cross*). (*He kicked the ball. He crossed the finish line.*)

Active voice A characteristic of a sentence whose subject typically is an agent and whose direct object has a role such as theme. (*The dean fired our professor.*) Compare: **Passive voice**.

Activity verb A type of **dynamic verb**, expressing action that can go on for an indefinite period of time. The action may be one of continuity (*run, walk*) or inherent change (*decline, grow*). (*He was running along the road. That tree is growing bigger.*)

Actor See *Agent*.

Act-related adverb An **adverb** that provides background or motive for the action of the verb. (*deliberately, knowingly, voluntarily*)

Adjective A word that describes properties of nouns, whether as an attributive adjective or a predicative adjective. (*black, big, happy, heavy*)

Adjective phrase A **phrase** headed by an adjective. (*He's very tall.*)

Adverb A word that describes how, when, where, why, or to what extent some action occurs (*carefully, often*).

Adverbial relative clause A **relative clause** introduced by *where, when*, or *why* rather than by a relative pronoun. (*That's the gas station where I'm working now.*)

Adverbial subordinate clause A **subordinate clause** that has an adverbial function. An adverbial subordinate clause may be a clause of time, manner, purpose, reason, result, concession, or condition. (*She called as I was leaving. Since you've apologized, I'll consider the matter closed.*)

Adverb phrase A **phrase** headed by an adverb. (*She finished very quickly.*)

Agent The **thematic role** of doer. (*The boy kicked the ball.*)

Alternative question A question offering a choice between two or more options. (*Would you like eggs, pancakes, or waffles?*)

Antecedent The words a pronoun substitutes for, in relation to the pronoun. (*Alice* is the antecedent of *she* in *Alice heard the plan, and she didn't approve.*)

Appositive A noun phrase that defines the noun phrase it follows. (*Prague, the capital of the Czech Republic, is very beautiful.*)

Article A type of **determiner**, including the **definite article** *the*, the **indefinite article** *a/an*, and **zero article**.

Aspect How the speaker views the action of the verb, for example, as ongoing in the case of **progressive aspect** or as complete in the case of **perfect aspect**.

Atelic verb A verb expressing something with no logical end point. **Stative verbs** and **activity verbs** are atelic.

Auxiliary verb A verb – either *be*, *have*, or *do* – that precedes the main verb in a verb phrase (*They are watching the child*) or a **modal auxiliary verb**.

Bare infinitive A verb form without infinitival *to* or inflections for tense. (*We helped her clean the garage.*)

Benefactive The **thematic role** of the person for whom an action is performed. (*He did it for his children.*)

Cardinal number A type of **determiner** – *one*, *two*, *three*, etc.

Clausal coordination **Coordination** of clauses. (*John went to the party, but Felicia stayed home.*)

Clause A unit that includes a subject and a verb – either an **independent clause** (**main clause**) or a **subordinate clause** (**dependent clause**).

Cleft sentence A **focus structure** in which a constituent has been made prominent by splitting the sentence – either an *it* **cleft** or a *wh-* **cleft**.

Collective noun A noun designating a group of individuals. (*crowd*, *team*, *the Parkers*)

Comitative role The **thematic role** of someone who accompanies. (*Lee went with his wife.*)

Common noun A noun that refers to a general person, place, or thing (*boy*, *school*) – either a **count noun** or a **noncount noun**.

Comparative construction A sentence that compares two things, either in inequality comparisons as superior or inferior (*Bill is calmer than John*; *John is less tolerant than Bill*) or in equality comparisons (*The hat is as expensive as the sweater*).

Complement For a verb, a constituent that follows the verb and completes its meaning; used especially for a clause, which may be a **gerund complement**, **infinitive complement**, **interrogative complement**, or *that* **complement**.

Complementizer A type of **subordinator** whose only function is to introduce clauses – the *for* introducing an infinitive clause or *that* introducing a *that* clause. (*It would be hard for him to leave now. I hope that he will come, too.*)

Conditional free relative clause See *Indefinite free relative clause*.

Conditional sentence A sentence with a clause, usually beginning with *if*, expressing a condition and a clause expressing the result of the condition. A conditional sentence may be a **real conditional** or an **unreal conditional**.

Coordinate sentence Two or more independent clauses joined by a **coordinator**.

Coordinating conjunction See *Coordinator*.

Coordination The joining of constituents of the same type (e.g., noun phrases, verb phrases, clauses) by a **coordinator**. (*Your car keys are in your purse or on the dresser. John went to the party, but Felicia stayed home.*)

Coordinator A word used to join constituents in **coordination**. A coordinator may be a single-word coordinator or a multiword coordinator.

Correlative coordinator A two-part multiword coordinator, which generally adds emphasis to the conjoined constituents – *both . . . and*, *neither . . . nor*, *either . . . or*, *not only . . . but*. (*We neither planned for nor desired that outcome.*)

Counterfactual conditional An **unreal conditional** speculating about past events that did not obtain or impossible states or situations in the present. (*If he had been paying attention, he wouldn't have crashed.*)

Count noun A **common noun** that can be made plural. (*person, book*)

Dative verb See **For *dative verb*** and **To *dative verb***.

Declarative* yes/no *question A reduced *yes/no* question in the form of a sentence. (*You play hockey?*)

Definite article The **article** *the*, used before a count noun or a noncount noun considered to be specifically identifiable to the speaker and listener.

Definite free relative clause A **free relative clause** that begins with *what, where*, or *when*. (*Sally ordered <u>what Jim chose</u>.*)

Degree adverb An **adverb** that describes the degree to which a verb's action is carried out. (*barely, relatively, thoroughly*)

Demonstrative determiner *This/these* and *that/those* used to modify a noun. (*these hats*)

Demonstrative pronoun *This/these* and *that/those* used as a **pronoun**. (*Which ones do you like, these or those?*)

Dependent clause See ***Subordinate clause***.

Determiner A word that comes before and modifies a head noun by indicating characteristics such as definiteness/indefiniteness, possession, and quantity. Types of determiners include the **article, demonstrative determiner, possessive determiner, quantifier, partitive,** number, **multiplier,** and fraction.

Direct object A noun phrase that occurs after a verb and, often, functions as a **patient**. (*The batter hit <u>the ball</u>.*)

Discourse connector A word or words connecting a sentence or clause to a previous sentence or clause, establishing relationships such as ordering, addition, and contrast (*moreover, however, in addition, in other words*). (*If you adopt this procedure, you can increase your production. <u>Furthermore</u>, your manufacturing costs will be reduced.*)

Discourse marker Largely restricted to spoken English, a word or words that are not an integral part of a sentence and are used to, for example, indicate a pause or wrap up or signal a new phase in a conversation (*Well, I mean, you know, oh, okay. <u>Well</u>, let's get started.*)

Discourse particle See ***Discourse marker***.

Display question A question, usually with a *wh-* word not at the beginning, asked by teachers to get students to display their knowledge. (*So, this play is about what?*)

Dynamic verb A verb that, in terms of **lexical aspect**, expresses action, rather than a state. A dynamic verb may be an **activity verb, achievement verb,** or **accomplishment verb**.

Embedded question clause See ***Interrogative clause***.

Embedded* wh- *question A **wh- question** embedded in a sentence. (*I don't know <u>what he is doing</u>.*)

Ergative verb A verb whose subject undergoes or experiences the action expressed by the verb (*collapse, faint, suffer*). (*She has suffered a lot.*)

Exclamatory question A question that has the form of an exclamation. (*Isn't he big!*)

***Existential* there** See ***Nonreferential* there**.

Extraposed relative A **relative clause** moved away from the noun it modifies. (*Something happened <u>that I can't talk about</u>.*)

Extraposition structure A sentence that begins with nonreferential *it* and ends with a clause that could replace the *it*. (*It is easy <u>to understand this lesson</u>.*)

Finite clause A clause with a verb that is inflected for tense (e.g., a ***that* clause** or an **interrogative clause**). (*He thinks <u>that he needs a vacation</u>.*)

Focus structure A sentence in which some element of the basic version of the sentence is moved into a position of prominence, including a **cleft sentence**, a sentence with **fronting**, and an **inversion**.

For *dative verb* A verb that in a sentence with a **prepositional pattern** has the preposition *for* before the indirect object. (*buy, do, make*) (*He bought it for his sister.*)

Free adjunct An **adverbial subordinate clause** that has no subordinator or overt subject and begins with a present participle. (*Arriving at the scene of the accident*, the team immediately began treating the survivors. High waves swamped the boats, *sinking several and carrying others out into the bay*.)

Free relative clause A **relative clause** that stands alone rather than modifying a head noun – either a **definite free relative clause** or an **indefinite free relative clause**.

Frequency adverb An **adverb** that answers the question *How often does the verb's action occur?* (*always, often, regularly*)

Fronting A **focus structure** in which a constituent is made prominent by being moved to the beginning of the sentence. (*This I don't understand.* Compare: *I don't understand this.*)

Future conditional A **real conditional** expressing predicted future results of conditions. (*If you don't leave now, you'll miss your plane.*)

Generic conditional A **real conditional** expressing a fact that appears to be a scientific truth. (*If a gas is heated, it expands.*)

Generic reference Use of a noun to refer generally to members of a class. (*Tigers are dangerous.*)

Genitive relative clause See ***Possessive (POS) relative clause***.

Gerund A **present participle** that can function as the head of a noun phrase. (*Swimming is a great form of exercise. Inviting the neighbors was a mistake.*)

Gerund clause A **clause** with a gerund that can appear in subject and certain other noun phrase positions. (*Writing good poetry isn't easy.*)

Gerund complement A **gerund clause** that functions as a complement. (*He enjoys watching TV.*)

Get *passive* A **passive voice** sentence with *get* + past participle rather than *be* + past participle. (*My car got stolen.*)

Goal The **thematic role** of the place to which or the person to whom the action is directed. (*He went upstairs. He gave his daughter a necklace.*)

Habitual conditional A **real conditional** expressing situations or events as the usual result of a condition being met. (*If they play bridge, they get into an argument.*)

Hypothetical conditional An **unreal conditional** speculating about imagined possible events or states in the present or future. (*If I found a wallet, I would return it.*)

Imperative sentence A sentence with a bare infinitive and, usually, without a visible subject, used to convey commands, instructions, or requests. (*Look at me. Don't be lazy.*) Variations include the emphatic imperative, imperative with tag, imperative with visible subject, vocative imperative, and *I need you* imperative.

Indefinite article The **article** *a/an*, used before a singular count noun considered to be specifically identifiable to the speaker and listener.

Indefinite free relative clause A **free relative clause** that begins with *whoever, whatever, whichever,* or *whenever.* (*Fred eats whatever Alice offers him.*)

Indefinite pronoun A **pronoun** referring to an indefinite or unspecified entity, formed by combining *some, any, every,* or *no* with *-one, -body,* or *-thing.* (*someone, anything, everybody*)

Independent clause A **clause** that can stand on its own as a sentence. (*As he was running to catch the bus, John tripped and fell.*)

Indirect object (IO) A noun phrase that occurs between the verb and its direct object in the dative movement pattern and/or after the verb and its direct object following *to* or *for* in the prepositional pattern, usually functioning as a **goal** or **benefactive**. (*She bought him a ticket. She bought a ticket for him.*)

Indirect object (IO) relative clause A **relative clause** in which the relative pronoun is an indirect object. (*This is the store <u>that she bakes her cakes for</u>.*)

Inference conditional A **real conditional** in which the proposition in the result clause is inferred from that in the *if* clause. (*If the door was locked, he must have come through the window.*)

Infinitival relative clause A **relative clause** with a verb in its infinitive form. (*John is not the right person <u>to confide in</u>.*)

Infinitive The form of a verb in which it is preceded by *to*. (*to see*)

Infinitive clause A **clause** with an infinitive that can appear in subject and certain other noun phrase positions. (*<u>To write good poetry</u> requires considerable talent.*)

Infinitive complement An **infinitive clause** that functions as a complement. (*He wants <u>to watch TV</u>.*)

Information question The basic type of *wh-* **question**, used to request information not previously mentioned. (*What has he done?*)

Inseparable transitive phrasal verb A transitive phrasal verb whose verb and particle cannot be separated by an object. (*Don't <u>pick on</u> him.*)

Instrument The **thematic role** of tool or other thing with which the action is done. (*He chopped the wood with <u>a hatchet</u>.*)

Instrumental adverb An **adverb** that answers the question *By what means?* (*mathematically, mechanically*)

Interrogative clause A **clause** that begins with a *wh-* element and includes a tensed verb or a modal and that can appear in subject and certain other noun phrase positions (*<u>How he plans to do that</u> is not clear.*)

Interrogative complement An **interrogative clause** that functions as a complement. (*He wonders <u>what she is thinking</u>.*)

Intransitive verb A **verb** that does not take an object. (*run, talk*)

Inversion A **focus structure** in which the constituent made prominent is moved to the front of the sentence and the subject is moved after the verb. (*Down with the ball comes Roan.*)

It cleft A **cleft sentence** formed by adding *it* + *be* to the start of a sentence, moving the focused element to follow, and following that element with an added *that* + the rest of the sentence. (*It's an SUV that she wants.* Compare: *She wants an SUV.*)

Lexical aspect The properties of a verb that describe its action, thus conveying **aspect**. Lexical aspect divides verbs into two main types – **stative verbs** and **dynamic verbs**.

Location The **thematic role** of place where the action occurs. (*He hung it on <u>the wall</u>.*)

Long passive A **passive voice** sentence that has an agent *by* phrase. (*He was helped by his brother.*) A short passive has no agent by phrase. (*He was helped.*)

Main clause See *Independent clause*.

Manner adverb An **adverb** that describes how the verb's action is carried out. (*loudly, slowly*)

Marginal modal A **modal auxiliary verb** with only two of the characteristics of **pure modals** – contraction with *not* and subject–auxiliary inversion. The marginal modals are *dare, need*, and *ought to*.

Mass noun See *Noncount noun*.

Modal auxiliary verb A kind of **auxiliary verb**, used to express meanings such as ability, permission, and possibility (*can, may, might*) and advice and necessity (*should, must*), as well as to express future time (*will, be going to*). In form, a modal may be a **pure modal**, **marginal modal**, or **semimodal**.

Multiplier A type of **determiner** – *twice, double, three times*, and so on.

Negative polarity item A word that can appear in negative statements but normally does not appear in positive statements. (*any, anybody, much, yet*) Compare: **Positive polarity item**.

Nominal relative clause See *Free relative clause*.

Noncount noun A **common noun** that cannot be made plural. (*information, stuff*)

Nonfinite clause A **clause** that does not contain verb forms inflected for tense (e.g., an **infinitive clause** or a **gerund clause**). (*He wanted to go to the carnival.*)

Nonreferential it An instance of *it* that fills subject position but does not refer to anything. (*It is cold in here.*)

Nonreferential there An instance of *there* not used to refer to something. (*There is a rabbit in the garden.*)

Nonrestrictive relative clause A **relative clause** that does not restrict the reference of the noun modified. Nonrestrictive relative clauses add information about the noun they modify and are set off by commas. (*I have a brother and a sister. My sister, who lives in Canada, is a biologist.*)

Nonverbal negation Negation through words such as *nobody, nothing, no,* and *never* or negative affixes such as *un-* and *non-*. (*He did nothing.*)

Noun phrase (NP) A **phrase** with a noun head and any preceding modifiers. (*My brother eventually chose the big red car.*)

Object of a preposition A **noun phrase** that follows a preposition and hence is part of a prepositional phrase. (*We are meeting in the conference room.*)

Object of comparison (OC) relative clause A **relative clause** in which the relative pronoun replaces a noun phrase that follows comparative *than*. (*The girl who Susan was faster than won the 100 meter dash.*)

Object (O) relative clause A **relative clause** in which the relative pronoun replaces the direct object in the clause. (*He saw many people who he didn't know.*)

Object of the preposition (OP) relative clause A **relative clause** in which the relative pronoun replaces an object of a preposition in the clause. (*The mattress that he slept on wasn't comfortable.*)

Object personal pronoun A **personal pronoun** that occurs as an object of verbs and prepositions – *me, you, him, her, it, us, them.*

Opposite polarity tag question A **tag question** with a positive stem and negative tag or a negative tag and positive stem. (*You are going, aren't you? He isn't a vegetarian, is he?*)

Ordinal number A type of **determiner** – *first, second, third,* etc.

Paired ergative verb An **ergative verb** that has a transitive counterpart. (Ergative = *The ship blew up*; transitive counterpart = *They blew up the ship.*)

Participial adjective An **adjective** formed from a present or past participle. (*interesting, bored*)

Particle A word that combines with a verb to form a **phrasal verb**. (*up* in *set up* or *give up, in* in *hand in*)

Particle movement With a transitive phrasal verb, the movement of a particle to the position following the object. (*Maggie looked up the address.* → *Maggie looked the address up.*)

Partitive A type of **determiner** that is a multiword expression consisting of a count noun + *of*. (*glass of, loaf of, piece of, slice of*)

Passive voice A characteristic of a sentence in which the direct object of an active voice sentence has been moved to subject position and the subject, if retained, is part of an agent *by* phrase. A theme, rather than an agent, is typically in subject position. (*Our professor was fired by the dean.* Compare: *The dean fired our professor.*)

Past participle Verb + *-ed*. (*He has finished his novel.*)

Patient (theme) The **thematic role** of the thing affected by the action. (*He chopped the wood.*)

Perfect aspect The **aspect** expressing the action of the verb as complete, expressed by *have* + past participle.

Permanently separated phrasal verb A **phrasal verb** whose verb and participle must be separated by an object. (*The job is getting him down.*)

Personal pronoun A **subject personal pronoun** (*he, she, we*) or an **object personal pronoun** (*him, her, us*).

Phrasal coordination **Coordination** at the level of the phrase. (*Your keys are in your purse or on your dresser.*)

Phrasal prepositional verb A verb that has an obligatory particle and preposition. (*do away with* [*something*], *look up to* [*someone*], *put up with* [*something*])

Phrasal verb A verb with an obligatory particle (*look up, get down, take off*) – either a **transitive phrasal verb** or an **intransitive phrasal verb**.

Phrase A unit consisting of a head element and any modifiers – **adjective phrase**, **adverb phrase**, **noun phrase**, **prepositional phrase**, **verb phrase**.

Place adverb An **adverb** that answers the question *Where did the action occur?* (*abroad, here, inside*)

Positive polarity item A word that can appear in positive statements but normally does not appear in negative statements. (*some, somebody, a little, several, already*) Compare: ***Negative polarity item***.

Possessive determiner A **determiner** that shows possession – *my, your, his, her, our, their*. Possessive nouns (*Bill's, children's*) also function as possessive determiners.

Possessive pronoun A **pronoun** that replaces a noun phrase indicating possession – *mine, yours, his, hers, its, ours, theirs*.

Possessive relative clause A **relative clause** in which the relative pronoun replaces an element that expresses possession. (*I met a girl whose brother works with you.*)

Predicate nominal A **noun phrase** that follows *be* and refers to the sentence subject. (*My mother is a doctor.*)

Predicative adjective An **adjective** that appears after a verb and not in a noun phrase. (*She is insane. She found him dull.*)

Preposition A word that together with a following noun indicates a meaning related to location in space (*in, on*) or time (*about, at*), an instrumental meaning (*by, with*), or other such meanings.

Prepositional phrase (***PP***) A **phrase** with a preposition head and a following noun phrase. (*in the garage, through a long tunnel*)

Prepositional verb A verb that has an obligatory preposition. (*decide on, stare at, care for*)

Present participle Verb + *-ing*.

Primary verb negation A type of **verbal negation** in which *not* negates a clause with a tensed verb. (*They are not staying with us. We did not live there.*) Compare: ***Secondary verb negation***.

Progressive aspect The **aspect** expressing the action of the verb as ongoing, expressed by *be* + present participle.

Pronoun A word that substitutes in some way for a noun phrase or a clause. A pronoun may be a **personal pronoun**, **possessive pronoun**, **indefinite pronoun**, **reflexive pronoun**, or **demonstrative pronoun**.

Proper noun A **noun** that is the name of a specific person, place, or thing. (*John, Paris*)

Pseudo-cleft See **Wh- cleft**.

Pure modal A **modal auxiliary verb** that has all four characteristics of modals (contraction with *not*, subject–auxiliary inversion, repetition in tags, invariant form). The pure modals are *can, could, may, might, must, shall, should, will*, and *would*.

Quantifier   A type of **determiner** that indicates amount or number of something. Common quantifiers include *all*, *both*, *each*, *every*, (*a*) *few*, (*a*) *little*, *many*, *much*, *more*, *most*, *several*, and *some*.

Real conditional   A **conditional sentence** in which the condition and result can be fulfilled. A real conditional may be a **generic conditional**, **habitual conditional**, **inference conditional**, or **future conditional**.

Recipient   See *Goal*.

Reciprocal pronoun   A **pronoun** used in object position referring to subjects that mutually perform the action, each on the other – *each other*, *one another*. (*Alice and Joan admired each other.*)

Reflexive pronoun   A **pronoun** used obligatorily or optionally after certain verbs (*pride ourselves*, *behave yourself*) or refers to another NP within a clause or is used for emphasis (*I myself*). The reflexive pronouns are *myself*, *yourself*, *himself*, *herself*, *itself*, *oneself*, *ourselves*, *yourselves*, and *themselves*.

Relative clause   A **subordinate clause** that modifies a noun phrase. (*The girl who we met is Bill's sister.*) A relative clause may be a **restrictive relative clause** or a **nonrestrictive relative clause**.

Relative pronoun   *That*, *which*, *who*, *whom*, or *whose* used to introduce a **relative clause**.

Restrictive relative clause   A **relative clause** that restricts the reference of the noun phrase it modifies, rather than restricting its reference. (*I have two sisters. My sister who lives in Canada is a biologist.*)

Resumptive pronoun   In a relative clause, a pronoun that sometimes in spoken English is inappropriately included in the gap left by *wh-* movement. (**Usually, they give you a thing that you don't want it.*)

Reversed pseudo-cleft   See *Reversed **wh-** cleft*.

Reversed **wh-** *cleft*   An alternative version of a ***wh-** cleft*, in which the focused element occurs at the beginning followed by *be* + *what*. (*A vacation is what I need.* Compare: *What I need is a vacation.*)

Same polarity tag question   A **tag question** in which both the stem and the tag are positive. (*So that's your little game, is it?*)

Secondary verb negation   Type of **verbal negation** in which *not* negates a clause that has a verb in infinitive, bare infinitive, or present or past participle form and does not have a tensed verb. (*She promised not to leave early. He hates not knowing the truth.*) Compare: **Primary verb negation**.

Semimodal   A **modal auxiliary verb** that is a fixed idiomatic expression beginning with *have*, *had*, or *be*. The semimodals are *be going to*, *be supposed to*, *had better*, *had best*, *have got to*, and *have to*.

Separable phrasal verb   A transitive phrasal verb whose verb and particle may be separated by an object. (*He looked up her number* or *He looked her number up.*)

Source   The **thematic role** of place from which or person from whom an action originated. (*He took the book off the shelf.*)

Speech act conditional   A sentence that looks like a future conditional but is not a conditional, as its clauses do not have a condition–result relationship. (*If you're going my way, I could use a ride.*)

Stance adverb   A special category of **act-related adverb**, expressing the speaker's attitude or judgment regarding the content of the clause, including its degree of certainty, generality, or accuracy. (*foolishly*, *regrettably*, *undoubtedly*, *generally*)

Stative verb A verb that, in terms of **lexical aspect**, expresses a state or condition, rather than an action. (*be*, *have*, *know*, *like*, *need*, *own*)

Subject A noun phrase that comes before the verb and in many cases is an agent. (*The batter hit the ball.*)

Subject clause A **clause** in subject position in a sentence. (*That she didn't reply doesn't surprise me.*) An **infinitive clause**, **gerund clause**, ***that* clause**, or **interrogative clause** can function as a subject clause.

Subject (S) relative clause A **relative clause** in which the relative pronoun replaces the subject of the clause. (*The guy that hired Robert was the manager.*)

Subjunctive The **bare infinitive** form following a verb of request or demand (e.g., *ask*, *demand*, *insist*). (*I insist that you arrive on time.*)

Subordinate clause A **clause** that cannot stand on its own, for example, a **relative clause** or an **adverbial subordinate clause**. (*As he was running to catch the bus, John tripped and fell.*)

Subordinator A word or words introducing an **adverbial subordinate clause** (*after*, *although*, *as if*)

Superlative construction A sentence that singles out a particular thing in relation to all other group members, in terms superiority (*That's the easiest test I've ever taken*) or inferiority (*That's the least expensive watch in the store*).

Supplementive clause See ***Free adjunct***.

Tag question A question consisting of a stem, or statement, followed by a related tag, or short question – usually an **opposite polarity tag question** but can also be a **same polarity tag question**.

Telic verb A verb expressing something with a logical end point. An **achievement verb** or an **accomplishment verb** is telic.

Tense A feature of verbs – the time that an action occurs in relation to the moment of speaking. Tense has three dimensions – present, past, and future. English marks two tenses – present and past (future time is expressed with *will* or *be going to*).

That *clause* A clause that is introduced by the complementizer *that* and includes a tensed verb or a modal and that can appear in subject position and certain other noun phrase positions. (*That he managed to get his degree is truly remarkable.*)

That *complement* A *that* clause that functions as a complement. (*He thinks that he will watch TV.*)

Thematic role The semantic relationship of an NP to a verb, preposition, or adjective. Common thematic roles include **agent**, **benefactive**, **goal**, **instrument**, **location**, **patient**, and **source**.

Theme See ***Patient***.

Time adverb An **adverb** that answers the question *When did the action of the verb occur?* (*already*, *earlier*, *now*, *then*)

To *dative verb* A verb that in a sentence with a prepositional pattern has the preposition *to* before the indirect object. (*bring*, *give*, *tell*) (*He gave a nice going-away present to his sister.*)

Tough *movement structure* A sentence that has an ease/difficulty adjective (e.g., *tough*, *fun*, *simple*, *easy*, *pleasant*, *difficult*) followed by an infinitive whose understood subject is the subject of the main clause. (*John is easy to please.*)

Transitive verb A verb that must take an object (*sell*, *find*)

Unreal conditional A **conditional sentence** in which the proposition in the *if* clause is an imagined condition and the proposition in the result clause is its imagined outcome. An unreal conditional may be a **hypothetical conditional** or a **counterfactual conditional**.

Verbal negation **Negation** that uses the negative element *not* with a verb – may be **primary verb negation** or **secondary verb negation**. (*Lance isn't very happy.*)

Verb phrase (***VP***) A **phrase** consisting of a main verb, any preceding auxiliary verbs, and any following related noun phrase and/or other element(s). (*He <u>bought a new car</u>. Alice <u>walks very slowly</u>.*)

Vocative imperative An imperative beginning or ending with an address form. (*Ann, you go first.*)

Wh- *cleft* A **cleft sentence** formed by adding a *wh-* word, usually *what*, at the beginning of a sentence and *be* before the focused element. (*What she bought was a red sweater.* Compare: *She bought a red sweater.*)

Wh- *question* A question beginning with *who, what, where, when, where, how*, etc. (*What are you looking at?*) Based on function, a *wh-* question can be categorized as an **information question**, a *repeat please* question, or an *elaborate please* question.

Yes/no *question* A question that can be answered by *yes* or *no*.

Zero article An instance in which a noun has no preceding article. (*There's milk in the refrigerator.*)

Index of Words and Phrases

Note: The symbol "n" means that the information about the word or phrase is in an endnote rather than in the main text.

Index of Topics

Note: The symbol "n" means that the information about the topic is in an endnote rather than in the main text.

Art Credits